WEST ACADE
EMERITUS A~~DVISORY B~~

JESSE H. CHOPER
Professor of Law and Dean Emeritus
University of California, Berkeley

YALE KAMISAR
Professor of Law Emeritus, University of San Diego
Professor of Law Emeritus, University of Michigan

MARY KAY KANE
Late Professor of Law, Chancellor and Dean Emeritus
University of California, Hastings College of the Law

LARRY D. KRAMER
President, William and Flora Hewlett Foundation

JAMES J. WHITE
Robert A. Sullivan Emeritus Professor of Law
University of Michigan

PRINCIPLES
OF
EVIDENCE

Ninth Edition

Daniel J. Capra
Philip Reed Professor of Law
Fordham University School of Law

Stephen A. Saltzburg
Wallace and Beverley Woodbury University Professor of Law
The George Washington University Law School

CONCISE HORNBOOK SERIES™

WEST
ACADEMIC
PUBLISHING

The publisher is not engaged in rendering legal or other professional advice, and this publication is not a substitute for the advice of an attorney. If you require legal or other expert advice, you should seek the services of a competent attorney or other professional.

© 1978, 1987, 1996 WEST PUBLISHING CO.
© West, a Thomson business, 2006
© 2009, 2012 Thomson Reuters
© 2015, 2019 LEG, Inc. d/b/a West Academic
© 2022 LEG, Inc. d/b/a West Academic
    444 Cedar Street, Suite 700
    St. Paul, MN 55101
    1-877-888-1330

Printed in the United States of America

ISBN: 978-1-63659-460-6

DJC to Anne

SAS to Susan Lee

Preface to the Ninth Edition

This *Concise Hornbook* was first published in 1978 and was entitled, *An Introduction to the Law of Evidence*. Its sole author was Graham C. Lilly, a distinguished professor at the University of Virginia Law School. The aim then, as now, was to provide readers with a hornbook of manageable size that would enable them to understand the principles and rules of evidence that are usually studied in the basic evidence course in American law schools. Over the years, the explanatory text has increased in size, while the footnote documentation has been reduced, so that the book itself would remain relatively concise. The fact that the Law of Evidence is now largely codified has facilitated this transition, and allowed footnote material to be reduced without sacrificing essential documentation.

The two of us assumed editorial responsibility for the Sixth Edition and continue to exercise that responsibility. Our goal, which was also Professor Lilly's, is to assure that the book will remain a useful source of study for students and lawyers for many years to come.

DANIEL J. CAPRA
Philip Reed Professor of Law
Fordham University School of Law

STEPHEN A. SALTZBURG
Wallace and Beverley Woodbury
University Professor of Law
The George Washington University
Law School

October 18, 2021

Summary of Contents

Table of Contents

PRINCIPLES
OF
EVIDENCE

Ninth Edition

Chapter I

INTRODUCTION

The subject you are about to explore—the law of evidence—is a key component of litigation in American courts. Trial lawyers need to know the rules and be prepared to use them in a timely manner, but even lawyers who do not engage in litigation must know at least the fundamentals of this body of law. Competent attorneys understand that someday in the future their clients may become involved in controversies surrounding even garden-variety transactions. Should one or more of these disputes ripen into litigation, the law of evidence will take center stage. It will influence discovery and have a significant impact on the terms of settlement, because the strength of a case, and thus its settlement value, depends on what can be proved at trial. And of course the rules of evidence will profoundly affect the course and outcome of trial—including pretrial stages such as a motion for summary judgment, at which the evidence rules apply. Therefore, the ability to recognize, develop, and preserve admissible evidence is essential to becoming a competent lawyer.

It is not too early in your evidentiary studies to consider this fundamental question: Why do we have or even need rules of evidence? There is no single answer to this question, but certainly a major reason for the rules is to control the information that reaches the lay jury. The received wisdom is that juries must be shielded from evidence that would be inflammatory in order to decrease the likelihood of a verdict prompted by momentary passions or erroneous inferences. Although the rules of evidence apply in bench (i.e., judge) trials, many of them are not strictly enforced in that context, and appellate reversals of evidentiary rulings in bench trials are rare.[1] Some of the rules of evidence are also designed to expedite the trial— for example, by forbidding the introduction of irrelevant evidence.[2] Other rules are designed to improve the quality of the evidence that is introduced at trial, for example, by preferring the original of a document to a copy (or to testimony about the contents of the original document),[3] and requiring expert testimony to be reliable.[4]

---

[1]   The judge is rarely reversed for considering "inadmissible" evidence because her professional training prepares her to evaluate the evidence accurately, taking full account of possible defects. However, her refusal to consider evidence that was in fact admissible may lead to a reversal.

[2]   *See* Fed. R. Evid. 402.

[3]   *See* Fed. R. Evid. 1002.

[4]   *See* Fed. R. Evid. 702.

One of the most complicated rules you will encounter is the hearsay rule. It seeks to assure that hearsay statements are reliable enough to be admitted at trial. The rule generally forbids the introduction of statements offered for their truth that were made out of court and thus out of the presence of the trial participants.[5] The hearsay problem typically arises because the testifying witness wants to state what an out-of-court "declarant" said about the event in question. ("The declarant told me that the water was three feet over the deck of the bridge when P, going at least 60 miles an hour in his SUV, tried to cross it.") The problem is that the witness on the stand will be unable to answer the cross-examiner's questions about the declarant's opportunity to perceive the event described, to remember it accurately, and to faithfully portray it. The witness can only repeat what the declarant said to him. In other words, the cross-examiner cannot put questions to the "real witness" (the declarant) that might reveal that he was mistaken or lying. The cross-examining lawyer who wants the declarant placed on the witness stand will likely raise a hearsay objection. The proponent of the evidence who wants it admitted will have an opportunity to show that it fits within an exemption or exception that justifies its admission.

In addition to promoting the offer and admission of reliable evidence or protecting against unfair prejudice, some evidentiary rules implement various social policies such as the preservation of confidences between protected parties like attorney and client or spouses.[6]

Perhaps most importantly, many evidentiary rules work to preserve a fair balance in the adversarial system of trials. The Federal Rules of Evidence, for example, generally apply equally to plaintiffs and defendants in civil cases and to the government and defendants in criminal cases. The rules themselves are oblivious to whether a party is rich or poor, a human being or an artificial entity. The rules seek to further the concept of equal justice under law.

You will see, as we go forward, that there is a tension that exists in all evidence codifications. There is a desire to assure that the rules are applied even-handedly to all litigants and that no party or type of party is favored or disfavored. But there is also a desire to apply the rules in a particular case with due regard to the particular facts before a court. The tension is resolved in some cases with evidence being admitted while in other cases with different facts the same evidence might be excluded.

---

[5]   *See* Fed. R. Evid. 801–802.

[6]   *See* Fed. R. Evid. 501, which recognizes evidentiary privileges, but leaves it to federal judges (that is, to decisional or common law) to determine the existence and scope of federal privileges.

Today, the study of evidence focuses on the Federal Rules of Evidence which apply not only in the federal courts, but also serve as a model for state codes of evidence. Almost all of the states have now adopted the Federal Rules, often with modifications that serve to preserve or introduce some local rules to which the adopting state wishes to adhere. Until 1975, the year in which the Federal Rules of Evidence took effect in the federal courts, the vast bulk of evidence law was contained in state and federal judicial decisions. But since 1975, a major change has taken place: the law of evidence has been largely transformed from a common law to a code-based subject. With this transition has come increased (but by no means complete) uniformity throughout all American courts.

A final note in this introductory chapter concerns aids to interpreting the Federal Rules. As originally presented to Congress, the Federal Rules had been drafted and were to have been promulgated as judicial rules of court, prescribed by the United States Supreme Court for the governance of trials in lower federal courts. (The Supreme Court is aided in this rule-making task by an administrative body called the Judicial Conference of the United States).[7] However, Congress was dissatisfied with some of the proposed Rules. It therefore intervened by passing the initial body of the Federal Rules of Evidence as a statute, containing not only many of the rules proposed by the Supreme Court, but also the modifications and new rules approved by the House and Senate. Thereafter, Congress granted rule-making authority to the United States Supreme Court—though Congress also retained the power to amend the rules directly.[8]

Today, amendments to the Rules of Evidence, as a general rule, are proposed initially by the Judicial Conference Advisory Committee on the Federal Rules of Evidence. (The Reporter to that Committee is a co-author of this book). The rule proceeds through the Judicial Conference and the Supreme Court. If the Supreme Court approves the rule amendment, it becomes law if Congress takes no action for seven months. However, the rulemaking process is not the only

---

[7]   *See* 28 U.S.C.A. § 331 (1988). The Chief Justice of the United States presides over the Conference, which discharges most of its work through committees. The Conference itself is made up of federal judges, but non-judges, such as practicing lawyers and professors of law, routinely participate in committee work.

[8]   The current statute granting power to the United States Supreme Court to promulgate rules of evidence for use in the federal courts is 28 U.S.C.A. § 2072. A companion statute, 28 U.S.C.A. § 2073, sets out the procedures to be followed by the Judicial Conference. Rules that are finally approved by the Supreme Court must be transmitted to Congress for review. *See* 28 U.S.C.A. § 2074. If Congress takes no adverse action during the prescribed review period, the proposed rule or rules become effective. There is an exception for rules of privilege, which must be affirmatively enacted by Congress.

means of enacting an evidence rule. Congress occasionally bypasses the judicial rule-making process and enacts a statute that imposes upon the lower federal courts a new or modified rule of evidence.[9] Thus, the historical and contemporary background of the Federal Rules of Evidence consists of both congressional legislative history and the commentary generated by the Judicial Conference.

Also important in interpreting the Federal Rules is the common law background against which the Rules were crafted. Both the original Advisory Committee that drafted the Rules and the Congress were aware of the evidence law that had been developed in both federal and state courts. They often considered the common law as they were drafting and reviewing the proposed Federal Rules of Evidence. It should not be surprising that the Advisory Committee's Notes on proposed Federal Rules of Evidence frequently refer to the common law. This was more important when the Rules were new, because lawyers and judges who had long experience with common law precedents needed to know whether the Rules codified or modified the common law. Since the Rules have been in effect since 1975, common law antecedents have faded in importance. But, they remain important in the area of privileges, because Rule 501 makes specific adopts the federal common law.

It should come as no surprise that often reasonable minds could construe an evidence rule in more than one way. Judges are fully aware of this and generally are receptive to arguments based on the apparent intention of the Rules' drafters. Thus, this text refers periodically to historical materials which, among other things, indicate the intention of the drafters and trace the changes made in a particular rule from its initial draft to its final passage.

It should be noted that the Federal Rules of Evidence have been completely restyled, effective December 1, 2011. The restyling is intended to make the rules more internally consistent, easier to understand and apply, and essentially more user-friendly. The restyling is not intended to change any evidentiary result. When we cite the language of a rule, we will of course use the restyled version.

---

[9]   For example, Congress added Rules 413, 414, and 415.

Chapter II

THE FRAMEWORK

Table of Sections

§ 2.1   The Adversary System

Anglo-American evidentiary rules and principles are a product of the adversarial system of justice. The theory underlying the adversarial model is that the self-interest of each party to the litigation will produce the evidence and the competing arguments necessary for the trier to make a fair and rational decision. The adversarial system, therefore, is driven by the parties.

Each litigant, and not the judge, largely determines what evidence she will present at trial. The parties are responsible for gathering and proffering evidence; the judge decides if a given item of evidence is admissible when a party-opponent objects that the proffered evidence violates an evidentiary rule. This observation leads to a related point: in addition to controlling her own evidentiary presentation, a party can influence the evidentiary record by objecting to the evidence offered by an opponent. If her objection succeeds, she can block the admission of the objectionable portions of the opponent's evidence, which of course tends to tilt the evidentiary balance in her favor. The success of the objection will depend upon whether the judge determines that an exclusionary rule of evidence applies. But a party is not *required* to object to adverse evidence, even if an exclusionary rule is available to prevent its admission. If by careless omission or deliberate inaction, a party fails to object to inadmissible evidence, the judge will normally admit it. Once admitted, this evidence stands on the same footing as other admitted evidence. Only in extreme cases, and if then usually only on behalf of a criminal defendant, will the court intervene and exclude inadmissible evidence on its own motion (*sua sponte*). The judge's failure or refusal to exclude evidence *sua sponte* will almost never constitute reversible error, although there is the possibility that an appellate court will in exceptional cases rely on the concept of "plain error," which is recognized in Federal Rule of Evidence 103(e).[1]

§ 2.2 Phases of a Trial

The plaintiff in a civil case and the government in a criminal case typically have the burden of proof ("the burden of persuasion"), although there are civil cases in which the burden of persuasion is on the defendant (e.g., to prove suicide in a case involving a life insurance policy). The party bearing the burden of persuasion is accorded the right to make the first opening statement. The opposing party's opening statement usually follows, although sometimes the defendant "opens" just prior to putting on the defense case. In the discussion that follows we shall assume that the plaintiff or prosecutor has the burden of persuasion.

After the opening statement(s), the plaintiff or prosecutor makes the first evidentiary presentation (the "case in chief"). Next, the defendant makes an evidentiary presentation (defendant's "case in defense or chief"). Often there are further evidentiary presentations, usually called the plaintiff's or prosecutor's "case in rebuttal" and the defendant's "case in rejoinder." When the evidence-taking phases of the trial are over, in most jurisdictions the closing arguments proceed as follows: (1) the plaintiff or prosecutor makes the first closing argument; (2) the defendant then delivers closing argument; and (3) after the defendant's closing argument, the plaintiff or prosecutor is allowed a final closing argument to rebut the defendant's closing remarks. (In some jurisdictions the defendant closes first, followed by the plaintiff or prosecutor.)

The judge has considerable control over the order of trial and will not be reversed by an appellate court, in changing the traditional order, unless there is a clear abuse of discretion. That said, the sequence below is typical of most trials and for our purposes will suffice:

(a)   Jury Selection (Voir Dire)

(b)   Counsels' Opening Statements

---

[1]   Satisfying the test for plain error is not easy, as the Supreme Court emphasized in its opinion in *United States v. Olano*, 507 U.S. 725 (1993) (interpreting the plain error standard in Fed. R. Crim. P. 52(b), which is substantially identical to the standard provided in Fed. R. Evid. 103(e)).

(c)   The Presentation of Evidence:

Case in Chief

Case in Defense

Case in Rebuttal[2]

Defendant's Case in Rejoinder

(d)   Counsels' Closing Arguments

(e)   Judge's Charge[3]

(f)   Jury Deliberation and Verdict

A final important observation about the order of trial events: unless the judge rules otherwise, a party has the exclusive right during its "presentation phase" to proffer witnesses, documents, or other items of evidence. The opponent is limited to cross-examination, although the cross-examiner may use documents that were not used on direct examination as long as the questions asked about them and their contents are within the scope of the direct examination or the judge permits a wider cross-examination. In other words, the opponent generally must wait until his presentation phase begins before being able to call witnesses and offer his own evidence. This rule prevents the cross-examiner from destroying the continuity of the direct examiner's presentation of evidence.

§ 2.3   Offers of Proof and Objections

The Offer of Proof: Federal Rule 103

In a broad sense, every document proffered as evidence and every statement elicited from a witness on the stand is an offer of proof. Commonly, however, the term "offer of proof" is used more narrowly to refer to the dual showing a proponent must make when the admissibility of her evidence is challenged by objection. Under Rule 103, the offer of proof must include, (1) a presentation or description of the evidence that a party seeks to introduce and, (2) a statement of the fact or facts she wishes to prove with the evidence. (You can appreciate why offers of proof must often be made outside the hearing of the jury—if the jury hears the offer, then the evidence is effectively admitted.) Sometimes, the context in which the evidence is proffered makes its nature and purpose so clear that no

---

[2]   Although many trials have four evidentiary phases, some trials consist only of the case in chief or, more likely, the case in chief and the case in defense. Usually the judge allows each party to decide whether or not to present additional evidence.

[3]   In federal courts and in some state courts, the judge may instruct the jury before closing argument, after closing argument, or both times. *See, e.g.,* Fed. R. Crim. P. 30(c).

elaboration—that is, no formal offer of proof—is necessary.[4] If there is any doubt about the evidence and its intended purpose, however, counsel should supplement ("perfect") the record.

Perfecting the offer of proof has two advantages. First, counsel might ultimately persuade the trial judge that the proposed evidence is admissible. Second, even if the judge sustains the opponent's objection, counsel may challenge the judge's ruling on appeal should she (the proponent of the excluded evidence) lose her case at trial. With the offer of proof in the record, the appellate court can make an informed decision about the nature and importance of the evidence and assess the trial judge's evidentiary ruling. Note, also, that an offer of proof gives the opponent a clearer picture of the nature and purpose of the contested evidence, giving him the opportunity to refine, restate, or even withdraw his objection. A party who realizes that his objection is invalid has good reason to withdraw it, because if he wins at trial an appellate court might reverse on the ground that the trial judge sustained the invalid objection.

An offer of proof may take many forms. Sometimes counsel's question to a witness alone suffices because, in context, counsel's purpose in offering the evidence and the witness's expected response are clear. As noted above, however, if there is doubt or ambiguity about the offer, counsel should specify "for the record" precisely what evidence she seeks to adduce and the proposition to which she directs it. She may accomplish this, for example, by summarizing the expected evidence and its purpose or by interrogating the witness out of the jury's presence—that is, in the presence of the judge, opposing counsel, and the court reporter. If the proponent offers a document or tangible object, she should record its purpose and ensure that the writing or the object (or at least an adequate description of the object) becomes part of the trial record. The point is that the steps necessary to complete an offer of proof vary with the particular setting.

The following are the most common situations in which an offer of proof will be found to be sufficient:

(a) In the context in which evidence is offered, its purpose and nature is sufficiently clear without further elaboration;

(b) Counsel for each side and the court reporter approach the bench and the proponent states his offer out of the jury's hearing (a "side bar" conference);

---

4   Fed. R. Evid. 103(a)(2) recognizes this possibility by providing that a party whose evidence is excluded must "inform[ ] the court of its substance by an offer of proof, unless the substance was apparent from the context."

(c) The proponent states his offer in open court, a procedure that suffices when the evidence described is unlikely to improperly influence the jury;

(d) The jury is excused, and the proponent formally interrogates a witness "for the record."

Objections: Rule 103

Under Rule 103, the objection, like the offer of proof, must be sufficiently explicit to reveal to the adversary, the trial judge, and the appellate tribunal the basis for contesting the evidence.[5] In addition to being explicit, sound trial administration and fairness to the proponent dictate that the objection must be made as soon as the objecting attorney is able to perceive the defect in the proffered evidence. Usually, counsel will make the objection as soon as the question calling for improper evidence is asked (or as soon as an objectionable item is offered). Sometimes, however, there is insufficient time to object, as when a witness answers quickly or gives an answer that is not responsive to the question asked. In circumstances where the evidentiary defect is not apparent until after a response has been made, a motion to "strike the evidence" is the proper remedy. A successful "strike" is followed by the judge's instruction to the jury to disregard the stricken evidence. Of course, as a practical matter, the jury may find this instruction difficult to follow.

Because offers and objections serve important informational functions, it is not surprising that the rules governing these devices require the offeror and objector to state their respective positions accurately in order to preserve any claim of error on appeal. This demand for precision reflects the assumption that the opposing attorneys are familiar with the forthcoming evidence. The judge, who does not have equal familiarity with the evidence offered, is entitled to expect informed and succinct offers and objections. Thus, as we see below, the specific rules governing offers and objections favor the judge and operate against the attorney who fails to take appropriate, timely action.

When counsel objects to the admission of her opponent's evidence, the judge, of course, must rule. It is important to note that the trial judge rules on the *objection that is actually stated* by the opponent and on the *offer of proof that is actually presented* by the proponent. The correctness of the judge's ruling is determined by the articulated postures of counsel; it is not determined by the positions they might have but did not assume. Thus, the judge does not err if she rejects an offer of proof that is faulty or that by its terms indicates

---

[5]   Fed. R. Evid. 103(a)(1).

that the proffered evidence is inadmissible. The fact that a different or revised offer would have made the evidence admissible is beside the point. Likewise, the judge who overrules an erroneous objection, or an objection made on the basis of an inapposite rule, has not made an error. The fact that a different, proper objection would have resulted in exclusion of the evidence is, again, of no consequence on appeal.

ILLUSTRATIONS

(1) Peter sues a private golf club for negligent maintenance of its golf cart. Peter offers evidence of two other accidents during the month preceding Peter's accident in which other golfers were injured while using the defendant's carts. Peter (through his attorney) states that the purpose of the evidence is "to show that the defendant has been negligent in maintaining its carts on other occasions, which supports the proposition that the defendant was negligent regarding his (Peter's) accident." The defendant objects on the ground that evidence of other separate accidents cannot be admitted to prove negligence. The judge sustains the objection and excludes the proffered evidence.

if wrong proffer → your call

There is no error because, as we will find, a party cannot admit prior acts of negligence to prove negligence at the time in dispute. But as we will see, this evidence might have been admissible for another purpose, such as to prove the club was put on notice by the prior acts. That said, the fact that Peter might have cast his offer in different terms will be unavailing on appeal. The trial judge is entitled to address only the argument made by the party; an afterthought on appeal is to be discouraged.

(2) In the same suit, Peter starts to testify that Cousin, a golfer and mechanical engineer, told Peter after Peter's accident that he (Cousin) had used the same cart Peter was using when injured, and that the cart had a defective axle and a loose clamp in the steering column. Cousin had rented the cart only a day before Peter rented it. The defendant objects that the evidence is irrelevant, but the trial judge overrules the objection.

should have been suld now

Assume the testimony about Cousin's statements was inadmissible on hearsay grounds (Cousin, who is the declarant, is not on the stand), but the evidence is relevant as tending to prove that the cart was defective. The judge ruled correctly even though another objection (hearsay) would have resulted in exclusion.

While the foregoing illustrations suggest that the rules governing offers and objections are arbitrary and harsh, this unfairness is ameliorated because the parties (unlike the judge) usually have ample pre-trial opportunities to become familiar with the available evidence. Thus, the parties can anticipate what offers and objections are likely to be forthcoming at trial. In contrast, the judge does not have similar opportunities to anticipate and study the forthcoming evidence; she is likely to know comparatively little about the evidence until the trial begins.

Keep in mind, also, that even an erroneous evidentiary ruling may not result in an appellate reversal. The appellate court will not reverse the judgment below unless it concludes that the erroneous evidentiary ruling probably had a substantial effect on the trial outcome.[6]

§ 2.4   Examining Witnesses: General Rules

The Form of Questions

In this section, we examine briefly a cluster of rules that govern the interrogation of witnesses. Most of these rules are found in Federal Rule 611.[7]

Leading Questions

One of these rules generally prohibits attorneys from asking leading questions during direct examination. The rule rests upon

---

[6]   Fed. R. Evid. 103(a) (error must "affect[s] a substantial right"). When an erroneous evidentiary ruling results in a violation of the United States Constitution, a different standard of review applies. Generally speaking, an appellate court will reverse the judgment below unless it determines beyond a reasonable doubt that the constitutional error was harmless. *See Chapman v. California*, 386 U.S. 18, 22 (1967).

[7]   Before the presentation of evidence and the interrogation of witnesses begin, the trial judge often asks the parties whether they want to invoke "the rule." "The rule" refers to sequestration of witnesses. Fed. R. Evid. 615, the sequestration rule, provides that any party has the right to request that the judge order that witnesses be excluded from the trial until they testify. The rationale for sequestration is that attendance at trial could allow a witness to tailor her testimony to what has previously been presented. Rule 615 provides, however, that certain witnesses can never be excluded— most importantly, the parties in the case. An entity—the government, a corporation, a labor union, etc.—is entitled to identify one representative to be present in the courtroom (to put the entity party on the same level as the individual party). The judge may permit persons who are essential to assisting a party and counsel (often experts) to remain the courtroom during testimony of others. Rule 615 also recognizes that Congress may authorize individuals to be present to some extent during trial, and Congress has given victims the right to attend trial within certain limits in the Victim's Rights and Restitution Act of 1990, 42 U.S.C. § 10606, and the Victim Rights Clarification Act of 1997, 18 U.S.C. § 3510. Finally, Rule 615 provides that a trial judge may do more than just exclude witnesses—the trial judge also may enter an order that prevents parties from providing trial testimony to prospective witnesses and to prevent witnesses from accessing trial testimony. This aspect of Rule 615 recognizes the risk of tailoring trial testimony can exist even if a prospective witness is excluded from the courtroom.

three assumptions. The first, a factual assumption, is that the attorney who calls a witness has interviewed the witness and has concluded that the witness is willing and able to provide favorable testimony for the attorney's client. The second, also a factual assumption, is that the attorney has prepared the witness (often called "woodshedding") so that both the attorney and the witness know how the direct examination will proceed and do not need to rely on leading questions. The third assumption, a psychological one, is that, given the cooperative relationship that has developed between attorney and witness, if the direct examiner phrases his questions in language that implies or suggests the desired answer, the witness will respond by providing that answer in order to maintain the cooperative relationship even if the questioner's choice of words differs from those the witness would use.

The leading questions doctrine promotes the principle of neutrality in the adversarial system: the trier of fact should hear a witness's unadulterated testimony, not testimony that has been influenced by partisan counsel feeding information to the witness through leading questions. Although counsel are partisan and have the opportunity to influence a witness during trial preparation, partisan influence is at least reduced by prohibiting leading questions of witnesses who are either neutral or favorable to the questioning party. Essentially the goal is to have the witness, not the lawyer, providing testimony to the factfinder.

When Is a Question "Leading"?

A leading question is one that clearly suggests the desired answer. Determining whether a question is leading involves a contextual judgment that takes account of such factors as phrasing and, occasionally, voice intonation. For example, in a suit for breach of contract for the sale of goods, the question set out below would constitute a leading question. After establishing that the defendant had spoken with the plaintiff, counsel for the plaintiff asks his witness:

> "During your conversation with the defendant Neill Jones, didn't Mr. Jones declare that he would not deliver the merchandise?"

On the other hand, counsel could avoid leading his witness by rephrasing the question:

"Will you state what, if anything, the defendant, Neill Jones, said, during your conversation, relating to the delivery of the merchandise?"[8]

The rephrased question avoids the suggestiveness that makes the initial question leading. To generalize: the correct approach to the interrogation of a witness who is not hostile is to use non-suggestive questions, at least when asking about matters that are actually disputed by the parties.

Qualifications to the "Leading Questions" Prohibition

There are a number of qualifications to the general rule prohibiting leading questions during direct examination. First, a leading question may be allowed because the opponent decides not to object. (The judge will not ordinarily intervene.) For example, the opponent may conclude that the damaging effect of such question(s) is insufficient to justify the interruption, delay of the proceedings, and possible jury impatience caused by an objection. Second, as we will see below, there are situations outside the reach of the general prohibition against leading questions.

Leading questions are permitted to establish *preliminary, uncontested facts*, such as a witness's identity, address, and other incidental matters. This exception to the general rule is simply a concession to trial efficiency. Leading questions are also proper, at least for a brief period, if the *witness is forgetful*. Here the theory is that a leading question or two may spark the witness's recollection. For example, in stating his question, counsel may direct the witness's attention to an event or a conversation in issue and reveal a portion of it. There is, of course, some risk that if the leading questions do not revive memory, the witness may nonetheless give an answer based upon the implied suggestion in the examiner's question. Whatever the theoretical extent of this risk, however, it is minimized by two practical controls: first, the opponent can object on the ground that recollection has not been refreshed and, second, during cross-examination the opponent can attempt to prove the limited extent of the witness's recollection. For example, the opposing attorney could ask about other closely related features of the incident about which

---

8   Trial lawyers sometimes use language like "what, if anything, did he say" or "where, if anywhere, did he go" to avoid leading. The result is that the questions appear to lay jurors to be stilted. Experienced lawyers avoid such language and ask questions in language that lay jurors are used to hearing. For example, instead of asking the question set forth in the text, experienced lawyers might ask the witness: "Did the defendant say anything during your conversation about the delivery of the merchandise?" Upon receiving a "yes" answer, they would ask "Please tell us what the defendant said?" You might notice that this follow up "question" is not actually a question; it is a request. But court reporters know to put a question mark after the words.

the witness testified. If the witness has little or no recollection of these features, the judge or jury may find that her memory is not trustworthy.

Leading questions are also usually permitted in the *interrogation of a very young witness* or the *interrogation of a witness who has communication problems*. Again, some risk to the neutrality of testimony exists, especially because a youthful witness or one who has difficulty communicating effectively may be susceptible to suggestion. As a practical matter, however, leading questions may be the only effective method of eliciting the testimony of such a witness.

Finally, as developed below in greater detail, leading questions may be used during direct examination to *interrogate a hostile witness* or to *interrogate a witness identified with an adverse party*. When leading questions are allowed on direct, the trial judge has ample power to prevent abuse. On objection, or occasionally on her own initiative, she can restrict or terminate a leading inquiry.

In contrast to the general rule governing direct examination, the prohibition against leading questions is generally inapplicable during cross-examination. Here the assumption is that the cross-examiner and the witness are antagonistic, and that there has been no pre-trial preparation or testimonial rehearsal as to the matters covered on direct. Moreover, the risk of suggestive influence, is thought to be absent in the supposedly hostile atmosphere of cross-examination. The use of leading questions also aids the cross-examiner in controlling the damage that an adverse witness might inflict on his client's case. For instance, counsel can frame inquiries narrowly in order to limit the witness's range of response. Thus, the cross-examiner can question a hostile witness on the examiner's own terms, thereby minimizing the negative impact of the witness's testimony.

It should be apparent that the factual assumptions of cooperativeness (during direct examination) and hostility (during cross) that underlie the rule governing leading questions may not always be accurate. Many witnesses, for example, have no strong allegiance to either of the parties, and many have information that both parties find favorable to their cases. Furthermore, the direct examiner may need to call a hostile witness, or the cross-examiner may have the opportunity to interrogate a friendly witness. (An attorney's choice of witnesses is, after all, limited to those witnesses who have personal knowledge of the events to which they testify.) In these instances, the interrogating counsel or the opposing counsel may request a change in the mode of examination. The trial judge has the power to grant or deny counsel's request, depending upon her assessment of the actual relationship between examiner and witness.

Federal Rule 611 and Leading Questions

In administering the rules governing leading questions, the trial judge will be guided by the following provisions of Federal Rule of Evidence 611:

(a) Control by the Court; Purposes. The court should exercise reasonable control over the mode and order of examining witnesses and presenting evidence so as to:

> **(1)** make those procedures effective for determining the truth;
>
> **(2)** avoid wasting time; and
>
> **(3)** protect witnesses from harassment or undue embarrassment.

* * *

(c) Leading Questions. Leading questions should not be used on direct examination except as necessary to develop the witness's testimony. Ordinarily, the court should allow leading questions:

> **(1)** on cross-examination; and
>
> **(2)** when a party calls a hostile witness, an adverse party, or a witness identified with an adverse party.

Note that Rule 611 makes special reference to calling an adverse party (or a close associate). When a party calls the opponent to the stand, a hostile exchange is likely to ensue. Consequently, the general rule is that the sponsoring counsel can, from the outset, treat the adverse party as a hostile witness and conduct examination by leading questions. The Rule makes the same assumption as to hostility to close associates of a party.

Rule 611 recognizes that there are "hostile" witnesses who are neither adverse parties nor associates of adverse parties. As to these witnesses, counsel should ordinarily seek the court's permission before conducting an examination by leading questions and explain to the court the basis for the claim of hostility.

It sometimes happens that a witness who is called on direct examination has not been thoroughly prepared, perhaps because of schedule conflicts or the witness's aversion to meeting with counsel. Such a witness might take offense at questions during direct examination and might actually appear to become hostile to the direct examiner. In such a case, the direct examiner again should request permission from the court to ask leading questions.

Scope of Cross-Examination

Another rule governing the interrogation of witnesses prescribes the scope of cross-examination. There are two versions of this rule. Under the so-called English Rule, a cross-examiner can inquire into any relevant matter. Conversely, under the predominant American Rule, the cross-examiner is limited to the subjects or topics that were covered by the direct examiner *and* to matters relating to the witness's credibility.

The difference between the English and American Rule is illustrated by the following hypothetical: It's a wrongful death action, and the plaintiff is suing for injuries he suffered on account of his wife's death. His wife was run down outside her house by a car driven by the defendant. The plaintiff calls a neighbor who saw the accident. On direct examination, the neighbor testifies that the defendant was talking on a cell phone while driving down the road, and hit the plaintiff's wife when she was walking across the street. On cross-examination, the defendant wants to inquire into what the neighbor knows about the state of the marriage between the plaintiff and the decedent. If permitted to testify to these matters, the neighbor would state that the plaintiff and decedent often had violent arguments, and that he had called the police on them a number of times.

In the hypothetical, the cross-examination seeks information that is relevant to the case, as it bears on the damages suffered by the plaintiff—if the marriage was bad, then the emotional damage of losing his wife is substantially diminished. Under the unconstrained English Rule, defense counsel would be permitted to ask this question. But under the American Rule strictly applied, she would not, because the question addresses subject matter beyond that covered in the direct examination—simply stated, the direct was about liability, and the defendant wants the cross-examination to be about damages.

Federal Rule 611(b)

In Rule 611(b), the Federal Rules of Evidence adopt the (majority) American Rule:

(b) Scope of Cross-Examination. Cross-examination should not go beyond the subject matter of the direct examination and matters affecting the witness's credibility. The court may allow inquiry into additional matters as if on direct examination.

The rationale of the American Rule is that the party who calls the witness ordinarily should be allowed its own order of proof, and that cross-examination beyond the subject matter of direct would be an unwarranted disruption. Of course, the Rule does not mean that the witness can never be asked about unrelated subject matter. The solution is for the adverse party to call the witness during its own case-in-chief.

Obviously, situations arise in which it is debatable whether the cross-examiner is venturing outside the scope of direct examination. The mosaic of human events does not always permit sharp divisions between the various topics of descriptive testimony. Generally speaking, judges administer the American Rule in a practical fashion, allowing cross-examination on topics that are reasonably linked to the subject matter of direct examination. This permissive posture defeats the strategy of a direct examiner who attempts to elicit from a witness only a fragment of an event or conversation in the hope of confining the cross-examiner to the same arbitrarily restricted scope of inquiry.

Trial judges also have discretion to expand the scope of cross-examination in order to prevent witnesses from suffering substantial inconvenience. For example, in our hypothetical above, the neighbor will probably be called to the stand twice: first by the plaintiff to testify on liability and then by the defendant to testify on damages. If the neighbor would suffer great inconvenience by this sequencing, the trial court can allow the defendant to cross-examine on damages in the plaintiff's case-in-chief.

Rule 611(b) provides that when a cross-examiner seeks to go beyond the scope of the direct examination, "[t]he court may allow inquiry into additional matters as if on direct examination." The purport of this sentence is that the cross-examiner who seeks to interrogate on a new matter generally should do so by asking non-leading questions. The assumption is that the cross-examiner typically would not risk getting into new material unless she had an opportunity to do some pretrial preparation with the witness.

Questions Relating to Credibility

The American Rule, of necessity, permits the cross-examiner to ask questions related to a witness's credibility. Questions directed to the credibility (impeachment) of a witness are allowed even if those questions introduce new topics. For example, the examiner may ask the witness whether he holds a grudge against one of the parties, whether he has a financial stake in the outcome of the case, or whether he has been convicted of a kind of crime that raises doubts about his credibility—for example, perjury or fraud.

When a witness is called to testify, the party relying on the witness is asking a trier of fact to believe two things: (1) this is a witness who is credible and can be relied upon, and (2) the facts related by the witness are accurate. The central purpose of cross-examination is to weaken or negate the testimony given during direct examination. Sometimes this is accomplished by demonstrating that the facts to which the witness testifies are incomplete or inaccurate. But another way to cast doubt on the witness's testimony is by suggesting through impeachment that the witness is not a credible person and cannot be trusted to be truthful and accurate. Thus, the credibility of a witness is always implicitly at issue during trial.

The Lay Opinion Rule

We conclude this section with a brief discussion of the "opinion rule" which purportedly forbids a lay witness from giving opinion testimony. (A quite different rule applies to expert witnesses.)[9] The common law rule on lay witness testimony confined the witness to a statement of "facts." The rationale was that it is the jury's responsibility, and not that of the lay witness, to draw inferences from the evidence.

Note that the common law opinion rule is based on a tacit assumption—namely, that once the jury has heard the "bare facts" from the witness, it is in as good a position as the witness to draw reasonable inferences. Sometimes, however, the witness is in a superior position. The modern rule on lay opinion, embodied in Federal Rule 701, recognizes that lay opinions can be helpful to the jury in some instances. It also seeks to avoid the essentially pointless arguments made under common law as to whether the lay witness was testifying to an "opinion" or a "fact." For example, when a witness describes a tree as "gnarled and decaying," is he making a factual statement or is he giving his opinion? There is usually no clear division between the two. The difference, rather, is a matter of degree. Moreover, there are some matters that can't be reduced to a statement of fact—such as, "the bag weighed about 50 pounds." How can that be described in exclusively factual terms?

Federal Rule 701

Rule 701 rejects any rigid rule that prohibits lay witnesses from giving opinions. The question for admissibility is whether the opinion would be helpful to the trier of fact:

Rule 701.   Opinion Testimony by Lay Witnesses

If a witness is not testifying as an expert, testimony in the form of an opinion is limited to one that is:

> **(a)** rationally based on the witness's perception;

> **(b)** helpful to clearly understanding the witness's testimony or to determining a fact in issue; and

---

[9]   *See* Chapter XI for a discussion of expert witness testimony.

> **(c)** not based on scientific, technical, or other specialized knowledge within the scope of Rule 702.

Rule 701 properly recognizes that a lay witness's opinion can be helpful to the factfinder, indeed more helpful at times than the raw data on which the opinion is based. An opinion is often a convenient shorthand device. For example, testimony that a person was "excited" or "angry" is more evocative and understandable than a long, physical description of the person's outward manifestations. On the other hand, if the opinion is unfounded, or if the opinion is in the form of a legal conclusion (e.g., "he is guilty"), it will be excluded as unhelpful.

The more inference-laden and conclusive a witness's statement is, the more likely it is to be unhelpful. When a lay witness testifies, "Fog was so heavy that the cyclist ran off the pavement and lost control," he is stating his opinion as to causation. Would his statement nonetheless be allowed because it would be helpful to the jury? Probably not, although testimony that "the fog was very heavy and it was hard to see" would surely be allowed. The witness should be allowed to describe the conditions—this is helpful because the jury was not there. But it is left to the jury to decide whether lack of visibility caused the cyclist to lose control.

Consider the following statements of opinion:

(1) "When the party ended, Puck appeared to be drunk."

(2) "After several hours of searching for the child, Portia looked exhausted and worried."

(3) "I would say that he was old, probably 75 or more."

(4) "When Henry heard that Paulina had gone out with Duncan, he looked really angry."

(5) "The white Porsche then pulled into the left lane and passed all three cars at a high rate of speed—probably eighty or more miles an hour."

(6) "Yes, I do recognize that handwriting. It is my sister, Lillian's."

Assume that in each of these instances the witness has actually observed the event or condition to which he testified—as is required by Rule 701, which mandates that the witness's testimony must be rationally based on personal perception. Note that in many of these instances, it would be difficult or impossible for the witness to recite the constituent "facts" that underlie his testimony. For example, how can a witness convey her perception of speed without saying the driver was "going fast" or that the driver was going about "eighty miles an hour"? Even when it may be possible to reduce a statement to its underlying components (as, for example, in Illustration (1)), the witness's opinion is still helpful. Testimony that Puck slurred his words and lost his balance on the dance floor helps the jury (and by the way, these are probably opinions rather than facts, anyway). But so, too, does the witness's opinion, formed from his first-hand observation that he (Puck) appeared to be drunk. The reason this opinion is helpful is probably apparent: we often observe other persons as an integral whole, without a distinct awareness of each particular feature or trait. From this kind of observation, we characterize a trait (such as age) or activity (such as speeding). General perceptions and characterizations, such as those noting fear or anger, often aid the jury.

The foregoing testimonial samples are illustrations of allowable lay opinion because, in the words of Federal Rule 701, each is based on "the witness's perception" and each is "helpful to clearly understanding the witness's testimony or to determine a fact in issue." Rule 701 is judicially administered by asking the simple question whether the proffered form of testimony is *helpful*. The administration of the lay opinion rule rests largely in the discretion of the trial judge.

It is important to note that Rule 701 governs only the testimony of a lay witness. The Rule does not apply to a witness whose testimony is "based on scientific, technical, or other specialized knowledge. . . ."[10] Such a witness must be presented and "qualified" as an expert witness. Rule 701(c) was added to the original Rule 701 to emphasize this point. Thus, while a lay witness could testify that a substance on the victim's clothing appeared to be blood, he could not testify that blood loss was the cause of death, as that would be expert testimony.[11] The reason for the limitation in Rule 701 is that parties relying on expert witnesses are required by procedural rules to produce pre-trial disclosures of their experts' qualifications and the bases and methodology that they used to reach their opinions.[12] These requirements should not be evaded by calling a "lay" witness who will really be considered an expert by the factfinder.

§ 2.5 Examining Witnesses: When Memory Fails

Refreshing Recollection

We have already noted that examining counsel may ask leading questions to elicit testimony from a forgetful witness. There is

---

[10] *See* Fed. R. Evid. 702 (expert testimony).

[11] Fed. R. Evid. 701 Advisory Committee's Note (hereinafter ACN) to the 2000 amendment.

[12] *See, e.g.,* Fed. R. Civ. P. 26(a); Fed. R. Crim. P. 16(a).

another courtroom technique that attorneys use to stimulate memory. Counsel may attempt to refresh a witness's memory by showing him some object (usually a writing) or by having him listen to a recording. Indeed *any* object or device—such as a photograph, a map, a song, or even a scent—that will refresh the witness's memory is fair game. The important restriction is that the object or reminder, whatever its nature, serves *only* the purpose of stimulating the witness's recall: the object or device used to refresh recollection is *not* an independent source of evidence. If a witness regains her memory of the event by consulting, say, a writing that describes it, she may continue to testify, but not from the writing. For example, a witness who examines the minutes of a past committee meeting may thereafter recall the committee's discussions and the resulting committee action. However, it is her *testimony* given from restored memory, and not the committee minutes, that constitutes the evidence received. *inadmissible evidence but needed for recall*

The courtroom procedure for refreshing present recollection through the use of a writing or other memory aid often calls upon the trial judge to make a difficult judgment. The problem is most acute when the reminder—for example a writing or recording—describes the event the witness is asked to recall, and is not independently admissible. The judge must determine whether the witness's recollection has actually been refreshed or, alternatively, whether she is in fact merely reciting the contents of the writing or other memorial that she is consulting—in which case the party is engineering the introduction of hearsay through the guise of refreshing recollection. You should not be surprised that judges often have difficulty knowing whether a witness is testifying from memory of events or memory only of what was used to refresh recollection. When in doubt, judges often rely upon cross-examination (discussed below) to challenge a claim of refreshed memory and leave to the jury the determination of whether the witness has a genuine memory of events.

If the judge rules that the witness's recollection has not been restored, then of course her testimony cannot constitute the evidence received. The actual evidence is the reminder itself. For now, let us assume that the witness's present recollection is refreshed. The object used to refresh recollection, which has been marked as an exhibit and shown to opposing counsel, has served its purpose. The examining lawyer is not entitled to admit it into evidence, but she may, of course, continue to elicit testimony based upon the witness's restored memory.

At the end of the direct examination, opposing counsel may use the memory aid in conducting cross-examination and may try to show that the witness's present recollection is faulty, for example by demonstrating that she cannot recall important details contained in the writing. The cross-examiner may also expose discrepancies between the witness's testimony and the writing, raising a question about which is accurate. Finally, the cross-examiner may introduce into evidence the item used to refresh recollection. The limited purpose of this evidence is to allow the jury to compare it with the witness's testimony. Technically, the item may be used only for "impeachment" purposes, that is, to cast doubt on the witness's testimony.

Federal Rule 612

Rule 612 of the Federal Rules of Evidence is pertinent to the present discussion. It provides:

Writing Used to Refresh a Witness's Memory

(a) Scope. This rule gives an adverse party certain options when a witness uses a writing to refresh memory:

(1) while testifying; or

(2) before testifying, if the court decides that justice requires the party to have those options.

(b) Adverse Party's Options; Deleting Unrelated Matter. Unless [the Jencks Act[13]] provides otherwise in a criminal case, an adverse party is entitled to have the writing produced at the hearing, to inspect it, to cross-examine the witness about it, and to introduce in evidence any portion that relates to the witness's testimony. * * *

Under these provisions, there is no absolute right to compel production of a writing used to refresh a witness's memory *prior* to his courtroom appearance, but neither is such a writing invariably protected from disclosure. Access to the writing previously used to refresh recollection lies within the judge's discretion, influenced by such factors as the importance of the "refreshed" testimony and the nature of the document used to refresh. Rule 612 reflects a judgment that in view of other means, notably discovery, available to parties to gain access to pertinent materials in the adversary's hands, it suffices to leave to the judge's discretion the question whether the opponent is entitled to a writing used as a memory aid prior to trial. (Note that the presumption of access to information used to refresh recollection

---

13   The Jencks Act, 18 U.S.C.A. § 3500 (1970), gives the accused the right to inspect written or recorded statements of any prosecution witness—after the witness has testified on direct examination—if the statement has been adopted by the witness or if the statement is essentially a verbatim recording of the witness's prior oral statement. The Act does not apply unless the statement deals with the subject matter of the prosecution witness's testimony.

prior to trial is significantly weaker in criminal cases, where pre-trial discovery is limited—this counsels in favor of the judge allowing the adversary to inspect the underlying information under Rule 612.)

Past Recollection Recorded ʜɛɑʀˢɑᵥ ɛxɕɛρʀiᴏʀ 803 (5)

Let us now suppose that neither leading questions nor the use of a writing (or other stimulus) results in restoring memory. In other words, counsel's attempts to "refresh present recollection" have failed. Suppose, further, that the examiner has in his possession a writing (or other recording) prepared at an earlier time by the very witness on the stand. This setting raises the possibility of introducing into evidence the witness's prior statement describing the event that the examiner wishes to prove.

As you will more fully appreciate when we reach the chapter on hearsay, the difficulty with introducing this writing lies in the disadvantage suffered by the *cross-examiner*. As we will see, hearsay evidence is generally excluded (there are many exceptions) because the cross-examiner cannot test the credibility of the out-of-court speaker (the "declarant"). The declarant's statements are revealed to the trier of fact either through the testimony of a witness who heard them or by the introduction of a record, often a writing, that contains the declarations. If Davy tells Warwick that "Puck shot Victim," and Warwick so testifies in an effort to prove Puck was the assailant, a hearsay issue arises. Puck's lawyer wants to cross-examine the declarant, Davy, the person who actually observed the shooting. (Davy may be mistaken or lying.) The same hearsay problem arises if Davy's diary contains the accusation "Puck shot the victim" and the diary is introduced by the prosecutor. Only the author of the diary entry (Davy) can provide adequate responses to the cross-examiner's questions.

Now suppose Davy *is on the stand* but he simply cannot recall whether Puck or Peter or someone else fired at the victim. In other words, he has no present recollection of the event. Suppose, however, Davy is able to testify that he keeps a diary and that he made an accurate entry in his diary soon after the shooting in question, when his memory was fresh. In short, he can give testimony vouching for *the accuracy of the entry* even though he cannot recall the event it describes. The point is that Davy's testimony gives his earlier, out-of-court statement added credibility—and moreover he is on the stand subject to cross-examination about the record and its accuracy. The first key to admissibility is that the witness's past recollection has been preserved in a writing or some other recorded form (hence the descriptive label "past recollection recorded" or simply "recorded recollection"). The second key to admissibility is that the witness is able to testify that he recognizes the writing or other recording, that he recalls making it (or adopting it if it was prepared by another) soon after the event in question when his memory was fresh, and that he believes the earlier recorded statements are accurate.

The difference between present recollection refreshed and past recollection recorded should now be apparent. In the first setting, the witness's testimony is the actual evidence; in the second setting, the past recording is the actual evidence—the witness's testimony serves only to qualify the record for admissibility.

Federal Rule 803(5)

The key features of past recollection recorded are set out as an exception to the rule against admitting hearsay in Federal Rule of Evidence 803(5):

(5) ***Recorded Recollection.*** A record that:

(A) is on a matter the witness once knew about but now cannot recall well enough to testify fully and accurately;

(B) was made or adopted by the witness when the matter was fresh in the witness's memory; and

(C) accurately reflects the witness's knowledge.

If admitted, the record may be read into evidence but may be received as an exhibit only if offered by an adverse party.

A "recorded recollection" escapes the hearsay bar if the witness on the stand can testify that the statements in the prior recording were accurate when made, and were made or adopted by him when his memory was fresh. Note that the Rule permits the recorded recollection to be read into evidence but not received as an exhibit for the proponent. The reason is obvious: recorded recollection is no better (and perhaps not as good in many instances) as trial testimony; trial testimony is presented orally to the jury and not in writing, and there is no reason to give the jury a written version of recorded recollection given the risk that a writing might appear to be more weighty than oral testimony.

The witness need not have a total memory failure for recorded recollection to be admitted. Rule 803(5) requires only that the record "is on a matter the witness once knew about but now cannot recall well enough to testify fully and accurately."

Of course, the fact that the writing or other recording is admitted into evidence simply means that the trier may consider it along with all of the other evidence in the case. The trier—let us say the jury— might decide that Davy was mistaken when he recorded in his diary that Puck shot the victim. All trials, of course, have conflicting evidence and, ultimately, the trier must decide which portions of the evidence to believe.[14]

§ 2.6   Role of Judge and Jury: An Overview

Generally speaking, the jury decides questions of fact (including witness credibility) and the judge resolves questions of law. The rationale for such a division is clear: the judge, through training and experience, is particularly qualified to resolve legal questions, while the jurors, who bring to the courtroom the common experience of the community, are equipped to settle factual disputes. This general rule has several qualifications, however.

The first qualification to this general statement of functions is that the jury discharges its fact-finding role only in those cases where the state of the evidence reasonably justifies a finding in favor of either party. If from the evidence there is no *reasonable* dispute as to the pertinent facts, the judge may use an instruction, judgment as a matter of law, or some other appropriate procedural device to discourage or prevent the jury from making any finding contrary to the overwhelming, conclusive evidence. In civil cases, the judge's intervention may take the whole case from the jury or only a portion of it. In criminal cases, the judge may grant a judgment of acquittal in whole or in part; but the judge cannot prevent the jury from acquitting a defendant no matter how strong the government's evidence—because granting a verdict for the government would violate the accused's Sixth Amendment right to a jury trial.[15]

A second qualification to the allocation of judge-jury responsibility arises when, in rendering a general verdict, the jury applies a general legal standard (as described in the judge's charge) to the particular facts of the case. That is, the jury first determines the facts and then applies the applicable substantive law. In some instances, notably where community values and standards are particularly important, the substantive law is phrased in very general terms. A defendant is negligent, for example, if he fails to "act reasonably" or does not exercise "due care." Similarly, an employer is liable for his employee's conduct only if the employee was acting in the "scope of employment" and "scope" is determined in the context of each case. In cases like these, when the applicable law is expressed as a *general legal standard*, the jury must not only find the facts, but must also *characterize* or label these facts in light of the

---

[14]   Rule 803(5) is discussed again in Chapter VII at § 7.6.

[15]   *See, e.g.,* Fed. R. Civ. P. 50(a) (permitting judgment as a matter of law in civil cases); Fed. R. Crim. P. 29(a) (motion for judgment of acquittal). *See also Sullivan v. Louisiana,* 508 U.S. 275 (1993) (recognizing that trial judges are constitutionally prohibited from directing a verdict against an accused).

indeterminate standard.[16] In a sense, the jurors are giving substantive, particularized content to the legal principle involved by construing it in the context of the specific facts before them.

The judge, too, assumes functions that vary from the more familiar task of deciding questions of law. There are numerous occasions when she makes factual determinations. In the pre-trial process, the judge resolves factual questions pertaining to the jurisdiction of the court over the subject matter or over the parties. For example, in determining whether the court has personal jurisdiction over the defendant, the judge resolves any factual dispute that arises with respect to the defendant's activities or "contacts" with the forum state. The judge also settles factual disputes that may arise in connection with discovery proceedings. She resolves, for example, factual disagreements associated with issues concerning whether a privilege protects materials from discovery, or whether a party has intentionally destroyed information that would otherwise be subject to discovery. Furthermore, in the course of a (pre-trial) summary judgment proceeding or at a pre-trial conference, she determines which, if any, factual issues are reasonably in dispute. Even after a jury trial commences, the judge monitors the evidence and, as already noted, removes from jury consideration in civil cases and against the government in criminal cases any factual determinations that in light of the evidence before the jury could rationally be resolved in only one way.

Judge's Fact-Finding Role in Applying the Rules of Evidence

The judge also plays an important fact-finding role in administering the rules of evidence. Rules of evidence often require proof of a foundational fact before evidence can be admitted. The judge determines whether these foundational facts have been proved. For example, the "Best Evidence Rule"[17] states that when proving the terms of a writing, the original document must be produced unless it is destroyed or is otherwise unavailable. Suppose the proponent claims that the original was destroyed or lost, but the opponent contests this assertion, thus raising a factual dispute. The judge

---

[16]   There are control devices, including summary judgment, jury instructions, and judgment as a matter of law (directed verdict), that can be used to limit the jury's characterization. These devices ensure that the jury is not allowed to reach an irrational characterization of the conduct in question. For example, it would be irrational to characterize as negligent a hazardous, but correctly performed, surgical procedure if it were the only known means of saving the patient's life and the patient was fully informed of the risks involved. Nonetheless, substantial latitude is inherent in such imprecise terms as "reasonable" and "scope," and if the facts as well as the issue of reasonableness or due care are disputed, the jury's verdict normally is decisive.

[17]   See Fed. R. Evid. 1002, 1004.

makes the preliminary factual determination necessary to apply the rule of evidence—it can't be left to the jury, because the foundational facts are not necessarily probative of any ultimate question that the jury has to decide, so the risk of jury confusion over a collateral factual matter would be great. And if the jury is told that the reason for determining the foundational fact is so that evidence can be heard, then it is likely to find the foundational fact in order to be able to hear the evidence.

In some instances, the judge determines preliminary factual issues that relate to, but are distinct from, the events being litigated. (For example, the judge decides whether the proffered witness is an expert on, say, the subject of ballistics and is thus able to give testimony on this specialized topic.) In other instances, the judge determines preliminary factual issues that are closely associated with the litigated events. A striking example is the factual determinations a judge must make when ruling on the hearsay exception for "dying declarations." In a prosecution for murder, the victim's dying declarations pertaining to the cause or circumstances of her impending death are admissible over a hearsay objection[18] if she spoke while firmly holding the belief that she was about to die.[19] (The theory is that, facing death, she would be unlikely to lie or falsely accuse.) Whether she spoke with the sense of "impending death" and whether her statement addressed "the cause or circumstances" of her death are preliminary facts determined by the judge.

ILLUSTRATION

Just after a private aircraft touches the runway while landing, it lurches sharply to the left and crashes into an airliner that is awaiting take-off on an adjacent runway. Peter, a passenger on the waiting airliner, observes these events through the window next to his seat. Fifteen minutes later, Peter, who sustained minor injuries in the collision, relates what he saw to Airport Investigator. At a subsequent trial in which both the owner and pilot of the out-of-control aircraft are defendants, Investigator is called to the stand to testify as to what Peter told him. Defense counsel objects to Investigator's testimony about Peter's remarks, arguing that the proffered evidence is hearsay. The plaintiff's lawyer argues that Investigator's testimony falls within an exception to the hearsay rule that allows into

---

[18]   The hearsay problem arises because the opponent who seeks to have this evidence excluded cannot cross-examine the deceased victim, whose statements are likely to incriminate the accused.

[19]   Fed. R. Evid. 804(b)(2).

evidence "excited utterances."[20] Out of the jury's hearing, plaintiff presents evidence indicating that Peter spoke while in a state of excitement and shock—a state that was produced by witnessing the accident and being jolted and injured himself. Defense counsel produces rebuttal evidence that when Peter made his statements, fifteen minutes after the accident, he had regained his composure.

The rule of evidence governing this hypothetical permits the introduction of hearsay statements that relate to the event being litigated, if the person (the "declarant") making the statements spoke *while in a state of excitement, shock, or stress caused by the event.* (The theory is that under these circumstances, the declarant would be unlikely to deceive or lie.) The judge decides the disputed factual question whether Peter was under a continuous state of excitement between the time of the event and the time of the statement. Note that this preliminary fact closely relates to the events being litigated—the crash, its cause, and the results.

JUDGE DECIDES IF EXCITED

WHY

Why do we allocate to the judge the task of deciding preliminary facts that are integrally linked to the application of a rule of evidence? We do so primarily because it would be impractical and unwise to assign these factual questions to the jury. The typical juror is uninterested in the technicalities of the rules of evidence and their underlying policies; usually she simply wants to find out all she can about the case. Moreover, as we have observed, these preliminary facts are often closely linked to the very evidence in dispute, so that deciding the preliminary facts requires consideration of the disputed evidence. Consider, for example, the two rules of evidence that, respectively, admit dying declarations and excited utterances if certain conditions—that is, certain preliminary facts—exist. To make an informed, intelligent decision about preliminary facts, the decision-maker needs to consider the content of the dying declaration or of the excited utterance. (Recall that, to be admissible, dying declarations must *pertain to the cause or circumstances* surrounding the impending death; excited utterances must *relate to* the exciting event.) A juror would find it impossible, as a practical matter, to ignore the very statements in question once these statements were revealed as part of a preliminary fact-finding process. Thus, even if the evidence turned out to be inadmissible, the jury would be likely to rely on it.

Federal Rule 104(a)

Rule 104 of the Federal Rules of Evidence is captioned "Preliminary Questions." It provides in part:

---

[20]   Fed. R. Evid. 803(2).

(a) In General. The court must decide any preliminary question about whether a witness is qualified, a privilege exists, or evidence is admissible. In so deciding, the court is not bound by evidence rules, except those on privilege.

Rule 104(a) assigns important fact-finding responsibilities to the judge. Note also the last sentence of subsection (a), which frees the judge from the usual rules of evidence when she is deciding a preliminary fact. (The only exception is for rules of privilege, which are designed to prevent *any* coerced disclosure of the protected information.) We noted in Chapter I that a principal reason for the creation of rules of evidence is the existence of the lay jury; we also noted that the rules are not strictly enforced in trials to the bench.[21] Because the judge presumably understands the possible deficiencies in "inadmissible" evidence, she can take account of these weaknesses when she is determining preliminary facts. So the normal evidentiary rules are suspended by operation of Rule 104(a) when the judge is finding preliminary facts. In short, we trust the judge to make a reliable determination of preliminary facts, even though she considers evidence that is technically "inadmissible."

The standard of proof that the judge must apply in determining preliminary matters of admissibility is *a preponderance of the evidence*.[22] Thus, in our Illustration, the judge will not admit the airplane passenger's hearsay statement as an excited utterance unless the proponent of the statement proves to the judge's satisfaction that it is more likely than not that the passenger was still under the influence of the startling event at the time he made the statement. ILUSTRATION ~NIWUV.

§ 2.7 Shortcuts to Proof: Judicial Notice and Other Devices

Judicial Notice

In certain limited circumstances, counsel can invoke the doctrine of judicial notice to avoid the need for formal proof of a relevant fact. Courts will take judicial notice of facts that are beyond reasonable dispute, but that would have to be proved by one side (assuming no stipulation or admission by the adversary). Because these facts would normally be decided by a jury, they are often labeled "adjudicative facts" or "historical facts."

---

[21] *See* Chapter I, at n. 1.

[22] *See Bourjaily v. United States*, 483 U.S. 171, 175–76 (1987) (admissibility requirements determined by the trial court under Rule 104(a) by a preponderance of the evidence).

The core feature of judicial notice is the uniformly recognized requirement that this evidentiary device applies only to those adjudicative facts that, in the language of Federal Rule 201(a), are "not subject to reasonable dispute." It is helpful to think of two general categories of facts that are likely to be beyond reasonable dispute. The first category consists of facts either *widely known* throughout the country or widely known to persons living in the area where the court taking judicial notice is located. The winner of the World Series, an economic depression, or the location of the United States Capitol are examples of facts likely to be widely known throughout the country. And facts such as the area of a city where local government is housed, the main subway routes, the streets and highways that are likely to be congested during rush hours, and the general seasonal weather patterns are examples of local facts likely to be widely known in the vicinity where the court sits.

The second category of facts that are likely to be beyond reasonable dispute are those which can be *accurately determined* by consulting reliable sources such as maps, charts, tables, and reliable internet sites in such varied fields as engineering, biology, medicine, history, mathematics, astronomy, physics, and so forth. This second category consists of facts that are unlikely to be widely known but which—in the words of Federal Rule 201(b)—"can be accurately and readily determined from sources whose credibility cannot reasonably be questioned." For example, a court might consult a reliable source to determine the tides or the depth of a body of water. Similarly, a court might consult an appropriate reference to determine the effective date of a treaty and whether one of the signatories was at war when the treaty became effective. Another example: a court could consult Googlemaps to determine the location of a certain business.

When Judicial Notice Is Conclusive

Recall that a jury's role is to decide pertinent facts that the parties to the suit reasonably dispute. In other words, the jury deals with factual disputes that, on the basis of the admitted evidence, could reasonably be resolved in favor of either party. Because judicial notice is taken only of those facts that are not subject to reasonable dispute, it would seem to follow that once a fact is judicially noticed, the jury is bound by the court's action and cannot make a contrary finding. In civil cases, the jury is so bound and, accordingly, the judge will instruct the jury to accept the judicially noticed fact as conclusive.

In a criminal trial to a jury, however, the Constitution requires the government to prove each element to the *jury's* satisfaction. The judge is without power to direct a verdict of guilty *against* the accused, even if the evidence points strongly toward his guilt. This prohibition in criminal jury trials has led to a modification of the usual approach to judicial notice. Under Federal Rule of Evidence 201(f), a fact that is judicially noticed is conclusive *except* in criminal jury trials. In these proceedings, the judge takes judicial notice but then instructs the jury that it "may or may not accept the noticed fact as conclusive."

A court *may* take judicial notice of a fact on its own motion. Under Federal Rule 201(c)(2) a court *must* take judicial notice of an appropriate fact "if requested by a party and supplied with the necessary information." Of course, counsel may disagree on whether judicial notice is proper. Under Federal Rule 201(e), a party is entitled "to be heard on the propriety of taking judicial notice and the nature of the fact to be noticed." For example, the attorney opposing judicial notice may argue that the fact proffered for the court's notice is neither widely known nor verifiable through reliable sources. The judge makes the final decision as to the propriety of judicial notice, using as a guide the "indisputability" standard of Rule 201(b).

Legislative Facts

Federal Rule of Evidence 201 deals only with judicial notice of "adjudicative facts" which are the facts that collectively make up the litigated event—that is, those facts that deal with the contested occurrence. So-called "legislative facts," by contrast, are related to the disputed transaction but only in the sense that they constitute the context or background in which the case at hand arose and will be resolved. A particular labor dispute, for example, may arise in the context of depressed prices, high unemployment, widespread labor unrest, and an economy that is in transition from wartime to peacetime. An injury to a professional football player during a game may arise in the larger context of the combative nature and physical demands of professional football.

Courts necessarily make determinations or assumptions about the context or environment in which the case arose and in which the law declared by the court will be applied. These determinations or assumptions often influence the way a court interprets a statute or crafts a judge-made rule of law. A well-known example of judicial notice of legislative facts is the Supreme Court's consultation of sociological studies in *Brown v. Board of Education*[23] as part of its effort to determine the deleterious effects upon children of segregated public schools. The point is that courts, and particularly appellate courts (which have some latitude to modify legal rules) often need to acquaint themselves with the factual context in which the legal rule controlling the case before them will operate.

---

[23]   347 U.S. 483, 494 (1954).

The standard that courts use when they "find" or "notice" legislative facts is not the beyond-reasonable-dispute standard that applies to the judicial notice of adjudicative facts. Although we have no definitive answer to the question of what less restrictive standard does apply, it is very likely a standard of probability—that is, based on the available information, it is at least probable that the setting in which the case arose and in which this legal rule will operate has the characteristics identified by the court. For example, a court might conclude that the labor dispute before the court occurred "in a coal mining labor environment, where unemployment is very high, and strikes have been frequent and often violent."

Lawyers sometime make arguments in their briefs that draw upon legislative facts. This argumentative technique has a distinguished pedigree. In a famous case,[24] attorney (later Supreme Court Justice) Louis Brandeis successfully argued that a state could constitutionally restrict the number of hours women were allowed to work. Almost the entirety of his "Brandeis Brief" was devoted to medical and empirical evidence that showed the harmful effects on women of working long hours. Brandeis's ground-breaking brief introduced a mode of appellate argument that continues today. But the use of facts in such a brief does not present an evidentiary question and is not governed by the rules of evidence.

Legislative facts should not turn on the identity of the parties. They should be applicable to any dispute in which they might be relevant. It should be apparent, however, that over time courts might well decide that earlier judgments about the reliability of legislative facts must give way to new information, particularly where there are scientific, technical or other advances in knowledge.

---

[24]   *Muller v. Oregon*, 208 U.S. 412, 419 (1908).

Chapter III

RELEVANCE: GENERAL PRINCIPLES AND SPECIAL APPLICATIONS

Table of Sections

§ 3.1 Basic Concepts

Relevance is the basic principle underlying all of the evidentiary rules. The threshold test of admissibility is the test of relevance; if evidence is not relevant, it is not admissible.[1] Because the fundamental principle of relevance pervades the law of evidence, it serves as both the dominant and unifying theme.

---

[1] Fed. R. Evid. 402. Despite the language of Rule 402, a failure to object to irrelevant evidence usually will result in its admission. This is true of all the exclusionary provisions of the Federal Rules; evidence that must be excluded upon proper objection generally will be admitted when no proper objection is made. As we move forward, when we say certain evidence is inadmissible, we shall assume a proper objection is made.

Under the Federal Rules, Rule 401 defines the term "relevant" evidence. Rule 402 then provides that relevant evidence is admissible unless it is excluded by some other national procedural rule, statute, or the Constitution; it also makes explicit that if evidence is irrelevant, it is inadmissible. Rule 403 provides that even if evidence is relevant, it can be excluded if its probative value is substantially outweighed by the risks of unfair prejudice, jury confusion or undue delay.

The Definition of "Relevant" Evidence

What is meant by the term "relevant evidence?" In its simplest form, relevant evidence helps prove the existence (or nonexistence) of some fact that is pertinent to a legal dispute between parties. Drawing upon an observation of reformer and philosopher Jeremy Bentham, we can say that the effect of relevant evidence "when presented to the mind, is to produce a persuasion concerning the existence of some . . . matter of fact—a persuasion either affirmative or disaffirmative of its existence."[2] Of course, all evidence tends to prove or disprove *some* fact, but not all facts are relevant to a legal dispute. In a judicial trial, the substantive law determines those facts that have pertinent (*i.e.*, legal) consequences. Thus, evidence that a defendant charged with statutory rape reasonably believed that the person with whom he had sexual relations was above the age of consent is irrelevant in a jurisdiction that makes statutory rape a strict liability crime. The same evidence is relevant in a different jurisdiction in which a reasonable mistake as to age is a defense.

The purpose for which evidence is offered also has an impact on a relevance analysis. For example, evidence that V, the victim of a robbery, consumed four martinis during the hour before he was robbed tends to show he was intoxicated at the time he was victimized. And this fact—V's intoxication during the robbery—is relevant to prove that V's ability to identify the robber might have been impaired by the intoxication. Accordingly, if the defense seeks to offer evidence of the intoxication to prove impairment, a court would admit the evidence for that purpose.

The law rejects irrelevant evidence for several reasons. First, the exclusion of irrelevant evidence advances the goal of efficiency: it is wasteful to receive evidence that has no proper bearing on the case. Second, the exclusion of irrelevant evidence advances the objective of unbiased factfinding within the requirements of the substantive law: although irrelevant evidence does not logically assist the trier of fact

---

[2]   JEREMY BENTHAM, RATIONALE OF JUDICIAL EVIDENCE, SPECIALLY APPLIED TO ENGLISH PRACTICE 16 (1827).

in resolving *pertinent* factual issues, it may nonetheless pose a risk that the trier will use that evidence inappropriately.

Consider a statutory rape case involving an intoxicated victim. If the trier of fact strongly disapproved of excessive drinking, it might express that disapproval by acquitting *D*, the defendant, even if the relevant evidence tended to show that *D* was guilty of statutory rape. Suppose, for example, the intoxicated victim appeared at a fraternity party at a college even though she was still a high school student. The trier could believe that the victim "brought it on herself" by drink-induced imprudence, and refuse to convict *D*. The potential for this sort of misuse is precisely why irrelevant evidence is excluded. (Even some evidence that is relevant is sometimes excluded due to its potential for inflaming the jury or otherwise causing undue prejudice.) There is also a risk of jury confusion or incorrect determination if irrelevant evidence is admitted. Many jurors probably assume that everything they hear in the case has some bearing on the disputed facts. If some evidence does not, the juror will likely be confused and, even worse might well try to shoehorn the evidence into the case in some misguided or inappropriate way.

In sum, irrelevant evidence cannot assist a trier in reaching a sound, unbiased decision in a case. But such evidence can distort factfinding and undermine confidence that a verdict was fairly determined.

Definition of Relevant Evidence: Federal Rule 401

Federal Rule of Evidence 401 defines relevant evidence as follows:

TEST FOR RELEVANT EVIDENCE

Evidence is relevant if:

(a) it has any tendency to make a fact more or less probable than it would be without the evidence; and

(b) the fact is of consequence in determining the action.

Although we may loosely think of relevant evidence as that which "tends to persuade," it is important to note that the principle of relevance embodies two distinct relationships. First, relevance connotes the *probative relationship* between the *evidence proffered* and the *factual proposition* to which that evidence is addressed. In other words, one aspect of relevance is concerned with whether proffered evidence is logically probative of the proposition toward which it is directed.

Assume that a defendant is charged with an armed robbery committed by someone carrying a handgun. The prosecution wants to offer into evidence testimony that the defendant owned a handgun prior to the time the robbery was committed. Defendant claims the evidence is irrelevant, because lots of people have guns and it doesn't mean that they use them for robberies. Certainly this evidence, standing alone, is insufficient to prove that the defendant committed the crime; there are many innocent explanations. But it is a piece of evidence making it somewhat more likely that the defendant committed the crime than if there were no such evidence. The fair inference is that a person with a gun is more likely to commit an armed robbery than a person without a gun. Therefore the gun possession is relevant. A probative relationship between the gun and robbery is all that is required for the evidence to be relevant. Relevance does not require a more probable than not or a beyond a reasonable doubt relationship.

The second aspect of relevance is concerned with whether the factual proposition to which the evidence is directed is *consequential* under the substantive law. A fact is consequential only if it helps to prove (or disprove) an element of a charge, claim, or defense. We have seen an example of the importance of focusing on the substantive law of a jurisdiction in the previous discussion of statutory rape.

Determining Consequential Facts

Determining what facts are of consequence involves a careful analysis of the substantive law that applies to a particular case. The only factual propositions that legitimately govern the outcome of a lawsuit are those that constitute the elements of a criminal or civil charge, claim, or defense. Therefore, evidence is of consequence (or, under the older common law terminology, "material")[3] only if it tends to establish the existence or nonexistence of an element of the controlling substantive law. We dealt with an example of this in the previous discussion of statutory rape. Some additional examples should shed more light on consequential facts.

Suppose that in a suit filed by Prospero against Duncan for assault and battery, Duncan offers evidence that he mistakenly thought Prospero was another person, Puck. This evidence should be rejected if the factual proposition to which it is directed—mistaken identity—is of no legal consequence under the substantive law governing the case. In other words, if the law of intentional torts

---

[3]   At common law, the objection "irrelevant" addressed the probative relationship between the evidence proffered and the factual proposition to which that evidence is addressed, while the objection "immaterial" generally meant that the proffered evidence bore no relationship to the legal issues raised by the substantive law made applicable by the pleadings. Thus, common law lawyers would often object that evidence was irrelevant and immaterial to assure that their objection covered both aspects of relevancy. Today, an objection under Rule 401 that evidence is irrelevant covers both common law concepts.

imposes the same liability notwithstanding this kind of mistake, the judge should declare this evidence irrelevant.

Another example involves a suit against Davy for breach of a contract to build a walkway. Evidence that Davy had two illegitimate children would seem irrelevant in such a case in every jurisdiction. The principal elements necessary to recover for breach of contract are: (1) existence of valid contract; (2) plaintiff's performance of all conditions precedent; and (3) defendant's breach or non-performance. The fact Davy had two illegitimate children is unrelated to any of these three elements.

To summarize: evidence is relevant only if it, (1) tends to prove or disprove a proposition of fact that, (2) is of consequence under the substantive law that applies to the case. Bear in mind that even if evidence strongly supports a factual proposition, the judge (on objection) will reject the evidence unless the proposition is "of consequence" to the lawsuit in which the evidence is offered.

Fundamental Principles of Relevance

To illustrate the fundamental principles of relevance, consider a hypothetical posed by Professor Arthur Best: plaintiff sues the owner of an office building on the theory that inadequate maintenance of the lobby caused the plaintiff's injuries.[4] Three items of evidence are proffered:

(1) The office building is one story taller than permitted by the applicable zoning regulations;

(2) The lobby, once painted pink, was recently repainted yellow;

(3) The lobby was dimly lit.

Of these, only the third item is directed to a fact of consequence. In order to state a valid claim, the plaintiff must allege, among other things, that a hazardous condition was the proximate cause of her injuries. The excessive height of the building would be relevant in a dispute over a zoning violation, but has nothing to do with the maintenance of the lobby. Similarly, the color of the lobby probably has no bearing on its maintenance with respect to safety.[5] On the other hand, dim lighting does have a tendency to point toward an unsafe or hazardous condition and might show, for example, that lobby users could not see a step or a loose tile. Thus, because the evidence about lighting is offered to show that there was an unsafe

---

4　ARTHUR BEST, EVIDENCE 3 (5th ed. 2004).

5　If, however, the plaintiff's theory was that the yellow paint was so distracting that it resulted in the plaintiff's missing a step on a stairs, the paint color would be relevant.

condition in the lobby, it meets the definition of relevant evidence under Federal Rule of Evidence 401.

"Background" Evidence

Although evidence must normally be consequential under the substantive law, background evidence, having little or no consequence to the law governing the case, is routinely admitted. In order to convey fully the "story of a case" to the trier of fact—that is, to permit the jury or judge trying the case to comprehend fully and contextually the consequential facts that gave rise to the lawsuit—it is almost always necessary to present background information. For example, in the suit discussed above for failure to properly maintain the interior of an office building lobby, testimony that the lobby "is on the west side of the building and is entered from Chancellor Street by either a revolving door or a handicap ramp" might not have a tendency to affect the probability of any consequential fact. Nonetheless, evidentiary facts of this sort are usually admitted. The reason is that this kind of background evidence *aids the jury's understanding* of the evidence that is "relevant." It is also something that the jury would expect in the telling of any story, and failure to meet juror expectations is a bad idea.

Similarly, incidental (background) evidence about a witness may be admissible to provide context for the factfinder. Such details as the witness's address, occupation, or marital status may come into evidence simply as contextual information. And of course evidence about a witness may sometimes bear strongly on a consequential fact and thus easily satisfy the definition of relevance. For example, evidence that a witness has poor vision or impaired hearing might affect the jury's assessment of her account of the litigated event. Evidence that the witness has abnormal hearing or vision has a tendency to reduce the trier's belief in the existence of those facts of consequence to which the witness testifies. Evidence directed to the credibility of a witness bears on the trier's assessment of the truth or accuracy of her account of consequential facts, and thus is relevant because it has a tendency to make such facts more or less probable.

Relevance and Sufficiency

There is an important difference between the relevancy of evidence and the *sufficiency* of evidence. For example, suppose that in April a prison guard, *V-1*, is murdered and that in May another guard, *V-2*, is murdered. The investigation by authorities intensifies and, in late May, *D*, a prisoner, tries to escape from prison. In a subsequent trial for the murder of *V-1* in which *D* is named the accused, is *D's* attempted escape relevant?

Clearly the evidence of an escape attempt does not establish the accused's guilt—people try to escape from prison for any number of reasons, most commonly because they hate prison and don't want to be there anymore. However, it is the totality of evidence introduced that must be sufficient to justify a finding of guilt. A single item of evidence is relevant if it has *any* tendency to increase (or decrease) the probability of a consequential factual proposition. It is not even necessary to demonstrate that it is *more probable* that escape was motivated by the fear of detection in connection with *V-1's* murder than by other possible motives, such as feared detection in connection with *V-2's* murder or the simple desire to gain freedom. The question is whether the probability that the accused committed the murder for which he is on trial is to some degree increased by evidence that he attempted to escape.[6] If so, the evidence is relevant and it should be considered along with other circumstantial evidence (such as fingerprints, blood stains, and the like) in determining whether the defendant is guilty beyond a reasonable doubt.[7] It is then up to the jury to determine whether all the proffered relevant evidence, considered as a whole, is sufficient to convict. → *sufficiency* .

Common Sense Assessment

The foregoing examples suggest that the test of probative value is derived from commonplace experience. That is, the test usually involves no more than a common sense determination whether proffered evidence reveals events or conditions that increase or decrease the likelihood of other, associated, events or conditions. In the words of an early evidence scholar, Professor James Bradley Thayer, relevance is an "affair of experience and logic, and not at all of law."[8] Common observation teaches that if one fled the scene of a crime, his guilt is made somewhat more probable than it would be in the absence of flight. Similarly, human experience indicates that if one had a motive for murder, it is more probable that he murdered than it would be if no motive existed. The touchstone of relevance, at least in the first sense—probative value—is therefore the presence of a logical experience-based relationship between the evidence and the ultimate proposition to which it is directed. Of course, this logical relation may be established not only by common observation, but by the principles governing probabilities in specialized disciplines, such

---

6   One piece of relevant evidence might bolster the significance of another piece of relevant evidence. For example, suppose that *D's* attempted escape occurred one day after *D* was indicted for the murder of *V-1*. The timing of the indictment and the escape attempt might make it more likely that a jury would find a connection between the murder and the escape.

7   As you will see, however, the judge may exclude relevant evidence if other considerations, such as prejudice or jury confusion, substantially outweigh the probative value of the evidence.

8   JAMES THAYER, A PRELIMINARY TREATISE ON EVIDENCE 269 (1898).

as statistics, science, medicine, architecture, or engineering. In these latter instances, an expert witness might be called to testify to the probabilities or other causal relationships within the specialized field. The trier of fact, however, ultimately determines the probative force of even technical or "scientific" evidence.

Summary

Here, then, are the simple core principles of relevance, the unifying theme of evidence law:

- In order to meet the first part of the relevance test, counsel's proffered evidence must tend to increase or decrease (*i.e.*, affect) the likelihood of the fact to which it is directed. This tendency test is very mild. *Any* tendency to decrease or increase the probability is all that is required.

- In order to meet the second part of the relevance test, the fact to which counsel's proffered evidence is directed must be a *consequential* fact, that is, a fact placed in dispute by the substantive law governing the case. (Although these basic principles are denominated "first" and "second" the order of their application does not, of course, make any difference.)

§ 3.2   Exclusionary Counterweights

Federal Rule 402 provides that relevant evidence is admissible, unless otherwise provided by the Constitution, a federal statute, other Evidence Rules, or other rules of procedure prescribed by the Supreme Court. It is helpful to think of relevant evidence as "presumptively admissible," that is, admissible unless excluded by some other applicable evidentiary provision found in the Federal Rules or elsewhere. There are many such exclusionary provisions, including the rule against hearsay, and many of these provisions (particularly those found in the Federal Rules themselves) are quite specific. For example, evidence that one party to a suit offered to settle the case is generally inadmissible to prove the validity or amount of a claim.[9] The theory is that a party who offers a compromise should not be penalized (by evidence that he did not stand firmly behind his initial claim or defense) for his attempt to resolve the dispute. The law favors compromise agreements and the law of evidence is crafted to encourage offers of compromise.

Of course, the United States Constitution, and particularly exclusionary rules associated with the Fourth, Fifth and Sixth

---

[9]   *See* Fed. R. Evid. 408. The rule contains limited exceptions to the general prohibition. *See generally infra*, Chapter IV, § 4.3.

Amendments, might render relevant evidence inadmissible. The study of those constitutional rules of exclusion is fully explored in texts dealing with criminal procedure.[10] Statutory provisions, too, sometimes operate to exclude relevant evidence, but they vary in nature and are not addressed in this book.

In addition to numerous, specific exclusionary rules, the Federal Rules contain a general exclusionary rule that applies broadly to almost all proffered evidence. This rule, embodied in Federal Rule 403,[11] contains a balancing test. Because of its pervasive importance, the Rule is set out in full below:

Federal Rule 403

EXCLUDING RELEVANT EVIDENCE FOR PREJUDICE, CONFUSION, WASTE OF TIME, OR OTHER REASONS

The court may exclude relevant evidence if its probative value is substantially outweighed by a danger of one or more of the following: unfair prejudice, confusing the issues, misleading the jury, undue delay, wasting time, or needlessly presenting cumulative evidence.

Rule 403 has several noteworthy features. As its title indicates, the rule provides for the exclusion of relevant evidence on, essentially, three grounds: (1) unfair prejudice, (2) confusion (including misleading the jury), and (3) waste of time (including undue delay and the presentation of needless, cumulative evidence). As noted above, Rule 403 provides a balancing test that allows the judge to exclude relevant evidence if "its probative value is *substantially outweighed*" by one or more of the counterweights of unfair prejudice, confusion, or wastefulness. This test tips the scales in favor of admissibility: only if the "probative value is substantially outweighed" by one or more of the countervailing factors is the judge permitted to exclude relevant evidence. Finally, because the balancing test is necessarily an inexact one that takes into account the applicable law, the facts, and the evidence in each case, the trial judge has considerable discretion in applying this test. Her determinations under Rule 403 will not be reversed by an appellate court unless she has clearly abused that discretion.[12]

---

[10]   *See, e.g.,* SALTZBURG, CAPRA & DAVIS, BASIC CRIMINAL PROCEDURE (8th ed. 2021).

[11]   Rules 412, 609 and 703 each contain balancing tests that differ from the test contained in Rule 403. Each of these rules is discussed later in this book.

[12]   SALTZBURG, MARTIN & CAPRA, FEDERAL RULES OF EVIDENCE MANUAL, § 403.02 [18] (12th ed. 2019).

The Effect of a Proffered Stipulation on Rule 403 Balancing

Old Chief v. United States[13] is the most notable case construing Rule 403. Old Chief was charged with assault with a dangerous weapon and use of a firearm in a violent crime. Additionally, he was charged as a felon in possession of a firearm. To sustain the last charge, the prosecutor had to prove, first, that Old Chief had been convicted of a felony-grade offense and, second, that Old Chief had thereafter possessed a firearm. To establish the first point, the prosecutor, over a defense objection, introduced the record of the prior criminal judgment. It showed that Old Chief had been convicted of a criminal assault causing serious bodily injury, for which he received a five-year prison term.

Although the introduction of this evidence seems unremarkable, a problem arose because prior to trial defense counsel had offered to stipulate that Old Chief had been convicted of a felony-grade offense, thus removing this issue from dispute. Defense counsel also asked the judge to instruct the jury that the accused had a prior felony conviction (without stating the nature of that conviction), leaving as the sole issue his subsequent possession of a firearm. (Counsel was concerned about the jury's adverse reaction when it learned that the prior offense was a serious criminal assault.)[14] When the prosecutor refused to accept or join in this stipulation, the trial judge permitted the government to introduce the judgment of conviction, evidence showing the name and nature of the prior conviction.

The central question before the United States Supreme Court was whether the trial judge abused discretion by permitting the prosecutor's evidence of the prior offense given that the defendant had offered to stipulate to the fact of a felony. Before reaching that issue, however, the Court rejected Old Chief's contention that the proffered stipulation rendered the name of the prior offense irrelevant. Noting that the relevance of an item of evidence does not turn upon whether it bears on a *disputed* issue, the Court found that the type of past crime committed by Old Chief had probative value bearing on a consequential fact. The named prior offense had probative force to place the accused within the class of persons convicted of a type of felony-grade offense that was within the

---

[13]   519 U.S. 172 (1997).

[14]   The defense was concerned that, because Old Chief was charged with assault in the present case, the jury would use the prior assault conviction as evidence of propensity (i.e., Old Chief was the kind of person who committed assaults and therefore committed the charged offense). As you will see, propensity evidence is generally excluded under Rule 404, but evidence of specific acts may be admitted to prove knowledge and other matters. We reserve our discussion of character evidence for later, but you should be able to see why the defense was concerned that the jury might use the prior conviction to Old Chief's disadvantage beyond finding that he indeed had a felony record.

statutory category[15] of offenses raising a prohibition against future firearm possession. Nor was the name of the prior offense rendered irrelevant because there was alternative evidence, such as an admission or stipulation, that also placed the accused within the statutory ban on possessing a firearm. When a party concedes a consequential fact that his opponent's proffered evidence tends to prove, this concession does not render the evidence irrelevant. This concession does suggest, however, that the judge should consider excluding the evidence under Rule 403, because the probative value in light of the stipulation is *minimized,* and so may be substantially outweighed by the risk of prejudice. In other words, the availability of the stipulation has the effect of discounting the probative value and thereby affecting the balancing that the judge must do under Rule 403. The probative value of a piece of evidence must be evaluated by other evidence available to prove the point.

Next, in a wide-ranging discussion, the *Old Chief* Court emphasized and elaborated upon the general principle that a party normally has the right to choose the evidence with which she wishes to prove his case.[16] Ordinarily an opponent has no right to block the party's evidence by offering admissions or stipulations. The right of evidentiary choice, said the Court, has at least three grounds of support. First, an item of evidence very often is probative of more than one point—so that an opponent's attempt to concede one point will not justify excluding that evidence. For example, testimony about a shooting may tend to establish "capacity and causation," while at the same time it may tend to establish "the triggerman's motive and intent."[17] The party is entitled to use evidence that is not confined to narrow, abstract linear reasoning, but narrates the story of the case with "descriptive richness"[18] that may capture more than the one point that the adversary offers to stipulate. Second, an evidentiary narration (as opposed to a spare stipulation) aids the jury in drawing inferences, in faithfully adhering to the law governing the case, and in appreciating the moral foundations of the law. Third, the party's right of evidentiary choice helps ensure that the jury receives the evidence it is likely to expect—and counters against a negative inference that may be drawn when a jury is told what the facts are rather than presented with evidence of those facts. Through a carefully planned evidentiary presentation, the prosecutor usually can avoid both unexplained gaps and truncated narrative accounts in

---

[15]   *See* 18 U.S.C.A. §§ 921, 922.

[16]   While the Court's discussion was in the context of a stipulation offered by an accused to preclude the government's evidence, it is equally applicable to evidence offered by the accused or by a party in a civil case.

[17]   *Old Chief,* 519 U.S. at 187.

[18]   Id.

an evidentiary sequence, and can also meet jurors' expectations as to what they would hear at a trial.

Nonetheless, the Court held that the particular circumstances in *Old Chief* required a limited departure from the general practice of allowing the prosecutor ample latitude to select the evidence to prove an element of a charged offense. That latitude is restricted when, as in *Old Chief*, one or more of the counterweights contained in Rule 403 substantially outweighs the probative value of the proffered evidence. That probative value must be discounted when other evidence, equally probative but less prejudicial, is available: in this case, the stipulation. The Court's principal concern was the unfair prejudice likely to result when evidence of the nature of the prior conviction (assault causing serious bodily injury) was offered for the sole purpose of proving the *status* of the accused.

The status that had to be proved, of course, was that of a convicted felon who was prohibited from possessing a firearm. In *Old Chief* there was a substantial risk that the jury would not confine its use of evidence disclosing the exact prior offense to the permissible issue of Old Chief's status. Rather, the jury might have used evidence of the prior conviction to reason that he had a propensity to commit violent crimes such as assault with a dangerous weapon. In other words, the prosecutor's evidence, which was presumably offered to show only that Old Chief had "felon" status, might have had the strong, even primary, effect of tainting the jury's attitude toward the question of his guilt of the gun-related crimes with which he was charged. Given the fact that the stipulation provided all the evidence necessary of the only thing that could be permissibly proved, i.e., the defendant's felony status, it followed that the minimized probative value of the conviction was substantially outweighed by the risk of unfair prejudice.[19] Notably, the stipulation was just as probative as the conviction for the proper purpose, because the statute prohibited *any* felon from possessing a firearm. Thus the prosecutor was not losing any probative value in acceding to the stipulation.

The Supreme Court's opinion in *Old Chief* is a study in contrast. The dictum, which dominates the opinion, is decidedly favorable to the prosecution and, by extension, supportive of the general principle that parties may usually select the evidence they wish to present. The specific holding, however, favors the accused. In a narrowly tailored ruling, the Court held that the trial judge abused discretion by permitting the prosecutor to reject the accused's offer (to stipulate his prior felony conviction) and to introduce instead evidence

---

[19] The majority noted that Congress treated virtually all felonies alike with respect to the ban on gun possession, which meant that the nature of the felony was not a part of the statutory scheme. Id. at 186.

[margin, left side: ISSUE + HOLDING]

revealing the name and nature of the prior offense. The key to the holding is that the only *legitimate* use of evidence pertaining to the prior conviction was to establish the accused's status as a felon prohibited from possessing a firearm. Furthermore, using the accused's stipulation or admission does not impede the flow of the prosecutor's narrative (because it is proof of a fact that is essentially unrelated to the central dispute, which was whether Old Chief actually possessed a gun); nor does it frustrate the expectations of the jury (because the mode of proof by stipulation is not essentially different from the mode of proving a prior conviction through the document indicating a judgment, so the jury is not deprived of live testimony or an interesting factual description). Because Old Chief was not on trial for his past crime, the jury would not expect to receive evidence concerning its details; it would only need to know whether the prior conviction raised a bar against firearm possession.

A broader lesson of *Old Chief* is that under Rule 403, proffered evidence cannot be evaluated in a vacuum. If there is other available evidence that is equally probative but less prejudicial, then the proponent must use that evidence. That principle prohibits a proponent from offering proof that is *unnecessarily* prejudicial.

The Meaning of "Prejudice"

Rule 403's reference to "unfair prejudice" *does not refer* to evidence that simply damages the opponent's case. Evidence favorable to one side is usually damaging to the opponent—but that doesn't make it "unfairly prejudicial" within the meaning of Rule 403. The rule refers to prejudice that is likely to result from the trier's *misuse* of the evidence—in other words, the rule is concerned only with evidence that is likely to distort the trier's proper evaluation. In *Old Chief*, there was a risk that evidence of the prior convictions, introduced for the sole legitimate purpose of establishing the accused's status, would be used improperly by the jury. In contrast, eyewitness testimony that Old Chief possessed a gun would certainly be damaging to Old Chief's case—but it would not be *unfairly* prejudicial.

Rule 403 Rulings Depend on Context and Evidentiary Alternatives

As suggested above, the opinion in *Old Chief* teaches that a Rule 403 determination is contextual in nature. That is, the trial judge must assess the challenged evidence not in isolation, but rather in the "full evidentiary context of the case. . . ."[20] This means that the probative force of the proffered evidence (in *Old Chief*, the criminal judgment) and its potential for unfair prejudice must be evaluated in

---

[20]   Id. at 182.

light of the importance of the evidence, its place in the narrative of the evidentiary presentation and, notably, in light of the availability of other evidence (in *Old Chief*, the stipulation) directed at the same point. If "alternative evidence" has the same or greater probative value but a lower danger of unfair prejudice, the probative value of the proffered evidence is discounted.

The Moral Foundation of the Law

Old Chief makes clear that trial judges should be wary of forcing stipulations of fact in a criminal case if they might drain the moral foundation of a law from the case and leave jurors confused about the reasons for prosecution. Consider, for example, if Old Chief had not simply offered to stipulate that he was a convicted felon but instead said the following to the trial judge: "Your Honor, there is no dispute in this case that I have a felony conviction. The only dispute on the gun charge is whether I possessed it. So, I ask that you instruct the jury that the only thing it needs to decide is whether the prosecution has proved beyond a reasonable doubt that I possessed a gun, and if the jury decides that this is proved beyond a reasonable doubt then I am guilty." It is doubtful that any judge would impose upon the prosecution a restriction that excluded the *fact* of a felony conviction from the case. The reason is that jurors (some of whom might have strong Second Amendment beliefs) might fear that the law was making gun possession itself a crime and acquit Old Chief on the gun charge because of concern about an overbroad law. In short, the suggested approach would pose a substantial risk of draining the moral underpinnings of the law from the case, something that *Old Chief* cautions against.

Other Negative Factors Considered Under Rule 403

While the *Old Chief* case focuses primarily on unfair prejudice as a counterweight to probative value, there are other counterweights contained in Federal Rule 403. Two of these— "confusing the issues . . . [and] misleading the jury"—bear a kinship to unfair prejudice in that they are designed to safeguard the factfinding process. The remaining counterweights—"undue delay, wasting time, or needlessly presenting cumulative evidence"—are simply time-saving factors that promote judicial efficiency. These latter counterweights substantially overlap as each bears upon the dispatch and efficiency with which the trial moves forward.

Suppose that in a civil trial involving a pedestrian (the plaintiff) who was hit by the defendant's car, counsel for the plaintiff requests that the jury be taken to the scene of the accident so that the members can view the physical surroundings. Assume that the scene of the accident is forty miles from the courthouse. If the physical surroundings can be accurately depicted by testimony, photographs, diagrams, or other means, the trial judge would probably deny this request on the ground that allowing a jury view would be a waste of time or would unduly delay the trial.

Under the terms of Rule 403, a court may also exclude evidence on the ground that it is needlessly cumulative. The emphasis here is on the term "needlessly," as parties may often choose to emphasize a particularly crucial fact by introducing more than one item of evidence to support it. Needlessly cumulative evidence often relates to a minor or undisputed issue. For example, if the parties to the traffic accident (above) do not seriously dispute the facts that the defendant was driving a European sports car capable of high speeds and that the accident occurred at noon on a clear day, the trial court may decline to allow several witnesses to be called to the stand simply to testify as to these facts. Similarly, a trial judge may pull the plug on a party's attempt to call five of the same kind of experts to testify to the same conclusion. On the other hand, if a defendant in a criminal trial denies involvement with a charged robbery, a trial court would likely allow several or more of the prosecution's witnesses to testify that they saw the defendant at the scene of the crime and several or more of the defense witnesses who support the defendant's alibi.[21]

Bench Versus Jury Trials

Although Rule 403 is equally applicable in bench and jury trials, the reality is that many trial judges take offense for two reasons when an objection is made that evidence is unfairly prejudicial or confusing. First, they believe that, unlike jurors, their training and experience will enable them to use evidence only for its probative value, to disregard both any inflammatory aspects of the evidence and any prohibited uses of the evidence, and to avoid confusion by asking questions when necessary. Since judges are human and may respond emotionally to evidence, there is reason to doubt whether such judicial confidence is always warranted, which brings us to the second reason: generally, in order to rule on evidence judges will have to see or hear it, which means they will always see the Rule 403 evidence that is purportedly unfairly prejudicial or confusing. So, whatever unfair prejudice or confusion might exist, it has already happened.

You might wonder whether a trial judge who sits on a multi-judge court and is asked to make a Rule 403 ruling could ask another judge on the court to decide the admissibility of the evidence so that

---

[21]   The fact that more than one eyewitness identified an accused makes the accuracy of each identification more convincing than if only one witness made an identification.

the trial judge will only see what the other judge has determined to be admissible. The answer is that in some courts in exceptional cases, judges have done this. But, it is not a common practice because judges believe it is unnecessary and that another judge who does not know the case well will have greater difficulty than the trial judge in assessing the relative need for the evidence.

While unfair prejudice and confusion are therefore not a reason to exclude evidence in a bench trial, trial judges do exclude evidence if it is cumulative or excessively time consuming. Judges like bench trials to proceed efficiently, are often likely to believe that they need to hear from fewer witnesses than jurors who are not trained to listen to evidence, and sometimes will be willing to review documentary evidence or exhibits in camera rather than to take court time to do so.

§ 3.3   Evidentiary Foundations

Rules of evidence require evidentiary foundations or predicates—that is, evidentiary steps that precede the introduction of testimonial, real, or demonstrative proof. Often, these foundations fit so naturally within the customary scheme of introducing evidence that they blend into the trial proceedings without notice or attention. Consider, for example, the foundational requirement of *Federal Rule 602*, which states in part:

NEED FOR PERSONAL KNOWLEDGE

A witness may testify to a matter only if evidence is introduced sufficient to support a finding that the witness had personal knowledge of the matter. * * *

Yet a trial attorney does not routinely ask a witness "do you have personal knowledge of the matters to which you will testify?" The witness's personal knowledge is ordinarily revealed by her preliminary testimony establishing her presence at the event to which she will testify. In the course of her preliminary testimony, the witness will quite naturally disclose that she was in a position to perceive the relevant occurrence. For example, a witness to an automobile accident may be called by the plaintiff and asked, "while you were standing on the corner of 20th and Main, what did you see?" If the witness answers, "I saw the defendant's car go through a red light," the witness is claiming personal knowledge without being specifically asked whether she has such knowledge.

Should there be a "foundation" objection, the judge has only to determine whether the trier of fact (here, let us assume, a jury) could reasonably find that the witness had perceived—that is, had first-hand knowledge—of the event or condition she describes in her testimony. Observe that in this instance the judge acts in a supervisory or "screening" capacity: the judicial role is to ensure that the jury has before it sufficient evidence to reasonably conclude that the witness saw or heard the occurrence in question. The assumption is that if the jury concludes that the witness lacks personal knowledge, it will ignore her testimony; consequently, the gatekeeping by the judge need not be as strict as it is for, say, determining whether an expert is reliable. FACT FINDER IS JURY

It is a rare case in which a judge finds that a rational jury could not believe a witness who claims personal knowledge. In the automobile accident case, suppose the witness is asked on cross-examination, "how far were you from the intersection where you say the defendant ran a red light when you made your observation?", and the witness answers "100 yards." Even though one might question whether a witness could observe the light from 100 yards away, the fact that the witness says she did is probably enough for the judge to let the jury decide whether to believe the witness. If, however, the witness said "ten miles," a judge would probably decide that no reasonable jury could believe a personal account of the accident under those circumstances, and thus the judge would exclude the testimony to save the time associated with further examination of the witness. 10 MILES V. 100 YARDS FROM ACCIDENT

In contrast, most rules of evidence call upon the judge to determine the preliminary or foundational facts to her own satisfaction. In these instances, the judge does not merely screen the evidence; instead, the judge makes the necessary factual determination. Recall, for example, the hearsay exception for recorded recollection.[22] In administering this rule of evidence the judge determines the preliminary (foundational) facts by a preponderance of the evidence as mentioned in Chapter II. These foundational components consist of determinations, (1) whether the witness is unable to testify fully and accurately from present memory, (2) whether the witness once had knowledge of the event in question, and (3) whether the witness made or adopted a record of the event when his memory of it was fresh. If the judge admits the record into evidence, the jury decides what probative weight to give it. The foundational or preliminary facts, however, must be determined by the judge.

ILLUSTRATION

The plaintiff, Paulina, brings suit against Dora, claiming that Dora, a dealer in fine art, is liable to the plaintiff on grounds of fraud, or breach of warranty, or both.

---

[22]   Supra Chapter II, § 2.5.

Paulina's complaint alleges that Dora sold to the plaintiff an expensive painting which Dora represented was the work of the Swiss painter, Paul Klee. In fact, Paulina claims, the work was by an unknown artist, most likely one who had worked as Klee's understudy. Dora, however, contends that the painting in question is actually one of Klee's early works.

During Dora's case in defense, her attorney calls Ella to the witness stand. Ella gives her name, address, and college major (commercial art); she then testifies that she has worked for more than twenty years for the Phillips Gallery of Art, where she specializes in arranging and conducting private tours of the gallery. Dora's attorney then asks Ella if she has examined the painting in question. Receiving an affirmative answer, the attorney asks Ella whether she has an opinion as to who painted the disputed piece of art. The plaintiff objects, arguing that Ella is testifying as an expert and the defendant has not established the necessary foundation for this expert testimony.

Federal Rule of Evidence 702 permits testimony by an expert if her knowledge will "help the trier of fact" and if she is qualified "by knowledge, skill, experience, training, or education" to address the specialized topic in question. The party calling an expert must provide a proper foundation before she testifies regarding a technical or scientific topic. The judge alone determines whether the foundation is adequate, because under Rule 104(a) it is the judge who determines whether the witness may provide expert testimony. Under Rule 104(a) the proponent must establish these foundation requirements by a preponderance of the evidence. The foundation needed here requires[23] evidence that the topic to be addressed is within the realm of "scientific, technical, or other specialized knowledge" *and* that the proposed witness has the necessary expertise. In this Illustration, the foundation is inadequate. The principal defect is defense counsel's failure to adduce evidence that Ella was qualified by training or experience to determine the authenticity of a painting by an early twentieth-century European painter. Majoring in commercial art and serving as a director and guide of private tours do not, standing alone, establish by a preponderance that she has the expertise necessary for her to render an opinion of the genuineness of the disputed work.

---

[23]   For a full explanation of the foundational requirements for expert testimony, *see* Chapter XI, §§ 11.3–5.

Notice again that in some instances, such as a claim by a lay witness to have personal knowledge, foundational requirements are fulfilled if the judge determines that the evidentiary predicate is *sufficient* for a jury to conclude that the foundational facts exist. The judge only screens the evidence to ensure that it is adequate to support the jury's determination. In other instances, as in the Illustration, the judge determines the existence (or nonexistence) of the foundational facts. In the next section, we will examine more closely the roles of judge and jury in foundational fact-finding. For now, it suffices to recall that subsection (a) of Federal Rule 104 assigns to the judge, and not to the jury, fact-finding responsibilities concerning "whether a witness is qualified, a privilege exists, or evidence is admissible."

Authentication

The term "authentication" denotes a particular foundational requirement that emerges in many trials. Its most frequent application is to documents and other items of real proof, but the requirement of authentication is not limited to tangible items. Under FRE 901, whenever a lawyer offers evidence that she asserts is genuine (e.g., an e-mail from *X* to *Y*), she must upon objection provide a foundation sufficient for a reasonable trier of fact to conclude that the evidence is authentic—that it is what the proponent claims it to be. Generally speaking, if an item of evidence is not authentic, it is not relevant. For example, if the prosecution wishes to admit a purported Facebook post by the defendant admitting to the charged crime, that entry is clearly relevant—but only if it is actually the defendant's Facebook post.

The evidentiary foundation ("authentication") required by Rule 901 to help assure authenticity is somewhat more demanding than daily experience might lead us to expect. In everyday affairs, if we receive an e-mail from a particular person, we normally assume that it was that person who sent the e-mail. Likewise, when the telephone rings and an unfamiliar voice says, "This is Alena Leitner calling," we normally assume it is she.

The law of evidence is more circumspect, however, for it operates in a milieu of conflict with a lay jury often acting as the factfinder. Under evidentiary principles, for example, the presence of a signature on a proffered document is not, standing alone, sufficient to satisfy the requirement of authentication; the same is true of an e-mail purportedly sent by someone. The proponent of the item must provide additional evidence that helps confirm its authenticity. Similarly, self-identification by a telephone caller—or by someone posting on a Facebook page—is not, standing alone, sufficient to meet the requirement of authentication. The party wishing to show that the caller or poster who identified herself was in fact that person must provide additional confirming ("foundational") evidence.[24]

All that said, the requirement of authentication (which includes identification) *is not stringent.* All that is needed is evidence sufficient for the judge to conclude that a reasonable jury *could* find that the evidence in question (*i.e.,* the evidence being authenticated) is what the proponent claims it to be. Furthermore, there are no fixed rules of authentication that require a specific evidentiary procedure or routine. This flexible approach allows trial attorneys to think creatively about how to provide the evidentiary clues that meet the authentication requirement.

To take an example in a case involving self-identification by a telephone caller, authentication would be satisfied if the person receiving the call testified that she recognized the caller's voice as that of Alena Leitner. The authentication requirement would also be met by evidence that the caller revealed information likely to be known by Alena Leitner. Similarly, authentication could be achieved by evidence that Alena Leitner frequently stutters and so did the caller—or that the caller acted in a way after the call that Alena Leitner would act. And as to the posting on Facebook, sufficient authentication would be found by evidence presented about the use of a log-in and password, or by something in the post (like the use of a nickname or endearment) linking the posting to the particular person asserted to have posted it.

You should think of authentication as simply the process of providing evidentiary confirmation that a proffered item of evidence is in fact what it appears to be.

In a bench trial, after the judge hears evidence supporting authentication and any contrary evidence introduced by the opponent, she decides if the proffered evidence (to which authenticating evidence is addressed) is genuine. However, in a jury trial, the judge simply *screens the authenticating evidence* in order to determine whether the evidence *supporting* authentication, if believed by the jury, is sufficient to allow it rationally to conclude that the proffered evidence is genuine.[25] Whether the judge

---

[24]   But if the proponent is trying to prove *that a person called* was in fact the person reached (respondent), it suffices for purposes of identification (authentication) to show that the caller dialed the number in the telephone directory that was assigned to the respondent and that the person reached identified herself as the respondent or provided other clues that confirmed her identity. *See* Fed. R. Evid. 901(b)(6).

[25]   This is the same task the judge performs in deciding whether a witness has personal knowledge. Generally, the trial judge is a screener rather than fact finder or final decision maker in the following limited situations: Fed. R. Evid. 104(b) (conditional relevance), Fed. R. Evid. 602 (personal knowledge), Fed. R. Evid. 901 (authentication), or Fed. R. Evid. 1008 (three specific "best evidence" questions).

personally believes the proffered evidence is authentic is of no consequence. If the process of authentication is satisfactory, the evidence in question is introduced; the jury evaluates it; and the jury ultimately decides if it is genuine. If the jury concludes it is not—for example, if it concludes that Alena Leitner did not make the telephone call in question, or that the Facebook posting was made by a hacker—it will then ignore the evidence, for it has no probative value. It is only probative if it is what the proponent says it is.

ILLUSTRATION *example of authentication*

In a dispute over the value of an antique clock, counsel for the plaintiff, Howard Carter, wants to introduce a business letter from one Duncan Pearce, a reputable antique dealer, who appraised the clock and offered to buy it. Pearce has since closed his business, retired, and moved to a foreign country. There are, nonetheless, a number of possibilities for satisfying the requirement of authentication:

(a) A lay witness who is familiar with Pearce's signature could testify that the letter was signed by Pearce.[26] (Thereafter, the letter would be introduced into evidence and read or shown to the jury.[27])

(b) An expert on handwriting identification, having been qualified by the required foundational questions,[28] could compare Pearce's signature on the exhibit with specimens of Pearce's signature (or his handwriting) that have been authenticated.[29]

(c) The jury could compare Pearce's signature on the letter with specimens of Pearce's signature (or his handwriting) that have been authenticated.[30]

(d) If Pearce's letter containing the offer was responsive to an earlier letter from, say, Howard Carter to Pearce, then Carter could take the stand, authenticate his

---

[26] Fed. R. Evid. 901(b)(2) permits authentication by a "non-expert's opinion that handwriting is genuine, based on a familiarity with it that was not acquired for the current litigation."

[27] As you will see in Chapter V, this letter also presents a hearsay question. Perhaps that question can be answered by invoking Fed. R. Evid. 803(6) or, possibly, 804(b)(3).

[28] See the immediately preceding Illustration on foundational requirements for experts.

[29] Fed. R. Evid. 901(b)(3) permits authentication by "comparison with an authenticated specimen by an expert witness * * *."

[30] Fed. R. Evid. 901(b)(3) also permits authentication by "comparison with an authenticated specimen by * * * the trier of fact."

letter (or a copy thereof) and testify that the contents of
Pearce's letter were responsive to his (Carter's) earlier
letter.[31] This means of authenticating Pearce's letter
invokes the *reply doctrine*. The theory of this doctrine is that
if *A* writes to *B*, and a reply letter that purports to be from
B is responsive to *A's* letter, a reasonable jury could find
that *B* actually wrote the reply letter.

The techniques set out above are simply possibilities, and are
not intended to foreclose other means of authentication. For example,
there might be circumstantial evidence that supports authenticity,
such as that the letter is written with a turn of phrase that Pearce
always used, or the writer uses a nickname for Carter that is
relatively unknown. The basic standard is always whether a
reasonable juror could believe, given the evidence presented, that the
challenged item is what the proponent says it is. Counsel's task is to
provide confirming evidence. Note that in the examples above,
authentication is often achieved by the introduction of evidence
extrinsic to the proffered document.

There are two major patterns of authentication. The first
pattern involves the introduction of evidence extrinsic to the
proffered item—evidence that tends to confirm that the item is
authentic. The second pattern, which we will consider shortly,
involves only the limited step of showing that the item in question
contains on its face the necessary indicia of authenticity.

Pattern One Authentication: Extrinsic Evidence

Federal Rule 901(b) sets out non-exclusive illustrations of
pattern one authentication. An authenticating process conducted in
conformity with one of these illustrations satisfies "the requirement
of authenticating or identifying an item of evidence * * *"[32]

A common example of pattern one authentication is found in
Federal Rule 901(b)(9). That subsection provides that an item of
evidence may be authenticated as follows:

> **Evidence About a Process or System.** Evidence
> describing a process or system and showing that it produces an
> accurate result.

This illustration is within the pattern-one category because the
proponent of an item of evidence must produce extrinsic evidence
that shows the accuracy of the process or system that produced the

---

[31]   Fed. R. Evid. 901(b)(4) permits authentication by evidence that shows
"distinctive characteristics" by revealing such features as "appearance, contents,
substance, [and] internal patterns * * * taken together with all the circumstances."

[32]   Fed. R. Evid. 901(a).

proffered evidence. Suppose, for example, a trucking company wanted to introduce evidence in the form of a computer printout that displayed the average monthly cost of service, maintenance, and repairs on its fleet of 200 trucks over the last five years. Evidence showing how the basic data were collected, how this information was arranged for computer processing, and the basic features of the company's software program would provide an adequate foundation to authenticate the resulting product—for example a printout displaying average monthly costs.

ILLUSTRATIONS

(1) Law enforcement officers have been trying to secure evidence that Dromio is a drug dealer. So far, they have been unsuccessful in their attempts to entice Dromio to sell drugs to a police undercover agent. The authorities have, however, identified a parking lot adjacent to a storage building that is thought to have been used by Dromio to make two narcotics sales. A surveillance officer equipped with night-vision binoculars is posted on the second story of a nearby building.

Several days later, at 2:00 a.m. a man wearing a cap and carrying a leather or vinyl pouch emerges from a parked car and greets another man, later identified as Davy, who enters the parking lot from an adjacent sidewalk. After a brief conversation, the men stroll around the side of the storage building, out of the sight of the observing officer. Unbeknownst to the two men, law enforcement officers have installed a small camera behind the gutter of the storage building. The camera is activated by the motion of a subject within the range of its lens. When activated, it runs for twenty minutes and records the date and the time frame during which it was operative. Video from the hidden camera shows two men exchanging cash for packages taken from a pouch. The packages, which are examined by Davy, appear to contain a white powder. On the video, the man delivering the packages and receiving the money appears to be Dromio.

At the trial of Dromio for selling a narcotic, the prosecutor could authenticate the video—and thus identify Dromio as the seller—by calling witnesses who could establish the installation of the video camera and the technical details of how it works. This testimony would then be linked with the testimony of someone familiar with Dromio's appearance. (Of course, the prosecutor could simply allow the jury to compare the features of the man shown in the film with the features of the accused, Dromio.) Because the ultimate goal of the prosecutor is to convince the jury that the seller was Dromio, the prosecutor would probably first obtain the testimony of the surveillance officer who, even if he could not identify Dromio, would provide the context for the jury to believe that Dromio was the person depicted in the video.

(2)   Twenty minutes after the transaction described in Illustration (1), law enforcement officers arrest Davy in his car. They seize a bag containing plastic packages—and these contain a white powdery substance.

Critical to the prosecution of both Dromio and Davy is proof that the plastic packages contained a narcotic. Suppose laboratory tests confirm that the substance in question is cocaine. At trial, the prosecutor wants to introduce the packages of white power along with expert testimony from the lab technician who ran the tests that the packages contain cocaine. By what means can she authenticate the powdery substance in the plastic bags as having been the substance seized after the transaction?

Chain of Custody Authentication

Items such as seized drugs, a blood sample, a glove, or a broken cable pose special problems of authentication. The difficulty is that these items—and many others—usually bear no distinctive features, such as a peculiar appearance or a serial number, that allow them to be differentiated from similar items of the same variety. Of course, when potential items of evidence come into the possession of law enforcement personnel, these authorities usually assign numbers, names, or other identifying data to the items. Nonetheless, the lawyer proffering these tangible items in court usually has to employ an authentication technique called "chain of custody."[33] This simply means that counsel offers authenticating testimony or, perhaps, official (public) or business records, that account for the whereabouts of the proffered item from its original seizure to its presence in the courtroom. The chain of custody technique is also useful when it is important to show that the evidence in question is in the same condition (at trial) that it was at the time of the litigated event. For example, it may be important to show that the evidence has not been subjected to climatic extremes, tampering, or some other source of alteration or contamination between the time of seizure and the courtroom presentation. (Evidence of a chain of custody might show

---

[33]   Although the Federal Rules of Evidence do not expressly mention chain of custody, the technique is everywhere recognized. It is simply an example of using circumstantial proof to establish genuineness. Fed. R. Evid. 901(b)(4).

the item in question was stored in a secure place, thus reducing or eliminating the opportunities for alteration or change.)

A chain of custody need not be flawless—it is commonly held that gaps in the chain of custody (e.g., a period in which the authorities lost track of the object, or left it in a place in which it could have been tampered with) present questions of weight and not admissibility. However, the custodial chain must at least be sufficient to allow a jury to find, first, that the item proffered in evidence is the same one that was involved in the events being litigated and, second, that its condition has not changed to a degree that makes it misleading.

Evidence, the Internet, and Modern Communications

How do the traditional forms of authentication, discussed above, get used when it comes to authenticating modern communications that occur over e-mail, text, and social media? The same kinds of authentication issues that arise when letters or testimony about telephone calls is offered at trial also arise when a party seeks to offer electronic forms of evidence. Suppose, for example, that a defendant is charged criminally for making a threat via e-mail. It will not be sufficient for the prosecution to offer a printout of the e-mail bearing the e-mail address of the defendant in the "send" line of the e-mail. Just as someone could write a letter and falsely sign another's name, someone could use an e-mail address of another person to make a threat. So how would the prosecutor authenticate the e-mail? As with other evidence, there is no one required method. The prosecutor would have to adduce sufficient foundational evidence for the jury to be able to find by a preponderance of the evidence that the defendant sent the e-mail.

A witness testifying that she saw the defendant send the e-mail would be sufficient, as would a witness testifying that the defendant admitted sending the e-mail. That authentication would be established under Rule 901(b)(1) which provides, as an example of authentication, "[t]estimony that an item is what it is claimed to be." Another possibility is that the threatening e-mail followed closely upon the heels of an argument between the defendant and the e-mail recipient and the e-mail made reference to the argument, or that the recipient of the e-mail telephoned the defendant after receiving it and the defendant did not deny making the threat. Or the proponent could show that the e-mail contained words or symbols that the defendant commonly used in his communications. In some cases expert testimony might be used to assist in identifying the sender of e-mail. All of these examples are grounded in Rule 901(b)(4), which provides as an example of authenticity "[t]he appearance, contents, substance, internal patterns, or other distinctive characteristics of the item, taken together with all the circumstances." That is, the proponent can authenticate by introducing circumstantial evidence that the e-mail was sent by the defendant.

Similarly, the contents, appearance of internal patterns of e-mail might also provide a means of authentication. If e-mails are sent back and forth discussing a business proposition, the substance of the e-mails may provide a sufficient basis to identify the communicators. Authentication by a showing of circumstantial evidence is probably the predominant method for authenticating electronic information in the courts today.

The anonymity available on the Internet makes authentication of some postings difficult, but not impossible. Some creative sleuthing is often required. An example is *United States v. Bynum*.[34] There, an FBI Special agent was working undercover and using an informant's password to enter a child-pornography online chat group administered by Yahoo. He observed on two occasions that someone using the moniker "markie_zkidluv6" had uploaded to the group's website a dozen photos depicting children engaged in sexual acts. The agent testified to the following steps—a subpoena to Yahoo to obtain subscriber information on "markie" and IP addresses associated with the uploads; use of a free, public website that directed him to the Internet Service Provider associated with those addresses; a subpoena to the provider which indicated that "markie" had used a phone-based dial-up service to access the internet; and another subpoena to the phone and internet companies providing the service. By this process, the agent obtained Bynum's name and address (which was his parents' home). The agent returned to the online chat group, saw a new posting of a video by "markie," and by accessing "markie's" profile information he found a photo of Bynum and a statement that Bynum, a 24-year-old single male living in North Carolina, "want[s] to chat with any cute girls that live close by that's [sic] up for a little fun." The FBI obtained a search warrant and found 5,074 photos and 154 videos of child pornography on a laptop computer.

It is hardly surprising that Bynum did not challenge authentication. The government's investigation tied the computer and the images to him, and his posting of his photo along with a statement as to his age and gender surely would have been sufficient authentication. Bynum did argue that there was insufficient evidence to prove beyond a reasonable doubt that he, rather than another occupant, resident or friend was the person responsible for

---

[34]   604 F.3d 161 (4th Cir. 2010).

the images. The court of appeals found substantial evidence to support the jury's verdict of guilty.

What if a proponent wants to prove what was on a web page on a particular day? Because web pages are dynamic, issues of authenticity are raised. But courts have recognized that a non-profit organization named the Internet Archive has established a "Wayback Machine" with which information posted on the Internet can be retrieved. Testimony from a person with knowledge about how the Wayback Machine retrieved a particular web posting (or a certification to that effect in lieu of the person's testimony) will be sufficient to authenticate the item. And some courts have taken judicial notice that the Wayback Machine reliably retrieves website postings, making testimony on the point unnecessary.[35]

Foundational Evidence of Authenticity Must Be Admissible at Trial

Because the ultimate determination of authenticity is made by the jury, it follows that any foundational evidence for authenticating an item—before the judge under Rule 901 as well as before the jury at trial—must itself be admissible. For example, assume the government wants to admit a criminal defendant's diary at trial. For authenticity purposes the government must show the judge enough evidence for a reasonable jury to believe the item is the defendant's diary. If the government's authentication evidence is an affidavit of an unavailable witness, then the judge cannot admit the diary. That is because the foundation evidence is hearsay—evidence that the jury would not be able to consider, and if in the absence of that evidence there is no foundation of authenticity, then the jury has no basis for determining the genuineness of the diary.

Pattern Two Authentication: Self-Authentication

Federal Rule 902 lists fourteen categories of documents that are "self-authenticating." These items have sufficient indicia of genuineness "within their four corners," so to speak, to pass the threshold test of authentication. Of course, compliance with the requirement of authentication means only that the judge admits the authenticated item into evidence; the opponent can still dispute its authenticity before the jury. A generous sample of Rule 902's self-authenticating documents includes:

---

[35] Useful discussions of authentication issues arising from the Internet, e-mail, social networks, blogs and text messages can be found in SALTZBURG, MARTIN & CAPRA, FEDERAL RULES OF EVIDENCE MANUAL, § 901.02 [9] (12th ed. 2019) and Grimm, Capra & Joseph, *Best Practices for Authenticating Electronic Evidence,* 69 BAYLOR L. REV. 1 (2017).

—Domestic public documents[36]

—Foreign public documents[37]

—Certified copies of public records[38]

—Official publications[39]

—Newspapers and periodicals[40]

—Trade inscriptions and the like[41]

—Acknowledged documents[42]

—Commercial paper[43]

In the year 2000, an amendment to Rule 902 added two additional categories—eleven and twelve—of self-authenticating documents. These additions allow domestic and foreign business records to be authenticated by certification. Generally speaking, authentication is satisfied when a qualified person, such as the custodian of the proffered records, provides a written declaration that the records were properly prepared in the regular course of business.

In 2017, another amendment to Rule 902 added two more categories—thirteen and fourteen—of self-authenticating documents. Rule 902(13) deals with certified records generated by an electronic process or system, and Rule 902(14) with certified data copied from an electronic device, storage medium, or file. The Rule follows the lead of the 2000 amendment regarding business records—allowing authentication to be established by a certification of a qualifying witness. The goal of the amendment is to lessen the cost of authenticating electronic evidence, because the authenticating witness need not be produced at trial.

Each of the fourteen categories of documents enumerated in Rule 902 has some intrinsic feature that provides the necessary degree of assurance of authenticity. Unlike Rule 901, which provides a *nonexclusive* list of authentication possibilities, Rule 902 provides a *closed* list of specific categories that meet various criteria for self-authentication. Many of the categories, such as public documents, describe records and instruments that bear a public seal or attestation (including certification) by a public official. Other

---

[36]   Fed. R. Evid. 902(1), (2) (sealed or signed by a public officer).

[37]   Fed. R. Evid. 902(3) (attested by a foreign official).

[38]   Fed. R. Evid. 902(4) (documents filed in a public office, certified by custodian).

[39]   Fed. R. Evid. 902(5) (books, pamphlets, etc. issued by public authority).

[40]   Fed. R. Evid. 902(6) (printed materials).

[41]   Fed. R. Evid. 902(7) (labels, signs, etc., affixed in course of business).

[42]   Fed. R. Evid. 902(8) (*e.g.*, a notarized document).

[43]   Fed. R. Evid. 902(9) (*e.g.*, a bond or bill of lading).

categories, such as those providing for the authentication of newspapers and trade inscriptions, describe writings that carry little risk of forgery or other alterations; furthermore, in these latter categories it is usually easy for an interested party to confirm genuineness or reveal falsity. Consider, for example, how easy it would be to expose as a forgery an article falsely claimed to be from the January 12, 2020 edition of the New York Times.

The previous sentence is a reminder that self-authentication under Rule 902 is sufficient to warrant admission of the authenticated evidence. But an opposing party may challenge the genuineness of the evidence at trial, and a trier of fact might find that it is in fact not genuine.

Illustrative Aids

A party at trial may seek to use "illustrative aids" for a number of purposes. Such aids can be used to add clarity or vividness to a witness's testimony; or to aid in argument to the jury. For example, a digital model of a portion of the human body might be employed in a medical malpractice case; or a chart or a PowerPoint might be displayed to remind the jury of the key evidence in a business conspiracy case. If a party is seeking to use an illustrative aid, it is not offering the information as proof of a fact.

Common sense will usually suggest the proper foundation for an illustrative aid—it must be a fair presentation, and one that will not trick the jury into thinking that it is evidence of a fact. So for example, a PowerPoint purporting so summarize relevant transactions will be objectionable it if "cherry-picks" the transactions favorable to the proponent. Finally, if the judge allows the party to use an illustrative aid, that aid can not be submitted to the jury for its deliberations. That is because it is not evidence.

§ 3.4   Conditional Relevancy

The relevance of one item of evidence (Item A) sometimes depends upon another connected item of evidence (Item B). Suppose, for example, Puck sues Dora for breach of an oral contract, claiming that, in response to his classified ad in the "wanted to buy" column, Dora telephoned him and offered to sell a four-piece bedroom suite for $3,500. Puck alleges he accepted the offer. Dora, in her answer, denies making (or authorizing) such a call—or any call whatsoever—to Puck.

At trial, Puck takes the stand and starts to testify about the terms of the offer. Dora objects on the ground that this testimony is irrelevant because she did not telephone Puck. It is true that Puck's evidence of the terms of the contractual offer is relevant only if Dora (or her agent) made the offer. This evidentiary deficiency becomes even more obvious if you imagine that the call was made by a complete stranger—a third person whose name happened to be Dora. Since that person is not the defendant, Puck's testimony about the content of the offer is irrelevant. Simply put, testimony about the offer supports a consequential fact if, and only if, defendant (and not a third party) made or authorized the offer.

Puck's problem stems from the fact that trials consist of an evidentiary sequence in which events portrayed by the evidence necessarily unfold one at a time. Puck must produce evidence not only of the terms of the offer, but also of the identity of the offeror— that the offeror was *defendant* Dora. The problem can be quickly resolved if Puck can testify, for example, that he recognized the voice of the defendant and, having provided the necessary authentication, he then proceeds to describe the offer. Suppose, however, his only evidence of identity (authentication) comes from a witness, W, who overheard Dora making the telephone call. Suppose, further, that W's testimony is scheduled for later in the trial. The relevance of Puck's testimony concerning the terms of the telephone offer *is conditioned* on the connected fact (not yet supported by evidence) that the defendant made the offer.

When the relevance of proffered evidence depends upon (*i.e.* is conditioned upon) a related fact that must be supported by other evidence, we say that the proffered evidence is *conditionally relevant*. The probative force (*i.e.*, relevance) of the evidence is conditioned upon a fact that is shown by other evidence. That "other evidence" must be sufficient to permit the trier to conclude by a preponderance of the evidence that the connected fact exists. To return to our example, the judge would admit evidence of the terms of the offer conditioned upon the assurance of Puck's lawyer that he would subsequently produce evidence that the offeror was Dora.

Federal Rule 104(b)

Federal Rule 104 is concerned primarily with the allocation of fact-finding responsibilities between judge and jury. In making this allocation, the rule addresses conditional relevancy in subsection (b). As we have seen, subsection (a) of this rule states that the judge alone must determine "preliminary [factual] questions about whether a witness is qualified, a privilege exists, or evidence is admissible." In other situations, such as the reception into evidence of authenticating testimony, the judge does not determine facts from the evidence presented. Rather, under Rule 104(b) the judge screens or monitors the evidence in order to ensure that it is sufficient to support a jury finding. (It is sufficient if a reasonable jury could find by a more-likely-than-not standard or, put otherwise, by a preponderance of evidence, that the supported fact—for example, that Dora made the offer—exists.) The judge assumes this monitoring role in situations involving conditional relevancy. *Rule 104(b)* states:

> **Relevancy That Depends on a Fact.** When the relevance of evidence depends upon whether a fact exists, proof must be introduced sufficient to support a finding that the fact does exist. The court may admit the proposed evidence on the condition that the proof be introduced later.

Applying Rule 104(b) to our illustrative contract dispute is simple and straightforward. The judge will allow Puck's testimony about the terms of the telephone offer either, (1) upon his testimony that he recognized or otherwise identified defendant Dora's voice, or (2) subject to the condition that other (forthcoming) evidence will be sufficient to support a jury finding that the caller was Dora.

Questions of authenticity thus are ones of conditional relevancy—the relevance of an item is dependent on it being the item that the proponent says it is. As such, authenticity disputes are resolved by the court under the low standard of whether there is sufficient evidence for a juror to find that the item is genuine. Even if the judge has doubts, she will admit the evidence over an authenticity objection if she determines that a reasonable person could find the item genuine.

ILLUSTRATION

Each of the following examples presents a problem of conditional relevance. The fact supported by the evidence in Column A is conditionally linked to the fact supported by the evidence in Column B. The judge must ensure that, at some point in the trial, the proponent produces sufficient evidence of the factual condition(s) [Column B] on which relevance depends. Note that the order in which the evidence supporting the connected facts is presented does not matter. For example, in Illustration (1) below, evidence that D was driving a black sedan might be offered first, subject to the later "condition" that the black sedan was speeding.

1. Proposition: Defendant was speeding through the intersection.

A.	B.
Witness testifies that a black sedan sped through the intersection	D was the driver of the black sedan

2.   Proposition: Accused shot victim with a handgun.

Ballistics expert testifies that the fatal bullet was fired from a particular handgun proffered as Prosecutor's Exhibit 1	The handgun was owned or possessed by the accused

3.   Proposition: Defendant Duncan sold his stock after illegally receiving "inside information" that Company would sustain huge losses.

Confidential memorandum from Company President to Chairman of Board of Directors expressing fear that outside accountants had apparently discovered questionable transactions and false entries overstating company's profits	Prior to the sale of his stock, defendant saw the memorandum or otherwise learned of its contents

4.   Proposition: Alena ran away from boarding school because she was depressed about her poor grades and hated her coursework.

A crumpled, detached diary page, discovered in the drawer of a desk used by Alena and her roommate. The author of the diary entries expresses remorse about low grades and antipathy toward her courses and teachers	Alena made the diary entries

5.   Proposition: Plaintiff, a delivery man, was contributorily negligent when he was injured by a dynamite blast at a construction site.

The construction supervisor yelled a warning when he saw plaintiff driving a truck toward the blast site	The plaintiff heard or should have heard the warning in time to stop

In Section 3.3 of this Chapter, we examined the requirement of authentication. In essence, this foundational requirement states that when a proponent proffers an item of evidence that she claims is genuine or authentic, upon objection she generally must offer additional evidence to confirm its authenticity. Thus, if the prosecutor proffers the accused's glove stained with the victim's blood, she must produce evidence that is sufficient for the jury to find,

(1) there is blood on the glove and it came from the victim and, (2) the glove belonged to or was in the possession of the accused.

You can see from this simple example that authentication is a form of conditional relevance. The authenticating evidence supplies the factual predicate that makes the glove relevant. A glove—even the defendant's glove—stained with ketchup has no relevance to show *D* was the murderer; neither does a blood-stained glove that was never in the possession of the accused.[44] The jury must have before it evidence that, if believed, is sufficient to support its conclusions that the victim's blood stains are on the accused's glove. The usual standard governing factual determinations by the jury applies: the jury ordinarily finds facts using a more-likely-than-not ("preponderance-of-the-evidence") standard.

Even in a criminal trial, a judge will not apply a higher standard of proof to questions of conditional relevance. Do not make the mistake of applying the "reasonable doubt" standard to individual items of evidence in a criminal case. The standard of reasonable doubt applies to the *aggregate* evidence that is available to the jury.[45]

"Connecting up" Evidence at Trial

We conclude this discussion of conditional relevance with a practical consideration. Suppose the plaintiff wishes to introduce evidence that the defendant, Drake, drove the black car that sped through the intersection in violation of the stop sign and struck Victim, a pedestrian. Wolsey can testify as to the speeding black car; Windsor can testify that Drake (the driver) was the only person in the car when, prior to the accident, it stopped at a gas station three miles from the intersection. Suppose that when Wolsey starts to testify about the speeding black car, Drake's counsel objects that the evidence is irrelevant because Wolsey did not see who was driving. Although that objection may on the surface appear meritorious, we have seen that the plaintiff can meet the objection by assuring the judge that she will "connect up" or link this evidence with forthcoming evidence showing that Drake was driving the black car. Thus, as we have also seen, the evidence of the speeding black car is admitted "on the condition that the proof will be introduced later"[46]

---

[44] Of course, this evidence is relevant to the accused's claim that he was not the killer.

[45] For example, in a prosecution for breaking and entering a home during the evening hours for the purpose of committing a serious crime, the prosecutor would ordinarily have to produce evidence sufficient to justify a "beyond-reasonable-doubt" finding that the accused *broke into* and *entered* a *dwelling place* in the *nighttime* with the *intent of committing a felony* therein. The reasonable doubt standard would apply to each element, but any particular piece of evidence proffered as proof of each element need only be probative and satisfy Rule 403's balancing test.

[46] Fed. R. Evid. 104(b).

that Drake was driving the black car. If the proponent fails to provide the necessary connecting evidence, the objector is entitled to strike the conditionally admitted evidence and to an instruction to the jury to ignore the evidence that was struck.

Judge-Jury Functions Under Rule 104

Rule 104(b) allocates to the jury the determination of whether the connected or "conditioning facts"—that is, those that form a predicate for the proffered evidence—actually exist. Why is this responsibility given to the jury when Rule 104(a) allocates to the judge the task of determining preliminary facts bearing on the admissibility of evidence? The answer lies in the nature of the question to be allocated to either judge or jury. There is very little chance that the jury will be misled or act irrationally in discharging its task under Rule 104(b)'s provision governing conditional relevance. The only issue for the jury is a common-sense relevance question. To return to an earlier Illustration, if the question is whether Alena was depressed, and the jury finds that the diary entry indicating depression was not written by Alena, it will ignore the entry. Similarly, if the question is whether Drake drove the speeding black car that struck the pedestrian, and the jury determines that Drake was not driving the offending vehicle, it will not hold him responsible. Thus, when the jury's task in dealing with evidence *is confined to a determination solely of conditional relevance*, there is virtually no risk that it will misuse the evidence.

These conditional relevance determinations, governed by Rule 104(b) and assigned to the jury, are quite different from determinations governed by Rule 104(a) and allocated to the judge. Rule 104(a) is concerned with findings of fact that pertain to the applicability of an exclusionary rule of evidence—including, for example, the qualifications of an expert witness and the factual predicates of a hearsay exception. If the judge did not make these factual findings, the exclusionary rules would be ineffective. For example, if the judge did not herself determine the factual issues related to admissibility, but merely "screened for sufficiency" she would often have to provisionally admit evidence that might ultimately be excludable. She would also have to instruct the jurors on the rules of evidence and tell them to ignore the evidence they have heard if they find that it is inadmissible under the exclusionary rules that the judge has explained to them. This evidentiary task is beyond the jury's capacity for two reasons: (1) the jury has no interest in technical exclusionary rules and probably will not understand their substance of how to apply them, and (2) jurors are unlikely to ignore "inadmissible" evidence that they have heard because they lack the experience and training we expect of judges.

Note also how intolerably complex the jury's task would become if the jurors had to apply the technical exclusionary rules, such as the hearsay rule, the rules governing privilege, and so forth. For example, assume a case in which the victim made a hearsay statement that the defendant shot him. The government offers the statement under the excited utterance exception to the hearsay rule. If the judge were to leave the factual predicate of the exception—that the declarant was under the influence of a startling event when making the statement—to the jury, then it would have to instruct the jury not to consider the victim's accusation unless it found the predicate fact. But the jury is unlikely to be able to so discriminate, and is at any rate likely to rely on the accusation even if they find that the victim was speaking calmly at the time. They wouldn't care whether an admissibility requirement of the Rules of Evidence was or was not met since they do not know why there is a hearsay rule and why there is an excited utterance exception. Jury confusion and incapacity would be inevitable.

The Application of Relevance Principles to Evidence of Similar Events

Suppose the plaintiff, attending her favorite play, slips on the theater stairs during intermission. She subsequently brings suit against the theater, alleging its negligence in allowing the carpet on the stairs to buckle. At trial, the attorney for the plaintiff offers evidence that two weeks prior to the plaintiff's fall, another patron slipped and fell on the same stairway.

Whether the evidence is admissible depends upon the circumstances surrounding each event—the principal (litigated) event and the collateral one. More to the point, the admissibility of evidence of "similar events" depends upon the trial judge's careful application of Rule 403. Collateral events, similar to the one that is the subject of a trial, sometimes have probative value to show a dangerous condition, that the defendant had "fair warning" or notice that a hazardous condition might exist, or that the condition in question was the cause of the plaintiff's harm or injury. On the other hand, the judge must take account of dissimilarities between the events, the possibility of conditions having changed between the collateral and principal event, jury distraction, and the consumption of trial time in proving up the collateral event—especially if that event is in dispute. In the example above, for instance, there may be significant differences in lighting on the two occasions, the number of persons using the stairs, the youth and agility of the two persons who fell, and the probability of other explanations for the two mishaps, such as a beverage spilled on the carpet in question. Sometimes, changed conditions diminish the probative value of a similar event, as where vegetation that blocked visibility at an intersection in July has been cut back by the highway department or has simply lost its leaves by November, and so is no longer an obstacle to observing oncoming traffic.

The judge must determine whether the probative value of evidence of the similar event(s) is substantially outweighed by Rule 403's counterweights to admissibility, such as jury confusion, time consumption, and prejudice. If the other act is offered to prove causation—i.e., that both acts are attributable to the same cause—it is generally the case that the evidence of the other event must be "substantially similar" in order to be admissible under Rule 403. Moreover, if the cause of the collateral act is itself in dispute, it is unlikely that evidence of the act will withstand an objection, because the court will be concerned about "a trial within a trial." On the other hand, if the other event is offered to prove that the defendant had or should have had *notice* of the dangerous condition, then strict similarity is not required—because anything close should have put the defendant on a duty of inquiry. Then there will be another Rule 403 balancing required, to determine whether the probative value of the other act in proving notice is substantially outweighed by the risk that the jury will mistakenly consider the other act as proof of causation.

§ 3.5   Direct and Circumstantial Evidence

Attorneys and judges often speak of evidence as being "direct" or, alternatively, "circumstantial." The difference between these types of evidence is straightforward: direct evidence, if believed, proves the fact without the need to draw any inference. The classic example is eyewitness testimony of a disputed event, offered to prove the event: "I saw Dali thrust a knife into Picasso's chest." Circumstantial evidence, if believed, requires the factfinder to draw one or more inferences in order to reach the fact in dispute. The classic example is testimony that is not a description of the disputed event but rather about a fact that is somehow related to it: "I saw Dali flee the scene of the stabbing and throw a knife into the river." For direct evidence, the trier's only task is to decide whether it is accurate (*i.e.* believable). In the imagined case above, the trier would have only to decide whether to believe the witness who testifies that she saw Dali stab Picasso. The judge has essentially no screening role as to direct evidence because it is the jury, and not the judge, that decides credibility.

The testimony about flight and discarding the knife, however, calls for a different mental process by the trier. As with direct evidence, the first step is to determine whether the proffered testimony is credible. (Should the witness who testifies that Dali fled and threw a knife into the river be believed?) Assuming the trier believes the testimony, (i.e., determines that more likely than not, it is true), it then becomes necessary for the trier to draw inferences to determine how strongly the evidence increases the probability that Dali stabbed Picasso. For example, the trier might draw inferences such as these: flight is associated with guilt; disposal of the knife points toward a cover-up; a cover-up suggests guilt, and so forth. Note that in order to be relevant, the circumstantial evidence, once believed, does not have to establish by a preponderance of evidence (or beyond a reasonable doubt) that Dali stabbed Picasso. The evidence need only increase the probability that he did so. Of course, when all the evidence has been received, the judge must decide whether or not, taken collectively, the evidence justifies a jury finding by a preponderance of the evidence (in a civil case) or beyond a reasonable doubt (in a criminal case). If it does not, the judge herself will rule in favor of the defendant.

Circumstantial evidence is not intrinsically inferior to direct evidence. Suppose, for example, that *D* is accused of breaking into *V's* apartment in the nighttime and stealing a diamond watch and other items of jewelry. He denies the offense and claims that he was in another city on the night of the crime. Nonetheless, *D's* fingerprints are found on *V's* windowsill and on her jewelry box, and there is testimony that during the afternoon preceding the crime, *D* was seen near *V's* residence. This circumstantial evidence may be more convincing than testimony by *V's* husband that he saw *D* take the jewelry, particularly if the lighting were bad, the time for observation fleeting, or *D's* physical or facial features were partially obscured. The weight to be accorded both circumstantial and direct evidence is determined by the jury, and it is dependent on the particular evidence presented and the surrounding circumstances, not by a formal classification.

§ 3.6   Rules of Relevance Related to Character

Introduction: Protective Rules

Over the years, certain relevance questions recurred with such frequency that appellate courts began to forge definite principles and rules to control trial courts' evidentiary decisions. Over time, these judicial principles and rules became fairly uniform across American courts and, in 1975 when the Federal Rules of Evidence were adopted, these appellate determinations were crafted into specific provisions of the Federal Rules. These rules, known as "relevance rules" appear in Article IV of the Rules, specifically Rules 404–415.[47] The rules that are key to the discussion here are Rules 404, 405, and 412–415.

Various policies and practical concerns undergird the "fixed" or "determinate" relevance rules but, broadly speaking, two themes predominate. One cluster of rules—the group discussed here in § 3.6—is concerned primarily with fairness in the trial process. The central issue is whether to admit evidence that a party has a particular character trait or propensity that increases (or decreases) the likelihood that he acted in conformity with that trait on a particular occasion. Suppose, for example, John Claggart, who is prosecuted for assaulting Billy Budd, is a man of violent, aggressive temperament. Should the court receive evidence of other occasions on which Claggart had been aggressive and violent? Alternatively, should the court receive testimony of witnesses who know Claggart, each of whom will give his opinion that Claggart is an aggressive, violent man? Finally, should the court permit witnesses familiar with Claggart's reputation to testify that he is reputed to be aggressive and violent? Whatever the *form* of the testimony (that is, whether it reveals other incidents, the opinion of associates, or Claggart's reputation), evidence depicting Claggart's violent disposition (a character trait) would be at least somewhat probative of his action on the day in question.

However, a basic tenet of American justice is that a trial is focused on the litigated event and not upon other misdeeds or upon the character traits of the parties. It is said: "We try cases, not people." The purpose of a trial is to resolve the event in question, and not to rectify other wrongs or redress undesirable features of a party's character. Furthermore, common observation suggests a person may sometimes act inconsistently with a particular character trait. Note also that judicial inquiry into character carries with it the price of distraction from the principal event and the consumption of trial time. Quite aside from these considerations, however, evidence of character or propensity raises a genuine risk that the trier of fact may base its decision upon a party's "good" or "bad" character and not upon the strength of the evidence concerning the litigated event. Thus, the rules and principles that appear in this subsection are designed to strike a balance between probative character evidence, on the one hand, and countervailing concerns, especially trial fairness, on the other.

---

[47] Rules 404–411 were part of the Federal Rules of Evidence enacted by Congress in 1975. Rule 412 was added later by a separate act of Congress, as were Rules 413–415.

Chapter IV, which follows this subsection (§ 3.6), deals with additional determinate rules of relevance. Generally speaking, these latter rules control admissibility in circumstances in which probative value (suggesting admissibility) comes into conflict with public or social policy (suggesting inadmissibility). An example would be proffered evidence that the defendant, an alleged tortfeasor, paid the hospital bill of the injured plaintiff. Although defendant's voluntary payment might suggest that he felt that he was legally liable, the law has sought to encourage "Good Samaritan" acts. The rule of evidence[48] that rejects disclosures that the defendant paid the plaintiff's medical expenses is designed to protect the benefactor from adverse evidentiary consequences.

Character Evidence: In General

In everyday affairs, we often rely on assessments of character. Consider, for example, the likelihood that a character appraisal will affect the decision of an employer who is selecting a new employee; or the decision of a lender who is deciding whether to make a loan; or the decision of a professional sports executive who is considering whether to bid on or trade for an athlete; or the decision of the character and fitness committee concerning a candidate for admission to the Bar. And, note again the sources of information available to one who is attempting to determine the character of another (X). First, witnesses could testify that X has a reputation for a certain character trait in his residential or employment community; second, witnesses acquainted with X could each give his opinion about X's character; and third, witnesses who have observed X's conduct on various occasions could describe his actions. Arguably, this third source of information is the most accurate; the second less so, and the first the least accurate.

These possibilities of the use of character in ordinary affairs are pertinent to the use of character evidence in the courtroom. As you will see, one set of specific evidentiary rules revolves around the central question in the area of character evidence, namely, whether evidence of a person's character trait is admissible to prove conduct in accordance with that trait. (Here, for example, one of several determinants is whether the issue arises in a criminal, as opposed to a civil, case.) A second set of rules revolves around the question of *what kind* of evidence is acceptable for the purpose of proving character in those instances where proof of character is permitted. For example, a rule might allow "reputation evidence" and "opinion evidence," but disallow "conduct evidence" because evidence describing particular instances of conduct, despite its possibly

---

[48]   Fed. R. Evid. 409.

superior probative value, is often unduly distracting and time-consuming. Indeed, as you will see, opinion and reputation evidence are the preferred means of proving character, although in one circumstance, evidence of past conduct is also available.

The materials that follow contain a number of subtle distinctions. Perhaps these fine distinctions are a reflection of the law's ambivalence about character. As you make your way through the text immediately ahead, be especially attentive to the purpose for which character evidence is being offered. Purpose is the most important determinant in the admissibility of character evidence, although—as you will see—it is not the only one. As noted above, another important determinant is whether the case in which character evidence is proffered is criminal or civil. The use of character evidence in civil cases is severely restricted.

Character Evidence: When Character Is an Essential Element

Sometimes (but as you will see, infrequently) the substantive law makes the nature of one's character a dispositive issue at trial. That is, the existence or nonexistence of a character trait is itself an issue that determines the outcome of the trial. Lawyers and courts refer to this situation as one in which character is "in issue."

Consider the following hypothetical case:

> Shylock files a character defamation suit against Antonio. In the complaint, the plaintiff alleges that Antonio, in the presence of third persons, referred to Shylock as a "usurious cheat." In his answer, Antonio asserts the defense of truth and at trial he offers a witness who will testify that Shylock has a *reputation* as a lender who charges exorbitant interest rates and cheats uninformed borrowers by making misleading and false statements. Antonio also offers two witnesses (former employees of Shylock) who are familiar with Shylock's business practices and each will testify that in his *opinion* Shylock is deceptive and dishonest in his lending practices. Finally, Antonio offers three witnesses who will testify as to specific *past events*; namely that each of them had received loans from Shylock only to discover later that Shylock had provided false information about the true rate of interest.

Notice the role that character plays in this hypothetical. The task of the trier of fact is to decide if Shylock's character is in fact that of a "usurious cheat." They *do not have to go on to decide whether on a particular occasion Shylock cheated one of his borrowers.* Shylock's character, in other words, is an end in and of itself—an ultimate issue. When that is the case, it stands to reason that concerns about character evidence evaporate—the substantive law *requires* the parties to proffer character evidence.

Federal Rule 405(b)—Proving Character When It Is in Issue

Federal Rule 405 is entitled "Methods of Proving Character." In those cases where character is allowed to prove conduct in accordance with the character, Rule 405(a) restricts the kind of evidence that may be used to prove the character trait. First, witnesses familiar with the reputation of the subject (the person whose character is in question) may testify as to that reputation. Second, witnesses who know the subject may give an opinion as to his character. Evidence of specific instances of conduct, however, is normally disallowed when character is offered circumstantially to prove conduct. The reason for restricting the allowable types of evidence to reputation and opinion is that presentation by those two methods does not require a significant expenditure of time. In contrast, proof of character by evidence of specific instances of conduct is usually time-consuming and distracting, and for these reasons is normally rejected.

However, *Rule 405(b)*, which reads as follows, suspends the usual restriction concerning modes of proof *in cases where character is in issue*:

> **(b) By Specific Instances of Conduct.** When a person's character or character trait is an essential element of a charge, claim, or defense, the character trait may *also* be proved by relevant specific instances of the person's conduct. [emphasis added]

Thus, in the imagined case above, *all three methods of proof* are available to Antonio. Obviously, this is because Shylock's character takes center stage as an ultimate issue; in the words of Rule 405(b), it is an "essential element" of the claim and defense. His character is not being used to prove conduct on a particular occasion, for example, by drawing the inference that because Shylock has the character of a cheater, he probably cheated the plaintiff to whom he lent money. The suit is not brought by a plaintiff who claims he is a victim of Shylock's dishonest lending practices. The key to the hypothetical is that because character is an essential element of Antonio's defense of truth, he is entitled to prove character by reputation evidence, opinion evidence, or specific instances of conduct. The rationale is that if a person's character is the fact in dispute in the case, the importance of the character is such that the parties should be able to prove it in any probative way.

Cases in which character "is an essential element of a charge, claim or defense" and thus important enough to be within the embrace of Federal Rule 405(b) are *infrequent*; it is rare that the substantive law requires proof of a person's character, as the substantive law is generally more concerned with conduct than with personality traits. In addition to cases based on defamation of character (where truth is a defense), there is a cluster of cases involving a claim against an employer or principal for hiring an unfit employee or agent. Typically, the defendant's liability hinges on proof that he negligently hired a person of unfit character. In practical terms, the employer will be liable *only if he* hired a person whose character made her unfit for the position she filled and, further, *if the* employer knew or should have known about her unfit character. In criminal cases, the most common situation in which character becomes an issue is when a defendant claims entrapment in a jurisdiction in which the entrapment defense is dependent on whether the defendant was predisposed to commit the crime.

ILLUSTRATIONS

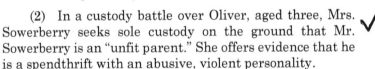

(1) Henry, Jr., a ten-year-old, is injured while aboard a carnival ride called Whip-A-Roo. Through a guardian, he brings suit against Carnival Inc., the owner and operator of the carnival. The complaint alleges that Carnival was negligent in hiring and retaining one Hyde, the operator of the Whip-A-Roo, because Hyde was "an intemperate vagabond who was addicted to drugs and the excessive use of intoxicating beverages. . . ."

(2) In a custody battle over Oliver, aged three, Mrs. Sowerberry seeks sole custody on the ground that Mr. Sowerberry is an "unfit parent." She offers evidence that he is a spendthrift with an abusive, violent personality.

Illustration (1) is a straightforward application of the type of case just described in the text: the employer's liability hinges on proof that he hired a person of "intemperate character." That person's character is essential to the plaintiff's claim and thus all three types of character evidence are available to the plaintiff.

Illustration (2) is more subtle and requires a more precise analysis. If the plaintiff's evidence pertaining to character—evidence such as reputation, opinion, or specific events—is offered solely to prove Sowerberry's *traits* of profligacy, violence, and abuse, it is admissible. His character is alleged to be "unfit" and Mrs. Sowerberry's evidence supports this proposition. However, were this same evidence offered for the purpose of showing, by a process of inference-drawing, Sowerberry's conduct on a particular occasion, then Rule 405(b) would not apply. (For example, suppose Mrs. Sowerberry offered evidence of Mr. Sowerberry's violent character to support her claim that on Christmas day he beat Oliver with a belt.) Furthermore, as you will see, the rule in *civil* cases is that character evidence, *no matter what its type, is only admissible when character is in issue, and is inadmissible to prove conduct on a particular occasion.* Thus, we are reminded that when a party offers character evidence, the opponent must consider whether character evidence is admissible at all and, if it is, what type of character evidence is permissible.

Notice how the principle of relevance applies to proving character. When a proponent is allowed to prove character, there are two separate relevance questions. First, is the proffered character *evidence* probative of the character trait alleged? Second, is the alleged character trait a consequential proposition or probative of some consequential proposition? As to the second inquiry, suppose the plaintiff sues a small loan company for hiring a dishonest employee (whose actions were the immediate cause of the plaintiff's loss). The consequential character trait at issue is dishonesty, rather than carelessness, intemperance, or violence. The trait of dishonesty, an essential component of the plaintiff's claims is clearly a consequential fact. As to the first inquiry, evidence demonstrating that the employee became angry and truculent when under stress should be rejected as irrelevant. Such evidence is not probative of the character trait at issue: dishonesty.

To summarize: you must determine whether a character trait is itself in dispute ("in issue") or whether it is offered as circumstantial evidence of conduct. Next, you must determine whether the proffered character evidence has probative value to establish the trait in question. Of course, it is comparatively rare for a character trait, standing alone, to be an ultimate proposition—that is, a core element of a claim or defense. More frequently, a character trait has probative value to prove conduct on a particular occasion. However, as you will see, the law of evidence allows the circumstantial use of character only in criminal cases, and only in limited circumstances in criminal cases.[49]

§ 3.6–1   Character Evidence: Criminal and Civil Cases Distinguished

The "Circumstantial" Use of Character

We turn now to what is sometimes called the "circumstantial use of character." More precisely, in the language of Federal Rule 404(a), circumstantial use refers to the use of "[e]vidence of a person's

---

[49]   Note that different rules apply when a party is impeaching a witness—in those circumstances, the witness's character for truthfulness can be proved, subject to the limitations of Fed. R. Evid. 608 and 609. *See infra* Chapter IX, § 9.3.

character or character trait * * * to prove that on a particular occasion the person acted in accordance with the character or trait." Use of one's character to prove his conduct at a specific time or on a particular occasion is disfavored. The traditional justification for rejecting character evidence offered to prove conduct is that its probative value is substantially outweighed by the introduction of collateral issues, by the consumption of time, and by the risk of unfair prejudice. The last factor carries particular weight. There is, for example, a risk that the character of one of the parties (either good or bad character) may unduly sway the jury and deflect its attention from evidence of the *conduct* that is the subject of the trial. Furthermore, there is a risk that the jury may conclude that even if there are doubts about liability or guilt, the party with bad character "deserves" to lose, or, in a civil case, the party with a good character "deserves" to win. The risk of prejudice is especially high in a criminal prosecution in which the government portrays the accused as a person of unsavory disposition.

Federal Rule 404

Use of character evidence to prove particular conduct (usually, conduct during the litigated event) is controlled by Federal Rule 404. It reads as follows:

CHARACTER EVIDENCE; OTHER
CRIMES, WRONGS, OR ACTS

(a) Character Evidence.

  (1) Prohibited Uses. Evidence of a person's character or character trait is not admissible to prove that on a particular occasion the person acted in accordance with the character or trait.

  (2) Exceptions for a Defendant or a Victim in a Criminal Case. The following exceptions apply in a criminal case:

   (A) a defendant may offer evidence of the defendant's pertinent trait, and if the evidence is admitted, the prosecutor may offer evidence to rebut it;

   (B) subject to the limitation in Rule 412, a defendant may offer evidence of an alleged victim's pertinent trait, and if the evidence is admitted, the prosecutor may:

    (i) offer evidence to rebut it; and

    (ii) offer evidence of the defendant's same trait; and

   (C) in a homicide case, the prosecutor may offer evidence of the alleged victim's trait of peacefulness to rebut evidence that the victim was the first aggressor.

(3) Exceptions for a Witness. Evidence of a witness's character may be admitted under Rules 607, 608, and 609.

(b) Other Crimes, Wrongs, or Acts.

(1) Prohibited Uses. Evidence of any other crime, wrong, or act is not admissible to prove a person's character in order to show that on a particular occasion the person acted in accordance with the character.

(2) Permitted Uses. This evidence may be admissible for another purpose, such as proving motive, opportunity, intent, preparation, plan, knowledge, identity, absence of mistake, or lack of accident.

(3) Notice in a Criminal Case. In a criminal case, the prosecutor must:

(A) provide reasonable notice of any such evidence that the prosecutor intends to offer at trial, so that the defendant has a fair opportunity to meet it;

(B) articulate in the notice the permitted purpose for which the prosecutor intends to offer the evidence and the reasoning that supports the purpose; and

(C) do so in writing before trial—or in any form during trial if the court, for good cause, excuses lack of pretrial notice.

Observe that Rule 404(a)(1) begins with a general prohibition, followed by three exceptions in (a)(2) and an additional exception, Rule 404(a)(3), which deals with witnesses. You will see in Chapter IX that Rules 608 and 609 permits, under certain conditions, evidence pertaining to a witness's character for truthfulness—the factfinder can consider that because if the witness has an untruthful character, the witness may be acting in accordance with that character while testifying. This evidentiary process ("impeachment" and "rehabilitation") involves casting doubt on the truthfulness of a witness's testimony (in other words, her testimonial "conduct" at trial) and rehabilitating the credibility of a witness who is attacked. The rules of impeachment and rehabilitation apply, with minor variations, in *both criminal and civil cases*.

So, we put aside impeachment of witnesses until Chapter IX and are about to examine the remainder of Rule 404(a) in some detail. But, before doing that it is important to note that the major "exception" to the general prohibition in Rule 404(a)(1) is not found in 404(a)(2) but is contained in Rule 404(b). Close examination of this subsection reveals that it does not provide an exception at all, but rather it draws a *distinction*. After reaffirming the general prohibition against the use of character to prove particular conduct, Rule 404(b) generally permits evidence that is offered to show distinct features of the crime charged in a criminal case or a disputed issue in a civil case, such as motive or identity—that is, it permits evidence to be admitted when it is offered for a purpose other than proving a person's propensity to act in a particular way.[50]

Imagine, for example, that *D* is charged with extortion and money laundering. The government convinces *D's* henchman, Cairo, to testify for the prosecution. Two weeks before *D's* scheduled trial, Cairo disappears; three months later his body is found and, thereafter, *D* is charged with homicide. At *D's* homicide trial, the judge admits evidence of *D's* illegal commercial activities and Cairo's intention to testify against him in the extortion trial. Although a by-product of this evidence is to prove *D's* character (for it shows he has engaged in other criminal activities), the proper purpose of this evidence is to establish *D's* motive for murdering Cairo. The key to admissibility lies in the purpose for which the evidence is offered. It cannot be offered on the ground that since *D* engaged in other crimes he has a "criminal disposition or character" and therefore it is more likely that he murdered Cairo. Rather, the evidence, to be admissible, must be offered to prove a specific point separate from propensity: motive. We will examine Rule 404(b) in greater detail, *infra*, but include it here to emphasize how important it is, especially in the prosecution of criminal cases.

Let us now return to the major exceptions contained in Rule 404(a), found in subsection (a)(2). Observe that these exceptions are *confined to criminal trials*. It is never permissible in a civil case to prove a person's character in order to prove conduct in accordance with that character. Note also that these subsections do not apply unless the accused, in his evidentiary presentation, makes the first or opening move. We will take up the details of these provisions in the material that follows. The picture that is emerging, however, is that, aside from character evidence used to impeach a witness, there is general reluctance to admit character evidence to prove a person's conduct. In criminal cases, this reluctance gives way to the accused's right to present character evidence (known as the "rule of mercy"). In civil cases, however, this reluctance is firm. Thus, the *circumstantial* use of character evidence is prohibited in civil cases. Furthermore, the permitted types of character evidence to prove conduct are opinion evidence and reputation evidence. However, in those

---

[50]   Although Fed. R. Evid. 404(b) is used much more frequently in criminal cases than in civil cases, it is applicable in all cases. Character evidence offered under Rule 404(a)(2) to prove conduct is confined to criminal cases, it can only be raised in the first instance by the accused, and it is subject to limitations as to form. *See* Fed. R. Evid. 405(a).

comparatively rare cases where character is "an essential element of a charge, claim, or defense"[51] evidence revealing specific instances of the subject's past conduct may also be used to prove his character.

§ 3.6–2   Character Evidence: Circumstantial Use of Character in Criminal Cases

Because most criminal acts involve calculated, deliberate conduct, the character of the accused often has probative value. If, for example, *D* has engaged in false advertising and embezzlement in the past, his deceitful character (as shown by this misconduct) increases the likelihood of his guilt when he is subsequently indicted for insurance fraud. However, as we saw in the last subsection, there are countervailing considerations that push against admitting evidence of *D's* character. For example, the trier of fact might accord undue probative force to evidence of *D's* character, paying little heed to the evidence directly bearing on his conduct in connection with the charge of insurance fraud. That is, the jury might use his "bad character" as the major determinant of his guilt. Or perhaps the trier will de-emphasize the consequences of a false determination that the accused committed the crime charged (insurance fraud) because evidence of his unfavorable character has provoked the trier's belief that he deserves to be confined or otherwise penalized—not only for the prior act, but for what he might do in the future, given his propensities.

These dangers of unfair prejudicial effect, when combined with other counterweights to admission, such as misleading the jury and time consumption, have led to the general prohibition embodied in Rule 404(a): Character evidence is not usually admissible to prove *D's* (or, for that matter, any other actor's) conduct on a particular occasion. What this prohibition means in the present context is that the prosecutor cannot introduce evidence of *D's* character for the purpose of helping to prove that *D* committed the crime with which he is charged.

The Accused's Right to Introduce Character Evidence

The first major exception to the general exclusionary principle as to circumstantial use of character evidence (Rule 404(a)) is set out in Rule 404(a)(2)(A), which allows the defendant in a criminal case to introduce evidence of a "pertinent" trait of character. This means that the defendant may introduce evidence of a character trait that would affect his conduct in such a way as to make it less likely that he committed the crime charged. A character trait that is not inconsistent with the crime charged has no probative value to

---

[51]   Fed. R. Evid. 405(b).

demonstrate that the accused did not commit the alleged offense. For example, in a prosecution for aggravated assault, the defendant would not be permitted to introduce evidence of his character trait for honesty. In the words of Rule 404, evidence of honesty would not be a "pertinent" character trait.

Why is it that the criminal defendant is excepted from the general prohibition against the "circumstantial" use of character evidence (*i.e.*, use that entails inferring specific conduct)? This concession—called the "rule of mercy"—is part of the deeply embedded American tradition favoring the accused in a criminal trial. In general, the American Constitution and the judicial systems that operate under it take special precautions to reduce the risk that an innocent defendant will be falsely convicted. This is especially so because the prosecution is the party with all the resources for discovering and preparing evidence—in some cases the defendant may only have his "good name" for a defense. Furthermore, because a major ground for excluding character evidence is apprehension about its prejudicial effect, the accused's use of evidence of good character can be justified because, in this context, there is a reduced risk that the trier will evaluate the evidence irrationally or emotionally.

Evidence of the Victim's Character

In addition to the right to portray his own character, Rule 404(a)(2)(B) extends to the criminal defendant the right to introduce evidence regarding the victim's character when this evidence is relevant to the defense. Again, however, the principle of relevance applies with full force: it is essential that the victim's character trait raised by the defendant is, in fact, relevant to the defense. Suppose in a criminal assault case the accused defends on the ground of self-defense. It would be relevant to show that the victim was a violent, aggressive person; it would not be relevant to show that the victim was a cheat or a drug addict.[52]

It will come as no surprise that the victim's character is irrelevant in the vast array of criminal cases. Cases in which self-defense is claimed are the major exception, in which case the victim's propensity for violence would be pertinent. Another possibility could theoretically arise with respect to victims in sexual assault cases; but

---

[52] Although a defendant could not defend on the basis of self-defense by offering character evidence showing that the victim was a cheat or a drug addict, such evidence could be admitted for another purpose. Suppose, for example, the defense claimed that the defendant had publicly accused the victim of being a cheat and/or a drug addict and the victim responded by assaulting the defendant. The evidence of the defendant's public accusation would not be character evidence; it would be evidence that is relevant to the defense theory that the victim had a motive to assault the defendant.

in those cases Rule 404 takes a back seat to the "rape shield" protection provided by Rule 412.[53]

The Prosecution's Rebuttal

A feature common to the exceptions in Rule 404(a)(2) is that, with one minor wrinkle,[54] it is the exclusive right of the criminal defendant to initiate the use of character evidence to prove conduct. But once the defendant has made the first move on character during his evidentiary presentation, the door is open for the prosecution to respond to the defendant's character evidence. Two attacks are available to the prosecutor: the first is to rigorously cross-examine D's character witness(es);[55] the second is to offer one or more character witnesses who offer a different take on character from that offered by defense witnesses. For example, if D's character witnesses have testified to his peaceful, nonviolent nature, the prosecution's character witnesses could testify to D's violent and bellicose disposition.

The defense offer of reputation or opinion evidence regarding the defendant's pertinent character trait permits the prosecution to offer rebuttal character evidence regarding the defendant, but does not permit the prosecution to offer character evidence relating to the victim. That is because, by bringing evidence of his own character only, the defendant has not opened the door to the victim's character. The prosecution's rebuttal right is broader when the defendant presents character witnesses who testify the victim's pertinent character trait. Suppose, for example, in a prosecution for criminal assault, D pleads self-defense and presents character witnesses who testify that V has a violent, aggressive character. It is clear that the prosecutor can present rebuttal character witnesses who portray V as nonviolent and peaceable. But suppose the prosecutor goes further and offers character evidence that D is a violent, aggressive individual. In terms of Rule 404, the issue is whether the accused's use of character evidence to establish a relevant trait of the alleged victim triggers the prosecutor's right to use character evidence to prove that the defendant has the *same* character trait. The current version of Rule 404(a)(2)(B) (reflecting an amendment in 2000) yields an affirmative answer.

In short, when D's evidence of V's character trait is admitted under Rule 404(a)(2), the prosecutor, in addition to being able to

---

[53]   See § 3.6–7.

[54]   *See* Fed. R. Evid. 404(a)(2)(C), discussed *infra*.

[55]   These would either be opinion witnesses or reputation witnesses. Recall that witnesses proffered to testify to specific instances of the subject's past conduct to prove the subject's character trait(s) are disallowed unless character "is an essential element of a charge, claim, or defense." Fed. R. Evid. 405(b).

rebut evidence concerning *V's* character, can introduce evidence that *D* has the same trait that *D* attributed to *V*. The common sense underlying this rule of parity is obvious enough: if the trier is made aware only of the victim's bad character trait and shielded from evidence that the accused has the same character trait, there is an increased risk that the trier will draw an erroneous inference about who provoked the violent encounter.

Homicide Cases

A difficult question arises when the accused makes an "indirect attack" on the victim's character *in a homicide case*. That is, the accused does not call witnesses to testify about *V's* character, but through other evidence, the defense portrays *V*, the deceased, as the first aggressor. Since *D* has not called to the stand any character witnesses, it can be argued that *D* has not opened the door to (rebuttal) *character* evidence by the prosecutor. It is, as we have seen, generally true that the prosecution cannot call character witnesses unless the accused has first done so.

A close reading of Rule 404(a)(2)(C), however, reveals that if the accused introduces evidence (not necessarily character evidence) in a homicide prosecution for the purpose of showing that the victim was the first aggressor, the door is partially open.[56] That is, the prosecutor is now entitled to introduce "evidence of the alleged victim's trait of peacefulness. . . ." This rule governing rebuttal recognizes that in murder cases where the central question is who was the initial aggressor, a character trait such as peacefulness or aggressiveness can have significant probative force. In order for the trier to assess these traits accurately, it seems fair to allow the prosecution to counter the accused's evidence that the victim was the first aggressor. As the alleged victim is now dead, the prosecutor's only available means of rebutting *D's* evidence may be to call witnesses who will testify that *V* was a peaceful, nonviolent person. The risk of prejudice to the accused is limited, first, because the prosecution's character evidence is confined to *V's* (not *D's*) character, and, second, because the allowable evidence is restricted to *V's* peaceful nature and does not include other admirable traits. In sum, the evidence of *V's* peaceful character is allowed on the grounds of evidentiary balance and the unlikelihood that the trier will use this evidence irrationally. The expectation is that the trier will use

---

[56] Even in this limited instance, the prosecution's use of character evidence must be triggered by the defendant's presentation of some evidence, i.e., the defendant must "open the door" before the prosecution can introduce character evidence to prove conduct. The door is opened when the defense puts on evidence that the deceased was the first aggressor.

evidence of *V's* peaceful character for its intended purpose, namely, to determine who initiated the deadly encounter.

Presenting and Cross-Examining Character Witnesses

Recall that Federal Rule 405 restricts the form of evidence by which a subject's character can be proven. When character is offered for the inference that the subject acted in accordance with character on a particular occasion, Rule 405(a) provides that proof is limited to testimony in the form of reputation or opinion. The "reputation witness" must be familiar with the subject's reputation in a setting (such as the subject's community or work environment) that is sufficiently communal for her reputation to develop. The "opinion witness" must be sufficiently acquainted with the subject to be able to form a well-founded opinion concerning the latter's character. The attorney presenting a character witness must initially elicit "foundation" testimony that establishes the required familiarity.

A reputation witness testifies as to the subject's reputation for the trait in question (for example, honesty); an opinion witness testifies that in her opinion the subject possesses the trait in question (for example, nonviolence). As we have seen, evidence of *specific instances* of the subject's actions for the purpose of inferring that she has the character trait in question is disallowed when offered to prove the subject's conduct.[57] Although such evidence is often the most accurate measure of the subject's character, its introduction is both time-consuming and a source of significant jury distraction.[58] Therefore, Rule 405(b) allows evidence of the subject's specific conduct only in cases where character is in issue, that is, *only* in cases where the subject's character is "an essential element of a charge, claim, or defense." In these relatively rare lawsuits, character may be proven by any of the available means: reputation, opinion, or specific instances of conduct.

All witnesses, including character witnesses, are subject to cross-examination and impeachment. One technique for attacking the credibility of a character witness is to weaken or negate the character witness's assertion that she is familiar with the subject's reputation or—in the case of an opinion witness—that she is well acquainted with him. The cross-examiner can, of course, ask straightforward questions that probe, for example, how long the reputation witness and the subject have lived or worked in the same community. Such a question would test the validity of the propositions underlying the witness's direct testimony, namely, that the subject has been a member of the community long enough to have

---

[57]   Fed. R. Evid. 405(a), (b).
[58]   There is often disagreement about the specific events.

developed a reputation and that the witness is familiar with it. A parallel question, appropriate for the opinion witness, probes the length and closeness of the witness's acquaintance with the subject.

Beyond these obvious inquiries, however, the cross-examiner can ask the reputation witness questions about events involving the subject that would be likely to affect the subject's reputation for the trait(s) in question. Correspondingly, the cross-examiner can ask the opinion witness about events that would be likely to affect her opinion about the subject's character for the trait(s) in question. The questions take either the form of "Have you heard that. . . ?" (appropriate for the reputation witness) or "Did you know that . . . ?" (appropriate for the opinion witness). Suppose, for example, an opinion (character) witness testifies that in her estimation the defendant is very brave and would never have deserted the Army. The cross-examiner might ask the witness if she knew that during a training exercise in which live ammunition was used, the defendant left his squad and hid in a storage building. If the witness answers "no," the cross-examiner has weakened her assertion (made during direct) that she is knowledgeable about the defendant's character for bravery. If the witness answers "yes," the cross-examiner has raised doubts about the standard the character witness used on direct when she characterized the defendant as "very brave."[59] Similarly as to a reputation witness, if that witness has not heard about a defendant's bad activity, the witness might not be plugged into the community; and if the witness has heard about the bad activity and yet still testifies to good reputation, then the judgement of the community is called into question.

ILLUSTRATION

Benedict Arnold is charged with spying for a foreign country and planting false evidence that was designed to incriminate a CIA agent, Iago, for Arnold's deceitful acts. Arnold defends on the ground that in fact *he* was framed by Iago, the alleged victim, who was scheming to advance his own career. In addition to his own testimony, Arnold calls a reputation witness, Lord Venice, and an opinion witness, Cassio, who will each provide character evidence that Arnold is law-abiding and honest. The accused also calls Roderigo, an ex-CIA agent who served as a subordinate to Iago for over ten years. Roderigo testifies that Iago is "deceitful, treacherous, and obsessively ambitious."

---

[59] The cross-examiner would also cast doubt on the character witness's truthfulness, at least in the context of this imagined case.

What evidentiary opportunities are available to the prosecutor as a result of the testimony presented by the defense?

First, *any* witness (e.g., Arnold, Venice, Cassio, and Roderigo) is subject to the traditional impeachment techniques described in Chapter IX. For example, by testifying on his own behalf, Arnold runs the risk that the prosecutor will present evidence that Arnold has been convicted of crimes that involve deceit and thus reflect adversely on his character for truthfulness. The prosecutor could also present evidence that Arnold has made prior statements that are inconsistent with his courtroom testimony. Furthermore, during his cross-examination of Arnold, the prosecutor can inquire about prior "bad acts" (not resulting in a conviction), such as falsifying an application for a business license or filing a false insurance claim, that cast doubt upon Arnold's character for truthfulness. These techniques of impeachment are discussed in Chapter IX. They can be used to impeach any witness who testifies at trial.

Second, the prosecutor can try to weaken the testimony of Lord Venice (Arnold's reputation witness) and Cassio (Arnold's opinion witness) by exposing their lack of familiarity with Arnold's reputation or with Arnold himself. One means of achieving this end is to ask "have you heard" or "did you know" questions. Note that these questions test not only the character witnesses' familiarity with the subject's reputation or the subject himself, but also the standard these witnesses are using when they assert that Arnold is law-abiding and honest. For example, the prosecutor might ask Cassio, the opinion witness, whether he was aware that Arnold had falsified his travel expenses when seeking reimbursement from his government employer. Observe that by using witnesses to portray his character as "law-abiding," Arnold presents the prosecutor with a considerable range of possible did-you-know (or have-you-heard) questions, because any number of activities might be inconsistent with Arnold's reputed "law-abiding" character. (For example, the prosecutor could ask Cassio, "Did you know that Arnold was convicted of reckless and drunken driving on August, 15, 2010?")

Third, by introducing character evidence that the victim, Iago is "deceitful, treacherous, and obsessively ambitious," Arnold triggers the prosecutor's right to present character witnesses who will testify that Iago is, say, truthful, fair, and honest. Moreover, the prosecution will be allowed to present character witnesses to testify that *Arnold* is deceitful, treacherous, and obsessively ambitious. This is because, by proving a negative character trait of the victim, the defendant opens the door to testimony that he has the same character trait. See Rule 404(a)(2)(B)(ii). If the trier of fact believes this evidence bearing on Arnold's bad character, it might draw the inference that Arnold was guilty of the charged spying and planting false evidence.[60]

Evaluation of Rules Governing the Cross-Examination of Character Witnesses

The allowance of "have-you-heard" and "did-you-know" questions during the cross-examination of the accused's character witnesses may result in juror confusion and unfair prejudice in some cases. Although such questions are purportedly designed to test the knowledge of the character witness and the standard he is using in his assessment of the subject's character, these inquiries necessarily describe the subject's unfavorable conduct. ("Have you heard that the accused, Arnold, inflicted physical injury on his wife?") One judicial safeguard against abuse is the requirement that the prosecutor's questions to the character witness must be in good faith. In practical terms, this good-faith requirement means that the prosecutor, after a reasonable investigation, must be satisfied that the event that is the basis for the cross-question actually occurred before asking a "did you know" question. Similarly, the prosecutor must be satisfied that there are rumors in the community which the character witness represents concerning the actions of the accused. Since reputation can be adversely affected by rumors that are untrue, the good faith basis required to question a reputation witness need not rest on evidence that the accused did what the rumors allege. In the case of a reputation character witness, the prosecutor must also be satisfied that the actual or rumored conduct would have been widely enough known to have affected the subject's reputation. Nonetheless, there is a risk that the trier, especially a jury, will be unduly influenced or even inflamed by the accused's past conduct. Of course, the defense is entitled to an instruction that the sole purpose of asking a character witness about alleged conduct of the accused is to test the witness's familiarity with the accused (or his reputation) and to reveal the witness's standard of evaluation. The instruction will go on to direct the jury not to consider these past events as evidence of guilt in the present trial. Such an instruction, however, may at best be only modestly effective.

There is another problem with the "have you heard" and "do you know" questions that is unlikely to be solved by a judicial instruction to the jury. Indeed, the instruction the judge gives to the jury is more likely to confuse than help it. The problem arises from the fact that questions are not evidence unless a witness adopts in an answer whatever is suggested in a question. So, when a prosecutor asks a defense character (reputation) witness "have you heard that the

---

[60] The traits of deceit and treachery also bear on impeachment, that is, these traits cast doubt on the credibility of Arnold and also Iago—assuming he testifies.

accused inflicted physical injury on his wife," and the character witness answers "no," the standard assumption seems to be that the jury will discount the character witness's testimony because it appears that the witness is not fully familiar with the defendant's reputation. Any jury discount should be questionable, however, because the jury is not supposed to assume that what the prosecutor asked about it true. The same issue arises with opinion character witnesses. If the prosecutor asks a character witness "did you know that the accused inflicted physical injury on his wife," and the witness says "no," there will be no evidence admitted to inform the jury whether the accused actually did hurt his wife and thus no basis for the jury to decide whether or not the witness is fully informed. Upon request, judges will usually instruct jurors that questions are not evidence. So what do we expect the jury to do in this scenario? There are no good answers, and it is unclear exactly what the jury does. One possibility is that it assumes that the information in the question is true, and that is a violation of the instruction that questions are not evidence.

It should be noted that when the character witness answers "yes" to either a "have you heard" or "did you know" question, the jury might be in a position to evaluate the accuracy of the reputation or the reliability of the opinion testimony. But, the fact remains that the jury will still not know whether the conduct of the accused actually did occur. So, if the reputation character witness says that no one in the relevant community believed the allegation and it had no negative impact on reputation, or the opinion witness says he did not believe the allegation and thus it did not affect his opinion, the jury still might find it difficult to decide how much weight to attach to the question, the "yes" answer, and the explanation.

Consider the evidentiary options available to the prosecutor if the rules of evidence disallowed cross-questions in the form of have-you-heard or did-you-know inquiries. The prosecutor would still be entitled to impeach the accused's character witnesses by any of the standard techniques of impeachment, such as revealing a prior criminal conviction that bears on credibility, producing evidence of bias, or disclosing prior statements inconsistent with the witness's present testimony. The prosecutor could also ask straightforward questions that probe how familiar the witness really is with the accused (or his reputation). For example, the prosecutor could ask the opinion witness how long he has known the accused and how often (and under what circumstances) they have associated with each other. Finally, the prosecutor could call her own character witnesses to testify that the accused has character traits consistent with the crime charged.

These available counterattacks appear quite adequate; sufficient, indeed, to justify the elimination of the prosecutor's right to ask such questions as, "Did you know that in September, 2015, the accused committed assault with a deadly weapon?" There are, however, arguments in favor of the present rules governing the prosecutor's cross-examination of the accused's character witnesses. Recall that it is the accused who has the right to control the introduction of character evidence. When he elects to introduce evidence of his own "good" character, he is likely to select character witnesses whose personal histories are not tainted by the kind of misconduct that will allow them to be impeached by the traditional methods.[61] Furthermore, the accused is likely to choose character witnesses whose *familiarity* with her or her reputation cannot be effectively challenged. Thus, the prosecutor's cross-examination may be ineffectual unless he can ask questions about the character witness's knowledge of prior instances involving the accused. But on the other hand, the rule allowing such questions leaves room for abuse—the prosecutor can, in the guise of "testing the witness," waft innuendoes into the jury box regarding the defendant's commission of bad acts.

Ultimately the threat of introducing the accused's bad acts on cross-examination of character witnesses is likely to deter many criminal defendants from raising character issues in the first place. This is part of the compromise inherent in the character rules—there is a recognition that character evidence may be necessary in criminal cases, but also that character evidence raises difficult questions of prejudice, jury confusion, and delay. The character rules appear to be geared toward allowing character evidence only where the accused finds it absolutely necessary to present such evidence.

In view of the problems associated with character evidence, Justice Jackson's opinion in *Michelson v. United States*[62] seems an accurate statement of the rules regarding such evidence:

> Thus the law extends helpful but illogical options to a defendant. Experience taught a necessity that they be counterweighted with equally illogical conditions to keep the advantage from becoming an unfair and unreasonable one. The price a defendant must pay for attempting to prove his good name is to throw open the entire subject which the

---

[61] The only standard technique of impeachment that is likely to be available is bias. The prosecutor may be able to show, for example, that the character witness's close ties to the accused motivated her favorable testimony.

[62] 335 U.S. 469 (1948).

law has kept closed for his benefit and to make himself vulnerable where the law otherwise shields him.[63]

The Bar on Circumstantial Use of Character Evidence in Civil Cases   ᴏɴʟʏ ᴄʀɪᴍɪɴᴀʟ ᴄᴀѕᴇ ₸

Except for allowing character evidence that bears on a witness's credibility (404(a)(3)), Rule 404's exceptions to its general prohibition against admission of character evidence to prove conduct on a particular occasion are confined to criminal cases, which means that such evidence is inadmissible in civil cases. The rationale is that character evidence offered circumstantially in civil cases is not worth its cost in time consumed, distraction of the trier, and potential prejudice. The justification underlying the admission of circumstantial character evidence in criminal cases—special precautions against an erroneous conviction and the accused's right to make a full defense—are absent in civil trials. In addition, many civil trials are based on a party's unintentional behavior, such as negligent conduct. In lawsuits involving careless behavior, character evidence has weak probative value.[64]

§ 3.6–3 Evidence of Habit Distinguished from Evidence of Character

Habit is related to, but different from, character. The term "habit" refers not to a general character trait such as cautiousness, but rather to a specific, repeated response to a particular situation, such as always fastening one's seatbelt when driving. If evidence of the regular use by *X* of her seatbelt were offered to show she was a careful person, it would be excluded. However, if her regular use was shown for the inference that on the day in question she fastened her seatbelt, it would be admissible "habit evidence." Similarly, *X* may have a *character trait* for punctuality and a *habit* of returning to her office from lunch between 12:50 and 1:00 p.m. Evidence of the former would be rejected, while evidence of the latter would normally be received. Evidence of a regularly repeated response to a particular situation (habit) has probative value that generally exceeds the probative force of evidence of a character trait—because it is more specific and less volitional. Furthermore, evidence of habit is less

---

[63]   Id. at 478–479.

[64]   As we have seen, however, character evidence is admissible in civil cases when character "is an essential element of a charge, claim or defense. . . ." Fed. R. Evid. 405(b). Furthermore, as suggested earlier, in instances involving a witness's credibility, the Federal Rules allow various kinds of evidence designed to reveal bad character for truthfulness. *See e.g.,* Fed. R. Evid. 608(a) (opinion and reputation evidence admissible). Observe that when character evidence is used to attack credibility, the specific conduct to which the evidence is directed is the witness's character for truthfulness. *See generally* Chapter IX.

likely to be unfairly prejudicial than evidence of character—less likely to turn the case into a popularity contest.

Federal Rule 406

Federal Rule 406 states:

HABIT; ROUTINE PRACTICE

Evidence of a person's habit or and organization's routine practice may be admitted to prove that on a particular occasion the person or organization acted in accordance with the habit or routine practice. The court may admit this evidence regardless of whether it was corroborated or whether there was an eyewitness.

Note that the Rule makes specific reference not only to evidence of the habit of a person, but also to the "habit" (more specifically a custom or routine practice) of an organization such as, for example, a business entity, fire department, hospital, library, or government office. Because organizations generally adhere to prescribed routines and procedures, it is comparatively easy to discover established organizational practices. For example, a hospital may have a routine practice of isolating patients with certain highly contagious diseases; a business may have a routine practice of responding to complaints, and so forth.

Proving a Habit or Practice

The reality is that even if there were no Rule 406, habit and custom evidence should be admissible when relevant pursuant to Rule 402. But, the Rule was included to assure that judges and lawyers distinguished between admissible habit evidence and inadmissible character evidence and to reject certain common law restrictions on habit and custom evidence.

Rule 406 does not specify how a habit or an organizational practice (custom) is to be proved. The rule does, however—in a change from the common law—specify that admissibility is not conditioned upon the absence of eyewitnesses to the event in question or the presence of other corroborative evidence. (Both of those conditions existed under common law and are rejected under the federal rule). Such evidence should not be required, for if the habit or custom evidence has probative force, it should be admitted regardless of whether it is corroborated and even if there is eyewitness testimony.

The proponent of habit evidence needs to convince the trial judge that a person repeatedly reacted to a specific setting or stimuli with sufficient uniformity to establish a habitual response. The usual means of establishing this foundation is by presenting witnesses who have observed the actor's consistent behavior over a significant time period. (In the case of a business or other organization, written rules, standards, or procedures are also probative.) The greater the number of observations or samples, the more likely it is that a uniform pattern can be shown. This is not to suggest that there can never be a deviation from habitual conduct; it is to say, however, that foundational evidence is weakened by variable conduct, as well as by eyewitness observations that span only a short period of time, or include only a small number of instances. Obviously, the trial judge must be allowed considerable discretion both in determining whether conduct is narrow and specific enough to constitute a habit (as opposed to a character trait) and whether the foundational evidence of repetitious activity suffices to establish a habit or practice.

ILLUSTRATION

Two days after Alice visited her Uncle Herbert and Aunt Louise, Herbert died of a sudden, unexpected heart attack. The present suit, Aunt Louise v. Alice, concerns ownership of a valuable oriental vase (worth $25,000 or more) that had originally belonged to Herbert's great grandmother.

Louise claims that Alice stole the vase in question at the conclusion of the latter's week-long visit with Herbert and Louise. Alice, however, says that the vase was a gift. She claims that Herbert gave it to her when she went into his study to thank him for the visit and to say goodbye.

A week before trial, the presiding judge calls a pretrial conference. At the conference, Alice's attorney indicates he expects to put on the witness stand friends and family members who knew Herbert prior to his death. They will testify that he was exceedingly generous, and was especially so with his nieces and nephews as he and Louise had no children. Each witness has observed one or more instances over the years during which, especially at Christmas, Herbert made generous gifts to his nephews and nieces, such as weekend vacations, gold wristwatches, gift certificates for expensive clothing, and season tickets to sporting and cultural events. Alice is prepared to testify that she has visited Herbert and Louise twice each year for ten years. At the conclusion of each visit, Herbert gave her a valuable item of china or jewelry that was a family heirloom.

Louise's attorney argues to the judge that none of this evidence is admissible. Is he correct?

Because this is a civil case, Rule 404 renders inadmissible evidence of character offered to prove particular conduct when character is not an essential element of a claim or defense, as in the Illustration.

Alice's best argument therefore rests not upon character evidence, but upon evidence of habit. But the testimony of family members and friends that Herbert is generous and has made various gifts to his relatives, especially his nieces and nephews, probably falls short of the specificity and regularity that is the essential foundation for habit evidence. The judge will probably characterize this evidence as tending to establish a character trait (generosity), rather than a habit. On the other hand, Alice's own testimony of her uncle's practice of giving her a valuable heirloom at the conclusion of each of her semi-annual visits does come closer to establishing a specific, repeated response to a particular situation (the conclusion of Alice's visit). Trial courts might differ on whether the conduct constitutes habit, and would probably not abuse discretion however they rule. But the better ruling is probably that there are not enough instances of gift-giving to establish a foundation of habit.

The fact that Alice is a self-interested witness might affect her credibility with the jury, but does not affect admissibility. And if the conduct is habit, the testimony cannot be excluded for lack of corroboration.

§ 3.6–4 Other Crimes and Wrongful Acts

Federal Rule 404(b)

The focus of this section is on Rule 404(b). It states:

(b) Other Crimes, Wrongs, or Acts.

(1) Prohibited Uses. Evidence of any other crime, wrong, or act is not admissible to prove a person's character in order to show that on a particular occasion the person acted in accordance with the character.

(2) Permitted Uses. This evidence may be admissible for another purpose, such as proving motive, opportunity, intent, preparation, plan, knowledge, identity, absence of mistake, or lack of accident.

(3) Notice in a Criminal Case. In a criminal case, the prosecutor must:

(A) provide reasonable notice of any such evidence that the prosecutor intends to offer at trial, so that the defendant has a fair opportunity to meet it;

(B) articulate in the notice the permitted purpose for which the prosecutor intends to offer the evidence and the reasoning that supports the purpose; and

(C) do so in writing before trial—or in any form during trial if the court, for good cause, excuses lack of pretrial notice.

Most commonly, Rule 404(b) is used in criminal cases by the government to prove a bad act of the accused *for some purpose other than the accused's bad character.* Of course, evidence disclosing a uncharged offense or wrongful act also reflects negatively on the accused's character, but if the trier can use this evidence properly without traveling the forbidden inferential route from (1) character evidence to (2) propensity to (3) conduct, then the proscription on character evidence is inapplicable. Evidence of the collateral misconduct can in such cases be permissibly used to draw inferences about some particular feature of the present crime. Typically that feature points either *to the accused's conduct (including identity)* during the charged crime or his *state of mind* during the charged crime.   ιｗｎｎＴＹ : ｓＴａｒｏ ｏＴ   ｈ ｉ Ｌ ｃＩ .

A simple example will set the stage for the discussion that follows. Suppose the accused, *D*, an accountant, is charged with embezzling money from the American charity that employed him. The indictment alleges that *D* attempted to hide his theft by making false financial entries in his employer's accounts. *D* defends on the ground that he did not misappropriate the funds in question and that any false entries were an innocent mistake. The prosecution offers evidence that five years earlier, *D's* Canadian employer had fired him for misappropriating company funds and covering up his theft by making false accounting entries. Subsequently, Canadian authorities successfully prosecuted *D*, who was fined and given a suspended sentence.

This evidence would be admitted, in the words of Rule 404(b), to show intent and the absence of mistake or accident. The point to emphasize is that the prohibition *barring the introduction of collateral crimes evidence is limited to situations where the only use of that evidence is to establish D's unfavorable character trait* as a way of proving the defendant's conduct during the charged crime. Think of the prohibition as a rule that rejects evidence of uncharged misconduct if its only probative value is to show propensity or predisposition.[65] If the prosecution can show that it is offering

---

[65]   Rule 404(b) is applicable in other instances, such as in civil cases. But as the vast majority of Rule 404(b) cases involve government proffer of bad acts against the accused, the discussion here will focus mainly on that context—thus reference will be made to the accused, the crime charged, etc. The reader should keep in mind, though,

collateral crimes evidence for a non-propensity purpose, then the court will analyze, under Rule 403, whether the probative value of the evidence for the proper purpose is substantially outweighed by the risk that the jury will misuse the evidence to make a judgment as to the defendant's character.

ILLUSTRATION

Assume that in the embezzlement trial described above, *D's* defense is that any misappropriations or false financial entries were made not by *D*, but rather by *X*, a part-time accountant who periodically worked for *D's* employer. The prosecutor offers evidence that five years ago, *D* was fired by his Canadian employer for misappropriating funds and making false entries and that *D* was subsequently convicted of embezzlement. *D* objects.

Should this evidence be admitted?

The defense is not mistake, but mistaken identity. Even though Rule 404(b)'s list of "purposes" for which evidence of other crimes or wrongs may be admissible is illustrative only, the list does include the most frequently encountered purposes for which this evidence is received. One of these permissible purposes is to show identity. However, identity cannot be established simply by showing that the accused has committed collateral offenses similar to, or the same as, the charged offense. To allow that would make the rule against circumstantial use of character evidence meaningless. Thus, if *D* is charged with bank robbery and denies that he was the robber, the prosecution cannot introduce evidence that before (or after) the charged crime, *D* robbed a bank to prove the identity of the robber. The reason this evidence is rejected is because in order to use it, the trier will necessarily draw the following inference: because *D* has committed a similar collateral crime, he has a propensity to commit bank robbery, and thus he is more likely to have committed the robbery in question.

This forbidden line of reasoning is even more apt to occur if *D* has committed *multiple crimes similar to or the same as* the charged crime. If evidence of similar collateral (uncharged) crimes were freely admissible, prosecutors could obtain convictions more easily, even in the face of weak evidence that *D* committed the offense charged. Furthermore, a person with a criminal record, especially one reflecting offenses similar to the offense being investigated, is likely

---

that Rule 404(b) can be used more broadly. In the example regarding *D*, the accountant, the American charity might bring an action against *D* to recover the stolen funds. In such an action, the charity would offer the Canadian theft evidence for the same purposes as the government in a criminal case.

to be the focus of a police investigation and is more likely than is a person with a "clean" record (or even a record involving *dissimilar* crimes) to be arrested and charged. Thus, having a criminal record can haunt the accused throughout the entire process of enforcing the criminal law, that is, from the police investigation through final judgment.

In the Illustration, the jury will be required to decide whether it was *D* or *X* who committed the crime, and the prosecution will contend that evidence that *D* has knowledge of how to embezzle and cover up by making false entries is probative of the fact that *D* in fact committed the crime. *D's* response is likely to be that any accountant, including *X*, would know how to make financial entries into business records, it is as easy to make a false entry as a true one, and the jury will have no difficulty in believing that both *D* and *X* had sufficient knowledge to commit the crime. If the trial judge is asked to admit the evidence to prove knowledge, it is difficult to predict what the ruling would be. Because the question is relatively close, it would not be an abuse of discretion to either admit the evidence or exclude it. But the better ruling is that the probative value of the evidence proceeds through a propensity inference, and so the evidence should be barred under Rule 404(b)—or, alternatively, that its probative value is substantially outweighed by its prejudicial effect under Rule 403.

Suppose, however, in the Illustration above, the accounting "cover-up" scheme used in the collateral Canadian theft was the same as the one used in the crime charged. And suppose further that the pattern of false entries was unusual—that is, the accounting scheme used to conceal the missing funds was uncommon enough to strongly suggest that the same accountant conceived and executed both cover-ups. When the collateral crime and the charged crime bear the same unusual characteristics or earmarks, evidence of the collateral offense *can* be used to prove identity. The evidence has specific probative value to prove identity and the trier can draw legitimate inferences that move directly from the evidence of the collateral misconduct (patterned false entries) to identity without the necessity of moving from "other crimes" evidence, to propensity, to conduct. This kind of evidence is often referred to as an accused's "signature" or "modus operandi" to indicate that the accused commits acts in an identifiable way particular to the accused.

While, as we have noted, evidence of collateral misconduct does taint the accused's character, this ancillary effect is tolerated if the evidence has significant probative force, independent of character, to establish an element of the crime charged. The court must assess the evidence under Rule 403: unless the probative value in proving identity is substantially outweighed by the risk that the jury will misuse the evidence to impugn the defendant's character, the evidence will be admissible—and the defendant will be entitled to have the jury instructed that the prior act cannot be used as evidence of the defendant's character.

Certainty with Which Collateral Misconduct Must Be Shown

A preliminary issue sometimes arising in connection with an offer of evidence of uncharged misconduct is the degree of certainty with which the commission of the other act must be shown. Remember the basic principle that individual items of evidence need not meet the standard of proof that applies to the totality of the evidence. Although the sum of all the evidence in a criminal case must support belief of the accused's guilt beyond a reasonable doubt, this standard of proof is not applied to individual items of evidence. Indeed, if it were, the prosecution would find it virtually impossible to obtain a conviction.

Observe that the use of misconduct evidence not charged in the case is yet another illustration of the principle of conditional relevance. Suppose *D* is prosecuted for lying to customs officials and concealing behind the lining of her suitcase an undeclared, expensive diamond bracelet. Her defense is that she placed the bracelet in a secure place to prevent its theft, and then forgot to declare it. The prosecutor now offers evidence that a year prior to the present offense, *D* failed to declare on her customs declaration a valuable diamond ring that was hidden inside the toe of one of her shoes. In order to use this evidence to infer knowledge or the absence of mistake, the trier of fact first must find that *D* actually concealed and failed to declare the diamond ring. If the defendant did not do the other act, it is not probative of knowledge or absence of mistake— because you can't learn from something that never happened. The relevance of the prior bad act for these proper purposes is *conditioned upon* it having occurred.

Under Rule 104(b), which governs conditional relevance, the proponent of other bad act evidence must produce evidence that is sufficient "to support a finding"[66] of its existence. The judge screens the evidence to ensure its sufficiency; the jury, using a more-likely-than-not standard, determines if the collateral event did in fact occur. The judge determines whether a reasonable juror could find that the act occurred more likely than not.

The leading case, which determined that the Federal Rules require only sufficient evidence to support a finding the uncharged

---

[66]   Fed. R. Evid. 404(b).

misconduct occurred, is *Huddleston v. United States.*[67] The *Huddleston* Court determined that under Rule 104(b), the trial court's task is to determine whether a reasonable person could find, by a preponderance of the evidence, that the defendant committed the act of uncharged misconduct. As discussed previously in § 3.4, the standard of conditional relevance is not difficult to meet. For example, if the government could present an eyewitness to the prior event, this will ordinarily satisfy the standard of conditional relevance even if the judge personally is not convinced that the witness's recollection is accurate. Under Rule 104(b), the proponent does not have to convince the *judge* that the act more likely than not occurred; the proponent simply needs to present enough evidence that *some reasonable person* could believe it more likely than not that it occurred.

Acquittal of the Collateral Crime

A special difficulty arises if the accused has been tried and acquitted of the collateral crime. In a technical sense, an acquittal means only that the jury (or the judge, in a bench trial) decided that the evidence admitted was insufficient to convince it beyond a reasonable doubt of the existence of each essential element of the collateral offense. This negative determination does not preclude a subsequent finding of the criminal conduct by the significantly less stringent standard of conditional relevance. Accordingly, courts reject the position that an acquittal of the collateral offense bars relevant evidence pertaining to it in the trial of another offense.[68]

The Probative Value of Multiple Similar Acts of Uncharged Misconduct

Cases arise in which a series of related events or acts, when considered cumulatively, have strong probative value with respect to some feature of the charged crime, and are accordingly not barred by the rule against character evidence because they are probative of something other than propensity. In one such case,[69] the accused was charged with infanticide when a child in her care died of cyanosis. She claimed that the child's death was accidental. The prosecutor offered evidence that over an extended period, children in the accused's care had suffered twenty cyanotic episodes. The extraordinary frequency of these unlikely incidences, argued the prosecutor, had the cumulative effect of increasing the likelihood that they were accompanied by purposeful conduct. On this theory, the judge admitted evidence of these collateral events. What is at work

---

[67]   485 U.S. 681 (1988).

[68]   *See Dowling v. United States*, 493 U.S. 342, 347–354 (1990).

[69]   *United States v. Woods*, 484 F.2d 127 (4th Cir. 1973).

here is the *doctrine of chances*—it is unlikely that so many unusual and yet similar events happen by chance. Another example: in a case involving insurance fraud for collecting on fire insurance for fires deliberately set, the defendant argues that the house caught on fire by accident. The government can respond with evidence that the defendant lived in four houses in the past two years, and each of them burned to the ground after he obtained fire insurance. What the doctrine of chances means is that there are only so many accidents.

Professor Edward J. Imwinkelried observes that,

> Under the doctrine of chances, the trier need not focus on the accused's subjective character. Under the doctrine of chances, the initial decision facing the trier is whether the uncharged incidents are so numerous that it is objectively improbable that so many accidents would befall the accused. . . .[70]

In the text ahead, which deals with the trial court's obligation to protect the accused from undue prejudice from evidence of bad character, you will see the critical role played by the trial judge in protecting the accused from unwarranted disclosures of his alleged participation in prior misconduct.

Proper Purposes for Admitting Evidence of Uncharged Misconduct: Illustrations

Rule 404(b)(2) sets out a number of purposes for which evidence of uncharged misconduct is often received. Although the purposes listed in this subsection are illustrative only, many of the decided cases focus on one or more of the purposes listed. Nonetheless, it is clear from the language of the rule, as well as its legislative history, that the drafters of subsection (b) created an open-ended system in which evidence of uncharged misconduct is admissible (subject to Rule 403) whenever the proponent can establish the uncharged misconduct is probative of something other than character.[71]

The examples below set out a sampling of circumstances in which consequential propositions normally *can* be established by the introduction of uncharged misconduct evidence. The chain of inferences based upon this evidence usually leads to an inference about either the *actor's conduct, or his state of mind, or both*; that is,

---

[70] Edward J. Imwinkelried, *The Use of An Accused's Uncharged Misconduct to Prove Mens Rea: The Doctrines which Threaten to Engulf the Character Evidence Prohibition*, 51 OHIO ST. L.J. 575, 586–87 (1990). For a thoughtful argument that the doctrine of chances is not an escape from the rule forbidding propensity evidence, but in fact violates the rule, *see* Paul F. Rothstein, *Intellectual Coherence in An Evidence Code*, 28 LOY. L. A. L. REV. 1259, 1261–65 (1995) (actor's propensity accounts for the unusual frequency of his involvement in the series of events).

[71] Fed. R. Evid. 404(b) ACN.

the evidence is probative without having to assume that the defendant was acting in accordance with a bad character trait. For example, suppose evidence of the uncharged crime, such as the illegal acquisition of explosives, indicates *D's* plan or preparation for the crime charged, such as detonating a bomb in a crowded public square. The uncharged misconduct evidence allows the trier to infer plan or preparation, which in turn allows it to infer conduct or identity. Other illustrations appear below:

(1)   In the prosecution of *D* for the murder of *V*, evidence that *V* had threatened to expose *D's* participation in a land fraud scheme is relevant to show *motive*—in other words, to reveal the reason why *D* might have committed the criminal offense charged. Existence of a motive usually supports an inference about conduct. A motive to do the charged act makes it more likely that the defendant committed that act, regardless of the defendant's propensity. If, on the other hand, the prosecutor offers evidence of a prior similar act, arguing that "because the defendant did it before, he had a motive to do the charged act", the evidence should be excluded because the stated probative value proceeds through a propensity inference.

(2)   In the trial of *D* for car theft, the defendant asserts that he was in a distant city on the day in question. Evidence that on the same day as the car theft, *D* purchased illegal drugs from a supplier in the city where the car was stolen is relevant to show that *D* had the *opportunity* to commit the theft. (Though query whether it is necessary to prove up the drug transaction—the defendant has a good argument that evidence of his location in the city is enough—so the evidence of a drug transaction might well be excluded under Rule 403). To continue with the car theft example, if the thief had used specialized tools to deactivate the stolen car's alarm system and to rig the electrical system so the engine would start, evidence that *D* possessed such tools during the period in question would be relevant to show he had the *capacity* to commit the theft.[72]

(3)   In the prosecution of *D* for the theft of a rented automobile, he asserts that he intended to return the car. Evidence of the theft of other rented cars by *D* is relevant to establish *D's* intent. The term "intent" is, generally speaking, synonymous with "purpose"; it denotes the desire to achieve a particular end and an awareness that

---

[72]   In this example, possession of the tools may not constitute a criminal offense; nonetheless, the jury would probably draw unfavorable inferences about the defendant's character from *D's* possession of these specialized tools. The protection against introducing evidence of character extends to any "bad" act, i.e., any act that could raise an inference of bad character—which as a practical matter means, any act the admission of which raises an objection by the opponent. The rule specifically prohibits evidence of "any other crime, wrong, or act" that is offered to prove propensity—so the act need not be a criminal act to be covered by the rule.

the action undertaken is likely to produce it. Thus, because the crime of theft is usually defined to require a taking of goods with the purpose of depriving the owner (either permanently or for a substantial period of time), evidence of other thefts bears upon the mental element of intent. If he had no intent to return the other cars it makes it less likely that he had an intent to return the car at issue. Though, admittedly, an argument that "because he intended the prior act it makes it more likely he intended the charged act" is not much different from "because he committed the prior act it makes it more likely he committed the charged act." Thus, the line between "intent" and "propensity" is a fine one. This means that it is important for intent to be disputed by the defendant, before other bad acts can be offered to prove intent. If similar acts are admissible to prove intent in every case, then the protection offered by Rule 404 would be negated.

(4) In the prosecution of D, a nurse, for murdering V by a lethal dose of morphine, evidence that prior to the murder D stole from the hospital dispensary enough morphine to cause death is relevant to show *preparation*. Preparatory steps increase the likelihood that the act charged was performed. Preparation may also reveal the accused's state of mind, *e.g.*, by showing deliberateness or purposefulness.

(5) In the prosecution of D for arson of building A, evidence that D had wrongfully burned building B covered by similar fire insurance is relevant, if coupled with other evidence, to show that D had a *plan* (scheme or design) to destroy these buildings in order to collect insurance proceeds. An inference can be drawn that the act charged is part of the larger scheme. From this conclusion, further inferences can be made about the actor's conduct or mental state in connection with the offense charged. In other words, when there is no direct evidence of a plan, the prosecution can prove circumstantially the existence of a plan by the separate but related prior bad acts, and then try to connect the charged incident to the plan. But the acts must in fact be part of a single, overarching plan—otherwise the prosecution is simply arguing that because the defendant did a lot of bad things, he had a propensity to do the bad thing charged.

(6) In the trial of D for receiving stolen property from A, evidence that on other occasions and under similar circumstances A had supplied D with goods (probably known by D to have been stolen) is relevant to show that D had *knowledge* that the goods in question were stolen. It is necessary that the prosecutor provide sufficient evidence for the trier of fact to conclude that D knew or should have known that the other goods were stolen. Perhaps, for example, the sale of the other goods was attended by suspicious circumstances

such as a price far below market value, "after-hours" delivery, or the absence of proper documentation. The element of knowledge is closely related to and frequently overlaps that of intent (or purpose) because both require awareness. But there is a difference between knowledge and intent. The element of knowledge appears to require only an awareness of wrongfulness or criminality (such as knowing that drugs are hidden in a car), whereas the element of intent seems also to call for a purpose or desire to achieve a particular end (such as intending to distribute the drugs).

(7)   In the prosecution of *D* for murder, committed by poisoning his wife with an herb that is only found on a remote island in the Pacific, a prior poisoning by the defendant, using the same herb, with his prior wife as the victim, is relevant to *identify D* as the actor in the offense charged. There must be more to link *D* to both the charged and uncharged crime than the fact that it is the same criminal offense. Evidence of other crimes is admissible to prove identity when identity is in question (that is, when the accused denies that he participated in the charged crime) *and* when the modus operandi of the two crimes is *sufficiently distinctive and similar to be substantially probative of identity.* It is often said that the conduct associated with the collateral and principal act must be so *similar* and *distinctive* that the resulting pattern is the "perpetrator's signature," a point made earlier. This may overstate the requirement, but it is quite clear that a mere showing that *D* has committed other crimes in the same class as the offense charged is insufficiently probative of identity to justify admission (e.g., a prior bank robbery to show that the defendant is the person who committed the charged bank robbery is not a sufficient showing for identity as a proper purpose). However, even when the principal and collateral crimes are largely dissimilar, it may be possible to introduce evidence that a distinctive feature linking the defendant to the collateral crime(s) is also involved in the crime charged. For example, it may be possible to show that a certain unusual weapon was used in committing both crimes or that some object acquired during the collateral crime (*e.g.*, a check-writing machine) was used to commit the crime charged (passing forged checks).

(8)   In the trial of *D* for the murder of his wife, *V-2*, he claims that the shooting was accidental and occurred when he was preparing to clean his pistol and pulled the trigger to ensure that the gun was "decocked" so he could disassemble it. Evidence that *D* had shot and killed his first wife, *V-1*, while claiming to have dropped his pistol as he was preparing to clean it, thus causing its accidental discharge, is relevant to show lack of accident or mistake. That is the doctrine of chances at work.

(9) In the trial of *D*, a firearms dealer, for selling assault weapons that were banned from importation and sale, evidence that *D* destroyed invoices and sales receipts and altered his financial statements is relevant to show consciousness of guilt. Other conduct, such as bribing or threatening witnesses, would be relevant for the same purpose.

Acts That Are "Inextricably Intertwined" with the Crime Charged

Rule 404(b) does not apply to evidence of the charged crime itself. But there are difficult questions about just what acts are bound up in the charged crime. For example, sometimes two criminal acts are so closely related by causation, geographic closeness, or (especially) time, that it is necessary to reveal the bad act in order that the trier of fact can fully understand the event charged. For example, suppose *D* is charged with reckless driving that resulted in the death of an elderly pedestrian who was crossing the street. Assume that just before the accident, *D* was leaving a nearby department store when the alarm buzzer sounded, indicating that he was carrying "unpaid-for" goods. As the security guard approached, *D* ran. The incident at the department store is clearly relevant to show why *D* was driving at a high rate of speed. Furthermore, the incident suggesting *D's* shoplifting could be viewed as so intertwined with the reckless driving charge that it does not constitute a "collateral" offense. If the act is "inextricably intertwined" with the charged crime, then many courts have held that evidence of the act is not governed by Rule 404(b), which by its terms applies to evidence of "other crimes wrongs or acts." Admissibility of an intertwined act would be evaluated under Rule 403, and obviously it is unlikely to be excluded. Most courts construe "inextricably intertwined" narrowly— and a few have rejected it entirely—as it is an exceedingly imprecise doctrine, and its only practical effect is to excuse the government of its notice requirement under Rule 404(b).[73] In the example given above, the department store evidence would be admissible under Rule 404(b) for the not-for-character purpose of showing motive or context, and Rule 403 would be applied to the evidence in any event— so there is little cause ever to apply the "inextricably intertwined" doctrine. But that has not stopped most of the courts from doing so.

Criminal and Civil Cases

In all of the examples and illustrations discussed in this subsection, other crimes evidence has been offered by the prosecution

---

[73]   Because of the potential impact of evidence involving collateral bad acts, as well as the need for full consideration of the evidentiary issues, Rule 404(b) entitles the accused to receive notice from the prosecution that it intends to offer evidence of uncharged misconduct.

against the accused. This is the typical setting, although Rule 404(b) is not confined to this pattern: it speaks simply of the admissibility of other bad act evidence not offered for the purpose of proving character or propensity, but offered instead for purposes such as motive, intent, or identity. The rule is broad enough to include civil cases, as well as the comparatively rare cases in which an *accused* invokes Rule 404(b). (The so-called "reverse 404(b) case.") Suppose, for example, two crimes, C-1 and C-2, bear so many similarities that it is likely they were committed by the same person. *D*, who is prosecuted for C-2, has evidence that the victim of C-1 identified another person, *X*, as the perpetrator of that crime. This evidence is relevant to show mistaken identity—that is, to show that *D* is innocent of C-2, the crime with which he is now charged. *D* is not attempting to prove the "criminal" character of the perpetrator of C-1, but is introducing the evidence on the specific point of identity—a signature crime of another person. Furthermore, the risk of prejudice, with which we are very concerned when other crimes evidence is offered against the accused, shrinks from importance in the reverse Rule 404(b) case. Any anger or passion aroused in the jury is directed not at *D*, but toward a third person, *X*.

A common example of Rule 404(b) applied to civil cases arises in employment discrimination cases. Assume the plaintiff claims that she was fired because she is a woman. The defendant contends that it had no discriminatory intent and the plaintiff was fired for insubordination. The plaintiff wants to introduce evidence that the defendant fired other similarly situated women and each time gave the same excuse, that the employee had been insubordinate. These other firings are not being introduced to prove character—they are offered for the not-for-character purpose of proving that the defendant had a discriminatory intent. The court would then, under Rule 403, determine whether the risk of unfair prejudice and confusion in admitting the evidence substantially outweighs its probative value in proving intent.

§ 3.6–5 Rule 403 Balancing with Respect to Other Bad Act Evidence

Evidence of uncharged misconduct to prove a particular point, such as intent, motive, or identity, carries a considerable risk of prejudice, because a jury might misuse the evidence in one of two impermissible ways: 1) for the forbidden "propensity purpose" (i.e., "once a bank robber always a bank robber"); or 2) for the inference that the defendant is a bad person who should be punished regardless of propensity and even if he did not commit the charged crime. Judges recognize the danger of unfair prejudice, and are called upon to undertake Rule 403 analyses in deciding whether to admit or exclude such evidence.

The general requirement that evidence of collateral offenses must have probative force above the propensity level begins our inquiry, but does not end it. In all cases in which evidence of uncharged misconduct is admitted for a purpose other than proving character, the trial judge must nonetheless determine whether the evidence is sufficiently probative for the permissible purpose for which it is offered. If the probative value for the permissible purpose is substantially outweighed by the risk of prejudice, jury confusion and delay, then the uncharged misconduct evidence will be excluded under Rule 403.

One critical factor in assessing the probative value of uncharged misconduct evidence is whether there is other available and less prejudicial evidence bearing on the not-for-character purpose, so that resort to bad-act evidence is unnecessary. Thus, if the circumstances of the case themselves indicate clearly that the accused intended to fire a gun, evidence of uncharged similar misconduct is not very probative because it doesn't further the government's case—it is cumulative.

Critical factors in assessing prejudice include the inflammatory nature of the uncharged misconduct. A prior murder is more likely to cause unfair prejudice than a minor theft. Special caution is also warranted when the collateral bad act bears a close resemblance to the crime charged (e.g., another bank robbery). This similarity increases the likelihood that the trier of fact will resort to a propensity inference. All of these factors must be taken into account when a judge rules on the admissibility of uncharged misconduct evidence.

It is also important to consider whether the accused has interposed a defense that heightens the probative importance of the uncharged misconduct evidence. Suppose, for example, the accused, a retailer, is charged with knowingly receiving stolen property. He offers the defense that he had no knowledge that the goods were stolen. Evidence that he has received other goods from the same supplier under suspicious circumstances (e.g., unaccompanied by a bill of sale, priced far below market, large volume purchase, delivered after hours, etc.) would be admissible to rebut this defense. The probative value is high because the defendant has raised the issue and the prosecution surely has the right to contest it.

Or suppose that the defendant is charged with possession of cocaine with intent to distribute. His defense is that he intended to use the cocaine himself. Evidence of a prior similar situation in which the defendant distributed the cocaine becomes probative to rebut the defendant's argument. The case for admission is strengthened because the government can not be accused of dressing up propensity evidence under the guise of "intent"—when the defendant actively contests intent, the prosecution surely has a right to respond.

On the other hand, if the defendant simply denies that he had any drugs on him at all (i.e. denies the charged act itself) the prior act of drug distribution is far less probative for any proper, non-character purpose—the prosecution is more likely to be introducing the evidence for the defendant's propensity to be involved with cocaine. Even though the prosecutor has the burden of proof as to intent whether the defendant actively contests it or not, the evidence is much more probative for intent when there is an active dispute as to that element. When intent is not contested, evidence of intent is not very probative because it does not advance the ball on an issue in dispute.

The general point is this: in each case posing the issue of uncharged misconduct evidence, the judge must take full account of the circumstances before her. Major factors that counsel against the admission of uncharged misconduct evidence (although one or even several may not be decisive) include the following:

(1)   The inflammatory nature of the bad act;

(2)   The similarity of the collateral bad act to the charged crime;

(3)   The availability of other, less prejudicial, evidence to prove the particular point toward which evidence of the collateral bad act would, if admitted, be directed;

(4)   The defensive claims of the accused, including whether or not the point to be proved by the collateral evidence is actively disputed;

(5)   The length of time between the act of uncharged misconduct and the act charged—generally speaking, the greater the time gap, the less probative is the act of uncharged misconduct in proving matters such as intent, plan, knowledge, etc.

Trial courts vary in the attention and care they take in evaluating Rule 404(b) evidence and making Rule 403 rulings with respect to it. Since appellate courts use an abuse of discretion standard in reviewing trial court decisions, the decisions of trial courts often are affirmed even where the record does not reveal in depth the mental processes of the trial judge, and even where the trial judge admits the evidence for a "laundry list" of proper purposes without analyzing whether the evidence is probative for any of those purposes without proceeding through a propensity inference.

For many years, federal appellate courts have set forth a four-part test for admissibility of Rule 404(b) evidence:

> To determine if such evidence is admissible, the district court must engage in a four-pronged analysis and evaluate whether (1) the evidence is directed toward establishing a matter in issue other than the defendant's propensity to commit the crime charged, (2) the evidence shows that the other act is similar enough and close enough in time to be relevant to the matter in issue, (3) the evidence is sufficient to support a jury finding that the defendant committed the similar act, and (4) the probative value of the evidence is not substantially outweighed by the danger of unfair prejudice.[74]

Under this test, most courts admitted evidence of uncharged misconduct with minimal consideration of whether the evidence was really being used for propensity, and without considering whether the so-called proper purposes were being disputed by the defendant.

But there is an indication over the last few years that some courts are tightening up their Rule 404(b) analysis, providing the criminal defendant with more protection from evidence of uncharged misconduct. For example, the Seventh Circuit, one of the courts that used this test for decades, repudiated it in *United States v. Gomez*, stating that "[e]specially in drug cases like this one, other-act evidence is too often admitted almost automatically, without consideration of the legitimacy of the purpose for which the evidence is to be used and the need for it."[75] In its place, the court determined that its more recent cases establish the following:

> [T]he district court should not just ask *whether* the proposed other-act evidence is relevant to a non-propensity purpose but *how* exactly the evidence is relevant to that purpose—or more specifically, how the evidence is relevant without relying on a propensity inference. Careful attention to these questions will help identify evidence that serves no permissible purpose.[76]

In *Gomez* the defendant was charged with selling drugs, and he claimed the sale was by his cousin. The trial court admitted evidence of Gomez's prior drug transaction to prove identity. But the court of

---

74   *United States v. Zapata*, 871 F.2d 616, 620 (7th Cir. 1989).

75   763 F.3d 845, 853 (7th Cir. 2014) (*en banc*).

76   Id. at 856.

appeals found error because the only way that the prior act was probative of identity was through a propensity inference. It proved that the defendant was more likely to do the charged act than was his cousin, *because the defendant did the act before.*

The *Gomez* court emphasized that even if other act evidence is relevant without relying on a propensity inference, Rule 403 applies with full force, and that under Rule 403 the evidence should not be admitted when offered for a purpose *that is not actively disputed by the defendant.* Under this view, it is not enough that the defendant has pled not guilty—if that were all that were required for an active dispute, then Rules 404(b) and 403 would provide little if any protection. Thus, a bad act offered to show intent, when intent is not actively disputed, "is not admissible to prove intent because its probative value will always be substantially outweighed by the risk of unfair prejudice." In contrast, when a proper purpose for the evidence (like intent or knowledge) is actively disputed, the bad act evidence *may* be admissible to prove intent, *"but it must be relevant without relying on a propensity inference*, and its probative value must not be substantially outweighed by the risk of unfair prejudice."[77]

The *Gomez* court also suggested an improvement in its standard jury instruction on Rule 404(b) evidence—that the judge should tell the jury *why* the bad act evidence cannot be considered for propensity—because we try cases, not people.

The Seventh Circuit's protective approach toward Rule 404(b) can also be found in the Third Circuit and in some new case law in other circuits.[78] It remains to be seen whether more courts will agree that care is required when trial judges are faced with Rule 404(b) issues, and if they do whether they will follow the lead of the Seventh Circuit. Under this more careful approach, prosecutors will have to wait to admit bad act evidence for purposes such as intent, knowledge, and identity, until it is determined that the defendant actually contests such issues. And courts will not be allowed to admit a bad act if its probative value for an asserted proper purpose is dependent on the defendant having a propensity to commit the charged crime.

The Advisory Committee on the Federal Rules of Evidence drafted an amendment to Rule 404(b) that is now Rule 404(b)(3)(A) and (B). The amendment is intended to apply the *Gomez* principle.

---

[77]   Id. at 859.

[78]   For a full discussion of the case law trend providing more protection—limiting the use of uncharged misconduct evidence under Rule 404(b)—*see* Capra and Richter, *Character Assassination: Amending Federal Rule 404(b) to Protect Criminal Defendants,* 118 COLUM. L. REV. 769 (2018).

Now under Rule 404(b), the prosecutor, in advance of trial, must articulate, in its pretrial notice, the non-character purpose for which the bad act evidence is offered and explain how the bad act evidence is probative for that purpose without assuming that the defendant has a propensity to commit the act. The new rule became effective in December, 2020. It should make it easier than before for trial judges to determine whether prosecutors are actually offering evidence that relies on forbidden propensity reasoning.

§ 3.6–6 Reputation, Threats, and Collateral Incidents Affecting the Defendant's State of Mind

A criminal defendant who pleads self-defense raises the issue whether, in light of all the circumstances, he acted reasonably in defending himself against the alleged victim (*V*). A similar issue is posed in a civil suit for battery in which the defendant pleads self-defense. The trier of fact considers not only the conduct of *V* and the defendant (*D*), but also the question of *D's* apprehension of harm. Of course, *V's* conduct toward *D* at the time of the offense is a major factor in determining whether the latter took reasonable steps to defend himself. But this conduct may not be the only factor. For example, suppose *V* had threatened *D* on an earlier occasion; or perhaps *D* knows that *V* is reputed to be a violent, dangerous person. In the present context, the key to admitting evidence of *V's* reputation, his prior threats to harm *D*, or *V's* violent conduct directed toward others, is *D's knowledge* of *V's* reputation, threats, or violent activities. The purpose of the evidence disclosing *V's* violent or threatening nature is to demonstrate that *D* had a reasonable basis for fearing *V*, and thus was justified in taking protective steps. Consequently, the evidence in this instance is not offered to prove any person's character and is not barred by Rule 404.

As we noted, the evidentiary use described above requires that *prior to* the litigated incident, *D* had knowledge of *V's* threats, aggressive conduct toward others, or reputation for violence. Knowledge does not work backward, so awareness obtained during or after the event is not relevant to *D's* knowledge of *V's* violent disposition.

To this general requirement of *D's* awareness, there is a notable exception: evidence of a threat by *V* to harm *D* is generally admissible even if it was disclosed to a third person and not to *D*. Even if *D* was unaware of *V's* statement, the threat increases the probability that the party making the threat carried it out. It is probative of the not-for-character purpose of proving *V's intent*.

Confirm your understanding of these evidentiary principles with the following hypothetical. *V* confides in *W* that he (*V*) is going to kill *D*, who is living with *V's* former girlfriend. Subsequently, *V* is killed or seriously injured and *D* is prosecuted; he pleads self-defense. Counsel for the accused (*D*) calls *W*, who will testify that *V* threatened to kill *D*. As we have seen, the relevance of this testimony is apparent. Recall that Rule 401 says that evidence is relevant if it has "any tendency to make the existence of any fact that is of consequence . . . more probable or less probable. . . ." *V's* threat meets this test, because an expressed intent to do an act makes it more likely that the person will commit the act. Of course, relevant evidence is excludable if its admission would contravene another rule of evidence. The evidence of *V's* threat would be rejected, for example, if it constituted inadmissible hearsay. As you will see in Chapter VII,[79] however, an assertion by an out-of-court speaker (the "declarant") that he will take certain action in the future is admissible under an exception to the hearsay rule.[80] And, as discussed above, the evidence does not run afoul of the bar on character evidence, because it is offered to prove intent. Thus, *V's* threat against *D* is admissible even though *D* was unaware of it.

Equally admissible would be *W's* statement to *D*: "Be careful *D*, *V* told me he was going to kill you." This would be admissible on the reasonableness of self-defense by *D* when confronted by *V*, whom he had good reason to fear. The evidence is admissible even if, in fact, *V* is a peaceable person—it is offered not to prove *V's* character but rather to show that *D* could have thought that *V* posed a threat.

§ 3.6–7 Special Rules: Cases Involving Sexual Misconduct

Introduction

Certain kinds of sexual offenses, namely sexual assault and child molestation, are specifically addressed in Federal Rules 412–415. These rules apply generally to both criminal and civil cases, although different provisions may be applicable depending on whether the case being tried is criminal or civil. A word of caution: although state jurisdictions usually have special evidentiary rules that apply in cases involving sexual misconduct, you should expect considerable variation from state to state, including significant departures from the federal evidentiary scheme.

---

[79]   *See* Chapter VII, § 7.2(c) in particular.

[80]   The applicable exception allows into evidence statements that reflect the declarant's then-existing state of mind, provided it is not offered to prove the declarant is accurately recounting a past event. *See* Fed. R. Evid. 803(3).

Rules 412 through 415 contain a number of technical provisions, but the overarching scheme is fairly straightforward. It is helpful to think of Rule 412 as a "rape shield provision" designed to protect the alleged victim of a sexual assault from unwarranted disclosures of her reputation or sexual history, particularly as that history pertains to sexual behavior with persons other than the accused. It is useful to think of Rules 413 through 415 as "sexual predisposition" provisions, because the premise underlying these rules is that an alleged offender's collateral sexual behavior of the same type that is claimed or charged in the case being tried has strong probative value. Rule 412 is essentially an exclusionary rule with respect to evidence of a *victim's* sexual behavior or predisposition. In contrast, Rules 413–415 are essentially *inclusionary* rules with respect to evidence of a *defendant's* sexual behavior or predisposition.

Rules 413–415 reject the general principle of Rule 404 that excludes evidence of uncharged misconduct (such as a crime) when its only probative value is to demonstrate a character trait or predisposition. As we have already observed, the premise of Rule 404 is that evidence of character offered to prove particular conduct is generally excluded because its probative value is insufficient to overcome countervailing considerations such as unfair prejudice, confusion, and time consumption. But Congress overrode Rule 404's exclusionary principle when it enacted Federal Rules 413–415—thus under these Rules the factfinder is allowed to consider prior bad (sexual) activity as proof that the defendant has a propensity to commit such acts.[81]

Background

Suppose *V* has consensual sexual relations with *A*. On another occasion, *V* has sexual intercourse with *D*. *V* claims *D* raped her; *D* claims *V* consented. At *D's* trial for sexual assault, defense counsel offers evidence supporting the fact that *V* consented to sexual intercourse with *A*. This is offered for the proposition that because *V* had consensual sex with *A*, it is more likely that the sex with *D* was consensual. How should the judge rule when the prosecutor objects?

During the first half of the Twentieth Century, judges would have usually admitted this evidence. Furthermore, they would usually have allowed reputation evidence that *V* had an "unchaste" or promiscuous character.

The last half of the Twentieth Century ushered in new attitudes, a critical reappraisal of the judicial practice of allowing evidence of

---

[81]   Congress decided to enact these rules, even though they were rejected by the Judicial Conference of the United States (the body that proposes to the United States Supreme Court additions and modifications to the Federal Rules of Evidence).

the victim's collateral sexual behavior, and legislative reform efforts ("rape shield statutes") that eventually prevailed in all jurisdictions. There was a growing acknowledgment that in sexual assault prosecutions, evidence of the victim's reputation or sexual behavior with third persons had marginal or no probative value. *V's* consensual sexual behavior with *A* (as in the example above) usually tells us little or nothing about whether her sexual behavior with *D* was consensual. After all, the victim did not accuse her other partner or partners of rape, but she *has* accused the defendant.[82] Moreover, admitting evidence of the victim's sexual behavior or predisposition runs the risk of the jury thinking that the victim "asked for it" or is simply not worthy of protection. Beyond this, there is the pragmatic concern that publicly subjecting *V* to embarrassing public disclosures and innuendoes has a chilling effect on her willingness to come forward and report a sexual assault to law enforcement authorities, and to testify at trial. It became acknowledged that sexual assault cases were often particularly hard to prove, and a virtual impossibility without the participation of the victim. Thus steps had to be taken to protect against two negative consequences that can occur when the victim's sexual behavior is admitted—unfair prejudice to the case, and psychological harm to the victim.

Federal Rule 412

Federal Rule 412 begins, in subsection (a), by generally prohibiting specified kinds of evidence in any civil or criminal proceeding involving alleged sexual misconduct. The term "sexual misconduct" encompasses a broad range of cases, including employment discrimination cases alleging sexual harassment.[83] The evidence generally forbidden is, first, that which shows that the "victim engaged in other sexual behavior" and, second, that which portrays the "victim's sexual predisposition."

The Rule's limitations apply equally to reputation evidence, opinion evidence, and evidence of specific sexual acts. As we shall see below, there are limited exceptions to Rule 412's general exclusionary provision, but these exceptions are specified in the body of the rule itself. Thus Rule 412 is a "gatekeeping" provision and *if evidence of a victim's sexual predisposition or collateral sexual behavior is to gain admissibility, it must pass through the portals of Rule 412.* This means that the evidence must fall outside the broad exclusionary ban

---

[82]   "[W]e would not expect a person—regardless of whether she is sexually active—to claim falsely that a consensual sexual act in which she participated was actually a rape." Sherry F. Colb, *"Whodunit" Versus "What Was Done": When to Admit Character Evidence in Criminal Cases*, 79 N.C.L. REV. 939, 974 (2001).

[83]   Fed. R. Evid. 412 ACN.

of Rule 412.[84] Before we turn to the exceptions to exclusion we should take up a procedural point.

Rule 412 has a procedural component, set out in subsection (c). The prescribed process must be followed in both criminal and civil cases. The party who seeks to escape the general exclusionary rule of subsection (a) must file a motion describing the evidence to be offered and its purpose. Thereafter, the court conducts an *in camera* hearing at which the proponent, the victim, and all parties may appear and advance their respective arguments. On the basis of the materials and arguments presented at this proceeding, the judge rules on the admissibility of the proffered evidence. The "motion, related papers, and the record of the hearing"[85] are thereafter sealed and, absent a court order of release, remain so. The general purposes of these required procedures are to facilitate an informed decision by the judge and to protect the victim from unwarranted public disclosures and innuendoes.

We turn now to the exceptions to the broad prohibition contained in Rule 412(a). These exceptions, set out in subsection (b) of Rule 412, are divided into two broad categories: criminal cases and civil cases.

In *criminal cases* there are three exceptions to the general exclusionary rule of Rule 412(a):

First, Rule 412(b)(1)(A) allows evidence of "specific instances of a victim's sexual behavior" when the accused offers this evidence in an effort "to prove that someone other than the defendant was the source of semen, injury or other physical evidence." For example, the accused might offer evidence that someone other than the defendant committed the crime or was the cause of her pregnancy, venereal disease, or physical injuries such as bruises or fractures.

Second, Rule 412(b)(1)(B) allows "evidence of specific instances of a victim's sexual behavior with respect to the person accused . . . if offered by the defendant to prove consent or if offered by the prosecutor." Collateral (uncharged) sexual encounters between the accused and the victim have more probative force on the question of consent than do sexual encounters between the victim and third persons. Note that "consent" is the only allowable purpose for which

---

[84]   The prohibition, as noted above, embraces *V's* "sexual behavior" as well as *V's* "sexual predisposition." Fed. R. Evid. 412(a)(1), (2). It is clear that sexual behavior includes physical contact. It also includes, according to the Advisory Committee Note, "activities of the mind." Courts are in dispute about whether a prior false claim of rape is evidence of sexual behavior or predisposition. Most courts have found evidence of false claims to be barred by Rule 412. *See* SALTZBURG, MARTIN & CAPRA, FEDERAL RULES OF EVIDENCE MANUAL § 412.02[4] (12th ed. 2019).

[85]   Fed. R. Evid. 412(c)(2).

the accused may offer evidence of other sexual activity with the victim.   ‚ ℓ (σ

Third, Rule 412(b)(1)(C) allows any evidence, "whose exclusion would violate the defendant's constitutional rights." Because the Constitution would override any contrary statute or evidentiary rule, this provision is, technically, superfluous. Nonetheless, it serves to remind trial judges, and defense counsel, that occasionally a rejection of the defendant's proffered evidence would violate what has been called the constitutional right to an effective defense.

The occasions when the exclusion of evidence would comport with the Federal Rules of Evidence, yet violate the constitutional rights of the accused, are infrequent. This comparative rarity is explained by the fact that the drafters of the Federal Rules were alert to the possible impact of constitutional principles on evidentiary rules, particularly in criminal cases. As a result, they crafted the Rules so as to minimize constitutional concerns.[86] Nonetheless, there are circumstances in which application of Rule 412 or other (state) versions of rape shield statutes may have such a restrictive effect on the accused's ability to defend himself that constitutional principles override the statutory prohibition that usually disallows evidence revealing the victim's sexual behavior. This will only happen, however, if the evidence proffered by the defendant is strongly probative of his innocence.

ILLUSTRATIONS

(1)   *V* testifies that *D* used false statements to lure her from a barroom and that he thereafter sexually assaulted her. Following this alleged sexual assault, *D* drove *V* to *X's* (her boyfriend's) home where she was permitted to leave the car. *X* testified that he was standing outside the home and observed *V* as she left *D's* car and that she immediately complained to *him* that *D* had raped her.

D's defense to charges of rape and forcible sodomy is consent. He also offers evidence that *V* and *X* were lovers and that *V* had fabricated the rape story in order to preserve her relationship with *X*, who grew suspicious when he observed *V* leaving *D's* car. Additionally, *D* offers evidence that by the time his trial began, *V* and *X* were living together.

---

[86]   *See, e.g.,* Fed. R. Evid. 201(f) (fact judicially noticed is not conclusive in criminal cases).

D's proffered evidence is excludable under Rule 412 and many state rape shield statutes *unless* the Constitution requires that *D's* evidence be received.[87] How should the trial judge rule?

In Illustration (1), the accused can successfully argue that rejection of his proffered evidence would violate what the Supreme Court has referred to as the constitutional right to an effective defense—an amalgam of rights including the right to "confront" an adverse witness.[88] This right can be violated by a court's preclusion or undue restriction of cross-examination, when the witness is important to the case and the cross-examination, if allowed, would substantially impair the adverse witness's credibility—and where the interests promoted by the rape shield rule are not compelling under the circumstances. The prevailing argument in Illustration (1) is that *D* has a right to ask questions that would reveal strong evidence of *V's* motive to lie, which grows out of her past and current sexual relationship with *X.* This is especially so where the dispute is one grounded in credibility—"he said, she said." Moreover, on the state side the interests are, relatively, not high. The jury is unlikely to be prejudiced severely by the fact that the victim is living in a sexual relationship with another person. The defendant is not seeking (and not entitled to seek) any details about *V's* sexual activities. And so neither prejudice to the case or harm to the victim is seriously at stake.

It would be a mistake, however, to conclude that the right to effective defense allows the defendant generally to impeach the alleged victim's credibility. Constitutional protection surrounds only evidence of those events or statements that bear a *close relationship* to the case being tried, such as evidence revealing *V's* bias or ulterior motive—and such evidence must be strongly probative, so that, for example, evidence that *V* and *X* had only been on a single date before the events in issue could probably be excluded as insufficiently probative of a motive to lie.[89] Moreover, general attacks on *V's* credibility, assuming they reveal *V's* sexual behavior or sexual predisposition, fall within the *general* prohibition of Rule 412(a) and are not considered important or probative enough to trigger the defendant's constitutional right to an effective defense. That is because sexual behavior or predisposition have very little to do with truthfulness in the ordinary case.

---

[87]   The facts in this Illustration are drawn from *Olden v. Kentucky,* 488 U.S. 227 (1988).

[88]   The Confrontation Clause is contained in U.S. Const. Amend. VI. There is also an argument that the judge's restriction violated the Constitution's "due process" clause, contained in the Fourteenth Amendment. See *infra,* text at notes 96–100.

[89]   *See Boggs v. Collins,* 226 F.3d 728, 736–39 (6th Cir. 2000) which contains a helpful discussion of the leading Supreme Court decisions.

(2)   Prosecution for attempted rape. *V* testifies that *D* knocked on her door and, after she invited him into her home, he became sexually aggressive. As *D* was forcibly removing *V's* clothing, she was able to free herself and run (screaming) into a nearby room where relatives were sleeping.

D testifies that after a period of talking and sexual foreplay, he and *V* had consensual sex. He then offers to testify that while engaged in sexual intercourse, ~~*D* had asked *V* whether she liked a particular~~ sexual position, ~~remarking that a mutual male acquaintance, *X*,~~ had told *D* that she did. *D* then made a remark about *V* "switching partners." *V* thereupon angrily ordered *D* to get dressed and leave at once.[90]

At *D's* trial, he offers the defense of consensual intercourse. How should the trial judge rule on the prosecutor's objection to *D's* testimony concerning what he said to *V*?

Illustration (2) is a close case and the answer is uncertain. Certainly, the Constitution would accord to the accused the right to introduce evidence that he made remarks to *V* that angered her. As stated above, several Supreme Court decisions, taken together, support the general proposition that the Constitution guarantees to accused persons "a meaningful opportunity to present a complete defense."[91] This "meaningful opportunity" includes, of course, the accused's right to present witnesses and to testify himself. Suppose, however, the judge applies evidentiary rules that severely circumscribe the accused's testimony. In the case[92] on which Illustration (2) is based, the trial judge restricted *D* to testimony that "he had said something to . . . [*V*] that angered her and caused her to fabricate the attempted rape charge."[93] Testimony about *V's* preferred sexual position as reported by *X* and about switching partners was excluded under Rule 412.

A closely divided federal appellate court, sitting en banc, found no constitutional violation. The majority held that the trial judge's ruling was not arbitrary and that he had struck a fair balance

---

[90]   The facts in this Illustration are drawn from *Stephens v. Miller*, 13 F.3d 998 (7th Cir. 1994) (*en banc*).

[91]   *Crane v. Kentucky*, 476 U.S. 683, 690 (1986). The right to make a complete defense is usually traced to *Chambers v. Mississippi*, 410 U.S. 284 (1973), where the Court relied on the due process clause of the Fourteenth Amendment, and *Washington v. Texas*, 388 U.S. 14 (1967), where the Court relied on the compulsory process clause of the Sixth Amendment.

[92]   *See Stephens v. Miller*, 13 F.3d 998 (7th Cir. 1994) (*en banc*).

[93]   Id. at 1002.

between the defendant's constitutional right to tell his story and victim's statutory right to be shielded from invasions of privacy and public denigration.

Rule 412: Civil Cases

Subsection (b)(2) of Federal Rule 412 applies to civil cases and governs the admissibility of evidence bearing upon the "sexual behavior or sexual predisposition" of the alleged victim. Usually, but not always, *V* is the plaintiff.

The proponent of evidence that discloses *V's* sexual behavior or sexual predisposition faces imposing obstacles. First, as is generally true when evidence is admitted under Rule 412, that evidence must be admissible under any other evidentiary rule that might apply, e.g., the rule against hearsay. Second, that evidence must surmount a special balancing test that is contained in, and specific to, Rule 412(b)(2). Under this special test governing civil cases, the proponent of the evidence must convince the judge that the probative value of the evidence of sexual behavior or predisposition *substantially outweighs* "the danger of harm to any victim and of unfair prejudice to any party." This is a different balancing test than the one of general application which favors admissibility and is contained in Federal Rule 403. Under Rule 403, evidence is admissible unless the *opponent* convinces the judge that its probative value is *substantially outweighed* by the counterweights of undue prejudice, jury distraction or confusion, or waste of time. Essentially Rule 412 calls for a "reverse-403" balancing test—tilted heavily toward excluding evidence. Furthermore, as the Advisory Committee notes, the special balancing test of Rule 412(b)(2) puts "harm to the victim" on the scale favoring exclusion, in addition to prejudice to the parties.[94]

Another feature of Rule 412(b)(2) addresses the admissibility of reputation evidence that portrays the victim's sexual predisposition. Such evidence is inadmissible unless *V* opens the door by introducing her reputation—presumably one for a virtuous or chaste character. She might, for example, offer evidence of her "good" reputation as bearing on the issue of damages.[95]

---

[94]   Fed. R. Evid. 412 ACN (1994 Amend.).

[95]   Such evidence would not violate the general rule that evidence of character is inadmissible in civil cases. That rule of inadmissibility applies only if evidence of character is being used to prove conduct on a particular occasion. *See* supra Chapter III, § 3.6–1.

Admissibility of Prior Acts of Sexual Misconduct in Cases of Sexual Assault or Child Molestation

Congress enacted Federal Rules 413 through 415 in 1995, bypassing the usual rulemaking process.[96] Building upon a line of cases that had shown increasing receptivity to admitting evidence of collateral sexual misconduct similar to the charged sexual offense, Congress took bold—and many would say unprincipled—steps to facilitate the admission of similar sexual offenses. The legislative history of Rules 413–15 reflects a congressional concern that "too often, crucial evidentiary information is thrown out at trial because of technical evidentiary rulings."[97] The "corrective" measures taken by Congress and embodied in Federal Rules 413–415 are far-reaching. Although we will examine these rules in detail, do not expect to find that they have been widely adopted by the states, for these rules remain highly controversial.

Under these Federal Rules, evidence of similar sexual offenses is admissible in both civil and criminal cases when specified sexual misconduct is alleged.

Rule 413(a) provides:

SIMILAR CRIMES IN SEXUAL-ASSAULT CASES

(a) **Permitted Uses.** In a criminal case in which a defendant is accused of a sexual assault, the court may admit evidence that the defendant committed any other sexual assault. The evidence may be considered on any matter to which it is relevant.

timely notice

The rule goes on to require that the government must give timely notice to the accused of its intention to offer evidence of similar sexual offenses, including a disclosure of what evidence will be offered.[98] Note that Federal Rule 413, like its companion rules, 414 and 415, limits "other offense" admissibility to sexual offenses of the same type as the charged offense. Because Rule 413 addresses only *sexual assault* prosecutions, it lets in only evidence of other *sexual assault* crimes. The rule would not, for example, allow evidence of a prior sexual assault committed by one who was being prosecuted for homicide or armed robbery. Similarly, the rule would not allow evidence of dissimilar offenses (such as a criminal battery) in a prosecution for sexual assault. The issue of admissibility in these other settings continues to be governed by Rule 404(b) or, in the case of impeachment, by Rules 608 and 609. Sexual assault is, however,

---

[96]   Pub. L. No. 103–322, 108 Stat. 2135–2137 (effective July 9, 1995).

[97]   113 Cong. Rec. S15072–3 (1993) (statement of Senator Dole).

[98]   Fed. R. Evid. 413(b).

broadly defined in Rule 413(d) and includes any nonconsensual sexual contact between the defendant and the victim, any violent act toward the victim from which the defendant derived sexual pleasure or gratification, and any attempt or conspiracy to engage in this prohibited sexual behavior. Thus, the Rule is written broadly so that evidence of attempts that do not result in completed offenses are admissible.

What is most striking about Rule 413 (and the companion Rule 414 dealing with child molestation) is its nullification of the established evidentiary principle that an accused should be shielded from the prosecution's use of character or propensity evidence. In the words of Rule 404(b), which embodies that longstanding principle, "[e]vidence of any other crime, wrong, or act is not admissible to prove a person's character in order to show that on a particular occasion the person acted in accordance with the character." Rule 413(a), in contrast, allows admission of evidence of a collateral sexual assault "on any matter to which it is relevant," *including propensity.*

Rule 413 is subject to other evidentiary rules that would deny or qualify admissibility, of which the most notable is the now familiar Rule 403.[99] Thus, the trial judge has some discretion in deciding whether the probative value of the other sexual assault(s) is substantially outweighed by undue prejudice or other counterweights, such as jury confusion or time consumption. Many factors, such as the similarity of the collateral sexual assault(s) to the charged offense, the recency and the other offense(s), the number of collateral offenses, the strength of the evidence supporting the collateral offense(s), and the similarity of the other acts to the charged crime, should bear on the trial judge's Rule 403 determination.

It is important to note, though, that the Rule 403 test applies differently to uncharged misconduct evidence under these rules than it does to evidence offered under Rule 404(b). Under Rule 404(b) and Rule 403, the trial court must balance the probative value of the uncharged misconduct for the not-for-character purpose; it cannot consider, and weigh in favor of admissibility, the probative value for the forbidden propensity inference. In contrast, Rules 413–415 provide that the trial court *must* consider the prior act of sexual assault as probative of the defendant's propensity to commit the crime charged. Thus the propensity inference is part of the probative value that the judge must balance under the Rule 403 test. Moreover, under Rules 404(b) and 403, the trial court, in weighing the risk of prejudice, must consider the possibility that the jury will convict the

---

[99]   *See* supra Chapter III, § 3.2.

defendant because of his propensity to commit the crime charged—this is "prejudice" because those Rules do not permit the jury to draw the propensity inference. In contrast, under Rules 413–415, the jury is allowed to draw the inference that because the defendant has committed sex crimes before, he has a propensity to commit them and therefore is more likely to have committed a sex crime on the occasion in question. Thus, the risk of drawing the propensity inference cannot be considered "prejudicial" when the trial judge conducts the Rule 403 balance in sexual misconduct cases under Rules 413–415. Essentially, under these rules the propensity inference transfers from the prejudicial effect to the probative value side of the scale, making it highly unlikely that a prior act of sexual misconduct will be found inadmissible.

It is the jury and not the judge that decides whether or not an alleged collateral assault actually took place. That is, the judge will treat evidence of the other sexual assault under the usual approach to issues of conditional relevance,[100] and thus screen evidence of the collateral sexual assault only to ensure that there is sufficient evidence of its existence to allow a reasonable jury to conclude (by a preponderance of the evidence) that it did occur.[101] This is the approach that is taken with regard to uncharged misconduct evidence under Rule 404(b).[102] The dispositive case under Rule 404(b) is *Huddleston v. United States*.[103]

Federal Rule 414, which applies to cases of child molestation, parallels Rule 413 in its general content and structure. It provides in subsection (a):

SIMILAR CRIMES IN CHILD-MOLESTATION CASES

(a) Permitted Uses. In a criminal case in which a defendant is accused of child molestation, the court may admit evidence that the defendant committed any other child molestation. The evidence may be considered on any matter to which it is relevant.

Note the "similarity" requirement: in prosecutions for child molestation—the collateral offense evidence is limited to incidents of child molestation; any other act of sexual misconduct would have to be analyzed under the traditional constraints of Rule 404(b).

---

[100]   *See* supra Chapter III, § 3.4.

[101]   *Johnson v. Elk Lake School District*, 283 F.3d 138 (3d Cir. 2002) (holding that under Rule 415, dealing with civil cases of sexual misconduct, judge's role is to screen evidence for sufficiency).

[102]   *See* supra Chapter III, § 3.6–4.

[103]   485 U.S. 681 (1988).

The other subdivisions of Rule 414 generally track their Rule 413 counterparts. For example, Rule 414(b) provides for the government's notice and disclosure of evidence of other offenses of child molestation that it intends to proffer. It will thus be seen that in most respects Rule 414 is the mirror image of Rule 413; the major difference is that Rule 413 applies to a charge of sexual assault, whereas Rule 414 applies to a charge of child molestation.

Civil Cases Involving a Sexual Assault or Child Molestation

Rule 415 addresses the admissibility of evidence of other offenses of sexual assault and child molestation in civil cases. Rule 415(a) provides:

SIMILAR ACTS IN CIVIL CASES CONCERNING SEXUAL ASSAULT OR CHILD MOLESTATION

(a) Permitted Uses. In a civil case in which a claim for relief based on a party's alleged sexual assault or child molestation, the court may admit evidence that the party committed any other sexual assault or child molestation. The evidence may be considered as provided in Rules 413 and 414.

Rule 415(b) contains the "notice and disclosure" provisions found in subsection (b) of Rules 413 and 414. As you will now anticipate, other rules of evidence may deny or qualify the admissibility of evidence within the ambit of Rule 415. As we have elsewhere observed,[104] character evidence is almost always disallowed in civil cases, except where it is an essential element of a charge, claim, or defense.[105] Under Rule 415, however, evidence of other acts of sexual assault or child molestation of the same type alleged in the civil case come into evidence as proof of propensity and for any other purpose for which it is relevant. Thus Rule 415 allows use of certain other acts to prove a character trait or predisposition and ultimately to prove the sexual misconduct in question.

---

[104]   *See* supra Chapter III, § 3.6.

[105]   Fed. R. Evid. 405(b).

Chapter IV

RELEVANCE: SPECIAL APPLICATIONS DRIVEN BY SOCIAL POLICY

Table of Sections

§ 4.1   In General

In this chapter, we continue our examination of special relevance rules, that is, determinate rules of relevance that yield solutions to recurring patterns of evidentiary issues. In the preceding chapter, such fixed rules responded primarily to considerations of whether or not the probative value of the evidence in question was overcome by factors such as unfair prejudice, jury confusion or distraction, or misuse (waste) of trial time. Some of these same factors surface in connection with the evidentiary rules under consideration in this chapter.

The unifying theme in this chapter, however, is that social policy can play an important role in resolving the issue of admissibility. In other words, a significant and often principal goal of the evidentiary rules examined here is to avoid discouraging socially beneficial behavior. This goal is presumably accomplished by excluding evidence that is offered for the *forbidden purposes specified* in the various rules we will encounter.[1] Generally speaking, however, the same evidence offered for another purpose—one that is not forbidden—usually falls outside the exclusionary ban and is admissible unless barred by some other evidentiary rule or principle—most importantly, Rule 403. Often, a critical issue in

---

[1] As you will see, there are questions regarding whether or not some of these exclusionary rules actually affect the behavior of the individuals who are their beneficiaries.

deciding whether evidence is admissible for some permissible purpose is whether or not the parties have a genuine dispute about the permissible purpose for which the evidence is ostensibly offered.

Suppose, for example, a rule states[2] that evidence that a party took remedial steps following an accident or injury is inadmissible to prove *that the party was negligent* in not taking such steps prior to the harmful event. Aware of this exclusionary rule, the plaintiff's lawyer offers evidence that following an accident in the defendant's machine shop, the defendant added safety devices designed to reduce or eliminate the occurrence of similar accidents. In making his offer of proof, the plaintiff's lawyer states that evidence of the newly installed safety devices is not offered for the purpose of proving the defendant's negligence, but rather for the limited purpose of showing that safer devices were feasible. If the defendant concedes the proposition that it was feasible to make his machines safer, the judge will reject the plaintiff's evidence. The protective rule of exclusion would be undermined if a party could successfully avoid it by offering the forbidden evidence for a "different" purpose that was not even contested.

§ 4.2   Subsequent Remedial Measures

Federal Rule 407 addresses evidence of remedial measures taken after an event that has caused harm or injury. The policy-based assumption underlying Rule 407 is that admitting evidence of subsequent remedial measures would discourage potential defendants from taking precautions that are in the public interest. Such remedial measures take a variety of forms such as repairs, design changes, new or amended safety regulations, warnings to users, product recalls, new or amended instructions, disciplinary action against the employee causing the harm, closing the particular geographic area which was the site of injury, and so forth.

The policy-basis for the rule is undermined somewhat by the fact that some persons taking remedial steps after an injurious event are unaware of the rule—so it would have no effect on their conduct. It is true, though, that some actors (especially business enterprises) are aware of the principle embodied in Rule 407—or made aware by counsel. Yet the public policy rationale is also countered by the fact that there will probably be an incentive to make changes after an accident or injury occurs, even knowing that it could be used by an opponent at trial—because failing to do so could lead to serious consequences should another accident or injury occur. For example, punitive damages may be assessed for failing to correct a condition of which the party was made aware by a prior accident. Thus, the

---

2   *See* Fed. R. Evid. 407, discussed in § 4.2.

assumption that defendants would not make changes without the protection of Rule 407 is dubious—they are likely to make them anyway.

Whether or not Rule 407 makes it more likely that safety measures will be taken, the Rule finds other support in the fact that the probative force of evidence of post-accident remedial measures is usually weak. The proponent of remedial-measure evidence is attempting to raise the inference that subsequent remedial steps were taken because the actor thought the prior condition was hazardous or harmful; therefore (the further inference goes), it is more likely that it was. Note, however, that the potential defendant who takes precautionary measures after an injury-causing event is usually acting on the basis of new information. Put otherwise, "the rule [barring evidence of remedial measures] rejects the notion that because the world gets wiser as it gets older, therefore it was stupid before."[3] There also exists the possibility that the person taking remedial steps is exercising extraordinary caution to avoid any possibility of future injuries, or is making the change for public relations purposes—not necessarily as a recognition that the prior condition was a dangerous one.

Without Rule 407, juries might well confuse the *ex ante* and the *ex post* analyses of an event. For example, a jury in a negligence case that is supposed to ask itself whether the defendant exercised reasonable care prior to an event (i.e., before the defendant knew that an accident or other problem arose), might be inclined to treat a subsequent remedial measure as an admission of a lack of reasonable care when in fact the measure is a response to an accident or other problem that a reasonable person would not have foreseen prior to its occurrence.

Text of Rule 407

Observe carefully the text of Federal Rule 407. It reads:

Rule 407.   Subsequent Remedial Measures

When measures are taken that would have made an earlier injury or harm less likely to occur, evidence of the subsequent measures is not admissible to prove:

- negligence;
- culpable conduct;
- a defect in a product or its design; or

---

[3] Rule 407 ACN quoting Baron Bramwell's statement in *Hart v. Lancashire & Yorkshire Ry. Co.*, 21 L.T.R.N.S. 261, 263 (1869).

- a need for a warning or instruction.

But the court may admit this evidence for another purpose, such as impeachment or—if disputed—proving ownership, control, or the feasibility of precautionary measures.

The rule states the purposes for which evidence of subsequent remedial measures is not admissible, including proving negligence *or a defect in a product or its design.*[4] But it goes on to say that such evidence may be admissible if offered for other purposes. This structure is typical of most of the various "public policy" rules that are the subject of this chapter. The intention of the drafters of Rule 407 and kindred rules is to foreclose specified evidence (such as remedial measures) if offered for particular, forbidden purposes (such as proving that a product was defective), while leaving open the possibility that the specified evidence might be admissible if offered to prove other propositions in the case. Of course, evidence offered for permissible purposes may encounter other evidentiary rules that foreclose admissibility—most importantly, the possibility that its probative value for a permissible purpose is substantially outweighed by the risk that the evidence will be misused by the jury for impermissible purposes (in which case the evidence will be excluded under Rule 403).[5]

Construing Rule 407: Pre-Injury Changes

Rule 407 speaks of taking remedial measures after an "earlier injury or harm." Remedial or precautionary measures taken prior to the injury-causing event are outside the protection of the rule.

ILLUSTRATION

Suppose that in year *one* the defendant company (*D*) manufactures and sells a new model in its line of electric circular hand-saws. In year *two* company officials learn that under certain unusual conditions, the axle bolt that secures the circular saw blade can break, causing the blade to dislodge and, sometimes, to be propelled through the air. To eliminate this hazard, the defendant begins using axle bolts made of more durable metal, coupled with a specifically

---

[4]   As currently written, Rule 407 (amended in 1997) expressly prohibits evidence of subsequent remedial measures in order to prove the defendant's product was defective. Some state jurisdictions allow remedial measures in product liability cases. The theory is that the manufacturer has strong incentives to correct defects and contain or prevent injuries by product modifications, warnings, recalls, and the like so that a rule that blocks evidence of post-accident remedial measures is not needed.

[5]   In most instances, the principal impermissible purpose about which a court will be concerned is one forbidden by the Rule—for example, that evidence offered for a purpose other than to prove negligence will actually be used by the jury to prove negligence despite a cautionary instruction by the trial judge.

designed washer that reduces the tension on the axle bolt. In year *three* the plaintiff (*P*) is injured when the circular blade on his saw (manufactured by *D* and purchased by *P* in year *one*) dislodges, takes a downward course, and inflicts serious injuries to *P's* knee and lower leg.

At trial *D* claims that its product is reasonably safe and that *P's* injury was occasioned by his misuse of the saw. *P* responds by offering evidence that *D* made design and material modifications to the model purchased by *P*, and argues that this is probative that the product he purchased was defectively designed. Should the trial judge exclude the evidence under Rule 407? Would the judge rule differently if *P's* injury from the saw occurred in year *one*?

Here the defendant made remedial changes in year *two*, but the event immediately causing the harm occurred later in year *three*. Thus, Rule 407 does not bar the proffered evidence. The practical effect of this limiting feature of Rule 407 is to increase the pressure on persons and enterprises taking remedial measures to protect persons, such as a prior purchaser, who have exposure to a potential harm or injury that has not yet materialized. That is a good thing, so the social policy works in favor of *not* applying the Rule.

Had the plaintiff sustained his injuries in year *one*, evidence of the defendant's remedial measures, taken in year *two* would have been excluded because it was offered to prove the product was defective—an impermissible purpose under Rule 407.

Measures Taken by Parties Not Responsible for the Harm

Guided by the policy underpinning of Rule 407, most courts have held that remedial measures taken not by the defendant but by a third party not responsible for the harm are not protected by the rule. When such a third party takes remedial action, evidentiary disclosure does not harm him (he—the actor—is not the defendant). Put otherwise, disclosure of the remedial measures does not exact a penalty from the one who took the socially responsible action that the defendant failed to take. Of course, cases of third-party remedial interventions are infrequent. But suppose, for example, there is a bicycle accident on a riding trail owned by *X* city. Subsequently, members of a private bicycle club post a warning sign, "Steep Rough Grade. Walking Advised." In a suit against *X* city filed by the injured bicyclist, evidence of the warning sign would not be banned by Rule 407,[6] although other exclusionary rules might apply.[7]

---

[6]   *See Pau v. Yosemite Park & Curry Co.*, 928 F.2d 880, 887–88 (9th Cir. 1991).

[7]   One concern a court may have is that introducing evidence of a third party's actions may lead the defendant to challenge the necessity of such actions and could

The Principal Escapes from Rule 407: Ownership, Control, Feasibility, and Impeachment

Rule 407 states explicitly that its exclusionary ban applies only when evidence of post-accident remedial measures is offered, essentially, to prove fault in the defendant's conduct or product—either as a recognition of negligence or that a product was defectively designed or manufactured. Other purposes for which evidence of such measures might be offered, "such as impeachment or—*if disputed*—proving ownership, control, or the feasibility of precautionary measures"[8] are not within Rule 407's proscription. Although the enumeration in Rule 407 of the purposes that fall outside its exclusionary ban is illustrative only, the bulk of case law addressing excepted purposes has focused on the ones enumerated in Rule 407,[9] especially the troublesome "feasibility" purpose.

The first thing to note is that three out of the four illustrative purposes do not escape the exclusionary ban of Rule 407 unless "disputed" by the parties. If the existence of a dispute or controversy were not required, it would be relatively easy for the proponent of the remedial evidence to offer it as bearing on some permissible purpose such as the feasibility of improving the product in question or making the premises in question safer. Of course, it is often a close question whether a defendant's pleadings and evidence actually dispute ownership, control, or feasibility. If the plaintiff's complaint does not specifically allege that the defendant owned and controlled an item and that improving it was feasible, the defendant's answer likely will not address these issues. This may leave open the question whether they are in dispute. Discovery often makes things clearer, and it is to the defendant's advantage to make clear that there is no dispute as to these matters in order to assure that the exclusionary portions of Rule 407 will be enforced.

---

lead to a trial within a trial. A court could conclude that this would waste time or perhaps confuse a jury as to whose conduct really matters and therefore decide to exclude the evidence under Rule 403. A court might also be concerned that a third party's action may have lacked sufficient expertise, and that the third party is unavailable for cross-examination.

8   Fed. R. Evid. 407 (emphasis supplied).

9   One unenumerated purpose (supporting the introduction of "remedial" evidence) that has found approval in the cases is rebutting the defendant's claim that the plaintiff was contributorily negligent. Suppose, for example, the defendant asserts that the plaintiff contributed to her injury for the reason that the danger about which the plaintiff complains would have been apparent to a reasonable person. The defendant's implementation of a subsequent remedial measure (taken after the plaintiff's injury) weakens this assertion. *See* SALTZBURG, MARTIN & CAPRA § 407.03 [11][a] (12th ed. 2019).

Ownership and Control

Sometimes the defendant disputes whether it owns or controls the premises, product, instrumentality, or process alleged to have injured the plaintiff. Suppose, for example, in a suit against a highway contractor for failing to erect warning signs at a road construction site, the defendant contends that it did not control the portion of the road where an accident occurred. The plaintiff could introduce evidence that after the accident, the contractor erected warning signs on that portion of the road. The purpose of the evidence would, of course, be limited to proving that the contractor had control over the location. The contractor could request the court to instruct the jury that evidence that the contractor erected the warning signs may only be used on the issue of control and not on the issue of negligence. The contractor might doubt, however, that the jury would understand the instruction and fear that it would call undue attention to the signs—in which case the contractor would prefer that no such instruction be given.

Feasibility of Precautionary Measures

The purpose most frequently invoked by litigators to elude the prohibition of Rule 407 is "feasibility of precautionary measures."[10] The issue most often faced by the trial judge is whether "feasibility" is "disputed" as required by Rule 407. The difficulty begins with the meaning of "feasibility," or in its adjectival form, "feasible."

To say that something is not feasible means, as one court put it, that it is not "physically, technologically, or economically possible."[11] It is theoretically possible that a remedial measure that was taken subsequent to the litigated event was not feasible (in the sense just noted) at an earlier time—for example, when the product or medical procedure causing the injury was first manufactured or instituted. If a defendant asserts, for example, that a safer design was not possible at this earlier time, the issue is joined. The plaintiff will try to show that the post-accident remedial measure or at least an equivalent measure was possible at the earlier date, and Rule 407 would not prohibit the evidence if offered to prove feasibility in this instance. The cases are truly rare, however, in which a defendant contests feasibility but in fact made the change that is claimed to be infeasible.

The far more usual situation is where a given design, production process, security measure, medical protocol, or other feature under consideration involves a trade-off in which the ideal product or procedure is compromised because of constraints such as costs,

---

[10] Fed. R. Evid. 407.

[11] *Tuer v. McDonald,* 347 Md. 507, 701 A.2d 1101, 1109–11 (1997) (discussing divergent approaches to what is meant by "feasible.").

availability of labor, or other practicalities. In other words, a person—for example, the defendant—weighs all the factors, including hazards, risks, and costs, and settles on the course of action he believes is preferable—recognizing that there may be other courses of action that are equally reasonable, with different trade-offs. The decision to take one course of action does not mean that the alternative later chosen was infeasible at the time, and so in these cases the defendant would concede feasibility and Rule 407 would bar the subsequent remedial measure—if the defendant does not so concede, then it opens itself up to proof of a subsequent remedial measure.

ILLUSTRATION

The defendants, Carl and his wife, Janet, own and operate a motel in a small town. Prior to opening their business, they consult the village police chief about security measures.[12] The police chief recommends additional lighting (which the owners install), but declines to suggest the installation of peep holes and chain locks on the entry door to each room. Because each room has a six-foot picture window adjacent to a solid entry door and standard (Triple A) door locks, the police chief advises the owners that additional security devices are unnecessary.

Subsequently plaintiffs, Husband and Wife, check into the defendant's motel. During Husband's brief absence, Stranger knocks on the plaintiffs' door; Wife responds by opening it, whereupon Stranger enters the room and rapes her. Eventually Husband and Wife sue Carl and Janet, claiming that the defendants breached their warranty to provide safe lodging and were negligent in failing to provide the plaintiffs with a room that was reasonably safe.

At trial, Carl testifies during cross-examination that because the picture window in each motel room afforded a view of the area outside the entry door, the installation of safety chains and peep holes was "unnecessary" and would have "provided false security." The trial judge thereafter excludes under Rule 407 the plaintiffs' evidence that, following the rape of Wife, the defendants installed safety chains and peep holes. At the conclusion of the trial, the defense lawyer, in his closing argument, asserts that in following the advice of the police chief, the defendants had

---

[12] The facts in this case are based on those in *Anderson v. Malloy*, 700 F.2d 1208 (8th Cir. 1983).

done all they "could or should have done." He then asks rhetorically, "What more can they do?"[13]

Did the trial judge err in rejecting the plaintiff's evidence of the defendants' subsequent remedial measures?

A defendant can always protect himself from evidence of subsequent precautionary measures bearing on feasibility by stipulating that other arrangements, designs, or protocols were feasible.[14] But in this case, Carl testified, in essence, that the addition of peep holes and safety chains would have been redundant, of no utility, and would have amounted to "false security" and the lawyer argued that nothing more could be done.

In the case on which this Illustration is based, Court of Appeals held that the trial judge abused his discretion when he rejected evidence of the defendants' subsequent precautionary measures. The court held that the defendants' evidence placed feasibility in dispute because the defendants contended, in essence, that peep holes and safety chains could not have been successfully employed—and the defendants never explicitly conceded that those changes were feasible.

feasibility in dispute

When a defendant claims that "our safety precautions were reasonable" and explains why additional measures were not employed, the defendant should specifically concede that it is not claiming that additional measures were impossible. Rather the defendant is claiming, "the suggested change is feasible, but I had no duty to do it." All that the defendants had to do was stipulate that the subsequent remedial measures were feasible, and then proceed to make the same arguments. But this they did not do.

Moreover, in this case, the closing argument by defense counsel essentially was a "not feasible" argument that might well have taken unfair advantage of the trial judge's exclusionary ruling. It is important when a defendant successfully argues that feasibility is not in dispute for the plaintiff to request that the judge assure that the defense does not thereafter make a "not feasible" argument.

---

[13]   Id. at 1214. Although the trial judge would have ruled on the admissibility of the evidence prior to the closing argument, the defense lawyer's argument that Carl and Janet did all they "could" have done as well as all they "should" have done confirmed that Carl was claiming that nothing more "could" have been done—which opened the door to the evidence otherwise barred by Rule 407.

[14]   Many courts have taken the position that a stipulation is essential in order to render evidence of subsequent precautions inadmissible. *See, e.g., Herndon v. Seven Bar Flying Service, Inc.*, 716 F.2d 1322, 1329 (10th Cir. 1983).

Impeachment

Rule 407 lists impeachment as one of the illustrative purposes for which evidence of subsequent measures is admissible. The key to admissibility is a showing that the testimony of a witness called by the defendant is contradicted by a subsequent remedial measure. Note that the "in dispute" requirement of Rule 407 applies to evidence of subsequent precautionary measures introduced to show ownership, control, or feasibility; the requirement does not, however, apply to evidence of such measures introduced to impeach a witness. This is because the application of the "in dispute" requirement to impeachment would be superfluous: a witness's credibility is always implicitly an issue.

The problem is that almost any testimony given by defense witnesses could be contradicted at least in some minimal way by a subsequent remedial measure. If the defendant's expert testifies that the product at issue was reasonably safe, a subsequent remedial measure could be seen as contradicting that testimony. If "impeachment" means simple contradiction, then the impeachment exception to Rule 407 would threaten to swallow the Rule itself. Accordingly, most courts have held that a subsequent remedial measure is not admissible for impeachment if it is offered for simple contradiction of a defense witness's testimony.[15] Essentially, the limited probative value of the evidence for impeachment is substantially outweighed by the risk of prejudice and confusion resulting from the possible misuse of the subsequent remedial measure by the jury. If the defense witness simply testifies that a product was reasonably safe, a subsequent remedial measure might contradict that testimony, but not very much so—there could be many reasons, other than a recognition of safety concerns, for the decision to change a product or condition after an accident.

On the other hand, if the defendant's witnesses testify in superlatives—e.g., "this is the safest product on the market"—then the evidence of a subsequent remedial measure provides more than simple contradiction. It shows that the witness puffed and exaggerated while on the stand. As such, the remedial measure provides a more direct and probative form of impeachment, which justifies a limited exception to the Rule.

§ 4.3   Compromise and Offers to Compromise

Rule 408 is designed to allow parties to a dispute to make offers and statements in compromise, without having to worry about

---

[15]   *See Flaminio v. Honda Motor Co.*, 733 F.2d 463 (7th Cir. 1984) (no impeachment with subsequent remedial measures was permissible where defense witnesses merely testified to the safety of the product under normal circumstances).

whether such offers and statements might later be admissible as some recognition of the validity or value of their claim or defense. Of course, the vast majority of lawsuits filed are settled prior to trial. If not for all the settlements, our judicial systems would have to be revamped in order to accommodate the large increase in trial activity. Quite aside from the effect of settlements on caseloads and public expenditures, the private resolution of disputes is generally more desirable than one forced upon the parties through state authority.

Suppose that Plato sues Descartes for $100,000, claiming plagiarism. Descartes offers to settle the suit for $75,000, but Plato declines the offer. At trial Plato offers testimony and documents that detail Descartes' rebuffed offer. Because of the substantial amount of the offer, it has probative value to indicate that Descartes thought his defense to Plato's claim was weak. In other words, the evidence of the offer is relevant. Contrast the foregoing offer with an offer by Descartes of $500 to settle the case. Here, probative value pointing toward Descartes' liability is weak to nonexistent. The sum offered is such a small percentage of the damage claimed that the most plausible inference is that Descartes simply wanted to avoid the time and expense necessary to defend against Plato's claim.

Now suppose Descartes offered a settlement of $25,000. Here a reasonable jury might draw the inference that Descartes thought he might incur significant liability—in other words, that Descartes had concluded that there was some risk in going to trial. On the other hand, Descartes might have had other reasons for making a settlement offer. Perhaps negative publicity was affecting the sales or general acceptance of his book that, you will recall, Plato claims contains plagiaristic materials.

What if Descartes offered into evidence his $500 settlement offer to show his confidence in his defense? If such offers were admitted, surely plaintiffs like Plato would respond by demanding $99,000 to show their confidence. In the end, admitting settlement offers would likely result in both plaintiffs and defendants making offers to create affirmative evidence for trial rather than making genuine offers intended to settle a case.

You can see that, generally speaking, probative value increases or decreases in proportion to the percentage of the amount in dispute in a case offered by a plaintiff or defendant.[16] However, other factors, such as negative publicity or the high cost of taking a case to trial,

---

[16]   A plaintiff who offers to take a small percentage of the amount in dispute appears to lack confidence in the case as does a defendant who offers to pay a large percentage of the amount in dispute. A plaintiff who offers to take a large percentage of the amount in dispute or a defendant who offers to pay only a small percentage of the amount in dispute appear to have confidence in their cases.

may influence a party's "settlement behavior." In the end, the best rule to encourage offers of compromise is one that disregards the amount of the offer and simply declares that evidence of an offer of compromise is inadmissible:

(a) If made by the plaintiff and offered by the defendant to show that the plaintiff's claim is weak, or if made by the plaintiff and offered by the plaintiff as evidence of a strong claim;

(b) If made by the defendant and offered by the plaintiff to show that the defense is weak, or if made by the defendant and offered by the defendant as evidence of a strong defense.

Federal Rule 408

With this brief introduction in mind, examine carefully the text of Rule 408, which was amended in 2006:

COMPROMISE OFFERS AND NEGOTIATIONS

(a) Prohibited uses. Evidence of the following is not admissible—on behalf of any party—either to prove or disprove the validity or amount of a disputed claim or to impeach through a prior inconsistent statement or a contradiction:

(1) furnishing, promising, or offering—or accepting, promising to accept, or offering to accept—a valuable consideration in compromising or attempting to compromise the claim; and

(2) conduct or a statement made during compromise negotiations about the claim—except when offered in a criminal case and when the negotiations related to a claim by a public office or agency in the exercise of regulatory, investigative, or enforcement authority.

(b) Exceptions. The court may admit this evidence for another purpose, such as proving a witness's bias or prejudice, negating a contention of undue delay, or proving an effort to obstruct a criminal investigation or prosecution.

Rule 408 has a number of noteworthy features. First, the rule protects not only offers of compromise, but also compromises that were agreed to but not implemented. The rule also includes settlement activity between a party and a third person on a related matter. The rationale for that protection is that a party might be reluctant to settle one litigation if the settlement could be used as a concession in a related litigation.[17] Second, the rule protects evidence of "conduct or a statement during compromise negotiations," thereby making it unnecessary for a negotiating party to constantly resort to such protective statements as "assuming arguendo my client was speeding . . .," or alternatively, employing such prefatory remarks as "without prejudice" or "hypothetically speaking." Prior to the widespread adoption of the Federal Rules of Evidence, lawyers routinely used these cautionary phrases during negotiations in order to avoid making an inadvertent statement of "fact" that could be used against their clients should there be a trial. Federal Rule 408 renders unnecessary these awkward precautionary remarks by protecting statements made during "compromise negotiations" whether or not they are couched in hypothetical terms.

A third noteworthy point about the text of Rule 408 is that it protects only statements or conduct made in an effort to compromise a claim that is disputed as to validity or amount. For example, suppose the plaintiff sues the defendant for $5,000, alleging that the defendant negligently failed to put a railing on a stairwell. During compromise negotiations the defendant's lawyer admits that his client's failure to erect a railing violated the applicable safety code. Even if such a violation were negligence per se, the lawyer's statement is nonetheless protected if he disputed the amount of damages to which the plaintiff was entitled. However, should the plaintiff's lawyer acknowledge that his client was negligent and also admit that the plaintiff has suffered at least $5,000 in damages as a result of the stairwell accident, this statement, as well as an offer to settle for, say, $3,000, would be outside the evidentiary protection of Rule 408. The policy underlying Rule 408—to encourage the resolution of disputes—is not served by protecting a party who simply refuses to satisfy a claim that he acknowledges is valid.

Note that the validity or amount of a claim can be "disputed" even before litigation has begun. Thus, statements and offers made to resolve a dispute before litigation are protected by Rule 408 if litigation ultimately ensues.

Purposes for Which Evidence of Compromise Is Not Forbidden by Rule 408

Rule 408(b) contains a familiar theme: the protective provisions of the rule do not apply when evidence concerning a compromise is offered for purposes other than to show that a claim or defense is weak. The rule gives some illustrations, such as proving bias or prejudice of a witness, negativing a contention of undue delay, or

---

[17]   Suppose, for example, *A*, *B*, and *C* are involved in a three car automobile accident. In the *A v. B* suit, *A* offers evidence that *B* paid *C* $30,000 to settle *C's* claim. Rule 408 applies to protect the compromise.

proving an effort to obstruct a criminal investigation or prosecution. Suppose, for example, *P* sues *A*, a truck driver, and *B*, the truck company. Prior to trial, *P* and *A* settle *P's* claim against *A*, and *A* agrees to testify for *P* in his trial against *B*. After *A* testifies, *B* could disclose *A's* possible bias by introducing evidence of his (*A's*) compromise (i.e., his financial relationship) with *P*.

ILLUSTRATION

Following American Credit card's termination of its contract with Universal Credit card, Universal sues American for breach of contract.[18] American's defense against Universal's claim is that Universal breached their agreement by steering its (Universal's) customers to American's competitors through a process called "rolling over accounts." Universal's position was that the rollovers occurred only after Universal thought it had reached a settlement agreement with American under which the rollovers to other banks were permitted. (The settlement under which Universal claimed it was acting was never finalized.) After the settlement was abandoned and litigation was resumed, Universal stopped rolling over accounts to American's competitors.

When, at trial, Universal's president starts to testify about the tentative agreement under which his bank engaged for a period of time in rollovers, American objects, citing Rule 408. How should the trial judge rule?

Universal offered evidence of the failed compromise for the purpose of explaining why it rolled over accounts in an apparent violation of the contract between Universal and American which American, the defendant, terminated. It was this termination, of course, that led to Universal's claim that American had breached their contract, which in turn led to American's claim that Universal should be denied a recovery because it had violated their contractual provisions through its rollover practices. When this lawsuit appeared to have been settled, Universal began to shift accounts to other banks as it thought it was entitled to do under the terms of the compromise. It would be unfair to allow American to cite Universal's rollover practice as the reason for denying Universal's breach of contract claim, while at the same time allowing American to foreclose "compromise" evidence that explained and perhaps justified the practice. From a policy standpoint, settlements are not encouraged when one party uses settlement discussions to lead his opponent into

---

[18]   The facts in this Illustration are based on those in *Bankcard America, Inc. v. Universal Bancard Systems, Inc.*, 203 F.3d 477 (7th Cir. 2000).

a contractual breach, and then uses the breach to escape liability. Consequently, the settlement evidence is admissible.

Impeachment

As discussed above, a witness may be impeached with evidence that he compromised a related matter—this could show a motive to falsify in the matter in which he is testifying—i.e., that he is biased. Evidence of compromise might be relevant for two other forms of impeachment. First, it might be relevant to contradict a testifying party's assertion about the validity or amount of the claim—e.g., if the plaintiff is testifying that his claim is worth $100,000, then why did he offer to terminate the case for $50,000? Alternatively, statements made in compromise negotiations might be relevant as prior inconsistent statements.

It can be seen, however, that if compromise evidence could be used for contradiction or prior inconsistent statement impeachment, then much of the protection of Rule 408 would be lost. As to contradiction, the same evidence that could not be admitted in the case-in-chief would be admitted for "impeachment" whenever the party who made the offer testifies, which presumably is every case. And as to prior inconsistent statements, parties would be reluctant to say or have their lawyers say anything during compromise negotiations for fear that it might in some way be inconsistent with future trial testimony. Accordingly, the 2006 amendment to Rule 408 specifically prohibits statements and offers in compromise to be admitted for purposes of impeachment by way of contradiction or prior inconsistent statement. The Advisory Committee Note to the amendment reasons that "[s]uch broad impeachment would tend to swallow the exclusionary rule and would impair the public policy of promoting settlements."

Use of Evidence of Civil Compromises in Subsequent Criminal Cases

Assume a defendant is sued by consumers for fraud. He settles the matter for $100,000 and, as part of the settlement, he signs a statement accepting the wrongfulness of his conduct. Subsequently he is criminally charged for the same fraud. Is his civil settlement, and his statement, admissible as evidence of guilt?

The 2006 amendment to Rule 408 provides that civil settlements are inadmissible in subsequent criminal cases. Moreover, statements made in an effort to settle a civil case are also inadmissible, with one exception: where the accused previously made a statement admitting criminal liability in the course of settlement discussions *with a government regulator*, that statement can be offered as an admission of guilt. The Advisory Committee Note to the 2006 amendment explains that admitting evidence of civil compromises in subsequent criminal cases "could deter defendants from settling" a civil action. In contrast, when an individual "makes a statement in the presence of government agents, its subsequent admission in a criminal case should not be unexpected." Moreover, an individual "can seek to protect against subsequent disclosure through negotiation and agreement with the civil regulator."

§ 4.4   Payment of Medical Expenses

Suppose that at the annual Spartan Township Memorial Day Picnic, there is always a "fathers against sons" softball game. When Phil attempts to steal second base, he collides with the second baseman, Drew, and sustains serious head injuries. Drew, who is clearly upset, declares "I'm so sorry. It was all my fault and I want to pay your medical bills."

Subsequently, Phil sues Drew, alleging negligence. Drew, who has had several months to think further about how the accident happened, denies negligence and asserts Phil's contributory negligence.

As you would anticipate, Phil wants to offer testimony that reveals what Drew said after the two collided. Drew's statement is clearly relevant and it would normally be considered a "statement of a party-opponent" and thus admissible against him. However, Rule 409 states that "[e]vidence of furnishing, promising to pay, or offering to pay medical, hospital, or similar expenses resulting from an injury is not admissible to prove liability for the injury." This provision renders inadmissible at least that portion of Drew's statement relating to his desire to pay Phil's medical bills. The exclusion of this evidence serves the policy objective of not penalizing one who engages in humane acts.

Rule 409 does not protect collateral statements made together with offers to pay medical bills. Thus, that part of Phil's statement admitting fault for the accident gains no protection from Rule 409; nor does it gain any protection from Rule 408 because, at the time of Drew's statement, Phil and Drew were not compromising a "disputed claim."[19]

§ 4.5   Pleas and Related Statements

Federal Rule 410, which applies to pleas and the plea-bargaining process in criminal cases, bears a relationship to Federal Rule 408, which applies to the compromise process in civil cases. Both rules facilitate the voluntary resolution of disputes by the adverse parties.

---

[19]   Fed. R. Evid. 408.

Rule 410 protects withdrawn guilty pleas and pleas of nolo contendere; the rule also protects statements regarding those pleas made at plea hearings or proceedings. Finally, it protects statements during the course of plea discussions between defendant (often speaking through his counsel) and the attorney for the prosecution, where those statements do not result in a guilty plea, or which result in a plea of guilty later withdrawn. Without these protections, the process of plea discussions and negotiations would be hampered by a lack of candor. Furthermore, unfair practices would probably develop as, for example, when the prosecutor produces evidence at a criminal trial that the defendant offered to plead guilty to a lesser offense. The jury might view evidence that the defendant was prepared to enter a guilty plea to a lesser offense as a convincing indication that he was guilty of the crime charged. It is a fact, however, that some people might plead guilty even if they are innocent, for a variety of reasons that include a quick release from incarceration or protecting a family member or friend who is actually guilty.

Text of Federal Rule 410

Rule 410 provides as follows:

Pleas, Plea Discussions, and Related Statements

(a) Prohibited Uses. In a civil or criminal case, evidence of the following is not admissible against the defendant who made the plea or participated in the plea discussions:

(1) a guilty plea that was later withdrawn;

(2) a nolo contendere plea;

(3) a statement made during a proceeding on either of those pleas under Federal Rule of Criminal Procedure 11 or a comparable state procedure; or

(4) a statement made during plea discussions with an attorney for the prosecuting authority if the discussions did not result in a guilty plea or they resulted in a later-withdrawn guilty plea.

(b) Exceptions. The court may admit a statement described in Rule 410(a)(3) or (4):

(1) in any proceeding in which another statement made during the same plea or plea discussions has been introduced, if in fairness the statements ought to be considered together; or

(2) in a criminal proceeding for perjury or false statement, if the defendant made the statement under oath, on the record, and with counsel present.

Observe that the provisions of the rule that declare certain evidence inadmissible do so by addressing:

(1)   pleas and statements

(2)   civil and criminal proceedings

(3)   the party (namely, the defendant) entitled to the rule's protection.

What Pleas and Statements Are Protected and Why

Rule 410(a)(1) renders inadmissible evidence of "a guilty plea that was later withdrawn." Once the court accepts a guilty plea, the defendant cannot withdraw it without the court's permission.[20] The trial judge may grant permission to revoke on a number of grounds, including: the plea was coerced, the defendant was inadequately represented, the defendant did not fully understand the consequences of entering a guilty plea, or the factual basis underlying the plea was weak. The point is that if a guilty plea was improperly entered, evidence that it was entered and withdrawn should not be used against the defendant in subsequent criminal or civil proceedings. If the guilty plea cannot be used against the defendant, Rule 410 also provides that statements made in connection with the plea colloquy that accompanied the entry of the plea also cannot be used. Rule 410(a)(3).

Rule 410 also renders inadmissible evidence disclosing that the defendant entered a plea of nolo contendere. A "nolo plea," which is essentially a "no contest" plea, says, in essence, "I admit nothing, but I will not contest the charges against me." The court must approve the entry of this plea. A defendant wishing to enter a nolo plea is usually concerned about the effect that an adverse (criminal) judgment will have on a civil suit (or suits) based on the same conduct that is the subject of the criminal charge. If there were no opportunity for entering a plea of nolo contendere, the defendant might decide to contest the criminal charge simply to protect against civil liability. The nolo plea avoids what a guilty plea would not: the introduction of evidence in the civil trial that the defendant had pled guilty to a criminal charge based on the conduct that now forms the basis of the

---

[20]   This is the long-standing rule in the federal system—*see* Fed. R. Crim. P. 11(d)—but it does not prevail in all states. Those states that allow a unilateral withdrawal may decline to exclude evidence of the withdrawn guilty plea in future proceedings. Note that in the federal system, the accused has the unilateral right to withdraw a guilty plea that has not yet been accepted by the court.

plaintiff's civil claim.[21] Since the purpose of a nolo plea is to enable the court to enter a judgment of conviction and impose a sentence without the defendant's admitting anything, Rule 410(a)(3) provides that statements made in the plea colloquy accompanying entry of the nolo plea also are inadmissible.

Note that Rule 410's protection covers withdrawn guilty pleas, nolo pleas, and, as we will see, plea discussions between the defendant and the government's attorney that do not eventuate in a guilty plea. The *entry of a guilty plea that is not withdrawn* is outside the protective ambit of Rule 410. A defendant who elects to plead guilty usually enjoys the benefits of pleading to a lesser charge or a reduced sentence (or both). However, he is not entitled to the additional benefit of using Rule 410 to block the subsequent evidentiary use of the guilty plea or statements he may have made during "plea-bargaining" discussions with the prosecutor.

As we have just observed, Rule 410's protection extends to a defendant's statements made during his exchanges with the prosecutor and directed to the possibility of a plea bargain. Specifically, Rule 410(a)(4) renders inadmissible evidence of "a statement made during plea discussions with an attorney for the prosecuting authority if the discussions did not result in a guilty plea. . . ." Were it not for this protection, statements by the defendant or his agent (the defense attorney) could be used against him in any subsequent criminal or civil proceeding in which they were relevant. They might be used, for example, to prove his guilt or to impeach his testimony by showing the inconsistencies between his testimony and earlier statements made during the plea-bargaining stage. The accused would be taking an enormous risk in entering into guilty plea negotiations: if the negotiations were to end unsuccessfully, then every incriminating statement made to the prosecutor would be admissible at the criminal trial and beyond.

The protection afforded by Rule 410 as to statements is intended to promote candor and thus increase the productiveness of plea discussions. The rule does not apply to discussions between the defendant and persons, such as police, who are not acting as "an attorney for the prosecuting authority. . . ."[22] However, a few cases have found that the rule applies when a law enforcement officer who

---

[21]   A nolo contendere plea results in a conviction, and a defendant is sentenced in the same way as if he pleaded guilty. The nolo plea is not an "admission," however, whereas a guilty plea is an admission of guilt. Note also Fed. R. Evid. 803(22), which creates an exception from the hearsay rule for certain judgments but not those entered pursuant to nolo pleas.

[22]   Fed. R. Evid. 410.

held discussions with the defendant was in fact acting as the prosecuting attorney's agent.[23]

Admissible Statements

Rule 410 contains two exceptions to its general exclusionary sweep. The first is designed to avoid misleading the trier of fact. Suppose the *defendant* introduces evidence of a statement that Rule 410 would exclude if offered against the defendant. This opens the door for his opponent to introduce evidence of any related statement made in the course of the same plea or plea discussions when in fairness the statements should be considered together. Think of this exception as an application of the "completeness" principle that underlies Federal Rule 106. That rule provides that when a party introduces a writing, in whole or in part, "an adverse party may require the introduction . . . of any other part—or any other writing or recorded statement—that in fairness ought to be considered at the same time."[24]

The second exception contained in Rule 410 is designed to thwart a defendant's attempt to shield himself from a perjury prosecution. If during the plea process the defendant makes a statement under oath, on the record and in the presence of defense counsel and is later prosecuted for perjury or false statement, evidence of the statement is admissible in the trial for the allegedly false testimony. The formal requirements that attend this exception, namely the oath, a transcript, and the presence of counsel, largely confine it to prosecutions for false or perjurious statements made during a plea hearing conducted under Rule 11 of the Federal Rules of Criminal Procedure.

Waiver of Rule 410 Protections

We have seen that in the adversarial system of litigation, the parties largely control the evidence that comes before the court. This tradition of party control permeates the evidence rules. With this background in mind, consider whether a prosecutor could refuse to "plea bargain" with a defendant unless the latter waived some of the evidentiary protections afforded to him by Rule 410.

This issue came before the Supreme Court in *United States v. Mezzanatto*.[25] There, the defendant arranged to meet with the prosecutor to discuss cooperating with the government. At the outset of the meeting, the prosecutor set forth his conditions: the defendant had to be completely truthful and he had to agree that any

---

[23]   *See, e.g., United States v. Millard*, 139 F.3d 1200, 1205–06 (8th Cir. 1998).

[24]   Fed. R. Evid. 106.

[25]   513 U.S. 196 (1995).

statements made during the plea discussions would be admissible if a trial ensued to impeach the defendant if he gave testimony that contradicted his statements during the plea discussions. Further, the prosecutor stated that if the defendant declined these conditions, the plea discussions would not go forward. After conferring with his counsel, the defendant agreed to the prosecutor's demands.

During the ensuing discussions, the defendant made statements that the prosecutor knew were untrue. As a result, the prosecutor terminated the plea discussions and brought the defendant to trial. During his trial testimony, the defendant made statements that were inconsistent with some of the statements he had made to the prosecutor during their plea discussions. The prosecutor then introduced evidence of the earlier statements, as prior inconsistent statements, despite the defendant's objections that the protections afforded by Rule 410 could not be waived. To allow a waiver at the behest of the prosecutor, he argued, creates an unfair procedure, frustrates the goal of party settlement, and "invites prosecutorial overreaching . . . [because of the] gross disparity in the relative bargaining power of the parties to a plea agreement. . . ."[26]

Ultimately, however, a majority of the Supreme Court rejected these contentions and upheld Mezzanatto's waiver of Rule 410 protection. Speaking generally, the Court endorsed the view that evidentiary rules are "presumptively waivable."[27] In this case, the waiver resulted in an appropriate outcome: the trier was apprised that the defendant had made conflicting statements. The Court also noted that waiving Rule 410 could promote the defendant's interest in plea bargaining. A prosecutor might well decline plea discussions unless the defendant agrees to such a waiver—this would be particularly true when the prosecutor believes that a particular person will not be truthful in the proffer session, so that the prosecutor would just be wasting her time; such a defendant could waive Rule 410 protections as a sign of good faith. Thus, the defendant's power to waive Rule 410 protection allows the possibility of a deal with the government that might not otherwise be reached. As to the defendant's claim that allowing waivers will lead to prosecutorial abuse, the Court was unwilling to endorse the belief that there would be widespread misconduct. It suffices, said the Court, "to permit case-by-case inquiries into whether waiver agreements are the product of fraud or coercion."[28]

---

[26]   Id. at 209.

[27]   Given the fact that the defendant may waive *constitutional* protections such as the right to counsel and the right to trial, it would have been odd if the Court had held that evidentiary protections are not waivable.

[28]   Id. at 210.

Subsequent lower court case law indicates that plea bargaining statements can be admitted not only to impeach the defendant at trial but also in the government's case-in-chief as substantive evidence of guilt—if the defendant knowingly and voluntarily agrees to such an arrangement.[29] Such arrangements are left to the marketplace of plea bargaining, as the Court directed in *Mezzanatto*.

Statements by the Prosecutor in Plea Negotiations

Recall that Rule 410 is a one way street: it confers evidentiary protections upon the defendant, but not upon the prosecution. There are occasions, however, when statements by the prosecutor during plea discussions would be useful to the defendant at a subsequent trial. Suppose for example the prosecutor during a plea bargaining discussion admits that there are gaps in his evidence, or that his witnesses may not be credible, or that in light of the entire evidentiary record he is willing to reduce the charge to a lesser offense if the defendant will then plead guilty. If the defendant offers evidence of statements like these at his subsequent trial, Rule 410 appears inapplicable. However, routinely allowing this kind of evidence would appear to discourage prosecutorial candor in plea negotiations.

ILLUSTRATION

Prosecutor (*P*) convenes a grand jury that returns an indictment charging Defendant (*D*) with armed robbery. Subsequently, *P* and *D* enter into plea bargaining discussions. At the conclusion of these talks, *P* offers to reduce the charge to grand theft if *D* agrees to plead guilty to this lesser charge. *D* refuses.

At *D's* trial for armed robbery, defense counsel offers evidence that *P* offered to reduce the charge against *D* from armed robbery to grand theft. *P* objects. How should the trial judge rule?

Rule 410(a) states that specified evidence that is adduced during various plea proceedings is not admissible "against the defendant." The rule does not protect the prosecution from adverse evidence. However, case law generally excludes evidence of a prosecutor's offer and statements made by the prosecutor in plea negotiations. The concern of these courts is that allowing "plea-bargaining" evidence

---

[29]   *See, e.g., United States v. Barrow*, 400 F.3d 109 (2d Cir. 2005) (upholding the defendant's waiver that permitted the government to admit defendant's plea negotiation statements as substantive evidence of guilt; noting that upholding such a waiver provided assurances that the defendant was being truthful by making deceit costly, and therefore the rule promoted the policy of plea bargaining).

against the prosecution will have an adverse effect on plea discussions and plea offers by the prosecutor.[30]

Perhaps Rule 403 is the proper rule under which to accept or reject the defendant's proffered evidence. That rule gives the trial judge considerable discretion in ruling on the defendant's offer of proof. There are a number of reasons why a prosecutor might wish to conclude a plea arrangement, other than recognition of a weak case. For example, she may be willing to reduce the charge against the defendant and reach a plea agreement because she has other cases of greater significance that she wishes to bring to trial. Or perhaps she offers to reduce the charge against the defendant because she wants to gain his cooperation with respect to gathering evidence against other persons who may have been involved in the offense charged. Other reasons could be suggested, but the point is that the jury might conclude that the prosecutor had a weak case against D when, in fact, she offered to reduce the charge for an entirely different reason. Moreover, a prosecutor's statements made in the give-and-take of plea negotiations should probably not be taken as very probative of the prosecutor's actual assessment of the strength of the government's case.

Rule 403, you may recall, empowers the judge to reject relevant evidence when its probative value is substantially outweighed by the danger of confusing of the issues, or misleading the jury. An additional difficulty stems from the long tradition, often implemented by a specific rule of professional responsibility, that it is generally inappropriate for a lawyer who represents a party to litigation to act as a trial witness. Thus, if the accused introduces evidence that the prosecutor offered to reduce the charge, the jury may never learn what actually motivated the offer. The judge, however, in exercising her authority under Rule 403, may hear arguments from both the prosecution and the defense outside the jury's presence, and then make her ruling.

§ 4.6   Liability Insurance

Federal Rule 411 prohibits evidence that "a person was or was not insured against liability" when this evidence is offered as bearing on whether the person "acted negligently or otherwise wrongfully." Rule 411 draws support from at least two sources. The first—and most important—is the concern that if jurors were made aware that a party charged with liability was insured, they might think about a

---

[30]   *See, e.g., United States v. Verdoorn*, 528 F.2d 103, 107 (8th Cir. 1976) (evidence of prosecutor's plea-bargaining stance as proof of government's weak case is inadmissible); *United States v. Delgado*, 903 F.2d 1495, 1499 (11th Cir. 1990) (Rule 403 supports rejection of defense evidence of statements of prosecutor and plea offer because reasons other than weakness in government's case may be explanatory).

"deep pocket" and impose liability when they otherwise would not or, perhaps, increase the damage award.[31] The second justification for the rule is the marginal relevance that the presence or absence of insurance is likely to have on a person's conduct. In cases involving negligent conduct, probative value would appear to be either very weak or nonexistent—a rational person is unlikely to act more carelessly simply because she is insured.[32] A possible third justification is that without the rule the incentive to purchase insurance might be weakened and the price of insurance might rise. The insured would have to consider the possible impact of this evidence in litigation, and the insurer would have to consider the impact of this evidence on premiums it charges.

The prohibition of Rule 411 is not absolute. Exclusion is not required when evidence of liability insurance is offered for "another purpose, such as proving a witness's bias or prejudice or proving agency, ownership, or control." Suppose, for example, a witness for the defendant is an employee or agent of the defendant's liability insurer. Evidence of this relationship is admissible to impeach the witness, even though it incidentally reveals the fact that the defendant has liability insurance.

ILLUSTRATION

Plaintiff, a truck driver, sues both the owner and the lessee of a truck stop for injuries incurred when the plaintiff fell into a grease pit on the premises. At trial, there is conflicting evidence as to whether the owner, the lessee, or both were responsible for maintaining the premises. The owner testifies that the lessee had sole responsibility for maintenance. Plaintiff thereupon starts to cross-examine the owner concerning whether the latter had liability insurance that protected against damages for injuries sustained on the truck stop premises. The defense objects, citing Federal Rule 411. How should the trial judge rule?

The evidence probably falls within one of the enumerated exceptions to Rule 411's prohibition against the disclosure of liability insurance. Arguably, the evidence in question is offered on the issue of "control." However, because the list of exceptions (allowable purposes) in Rule 411 is illustrative, not exhaustive, it is unnecessary

---

[31] Of course, in some contexts insurance coverage is either quite common or mandatory, so it is reasonable to suppose that the jury probably assumes that there is some insurance coverage.

[32] Thus, rejection of evidence of liability insurance could rest on the justification of minimal probative value. But Rule 411 does not leave the issue of admissibility of evidence of liability insurance to a mere relevance determination and its attendant fluctuations from case to case.

to fit the evidence within one of the enumerated purposes. The evidence in the Illustration was not offered on the issue of the owner's negligence or wrongful conduct, but was addressed to the disputed issue of which defendant had responsibility (an adequate surrogate for "control") for maintaining the truck stop. Thus the judge should overrule the defendant's objection.

Chapter V

HEARSAY: WHAT IS IT?

Table of Sections

---

§ 5.1   Overview

The rule against hearsay is designed to exclude statements that are not reliable when offered to prove that what a person said was true. The classic hearsay situation is this: a witness testifies that someone else (whom we call the *declarant*) made a statement about an event that is in dispute at the trial. The witness relates the statement, but cannot verify that the declarant was telling the truth. If the statement is offered to prove that what the declarant said was true, then there is no way to verify it for accuracy. The declarant is not at trial. He is not speaking under oath. The factfinder does not get to view him and make its own assessment of whether he is speaking the truth. Most importantly, he is not subject to the crucible of cross-examination, so there is no opportunity to assess his sincerity, precision, perception, and memory of the event. Cross-examining the witness relating the statement in court is not a sufficient safeguard, because the witness cannot tell the factfinder about the declarant's sincerity, perception, etc. He only knows what he heard the declarant say.

But not all statements made by an out-of-court declarant are hearsay. To constitute hearsay, the repeated statement must be offered for the purpose of proving that what the declarant said is true. If the statement is offered for a not-for-truth purpose, then we are not concerned that the declarant may be lying, misperceiving, etc. The statement has probative force despite its testimonial infirmities.

Suppose, for example, Owner lends a painting by Alfred Sisley to Museum so that it can be included in an exhibit of Impressionist painters. During the exhibition, the painting is stolen and, subsequently, Owner sues Museum. A member of the maintenance crew testifies that as he walked past the entrance to the exhibit he caught a brief glimpse of a man in uniform. The man said to a person the witness could not see, "I made sure all the visitors had left the gallery area and then locked both doors." If this statement were offered to prove that the visitors were cleared from the gallery and the doors were then locked, it would be hearsay because it would be offered for its truth. However, if the witness's testimony were offered only to prove that the guard was at his station near the exhibit, the statement would not be hearsay.[1] The declarant's statement makes it more likely that he was a security guard, even if he was mistaken or lying about his actions. Note, however, that the principle of relevance confines the purposes for which an out-of-court statement can be offered. If the presence of the security guard near the exhibit did not bear on a consequential proposition, the statement of the speaker (declarant) could not be admitted for the "nonhearsay" purpose of proving he was on duty. To allow admission where the statement is not sufficiently probative for a not-for-truth purpose would gut the hearsay rule.

Rationale for Excluding Hearsay

Why do we confine the rule against hearsay evidence to out-of-court statements that are offered "to prove the truth of the matter asserted in the statement"?[2] The principal basis for the rule against hearsay is that a cross-examiner who is confronted with adverse hearsay evidence is denied the opportunity to cross-examine the "real" witness (the declarant) and to expose weaknesses in his statement. However, if his statement is not offered for its truth, the *only* question for the trier of fact is whether the declarant in fact made the statement to which the witness on the stand testifies. As to this question, the cross-examiner can conduct an effective cross-examination because he can ask questions of the witness that are designed to show that the witness is mistaken or lying about *the declarant's statement*—that is, exactly what, if anything, the declarant said. When the key question is whether the witness heard and reported something correctly, the witness is as able to explain what was heard as effectively as the witness can defend what the witness saw, felt, smelled, or touched.

ILLUSTRATION

Andy's Bar and Grill is located near an Air Force base from which soldiers often fly to their new duty station, sometimes located in a combat zone. On a particular Saturday night a group of soldiers who were about to be "shipped out" went to Andy's for drinks. Arguments ensued between the soldiers and anti-war protesters who were also

---

[1]   *See* ARTHUR BEST, EVIDENCE 66 (5th ed. 2003).

[2]   Fed. R. Evid. 801(c) (defining hearsay).

having drinks at Andy's Bar and Grill. A fight broke out; then another; and a melee ensued.

Your client, Hemmingway, suffered serious injuries to his head, which he thinks were inflicted, without provocation, by Corporals Buck or Spitz or both. Hemmingway says he unsuccessfully tried to fend off his attackers with an empty gin bottle and a wooden stick. Two eyewitnesses substantiate Hemmingway's account.

Unfortunately however, by the time Hemmingway consults you, most of the soldiers involved in the fray have been sent abroad and many of the protesters cannot be located. However, you do locate a reporter, Woodward, who wrote an article about the brawl for the local newspaper. Woodward interviewed Buck and Spitz before they left for the war zone; he also interviewed Bartender and Waitress, who observed the events in question. On the basis of the statements of these four "declarants," Woodward concluded that Hemmingway, who had drunk an entire bottle of gin, attacked Buck and Spitz from behind with an empty gin bottle and the leg of a broken chair. Subsequently, Buck and Spitz return to the base and you, on Hemmingway's behalf, file suit against them for assault and battery.

Suppose that during the trial the defense calls Bartender and Waitress. You cross-examine each of them before you learn that Buck and Spitz have suddenly been ordered to participate in a field maneuver in a remote section of the base. However, Woodward will testify in their place and will give their account of the relevant events of the brawl.

[handwritten margin note: ASK IF BUCK & SPITZ RECOLLECTION WAS CORRECTED?]

What kinds of questions, designed toward what ends, are useful to you when you cross-examine Bartender and Waitress, but are of little value to you in your cross-examination of Woodward? In other words, which practical limitations, not applicable in your cross-examination of Bartender and Waitress, seriously hamper your cross-examination of Woodward?

This Illustration is designed to encourage you to think about what ends are likely to be pursued by a cross-examiner. Often, she focuses on ways in which she can discredit the witness or at least raise doubts about the accuracy of his testimony. For example, she may ask questions designed to reveal that the witness was not in a good position to observe the event in question; that he has poor eyesight; that his memory is faulty, that he is being evasive or deceptive, and so forth. As we have seen, such questions are of limited value when the witness on the stand has recited what someone else— the declarant—has said about the event. The witness, who was not, himself, a first-hand observer can say no more than what he was told by the declarant. This is why hearsay testimony carries with it certain infirmities, often called hearsay "dangers" or "risks." These potential dangers to testimonial accuracy are:

(a) *Defects in Perception*: the declarant's statements may be unreliable because he did not observe or hear accurately.

(b) *Defects in Memory*: the declarant's statements may be unreliable because his memory (of the event about which he spoke) may have been weak, inaccurate, or incomplete.

(c) *Defects in Sincerity*: the declarant's statements may be unreliable because he purposefully gave a biased, incomplete, or false account.

(d) *Defects in Narration or Transmission*: the declarant's statements may be unreliable because his language was ambiguous, or because he inadvertently left out an important word or phrase, or because the meaning of his statement was dependent on tone and context.

The assumption underlying the hearsay rule is that cross-examination can test for and reveal these infirmities. Accordingly, the lack of opportunity to cross-examine the person with personal knowledge of the event that the statement is offered to prove is the fundamental reason for excluding hearsay evidence. This rationale is, of course, consistent with a major tenet of the adversary system: cross-examination is the essential means for testing the accuracy of testimony and discovering the truth. And of course the other two deficits are important as well—the declarant is not under oath and the jury has no opportunity to view the declarant's demeanor as a witness.

Despite the importance of cross-examination, oath, and demeanor however, an absolute exclusion of all hearsay statements would actually impede accurate fact-finding; this is because hearsay can, in some circumstances, be reliable (as you know from the fact that you often tell the truth, without the safeguards of oath and cross-examination). As the next two chapters demonstrate, there are numerous exemptions and exceptions[3] to the hearsay rule. Bear in

---

[3]   A statement falling within either an exemption or exception may be used to prove the truth of the matter asserted in the statement.

mind, then, that *classification of a particular statement as hearsay does not necessarily mean that the statement will be excluded.* Quite often, a declarant's hearsay statement is admissible because it falls within one of the various exemptions or exceptions.

§ 5.2   A Definition of Hearsay

We begin a detailed analysis of the hearsay rule by examining the "definitional" portions of Federal Rule 801. This rule first defines "statement" and then goes on to incorporate "statement" (as thus defined) into the definition of hearsay. Rule 801(a) says that "statement" is "a person's oral or written assertion, or nonverbal conduct, if the person intended it as an assertion." The crux of this definition is this: a person makes a statement when she asserts something either through the use of words or through conduct (such as nodding her head or using hand signals) that is intended as a substitute for words.

Rule 801(c) uses the word "statement" (as defined in subsection (a)) in its definition of hearsay:

    (c)   **Hearsay.** "Hearsay" means a statement that:

        (1)   the declarant does <u>not</u> make while testifying at the current trial or hearing; and

        (2)   a party offers in evidence to prove the truth of the matter asserted in the statement.

This definition captures the principle we have just discussed: the hearsay rule is concerned with an out-of-court statement (that is, a statement not made from the witness stand at this trial)[4] offered for the purpose of convincing the trier of fact that the statement is true. Of course, as we know, a declarant's statement must be probative of one (or more) consequential propositions or it would fail the basic test of relevance. However, a hearsay statement, even if relevant, is inadmissible unless it falls within an exemption or exception. This basic proposition is affirmed by Federal Rule 802, which declares that hearsay is not admissible unless an exception can be found in the Federal Rules, a statute, or other national rules prescribed by the Supreme Court.

---

    [4]   We often speak of hearsay statements as "out-of-court" assertions offered for their truth. This is a convenience; technically, however, any statement made anywhere other than from the stand in the *present* trial is hearsay if offered for its truth. For example, statements made during testimony rendered in another trial (and thus given "in court") would be hearsay; so too—at least ordinarily—would a statement made prior to trial by a *testifying* witness and offered for its truth. This is what the rule means when defining hearsay as a statement not made "while testifying at the current trial or hearing."

Machines and Animals

In its several subsections that define hearsay, Rule 801 consistently speaks of hearsay declarations *of a person*—the declarant. Machines or devices such as radar units, heart monitors, surveillance cameras, or clocks do not make hearsay statements; neither does an animal such as a tracking dog that follows the scent of the accused from the scene of the crime to his hiding place, or a parrot who calls out the name of the accused as someone (whose identity is in issue) enters the victim's house. Judges may sometimes exclude evidence derived from these various sources, but not because of the hearsay rule. Machines, parrots and bloodhounds cannot be cross-examined. They cannot take an oath. Evidence derived from devices or animals is tested for reliability by the cross-examination of persons who are acquainted with the operating principles and particular features of the device or the training and history of the animal. But machine and animal output is not hearsay.[5]

§ 5.3   Statements That Are Not Hearsay: A Sampling

"Not Offered for Truth"

As we have seen, if the proponent's probative purpose can be realized without the factfinder's reliance upon the truth of the declarant's statement, the hearsay rule is inapplicable. Thus, it is important to focus closely on the *purpose* for which the declarant's statement is offered. Sometimes it is readily apparent that a proffered statement is not being offered for its truth. Yet, at other times, the proffered statement appears to have its greatest probative force if its assertion is used for its "truth content," rather than for the other relevant (and permissible) nonhearsay purpose for which the proponent proffers it. In these situations, the trial judge must consider whether to exclude the evidence on the grounds set out in Rule 403, especially the ground of "unfair prejudice"—the unfair prejudice being the risk that the jury will misuse the evidence as proof of the facts related in it, i.e., for its truth content.

If the trial judge decides to admit the evidence for a nonhearsay purpose, the opponent of the evidence is entitled to have the judge instruct the jury members that they can consider the evidence only for its proper (nonhearsay) use and not for its forbidden hearsay use.

---

[5]   Human beings can use various instruments to make hearsay statements from simple ones like pencils and pens to more complicated ones like computers and smart phones. If a machine output contains human input, and that human input is offered for its truth, then the hearsay rule will be applicable. A simple example is a statement of a declarant that is videorecorded (as opposed to a videorecording of a car passing through an intersection).

Sometimes, however, the opponent declines to request the instruction, because he does not want to suggest the possibility that the statement could be used for its truth by calling that possibility to the jury's attention.

The material that follows contains examples of statements that are not hearsay. These nonhearsay "patterns" are based on the text of Federal Rule 801, as well as cases that involve the various nonhearsay exemplars that will be described. Of course, other patterns arise, but the central issue remains constant: Is the declarant's statement offered for its truth, or is it probative of a disputed fact without regard to its truth?

Verbal Acts (Words That Have Independent Legal Significance)

A statement that itself creates or shifts a legal relationship is not hearsay. Such a statement is often called a "verbal act"—suggesting the analogy between conduct that has legal significance (for example negligent conduct or criminal conduct) and words that have legal significance, quite independent of the declarant's perception, memory, sincerity, or narration.

Suppose the declarant runs into a Broadway play and excitedly yells, "fire, fire—there's a fire in the basement!" Later, he is prosecuted for giving a false alarm. A witness who was in the theatre testifies as to the defendant's actions and words. These words are not hearsay; they were a "verbal act"—they had *independent legal significance* because they constituted an offense, namely, giving a false alarm in a public place. The declarant's words are not being used for the hearsay purpose of proving there actually was a fire in the basement, because if there were a fire in the basement the declarant would be hero rather than a criminal. The fact that the words were uttered and were false is enough to constitute the crime. Another example is a prosecution for threatening a person. Evidence that the declarant made the threat is not hearsay, because *the threatening words constitute the crime.*

To illustrate further, suppose the issue at hand is whether *B* accepted *A*'s offer for certain painting services. A witness testifies that she heard *B* say to *A*: "I accept your offer to paint my porch for $500." Under the objective theory of contract formation, *B*'s statement resulted in a binding contract. Imagine that prior to *B*'s acceptance he had confided in his wife that he intended to tell *A* that he (*B*) accepted *A*'s offer, but that he would really be lying because he wanted to use the $500 to buy a kitchen appliance. *B*'s insincerity is of no consequence; there is still a contract; the words of acceptance completed the bargain. Similarly, a *contractual offer* is a verbal act because it shifts the legal relations between the parties by empowering the offeree to accept the offer.

Verbal acts can arise in both civil and criminal cases, as the following illustrations suggest.

ILLUSTRATIONS

(1) An issue at trial is whether Smith illegally impersonated a United States ambassador named Bruce. *W* testifies that when Smith met a representative of the Immigration and Naturalization Service, Smith said, "I am Ambassador Bruce."[6]

(2) An issue at trial is whether Father put a deposit in trust for Daughter or for Son. Bank Teller testifies that when Father handed him a check for $50,000, Father said, "I want the entire amount of this check put in trust for Daughter."[7]

(3) An issue at trial is whether *A*, an Army Officer, gave to *B* a Rolex watch or whether *A* simply put the watch in *B's* care during the time *A* was engaged in a dangerous combat mission. *W* testifies that when *A* handed the watch to *B* he (*A*) said, "We have been friends through thick and thin; whatever happens, I want to give you this Rolex."[8]

(4) An issue at trial is whether *D* spoke words that defamed a corporate vice-president, *P*. *W*, a witness for *P*, testifies that at a meeting of the Board of Directors, *D* appeared before the Board and said, "You should all know I have completed my investigation of *P's* activities; he has been defrauding the company."

(5) An issue in an adverse possession case is whether *D*, who claims adverse possession of Greenacre, held the property adversely and notoriously. *W* testifies that on several occasions *D* appeared before the local zoning board. On each occasion *D* identified himself as the owner of Greenacre.

(6) An issue at trial is whether *B*, a defendant bank, guaranteed to pay Hospital's bills for certain medical supplies should Hospital fail to pay the plaintiff, Supplier.

---

[6]   The words of impersonation constitute the offense.

[7]   In most jurisdictions, the father's statement would result in the deposit being held in trust for Daughter. Even in a minority jurisdiction, Father's declaration is *part* of a shift in legal relations, and as such, is not hearsay.

[8]   In most jurisdictions, a transfer of property accompanied by words of donation results in a gift, even if the donor did not intend to make a gift.

> *W* testifies that *B's* Vice-President said to Supplier, "Go ahead and ship the supplies to Hospital; we guarantee payment."

In Illustration (1), we have another example of a statement being offered because it is false, not true. You can readily see that in any case charging a person with a false or misleading statement— e.g., securities and other fraud cases—the statements constituting the offense will not be hearsay because they will not be offered for their truth.[9] So there are two reasons why the statement is not hearsay: 1) it is a verbal act; and 2) it is offered to prove that it is false, not true.

In the other Illustrations, the declarant's words either shift the legal relationship between the declarant and some other person or else the words are an operative part of a shift in relationship. In Illustration (2), the instruction creates the trust into which the money will be placed. In Illustration (3), *A's* words establish that a gift is being made. In Illustration (4), the declarant's words gave rise to *P's* cause of action for slander (obviously *P* is not trying to prove the truth of *D's* statement). In Illustration (5), the statements of ownership play an operative role in the legal rule governing adverse possession. Generally speaking, that rule requires that the adverse possessor hold the property in question for a specified number of years, and that he do so openly (notoriously) and adversely. Thus, *D's* assertions may be received as evidence that he openly claimed ownership. However, these same assertions would be hearsay if offered to show, for example, that *D* actually owned Greenacre aside from adverse possession. In Illustration (6), the Vice-President's words created Bank's obligation to cover Hospital's bill, (assuming the substantive law acknowledged a verbal, as opposed to a written, commitment).

The bottom line is that whenever a declarant's words, or conduct accompanied by words, affect the legal relationship between the declarant and another person (or entity), there is a non-hearsay rationale for admitting the declarant's statement. The only question at trial is whether the declarant actually made the statement—a question that can be addressed by cross-examining the witness who testifies that she heard the declarant make the statement.

---

[9]   When we turn to the exemptions and exceptions that justify admitting hearsay statements, you will see that any statement of a party (or certain agents) that is offered against that party is admissible under Rule 801(d)(2) even if offered for its truth. At this point, we are focusing on whether there is a need for an exemption or exception, and if a statement is not being used for the truth of its contents the answer is "no."

Statements Offered for Their Effect on the Listener

A statement is not hearsay when the purpose of admitting it is to show the probable effect of the statement on the state of mind of another person who heard (or read) it. Suppose, for example, a grocery store customer sues the store for injuries she sustained when she slipped on a broken bottle of olive oil that someone had dropped in the aisle. The plaintiff calls a shopper to testify that she heard another shopper report to the store manager, 30 minutes before the accident, that "a bottle of olive oil dropped in the aisle." This evidence is, of course, relevant because—whether or not it is true—the report put the manager on notice of a possible dangerous condition. Without relying on the truth of the shopper's statement, the factfinder can evaluate the reasonableness of the manager's conduct.

Another example of a "statement offered for its effect on the listener" appears in a British case involving a prosecution for the forbidden possession of ammunition in a battle zone.[10] The accused tendered the defense of duress. He claimed that he had been captured by enemy terrorists and forced to take up arms against the British. To establish his defense, he offered evidence of his captors' orders and threats. These statements were not hearsay because they were not offered to prove that their contents were true. They were not offered, for example, to prove that the terrorists would have carried out their threats to torture the accused or bury him alive should he refuse to join them. Instead, the statements were offered because their mere utterance was significant in establishing duress. Evidence that the threats were made enables the trier to assess the probable effect of the terrorists' words on the accused's state of mind and to judge his conduct accordingly.[11]

Further examples of statements that could be offered to show their probable effect on the listener:

> (1)   On the issue of whether *D* was negligent when he drove a car that had defective tires, a statement made to *D* by *X*, a service station attendant, who looked at the front tires and said, "Both of these front tires are bad and the one on the left front already has a tear."

> (2)   On the issue whether *D* was anxious and worried about his health, a statement to *D* by his physician (declarant) that "You have had a series of small heart

---

10   *Subramaniam v. Public Prosecutor*, 100 Solicitor's Journal 566 (Judicial Comm., Privy Council 1956).

11   It would be important to know whether the statements were made seriously or in jest. But the context and tenor of the statements can be testified to by the defendant, who was there when the statements were made. So the manner in which a statement was made does not present a hearsay concern.

attacks and strokes; one heart artery is closed and the others are badly congested."

(3) On the issue of whether D had purposely and fraudulently failed to file an estate tax return, a letter to D from his accountant stating that "Your available deductions will eliminate any concern about estate tax liability."

(4) On the issue whether Police Officer had probable cause to arrest X, a statement to the officer by an excited and angry woman, "that man (X) broke into my car and took the money out of my purse."

In each of these illustrations, there is a nonhearsay use for the declarant's statement. In the first example, the station attendant's statement warned D (i.e., put him on notice) that he had a defective tire. This statement would be hearsay if offered to prove that the tire was defective. It could not be used for this purpose unless it came within a hearsay exemption or exception, but it could be used for the nonhearsay purpose of showing that D was aware of the possibly dangerous condition of his tires. Other evidence, such as expert testimony (or the station attendant's testimony from the stand), would be required to prove the defective condition of the front tires.

In the second illustration, the physician's statement has probative force to prove that D was anxious and worried about his health. Note that we are assuming that D's state of mind is consequential under the substantive law governing the case. Perhaps, for example, D's mental state is relevant to whether he attempted suicide or whether he was justified in revoking a trust that he had established because he anticipated needing the trust proceeds to cover his medical expenses. (If D's mental state is not relevant, then the physician's statement could not be admitted for its effect on the listener because to do so would violate Rule 403—its probative value to prove D's mental state would be substantially outweighed by the risk that the jury would misuse the statement for its truth.)

In the third illustration, the accountant's assurance that no estate taxes would be due makes it less likely that D would have willfully and fraudulently failed to file an estate tax return. Even if the statement were not true, it would have had an impact on D's state of mind.

Finally, in the fourth illustration, the evidence helps to prove that the officer acted reasonably when he arrested X. This is because the arrest is legal if there is probable cause, and under that standard, it is not required that X actually committed the offense; it is enough for the officer to reasonably believe that X committed the offense. And a report of a victim would certainly be relevant to whether the officer had that reasonable belief.

It must be remembered that a statement that is probative for its effect on the listener might still be excluded under Rule 403. That will occur when the risk of prejudice (the jury's misuse of the statement for the truth of its content) substantially outweighs its probative value in explaining the listener's state of mind or conduct. A classic example arises in a prosecution for bank robbery. The prosecutor calls the police officer who arrested the defendant. The defendant denies involvement. The officer testifies that a few hours after the robbery, a confidential informant told him that the defendant robbed the bank. Over a hearsay objection, the prosecutor argues that the accusation is offered only for its effect on the listener—to explain why the officer decided to look for and arrest the defendant. In this example, the statement should probably be excluded under Rule 403. The case is not about the police officer's conduct. The government is offering the statement as part of the background of the investigation—but the contested issue is whether the defendant is the robber. And as to that issue, the accusation runs a substantial risk of jury misuse. The result would be different if the defendant attacked the quality of the police investigation, or argued that the police were out to get him and concocted a case against him. In these circumstances, the accusation is quite probative to show the bona fides of the investigation that the defendant has critiqued.

Implied Assertions

We often encounter statements that assert something ("New York City is intellectually and culturally exciting"), but carry an unstated message or implication ("I like New York City.") Someone who dominates the dinner conversation with animated accounts of the accomplishments of various baseball players is impliedly asserting that he likes baseball.

There is a rather indistinct line separating a declarant's statements that the trier can use circumstantially for their implication—thus avoiding the hearsay rule because the statement is not offered for the "truth of the matter *asserted*"—and statements in which the implied proposition is so close to the surface of the expressed statement that the declarant was probably aware that she was making two assertions: one explicit and the other implicit. If the declarant refers to *X* as a "dirty, lying cheat" and the issue is whether she disliked *X*, you can certainly argue that her statement is equivalent to "I hate *X*" and thus this statement is offered for its truth. Another example is a statement constituting an aphorism or metaphor, or statements clothed in irony or sarcasm, in which it is clear that the speaker is asserting something other than what is said in the specific words. In the following examples, the declarant is clearly aware of the assertion he is making and so the statement is hearsay:

"the clouds burst," (heavy rain)

"he was burning with desire," (passionate)

"the barber scalped him," (very close haircut)

"of course, *you* would never have eaten the rest of the cake," (you ate the cake)

"fools rush in where angels fear to tread," (you were foolish to do that)

"forget the trial—put him in the can and throw away the key," (he is guilty of the offense charged)

Before allowing a declarant's statement into evidence on a *nonhearsay*—circumstantial use—basis, the judge should be satisfied that the declarant did not intend to be asserting the proposition that is supposedly "implied." This requirement accords with the basis for classifying statements used circumstantially as nonhearsay: when a statement is implied by the declarant (or, put otherwise, inferred by the listener) the hearsay danger of insincerity is reduced because the declarant was not focused on the proposition for which his statement is offered at trial. Intentional assertions are more likely to be lies than unintentional implications.

A famous English case[12] considers in detail the issue of implied assertions. There, the proponents of a will proffered letters to the testator from X, Y, and Z to prove the competency of the testator. So far as the letters disclosed on their surface, the writers (declarants) intended only to communicate various business and social matters. The letters were not offered to prove anything expressly said within them. Rather, they were offered for the *implied assertion* that the writers believed the testator was competent. In other words, the writers' use of normal, unguarded language, coupled with the fact that the writers entrusted to the testator the discharge of certain business and social affairs, implied that they thought he was competent.

The English court ruled that the letters were hearsay—the court concluded that if a statement is offered for the truth of an implication, then it is hearsay, end of story. But American courts applying the Federal Rules of Evidence would classify the letters as nonhearsay— because there was apparently *no intent* on the part of the writers to communicate their belief that the testator was competent (rather the

---

[12]   *Wright v. Doe d. Tatham*, 7 Ad. & E. 313, 112 Eng. Rep. 488 (Exch. Ch. 1837).

intent was to communicate business and social matters). The Federal Rule provides that if a statement is offered for the truth of what the statement implies rather than expresses, it is hearsay only if the declarant intended to communicate the implication.

ILLUSTRATION

The police receive a reliable tip that *X's* house is being used for illegal bookmaking. When the police execute a search warrant at the house, several telephones in *X's* library ring and a policeman answers each of them. Each caller identifies himself and then places a bet ("put $100 on the Packers to win this Sunday"). At trial, the officer answering the phones testifies, over a hearsay objection, as to what the callers said. On appeal *X's* counsel argues that the trial judge made an error in allowing this "hearsay" evidence. Was the trial judge mistaken in her ruling?

[margin note left: IMPLIED ASSUMPTION MUST BE INTENTIONAL]

[margin note right: NOT A STATEMENT]

Under the Federal Rules, the trial judge's decision was correct. The callers were simply placing their bets; they were not making an intentional assertion that "*X's* house is used for gambling transactions." This latter assertion was implied, but implied assertions are not hearsay under Federal Rule 801 unless they are intentional. That rule defines a hearsay statement as an oral or written assertion (or conduct that substitutes for words) that is intended by the declarant to assert the proposition for which the statement is offered. Here, the declarants were not intending to communicate their belief that they were calling a betting parlor. Their intent was to make a bet. (This is why a statement giving directions—e.g., "slow down" or "check that person for a gun"—are ordinarily not hearsay).

On the other hand, if a police officer interviews such a caller and asks them if the house is used for gambling purposes, and the declarant says "you know how people like to gamble these days" it will be hearsay, even though the declarant did not specifically state that the premises were used for gambling. The declarant was intending to tell the officer that the house was used for gambling.

Non-Assertive Conduct

Conduct can also give rise to implied assertions. A witness, for example, sees a trucker stop for a stoplight. At the stoplight, the truck is flanked by a car driven by P. A minute or two later the truck driver accelerates and the truck slowly moves forward toward the intersection. *P's* car, which can move more swiftly, also starts, enters the intersection, and is struck from the side by *D's* car. At trial, the issue is who had a green light. The trucker cannot be found. From the angle at which the witness, a pedestrian, was standing, he could not see the green, yellow, and red lens on the stoplight. But he will testify as to the actions of the truck, followed by the actions of *P's* car on its flank.

The desired inference is that the light had turned green, prompting the trucker to start forward. Counsel for D objects, citing the rule against hearsay. He argues that the truck driver's actions are the equivalent of rolling down his window and saying to the witness and the driver of the plaintiff's car: "The light is green!" The decisive issue under the Federal Rules, however, is whether the truck driver intended to assert that the light had turned green. Because he was merely moving his truck forward and into the intersection, he probably did not intend to make an assertion about the color of the stoplight.

Sometimes, of course, conduct is intended as an assertion. Suppose, in the foregoing example, there had been construction at the intersection requiring traffic to merge into one lane. To facilitate the flow of traffic, the construction company assigns a worker to assist drivers. The employee uses arm gestures to move traffic forward when the light turns green and to point traffic toward the open lane. He is quite obviously making assertions. Other instances of using conduct to make an assertion include nodding or shaking the head, pointing a finger at a person to designate or identify him, and using sign language. When conduct is used as a substitute for words, all of the usual hearsay dangers attach. But where the "declarant" (that is, the person whose conduct is observed by the witness) does not intend to make an assertion, the danger of insincerity as to the unintended (implied) assertion is considered sufficiently minimized to escape the rule against hearsay. The assumption is that lies are more likely when a declarant intends to communicate a fact or idea.

Thus, under the hearsay rule, assertions are treated the same way whether they are verbal or by conduct—the question is whether the actor or speaker had the intent to communicate the assertion that is offered for its truth.

ILLUSTRATIONS

ISSUE	EVIDENCE
Had it started to rain?	Dc opened her umbrella.
Does the bus stop at the corner of Sixth and Main?	A number of people, some holding tickets or tokens, stood at the corner of Sixth and Main.

Is the ship seaworthy?	Dc, an experienced captain, examined the ship during the morning hours and set sail with his family after lunch.
Did X, while traveling abroad in a tropical climate, contract malaria?	Dc, a physician, prescribed a course of treatment that is the usual therapy for malaria.
Did A finish ahead of B, the favorite, in the local marathon?	Uncle, (Dc) who bet on B, paid his nephew (who bet on A) $25 as soon as the results of the race were known.

In all of the foregoing illustrations, the conduct in question apparently proceeds from the actors' belief that a certain condition exists. The actor does not, however, directly state this belief. Rather, his belief is implied by his action or, put otherwise, may be inferred by an observer. The key to treating implied assertions as nonhearsay is the reduction of the hearsay danger of insincerity when the fact that is impliedly asserted was not intended to be communicated.[13]

Ledgers, Inscriptions, and the Like

Suppose that in connection with a raid on X's house the police seize a bookkeeper's ledger containing the details and amounts of various gambling transactions. At X's trial, the prosecutor offers the ledger as proof that X engaged in gambling activities. If the prosecutor's offer is limited to showing the general nature of the entries as circumstantial evidence that gambling transactions took place in X's house, the ledger would not be hearsay because it is not offered for the truth of a particular entry.[14] In the same nonhearsay category as the ledger would be items such as X's address book listing Y's address and telephone number or a receipt showing that X had paid ten-thousand dollars to Y, if these items were offered for the

---

[13]   If a "declarant" intends her implied assertion, she could deliberately manipulate her conduct or statement to deceive others. Suppose, for example, the ship captain wanted to give the false impression that a ship was seaworthy. She could inspect the ship in the morning; set sail with her family in the afternoon; but go into port soon after she was out of the observer's (auditor's) sight. The judge decides if the declarant intended to make the relevant assertion. *See* Fed. R. Evid. 104(a).

[14]   *See, e.g., United States v. Alosa* 14 F.3d 693, 696–97 (1st Cir. 1994).

limited purpose of showing that X and Y were acquainted.[15] The key to avoiding a hearsay characterization of these entries is to offer them not for their truth, but as circumstantial evidence that X was acquainted with Y. Again, however, it is essential that X's acquaintance with Y be consequential (relevant) under the applicable substantive law. Suppose, for example, X were charged with illegal drug sales. If Y were involved in assisting persons such as X in "laundering" illegal drug proceeds, it would probably be relevant that X knew Y. Obviously, entries offered to prove what they assert (e.g., the receipt and sale of heroin) would be hearsay.[16]

[margin handwriting: must be consequential under substantive]

Keep in mind that the sole purpose of this chapter is to flesh out the definition of hearsay. In many of the foregoing illustrations and examples, the evidence, even if hearsay, might be admitted as an exemption or exception[17] to the hearsay rule. As a practical matter, the number of exemptions and exceptions allowing hearsay statements into evidence serve to limit the number of occasions in which a judge must make subtle distinctions between hearsay and nonhearsay. There is no practical reason for drawing a fine line between hearsay and nonhearsay if the proffered evidence, even if classified as hearsay, is admissible anyway.

ILLUSTRATION

An issue in a hit-and-run case is whether a certain truck belonged to X or Y. A witness will testify that a sign painted on the side of the truck in question said:

X's QUALITY MULCH

We Deliver

[margin handwriting: mechanical noise]

X's lawyer objects to evidence reciting the content of the sign on the ground that the statement is essentially that of some declarant, such as the person painting the sign, or the person who engaged him, who is asserting that the truck belong to X. How should the trial judge rule?

Although X's argument favoring a hearsay characterization is plausible, most courts would reject it. One rationale for a nonhearsay characterization is to view the sign as just another external feature of the truck, in the same category as size, color, make, and other identifying features. Another possibility is that a label or name on an

---

[15]   As you will see in Chapter VI, statements made by a party-opponent are admissible against them as an exemption from the hearsay rule and thus may be admitted for their truth.

[16]   Authenticated entries made by the *defendant* would be admitted as nonhearsay party exemptions.

[17]   As you will see, hearsay exemptions are essentially like hearsay exceptions. Both exemptions and exceptions allow assertions to be used for their truth.

object has probative value to show that it is owned by a person of that name—in this case, X. The sign is circumstantial evidence that the truck belongs to a person named X, as opposed to a person named Y or Z. Put otherwise: a person named X is much more likely to be responsible for the sign or label than someone not named X. Because the truck is labeled as belonging to one named X and the party we are interested in is also named X, there is an increased likelihood that "our X" and the X whose name appears on the truck are the same person. In addition to these nonhearsay bases for admissibility, there is a strong likelihood of invoking a hearsay exemption called "statements of a party-opponent." We will consider party-opponent statements in the next chapter.

Statements Revealing Awareness; Knowledge Derived from a Particular Source

In comparatively rare cases, a declarant's statement reveals knowledge that he must have acquired from a particular source. Even if the declarant is known to be a cunning dissembler, acquisition of the knowledge revealed by his statement allows us to infer that he has had access to the source of the information he discloses—and when the purpose for offering the statement is to show that it was derived from a certain source, it is not hearsay. Suppose, for example, there were a secret society of ten members. Rosenkreutz, the founder of the society, knows the names of the entire membership. As each member is inducted, he or she is given the means by which to signify membership in the society: a special handshake; three particular questions about international politics; and a handkerchief or tie that contain four specified colors.

At a dinner party, A, a society member, meets B who displays and performs all of the rituals signifying membership. If A can correctly assume that B had little or no chance of acquiring knowledge of the society's rituals unless B was a member, A can be confident of B's membership, regardless of what B says. Perhaps B is a liar or has a poor memory or is not a careful observer; still, A's assurance of B's membership would not be shaken. Without relying on B's credibility, A can confidently draw an inference that B, like himself, is one of the group of ten.

This thought experiment should facilitate your understanding of the well-known case of *Bridges v. State*.[18] There, a child was abducted by the defendant and taken to his house where she was sexually molested. Subsequently, the child described to her mother not only what the exterior of the house looked like, but also what the interior looked like, including the furnishings and various articles in the room

---

[18]　247 Wis. 350, 19 N.W.2d 529 (1945).

in which she was molested. At defendant's trial, the prosecutor introduced detailed evidence depicting the exterior and interior of the defendant's home. He also supplied evidence showing that it was extremely unlikely that the victim could have gained knowledge of these surroundings except through her transport there by the defendant. Next, the prosecutor called the victim's mother who testified to the detailed statements of her daughter's description of the premises to which she had been taken by the accused. The child's description, given to her mother, matched the actual appearance of the defendant's home.

The court held that the mother's testimony did not violate the hearsay rule. Her courtroom narrative of what her daughter had told her was not offered "for the truth" of what the defendant's home looked like. Rather, the child's description, repeated in her mother's testimony, was offered to show the congruence between the actual appearance of the defendant's house and the child's account of that appearance. In other words, the declarant's description showed her knowledge of the physical appearance of defendant's house—a knowledge that was derived from being there.[19]

Silence—Including Nondisclosure and Failure to Complain

Silence is usually within the nonhearsay category of nonassertive conduct. Sometimes one's inaction or silence—his failure to speak out or complain—has probative value to show that an alleged event did not occur or an alleged condition did not exist. Suppose, for example, a plaintiff sues the railroad on which she had taken a trip six months before. In her complaint, she alleges that during her trip the temperature in her passenger car dropped far below normal. As a result, she got sick. In its defense, the railroad offers the testimony of the conductor and the porter. Each is prepared to testify that no one else complained about the temperature in the passenger car. The hearsay rule should not prevent this testimony because the passive passengers were not making an assertion.[20]

---

[19]   No one really cares about the physical description of the house of the abductor except insofar as it matches the premises and the abductor; it is the fact that the child is able to offer descriptions of both that match the place and individual that matters, along with evidence that the child could not have obtained the specifics on any occasion other than the abduction.

[20]   *See Silver v. New York Cent. R. Co.*, 329 Mass. 14, 105 N.E.2d 923 (1952).

ILLUSTRATIONS

Issue	Evidence
(1) Was the restaurant's fish chowder spoiled?	Other customers ate the same chowder and no one complained.
(2) Did A, representing the ABC partnership, agree to license one of the partnership's patents to the X Company?	When A returned from a business trip and reported his activities (which included a meeting with X's president) to his partners, B and C, he made no mention of licensing patent rights to X.

[handwritten marginalia: "not hearsay", "not relevant", "not hearsay"]

[handwritten marginalia left margin: "not relevant", "probative"]

Although passive conduct, including silence, is not usually hearsay because no assertion is intended,[21] problems of relevance may arise. In order for inaction, failure to complain, or silence to be probative, persons who did not react or speak out must have been exposed to the event or condition that allegedly occurred or existed. In Illustration (1), for example, noncomplaining customers must have eaten chowder from the same pot or batch from which the plaintiff was served. Furthermore, silence has little probative value unless a complaint or protest can be made without undue difficulty. If lodging a complaint were onerous or impractical, the fact that other persons did not complain has little or no probative value because there is a likely alternative explanation for their passive behavior.

In Illustration (2), it is unlikely that A intended to assert anything by *failing* to mention the lease of the patent; so the omission is not hearsay because it is not a statement that there was no lease. If the *ABC Partnership* later claims there was a lease, the *X Company* may be able introduce the omission in evidence. But, because the subject might not have arisen *when* A reported on his trip, the probative value of the omission of the lease in *A's* report might be diminished when a jury considers the weight to give the evidence.

Prior, Out-of-Court Statements by the Witness on the Stand: Impeachment vs. Substantive Effect

A hypothetical case will reveal a central feature of the problem addressed in this subsection. Suppose Henry Ford sues Walter Chrysler and the main issue in the case is whether a particular car

---

[21] Consider, however, the following: "Keep talking into the cell phone until you see her enter; then remain perfectly silent for thirty seconds and hang up." You can see that the silence is intended to communicate that "she just entered."

was black or some other color. If Ford can prove the car was black he will win the suit, but if Chrysler can show that the car was another color he will prevail. The plaintiff, Ford, calls his key witness, Edsel, a freelance automotive journalist. To Ford's surprise, Edsel testifies that the car in question was green. Ford then introduces evidence that two months prior to the trial, Edsel told a Ford engineer that the car in question was black.

It appears that each party has now produced conflicting evidence on which a jury could make a finding one way or the other. But under the Federal Rules, if Ford has the burden of persuasion and if the only evidence he has that the car was black is Edsel's prior inconsistent statement, the judge will direct a judgment as a matter of law for the defendant Chrysler.

The explanation for this odd result is found in the definition of hearsay. Federal Rule of Evidence 801 defines "hearsay" as a statement that "the declarant does not make while testifying at the current trial or hearing" offered to prove the truth of the matter asserted in the statement. *Edsel's prior statement that the car in question was black meets the definition of hearsay—it was not made from the stand at the present trial* (It is considered hearsay even though the declarant, Edsel, is on the stand subject to cross-examination.) Therefore, unless it fits within an exemption or exception, it is inadmissible if offered for its truth. Yet, it seems plain enough that the trier of fact should be made aware of evidence indicating that Edsel had made an earlier inconsistent statement, for the earlier statement casts doubt on his credibility.

Common law judges did not hesitate to admit evidence of the witness's prior inconsistent statement, but, true to the hearsay rule, disallowed use of the prior statement to prove the truth of its content. This convoluted result was accomplished by instructing the jury (when requested by a party to do so) that the witness's prior statement could be used only to cast doubt on—that is, impeach—his trial testimony. The prior statement could not be used for its truth (i.e., as "substantive" evidence) In other words, because the witness has given inconsistent accounts of the same event, the jury may consider his prior statement only as bearing on whether the witness's trial testimony is unreliable.

Thus, in our imaginary case, if the jury members believe that prior to trial Edsel had said the car was black, they may consider this inconsistency in evaluating the credibility of his testimony that the car was green. But unless the prior statement comes within a hearsay exemption or exception, it cannot be used as the basis for a jury finding that the car was black. That is why Ford could not prevail if he had the burden of proving the car was black and if the only evidence supporting that fact was Edsel's prior statement.[22] Of course, if Ford had other admissible evidence sufficient to support a finding by the trier that the car was black, the judge would not grant a judgment as a matter of law (i.e., a directed verdict). And there would be no practical means of discovering whether the jurors had also (improperly) considered Edsel's prior out-of-court statement as proof that the car in question was black. But they probably did, because the limiting instruction is unlikely to have much impact, if it can be understood at all.

ILLUSTRATION

Federal Authorities bring charges against George Smith for illegally transporting his girlfriend, Mary Case, in interstate commerce for the purpose of prostitution. Prior to trial Mary, who had broken up with George, gave several statements to the police in which she disclosed her activities as a prostitute. However, the day before trial Mary and George reconcile. When Mary takes the witness stand for the government, she surprises the prosecutor by testifying that she has never engaged in prostitution. He thus proceeds to impeach her with evidence of her prior written and oral statements to the contrary. At the close of the prosecution's case, defense counsel moves for a directed verdict of acquittal and calls the court's attention to the fact that the only evidence that Mary had ever engaged in prostitution consists of her own prior inconsistent statements. How should the trial judge rule?

The judge should grant the motion under the Federal Rules of Evidence. The Federal Rules endorse the common law view that prior statements of a witness offered for their truth are hearsay. When the prior statements are inconsistent with the witness's trial testimony, they may, as we have seen, be introduced for purposes of attacking the witness's credibility. However, unless the earlier statements qualify for an exemption or exception to the hearsay rule, they cannot be used to prove the truth of the assertion they contain. This rule applies to both bench trials and jury trials. In jury trials, a party[23] may request that the judge instruct the jury regarding the restricted purpose for which evidence of the inconsistency is admitted.

---

[22]   We are assuming, of course, that the prior statement does not qualify under an exemption or exception.

[23]   The party requesting the instruction will almost always be the one trying to convince the jury to believe the truth of the witness's statements from the stand, and to disbelieve the prior inconsistent statement.

The hearsay characterization of a witness's own prior statements has been justly criticized.[24] Earlier statements are often made before the pressures of litigation, so they may be more reliable than trial testimony. And the earlier statements are made closer to the event in question, reducing the risk of memory loss. Most importantly, the cross-examiner can question the witness not only about the present testimony from the stand, but also about what the witness said prior to the trial. And the jury is able to observe the witness's demeanor as he responds to questions about both his trial testimony and his previous account. Thus, the typical hearsay problems of inability to cross-examine the declarant, and inability to view demeanor, are absent when the witness is himself the declarant.[25]

Over the years, the debate has continued over the hearsay classification of a witness's prior inconsistent statements. Many trial lawyers support the rule that such statements are hearsay and, absent an applicable exemption or exception, cannot be used "substantively"—that is, to prove the truth of the facts they assert. Apparently, some trial lawyers believe that a cross-examination directed to testimony a witness has just given is more effective than a cross-examination directed at the witness's earlier inconsistent statement. As it is sometimes put, cross-examination is best when it "strikes while the iron is hot." There is also an argument that cross-examination will be ineffective if the witness denies ever making the prior statement or claims no memory—because questions about why the witness made the prior statement, what the witness was thinking at the time, etc., would be forestalled by the witness's contention that he never made the statement in the first place or has no memory of it.

Our focus is on the Federal Rules, but it should be noted that a number of states have been persuaded that prior inconsistent statements should be admissible for their truth. As we shall see in Chapter VI,[26] the Federal Rules do provide a limited exemption from the hearsay rule for certain prior inconsistent statements, and where

---

[24] Early criticism, which has not lost its trenchancy, was offered by the late Professor Edmund M. Morgan in a classic article, *Hearsay Dangers and the Application of the Hearsay Concept*, 62 HARV. L. REV. 177, 192–96 (1948).

[25] Of course, if the witness's prior statements are consistent with his testimony, there is usually no need for the earlier statements and the trial judge can prohibit their introduction. Rule 403 permits the judge to reject relevant evidence that results in "undue delay, waste of time, or the needless presentation of cumulative evidence." The prior consistent statements of a witness, like his prior inconsistent statements, are hearsay. Thus, if the sole purpose of a witness's prior consistent statement is to bolster her testimony, evidence of the consistent statement generally will be excluded. *See* Chapter VI, § 6.2.

[26] Section 6.2.

that exemption applies the inconsistent statements are admissible both to impeach the testifying witness and as substantive evidence.[27]

[There is a short Hearsay Quiz in Appendix I.]

---

[27]   Fed. R. Evid. 801(d)(1)(A).

Chapter VI

HEARSAY EXEMPTIONS

(Definitional Nonhearsay)

Table of Sections

§ 6.1 Introduction

In the last chapter we defined and illustrated hearsay evidence. In this chapter we examine two classes of evidence that meet the basic definition of hearsay (that is, an intended assertion offered for its truth), yet under subdivision (d) of Federal Rule 801 they are treated as nonhearsay. Generally speaking, these *exemptions* from the hearsay rule were applied by common-law judges as *exceptions* to the hearsay rule. But the drafters of the Federal Rules thought that these particular common-law exceptions had characteristics that distinguished them from the other common-law exceptions. They decided, therefore, not only to address these two classes of evidence separately, but also to transform them from hearsay (under Rule 801(c)) to nonhearsay (under Rule 801(d)).[1]

Most courts and commentators refer to these two classes of evidence as hearsay *exemptions* or *exclusions,* and that is how they will be referred to in this book. The idea is that Rule 801(d) *exempts* two classes of evidence (that are hearsay under Rule 801(c)) from the hearsay category or, put otherwise, *statutorily redefines* them so as

---

[1]   It surely is debatable whether this judgment to "define" what otherwise is hearsay as nonhearsay was wise. There is a good argument that the common law approach of calling these hearsay exceptions was easier to understand and administer. After all, Rule 801(c) and Rule 801(d)(1) combine to create "non-hearsay hearsay." This oxymoron does not make life easier for trial lawyers, students and judges. Nonetheless, the Advisory Committee on Evidence Rules rejected a proposal to redesignate the exemptions as exceptions, on the ground that the "exemption" designation has become ingrained, and most importantly because it would not make any practical difference. Whether a statement is within an exemption or an exception, the result is the same: it is admissible for its truth despite the fact that it is hearsay.

to remove them from the basic definition of hearsay. The important point is that hearsay exemptions and hearsay exceptions have an identical effect: an out-of-court statement within either category overcomes a hearsay objection and thus the proponent may use the statement to prove the truth of the matter it asserts. At the *practical level*, therefore, *exemptions and exceptions operate identically*.

Two Categories of Exemptions

There are two broad categories of statements transformed into nonhearsay by Rule 801(d):

(1) [Certain prior statements by a testifying witness;⌉ and   1 ,   2 ,   3

(2) Statements made by a party or a party's representative offered in evidence by that party's opponent. ①

The first category (Rule 801(d)(1)) includes certain prior *inconsistent* statements made by a testifying witness, as well as certain prior ② *consistent* statements made by her. Also within the first category are out-of-court *identifications* made by a testifying witness.[2] Within the ③ second category (Rule 801(d)(2)) are statements *made by a party* as well as statements made by other declarants (such as a party's agent) *associated with a party*. This exemption is confined to statements that are offered *against a party by her opponent*. A party cannot introduce her own (presumably favorable) statements as nonhearsay under Rule 801(d). The party-statement exemption under Rule 801(d)(2) is, so to speak, "a one way street."

§ 6.2   Category I: Prior Statements of a Testifying Witness

We have already observed[3] that the hearsay rule applies to any statement other than one made by the declarant while testifying at the trial or hearing, offered in evidence to prove the truth of the matter asserted in the statement. Yet Rule 801(d)(1) removes from the hearsay category certain prior statements of a testifying witness. As we noted above, these exemptions from the basic definition of hearsay fall into three classes:

1. Specified Prior Inconsistent Statements (Rule 801(d)(1)(A))

2. Specified Prior Consistent Statements (Rule 801(d)(1)(B))

---

[2]   These may be inconsistent with trial testimony, consistent with trial testimony, or admitted even though the declarant/witness cannot remember enough to make an in-court identification.

[3]   Chapter V, § 5.2.

3.   Prior Identification of a Person (Rule 801(d)(1)(C))

We will take up each class in the order in which it is set out in Rule 801(d)(1). Note preliminarily that each of the three exempted classes of prior statements by a testifying witness has a basic requirement in common: the declarant must testify at trial and be "subject to cross-examination about the prior statement. . . ."[4] This requirement that the hearsay declarant (who has made a pretrial statement) take the stand and testify applies to all of the exemptions contained in Rule 801(d)(1), but not to the exemptions set out in 801(d)(2), which covers party-opponent statements.

① testify

② subject to cross examination about prior statement

Prior Inconsistent Statements

A prior inconsistent statement of a testifying witness can be used to impeach his credibility.[5] So used, the proponent of the statement offers it to show that on another occasion the witness gave an account that differed from, and is inconsistent with, his testimonial account. Therefore, the proponent will argue, the witness is not reliable. A prior inconsistent statement used *only to impeach* does not violate the hearsay rule because it is not offered for the truth of the assertion it contains. Rather, the earlier inconsistency is offered to show that at another time the witness has given a conflicting version of the same event and therefore his account from the witness stand is not reliable. We saw in the previous Chapter that there has long been controversy over whether prior inconsistent statements should be limited to impeachment rather than substantive use. In this Chapter we examine a specific and very narrow set of prior inconsistent statements, granted substantive admissibility as an exemption from the hearsay rule, by Rule 801(d)(1)(A).

1 BRICK

2 BRICK

Rule 801(d)(1)(A) exempts from the hearsay rule a testifying witness's prior inconsistent statement only if it "was given under penalty of perjury at a trial, hearing, or other proceeding or in a deposition."[6]

①

ILLUSTRATION

Rafael is prosecuted for transporting undocumented individuals into the United States. The grand jury's indictment alleges that he owned the van that carried eleven undocumented persons across the Mexican border, and that the driver, Miguel, was acting as Rafael's agent

---

4   Fed. R. Evid. 801(d)(1).

5   Certain requirements, imposed by Fed. R. Evid. 613, must be met.

6   Before the Rules were re-stylized, Rule 801(d)(1)(A) included an oath requirement. Its elimination was not intended to be substantive. The assumption is that a statement made subject to penalty of perjury is under oath or its equivalent.

Miguel [handwritten note in margin]

and coconspirator. After the Border Patrol stopped the van and apprehended its occupants, Miguel was taken to a nearby border patrol station. There, he gave sworn, tape-recorded statements implicating Rafael to Pearce, an investigator for the Border Patrol. Subsequently, Miguel testified before the grand jury that indicted Rafael and implicated him in the crime. *801(d)(1)* [handwritten note]

At Rafael's criminal trial, the prosecution calls Miguel, who unexpectedly testifies that he had borrowed Rafael's van on the pretense of hauling produce. Miguel also testifies that Rafael had no knowledge that Miguel was using the van to transport aliens across the border.

The prosecutor then impeaches Miguel with evidence of his prior inconsistent statements to the border patrol agent and to the grand jury. At the close of the evidence, defense counsel moves for a directed verdict of acquittal. *-No* [handwritten note] She argues that Miguel's prior inconsistent statements may only be used to impeach him, and hence do not constitute substantive evidence that Rafael was involved in the illegal transportation of immigrants. Because these prior statements cannot be used substantively, she argues, there is insufficient evidence for the jury to find beyond a reasonable doubt that Rafael was involved in the crime charged. How should the trial judge rule?

subject to penalty of perjury - under oath [handwritten note in left margin]

Rule 801(d)(1)(A) allows a prior inconsistent statement to be used substantively if it was made subject to the penalty of perjury (i.e., under oath) at a "trial, hearing, or other [formal] proceeding, or in a deposition."[7] Note that there is no requirement that the proceeding have been an adversary proceeding. Grand jury "hearings" or "proceedings" fall squarely within Rule 801(d)(1)(A): the witness who appears before a grand jury testifies under oath and is subject to a prosecution for perjury if he lies. Therefore, Miguel's statements before the grand jury are admissible as proof of a fact— that Rafael was involved in the illegal transportation. Whether a "hearing" or "proceeding" conducted by a member of the United States Border Patrol also fits within Rule 801(d)(1)(A) is a closer question.

The scope of Rule 801(d)(1)(A)—the "proceedings" that are covered—can be gauged by the Rule's requirement of exposure to a perjury charge. First, that requirement adds to the likelihood that

---

[7] Of course, a prior inconsistent statement not made under oath can be used substantively (i.e., to prove its truth) if it comes within another hearsay exception or fits within another hearsay exemption. And a prior inconsistent statement admissible under Rule 801(d)(1)(A) can be used both as substantive and impeachment evidence.

the declarant will tell the truth. Second, statements given under oath and subject to a perjury penalty are almost invariably recorded by a court reporter or some other official acting on the government's behalf. An official recording is generally a reliable means of proving that the declarant (who is a testifying witness at trial) actually made a prior inconsistent statement. Furthermore, the recordation is normally a reliable method of proving exactly what the declarant said on the prior occasion. The existence of a recording thus minimizes trial disputes that center on whether the witness even made a prior inconsistent statement at all or, if he did, what exactly he said on the earlier occasion. This avoids the problem of having to cross-examine the witness about a prior statement that he denies ever making. Finally, most prior statements that are made in a "trial, hearing, or other proceeding, or in a deposition" are made in formal settings in which there is little reason to question whether the circumstances in which the statements were made calls their trustworthiness into question.

Because Miguel made a sworn, recorded statement before the Border Patrol investigating officer, and was subject to a perjury charge if he lied, there is at least a plausible argument that his prior statement can be used to establish Rafael's guilt.[8] On the other hand, police interrogations do not qualify as "proceedings" under Rule 801(d)(1)(A). The language of the rule, which embraces prior inconsistent statements made "at a trial, hearing, or other proceeding, or in a deposition," implies a formal inquiry, officially sanctioned by statute, regulation, or court rule, and conducted by a person or body that routinely receives witnesses' testimony subject to the penalty of perjury. The border patrol proceeding is in a twilight area between, say, a grand jury hearing and a police investigation or proceeding. But even if the statements at the border patrol proceeding are not admissible to prove a fact, the court will deny the motion for judgment of acquittal—the statements at the grand jury are clearly admissible to prove Rafael's guilt, and provide enough evidence for a reasonable factfinder to find him guilty.

The foregoing discussion highlights the critical difference between a statement offered for impeachment and one offered to prove a fact (i.e. for substantive use). The defendant is right that if Miguel's two prior statements were admissible only for impeachment, then a directed verdict should be granted. In considering motions for a directed verdict, or a motion for judgment of acquittal, the trial judge may only consider the substantive

---

8   In circumstances similar to those in the Illustration, one court held that statements given before a Border Patrol agent could be used substantively. *United States v. Castro-Ayon*, 537 F.2d 1055, 1057–58 (9th Cir. 1976) (immigration hearing very similar to grand jury proceeding).

evidence that has been submitted. Impeachment evidence is for the jury to consider, once the court has found sufficient substantive evidence to create a jury question.

It should be noted that the hearsay exemption provided by Rule 801(d)(1)(A) is extremely narrow. A witness who has made a statement under oath at a formal proceeding is most unlikely to make an inconsistent statement at a later trial—that is essentially an invitation for a perjury charge. In contrast a number of states, such as California and Wisconsin, grant substantive admissibility to *all* prior inconsistent statements. The rationale is that the hearsay danger of such statements is minimal because the person who made the statement is testifying, and so is subject to oath, cross-examination, and the jury's opportunity to view demeanor.

Prior Consistent Statements

Prior consistent statements, like their counterpart, prior inconsistent statements, fall within the general definition of hearsay when they are offered to prove that the prior statement was true—to reiterate prior statements are hearsay when offered for their truth, even though the declarant is now testifying at trial.[9] Even if consistent statements were not hearsay, there would ordinarily be good reason not to accept them as evidence, because they usually add very little to the trial testimony. Suppose, for example, on the issue of the color of a car, the witness testifies that it was black. Prior statements made by the witness to the same effect probably add very little (a lie or mistake repeated often does not make it more likely true or correct); and their admission into evidence consumes trial time, especially if evidence of the prior consistent statements is provided by other witnesses. Furthermore, if prior consistent statements were freely admissible, parties would be motivated to enhance favorable testimony by having their witnesses generate out-of-court statements that would coincide with their subsequent trial testimony.

Despite reasons to doubt the general probative value of prior consistent statements, there are some circumstances in which a witness's prior consistent statement is useful to rehabilitate the credibility of a witness who has been attacked. Rule 801(d)(1)(B) provides that a prior consistent statement that rehabilitates a witness's credibility is also admissible as substantive evidence. Note that the Rule does not require that these statements have been made in a proceeding subject to penalty of perjury as is required of prior inconsistent statements.

---

[9]   Fed. R. Evid. 801(c).

The most important example (and the only one recognized under the original version of the Rule) arises when a cross-examiner directly or by fair implication charges that a witness's testimony is a "recent fabrication," or is the product of an "improper influence or motive." See Rule 801(d)(1)(B)(i). Under those circumstances a prior consistent statement may have probative force to rebut this charge. It is imperative, however, that the prior consistent statement(s) *predate* the alleged corrupting influence or purported fabrication.[10] If it was made before the motive to fabricate arose, it shows that the witness's consistent testimony was not a product of the bad motive or fabrication. [prepare motive arose to fabricate]

In sum, a witness's prior consistent statement is admissible *both* for its truth and to rehabilitate the witness's credibility if 1) the witness is attacked for recent fabrication or improper influence or motive; 2) his consistent statement predates the alleged corrupting influence; and 3) he is subject to cross-examination concerning the consistent statement.

ILLUSTRATION

In *D's* prosecution for distributing drugs, two of his former associates testify for the prosecution. On cross, *D's* attorney establishes that prior to trial, the two witnesses were incarcerated in the same jail cell; he then asks questions designed to show that during that incarceration they decided to frame *D* in order to minimize their own punishments. In rebuttal, the prosecutor presents a police detective who will testify that the two prosecution witnesses made statements consistent with their testimony after they were arrested and during a period (preceding their incarceration in the same cell) in which they were held in separate cells and could not communicate with each other. The defense attorney objects to the officer's testimony.[11]

motive

Pursuant to Federal Rule 104(a), the judge must determine whether a prior consistent statement predated the time at which a fabrication was allegedly conceived or some motive or improper influence attached. In the Illustration, the defense attorney charged that the witnesses' frame-up was conceived and planned while they

---

[10]   The leading case interpreting Fed. R. Evid. 801(d)(1)(B) is *Tome v. United States*, 513 U.S. 150, 156–60 (1995).

[11]   This Illustration is a variation of the facts addressed by the Third Circuit in *United States v. Anderson*, 303 F.3d 847 (7th Cir. 2002) (consistent statements admissible since they predated alleged frame-up). *See also United States v. Prieto*, 232 F.3d 816, 819–20 (11th Cir. 2000) (admissible prior consistent statements predated any discussion of cooperation with authorities).

were cellmates. The police detective's testimony rebuts this charge because he asserts that the two witnesses made statements consistent with their testimony prior to the time they were placed in the same cell where they could communicate with each other. So the prior statement should be admissible both to rehabilitate the witness and for its truth under Rule 801(d)(1)(B).

Other cases present more difficult factual questions for the judge. For example, suppose an arresting officer says to an arrestee, X, "If you cooperate with us and the prosecutor, you will get a lot lighter sentence." Subsequently, X agrees with the prosecutor to testify adversely to D in return for a reduced sentence. At trial, after X has given testimony damaging to D, the cross-examiner asks leading questions suggesting that X's testimony is unreliable because, in return for a lighter sentence, X gave a skewed and partially false account of D's activities. Later, the prosecutor proffers a police detective willing to testify that after X's arrest, but before X spoke with the prosecutor, he gave an account of D's activities consistent with his (X's) testimony.

The issue for the judge is whether it is more likely than not that X's consistent statement preceded his incentive to give false or misleading testimony; if this motive existed prior to his consistent statement, Rule 801(d)(1)(B) would not be satisfied (because it would then be subject to the same charge of bad motive and therefore would not rebut the attack on the witness) and the pre-trial consistent statement would be hearsay. In a case with strong factual similarities to this example, a federal court of appeals held that statements consistent with the witness's trial testimony did not precede his motive to give misleading or false testimony.[12] Initial conversations with the police had included police assurances about the benefits of cooperating with the prosecution; therefore any subsequent statements to prosecutors necessarily came after the motive for supporting the state's case had attached.

You can see from the examples discussed above that factual determinations of the trial judge are especially important under Rule 801(d)(1)(B). That is because it is often unclear exactly when the influence, motive, or incentive to falsify arose. The ruling of the trial judge on the issue of whether the prior consistent statement preceded the corrupting motive or event is not easily overturned on appeal. The appellate standard for overturning factual determinations by a trial judge is generous: normally, the trial court's findings of fact will not be reversed on appeal unless they were "clearly erroneous."[13]

---

[12] *United States v. Awon*, 135 F.3d 96, 99–100 (1st Cir. 1998).
[13] Fed. R. Civ. P. 52(a).

Rule 801(d)(1)(B) was amended in 2014 to add a provision admitting prior consistent statements over a hearsay objection, when they are offered "to rehabilitate the declarant's credibility as a witness when attacked on another ground." "Another" means a ground other than rehabilitating a witness attacked for having a bad motive or making a recent fabrication, with a prior consistent statement made before the corrupting influence arose. The Advisory Committee that drafted the amendment explained the problem it addressed as follows:

> Though the original Rule 801(d)(1)(B) provided for substantive use of certain prior consistent statements, the scope of that Rule was limited. The Rule covered only those consistent statements that were offered to rebut charges of recent fabrication or improper motive or influence. The Rule did not, for example, provide for substantive admissibility of consistent statements that are probative to explain what otherwise appears to be an inconsistency in the witness's testimony. Nor did it cover consistent statements that would be probative to rebut a charge of faulty memory. Thus, the Rule left many prior consistent statements potentially admissible only for the limited purpose of rehabilitating a witness's credibility.

The Committee explained that the amendment did not make any evidence admissible that was previously inadmissible, because it allows statements to be considered only if they rehabilitate a witness whose credibility has been attacked. The amendment recognizes that prior consistent statements, even if technically offered only for rehabilitation, would inevitably be used as substantive evidence by a jury, because if it believed that the trial testimony was true it would also have to believe a consistent statement:

> As before, prior consistent statements under the amendment may be brought before the factfinder only if they properly rehabilitate a witness whose credibility has been attacked. As before, to be admissible for rehabilitation, a prior consistent statement must satisfy the strictures of Rule 403. As before, the trial court has ample discretion to exclude prior consistent statements that are cumulative accounts of an event. The amendment does not make any consistent statement admissible that was not admissible previously—the only difference is that prior consistent statements otherwise admissible for rehabilitation are now admissible substantively as well.

So the bottom line is that if a prior consistent statement is admissible to rehabilitate a witness who has been attacked, on any *(margin note: CAN BE for BOTH ALWAYS (C))*

ground, it is also admissible substantively, i.e., for its truth. No longer does a trial judge have to give an instruction that is impossible for the jury to follow.

Prior Identifications

(margin note: ① DEC TAKE STAND ② CROSS-EXAM)

Federal Rule 801(d)(1)(C) exempts from the general definition of hearsay (contained in 801(c)) a statement that "identifies a person as someone the declarant perceived earlier." As with all of the exemptions contained in Rule 801(d)(1), it is essential that the declarant take the stand and be subject to cross-examination concerning the hearsay statement. Generally speaking, an earlier out-of-court identification is more reliable than one made in the courtroom. The earlier identification is, of course, closer in time to the event that is the subject of the litigation than is an identification made at the trial. Two other factors may affect the accuracy and reliability of courtroom identifications. First, the person who is the subject of the identification may have changed his appearance by the time of trial. Second, when that person is a party, his location within the courtroom (as, for example, at counsel's table) may suggest who he is.

(margin note: DOESN'T HAVE TO BE CONSISTENT/ INCONSISTENT)

Some technical points emerge from a close reading of Rule 801(d)(1)(C). Subsection (C) operates independently of subsections (A) and (B), so that it is immaterial whether the prior identification is consistent or inconsistent with an identification made in the courtroom. There is also no requirement that the prior identification be sworn to or recorded. Subsection (C) does not require that a *courtroom* identification precede evidence of a prior identification. Indeed, Subsection (C) does *not require* that there be a courtroom identification at all. The subsection simply requires that the prior "statement" (which could, of course, consist of pointing to the subject in question) be an identification, and that the person who made it is testifying and so subject to cross-examination.

(margin note: - NO PERJURY)

(margin note: - NO ORDER)

Of course, in criminal cases, law enforcement officials must be obedient to constitutional requirements such as the presence of counsel at a lineup (if conducted after the defendant is formally charged) and to the constitutional proscription against causing unduly suggestive identifications.[14]

ILLUSTRATION

After a brutal attack on John Foster, a federal correctional counselor, an FBI agent visits him in the hospital. Although Foster's head injuries have impaired his

---

[14] *See* SALTZBURG & CAPRA, AMERICAN CRIMINAL PROCEDURE chapter 4 (11th ed. 2018) for a discussion of the constitutional limitations on admitting identification evidence.

memory, he is able to identify his assailant, Owens, from an
array of photographs that display eight prison inmates who
were in the general proximity of the assault and thus in a
position to attack Foster. At Owens's trial for assault with
intent to kill, Foster takes the stand. Foster's recollection of
the attack is hazy and on cross-examination he admits that
he cannot now remember seeing Owens during the attack.
Foster does recall the visit of the FBI agent and he also
recalls identifying his attacker's picture from a group of
photographs. However, when Foster is shown the same
array of photographs, he cannot be certain whether he had
pointed out Owens or Ramsey, another pictured inmate.

Subsequently, the prosecution calls the FBI agent who
had visited Foster in the hospital. Over objection, the agent
is allowed to testify that when Foster was shown
photographs of the eight inmates, he identified Owens as
his attacker. On appeal, Owens' counsel argues that (1) a
photographic identification is not within Rule 801(d)(1)(C)
and, (2) because Foster's memory was still badly impaired
at the time trial was held, he was not effectively "subject to
cross-examination concerning the prior statement" of
identification, as required by Rule 801(d)(1). How should
the appellate court rule?

First, the photographic identification of Owens meets Rule
801(d)(1)(C)'s requirement that the prior statement be one that
identifies a person who was perceived by the identifier. Owens was
identified after an earlier perception, even though a photograph was
the means by which Foster made the identification.

Second, the fact that at trial Foster cannot recall seeing Owens
might affect Foster's credibility, but does not establish Foster's lack
of perception. The earlier identification was based on his recollection
of the assault and its perpetrator. Nor does it matter that it was the
FBI agent's testimony that established that Foster pointed out
Owens' picture. The same principle would apply if the identifier
picked *D* out of a lineup and stated that he (*D*) was the bank robber.
At trial, someone who saw and heard the identifier pick *D* could so
testify, even if the identifier could not point to or otherwise identify
D during his (the identifier's) testimony—so long as the identifier is
produced at trial and subject to cross-examination about the
identification.

The most important question in this problem is whether a
memory-impaired declarant is "subject to cross-examination" within

the meaning of Rule 801(d)(1). In *United States v. Owens*,[15] the Supreme Court examined this question. *Owens* bears a close factual resemblance to the Illustration above. There, the witness, who had suffered severe memory impairments after a brutal attack by a prison inmate, testified on direct that he only partially recalled the assault. Even though he could not now (at trial) remember seeing his assailant during the attack, he did recall making a photographic identification while in the hospital and in the presence of a particular FBI agent. However, he had little or no recollection of other relevant particulars of the basis for his identification, such as the names of other visitors or whether any of them had suggested Owens was his assailant.

Nonetheless, the Supreme Court held that Foster was "subject to cross-examination" as that term is used in Rule 801(d)(1).[16] It was sufficient, the Court said, that Foster was on the stand responding to cross-questions, even though his answers did not contain many of the "facts" the cross-examiner wanted to elicit. The Court did suggest that "limitations of the scope of examination by the trial court or assertions of privilege by the witness may undermine the process [of cross-examination] to such a degree that meaningful cross-examination within the intent of the Rule no longer exists."[17] But the trial court imposed no such limitations on the defendant in *Owens*. *Owens* yields the general impression that the presence of the witness on the stand coupled with his unrestricted responses to cross-questions will satisfy Rule 801(d)(1). Even an uncooperative witness should not nullify cross-examination, so long as he at least responds to cross-questions. Put another way, the Court's position is that "cross-examination" need not be perfect; it simply has to be adequate to trigger admissibility under Rule 801(d)(1).

The key to the *Owens* case is its premise that a poor performance on the stand by the witness who has made a prior identification usually has the effect of undermining the reliability of that identification. For example, when a witness testifies that he lacks memory about the prior statement or its underlying truth, this professed lack of memory could lead the factfinder to believe one of two things: 1) that the witness is feigning a lack of memory to avoid

---

[15]   484 U.S. 554, 561–64 (1988).

[16]   Owens unsuccessfully argued that a witness was "unavailable" for cross-examination because Rule 804(a)(3) defined a hearsay declarant as unavailable if he "testifies to not remembering the subject matter." The Court rejected the notion that unavailability for purposes of the hearsay exception was the same as "subject to cross-examination" under Rule 801(d)(1).

[17]   484 U.S. at 562. There may be other circumstances in which cross-examination will not be adequate, and the prior identification would then be inadmissible. One exception would arise if the witness refuses to answer cross-examination questions; another is where the trial judge improperly cuts off questions from the cross-examiner.

being confronted with the prior statement; or 2) that the witness is actually memory-impaired in general and so his prior identification might have been memory-impaired as well. The Court recognized that not every witness with a professed lack of memory is equally impeachable, however—for example, in *Owens,* the witness had suffered a head injury from the attack, which rendered his professed lack of memory quite plausible. But had *Owens* held that Rule 801(d)(1) required that the cross-examiner must *in fact* be afforded a thorough and effective cross-examination, trial judges would constantly have to measure the adequacy of a particular cross-examination under that subsection. *Owens* removes the need for such a difficult determination.   *personal knowledge requirement gone*

§ 6.3 Category II: Party-Opponent Statements: In General *-opponents words can be used against him*

The rationale for the Rule 801(d)(2) exemption from hearsay is that the party's *opponent* is entitled to admit statements of the adversary because that is part of the adversary system—what you say is fair game for the opponent. Such statements, while admissible for their truth, are in no way conclusive.[18] The party against whom the statement is admitted may produce rebuttal evidence that shows, for example, that there is a benign explanation for what was said or done. Think of party-opponent statements as simply manifestations of the adversary system: a party's past statements, which appear to weaken his contentions at trial, may be introduced against him by his adversary, over a hearsay objection. Another way to look at this is that the hearsay rule protects a party from unreliable statements made by declarants that cannot be cross-examined and are essentially outside the opponent's control—but that rationale does not apply to statements by a party, or those affiliated with a party. *rationale*

Not only are party-opponent statements admissible for their truth under the adversary theory, but even the pervasive principle of Rule 602, generally requiring that a witness or hearsay declarant[19] have personal knowledge of the event or condition about which he speaks, has no application to statements of a party-opponent. The assumption is that a party who makes an out-of-court statement about an event or condition must have had some basis for his assertions, and if not, then that is the party's problem, not the

---

[18]   Compare, for example, an admission made in a pleading such as the defendant's answer. This admission is conclusive (unless the pleading is subsequently amended) and removes the matter admitted from the parties' dispute.

[19]   This principle expressed in Rule 602 also generally applies to hearsay declarants.

adversary's.[20] The gist of the rule that exempts party-opponent statements from the hearsay ban is that a party bears the responsibility of having to confront in the courtroom evidence that he made statements or took other assertive actions that are inconsistent with his position at trial.

Note, also, that if a party, herself, (as opposed to a party's representative or agent) makes a statement and then raises a hearsay objection to its subsequent admission, she is saying, in essence, that she needs to cross-examine herself in order to expose a mistake or falsehood. This position, on its face, is untenable.

Possible Rules of Exclusion for Party-Opponent Statements

While party-opponent statements are exempt from the hearsay rule, it is a mistake to assume that these statements are always received into evidence. Sometimes they are excluded to avoid undue prejudice or because of an overriding social policy such as the exclusion of character evidence.

Suppose, for example, that an accused in a bank robbery prosecution (the crime charged) had admitted to an undercover agent that on another occasion he had sold drugs (a collateral offense). His statement, while exempt from the hearsay rule, would almost certainly be excluded in the trial for the principal crime under Rules 403 and 404(b).[21] Likewise, statements made by a party in the course of compromise negotiations or plea bargaining are not usually admissible against him.[22] The point is that although party-opponent statements escape the hearsay rule, they are sometimes rendered inadmissible by the application of an exclusionary rule or principle contained elsewhere in the Federal Rules—as is the case with any statement that is admitted under a hearsay exception, it is still subject to exclusion on other grounds.

---

[20] Of course, the party making the statement can take the stand and explain, for example, that he was mistaken as to the true facts, was simply guessing, or had been misled. The assumption is probably applicable to statements by authorized spokespersons, since the party authorizing the statement must have some basis for doing so. The assumption is more difficult to justify with respect to statements by agents and coconspirators, and the admissibility of these statements rests upon the notion that the party against whom they are offered is *responsible* for them and therefore cannot complain about the lack of an opportunity to cross-examine the declarant. This is not to say that agents and coconspirators will never be available for cross-examination; they may be but Rule 801(d)(2) does not require a showing of availability. If a declarant whose statement is admitted under (C), (D) or (E) of Rule 801(d)(2) is available, Rule 806 permits the party against whom the statement is offered to call the declarant and question them as if on cross-examination and to impeach them.

[21] See Fed. R. Evid. 404(b) and the discussion in Chapter III, §§ 3.6–4, 3.6–5.

[22] See Fed. R. Evid. 408, 410, and the discussion in Chapter IV, §§ 4.3, 4.5. See also Fed. R. Evid. 407 (evidence of subsequent remedial measures inadmissible), 409 (evidence of payment of medical expenses inadmissible).

Admissible Only Against the Party Who Made It

A party-opponent statement is admissible *only against the party* who, through his own action or the action of his agent or representative, made the statement. His statement is inadmissible against other parties who are merely aligned as co-plaintiffs or co-defendants. However, if these other parties are so closely associated with the party who made the statement that they can be deemed his principals or accomplices, then his statement is also admissible against them. For example, if one coconspirator makes a hearsay statement in connection with advancing the aim of the conspiracy, his statement is admissible not only against himself, but also against the other coconspirators.[23] Similarly, statements by an agent about a matter within the scope of his authority are admissible against both the agent and his principal—assuming the principal is a party.[24]

The rule that party-opponent statements are admissible only against the parties who are responsible for them flows from the fact that such statements, unlike most admissible hearsay statements, are not allowed into evidence because they are deemed trustworthy. As we have seen, the nature of the adversary system explains why party-opponent statements are allowed into evidence—if you are responsible for a statement, your adversary should be able to use it against you. Judges do not attempt to screen out "unreliable" statements made by a party or agent and offered against the party; rather the judges leave it to the party against whom the statement is offered to negate the probative force of the statement.

Because party-opponent statements are admissible only against the party or parties responsible for them, other ("nonresponsible") parties are entitled to a limiting instruction that directs the jury to confine its consideration of these statements to the party who made it or is responsible for it. An instruction to the jury usually suffices in a civil case, but in a criminal prosecution with multiple defendants, it may be necessary to hold separate trials in cases in which a hearsay statement of *D-1* also implicates *D-2*, yet is not independently

---

[23]   This is true even if the coconspirator who made the damaging statement is not joined as a party. This statement is attributed to his fellow conspirators and is admissible against those coconspirators who are made a party. But the declarant's statement would not be admissible against other parties to the suit who were not part of the conspiracy.

[24]   You should not assume that all coconspirators must be prosecuted in a single case or even that all must be prosecuted in some case. Many conspirators make deals with the government and become cooperating witnesses. Yet, as you will see, statements that qualify as coconspirator statements are admissible even though the declarant is not a party. Similarly, you should not assume that an agent and a principal must be joined as parties for the agent's statement to be admissible against the principal. The key to a party-opponent statement is that it is offered *against* a party and fits under one of the five categories set forth in Rule 801(d)(2).

admissible against *D-2*. If *D-1* and *D-2* were jointly tried, the jury might improperly consider *D-1's* statement as evidence not only of his guilt, but of *D-2's* as well.[25]

One-Way Admissibility

A party can never admit its own statements in its favor under Rule 801(d)(2). Admissibility of party-opponent statements is a one-way street. Consider a case where the defendant is charged with a murder in New York City. He wants to offer his own statement, made to a police officer, that he was dealing drugs in Buffalo on the day of the murder. This statement would help to establish an alibi, but it is not admissible as a party-opponent statement. It sounds like an "admission" but the simple fact is that a party's own statements are not admissible in his favor under Rule 801(d)(2). The rule is grounded in the adversary system, meaning that you are not entitled to protection *from* your own statements.

§ 6.4   Individual and Adopted Party-Opponent Statements

Suppose the owner of a machine shop told an insurance adjuster that one of the owner's employees was badly injured because the machine on which the latter was working was not equipped with a safety shield. Suppose next that the owner is subsequently sued by the injured employee and the owner contends that the machine was safe and that the accident was due to the employee's own carelessness. The employee can introduce the owner's statement against him—for example, by calling the adjuster to the stand and having him relate what the owner said. Federal Rule 801(d)(2) exempts from the hearsay rule a statement that "is offered against an opposing party and: (A) was made by the party in an individual or representative capacity; . . ."

Objections by the owner that he did not see the event (no personal or first-hand knowledge) or that he was merely offering an opinion would not preclude admission of the owner's hearsay statement. Of course, the owner can take the stand and explain that he was mistaken or misinformed when he made the statement in question. Note, also, that the quoted portion of the rule makes it clear that it is of no consequence whether a party made the statement in a personal (individual) capacity or in his capacity as a representative.

---

[25]   In criminal cases, the use of limiting instructions to protect non-admitting parties may not be sufficient to satisfy the right to confrontation. *See Bruton v. United States*, 391 U.S. 123 (1968), discussed in Chapter VIII.

Thus, if a trustee is a party to a suit, his hearsay statement may be used against him even though he made it in an individual capacity.[26]

ILLUSTRATION

Deuce is prosecuted for the possession of controlled drugs. He pleads not guilty and contends that the drugs in question belonged to his former roommate, a Columbian national who has returned to his native land. Anita, Deuce's estranged girlfriend, is willing to testify that Deuce once told her that "he made a hell of a good living moving drugs right under the nose of the cops." Deuce's lawyer objects to Anita's proffered testimony on the ground of irrelevance and on the further ground that Deuce has not testified, and probably will not take the stand. How should the trial judge rule?

own maximum

Deuce's statement increases the likelihood that the drugs in question were his, consequently it is relevant under Rule 401. And whether or not a party testifies has no bearing on the admissibility of his own hearsay statement. Thus the statement is admissible against Deuce under Rule 801(d)(2)(A).

There is one aspect of Rule 801(d)(2)(A) that also impacts the other four exemptions found in Rule 801(d)(2)[the trial judge is a factfinder under Rule 104(a) when an objection is made to a statement that a witness attributes to a party]Suppose, for example, that Deuce claims that his estrangement with Anita caused her to seek revenge and that she invented the statement upon which the prosecution relies. To admit the statement the trial judge must find by a preponderance of the evidence that Deuce *actually made the statement.* If the judge believes it is more likely that Deuce is correct and that Anita invented the statement, the jury will never hear it. Likewise if a Facebook post is offered as a statement of the defendant, the judge has to find by a preponderance that the defendant actually made that post. Upon first reading, this might seem wrong since the typical issue of authentication arises under Rule 901 and the trial judge under that Rule is a screener, not a fact finder, deciding only whether there is sufficient evidence for the jury to find that a particular person made a statement. But, when the objection is hearsay, the judge must decide whether a statement falls within Rule 801(d)(2), and the judge must decide disputed facts—in this example the disputed fact is whether the defendant made the post.

*104(a)
↓
heaviav
changes
me rule*

If the judge admits the statement, the jury will not know of the judge's finding. So in our example, Deuce can offer the same evidence about estrangement and revenge, and the jury can decide whether to

---

[26]   Rule 801(d)(2) ACN.

believe that Deuce made the statement and, if so, what weight to give it.

Adopted Statements

Sometimes a party will, in the words of Rule 801(d)(2)(B), manifest "that it adopted or believed" the truth of someone else's statement, thereby putting the statement on the same footing as a party's own statement. Suppose, for example, a patient uses the written opinion of a physical therapist to make an insurance claim; or a businessman distributes to current and potential customers or investors a newspaper article that describes his company as financially sound and increasingly profitable; or an evangelist "pro-life" minister distributes to his congregation a pamphlet in which the author, a doctor, claims that use of the "morning-after" birth control pill is the equivalent of murder.

These are examples of the adoption by one person of the statement of another. The law of evidence treats a statement adopted by a party as that party's own statement, and consequently exempts the adopted statement from the hearsay rule when offered against the party.

More troublesome, and often more problematic, are statements that a party "adopts" through tacit acquiescence in another person's statement. Sometimes, the other person's statement has an accusatory tone:[27] "Your insect control device wouldn't work and you knew it." Silence in the face of this kind of accusation often is found to be an adoption of the statement—on the ground that a reasonable person would deny such an accusation if it were untrue. The judge must decide if the statement in question (whether or not accusatory) 1) was heard and understood, and 2) whether, in the circumstances in which the statement was made, a reasonable person would have expressed his disagreement with it. The preferred, though not universal practice, is for the judge initially to determine whether an adoption was made, as that is a preliminary question concerning the admissibility of evidence and, as such, allocated to the judge (and not the jury) by Federal Rule 104(a).[28] The jury may then be instructed that the probative value, if any, that the jury attaches to the evidence depends on whether, upon hearing the statement, a reasonable

---

[27] However, this is not always true. For example, in *United States v. Beckham*, 968 F.2d 47 (D.C. Cir. 1992), *X*, a cocaine seller, said that he only had one bag left, but that the buyer (an undercover agent) could purchase another bag from supplier, *Y*. Upon hearing this, *Y* walked over to a container containing crack cocaine and opened it. Held: *Y* adopted *X*'s statement.

[28] For a discussion of the judge and jury problem, *see* SALTZBURG, MARTIN & CAPRA, FEDERAL RULES OF EVIDENCE MANUAL § 801.02[6][d] (12th ed. 2019).

person in the party's circumstances would have denied or protested its accuracy if he believed it was untrue.

Adoptions by silence are particularly troublesome when the accused fails to deny accusations by (or in the presence of) law enforcement officials. If the defendant is in custody, and has been given *Miranda* warnings, his right to remain silent is constitutionally protected[29] and failure to speak cannot be used against him. Of course, a defendant may waive his right to remain silent. If he does so knowingly and intentionally, and thereafter freely converses with the police, he runs the risk that he may tacitly acknowledge the truth of some of the statements made by the police or others in attendance. For example, he may firmly deny certain statements by the police, but remain mute as to others, in which case an adoption is likely to be found as to the latter.

Regardless of whether *Miranda* warnings have been given, a person's silence around police officers is not likely to be found an adoption of statements made by officers or others. There is a common understanding that silence around police officers is often the best course for a suspect, whether you are formally under arrest or not. That understanding is inconsistent with an adoption of any accusation in the presence of an officer.

§ 6.5   Statements by Authorized Spokespersons and Other Agents

Rule 801(d)(2)(C) exempts from the hearsay rule a statement made "by a person whom the party authorized to make a statement on the subject" about which the person speaks. This subsection simply says that when a party has delegated "speaking authority" to an agent, statements made in the course of exercising that authority are admissible against the party. Familiar examples of delegation are a client's authorization to a lawyer to speak for her in connection with a case or other legal matters, and her authorization to her accountant to speak for her with respect to financial matters.[30]

---

[29]   *Doyle v. Ohio*, 426 U.S. 610 (1976).

[30]   The courts are split on whether an expert witness's out-of-court statements may be used as a statement of the party retaining the expert. It is clear that when a party engages an expert to testify at trial, the agent has speaking authority. On the other hand, an expert is supposed to render an independent opinion. *Compare Collins v. Wayne Corp.*, 621 F.2d 777, 782 (5th Cir. 1980) (admissible as agent's statement against the party) *with Kirk v. Raymark Indust. Inc.*, 61 F.3d 147, 163–64 (3d Cir. 1995) (not admissible). Perhaps the correct answer lies in the circumstances of each case—the judgment should be contextual.

It should be clear, however, that the fact that someone consults a specialist on a matter does not mean that anything the specialist says is an authorized statement. Suppose, for example, that a patient goes to her doctor claiming chronic fatigue, and the doctor says to the patient at the conclusion of an examination, "you are a

[handwritten margin notes: "DESIGNATED AGENT CAN SPEAK FOR COMPANY"]

The business world is replete with instances in which designated agents are permitted to speak for their company, as, for example, where a construction company's manager is permitted to negotiate with suppliers of materials or a corporate CEO is given authority to initiate product recalls. Federal Rule 801(d)(2)(C) makes no distinction with regard to the persons with whom a "speaking agent" is communicating, so long as the agent is speaking within the range of his delegated speaking authority.[31] Thus, if the construction foreman of a general building contractor is given authority to render oral and written reports evaluating the work of subcontractors, the foreman's oral or written statements to anyone about this subject will constitute the general contractor's statements, thus admissible against the general contractor despite the fact they are hearsay. It is immaterial, for example, whether the foremen's statements were made to a fellow employee, corporate management, a sub-contractor, or someone outside of the construction business. The pivotal issue under Rule 801(d)(2)(C) is whether the putative principal had in fact delegated to the agent the authority to speak. If not, the agent's statement is not admissible against the "principal" *under this subsection*, but would, of course, be admissible against the agent if she were a party and if the statement were relevant to her claim or defense.

[handwritten margin notes: "JUDGE DECIDES WHO HAS AUTHORITY"]

The decision as to whether the purported agent had speaking authority is governed by Rule 104(a), which allocates to the judge questions concerning the admissibility of evidence, to be determined under the preponderance standard. Sometimes the very statement in question contains an assertion that supports the conclusion that the agent was authorized by the principal to speak for the latter. ("My company, *D*, has asked that I speak with you about selling your property before the EPA launches an investigation as to whether the underground water is contaminated by mercury.") Can such a statement be used by the judge as evidentiary support for her conclusion that the agent had speaking authority? Under Rule 801(d)(2), it can. However, Rule 801(d)(2) specifically provides that the statement "does not by itself establish the declarant's authority" to speak for the party-principal. Thus, the judge cannot conclude

---

malingerer." That statement is not the authorized statement of the patient. Similarly, when a prospective client consults with a lawyer and is told at the conclusion of the consultation, "you have no case," that statement is not an authorized statement of the client. You might wonder when you turn to the next exemption (D) whether the statements of the doctor and lawyer might be agents' statements. The correct answer is "no," since both the doctor and lawyer are acting as professionals making independent judgments and are not under any control of the patient and prospective client.

[31]   Rule 801(d)(2) ACN.

there was speaking authority unless there is at least some evidence of its existence other than the statement of the purported agent.

Statements by Agents About Matters Within the Scope of Their Employment

Common law judges had a very restrictive view on when a principal had delegated speaking authority to an agent. For example, agents hired to deliver goods (truck drivers) or services (ushers), or to engage in construction or repairs (electricians or masons) were usually regarded as lacking the authority to speak for the principal. The theory was that the agent was hired to perform various physical tasks, not to speak for the principal, and especially not to speak adversely to the principal's interests. Rule 801(d)(2)(D) expands the possibility for admitting agents' statements by declaring that a statement by a party's agent or employee "on a matter within the scope of that relationship and while it existed" constitutes a statement of the principal. Under the Rule, a party may not have authorized a person to speak on the party's behalf, but the person's statements are exempt from the hearsay rule as long as they related to the scope of agency or employment and were made while the agency or employment was ongoing.

[margin handwriting: wimir slope of employmen]

The judge decides whether the statement concerns a matter within the scope of the agency or employment, because that question controls the admissibility of the statement and thus implicates Federal Rule 104(a). In resolving this issue, the judge may consider any portion of the statement itself that is helpful, although the agent's statement, standing alone, is not sufficient to establish the scope of his duties.[32] In order to qualify as an agent's statement under the rule, the statement must have been made before the agency or employment relationship is terminated.[33] This limiting feature protects the principal from damaging statements by terminated agents who may bear ill will against their former employer.

[margin handwriting: 104(a)]

ILLUSTRATION

Alex was hired to perform maintenance services for the Draper Chemical Corporation. One of Alex's duties was to inspect daily certain pipelines that carried toxic chemicals, in order to ensure that there were no leaks. One Friday Alex decided to leave work before lunch in order to depart early for a weekend of fishing. That night a sensor alarm sounded, indicating the presence of toxic substances. Several night-shift employees were rushed to the hospital after inhaling fumes from the chemicals that had seeped

---

[32]   Fed. R. Evid. 801(d)(2).
[33]   Fed. R. Evid. 801(d)(2)(D).

from a leak in one of the pipes Alex was responsible for inspecting.

(margin note: YES →)

On Monday, when Health and Safety Authorities spoke with Alex, he admitted that he had not inspected the pipe in question on the preceding Friday. On Wednesday, Alex submitted his resignation (effective immediately) to Draper Chemical in order to be eligible for three weeks of "transition pay" which was not available to employees who were fired. On Friday, Alex visited one of the injured employees, Perrozzi, at the hospital. During their conversation, Alex remarked that the pipe in question was old and corroded and that he had twice told his supervisor it should be replaced.

(margin notes: YES AGAINST ALEX; NO →)

During Perrozzi's suit against Draper Chemical for personal injuries, Perrozzi offers to testify as to what Alex had told him about the defective pipe. Perrozzi also offers a co-worker who will testify that on the Monday before Alex quit he heard Alex admit to a Health and Safety Inspector that he, Alex, had not conducted the required pipe inspection on the Friday of the accident. How should the judge rule on these offers of proof?

Alex's statement to the Health and Safety Inspector, would be admissible under Rule 801(d)(2)(D), because Alex was speaking about a matter within the scope of his employment and he made the statement in question while still employed. Thus, Alex's statement is admissible against Draper Chemical as the latter's statement. Of course, if Alex were joined as a party defendant, his statement would also be admissible against him as an individual party-opponent statement.

Alex's statement to Perrozzi during their hospital conversation stands on a different footing. Because Alex's employment terminated prior to this conversation, neither Rule 801(d)(2)(C) (speaking authority), nor Rule 801(d)(2)(D) (scope rule) applies, and the statement would be inadmissible against Draper Chemical. If Alex were joined as a party defendant, his statement would be one of a party-opponent *if* Perrozzi offered it against him. But, in reality the effect of Alex's hospital statement that he had twice warned his supervisor about the old, corroded pipe is to *exonerate* Alex and place the blame on Draper Chemical. If Alex were the sole defendant, it is inconceivable that Perrozzi would seek to offer the statement. But in a joint trial Perrozzi might seek to offer the statement in the hope that a jury would use it against the company irrespective of any limiting instruction (because the statement is hearsay as to the company) that the judge might give.

Coconspirators' Statements

Federal Rule 801(d)(2)(E) provides that a statement made by a declarant during the course and in furtherance of a conspiracy is admissible for its truth against all the declarant's fellow conspirators. A conspiracy is tantamount to a partnership[34] in the sense that in each enterprise the members act in concert to further and achieve desired objectives. As coconspirators implement their plans, one or more of them may make statements that will be offered in subsequent litigation as a party-opponent statement. For example, suppose *A*, *B*, and *C* are accountants who conspire to embezzle funds from their corporate employer. Unbeknownst to *A*, a conversation he has with *X*, an accountant, is secretly recorded. During this conversation, in which *A* tries to persuade *X* to join the company's accounting section and embezzlement scheme, *A* enticingly describes certain activities of himself, and of *B* and *C*, which have resulted in huge financial gains. *A*'s recorded statements, subsequently produced at *A*'s criminal trial, are not only his statements; they also constitute statements of *B* and *C*—because they were made during the course of, and in furtherance of, a conspiracy in which *A*, *B*, and *C* are members. The justification for admissibility is that when you join a partnership, the acts and statements of other partners are properly attributed to you if they are made during the existence of the partnership and in furtherance of the partnership's goals.

Moreover, if *X* were to join the conspiracy, statements of his coconspirators made in furtherance of the conspiracy would be admissible against *X* under the coconspirator exemption. Even coconspirators' statements made by *A*, *B*, and *C* *before* *X* joined the conspiracy would be admissible against him. The rationale is that when *X* elected to join the conspiracy he took it as he found it; that is, he subscribed to both its potential for gain and its preexisting risks.

These broad, even breathtaking rules of admissibility, are tempered by three important restrictions, all of which track the substantive law of conspiratorial liability.[35] Those three requirements are (1) the declarant's statement must be intended to further the objectives of the conspiracy; (2) the declarant's statement must be made while the conspiracy is in operation; and (3) the declarant and the party against whom the statement is offered must in fact be members of the same conspiracy. All of these admissibility

---

[34]   The statements of one partner relating to the activities of the partnership are generally admissible against the partnership.

[35]   Fed. R. Evid. 801 ACN notes that the exemption for coconspirator hearsay is intended to track the substantive law of conspiracy, which determines which acts of conspirators can be attributed to others in the conspiracy. The intent of Rule 801(d)(2)(E) is to treat the words of conspirators in the same way as acts are treated.

requirements must be proved by a preponderance of the evidence under Rule 104(a). The judge is the factfinder as to these requirements.

Although the coconspirator exemption is most often encountered in criminal cases, it is applicable to civil cases as well. The proponent must convince the judge that his evidence meets the requirements listed above. It is not necessary that a conspiracy be charged in the indictment or, in a civil suit, alleged in the pleadings. It is immaterial whether a coconspirator's hearsay statement is made to another coconspirator or to an outsider. Furthermore, it does not matter whether or not the declarant-coconspirator is joined as a party to the civil or criminal trial.

The breadth of the coconspirator exemption sometimes causes parties and judges to rely on it unnecessarily. The exemption is needed only when a coconspirator's statement is offered for its truth. When the statement has a nonhearsay use, its admission need not rest on Rule 801(d)(2)(E). Suppose, for example, *A*, *B*, and *C* agree to extort money from local store owners by threatening injury to the owner or his family. A threatening statement by A to a shop owner ("If you don't pay weekly protection money your son will have an unfortunate accident") is a verbal act—it has independent legal significance because making the statement constitutes an offense. The statement comes in as nonhearsay; the substantive law of conspiracy determines whether *B* and *C* share *A's* criminal responsibility.

The "In Furtherance" Requirement

Courts usually take a generous view of what statements advance the conspiracy. But the in-furtherance requirement precludes use of the coconspirator exemption to admit simple narratives about past events, idle chatter, bragging, and the like (e.g., a statement from a conspirator to bank robbery, made to his brother: "I wish [defendant] hadn't shot the bank teller"). Even more obviously, statements that are designed to defeat the conspiracy are not made in furtherance of it—e.g., confessions to police officers.

On the other hand, statements in furtherance of the conspiracy should include those designed to launch the conspiratorial transaction, to recruit new members (as in the example above), to recount past conduct or events *in order* to plan future strategy, to keep members aware of progress, to reassure members or elicit their cooperation, to persuade non-conspirators to do business with the conspiracy, to intimidate straying conspirators so that they will not cooperate with the authorities, and so forth. The same can be said for transactional records, inventories, status reports, and other entries that are designed to track the financial condition or progress of the conspiracy. In all of these examples, the declarant-conspirator is intending to further the objectives of the conspiracy.

What if a seller in a drug conspiracy states to a buyer: "wait here, [the defendant] has the drugs, he will be here in ten minutes"—but the buyer is in fact an undercover police officer? The seller's statement does not actually further the conspiracy. Just the opposite. Yet it still satisfies the "in furtherance" requirement, because the seller *intended* for the statement to further a drug transaction.

The "During the Course" Requirement

[handwritten: DURING the cou]

As we have noted, the hearsay exemption for coconspirators' statements applies only to statements made during the course of the conspiracy. When the conspiracy is over, Rule 801(d)(2)(E) is no longer applicable. Determining when a conspiracy begins and ends can be difficult, for often there are no clear lines of demarcation. A conspiracy takes root when two or more persons agree to jointly seek a common end. The fact that additional persons later join the conspiracy does not affect the point in time at which the conspiracy originated. The conspiracy terminates when the conspirators achieve their objective or when they abandon their quest. Even if the conspiracy has not ended, a conspirator may withdraw from the conspiracy and once that happens any subsequent statements that a conspirator makes are no longer admissible against the withdrawn member as coconspirator statements. Invoking Federal Rule 104(a), the judge must decide when a conspiracy begins and ends or if and when a conspirator withdrew from the conspiracy.

ILLUSTRATIONS

In which (if either) of the following hypothetical problems has the conspiracy (comprised of *A*, *B*, and *C*) terminated?

(1) *A*, *B*, and *C* conspire to set fire to a building owned by *A* and *B*, and thereafter to collect the fire insurance proceeds. *C*, the coconspirator who actually sets the fire, is arrested one month after the building burns. Faced with the possibility of a long prison term, *C* (two weeks after his arrest) reveals to the prosecutor details about the conspiratorial plot of *A*, *B*, and *C*. Meanwhile, *A* and *B* have filed a claim for the insurance proceeds and threatened suit against the fire insurance company should it fail to honor their claim.

[handwritten: C DONE / yes to A·B]

(2) *A*, *B*, and *C* conspire to rob a bank. Several days after the successful heist, they have a conversation and

decide to break the get-away car into component parts and destroy it. Furthermore, because some of the stolen currency may be marked, the conspirators also agree that each of them will hide his separate share in a safety deposit box and leave it there for at least three years.

In Illustration (1), the first issue is when *C* effectively withdrew from the conspiracy. Once he terminates his membership in the conspiracy, his statements are no longer admissible as the statements of *A* and *B*, nor are *their* statements admissible against *C*. Generally speaking, a participant in the conspiracy remains a member until he takes affirmative steps to withdraw. *C's* decision to reveal the conspiratorial plot to the police signals a voluntary withdrawal. (Furthermore, these statements do not advance the conspiracy, because *C* is advancing law enforcement interests).

In Illustration (1), the trial judge would have to decide, based on facts peculiar to the case before him, when *C's* withdrawal became effective. The conspiracy itself survived *C's* arrest because the ultimate aim of the conspiracy was to collect the insurance proceeds and *A* and *B* were pursuing that end, even though *C* had been apprehended as a suspect. If, during the continuance of the conspiracy, *A* or *B* made statements that incriminated *C*, those statements would be admissible against *C only if they predated* his withdrawal by revealing the coconspirators' plot.

Illustration (2) also raises a question as to when the conspiracy terminated. In the federal courts (but not those of all the states), the coconspirator exemption from hearsay usually ceases to operate during the concealment phase—that is, when the members are trying to avoid detection—otherwise the conspiracy would be temporally unlimited as there will always be attempts to conceal it. However, the concealment phase does not begin until the principal goal of the conspiracy has been either achieved or abandoned. In crimes involving the illicit acquisition of money, the principal objective of the conspiracy is not realized until the money has been received *and* divided among the members. In the present Illustration, two separate acts, destruction of the car and secreting the money after it has been divided up, fall within the concealment phase and are not part of the initial conspiracy under the Federal Rules.

Coconspirator Hearsay: The Judge's Role

As stated above, the coconspirator exemption requires the proponent to show that the declarant and the defendant are members of the same conspiracy. The leading case on this admissibility requirement is *Bourjaily v. United States*.[36] The *Bourjaily* Court held

---

[36]　483 U.S. 171 (1987).

first that the judge must determine, under the provisions of Rule 104(a), whether the requirements of the coconspirator exemption have been satisfied. Thus the judge, not the jury, determines whether there was a conspiracy, whether the declarant and the party to the suit (usually, the defendant) were members of it, and whether the declarant's statement was in furtherance of the conspiracy. *Bourjaily's* second holding it that the judge is to use a preponderance-of-the-evidence standard in making her determination—this is the basic Rule 104(a) standard. Third, the burden of convincing the judge of the foundational facts lies with the proponent of the evidence—usually the government. **Bourjaily**

Fourth, the judge *must consider the declarant-coconspirator's statement itself* in resolving the issue of whether all of the requirements of the coconspirator exemption have been met. For example, in a case involving a drug conspiracy, assume that one of the low-level dealers complains about the low quality of the product. The declarant who supplies him says, "don't worry, we will be getting better product soon. My brother Bill is going to South America next week to pick up some great stuff." That statement is admissible against Bill if the government can prove to the judge by a preponderance that Bill and the declarant are in fact members of the same conspiracy. In deciding this question, the trial judge will consider not only any independent evidence of conspiracy (e.g., joint bank accounts, meetings between the declarant and Bill, etc.) but also the very statement that the government is trying to introduce under the coconspirator exemption.

It can be argued that it is circular to admit the statement only if there is evidence of conspiracy, but then to allow the statement itself to be the evidence of the conspiracy. But the Court in *Bourjaily* relied on Rule 104(a), which states that in making an admissibility determination, the judge is not bound by rules of admissibility (except those in regard to privilege, which are not applicable here). Of course, the judge may choose not to give the hearsay statement much weight as proof of conspiracy, for the very reason that it might be an unreliable statement by an unreliable declarant. But the statement itself is likely to be given considerable weight if it is supported by independent evidence. As the Court in *Bourjaily* noted, a hearsay statement that looks unreliable in isolation can be corroborated by other evidence of conspiracy.

The *Bourjaily* Court declined to decide whether the hearsay statement, standing alone, would be sufficient evidence upon which to base a finding that all of the requirements of the exemption were satisfied. This question was subsequently answered by an amendment to Rule 801(d)(2)[37] stating that the trial court must consider the statement as part of the proof of conspiracy, but that the statement "does not by itself" establish the foundation requirement that the defendant and the declarant are members of the same conspiracy.

In essence, the *Bourjaily* Court interpreted Federal Rule 104(a) as applying to the requirements of the coconspirator exemption because, in determining whether these requirements are satisfied, the judge is dealing with preliminary questions concerning the admissibility of evidence and therefore is not bound by the usual exclusionary rules, including the rule against hearsay—and so the judge may consider hearsay for what it is worth. As with other findings the judge makes under Rule 104(a), the jury is not informed that the judge has found any of the Rule 801(d)(2)(E) requirements to be satisfied. In fact, the jury never knows there is a coconspirator exemption from the hearsay rule. If the judge admits the statement, the jury decides whether to believe it and what weight to give it.

It must be remembered that a jury might find a defendant not guilty of conspiracy even though the judge has found that a conspiracy exists and the defendant was a member, which findings justified the admission of coconspirator statements. The judge's ruling was based upon a preponderance of the evidence, whereas the jury must decide whether the prosecution has proved the defendant's guilt beyond a reasonable doubt.

The Coconspirator Exemption: A Reprise

The traditional justification for the coconspirator exemption is founded on the analogy between a business partnership and a conspiracy. The analogy is imperfect, however, because there usually is actual authority for a partner to speak for the partnership, which has a separate legal identity from the individual partners.

Another possible justification for the coconspirator exemption is the difficulty of proving the existence of a conspiracy which, by its nature, is clandestine and covert. Furthermore, neither the courtroom testimony of a coconspirator nor the observable activities of the conspirators adequately reveals the true nature of the conspiracy. The Supreme Court has remarked:

> Because [coconspirators' statements] . . . are made while the conspiracy is in progress, such statements provide evidence of the conspiracy's context that cannot be replicated, even if the declarant testifies to the same matters in court. . . .

---

[37]   The amendment became effective December 1, 1997.

Conspirators are likely to speak differently when talking in furtherance of their illegal aims than when testifying on the witness stand. Even when the declarant takes the stand, his in-court testimony will seldom have the evidentiary value of his statements made during the course of the conspiracy.[38]

Thus, the argument goes, the coconspirator exemption is grounded in necessity. Of course, mere need cannot be enough for a hearsay exception, but the thought is that the foundation requirements for establishing conspiratorial liability provide at least some assurance that the statements are fairly attributed to the defendant.

---

[38]   *United States v. Inadi*, 475 U.S. 387, 395 (1986).

Chapter VII

HEARSAY EXCEPTIONS

Table of Sections

§ 7.1 Overview

The Federal Rules of Evidence contain twenty-nine "true" exceptions to the rule against hearsay (which we have distinguished from "exemptions"). Most of these are quite specific and state with particularity the requirements that must be satisfied in order to escape the rule. For example, Rule 803(2) contains an exception for a "statement relating to a startling event or condition, made while the declarant was under the stress of excitement that it caused." Two of the twenty-nine exceptions are more general in content. These exceptions are designed to address situations in which some flexibility is required. Rule 804(b)(6) allows into evidence statements of a declarant offered against a party who has wrongfully prevented that declarant from testifying. Rule 807, the so-called "catch-all" or "residual" exception, addresses hearsay statements that fit no categorical hearsay exception but the proponent argues that they are reliable under the circumstances.

The Rationale Underlying the Exceptions

The exceptions to the hearsay rule have been developed over many years. Most of the exceptions contained in the Federal Rules were first articulated by common law judges; many of these were

judicially modified and refined with the passage of time. The
exceptions are based on judicial experience rather than social science
methodology and investigation. Nonetheless, each of the exceptions
has at least one feature that serves to eliminate or reduce one or
several of the hearsay dangers, namely, insincerity, faulty
perception, deficiencies in memory, and errors in narration. For
example, Rule 803(2) allows into evidence statements relating to an
exciting event, but only if the declarant speaks while still under the
influence of the stress or excitement caused by perceiving the event.
Because the time between the event and the declarant's statement is
usually short, there is a reduced concern that she has a faulty
memory. More importantly, because she spoke excitedly, and
presumably unreflectively, it makes it less likely that she had the
opportunity and frame of mind to tell a lie.

The Layout of the Exceptions

The drafters of the Federal Rules divided the exceptions into two
major categories. Rule 803 contains the first group; Rule 804 contains
the second. The feature that differentiates these groups is this: the
twenty-three exceptions listed and defined by Rule 803 (with one
minor exception) may be used whether or not the declarant is
available to testify; conversely, the five exceptions listed and defined
by Rule 804 may not be used unless the proponent proves to the judge
that the declarant is unavailable as a witness.

All of the exceptions except one are conveniently placed in Rules
803 and 804. The only exception that appears elsewhere is the
residual or catch-all exception. In 1997, that rule, which had
appeared redundantly in both Rule 803 (as 803(24)) and 804 (as
804(b)(5)), was transferred to a new location where it now appears as
Rule 807.

§ 7.2   Federal Rule 803 Exceptions: In General

The courtroom availability of a Rule 803 declarant is
immaterial—with one minor qualification, the exceptions contained
in this rule are available whether or not the declarant testifies. The
justification is that these exceptions have admissibility requirements
that tend to guarantee that the hearsay statement is better than (or
at least different from) any testimony that the declarant could
provide on the matter at trial. For example assume that a plaintiff
sues for injuries suffered in a horrific accident in which he was hit by
a car that sped through a red light. The plaintiff introduces a
statement by a bystander to the accident, who was crying and yelling
"I can't believe the blue car ran the light and hit that poor guy!" This
statement is likely to be admitted under the hearsay exception for
excited utterances. A statement is admissible as an excited utterance

only if the declarant is under the influence of a startling event, and it must also relate to that event. These admissibility requirements tend to guarantee that the declarant is making the statement spontaneously and while the event is fresh in his memory. Compare that statement to trial testimony from the bystander about the event—which is long after the event and hardly spontaneous.

No single rationale explains or justifies the twenty-three exceptions set out in Rule 803. However, some factors that account for the legislative and judicial recognition of one or more of these exceptions include:

(1)   A motive for the declarant to speak truthfully;

(2)   The lapse of only a brief period of time between the declarant's perception of an event or condition and her statement(s) about the event or condition;

(3)   A state of mind, attributable to the declarant, that makes it unlikely that she could (or would) contrive a falsehood;

(4)   Scrutiny of the declarant's statement(s) by third persons (including the general public) who are in a position to detect falsehoods or inaccuracies;

(5)   A duty, imposed by law, to speak or report accurately;

(6)   Reliance by others on the accuracy of the declarant's statement;

(7)   A foundation requirement that provides a trier information to aid it in assessing reliability.

Sometimes more than one exception will apply to the same statement; likewise, an exemption (such as for party-opponent statements) may apply to a statement that also falls within a Rule 803 exception. It does not usually matter which exception or exemption a proponent invokes—the objective is to have the evidence in question admitted.

§ 7.3   Spontaneous Declarations: Excited Utterances and Present Sense Impressions

The term "spontaneous declarations" as used here includes two related but distinct hearsay exceptions for statements made under circumstances that minimize the hearsay dangers of insincerity and inaccurate memory. These exceptions are supported by reduced risks of insincerity and faulty memory, and require that the excepted statement address events or conditions that the declarant recently perceived.

Present Sense Impression—Rule 803(1)

This exception is of comparatively recent origin; it did not have widespread approval until it was included in the Federal Rules in 1975.[1] The exception is contained in Rule 803(1) which removes from the hearsay ban:

> **Present Sense Impression.** A statement describing or explaining an event or condition, made while or immediately after the declarant perceived it.

Reasonable people can—and do—disagree on the question of how much time may elapse between the event or condition and the declarant's statement for the statement to be within the exception. That judgment is contextual and it falls to the trial judge to make it. The judge has two guidelines: one is textual, the other is derived from the rationale supporting this exception. First, the text of the rule states that the declarant must make the statement as she is perceiving the event or condition in question or "immediately after" it. Thus, there must be a very close temporal nexus between the event (or condition) and the declarant's descriptive or explanatory statement. Second, the principal rationale for admitting a declarant's statement of her present sense impression is that the brief period between the declarant's perception and her statement allows very little time for devising a fabrication.[2] Taken together, the text of the rule and its supporting rationale establish that the lapse of more than just a few minutes between the declarant's perception and her descriptive statement renders the present-sense exception inapplicable. (It doesn't take much time to think up a lie.)

Note that the text of Rule 803(1) *confines the content* of the declarant's statement: it must *describe or explain* the event or condition that the declarant has just perceived. Suppose, for example, a declarant, caught in a late afternoon rush-hour traffic jam, observes a fire engine speeding down the highway in the opposite direction. She then remarks to her passenger, "Look how fast he is going—over ninety, I'll bet." This would be a descriptive statement that would qualify as a present sense impression. On the other hand, suppose the declarant said, "That reminds me. As I was driving to the airport to pick you up, I saw two brush fires down in Pleasant Valley, and no one was attending them." This statement does not describe or explain

---

[1]   The leading pre-Rules case supporting this exception is *Houston Oxygen Co. v. Davis*, 139 Tex. 1, 161 S.W.2d 474, 476–77 (Com.App. 1942).

[2]   Of course, the hearsay risk that the declarant's memory was faulty is also reduced or eliminated.

the declarant's observation of the speeding fire engine. Perhaps the presence of the fire engine reminded her of the brush fires or perhaps she is simply speculating about its destination. Note, also, that the lapse of time between what the declarant describes and the occurrence of the brush fires would preclude the application of Rule 803(1).

The simple example above suggests two additional observations about the present sense impression exception. First, this exception, like most hearsay exceptions, requires that the declarant have first-hand (personal) knowledge of the event or condition about which he speaks. (This pervasive requirement not only applies to all lay in-court testimony, but to most out-of-court hearsay declarations as well.[3]) Second, note that in the foregoing hypothetical, the driver was speaking to her passenger who, presumably, was able to make her own observations of the fire engine. When a declarant is speaking to someone who can also observe the event or condition she describes, she is less likely to speak falsely or inaccurately. Nonetheless, the exception for present sense impressions does not *require* the person to whom the declarant speaks to also observe the event or condition the declarant describes. It has been held to require, however, some indication other than the statement itself that the declarant's assessment was accurate.

ILLUSTRATION

Lena has disappeared and at Frank's trial for her murder, the prosecutor wants to establish that Frank and Lena were together the night of her disappearance. Janet will testify that on the night in question Lena called her at about 7:15 p.m. During their conversation Lena said that she was waiting for Frank at the Skylight Lounge, but that he was so late they would probably have to skip dinner and go directly to the theater. Lena then said to someone, "Well finally! Where have you been?" Janet then heard an indistinct male voice, and Lena said to her, "Frank just came in and our cab is waiting outside. Got to run. I'll call you tomorrow."

Should the judge sustain or overrule defense counsel's hearsay objection to Janet's testimony?

Let us assume that Janet is familiar with Lena's voice and is thus able to authenticate her caller's identity. The remaining issue is whether the prosecutor can overcome the defendant's hearsay objection. Rule 803(1) requires that the declarant perceive an event

---

[3]   As we have seen, however, this requirement does not attach to party-opponent statements. *See* Chapter VI, § 6–3.

or condition and contemporaneously or immediately describe or explain it. In making a determination of the facts that pertain to this evidentiary rule, the *judge* must necessarily find that (1) there was an event or condition, (2) the declarant perceived it—or, put otherwise, had personal knowledge of it, (3) the statement describes or explains the event, and (4) the statement was made at the time of the event or immediately thereafter.

The usual standard of proof, preponderance of the evidence, applies to these determinations by the judge and the burden is on the proponent to convince the judge of these preliminary facts.[4] However, the proponent is aided by a provision in Rule 104(a) stating that when finding facts pertaining to an evidentiary rule of admissibility, the judge is not bound by the rules of evidence except those with respect to privileges. Thus, the judge is free to consider the declarant's statement itself for whatever probative force it may have on (1) the existence of an event (or condition), (2) the declarant's perception of it, and (3) the immediacy with which the declarant spoke. The statement alone may in a few courts provide a sufficient evidentiary basis for the judge to conclude there was an event (or condition). But this is unlikely—most courts are concerned about potential unreliability, *and so require independent evidence of the event before the statement can be admitted as a present sense impression.* Otherwise, the statement proves its own admissibility requirement— which would be a result inconsistent with other evidence Rules, such as Rule 801(d)(2) (discussed in Chapter 6) which requires that evidence independent of the statement must be submitted to prove that the declarant was an agent or co-conspirator of a party.

An example of the kind of independent evidence necessary to satisfy the present sense impression exception is *United States v. Blakey.*[5] The defendants were charged with extortion. The government offered the victim's hearsay statement that "stuff like tonight cost me a thousand dollars." The statement was made immediately after the victim and the defendants came out from a short meeting in the back of the victim's shop. The defendants argued that the statement could not be admitted under Rule 803(1) because there were no witnesses, other than the declarant and the defendants, to the relevant event—the purported exchange of money in the back of the declarant's shop—and the declarant was not available to testify. The court held that the statement was properly admitted, however, because "there were several witnesses who could testify to the events leading up to and following the meeting" in the back of the shop. These witnesses would testify that the defendants

---

[4]   *Miller v. Keating*, 754 F.2d 507, 510–11 (3d Cir. 1985).

[5]   607 F.2d 779 (7th Cir. 1979).

acted in a very intimidating manner before going to the back of the shop and that after the meeting, the defendants came out looking "satisfied." The court recognized that the hearsay exception did not require "that the witnesses be in the same position to observe as the declarant." But it was necessary "that the witnesses be able to corroborate the declarant's statement." That is, the declarant's statement is not itself enough to prove by a preponderance of the evidence that the event occurred.

In the Illustration, Janet can testify that Lena complained to her that Frank was very late, that Lena then made a statement to someone about being late, and then Janet heard a man's voice (although indistinct). This might be sufficient corroboration of Lena's report to Janet that it was Frank, given the context. But it is more likely that a judge would rule that the evidence can be offered to prove only that Lena met a man; Janet does not in the problem have familiarity with Frank's voice, and so she can only verify that it was a man, not Frank. Suppose, however, that Janet has personal knowledge that Lena has been dating Frank for months and that they typically go to the theater on Wednesdays (the day in which Lena called Janet). That might be sufficient corroboration to support introduction of Lena's entire statement.

Excited Utterance: Rule 803(2)   ~~Broader~~

Rule 803(2) provides a hearsay exception for the following kind of statement:

> **Excited Utterance.** A statement relating to a startling event or condition, made while the declarant was under the stress of excitement that it caused.

A close reading of the text of this rule suggests several contrasts between the exception for an excited utterance and the exception for a present sense impression. The latter confines admissibility to statements that *describe or explain* the event or condition in question. The subject-matter ambit of an excited utterance is broader: the declarant's statement need only *"relate to"* the exciting event.[6] In addition, the exception for excited utterances requires that the declarant speak while under the influence of stress or excitement; no such requirement attends a present sense impression.

The fact that an excited utterance, as the name suggests, is grounded on the declarant's mental state (excited, startled, stressed) suggests that the time lapse between the event and the declarant's statement relating to it is not always the central issue. It is true that

---

[6]   Suppose, for example, the excited declarant who witnessed a car bombing makes a statement about the late arrival of medical personnel. Her statement would "relate" to the explosion—the cause of the excitement.

people get less excited as more time passes after a startling event. But the fundamental question is whether the declarant was in a continuous state of emotional upheaval between the occurrence of the event and the time when she spoke. It is this feature—"excitement," broadly defined—that reduces the risk that the declarant is lying or consciously misleading the listener. The risk of inaccurate memory is also reduced because, as a practical matter, the declarant's emotional state will subside before her memory significantly declines.

Note, however, that the hearsay danger of inaccurate perception is probably increased: emotion and stress are associated with faulty perception.[7] The question, however, is not whether this or any other hearsay exception is flawless. The issue is whether allowing the trier of fact to evaluate the evidence in question is preferable to excluding the evidence and thus depriving the factfinder of relevant material. The party who unsuccessfully opposes the admission of hearsay evidence remains free to try to discredit its reliability.

Under the provisions of Rule 104(a), the judge, not the jury, decides if the declarant's statement satisfies the requirements of Rule 803(2). The essential elements are (1) an exciting event, (2) followed by the declarant's statement that relates to it, and (3) which was made while still under the stress caused by the exciting event, before there was opportunity for reflection and (hence) fabrication. The familiar requirement of personal knowledge also applies. The statement itself usually has considerable probative force in establishing these elements. As we have seen, the judge (freed from the usual rules of evidence under Rule 104(a)) may consider the declaration itself in ruling on the admissibility of the proffered statement. Suppose, for example, the driver of a car calls 911 and says,

> There has been a terrible accident on Route 340 at Jacob's Creek Bridge! Get help right away. A cement truck crossed into the wrong lane and hit a motorcycle. He's in the water—I mean the motorcyclist—may be dead. The truck just kept going. Hurry!

In this case, the statement strongly points toward an exciting event; the recitation of the details of that event suggest that the caller observed it; and his manner of speech and the phrasing of his report to the operator have considerable probative force to show that the

---

[7] In *United States v. Boyce*, 742 F.3d 792 (7th Cir. 2014), the court held that the trial judge did not abuse discretion in admitting as excited utterances statements made in a 911 call by a victim of domestic violence. Judge Posner concurred and expressed skepticism about both present sense impressions and excited utterances, arguing that there is no empirical basis for assuming that 1) it takes time to lie, and 2) you can't lie when you are excited. There are studies indicating, however, that it *does* take time and a calm mindset to craft a lie of the type that could be used in court.

accident caused the requisite emotional state in the observer-declarant. Moreover, any question about the existence of the event is satisfied by evidence of the event itself—in this case, the physical evidence of the accident. Exciting events tend to leave evidentiary traces. Furthermore, there would be evidence, perhaps supplied by the declarant, of the approximate period of time between the accident and the declarant's telephone call. And finally, the 911 operator could testify that the declarant seemed distressed and excited, or a recording of his call, if available, could be offered in evidence. It goes without saying that courts are much more comfortable admitting hearsay as an excited utterance when there is some evidence other than the statement itself to prove that the startling event occurred. One can assume that independent evidence supporting the statement will be required, but will also be abundant.

Now suppose the motorcyclist was unconscious when rescue workers pulled him from the water. Ten hours later, in the presence of his physician and his wife, he regains consciousness in the hospital. His wife says, "You are going to be all right; the doctors all say so. You are going to be all right. Do you know what happened?" He replies, in an excited manner, "I. . . ." "I was on the bridge, and a truck—a big cement truck—came right at me, right in my lane." The fact that the motorcyclist's statement came ten hours after the exciting event does not necessarily preclude the application of the excited utterance exception. Neither does the fact that the declarant spoke in response to a question. The now-familiar issue is whether the declarant spoke while still under the stressful influence of the startling event. The required immediacy, indispensable to the application of the exception for a present sense impression, is not always an operative feature of an excited utterance. Of course, had the declarant not been unconscious during the intervening ten-hour period, his statement would not be within the excited utterance exception. At some point, fairly soon after the accident, he would have regained sufficient composure to be capable of making up a false or misleading statement. In the present example, however, the declarant appears to have been in the requisite mental state of stress and shock when he spoke.

Observe, also, that the declarant in the example just above—the motorcyclist—was also a participant in the exciting event. Generally speaking, participant-observers are likely to maintain the required emotional state of excitement for a longer period than mere observers—personal involvement will add to the state of excitement. Other factors bearing on the duration of the state of excitement include the declarant's age (children, for example, are likely to be under the influence of a startling event for a longer time than adults), her physical and mental state, and the probable emotional impact of the event itself (e.g., a murder is likely to be upsetting for a longer period of time than a fist fight).

An additional feature that might bear on admissibility is whether or not the declarant can be identified. Suppose someone who is walking past a liquor store sees a robbery in progress. He dashes down the street to a shoe repair shop and says to the owner, "Quick! Call the cops. Two teenage kids with an assault rifle are robbing the liquor store." The call is made, but the declarant is never identified. Subsequently, *A* and *B*, two teenagers, are arrested and placed on trial for robbery. Should the fact that the declarant cannot be identified preclude testimony by the shoe repairman as to what the declarant said? The prevailing view is that an inability to identify the declarant is not, standing alone, fatal to the applicability of Rule 803(2). One risk is that the declarant never even existed, and is being made up by the witness—but that is a problem for cross-examination. The hearsay rule is concerned with whether a declarant is lying; if it is the *witness* that is lying, the remedy is cross-examination under oath. That said, courts proceed with more caution when the declarant is anonymous, because it can be difficult for the objector to demonstrate that the declarant lacked first-hand knowledge or to introduce impeaching evidence (such as bias) designed to weaken the probative force of the declarant's statement.

Sometimes, days or months after an emotional event such as a sexual assault or a carjacking, the declarant encounters something (e.g., the crime scene), or some person (e.g., the perpetrator), that vividly renews the memory of the exciting event and reignites the emotion and nervous stress that accompanied it. ("There he is—that's the man who tried to lock me in the car trunk and kidnap me!") Although the risk that the declarant's memory may be inaccurate is somewhat increased, the exception for excited utterances is ordinarily applicable in situations such as this because its essential requirements are usually satisfied.[8] The startling event is not the original event, because the declarant was not under a continuous state of excitement between that event and the statement. Rather, the startling event is the shock of seeing the perpetrator (or some other trigger) in such unexpected circumstances. And the statement (referring to the original trauma) is sufficiently "related" to this new startling event.

---

[8]   *State v. Brown*, 112 Ohio App.3d 583, 679 N.E.2d 361, 373 (1996) (child experienced nervous excitement when he returned to the crime scene where, three days earlier, he had witnessed his brother's murder).

§ 7.4 Physical or Mental Condition (the "State of Mind" Exception)

The hearsay exceptions for a declarant's statements concerning her physical or mental condition are well established. Their recognition is based in part on primacy: a principal means of learning about a person's bodily or mental condition is through her own statements. The declarant is usually in a favorable position to perceive and report her own physical or mental condition ("There is sharp pain in my lower back" or "I am depressed"). Even if the declarant is not always a reliable source of information, her declarations are nonetheless likely to facilitate evaluations by health care professionals and even family members. The emphasis in this section, of course, is upon using the declarant's statements for their truth. The danger of mistaken perception is arguably low, because it is the declarant assessing her own internal feeling. And the danger of inaccurate memory, at least when the exception is applied to statements disclosing a presently existing state of mind or bodily condition.

The "State of Mind" Exception: Rule 803(3)

Rule 803(3) provides that the hearsay rule will not exclude:

Then-Existing Mental, Emotional, or Physical Condition. A statement of the declarant's then-existing state of mind (such as motive, intent, or plan), or emotional, sensory, or physical condition (such as mental feeling, pain, or bodily health), but not including a statement of memory or belief to prove the fact remembered or believed unless it relates to the validity or terms of the declarant's will.[9]

ILLUSTRATIONS

Suppose a nurse is willing to testify concerning the following statements made by her late friend and patient, Thomas:

(1) "Today, the pain in my lower back is very acute."

(2) "I am so discouraged and depressed. For me, life is no longer worth living."

---

[9] The drafters of the Federal Rules concluded that a declarant's statement concerning his will falls into a special category. The unavailable declarant is the person who presumably knows the most about his will: typically his declaration concerns his own conduct, and normally a testator considers the execution or revocation of his will a serious matter. These considerations, coupled with the need to at least consider evidence concerning the testator's relevant statements, have carved out a special qualification to Federal Rule 803(3)'s general requirement that the statement cannot be offered to prove the truth of a past event.

(3) "I am not in this business just to be competitive—
as soon as I recover, I'm going to drive Cartwright, my last
competitor, out of business."

(4) "Don't try to convince me of Fred's redeeming
features! I can't stand the guy. When I revised my will last
month I left every nephew $50,000—except Fred. For him,
zero."

(5) "I vividly recall the year 2008; I was miserable for
most of it—migraine headaches every day or two."

(6) "Didn't I tell you? Don Purcell has quit his job with
Benchmark and will start working for me in January."

(7) "When I saw firsthand the way Edgar abuses
Alice—even batters her—that's when I decided not to leave
him a cent."

The first four illustrations appear to fit within the language of
Rule 803(3); the next two (5 and 6) do not; and the last (7) is
problematic. As always, of course, the initial question is the now
familiar one of relevance: does the proffered evidence tend to prove
or disprove a consequential fact? If we assume, for example, that the
proponent of the evidence in Illustration (1) needs to prove that the
declarant suffered back pain, evidence of the declarant's statement is
relevant and, under Rule 803(3), admissible. Likewise, if we assume
the declarant's depressed state of mind is relevant in Illustration
(2)—as it would be, for example, if the issue were suicide—the
declarant's statement also fits within the terms of Rule 803(3).

Let us assume, then, that each statement in the Illustration is
relevant. Illustration (3) has probative value to show the declarant's
presently held intention to drive his competitor out of the market; it
makes it more likely that he acted in accordance with his intent.
Illustration (4) falls within the special provision of Rule 803(3)
dealing with wills. Illustration (5) is a statement about a *past* state
of mind and physical condition—it fails the admissibility
requirement of Rule 803(3) that the statement reflect the declarant's
"then existing" state of mind at the time it was made.

In Illustration (6), the declarant expresses his belief or state of
mind regarding a past event (Don has quit). As such it is "backward
looking," so to speak, and is simply a statement of the declarant's
memory or belief. Thus, it is not within Rule 803(3) if offered to prove
the fact remembered or believed (with the only exception being a will
case). If statements of a past fact remembered or believed were to
qualify generally for admission under Rule 803(3), there would be
nothing left of the rule against hearsay (because every assertion that

is hearsay is offered for the truth of the fact remembered or believed by the declarant). Note that the statement also predicts a future event (Don will start working for me in January). But the predicted future event primarily concerns *not the declarant's state of mind, but the conduct of another*. Therefore, assuming this evidence is offered to prove that Don quit his job at Benchmark and went to work (or intended to go to work) for the declarant, it is hearsay as to both propositions and is not admissible under Rule 803(3).

The last Illustration is problematic because it is unclear what relevant fact the proponent is trying to prove. If the hearsay declaration is offered to prove that Edgar abused Alice, it is hearsay and not admissible under Rule 803(3)—it looks backward and is not a statement of the declarant's state of mind. However, if it is offered to prove that the declarant intentionally omitted Edgar from his will, at least the last portion of the statement would fit the special provision of 803(3) dealing with wills. The judge would have to decide whether to admit the entire statement (so that the jury can better understand what the testator was thinking) or, perhaps, exclude the first portion as prejudicial to Edgar, assuming he is a party.[10]

Rationale and Applications of the State of Mind Exception

When a declarant is speaking about her current state of mind, the hearsay dangers of mistaken perception and faulty memory are minimized. Furthermore, the frequency with which state of mind is an issue in litigation adds a practical need for this evidence. Often, the most convincing evidence of a declarant's state of mind is her own declaration. Thus, at an early date, common-law judges began admitting into evidence a declarant's statement concerning her own mental (or physical) condition. This is so even though there is a serious argument that such statements might be unreliable—i.e., they do not accurately reflect the declarant's state of mind, either because the declarant is confused about her own state of mind or is simply lying about how she feels.

Note the various contexts in which one's mental state becomes a relevant issue in litigation, both criminal and civil. For example, a crime is normally defined so as to require a particular mens rea or state of mind;[11] the measure of civil damages sometimes depends on the mental suffering of the victim or the malicious intent of the

---

[10]   The best argument for admitting the entire statement is that the first portion explains and strengthens the latter proposition that Edgar was intentionally omitted from the will.

[11]   Note that statements by an accused reflecting his state of mind are admissible against him as party-opponent statements, so resort to the state of mind exception is unnecessary for the prosecution. But Rule 803(3) is a potential ground of admissibility for statements by the defendant reflecting an *innocent* state of mind.

defendant (e.g., intentional infliction of emotional harm). The cases are replete with other instances in which mental state is an issue: the question of where one is domiciled is answered in part by a person's intention; the issue of whether a will was validly executed (or revoked) may turn upon intent; the question of whether one fraudulently conveyed assets turns primarily on his intention; and a business tort is usually defined to include the intention of the alleged wrongdoer. In these and similar instances, the substantive law itself specifies a particular state of mind and thus an actor's mental state often becomes a pivotal element at trial. In other words, mental state is often an ultimate proposition to which the parties address their conflicting evidence.

State of mind can also serve as circumstantial evidence of behavior. In this context, the declarant's state of mind is not itself an element of the case or an ultimate proposition; rather, a person's state of mind may be probative of that person's conduct. Suppose, for example, there is an issue at trial concerning whether an individual has left the United States and returned to his native country. Evidence that he often expressed deep affection for his homeland and that he also declared that he intended to return there permanently provide a basis for the inference that in fact he did.

Observe that even though the state of mind exception is limited to the expression of a *presently existing* state of mind, the trier can make reasonable inferences that the same state of mind existed at an earlier or later date. Thus, if a declarant stated in August that he loved his girlfriend, the trier could draw an inference that he loved her in July and September—that's a question of probative value. On the other hand, if the declarant makes a statement in August, "I fell in love with my girlfriend last month" this would not be admissible under the state of mind exception, because it is not a statement about the declarant's current state of mind.

The Hillmon Doctrine

In Illustration (3) above, the declarant expresses his intention to take certain action in the future—that is, to drive his competitor, Cartwright, out of business. We noted that the declarant's statement was within Rule 803(3)'s exception. This application of the state-of-mind exception to the hearsay rule—that is, using statements of a declarant's current state of mind to prove subsequent conduct in accordance with that state of mind—was first articulated by the United States Supreme Court in a famous case, *Mutual Life Ins. Co. v. Hillmon.*[12]

---

[12]   145 U.S. 285 (1892).

The central issue in *Hillmon* was whether a body discovered at Crooked Creek, Kansas, was that of Hillmon, the insured, or that of Walters, a companion. In an effort to prove that Walters was present at Crooked Creek (and thus the body could have been his), the defendant insurance company offered as evidence several letters written by Walters to his family and fiancée. In these letters Walters declared his intention to leave Wichita, Kansas, and travel with a new acquaintance, a sheepherder named Hillmon, to the vicinity of Crooked Creek. The Supreme Court held that Walters' written statements were admissible under the state of mind exception to prove that Walters was at Crooked Creek, because they showed his presently held intention to travel there with Hillmon. This intention was, of course, relevant because it increased somewhat the probability that Walters embarked upon his intended journey, reached his destination, and that the body was his. Notably, there was no issue in the *Hillmon* case concerning whether or not Hillmon was present at Crooked Creek; the parties agreed that he was there.

Assume, however, that the issue in the case had been whether *Hillmon* was at Crooked Creek at the time of the death in question. The problem we confront is whether Walters' declaration—I am going with Hillmon—is admissible under the state of mind exception to prove the conduct of the non-declarant, Hillmon.

In the course of the *Hillmon* opinion, Justice Gray, its author, stated:

> The letters in question were competent . . . as evidence that, shortly before the time when other evidence tended to show that he went away, he had the intention of going, and of going with Hillmon, which made it more probable *both that he did go and that he went with Hillmon* than if there had been no proof of such intention.[13]

Thus, at least in dictum, the Court approved of the evidentiary use of Walters' declaration for proof not only of Walters' future conduct, but Hillmon's as well. This apparent extension of the *Hillmon* doctrine, exceeding the facts actually before the Court (because there was no dispute as to Hillmon's presence at Crooked Creek), would allow the declarant's statement not only to prove his own future conduct, but also the cooperative conduct of another. But the problem with this extension is that it allows the proponent to prove not only the *declarant's* state of mind but also the state of mind of another (i.e., that *Hillmon* intended to go to Crooked Creek). And there is nothing in the state of mind exception that guarantees the reliability of the declarant's opinion about a state of mind that is not his own.

---

13   *Hillmon*, 145 U.S. at 295–96 [emphasis supplied].

ILLUSTRATIONS

(1) Larry, a high school student, was apparently kidnapped—at least his father received demands for a ransom. Even though Larry was never found, Angelo is brought to trial on a kidnapping charge. The prosecution calls several of Larry's friends who testify that, on the day Larry disappeared, he told them he was going to meet Angelo at 9:30 p.m. in the parking lot of Sundown's Restaurant to pick up a package of marijuana. One friend, for example, testified over objection that while he and Larry were sitting at a table in Sundown's, Larry said that it was "time to pick up the pot from Angelo in the parking lot" and that he "would be right back."[14]

Assuming there was no evidence of Angelo's whereabouts, is this testimony admissible?

(2) Assume the same facts as in (1), except there is other evidence from which the trier of fact could reasonably conclude that Angelo was in Sundown's parking lot at the appointed hour.

Should this be the decisive factor in the trial judge's ruling?

The difficulty in Illustration (1) is apparent: Larry's statement really has two assertions: "I am going to meet Angelo" and "Angelo is going to meet me." Implicit in these assertions is some prior arrangement between Larry and Angelo by which Angelo agreed to meet Larry in Sundown's parking lot to deliver a package of marijuana. A statement such as "Angelo and I agreed that we would meet at nine o'clock in Sundown's parking lot" does not fit within the state-of-mind exception. It is a statement of memory or belief about a past fact. Furthermore, Larry's statement in Illustration (1) is, at least in part, a declaration *about what someone else—Angelo—will do in the future.*

Some courts admit statements by *X* that he intends to do something jointly (or in cooperation) with *Y,* at least under certain conditions.[15] In other words, Justice Gray's dictum in the *Hillmon* case has sometimes proved decisive. Many of these courts, though, paradoxically attempt to confine the state-of-mind exception by instructing the jury, for example, that the declarant's statement may

---

[14]   This Illustration, with only minor departures, tracks the facts in *United States v. Pheaster,* 544 F.2d 353 (9th Cir. 1976).

[15]   Id. at 376–80; *State v. Terrovona,* 105 Wash.2d 632, 716 P.2d 295, 298–301 (1986) (victim tells girlfriend that he is going to help accused who ran out of gas at 116th St.; subsequently victim's body found at 116th St.); *People v. Alcalde,* 24 Cal.2d 177, 148 P.2d 627, 631–32 (1944) (victim states she is "going out with [the accused] Frank tonight;" victim is murdered that night).

be used only as evidence of his own intention and conduct[16] (which is to say, the *Hillmon* dictum is not in fact followed, because the evidence is not in fact admitted to prove the conduct of someone other than the declarant). Others that admit such statements provide a protective requirement that the declarant's statement is admissible only if there is evidence corroborating the conduct of the other person.[17] Others simply find that the hearsay statement of a declarant is never admissible under the state of mind exception to prove the subsequent conduct of another person.

The first restriction noted above—admitting the statement only to prove the declarant's conduct and not that of the other actor—is too technical for the jury to adhere to or even understand. If X says "I'm going out with Y tonight" and the jury is allowed to hear the entire statement, it is difficult, to say the least, for the jury to ignore the portion of the statement referring to Y's participation. On firmer ground is the requirement enforced by some courts that there be other (corroborative) evidence of Y's conduct. Independent evidence of Y's conduct makes it more likely that the statement is accurate. Concerns about unreliability will be assuaged if there is enough corroborative evidence to sustain independently a jury finding of Y's conduct. As in Illustration (2), the jury now has before it evidence of the declarant's (Larry's) future conduct (his declaration) and independent evidence that is sufficient to uphold a jury finding of Angelo's conduct. But the problem is that the corroboration analysis can be flimsy; and in the end the state of mind exception simply does not allow admission of the state of mind of someone other than the declarant. Nor does the text of the rule embrace, or even mention, a corroboration requirement. So courts allowing corroboration are reading a factor into the rule that is not there.[18]

Bear in mind that the principal dispute over the boundaries of the *Hillmon* doctrine center on statements in which X declares her intention to meet Y or to undertake some joint activity with Y, and X's declaration is offered not only as proof of her conduct, but of Y's as well. Even the expansive version of *Hillmon* does not permit the use of a declaration by X that does not embrace her own conduct, but simply predicts Y's future conduct. Thus, Larry's statement, "Angelo is doing a drug deal tonight" is in no way admissible under the state

---

[16]   *Alcalde*, 148 P.2d at 632.

[17]   *United States v. Delvecchio*, 816 F.2d 859, 863 (2d Cir. 1987).

[18]   For an application of the corroboration requirement, *see People v. James*, 93 N.Y.2d 620, 695 N.Y.S.2d 715, 717 N.E.2d 1052 (1999). The question in the case was whether James was at a meeting in which answers to an exam were unlawfully handed out in advance. Corroboration was found mainly by the fact that when he took the exam the day after the meeting, he got every question right. Then, when the results were invalidated (due to suspicion of taint) and a new exam was given shortly thereafter, James took it again and flunked.

of mind exception. If it were, that would be the exception that
swallowed the hearsay rule, because every statement is in some way
a reflection of a person's state of mind.

ILLUSTRATIONS

Examine the following hearsay statements and
determine whether either (or both) of them should be
admitted under Rule 803(3)'s exception for state of mind (or
bodily condition):

(1)   In the prosecution of husband (Y) for the murder
of wife (X), the latter's statement, "I'm so afraid of what Y
will do. He has threatened to kill me and I know he will as
soon as he thinks he can get away with it."

NO

(2)   In the prosecution of Y (an illegal drug dealer) for
the murder of X (a drug distributor), X's statement to his
girlfriend, "I'll be back in about an hour and we can go out;
first, I need to see Y and I'm going over to his condo now."

YES

In Illustration (1), assume that Y's defense is that he did not kill
his wife, X, but someone else did. In this event, as in many cases of
murder, the *victim's* state of mind is irrelevant under the substantive
law; that is, her state of mind is not an element of the crime.
Therefore, the only relevant purpose of the evidence is to show what
Y did and for this purpose the wife's statement is inadmissible
hearsay.

Of course, the victim's mental state sometimes bears on her
relevant conduct. Suppose the victim says, "Tonight I'm going to tell
him it's over—that I'm leaving and I'm taking the kids." Such a
forward-looking statement is within the *Hillmon* doctrine. The
declarant is stating what *she* intends to do (confront the other person
and announce her departure), which makes it more likely that she
did that very thing.

YES - ILLUSTRATION #1

However, as we noted above, the victim's statement in
Illustration (1) is relevant only for its bearing on what the husband
allegedly said and did. Therefore it is inadmissible hearsay. X's
statement that Y threatened to kill her is simply a statement of her
recollection. Furthermore it carries another hearsay difficulty: there
is no way to cross-examine the deceased, X, as to whether or not Y
actually made these threats. X's statement that she held the belief
that in the near future Y would kill her is forward-looking. However,
it is not a declaration of *her* intended conduct, but rather that of her
husband. There is no dispute about X's conduct and therefore there
is no justification under *Hillmon* to use a statement about her state

of mind to prove her conduct. Thus, the statement in Illustration (1) should be inadmissible, and most courts would so hold.[19]

Illustration (2) falls comfortably within the *Hillmon* doctrine. The declarant, *X*, states his presently-held intention to go to *Y's* condominium and return. There is no statement about *Y's* activities or even his presence in the condominium. If it is relevant that *X* was there—for example, because it provided *Y* or *Y's* henchman with the opportunity to kill *X*—the statement is admissible. *X's* assertion avoids the hearsay rule because it is excepted from it by Federal Rule 803(3). There is no doubt that Rule 803(3) includes the declarant's statement of what he intends to do; difficulties arise only when the declarant's assertion includes what he intends to do in association with another.

Statements That Look Backward: The Shepard Rule

The Supreme Court had occasion to revisit the famous *Hillmon* doctrine in *Shepard v. United States*,[20] decided four decades after *Hillmon*. In this case, Dr. Shepard was prosecuted for the murder of his wife by poisoning her. There was evidence that shortly before dying, Mrs. Shepard summoned her nurse and asked to examine the contents of a whiskey bottle. Stating that this was the liquor she drank just before collapsing, she asked whether there was enough remaining in the bottle to permit a test for the presence of poison. After remarking that the taste and smell were strange, she concluded, "Dr. Shepard has poisoned me."

At trial, Mrs. Shepard's statements were admitted under the hearsay exception for dying declarations.[21] On appeal, however, it was held that the prosecution had failed to provide adequate evidence of an essential feature of that exception, namely, that the declarant spoke while believing that her death was imminent. There remained, however, two possibilities for upholding the trial court's decision to admit Mrs. Shepard's statements. First, admission of this evidence might be sustained on the ground that her statements had probative value to rebut defense evidence that Mrs. Shepard was depressed and had suicidal intentions. (The government pressed this contention.) Under this theory, the evidence would not be used to prove any fact stated or suggested by Mrs. Shepard's statements, but only for the limited purpose of showing that her state of mind was consistent with a will to live. Second, even if Mrs. Shepard's statements were hearsay, the government argued that the statements were within the

---

[19]   *See, e.g., United States v. Joe*, 8 F.3d 1488, 1492–93 (10th Cir. 1993); *United States v. Brown*, 490 F.2d 758, 763–64 (D.C. Cir. 1973). *Contra State v. Alston*, 341 N.C. 198, 461 S.E.2d 687, 704 (1995).

[20]   290 U.S. 96 (1933).

[21]   *See* Fed. R. Evid. 804(b)(2), discussed later in this Chapter.

state-of-mind exception to the hearsay rule—to prove her state of mind of memory or belief that Doctor Shepard had poisoned her.

Justice Cardozo's opinion for the Supreme Court rejected both of these possibilities. He found unconvincing the argument that Mrs. Shepard's statements could have been properly received for the limited, non-hearsay purpose of showing her will to live. The overriding feature of her statements was their accusatory thrust, directed toward the defendant's conduct and guilt. Even a carefully crafted limiting instruction to the jury, restricting its members to a consideration of Mrs. Shepard's statement solely to determine her state of mind, could not overcome "[t]he reverberating clang of those accusatory words, [which] would drown out all weaker sounds."[22] Most importantly, no such instruction was actually given at trial— which is not surprising, because Mrs. Shepard's declaration was admitted for its truth at the trial.

The final question was whether Mrs. Shepard's statements might qualify for admission under the exception for a declarant's expressions of her state of mind.[23] Here, of course, the theory was that although the statements were hearsay, they could nonetheless be admitted for their truth because the applicable exception renders cross-examination of the declarant unnecessary. Observing that the principal probative force of the statements in question was directed toward *past* acts of *another* person, Justice Cardozo emphasized the limits of the *Hillmon* doctrine and the state of mind exception to the hearsay rule:

> Declarations of intention, casting light upon the future, have been sharply distinguished from declarations of memory, pointing backwards to the past. There would be an end, or nearly that, to the rule against hearsay if the distinction were ignored.

> The testimony now questioned faced backward and not forward. This it did, in at least its most obvious implications. What is even more important, it spoke to a past act, and more than that, to the act of someone not the speaker.[24]

The *Shepard* opinion reaffirms the principal limitations on the *Hillmon* doctrine. Generally speaking, that doctrine, now embodied in Federal Rule 803(3), is restricted to proof of forward-looking

---

[22]   *Shepard*, 290 U.S. at 104. This was essentially a Rule 403 analysis, conducted before there was a Rule 403.

[23]   Under the government's argument, this particular switch of admissibility theories did not prejudice the defendant, because it would justify using Mrs. Shepard's declaration for its truth, as it was used at trial.

[24]   Id. at 105–106.

declarations in which the declarant states his intention to undertake a course of conduct in the future. A statement of memory or belief cannot be admitted under the state of mind exception to prove that the fact remembered or believed is true. Thus, "I went to the store yesterday" cannot be admitted under Rule 803(3) to prove that you went to the store yesterday. In contrast, "I am going to the store tomorrow" can be offered, under *Hillmon*, for the inference that you acted in accordance with your intent to go.

As we have seen, however, statements by the declarant about his will fall into a special category: such statements not only may look to the future ("I intend to execute a codicil tomorrow."), but may refer to the past as well ("After Emma died, I tore up my will."). The assumption of Rule 803(3) is that in a will contest the testatrix's absence justifies the admission of all relevant information that would inform her intent.

Polls or Opinion Surveys

Persons conducting surveys and opinion polls often ask their respondents questions that are designed to elicit responses concerning their state of mind. For example: "Do you think the country is moving in the right direction?", or "Who do you think makes this handbag?" These responses raise hearsay issues, but most courts find that the statements are admissible under the state of mind exception when the results are offered to show what the respondents thought.[25] If, however, the poll results are offered as proof of an underlying fact—e.g., how many people purchased a handbag or voted in an election—the state of mind exception would not be applicable, because (as we saw in *Shepard*) the hearsay exception cannot be used to admit statements offered to prove the truth of a past fact (such as "I voted"). But surveys collecting facts may be admissible under some other hearsay exception, most likely the "residual" exception discussed later in this chapter.

Of course, for polling results to come before the trier of fact, the proponent must show that the survey employed a reliable methodology. Such features as the selection of a sampling area, the determination of a random selection within it, the design of the questions, and the execution of the interviews can be important factors in the survey's accuracy. The survey methodology must be established as reliable under Federal Rule 702, governing expert testimony. Issues related to the reliability of expert testimony are discussed in Chapter XI.

---

[25]   *See Schering Corp. v. Pfizer Inc.*, 189 F.3d 218 (2d Cir. 1999) (results of opinion poll should have been admitted under the state of mind exception).

§ 7.5   Statements for Purposes of Medical Diagnosis or Treatment

The traditional basis for this exception rests on the assumption that persons seeking medical treatment have an incentive to be truthful: proper treatment may depend on the patient's accurate description of his condition and symptoms. In addition, a lay person is likely to assume that a physician, trained in medicine, might easily detect a patient's exaggerations and falsehoods. Finally, a statement to be admissible under this exception must be pertinent to a doctor's treatment or diagnosis. And if a doctor would take such a statement into account in treating or diagnosing a person, that should mean that the statement is reliable enough to be considered by a jury.

Federal Rule 803(4)

Rule 803(4) excepts from the hearsay rule:

(4)   *Statement Made for Medical Diagnosis or Treatment.* A statement that:

>   **(A)**   is made for—and is reasonably pertinent to—medical diagnosis or treatment; and

>   **(B)**   describes medical history; past or present symptoms or sensations; their inception; or their general cause.

The central requirement of this hearsay exception is that the statement in question be made for purposes of medical diagnosis or treatment—including medical history, past as well as present symptoms, and the external cause of the patient's condition if relevant to the diagnosis or treatment. Frequently, statements falling within Rule 803(4) will be made by the patient to her physician. The rule, however, is not limited to this typical setting.

ILLUSTRATION

A mother takes her tearful and injured six-year-old daughter to the hospital emergency room. When she arrives at the desk of the intake nurse, the mother says, "Please have her examined right away. She lost control of her bicycle and went over the curb and into the street. An old man who wasn't looking where he was driving sideswiped the bike, and she hit the pavement really hard. She was unconscious—then in a few minutes she came to and started crying."

A close reading of Rule 803(4) leads to the conclusion that, with the exception of one portion, the mother's statements qualify for admission. Her account makes it reasonably clear that she had firsthand knowledge. Her statements about her daughter's injury are made to the nurse for purposes of diagnosis and treatment—it need not be the declarant getting the treatment. And a statement need not be made to a doctor; if for purposes of obtaining treatment or diagnosis it could be made to anyone in the medical care field or even to a family member or colleague. (For example: "Quick, get me to the hospital—I have severe pains in my chest and my arms feel numb.")

The language of Rule 803(4) includes within the exception statements pertaining to the "general cause" of the patient's condition if they are reasonably pertinent to diagnosis or treatment. The facts that the child was thrown from her bicycle and onto a hard surface after being obliquely struck by a car are pertinent to diagnosis or treatment. (For example, the attending physician would be more alert to serious internal injuries.)

The only portion of the mother's account that falls outside the boundaries of Rule 803(4) is her remark that her daughter was hit by "an old man who wasn't looking where he was driving." As the Advisory Committee states, Rule 803(4) is broad enough to include "a patient's statement that he was struck by an automobile . . . but not his statement that the car was driven though a red light."[26] A statement that the man was at fault does not further any treatment or diagnosis. Consider, however, the possibility that the portion of the mother's account not within Rule 803(4) might qualify as an excited utterance. It is certainly plausible to argue that the mother was still stressed and excited when she spoke to the nurse and that her statement about the old man's inattention "relates to" the exciting event.[27]

Statements in a Medical Record

Very often, statements that are within Rule 803(4)'s purview are contained in a medical record. Where that is so, the proponent will offer the record to prove what the declarant's words were, and then invoke Rule 803(4) in order to permit the trier to use the declarant's statement for its truth. This process involves linking two hearsay exceptions. Normally, we require that the witness to the hearsay statement take the stand and testify as to what the declarant (e.g., the patient) said. The presence of the witness permits the opponent to cross-examine regarding whether or not the declarant did in fact make the statement that the proponent claims. When the proponent uses a medical record in lieu of the live witness, it is necessary for her to invoke a hearsay exception that permits the trier of fact to find that the statement was made. In other words, because the opponent cannot cross-examine the medical record in an effort to disprove any

[26]   Fed. R. Evid. 803(4) ACN.
[27]   *See* Fed. R. Evid. 803(2).

statement allegedly made by the declarant (or to show that the statement actually made was different from the one recorded), the record itself must comply with the terms of a hearsay exception.[28] The exception that usually facilitates this line of proof is contained in Rule 803(6); that exception covers statements contained in regularly prepared and maintained business records.

ILLUSTRATION

In a civil proceeding in which a state agency sues to terminate the custody rights of a stepfather, Morris, the agency's lawyer proffers a medical record. The record was prepared by Dr. Wolf, who had examined Morris' stepdaughter, Hilda, age 12. After the examination, Dr. Wolf made medical-record entries indicating that his examination disclosed "vaginal ruptures, the presence of semen in the vagina, and psychological trauma." Another entry made by Wolf states that "Patient, Hilda, says that her stepfather, Morris, came into her bedroom last night around midnight and raped her."

How should the trial judge rule on Morris' hearsay objection?

The physician's medical findings were made in the regular course of business and, as we shall later see, should qualify for admissibility under Rule 803(6). Dr. Wolf's entry recording Hilda's account of the events of the preceding night was also made in the regular course of the doctor's (or hospital's) business, thus permitting the use of the medical record to prove what Hilda told Wolf. Rule 803(4)—statements for purposes of medical diagnosis and treatment—permits the trier to use Hilda's statement for the truth of its contents—that she was sexually assaulted by Morris.[29] In many situations, the identity of perpetrator or tortfeasor would not be pertinent to diagnosis or treatment. In the Illustration, however, Morris's identity *would* be pertinent. Proper psychological counseling (or proper referral by the examining physician) would be influenced by the nature of the relationship (stepfather and stepdaughter) between Morris and Hilda. Furthermore, proper treatment hinges in part on not returning Hilda to Morris's care.

---

[28]   Rule 805 provides that "[h]earsay within hearsay is not excluded by the rule against hearsay if each part of the combined statements conforms with an exception to the rule."

[29]   If this were a criminal case, and if Hilda were not available as a witness (and thus could not be cross-examined by Morris), there would be an issue as to whether the Sixth Amendment's Confrontation Clause should bar Hilda's declarations about Morris. As we will see, this particular statement probably would not violate the Confrontation Clause because it is not "testimonial." *See generally* Chapter VIII.

Statements Made for Litigation Purposes

We have noted that Rule 803(4) removes from the hearsay ban statements made solely for the purpose of a medical *diagnosis* (even though not for the purpose of treatment). Some doctors diagnose a condition for other doctors to treat, and it is clear that the exception should cover statements made to the diagnostician. But some doctors might diagnose a condition in anticipation of testifying at a trial. In the expert witness situation, the patient's statements of present and past conditions carry greater hearsay risks then would be present if the patient were also seeking treatment. The stimulus to truthtelling that presumably exists when the patient is aware that proper treatment or diagnosis depends in part on his candid disclosures to the physician is not operative where the patient seeks a diagnosis for partisan purposes.

The risk that the patient's statements to medical personnel might be false or misleading when made in anticipation of litigation caused most common law judges to hold that these statements could not be admitted for their truth. Nonetheless, under the common-law approach, the patient's statements of medical history as well as past and present conditions were admissible not for their truth, but rather to apprise the trier of the basis (or at least part of it) upon which the expert grounded his opinion.[30] Thus, the jury was made aware of the patient's remarks to, say, the examining physician, following which the jurors were instructed to consider the patient's statements solely for their bearing on the physician's expert opinion, and not for their truth.

Most jurors were probably bewildered by such an instruction and would have found it difficult to follow. Moreover, jurors can usually appreciate the potential for the patient's (typically, plaintiff's) suspect motivation and thus, when appropriate, can discount the probative value of his statement to the examining physician when made for purposes of litigation. Thus, the federal drafters took the pragmatic view that there was little or no practical gain in attempting to distinguish between statements for purposes of treatment or medical diagnosis and those for purposes of diagnosis in anticipation of litigation. As we have seen, Rule 803(4) includes descriptions of medical history, as well as past and present symptoms, when made for and reasonably pertinent to "medical diagnosis or treatment."

---

[30]   Typically, the expert's opinion will be based on medical tests and the patient's account of his medical history, including past and present symptoms.

§ 7.6   Recorded Recollection (Past Recollection Recorded)

At the beginning of this chapter, we made the observation that the hearsay exceptions are based more upon the commonplace observations of judges and lawyers than upon academic disciplines such as the social sciences. Most of us, for example, have had the experience of not being able to recall a particular fact or event, only to have it reenter conscious memory when someone—or something, like a writing—reminds us of the relevant historical context or points out some salient feature of the forgotten incident. This common experience of recovering memory in response to some stimulus or catalyst underlies the evidentiary rule that allows counsel to use leading questions, a writing, a sound recording, or some other means to refresh a witness's recollection. If one or more of these techniques is effective, then the witness's testimony (based on her refreshed recollection) constitutes the evidence for the jury's consideration. The technique or device used to prompt the now-revived recollection has served a useful function; it is not, however, evidence.

The hearsay exception for past recollection recorded (or simply, "recorded recollection") draws upon another widely-shared experience.[31] Most persons have had the experience of observing something, promptly making a record of the observed event, and, at a later date, having confidence that the recordation is accurate, even though the event itself has faded from memory.

Federal Rule 803(5)

Rule 803(5) removes from the hearsay ban:

(5) *Recorded Recollection.* A record that:

> **(A)** is on a matter the witness once knew about but now cannot recall well enough to testify fully and accurately;
>
> **(B)** was made or adopted by the witness when the matter was fresh in the witness's memory; and
>
> **(C)** accurately reflects the witness's knowledge.

If admitted, the record may be read into evidence but may be received as an exhibit only if offered by an adverse party.

The contrast between refreshing a witness's memory and having a witness affirm the accuracy of a prior recording becomes clear when

---

[31]   Rule 803(5) was introduced in Chapter II § 2.5.

Rule 803(5) is carefully examined. The "Rule 803(5) witness" either has no recollection of the event or condition in question or his partial recollection is insufficient to enable him to testify "fully and accurately." Thus, it is the record itself that serves as proof of the matter it describes. The witness's role is to provide foundational testimony that is akin to the testimony of an authenticating witness. When the proper foundation is complete, the memorandum or record is read (or played) in the jury's presence.

The record itself is not received into evidence as an exhibit, unless "offered by an adverse party." The intent of this latter provision is to reduce the chance that the jury will give undue weight to the record, because exhibits are not only examined by the jury when received in evidence, but also often carried to the jury room when the jury retires to deliberate. The rationale of the provision is that the past recollection recorded should be treated like any other trial testimony, and trial testimony is *not* accessible in the jury room during deliberations. (The opponent, of course, has the option of offering the record into evidence, which he would ordinarily not do unless he thought the writing or record was inaccurate and that this inaccuracy would be highlighted by the jury's further examination.)

The central features of Rule 803(5) are these:

1.   The witness once had personal knowledge of the event or condition in question, but by the time she takes the stand her memory has faded to the point that she is unable to testify fully and accurately.

2.   The witness made or adopted a record of the event or condition in question *when her memory was fresh*; there is no requirement that the record be made or verified "immediately" or "promptly" after the witness's observations.

3.   There must be evidence—and the testifying witness usually supplies it—sufficient for the judge to conclude that the record correctly reflects the witness's knowledge at the time the record was made or verified.

In the typical setting, the witness who prepared the writing or other record will take the stand and supply all of the necessary foundational conditions, including her present inability to recall sufficiently the event or condition in question. Indeed the witness *must* take the stand to testify to lack of present memory for this exception to be available.

Two-Person Transmissions

The evidentiary routine is essentially the same when a record is prepared by one person—for example, the secretary to a commission or committee—and verified as accurate by another, such as the Committee chair, when the latter's memory of the recorded event or condition was fresh. A slightly different evidentiary routine is followed when a declarant-observer reports her observations to another, who then records them but does not show the resulting record to the declarant for her verification.

ILLUSTRATION

Bystander sees a hooded man dash out of a bank and run quickly to a parked car in a nearby alley. As he speeds away, Bystander is able to read his license plate. When Bystander reaches the bank he is met by Security Guard who tells Bystander the bank has just been robbed and is closed until further notice. Bystander then reports what he saw and gives the license number and state of registration of the getaway car as "VA-YT468." The Security Guard records the information, as well as Bystander's name, address, and telephone number.

At trial, the prosecutor wants to show that the defendant's car (VA-YT468) was at the scene of the crime and was driven away by the robber. Both Bystander and Security Guard are available to testify. Bystander, who cannot now recall the license plate number, wishes to testify that he gave the plate number to Guard when his (Bystander's) memory was fresh and that the number he then gave was accurate. Guard will, if allowed, testify that he accurately recorded the license plate number that Bystander stated was on the getaway car.[32]

Should the trial judge allow the proffered testimony and admit into evidence Security Guard's memorandum as past recollection recorded?

Suppose that after observing the license plate number, Bystander promptly entered it on his smartphone. At trial he takes the stand and testifies that his memory was fresh when he made the entry, that the entry accurately records what he saw, and that he cannot now remember the license number. Bystander's record should be admitted as past recollection recorded as all the foundation requirements for the exception have been met.

---

[32] For similar facts, *see United States v. Booz*, 451 F.2d 719 (3d Cir. 1971); *see also United States v. Lewis*, 954 F.2d 1386 (7th Cir. 1992).

If this result is correct, then why should not the collaborative efforts of two persons with firsthand knowledge—one who saw and spoke, the other who heard and recorded—also satisfy the requirements of Rule 803(5)? Although a record is normally "made" by the observer, there is no reason why the two separate functions (observing and recording) cannot be carried out by two persons. As you might anticipate, however, *it is necessary that both participants take the stand and testify.* From an analytical perspective, there is one witness who once had reliable knowledge about the event observed (but who cannot now remember) and another witness who once had reliable knowledge about what he recorded (but who has no firsthand knowledge of what the person whose statement he recorded actually saw). Each, respectively, can testify that what was said or recorded was accurate. This is the essence of Rule 803(5).

Here are two final, but important points. First, suppose that in the Illustration above, Bystander was not available to testify. Security Guard is then able only to provide the foundation that he is confident that he recorded accurately what Bystander said. The problem is that Security Guard has no knowledge of whether what Bystander said is true. Yet it seems clear that Bystander's statement is being offered for its truth. This will be seen even more strikingly if Bystander said (and Guard had recorded), "The man who ran out of the bank was a very tall white man; he carried a black satchel, and he had a slight limp as he ran to a blue Lincoln, license 'VA-YT468' and sped away." All of the hearsay dangers are, presumably, present.

This means that Rule 803(5) cannot be the vehicle for admitting the Security Guard's record, because it contains underlying hearsay that is not admissible under any exception. Suppose, however, that Bystander's statement could be qualified as a "present sense impression"[33] or an "excited utterance."[34] If Security Guard recalls the statement, he could then testify to it and it would be admitted under one of the two hearsay exceptions. But, what if Security Guard does not fully recall the substance of what Bystander said? As long as Security Guard testifies that he wrote down accurately what Bystander said, his writing will itself qualify as recorded recollection.

The second, and closing, comment about the "recorded recollection" exception concerns the occasional difficulty of providing evidence sufficient to allow the court to conclude that the witness's earlier recordation accurately reflected his knowledge. Sometimes the foundational evidence is necessarily circumstantial, for the witness cannot recall making the particular entry in question. Suppose, for example, the witness, a security guard, is able to recall

---

[33]   *See* Fed. R. Evid. 803(1).

[34]   *See* Fed. R. Evid. 803(2).

only that when he checks the security system, he "always records the working condition of each alarm and, when he fills out his report, specifically notes any problems he detected." Although the guard may not recall the night in question, his systematic routine of checking and recording (habit or custom) should provide sufficient evidence for the court to conclude that his entries were correct.

§ 7.7   Business and Public Records

Introduction

This section covers two frequently used hearsay exceptions: business records and public records. Because these exceptions share some characteristics, it is useful to consider them in tandem. Each of these exceptions requires that the declarant's hearsay statements be contained in a writing or other record that can be accessed by persons in addition to those who created it. Furthermore, declarations within the purview of these exceptions are usually relied upon by others, who are often in a position to detect mistakes or false entries. Finally, the declarant is usually disinterested insofar as the *content* of the record is concerned and typically is motivated to be careful and accurate because unreliable entries may adversely affect job performance.

Note that a business document or public record is often a composite of several business or public entries made by different persons. Let us begin with an example from the business world. A "Statement of Current Inventory" reflecting items in a clothing store might be based upon entries from the receiving department, from accounting, from persons who stock the display areas, and from the sales and return departments. Generally speaking, if each person supplying the information for an entry did so in the regular course of business and had personal knowledge of the facts she supplied, the composite record is admissible. In other words, it suffices for admissibility that the business employee *supplying the information* had personal knowledge, even if the recorder did not. For example, if someone in the receiving department e-mails a clerk in the accounting department that a particular shipment of men's shoes is defective and is being returned to the distributor, subsequent entries by the accounting clerk are admissible. The person who was the source of the information had personal knowledge and (we will assume) was making his report in the regular course of business; the clerk also (let us assume) had a regular business duty to record returned shipments as reported by the receiving department.

This transaction and many others are likely to be reflected in the composite inventory tally that appears on the "Statement of Current Inventory." It is not necessary to call each person who contributed entries that appear in, or affect, the totals in the inventory report. (Such a requirement would make it almost impossible in many cases to admit business records—and cross-examination of all the people who had a hand in an unremarkable record would have little utility.) Nor is it required that the person who provides the evidentiary foundation for the current inventory statement have personal knowledge of each underlying transaction. It is, however, necessary that the person authenticating the inventory statement be familiar with the record-keeping procedures of the clothing store, for she must confirm that each statement or entry that contributed to the composite record was made in the regular course of business.

In due course, we will examine more closely the foundation required for the admission of business records, as well as the foundation required for public records. These requirements differ in some respects. Generally speaking, the proponent of a business record must provide testimonial or written evidence that the record was compiled in the regular course of business. The proponent of a public record must establish that it is the record of a duly authorized public office.

Business Records

The term "business records" embraces a wide variety of regularly conducted activities, including the activities of such disparate enterprises as hospitals, charities, fire departments, public utilities, and other regularly conducted activities, whether or not conducted for profit. The key is regularity and, in particular, regularity in record keeping. A business (or other enterprise) relies on its own records and, typically, so do third parties that interact with it. This reliance is one of the factors that justifies the business-entry exception to the hearsay rule. Those who place reliance on recorded facts and figures have an incentive to monitor the accuracy of their informational base.

Rule 803(6) provides an exception to the hearsay rule for:

(6) *Records of a Regularly Conducted Activity.* A record of an act, event, condition, opinion, or diagnosis if:

> **(A)** the record was made at or near the time by—or from information transmitted by—someone with knowledge;

> **(B)** the record was kept in the course of a regularly conducted activity of a business, organization, occupation, or calling, whether or not for profit;

> **(C)** making the record was a regular practice of that activity;

> **(D)** all these conditions are shown by the testimony of the custodian or another qualified witness, or by a certification that complies with Rule 902(11) or (12) or with a statute permitting certification; and
>
> **(E)** the opponent does not show that the source of information or the method or circumstances of preparation indicate a lack of trustworthiness.

You should be attentive to several features of the quoted text. First, the rule requires that the record be made "in the course" of regularly conducted activity and that the entry was made as a "regular practice." The Rule thus requires that the entry is routine and not one that is made for some special, nonrecurring purpose.

But the rule is not, by its terms, limited to records prepared by for-profit businesses. The term "business records" is often used in describing the exception, but in fact the exception covers records of any "organization, occupation, or calling, whether or not for profit"— so long as the activity recorded occurs regularly and the record is prepared as a regular practice. It follows that records of non-profit institutions, criminal enterprises, and even individuals can qualify for admissibility under this exception if they are regularly recorded records of regularly conducted activity.

Second, the rule demands that the entry be "made at or near the time" of the event, act, or observed condition that it records. This feature of the rule minimizes the hearsay danger of lapsed or faulty memory.

Third, a proviso at the end of the rule permits the judge to exclude an entry that appears suspicious or untrustworthy. This "untrustworthiness clause" gives the judge authority to exclude even a regularly maintained record if the opponent shows that the "source of information or the method or circumstances of preparation" render the record untrustworthy.[35] For example, the judge is likely to reject entries made in anticipation of litigation or by an employee with a motive to shift blameworthy conduct from himself to another. The rule makes clear that once the basic requirements of the exception have been established by the proponent, it is then the opponent's burden to show that the record is untrustworthy.

---

[35] An amendment to Rule 803(6)(E) established that the burden of showing untrustworthiness is placed on the opponent of the record. That is to say, records made in the ordinary course of regularly conducted activity are presumed to be trustworthy.

Circumstances Indicating Untrustworthiness

ILLUSTRATIONS

Assume that, at noon on a given day, there is a collision at a railway crossing between a train and a delivery truck. The driver of the truck, the engineer of the locomotive, and a bystander all witness the event. Within ten minutes of the accident, police officers Blue and Shield arrive at the scene. They conduct interviews and examine the physical evidence. Only Truck Driver is injured, and he is taken to the hospital.

Subsequently, Truck Driver and his employer, Trucking Company, file suit against Railroad Company, alleging that Engineer was speeding and, also, failed to blow the train whistle, which may have been in disrepair. (Engineer is not named as a defendant, as he has left Railroad's employ and his current address is unknown). Railroad denies negligence, claims the whistle blew several times, and asserts that Truck Driver was contributorily negligent because he was speeding and, also, failed to stop, look, and listen for an oncoming train.

At trial the following evidence is offered by the party indicated below. There is a hearsay objection to each of the proffered items of evidence. Nonetheless, the judge uniformly rules for the proponent and admits each item of evidence in question. Assume that the written statements below are accompanied by foundational evidence showing that they were routinely made in the regular course of business. Was the trial judge correct in ruling that all of the written entries described below were admissible?

(1) Railroad offers an accident report of a type that, in accordance with its by-laws, it routinely prepares after any accident involving personal injury, death, or property damage. A sentence in the report declares that Railroad's Chief Investigator (a railroad employee) inspected the locomotive whistle three hours after the accident and found it in good working order. The report also states that Investigator interviewed Engineer the day after the accident. Engineer declared that he blew the whistle twice before the train reached the intersection where the collision occurred. This statement was dutifully recorded by Investigator.

In Illustration (1), the first question is whether Railroad's accident report is a business record. An early, pre-Rules Supreme

Court opinion took the view that such a report was not a business record because it was prepared for the purpose of litigation, not for the purpose of operating a business.[36] But it is now generally accepted that business enterprises have a "business" reason to carefully investigate accidents because accidents, even in the absence of litigation, are costly events that businesses try to prevent. The Advisory Committee Note to Rule 803(6) indicates the Committee's belief that routine accident reports are business records. That conclusion, however, does not mean that an accident report (or selected entries within) is admissible. Even if an entry within the report was made in the regular course of business and contains information supplied by an employee (e.g., Engineer) with personal knowledge, it will be rejected by the judge if attending circumstances make the entry *untrustworthy*. Rule 803(6)(E), set forth above, expressly provides for this contingency. For example, Engineer certainly had motives to deny any fault: he might be fired if he were negligent or irresponsible in operating the train; furthermore, he knows that he is a potential defendant and thus may be reluctant to admit fault. Generally speaking, reports prepared in anticipation of litigation by a party to the case are inadmissible when the reports are favorable to the preparing party—the litigation motivation renders those reports untrustworthy.[37]

(2) Railroad offers a portion of a police report prepared by Officer Blue. The report states that when Blue arrived at the scene, he interviewed Bystander. According to Blue's report:

> Bystander had just finished a jogging workout. He says that he heard the train whistle twice, then saw the truck in question. The Truck Driver was going about sixty-five or seventy miles an hour. When the driver saw the railroad crossing, or maybe the train, he jammed on his brakes and the truck began to skid. Because the driver apparently couldn't stop before reaching the railroad crossing, he accelerated, but the train hit the back of the truck before the driver could clear the railroad.

In Illustration (2), Officer Blue records the statements of Bystander. The officer had a business duty to record, but the declarant (Bystander) did not have a business duty to speak. Courts

---

[36]   *Palmer v. Hoffman*, 318 U.S. 109, 113–14 (1943).

[37]   *See Scheerer v. Hardee's Food Sys., Inc.*, 92 F.3d 702 (8th Cir. 1996) (incident report on slip-and-fall, prepared by restaurant manager, was not admissible under Rule 803(6) because it was prepared in anticipation of litigation and was favorable to the preparer).

have consistently held that a business entry that contains a statement by an "outsider" with no business duty to speak cannot be used to prove the truth of the declarant's statement unless the statement can be shown to be reliable even though not within the business record exception—for example, reliability will be found if the outsider's statement is within some other exception or exemption to the hearsay rule.[38] In this case, there is at least a ten-minute gap between the accident and Bystander's statement to the police—too much time for the statement to be characterized as a present sense impression.[39] It might be possible for the proponent of this evidence to lay the foundation necessary to characterize Bystander's statement as an excited utterance. His statement does relate to the startling event, as required by Federal Rule 803(2). To successfully invoke this exception, Railroad would have to convince the judge that Bystander spoke while still under the influence of the stress and excitement caused by the collision. The fact that Bystander was not, himself, involved in the accident tends to strengthen his credibility (sincerity), but, on the other hand, his status as a nonparticipant suggests that he would regain his composure more rapidly than would the individuals who were actually involved in the collision. Success in admitting the evidence in Illustration (2) depends upon linking Officer Blue's duty to record with Bystander's excited utterance.

The Illustration thus presents a question of multiple hearsay. The problem with statements made by one without a duty to the recording entity is that there is no guarantee that they are telling the truth. Thus the risk is that you have a reliable recording of unreliable information. The record itself was regularly conducted, but the Bystander's statement in the record was not. Under Rule 805, if there is multiple hearsay, there must be an exception for each statement.

It must be noted that many courts find the unreliability problem solved if it can be shown that the person who made the business record was in a position to verify the accuracy of the statement made by the outsider. For example, assume that the government wants to prove that the defendant bought a controlled substance from a pharmacy. There is a pharmacy record indicating that he did, and the pharmacy policy is that before such a drug can be purchased, the buyer must present identification that is electronically checked for authenticity. This would be verification that the person listed in the record as the buyer is in fact the defendant. But if there is no

---

[38]   The Advisory Committee was aware of these court decisions, and approved of them. *See* Fed. R. Evid. 803(6) ACN. A leading case is *Johnson v. Lutz*, 253 N.Y. 124, 170 N.E. 517 (1930).

[39]   *See* Fed. R. Evid. 803(1), *supra*.

significant process of verification, then the outsider's statement, if offered for its truth, must satisfy an independent hearsay exception.

(3) Railroad offers another portion of the police report. In this portion, Officer Blue reports, "Officer Shield states that he just measured the tire (skid) marks that were made by the truck's wheels. The skid marks were 45 feet long, and formed an undulant pattern, indicating the rear of the truck was swinging back and forth during Driver's stopping maneuver."

In Illustration (3) both the speaker (Officer Shield) and the recorder (Officer Blue) had a business duty. The entry was made "at or near the time"[40] of Officer Shield's observation and measurement of the skid marks. After a proper foundation is laid,[41] this entry is admissible as a business record.

(4) During Truck Driver's cross-examination of Railroad's Chief Investigator (recorded by the court reporter), the Investigator admits that, following his investigation, Engineer was fired. Investigator also admits that before Engineer was dismissed, he told Investigator that he thought the train was "going about seventy-five or eighty miles an hour" when it hit the back of the truck. When asked why this statement was not in his accident report, Investigator states that interviews with other members of the train crew convinced him that Engineer's estimate of speed was "entirely too high—twenty-five or thirty miles an hour above the actual speed."

Illustration (4) does not really involve the business records exception, although Chief Investigator's concessions during cross-examination cast doubt on the accuracy of his report. Under the facts of this Illustration, the Engineer's pre-termination declaration is exempted from the hearsay rule because his statement concerned a matter within the scope of his agency and he made the statement while still employed by the defendant.[42] It is critical that Engineer's statement preceded the termination of his employment because, had it been made after his discharge, it would not have been exempted from the hearsay rule under that subsection. Note that there is no concern about the record being prepared in anticipation of

---

[40]   Fed. R. Evid. 803(6).

[41]   There must be testimony or other admissible evidence that the information in the entry was supplied by an individual with first-hand knowledge who had a business duty to speak and that the written record (the police report) was prepared in the ordinary course of business.

[42]   Fed. R. Evid. 801(d)(2)(D). The engineer might also have had delegated "speaking authority" under Fed. R. Evid. 801(d)(2)(C).

litigation—because the entries are *unfavorable* to the preparing party.

Medical Diagnoses in Business Records

Prior to the widespread adoption of the Federal Rules of Evidence, some courts were very skeptical of a hospital (business) record that contained a medical diagnosis. A recorded diagnosis of a routine medical condition, such as a broken limb or a kidney stone, caused no problem; neither did a diagnosis that was supported by "objective" findings such as an X-ray plate or the electronic images produced by magnetic resonance imagining (MRI). But some diagnoses, especially those that were not routine or rested heavily on "subjective" professional judgments,[43] were labeled "conjectural" or simply "opinions" and rejected.

The text of Federal Rule 803(6) states that the business records exception includes entries that record "an act, event, condition, opinion, or diagnosis." The textual language means that medical records containing opinions or diagnoses can be admissible. Recall, however, that Rule 803(6) permits the judge to exclude a business record when the opponent can show that the source of information or the method or circumstances of preparation indicate a lack of trustworthiness. Suppose, for example, a plaintiff claims that job-related stress and mistreatment by his employer had caused him to suffer "transient global amnesia."[44] Prior to trial, plaintiff had spent three days in the hospital where, according to his hospital record, he was diagnosed as suffering from the amnesia noted above. The hospital record did not elaborate on the nature of this infirmity, nor—more importantly—did the record indicate a causal connection between the plaintiff's work experiences and his transient global amnesia. This hospital entry would likely be deemed untrustworthy because of its cryptic nature, which left to sheer speculation the particulars of the disease and its causation, and failed to provide any basis for the doctor to make a conclusion.

Laying a Foundation for Business Records

The proponent of a business record must provide a proper foundation. That foundation includes evidence that the record in question was 1) kept in the course of regularly conducted activity, 2) recorded as a regular practice. The proponent must also show that the information contained in the record was transmitted by someone with personal knowledge and that the record was prepared in timely fashion—"at or near the time" of the recorded event.[45] In practice, the

---

[43]   For example, psychiatric diagnosis.

[44]   *See Fowler v. Carrollton Public Library*, 799 F.2d 976 (5th Cir. 1986).

[45]   Id.

various foundation requirements are often treated as a composite and satisfied by evidence that shows the record-keeping procedures of the business enterprise. For example, a custodian of the records or some other person familiar with the record-keeping routine can take the stand and give the required testimony. (The emphasis usually falls on whether the document in question is a regularly-kept business record.) A useful amendment to Rule 803(6), effective in 2000, permits the custodian or other qualified person to provide a written certification (in lieu of in-court testimony) that attests to the propriety of the proffered records.[46]

Today, of course, most businesses use computers to establish and maintain their business records. Although the general rule is that no special foundation is required for computer-generated business records,[47] it is usually necessary to lay a foundation that shows how data are gathered, stored, and retrieved. Sometimes, more detail is required, such as evidence about the software program used to manage the business data. Of course, if the opposing parties stipulate or otherwise agree to the introduction of specified business records, no further foundation is required.

Absence of an Entry in Business Record

If a regularly-kept business entry is admissible to show a fact or event, the absence of an entry that would normally record such a fact (or event) has probative force to show the unrecorded fact never existed. For example, if *X* company routinely records shipments of goods that are prepaid by the customer, the absence of such an entry pertaining to customer *Z's* order makes it less likely that he prepaid. Federal Rule 803(7) makes it clear that "[e]vidence that a matter is not included" in a business record that would normally record it, is admissible "to prove that the matter did not occur or exist." Again, however, as in the case of Rule 803(6), the judge is empowered to exclude this evidence if the opponent shows that it is untrustworthy.

Observe that the hearsay exception contained in Rule 803(7) is probably superfluous. When there is no entry pertaining to a particular matter or event, there is ordinarily no assertion being made by the declarant.[48] The Advisory Committee to the Federal

---

[46]　Certifications of domestic records must comply with Rule 902(11). *See* Fed. R. Evid. 803(6). Foreign business records that are offered in federal civil trials must comply with Fed. R. Evid. 902(12), and there is a comparable statute allowing for certification of foreign records in federal criminal cases.

[47]　*See, e.g., United States v. Linn*, 880 F.2d 209, 216 (9th Cir. 1989).

[48]　The inclusion of Rule 803(7) defeats the argument that a business record that indicates that certain events or transactions occurred is a statement that *only* they occurred and thus the record is inadmissible hearsay if offered to prove that something not listed in the record did not occur.

Rules recognized this, but, noting some contrary authority, proposed Rule 803(7) in order to ensure a uniform practice.[49]

Public Records: In General

The hearsay exception for public or governmental records rests upon a number of grounds. The first is an assumption that public officials will generally discharge their duties faithfully and honestly. The second is a recognition that the volume of public records makes it unlikely that a public official will have any recollection of the contents of most of the public documents within her responsibility. The third is that public documents are relied on by others, such as members of the general public, persons within the governmental agency that created the records, or members of another governmental business or department.

Generally speaking, but subject to an important qualification to be noted shortly, the information contained in a public record originates from a person with a public duty and first-hand knowledge. In this respect, the exception for public records is analogous to the exception for business records. It is also true that those who create public records are usually engaged in routine, systematic practices and that they typically record events shortly after their occurrence. However, *there is no* requirement under Rule 803(8), which is the principal Federal Rule governing public records, that a record be created *soon after* the event that it records. Nor does Rule 803(8) require that a public record be made as part of a *regular, systematic routine*. Thus, a non-routine entry by a government geologist about the composition, texture, or color of certain volcanic ash would be an admissible public record, even if it were not made soon after the official's observations. This is because public records are presumed reliable due to the public duty of those who prepare them—as distinct from the regularity-based foundation of business records.

While public records are presumed to be reliable, the last provision in Rule 803(8) authorizes the judge to exclude a public record or entry if the opponent establishes that the sources of information or other circumstances "indicate a lack of trustworthiness." This provision parallels a similar one in Rule 803(6) that deals with business records.

---

[49]   Fed. R. Evid. 803(6) ACN.

Public Records: Rule 803(8)

The Federal Rules of Evidence contain a number of provisions governing the admissibility of public documents.[50] Principal among these is Rule 803(8), which provides a hearsay exception for:

(8) ***Public Records.*** A record or statement of a public office if:

    (A) it sets out:

        (i) the office's activities;

        (ii) a matter observed while under a legal duty to report, but not including, in a criminal case, a matter observed by law-enforcement personnel; or

        (iii) in a civil case or against the government in a criminal case, factual findings from a legally authorized investigation; and

    (B) the opponent does not show that the source of information or other circumstances indicate a lack of trustworthiness.

There are three kinds of public records set out in subsections (A)(i), (ii), and (iii)—although there is some overlap. The public records within subsection (A)(i) bear a close resemblance to business records. Subsection (A)(i) includes entries such as those pertaining to payroll, personnel, inventories, disbursements, and, generally speaking, the internal or "office" operations of a governmental department, agency, or commission. Public records falling within subsection (A)(i) are admissible in both civil and criminal cases and may be introduced by or against any party. As you will see momentarily, criminal defendants are given special protection in subsections (A)(ii) and (iii), and, in some cases, public records within these two subsections cannot be introduced *against* such defendants.

Subsection (A)(ii) embraces records of matters observed pursuant to a public duty to observe and report. Typically, these observations are made outside an office environment—"in the field," so to speak. Recorded observations within subsection (A)(ii) would include, for example, a policeman's arrest of a suspect, the Weather Bureau's observations of weather conditions, an induction officer's observation that an inductee refused to take the required oath, a safety inspector's citation to an employer detailing safety violations, and an INS officer's report that he had deported a particular individual.

It is not always clear, however, whether a particular record should be characterized as within subsection (A)(i) because it

---

[50]   *See* Fed. R. Evid. 803(8), (9), (10), (12), (14), (22), and (23).

describes an activity of a public office or agency or whether the record more comfortably fits with subsection (A)(ii) because it records matters observed while under a legal duty to report. At least in civil cases, it is not at all important to classify a public report under a particular subdivision. The question in civil cases is essentially whether there are substantial indications that the public report is untrustworthy. If not, the report is admissible and the court will not spend any time worrying over the appropriate subdivision.

Classifying the record is sometimes important in criminal cases because Rule 803(8)(A)(ii) states that it does not apply to criminal cases if the proffered public report contains matters observed by law enforcement personnel. Suppose, for example, a Customs Service Agent finds a powdery substance hidden in the lining of a traveler's suitcase. Suspecting the substance is heroin, the agent sends the powder to a Customs Service forensic chemist, who tests it. The chemist then files a routine report that identifies the substance in question as heroin. An argument can be made that this report, filed by a chemist who routinely tests and identifies various substances, is simply a record of an office activity within Rule 803(8)(A)(i). However, in a case involving these essential facts,[51] a federal court of appeals found that the chemist's report was prepared pursuant to either Rule 803(8)(A)(ii) or, even more likely, pursuant to Rule 803(8)(A)(iii), to which we turn shortly. The court also found that the chemist could properly be included in the "law enforcement personnel" category to which subsection (A)(ii) makes specific reference.

Note that subsection Rule 803(8)(A)(ii) appears to state categorically that any "law-enforcement" report is inadmissible in criminal cases. Yet the intent of the drafters of this subsection was to protect the criminal defendant. Therefore, as most courts have wisely held,[52] subsection (A)(ii) excepts from the hearsay ban reports by police and other law enforcement agents that the *accused offers against the government*. In other words, the prohibition in this subsection applies only to reports offered *against the accused*. Thus, the accused would be able, under this subsection, to admit a law enforcement report concluding that the accused's fingerprints were *not* identified at the scene of the crime. This interpretation of Rule 803(8)(A)(ii) is consistent with the text of subsection (A)(iii), which shields the criminal defendant, but permits public records within

---

[51] *United States v. Oates*, 560 F.2d 45 (2d Cir. 1977). The *Oates* case has been criticized and, as discussed below, most courts have found ways to distinguish it or to depart from its construction of Rule 803(8)(A)(ii). *See, e.g., United States v. Baker*, 855 F.2d 1353, 1359–60 (8th Cir. 1988) (Chemist's drug analysis report is admissible).

[52] *See, e.g., United States v. Smith*, 521 F.2d 957, 963–68 (D.C. Cir. 1975).

that subsection to be introduced "against the government in a criminal case . . ."

Subsection (A)(iii) of Rule 803(8) generally confers admissibility upon investigative findings by a public official who is pursuing an official investigation, but again, there are limitations when such a report is offered against the accused in a criminal case. The text of subsection (A)(iii) provides a generally applicable hearsay exception for public records or reports that present "factual findings resulting from a legally authorized investigation." Public reports within subsection (A)(iii) should include, for example, an investigative report by the Army setting out the extent and causes of lost military supplies or a report of the Bureau of Mines detailing the probable cause of an explosion. The limitation on admitting such reports in civil cases lies in the untrustworthiness clause of the rule. So if, for example, the report appears biased, or the conclusions in an investigative report appear under-researched or speculative, a court has discretion to exclude the report as untrustworthy. It should be noted, though, that public reports are given a *heavy presumption of reliability*—the opponent has to make a strong case that the circumstances of preparing a particular public report clearly render it untrustworthy.[53]

With respect to criminal cases, the predominant view is that the exclusionary language of Rule 803(8)(A)(ii) and (iii) is not to be read literally. The drafters of the Federal Rules were concerned that police reports could be manipulated against a criminal defendant, without any possibility that the accused could cross-examine the officer who prepared the report. As to police reports prepared for a prosecution, the constitutional concerns, specifically the right of the accused to confront an adverse witness, are evident. Yet not all police reports are prepared for purposes of prosecution with a specific defendant in mind. If the exclusionary language of Rule 803(8)(A)(ii) and (iii) is read literally it would mean that even routine tabulations of information would be excluded, and the government would be hard-pressed to call a live witness who could testify to the same information. For example, to prove the defendant crossed into the United States by car on the day of a crime, the government may wish to introduce a routine tabulation of all border crossings that day. This report is obviously not prepared under adversarial circumstances; and to exclude it means that the proof is gone—it is unlikely that anyone will have a memory of the crossing of a particular car on a particular day. Accordingly, most courts have construed Rule 803(8)(A)(ii) and (iii) flexibly: the exclusionary language covers only

---

[53]   Rule 803(8)(B) was amended along with Rule 803(6)(E) in 2014 to make clear that the burden of showing untrustworthiness is on the opponent.

those police-generated reports that are prepared under adversarial circumstances, where there is a risk of manipulation by authorities bent on convicting a particular criminal defendant. Where the risk of manipulation and untrustworthiness is minimal—in particular where the report contains unambiguous factual matter prepared under nonadversarial circumstances—courts have held that the report should be admitted despite the apparently absolute language of the Rule.[54]

Remember, though, that while a report that is ministerial in nature and made without contemplation of specific litigation is ordinarily held admissible, those law enforcement reports that are adversarial and evaluative in nature are ordinarily excluded, consistent with the exclusionary intent of Rule 803(8)(A)(ii) and (iii).[55]

Information from Outside Sources

In conducting an investigation "pursuant to authority granted by law," the investigating officer frequently obtains information from persons who have no public duty to speak. They may, for example, be merely witnesses and not governmental officers or employees. When we examined the hearsay exception for business records, we saw that under that exception it was necessary that both the "speaker" (the source of the information) and the recorder have a business duty to act. Otherwise, the outsider's statement must fit within a hearsay exception or exemption, or the statement from the outsider must be verified for accuracy by the recordkeeper. The same hearsay on hearsay problem arises when a public official obtains information from a private individual (such as, a bystander's statement about an accident, made to a police officer who records it). Accordingly, the same requirements exist—the private individual's statements in a public record are not admissible unless they satisfy a hearsay exception or exemption, or their accuracy has been verified by the public recordkeeper. But while subsection (A)(iii) is not a license to admit records of hearsay statements by members of the general public, the officer's own findings—including findings based on

---

[54]   See, e.g., United States v. Enterline, 894 F.2d 287 (8th Cir. 1990) (computerized lists prepared by police of vehicles reported stolen were admissible despite the exclusionary language in Rule 803(8)(A)(ii) and (iii)).

[55]   See, e.g., United States v. Pena-Gutierrez, 222 F.3d 1080 (9th Cir. 2000) (trial court erred in admitting into evidence "the on-the-scene investigative report of a crime by an INS official whose perceptions might be clouded and untrustworthy"); United States v. Bohrer, 807 F.2d 159 (10th Cir. 1986) (an IRS contact card was excluded under Rule 803(8) because it was prepared under adversarial circumstances and because information included therein was subjective rather than ministerial in nature, thus subject to manipulation).

hearsay—are admissible unless the proponent can show they are untrustworthy.

"Factual Findings"

There is yet another salient feature of Rule 803(8)(A)(iii): its language apparently confines the admissible content of public investigative reports to "factual findings." But a narrow reading of "factual findings" would exclude significant portions of an investigator's report on the ground that they contain evaluations, opinions, or conclusions—not bare facts—and such an exclusion would rely on an evanescent distinction between fact and opinion. As the Illustration and discussion below indicates, the Supreme Court has rejected the notion that only "facts" can be admissible under Rule 803(8)(A)(iii).

ILLUSTRATION

During a Navy training exercise, one of the participating aircraft departs from the prescribed flight pattern. In an effort to avoid a collision with an adjacent aircraft, the pilot of the errant plane banks sharply. Thereafter, the plane plunges downward, crashes, and burns. The pilot and her student are both killed. Subsequently, survivors of the decedents file suit against the manufacturer of the doomed aircraft. The plaintiffs contend that the crash was caused by a defect in the plane's fuel system; the defendant contends that the accident resulted from errors made by the pilot as she tried to maneuver the plane back on course.

At trial, the defendant offers an investigative report prepared by a JAG officer who conducted an exhaustive post-accident investigation of the crash. The report contains numerous "factual findings" as well as a section labeled "Opinion." In the latter section, the investigator reconstructs the evidence bearing on pertinent events and concludes that the "most probable cause of the accident was the pilot's failure to maintain proper interval."[56]

The plaintiffs object to the admission into evidence of the "Opinion" section of the JAG report. How should the trial judge rule?

This Illustration is based on *Beech Aircraft Corp. v. Rainey*,[57] decided by the Supreme Court in 1988. The Court held that Rule 803(8)(A)(iii) does not exclude an investigative report merely because

---

[56]   *Beech Aircraft Corp. v. Rainey*, 488 U.S. 153, 158 (1988).

[57]   Id.

it contains opinions or conclusions. The Court noted that the language of Rule 803(8) is plainly addressed to the admissibility of *records,* and in the context of subsection (A)(iii), the requirement is that the *record in question* set out factual findings. So construed, Rule 803(8)(A)(iii) does not distinguish between facts and opinions by approving the former, but rejecting the latter—to do so would raise difficult and often untenable distinctions between what is an "opinion" and what is a "fact." It is enough that the record as a whole contains a factual finding, and if so the opinions in the same report are not automatically excluded. Finally, Rule 803(8) itself provides protection against the admission of speculative or unsubstantiated hearsay assertions. If the sources of information or other circumstances cast doubt on the reliability of statements in a report, the judge may exclude them. The trustworthiness clause of Rule 803(8) permits the trial judge to take full account of such factors as the expertise of the investigator, her possible bias or motive to distort, the thoroughness of her inquiry, and the strengths and weaknesses of the factual basis that underlies her report. Thus, if a public record contains a factual finding, the opinions in that record will also be admissible unless the opponent can show they are untrustworthy.

The Relationship Between Rule 803(8) and Rule 803(6)

We have seen that there is a rather close kinship between Rule 803(6), governing the admission of business records, and Rule 803(8), controlling the admission of public records. The term "business" is so broadly defined in Rule 803(6) that it surely embraces most public entities such as governmental departments, agencies, commissions, and the like. Therefore, many recorded hearsay declarations will meet the conditions of both Rule 803(6) and Rule 803(8). As to many of the hearsay statements contained in these documents, it is a matter of indifference whether the proponent offers his recordation as a public record or as a business record. The record will be admitted under the rule he cites, assuming the conditions of the rule are satisfied. Usually a proponent will invoke the public records exception because it is easier to do so: no foundation witness or affidavit is required to establish the foundation requirements of the exception, and there is no requirement that the record be regularly prepared or prepared at or near the time of the event.

However, as we have just observed, Rule 803(8) contains special protections for the accused in a criminal prosecution. This raises the question whether a law enforcement report that is inadmissible under Rule 803(8) in a criminal case might nonetheless be qualified as a business record. After all, a general governing principle of evidence holds that if evidence is admissible under the theory or rule cited by the proponent, it will not be rejected simply because it would be inadmissible if offered under another theory or pursuant to another evidentiary rule. Consider whether the following records should be admitted as public records, or business records, or under some other exception to the hearsay rule.

ILLUSTRATIONS

(1) In a prosecution for the possession and use of a dangerous weapon during the commission of a felony, the prosecutor proffers a police report that states, "When Abel [the accused] was arrested, approximately 20 minutes after the robbery, he had in his possession, encased in a shoulder holster under his jacket, a Beretta 92FS, 9mm, semi-automatic pistol, serial number BER400817."

The law enforcement report is inadmissible under Rule 803(8) because it was prepared under adversarial circumstances—after a crime has been committed and individualized to the suspect—and it favors the government. It is possible that the officer's adversarial motives could have affected the report—clearly the circumstances raise a question of trustworthiness that require cross-examination. As discussed above, the exclusionary language of Rule 803(8) has not been applied to exclude all law enforcement reports. Only those law enforcement reports that are subjective and made under adversarial circumstances—like the report in Illustration 1—are excluded, on grounds of trustworthiness. It follows that if a police report is of the kind that is excluded under Rule 803(8), *it must also be excluded under Rule 803(6)*. This is because records that are prepared in anticipation of litigation and favorable to the preparing party are excluded *under the trustworthiness criterion* of Rule 803(6); and those are, in effect, the only records that are excluded under the prevailing view of Rule 803(8).[58] Accordingly, under the predominant approach to Rule 803(8), the issue of whether a law enforcement report excluded under Rule 803(8) can nonetheless be admitted under Rule 803(6) does not arise. Such a report is by definition untrustworthy and inadmissible under both Rules.[59] Put another way, it would be silly for the government to argue that a report, though excluded

---

[58]   *See, e.g., United States v. Bohrer*, 807 F.2d 159 (10th Cir. 1986) (an IRS contact card, excluded under Rule 803(8) because prepared under adversarial circumstances, was also excluded under Rule 803(6) because adversarial circumstances of preparation show lack of trustworthiness).

[59]   *See, e.g., United States v. Brown*, 9 F.3d 907 (11th Cir. 1993) (property receipt properly held admissible under Rule 803(6); while Rule 803(6) cannot be used to evade the exclusionary language of Rule 803(8), a property receipt is not the type of law enforcement report that is excluded under Rule 803(8): "The police custodian in the instant case had no incentive to do anything other than mechanically record the relevant information on the property receipt. We believe that this is the type of reliable public record envisioned by the drafters of Rule 803(8).").

under Rule 803(8) because it is untrustworthy, should be admitted under Rule 803(6) despite the trustworthiness clause in that Rule.

> (2)   In a prosecution for a conspiracy to violate federal firearms laws, the government needs to prove that certain weapons were transported to Northern Ireland. The prosecutor proffers a routine inventory report prepared by the Northern Ireland police. Among the inventoried items are weapons seized by the police, some of which bear serial numbers that match weapons formally owned or possessed by the defendants.

Despite the broad exclusionary language of Rule 803(8), most courts, as discussed above, draw a distinction between non-adversarial (routine or ministerial) law enforcement reports and law enforcement reports that are prepared in an adversarial context in which the attention of law enforcement officials is fastened upon one or more suspects. A routine property inventory is ministerial, and thus the police report in Illustration (2) would be admissible under Rule 803(8) in most courts.[60]

> (3)   The police report in Illustration (1) is proffered as the past recollection recorded of the officer who prepared it. The officer cannot now recall what, if any, weapon was carried by the arrestee, Abel. However, the officer can verify that he prepared the report soon after the arrest, when his memory was fresh, and he is sure the entry is accurate.

The police report described in Illustration (3) is offered under Rule 803(5) as the officer's past recollection recorded. The author of the report is on the stand; his demeanor can be observed by the trier of fact; he can be cross-examined about what he can (and cannot) recall and about the circumstances surrounding the preparation of the record. In short, Rule 803(5), by its terms, requires that the author of the "recorded recollection" testify and, thus, be subject to cross-examination. This context is significantly different from one in which a public record is offered against the accused and the person or persons preparing the report do not appear and testify. This difference has persuaded most courts that the protective provisions of Rule 803(8) do not prohibit the introduction into evidence of a

---

[60]   *See, e.g., United States v. Grady,* 544 F.2d 598, 604 (2d Cir. 1976), on which Illustration 2 is based. Once it is determined that the protective provisions of Rule 803(8) are inapplicable, the proffered record may be received as either a public record or a business record. But as stated in text, the business records exception requires the testimony or affidavit of a qualified witness to establish that the record is authentic and the requirements of the exception are met. In contrast, no foundation is required for public records, and sealed public records are considered self-authenticating. *See* Fed. R. Evid. 902.

police report that meets the requirements of past recollection recorded.[61]

> (4) In a perjury prosecution, the District Attorney offers a transcript of the testimony of the accused in an earlier case. The purpose of this evidence is to establish the exact content of the accused's testimony and also, to establish that the accused had been sworn.

[handwritten margin note: No court reporter court reporter isn't court]

Illustration (4) raises the issue of whether a court reporter is included in the term "law enforcement personnel" which is used in Rule 803(8)(A)(ii) to generally identify those persons who enforce the criminal laws. This term should not be so broadly construed that it embraces purely administrative personnel. A court reporter has a clerical or ministerial role and should not be considered an officer or employee charged with enforcing the criminal laws.[62] Thus the record should be admitted under Rule 803(8)(A)(ii)(a matter observed by a public official).

> (5) In a "hit-and run" prosecution, in which the defendant is charged with colliding with an ambassador's car and leaving the scene, the government offers a police report. The report was prepared by an investigating police officer who, using skid marks and other physical evidence, estimated the speeds of the two vehicles involved, the point at which the cars collided, and the trajectories of the two cars before and after the collision. This kind of report is routinely prepared, and the officer who prepared it is on the witness stand. The prosecutor offers the report as both a public record and a business record.

Illustration (5) rests on the proposition that when the author (with personal knowledge) of a public report testifies, the concern that underlies the protective provisions of Rule 803(8)—the inability of the accused to confront adverse hearsay declarants—disappears and the report is admissible,[63] unless of course, the judge finds that it is untrustworthy. Note also the possibility of using the police report to refresh the officer's recollection

---

[61] *See, e.g., United States v. Picciandra,* 788 F.2d 39 (1st Cir. 1986).

[62] *See United States v. Arias,* 575 F.2d 253, 254–55 (9th Cir. 1978).

[63] *See United States v. Sokolow,* 91 F.3d 396, 404–05 (3d Cir. 1996). The concern underlying Rule 803(8) does disappear insofar as the author has first-hand knowledge of the matters recited in the public report. The concern is ameliorated if the other contributors to the report were operating under a public or business duty to speak. However, the fact that the author of the report is on the stand does not justify admitting the declarations of members of the general public, such as witnesses, for the truth of their declarations, unless, of course, some other hearsay exception (or exemption) applies.

The Absence of a Public Record

Rule 803(10) addresses the absence of a public record. For example, assume the government wants to prove that the defendant practiced medicine without a license. Rule 803(10) may be invoked to prove that there is no record of such a license being issued—from which the inference can be drawn that the defendant never had a license to practice medicine.[64] Under the exception, a public official must either testify—or provide a certification—that she has made a diligent search for the record. Note, however, that where the official does not testify, but merely submits a certification that she conducted a diligent, but unsuccessful, search, that is a declaration by a person not on the witness stand and it is offered for its truth. In order to be admissible as proof of the absence of a record, the certification must itself establish that a diligent search was conducted.[65]

§ 7.8   Miscellaneous Rule 803 Exceptions

Ancient Documents

We have seen that a document that is twenty or more years old, regular (unsuspicious) on its face, and located in a place where, if authentic, it would likely be, needs no additional foundational evidence in order to be admitted as authentic.[66] Of course, the opponent may continue to dispute its authenticity. The foundational facts of age, regularity, and location suffice, however, under the "ancient documents" authentication rule to permit a reasonable trier to determine that the document is genuine.[67] There is a second aspect to the ancient documents rule: it creates a hearsay exception for the declaratory content of old documents. As originally enacted, Rule 803(16) excepted from the hearsay rule:

---

[64]   Rule 803(10) relates to Rule 803(8) in the same way that Rule 803(7) relates to Rule 803(6) and defeats the argument that a public record that indicates that certain events or transactions occurred is a statement that *only* they occurred and thus the record is inadmissible hearsay if offered to prove that something not listed in the record did not occur.

[65]   We shall see below that certifications under Rule 803(10) are problematic in criminal cases due to the limitations imposed by the Confrontation Clause. Rule 803 (10) was amended in 2013 to include a "notice and demand" procedure for dealing with testimonial certificates in response to the Supreme Court's Confrontation Clause decision in *Melendez-Diaz v. Massachusetts*, 557 U.S. 305 (2009). That decision is discussed in Chapter VIII.

[66]   Fed. R. Evid. 901(8). *See* Chapter III, § 3.3.

[67]   This is not the only means by which an ancient document can be authenticated. For example, a witness with knowledge may testify that the document in question is genuine. Authentication requires only that there be foundational evidence sufficient to permit a reasonable trier to conclude that the proffered document is genuine.

Statements in Ancient Documents. A statement in a document that is at least twenty years old and whose authenticity is established.

The current version of the Rule excepts from the hearsay rule:

Statements in Ancient Documents. A statement in a document that was prepared before January 1, 1998, and whose authenticity is established.

The limitation on the ancient document rule, effective in 2017, resulted from the Advisory Committee's concern that electronically stored information (ESI) would be automatically admissible—even if unreliable—once it became 20 years old. The Advisory Committee determined that ESI can be easily and cheaply stored for 20 years, and so eventually the ancient documents exception would be an easy (too easy) means of admitting unreliable text messages, tweets, e-mails, etc. The Committee was aware, however, that many lawsuits have relied on and are currently relying on the exception to admit old documents—particularly cases involving latent diseases and environmental cleanups. The Committee did not wish to affect these cases and so, essentially, grandfathered admissibility for all documents prepared before 1998.

The Advisory Committee also explained how ancient documents might be addressed going forward:

Going forward, it is anticipated that any need to admit old hardcopy documents produced after January 1, 1998 will decrease, because reliable ESI is likely to be available and can be offered under a reliability-based hearsay exception. Rule 803(6) may be used for many of these ESI documents, especially given its flexible standards on which witnesses might be qualified to provide an adequate foundation. And Rule 807 can be used to admit old documents upon a showing of reliability—which will often (though not always) be found by circumstances such as that document was prepared with no litigation motive in mind, close in time to the relevant events. Finally, many old documents can be admitted for the non-hearsay purpose of proving notice, or as party-opponent statements.

Learned Treatises

Generally speaking, at common law an expert witness could be impeached by showing that an author, also an expert in the witness's field, held professional views that contradicted those of the witness. The Federal Rules of Evidence go much further in *Rule 803(18)*, which provides as follows:

***Statements in Learned Treatises, Periodicals, or
Pamphlets.*** A statement contained in a treatise, periodical, or
pamphlet if:

    (A) the statement is called to the attention of an expert
    witness on cross-examination or relied on by the expert
    on direct examination; and

    (B) the publication is established as a reliable authority by
    the expert's admission or testimony, by another
    expert's testimony, or by judicial notice.

If admitted, the statement may be read into evidence but not
received as an exhibit.

The Rule clearly provides that statements qualifying under Rule
803(18) are read into evidence, but are not received as exhibits. To
treat them as exhibits would normally entitle the jury to use the
learned volume, pamphlet, or periodical during its deliberations,
thereby affording these works more prolonged jury attention than the
expert testimony presented at trial. Even more importantly, if the
jury had access to a treatise or similar work during its deliberations,
jury members might attempt to interpret and apply the work without
the benefit of expert guidance.[68]

Before passages in a treatise (or similar publication) qualify as
an exception to the hearsay rule under Federal Rule 803(18), the
proponent of this evidence must establish that the work in question
is a reliable authority. Perhaps the expert being challenged by a
cross-examiner will admit that the work is authoritative. If not,
another expert can provide this foundational testimony. In some
instances, which will be rare, a court may take judicial notice that
the work is reliable. Suppose, for example, the work is widely adopted
by medical schools as a required text or the author is a renowned
authority. The problem for the court is how to be sure of the
reputation of the author or the number of medical schools using the
text. A witness might be necessary to inform the court, and the
witness's testimony might well moot the need for judicial notice.[69] In
any event, the judge must be persuaded by whatever foundational
evidence is presented that the proffered work is a reliable authority
before a proponent will be allowed to invoke Rule 803(18).

---

    [68]   Fed. R. Evid. 803(18) ACN.

    [69]   The proponent could offer a declaration of an expert since the court will make
a Rule 104(a) ruling on the purported learned treatise, but the court might insist on
admissible evidence.

Another signal feature of the present rule is that an expert on the stand must have the opportunity to interpret or comment upon the passages in the learned work that are read to the jury. This end is achieved by that provision in Rule 803(18) that directs that the work in question is admissible only to the extent "called to the attention of an expert witness on cross-examination or relied on by the expert witness in direct examination." Thus, as a practical matter, the rule ensures that the trier of fact will have the benefit of an expert's view of the validity of the textual passage in question and, just as importantly, how those passages bear upon the issue(s) in the case before the court.

Rule 803(18) avoids the woodenness of the common law as it developed in many jurisdictions. Two principal limitations on the use of learned treatises in many common law jurisdictions were (1) the expert on direct examination could not quote from a treatise for its truth because it was hearsay, and (2) a cross-examiner could not use a treatise to impeach an expert unless the expert either relied upon the treatise in reaching an opinion or conceded that the treatise was reliable. Rule 801(18) rejects both of these limitations and provides much greater latitude for the use of treatises by both direct and cross-examiners.

Finally, the rule is not limited to printed materials. Under the definitional section of the Restyled Rules of Evidence, effective December 1, 2011, any reference to written material in the Rules "includes electronically stored information."[70] So for example it is possible for a video presentation, or a website, if found authoritative and relevant, to be admitted into evidence under the learned treatise exception.

Judgment of a Criminal Conviction: Rule 803(22)

Rule 803(22) provides a hearsay exception for the following:

Judgment of a Previous Conviction. Evidence of a final judgment of conviction if:

(A) the judgment was entered after a trial or guilty plea, but not a nolo contendere plea;

(B) the conviction was for a crime punishable by death or by imprisonment for more than a year;

(C) the evidence is admitted to prove any fact essential to the judgment; and

---

[70] Fed. R. Evid. 101(b)(6).

(D) when offered by the prosecutor in a criminal case for a purpose other than impeachment, the judgment was against the defendant.

The pendency of an appeal may be shown but does not affect admissibility.

Rule 803(22) is concerned with using a prior criminal conviction in a subsequent criminal or civil trial as *evidence*. The rule is used when a proponent is trying to prove a fact that has already been proved in a prior conviction. Proof of such a fact through a conviction is considered reliable, because it has already been proved beyond a reasonable doubt in a previous proceeding.

When there has been a conviction and the subsequent litigation raises the same factual issues, it is possible that a party will not have to resort to Rule 803(22) to reprove those facts. Substantive law doctrines of issue preclusion (collateral estoppel) may operate to preclude any dispute as to the same facts. This hearsay exception does not address issue preclusion, which is not properly included within the law of evidence, but rather is part of the body of law generally known as the "law of judgments." Rule 803(22) is concerned with using a prior criminal conviction as an *evidentiary* tool employed in an effort to prove a "fact essential to the [prior criminal] judgment." The proponent of the prior criminal judgment would, of course, prefer that the law of judgments, and in particular issue preclusion, foreclose altogether the relitigation of the fact(s) claimed to underlie the prior conviction. But sometimes issue preclusion is not available, so the proponent turns to the evidentiary use of the prior conviction, and the possible application of Rule 803(22).

Note that under 803(22), it is immaterial whether the prior judgment rests on a guilty plea or upon a conviction after trial. It is essential, however, that the judgment represents a conviction of a felony grade offense—one that is punishable by death or imprisonment for more than a year, A conviction based on a plea of nolo contendere is not within the exception; "nolo pleas" are not an admission of guilt by the pleader.[71] A judgment of acquittal is also outside the scope of Rule 803(22), because it implies only that some factual element necessary to a conviction was not found to exist beyond a reasonable doubt.

---

[71] He agrees not to contest the government's case, in return for which he does not have to bear the adverse collateral consequences of the plea and resulting conviction.

The essence of Rule 803(22) is that it permits the introduction into evidence of a prior felony-grade conviction to prove any fact essential to sustain that judgment. The prior judgment is usually against a party to the present suit, but in a civil case this congruence of party identity is unnecessary—and the same is true in a criminal case where the accused offers a prior conviction of another person *against the government* in an effort to prove some exculpatory fact (e.g., that someone else committed the crime). Thus, imagine a civil suit in which *A's* executor (the plaintiff) claims that the defendant *B* (and not *C*) negligently shot and killed *A* while the three of them were hunting. *B* could introduce a criminal judgment showing that *C* was convicted of the involuntary manslaughter of *A*.

A final example illustrates a restriction appearing near the end of Rule 803(22). Suppose that the present trial (Trial 2) is a criminal prosecution in which *D* is charged with the receipt of rare and valuable (stolen) stamps. To prove that the stamps were in fact stolen, the government introduces a judgment, obtained in an earlier criminal trial (Trial 1), showing that *X* had been convicted of stealing the stamps in question. The prior judgment is offered for the hearsay assertion by the trier of fact in the first trial that the stamps were stolen. Rule 803(22) would disallow this evidence, because in criminal cases, the conviction offered must be a judgment against the defendant if offered to prove a fact. Here the previous criminal judgment was against a person other than the defendant in the present trial; and the evidence is not offered for the purpose of impeaching the credibility of a witness. The concern here is that the criminal defendant is unable to confront and cross-examine the witnesses in Trial 1. The Confrontation Clause of the United States Constitution (discussed more fully in Chapter VIII) accounts for this restriction in Rule 803(22)(D).[72]

Other Miscellaneous Rule 803 Exceptions: A Sample

We have addressed the Rule 803 exceptions most often studied in evidence courses and most often discussed in the reported cases. Recall, however, that Rule 803 has twenty-three exceptions, of which we have examined twelve. The remaining rules, some with a long common law history, are fairly narrow in scope and comparatively easy to grasp. A sample follows:

    1.   Rule 803(9) excepts from the hearsay rule records that contain statistics pertaining to "birth, death, or marriage." The strong analogy here is to public records, the subject of Rule 803(8). This helpful comparison will be readily seen by examining the provisions of Rule 803(9): the

---

[72]   Fed. R. Evid. 803(22) ACN.

vital statistics controlled by this rule must be reported to a public office "in accordance with a legal duty"—covering such persons as physicians, ministers, coroners, undertakers, and the like. Many of the persons required by law to file the report are not public officers, but they are performing a publicly imposed duty when they file the reports named in Rule 803(9).

2.   Rule 803(17) excepts from the hearsay rule compilations "relied on by the public or by persons in particular occupations."[73] Stock quotations, weather conditions, census statistics, commodity market reports, price and inflation indexes, and a host of other tabulations and quotations are admissible under this rule—including information on websites and the like, because Fed. R. Evid. 101(b)(6) provides that a reference to written material includes material in electronic form. The source of the published information may be either public[74] or private. Note that the person or entity that is the source of these published materials usually has an incentive to be accurate. Furthermore, falsity is likely to be detected by those who rely on the data. Thus, the combination of a disinterested source and public reliance justify this exception to the hearsay rule. The accuracy of the compilation, list, or directory may be challenged by the opponent. The admission of a Rule 803(17) report is not conclusive as to the accuracy of the reported data.

3.   Rule 803(19) is one of several hearsay exceptions contained in Rule 803 that allow evidence of reputation as an exception to the hearsay rule.[75] Under this subsection, reputation evidence is admissible to prove a person's "birth, adoption, legitimacy, ancestry, marriage, divorce, death, relationship by blood, adoption, or marriage, or similar facts

---

[73]   Fed. R. Evid. 803(17).

[74]   There will be instances in which a public record, admissible under Rule 803(8), will be published and thus also fall within Rule 803(17).

[75]   *See also* Fed. R. Evid. 803(20) (proof of boundaries), (21) (proof of character). Rule 804(b)(4) also contains a hearsay exception that pertains to family history. In the case of 804(b)(4), hearsay *declarations* by family members about family relationships are admissible.

You might want to pay particular attention to Rule 803(21) in connection with character evidence, When a character witness testifies to reputation evidence as permitted by Rules 405 and 608, the witness is saying that people in the relevant community report that someone possesses a pertinent trait of character. The witness's testimony is hearsay because it is offered for the truth of what people are saying. Rule 803(21) provides the relevant exception.

of personal or family history".[76] There are three sources from which relevant reputation evidence may be obtained: within the family, within the community, or among associates familiar with the reputation concerning persons whose relationship is in question. A witness who testifies concerning this reputation must have personal knowledge of the reputation, but need not have personal knowledge of the relationship in question. ("The reputation throughout the village is that she was Bert Grant's illegitimate daughter.")

§ 7.9   Rule 804 Exceptions—Requiring Unavailability of the Declarant

We have seen that Rule 803 exceptions apply whether or not the declarant is available to testify. This is not true of Rule 804 exceptions: The five exceptions set out in Rule 804(b) are applicable only if *the declarant is unavailable.*

As a general matter, the drafters of the Federal Rules thought that statements falling within the Rule 804 exceptions were not as reliable as live testimony, but superior to no evidence at all. Thus, they built in a preference for the declarant's live testimony. The drafters believed that the 803 exceptions, but not the 804 exceptions, were reliable enough that they should be admissible even if live testimony is also available. As you examine the 804 exceptions, you might wonder whether they are less reliable than those in 803.

Rule 804(a): Unavailability Defined

Because Rule 804's first preference is for the declarant to appear and testify, it becomes necessary to determine when she is unavailable. In an effort to give some consistency to judicial rulings on "unavailability," the drafters of Rule 804 provided, in subsection (a), the list of circumstances in which a witness may be considered unavailable for the purpose of all of the Rule 804(b) exceptions. Rule 804(a) states that a witness is unavailable if:

(1)   she successfully invokes a claim of privilege;

(2)   she refuses to testify in defiance of the judge's order to do so;

(3)   she testifies that she cannot remember the event in question;

(4)   she is unable to testify because of death, physical or mental illness or infirmity; or

---

[76]   Fed. R. Evid. 803(19).

(5) she is absent and the proponent of her hearsay declaration has been unable to procure the declarant's attendance "by process or other reasonable means."

Note that if the proponent's ground of unavailability is that the declarant is absent, he must surmount yet another hurdle. Before he is able to invoke the hearsay exceptions for dying declarations, statements against interest, or family history (all contained in Rule 804(b)), he must show that the declarant's *deposition* cannot be procured "by process or other reasonable means."[77] The preference for the declarant's deposition rests largely on the opportunity afforded the opponent to conduct a cross-examination. This second-level preference for taking the declarant's deposition does not apply to the Rule 804(b) exception for former testimony. First of all, the opportunity for cross-examination has already been afforded under the "former testimony" exception to the hearsay rule. Second, it is highly likely that the former testimony was recorded as part of the court reporter's transcript of trial or proceeding, so the reason to insist upon a deposition disappears entirely.

Finally, Rule 804(a) provides, reasonably enough, that a declarant cannot be found unavailable if the proponent "procured or wrongfully caused the declarant's unavailability as a witness in order to prevent the declarant from attending or testifying." This provision recognizes that a party may in some cases have an incentive to admit hearsay over the testimony of a declarant who is actually available to testify—perhaps the declarant won't communicate well on the stand, or is likely to make statements inconsistent with the hearsay. In these circumstances, a party may think about "making" the witness unavailable. But Rule 804(a) provides that such conduct disentitles the party from using the hearsay at trial.[78]

Former Testimony

The central feature of this exception is the principle that if a party has had the opportunity and similar motive to develop (by direct or cross-examination) a witness's testimony in the first trial (or proceeding), the witness's (trial-one) testimony should be admissible against that party in trial two. The hearsay dangers are minimized by the prior opportunity and similar motive to develop the testimony and by the fact that the testimony was made under oath. It can be argued that prior testimony is so reliable that it should be a Rule 803 exception, so that the declarant's availability is immaterial. But prior

---

[77]   Fed. R. Evid. 804(a)(5).

[78]   This provision works hand-in-hand with the forfeiture by wrongdoing exception found in Rule 804(b)(6). A party who engages in wrongdoing loses the right to offer statements of an unavailable declarant and gives up the right to complain when such statements are offered against him.

testimony is read from a record, and so is not as useful to the trier of fact as in-court testimony. It is a paler substitute of trial testimony and so is only admissible if the declarant is unavailable. A witness's demeanor is an important factor in the trier's assessment of the witness's credibility.[79]

Rule 804(b)(1)

Rule 804(b)(1) creates an exception from the hearsay rule for the following:

Former Testimony. Testimony that:

(A) was given as a witness at a trial, hearing, or lawful deposition, whether given during the current proceeding or a different one; and

(B) is now offered against a party who had—or, in a civil case, whose predecessor in interest had—an opportunity and similar motive to develop it by direct, cross-, or redirect examination.

Observe that the rule requires only an *opportunity* and similar motive to develop the witness's testimony in the first proceeding— thus, a party who chooses not to develop adverse testimony may nonetheless be bound by it in a subsequent proceeding. Furthermore, it is immaterial whether that opportunity is afforded at the juncture of direct examination or at the point of cross-examination. Thus, if, say, the plaintiff in Trial 1 calls *W*, asks only several questions and, following his opponent's cross, declines redirect, the rule is satisfied and *W's* testimony is admissible in Trial 2 against the Trial 1 plaintiff—so long as the motive for developing the testimony is similar in both trials. Even more clearly, the rule is satisfied if a cross-examiner (against whom *W's* testimony is subsequently offered) waived cross-examination—again assuming the motive for examining the witness was similar in both trials.

Recall that modern rules governing the interrogation of witnesses provide flexibility:[80] a direct examiner, faced with a hostile witness, may secure the court's permission to ask leading questions; a cross-examiner, who interrogates a friendly witness may, after a successful objection, be confined by the court to nonleading questions. These flexible approaches to witness interrogations are reflected in

---

[79]   Of course, if witnesses' testimony were routinely videotaped, some "demeanor evidence" would be available to the trier of fact in the second proceeding. But studies have shown that testimony of a live witness is more useful to the trier of fact than videotaped testimony—just like talking to your friends over Zoom is not the same thing as talking to them in person.

[80]   *See* Fed. R. Evid. 611.

Rule 804(b)(1), which draws no distinction between direct and cross-examination.

The "Party" Requirement

Under Rule 804(b)(1) the focus for admissibility is on *the party against whom the former testimony is now offered*. The central question is whether the prior testimony of a witness should be admissible against that party on the ground that he was adequately protected by an earlier examination of the witness or by an earlier *opportunity* to develop the testimony of that witness.

In criminal cases, there is a *"same-party"* requirement: the defendant against whom the former testimony is offered in the second proceeding must have also been a party to the first proceeding. This coincidence of parties is not required when the second proceeding is civil in nature. In some civil settings, a different party (from the one against whom the prior testimony is now offered) may have adequately protected the interests of the present party—by developing the witness's testimony in the same way as the present party would do if the witness were now available. When that is the case, the prior party will be considered a "predecessor in interest" of the present party—but that is so in a civil case only.

ILLUSTRATIONS

(1)   Pate and his passenger (and girlfriend) Pam, are both injured when Pate's car is struck by a train at a railroad crossing. Pate and Pam join as co-plaintiffs and sue the railroad company for installing a mechanically defective signal. Bystander testifies for the plaintiffs that the signal in question was not working, and he is cross-examined by the railroad. Although the plaintiffs win, the appellate court reverses and orders a new trial on the ground that the judge gave the jury an erroneous instruction. At the time of the second trial, Bystander is in the armed forces, stationed in a war zone and his presence as a witness cannot be secured. Pate and Pam offer a transcript of Bystander's former testimony against the railroad. Is it admissible?

Illustration (1) meets the requirements of Rule 804(b)(1). The railroad had the opportunity to "develop" Bystander's adverse testimony and, indeed, attempted to weaken that testimony by cross-examination. Its motive in the earlier proceeding is at the very least "similar" to its motive at the new trial; to show that the signal was operating properly at the time of the accident. Note that the issue to which Bystander testified is the same in both trials. Although Rule 804(b)(1) does not require identical issues in the first and second proceedings, similarity of issues is still a relevant concern in applying the rule. Similarity of issues sheds light on similarity of motive (how one would seek to develop the testimony) which is required by the rule. The greater the divergence of the issues in the first and second trials, the greater the likelihood that the similarity of motive required by the rule is lacking. Of course, the fact that, say, trial 1 and trial 2 have a number of different issues is not controlling: the *only* issue (or issues) of importance in the application of Rule 804(b)(1) is the issue *toward which the former testimony is directed.*

(2)   Assume the same car-train collision described in Illustration (1). Assume further, however, that Pate and Pam do not join as co-plaintiffs, but Pam alone brings the first suit alleging the railroad's negligence. Now imagine that in this first suit, Bystander is called as a witness by the *railroad* and he testifies that the signal was functioning properly. There is a verdict for the defendant.

Months later, Pate sues the railroad, alleging that the signal was defective and inoperative.[81] Bystander is in the armed services and unavailable. The railroad offers a transcript of Bystander's prior testimony (given in Pam's trial) against Pate. Should the trial judge admit it?

Illustration (2) tests the limits of the phrase "predecessor in interest" that appears in Rule 804(b)(1), and is applicable to civil cases only. In this Illustration, Pam had the opportunity to develop Bystander's adverse testimony, but the transcript of his former testimony is offered against Pate in subsequent litigation. Pam had the motive of weakening or discrediting Bystander's testimony that the signal was operating properly. Pate would have a similar motive if Bystander were available and the railroad called him to the witness stand. Nonetheless, the language of Rule 804(b)(1) disallows the use of Bystander's former testimony against Pate unless Pam is Pate's "predecessor in interest" as that term is used in Rule 804(b)(1). This phrase liberalizes Rule 804(b)(1)'s "same-party" requirement that applies in criminal cases.

The phrase "predecessor in interest," which some courts use interchangeably with the phrase "parties in privity," has an exasperating imprecision about it. At common law, the expression generally refers to a predecessor from whom the present party received the right, interest, or obligation that is at issue in the current litigation. For example, a decedent is a predecessor in interest to (or "in privity with") both her personal representative and those, such as heirs and legatees, who inherit from her. So, too, is the

---

[81]   Pate was not a party to the first suit, and thus could not be bound (issue precluded) by a finding that the signal was operating properly.

grantor of property a predecessor to the grantee. The terms "predecessor" or "privity" have also been used to characterize instances in which two parties are linked by representation, as where, for example, a trustee is a party to the first suit and a beneficiary is a party to the second suit.

The common law concept of privity is of limited value in the solution of evidentiary problems such as the application of the hearsay rule. In Illustration (2), Pam and Pate do not stand in a relationship of privity as that term has been historically used; no property interest has passed between them, nor was Pam, the plaintiff in the first suit, Pate's legal representation or fiduciary. Thus, if the trial judge equates "predecessor in interest" with privity, Bystander's former testimony is inadmissible against Pate, who is not a successor in interest.

But most courts have applied the predecessor-in-interest language more broadly, so that if the prior party had developed the testimony in a way that the new party would do in the current litigation, then the prior party will be considered a predecessor-in-interest of the new one.[82] The rationale is that if the previous development of the testimony was as effective as would be likely to occur in the subsequent trial, it is sufficiently reliable and there is no justification for excluding it—especially because the alternative is no evidence at all from that witness, who must be unavailable for the exception to apply. So most courts would find that Bystander's testimony is admissible against Pate, so long as Pam developed that testimony in the way that Pate would have if the witness were available for the second trial. Pam's motive to weaken or discredit Bystander's testimony is similar to Pate's, and Pam had the opportunity to do so. Unless some failure or inadequacy in that cross-examination is detected, most courts will rule that because both Pam and Pate had the common objective of showing that the signal malfunctioned, and because this is a common issue in both trials, Bystander's prior testimony is admissible against Pate. A court might be persuaded not to admit the testimony, however, if it could be shown that Pam, for whatever reason, *did a poor job* of developing the witness's testimony.

As discussed above, the "predecessor in interest" possibility is not allowed in criminal cases. Assume that two people are charged with a bank robbery. They are tried separately, and in the first trial, the bank teller testifies in a way that incriminates both defendants. If the bank teller is unavailable for the second trial, the government

---

[82] *See, e.g., Supermarket of Marlinton, Inc. v. Meadow Gold Dairies, Inc.,* 71 F.3d 119 (4th Cir. 1995) (core of Rule 804(b)(1) is not privity, but rather similarity of motives between predecessor party and present party).

is not allowed to admit the teller's testimony under Rule 804(b)(1). This is because the criminal defendant has a right to confront adverse witnesses, and it will not do to tell the defendant that his right to confrontation was satisfied by the cross-examination conducted by the other defendant. The right to confrontation is a personal right.

Similarity of Motive and Grand Jury Testimony

The Supreme Court has emphasized that similarity of motive in the first and second proceedings is an indispensable feature of Rule 804(b)(1). In *United States v. Salerno*[83] the Court addressed the issue of whether defendants in a criminal trial could introduce against the government the prior grand jury testimony of two (now-unavailable) witnesses, who testified favorably to the defendants at the grand jury proceeding. The admissibility of this testimony, the Court said, turns upon whether the prosecutor in the grand jury proceedings had a motive to develop the witnesses' testimony that was similar to the motive that would exist if the witnesses testified at trial.

On remand, the Second Circuit found that the government's motives were dissimilar.[84] The court concluded that generally the prosecutor at a grand jury proceeding does not have a similar incentive to attack the testimony of witnesses who testify favorably to the defendant as she would have at trial. This is because the standard of proof for obtaining an indictment (probable cause) is substantially lower than the beyond the reasonable doubt standard that will apply at a criminal trial. In most cases, a prosecutor is unconcerned about exculpatory testimony at the grand jury proceeding, because she has enough other evidence so that the indictment is not in doubt—therefore she will not spend time trying to attack or question the witness. But at a criminal trial, any exculpatory testimony could create a reasonable doubt, and so the prosecutor has a strong motive to develop the testimony at that point. These respective motives are, accordingly, dissimilar in most cases— the exception being where there is some doubt as to whether an indictment will be obtained.

It should be noted, though, that other courts do not agree with the Second Circuit's analysis and have found that an accused can have exculpatory grand jury testimony admitted under Rule 804(b)(1)—these courts emphasize that the requirement is that the

---

[83]   505 U.S. 317, 321–24 (1992).

[84]   *United States v. DiNapoli*, 8 F.3d 909, 915 (2d Cir. 1993). *Contra United States v. Miller*, 904 F.2d 65, 67–68 (D.C. Cir. 1990) (similar motive).

motive be "similar"—not identical in intensity, as the Second Circuit required.[85]

Contextual determination of the kind illustrated in *Salerno* must also be made in a related criminal context, namely, where the first proceeding is a preliminary hearing and the second proceeding is a criminal trial.[86]

In the foregoing Illustrations and discussion, it has been assumed that the statements contained in a witness's former testimony were shown by the introduction of a transcript. As we have seen, the transcript is a public record, and thus is admissible to show what the witness said. And we have noted that the former testimony exception—assuming its conditions are satisfied—allows the witness's statements to be received for their truth. Use of the transcript from the former proceeding is an efficient means of proving what the witness said and it has the added advantage of probable accuracy.

Dying Declarations

The hearsay exception for statements made in contemplation of death has the imprimatur of age, but remains, even in its modern form, rigid and arbitrary. During the Nineteenth Century, courts increasingly admitted *in criminal homicide prosecutions* the victim's dying statements identifying his slayer or otherwise revealing the cause of his impending death. Over the years, courts and commentators have advanced several justifications for this hearsay exception. The principal justification is that a declarant faced with what he believes is his certain death is unlikely to lie. The motivation to speak truthfully might be rooted, as the early cases said, in the religious belief that one "about to face his Maker" will not conclude his earthly activities with "a lie on his lips." Aside from this religiously-based notion, there is a current of psychological opinion that one facing death has nothing to gain by promoting a fabrication—though the response to this argument is that such a declarant also has nothing to *lose* by lying, either. Finally, in functional or pragmatic terms, the lapse of time between the relevant events and the declarant's declaration is likely to be short, thereby reducing the hearsay danger of a faulty memory. Memory problems are also reduced in many cases by the restriction for dying

---

[85]   *See, e.g., United States v. McFall*, 558 F.3d 951 (9th Cir. 2009) (exculpatory grand jury testimony admissible against the government under Rule 804(b)(1)).

[86]   *See, e.g., Glenn v. Dallman*, 635 F.2d 1183, 1186–87 (6th Cir. 1980) (preliminary hearing testimony admissible against accused). Note, however, that grand jury testimony may not be admitted against an accused under Rule 804(b)(1). This is because the accused is not present at the grand jury and has no opportunity to cross-examine grand jury witnesses.

declarations that limits their content to "the cause or circumstances" of what the declarant believed to be her imminent death.[87]

Federal Rule 804(b)(2)

The exception to the hearsay rule pertinent to the present discussion appears in Rule 804(b)(2):

> **Statement Under the Belief of Imminent Death.** In a prosecution for homicide or in a civil case, a statement that the declarant, while believing the declarant's death to be imminent, made about its cause or circumstances.

The exception applies in one and only one kind of *criminal* prosecution: homicide. However, the exception is available in all civil cases. The crux of the exception is the declarant's settled expectation that death is inevitable. ("I might be dying" does not qualify.) Observe, also, the restricted scope of the permissible subject of the dying statement: "cause or circumstances" of the "imminent death"— so a statement such as "I am sorry that I killed by brother when I was 12" is not admissible. As with all Rule 804 exceptions, the declarant must be unavailable. Obviously, this requirement is always satisfied in homicide prosecutions.

ILLUSTRATIONS

(1) Mrs. Shepard, who suddenly feels desperately ill, calls for her caretaker-nurse. "Call Dr. Knight immediately," she says, "because I am probably dying." And, she continues, "bring me the bottle of sherry my husband, Dr. Shepard, bought for me; he gave me a glass before dinner and I'm sure he poisoned me!"[88] The next day, Mrs. Shepard dies and, subsequently, her husband, Dr. Shepard, is prosecuted for murder by poisoning. The prosecution offers the decedent's dying declaration. Admissible?

(2) Mae is viciously assaulted and raped. In a statement to a member of the medical team that answered her 911 call, she says, "I'm dying" and then in a barely audible voice, she identifies her assailant as Troy. After two weeks in intensive care, Mae begins to recover. A month later, however, she dies from a brain aneurysm. Troy, who denies he was the assailant, is prosecuted for rape with

---

[87] Fed. R. Evid. 804(b)(2). It is possible that a victim will be shot on day 1, in a coma for two months, suddenly awake and told she is about to die, and says "X shot me." This is the kind of case in which memory issues are present, but the statement appears to qualify as a dying declaration.

[88] For a case that is similar on its facts, *see Shepard v. United States*, 290 U.S. 96 (1933).

intent to kill. The prosecutor offers the 911 medical assistant who will testify as to Mae's dying declaration. Admissible?

(3) Suppose Mae's husband, alleging assault and rape, sues Troy for civil damages. He offers Mae's dying declaration. Admissible?

In Illustration (1), the declarant does not have a firmly held conviction that she is about to die. That fact alone defeats the application of the exception for dying declarations. Furthermore, the declarant appears to be speculating about her condition (poisoned) and about the culprit (Dr. Shepard). Generally, a hearsay declarant's statement is inadmissible for lack of personal knowledge unless, from all the surrounding circumstances, a reasonable trier could conclude that the declarant had personal knowledge.[89]

The declarant in Illustration (2) does have a settled expectation of death, and the statement concerns the causes and circumstances of her death, so it would be admissible in a murder prosecution as a dying declaration. But the dying declaration exception applies to only one kind of criminal prosecution: homicide. In the Illustration, the prosecution is for rape with intent to kill, so the present exception does not apply.[90]

In the civil suit brought by Mae's husband in Illustration (3), the declarant's statement should be admissible. Mae thought she was about to die, although she did not die until later. The cause of her death seems sufficiently related to the sexual assault.

Note that if a hearsay statement is not admissible as a dying declaration, the proponent will explore other possible exceptions. One who speaks in circumstances involving the possibility of death is often under the influence of stress or excitement. Thus, statements not admissible as dying declarations may often be received under Rule 803(2), the exception for excited utterances. The use of this hearsay exception has an added advantage. Whereas dying declarations under Rule 804(b)(2) are limited to statements concerning the cause or circumstances of the declarant's impending death, excited utterances under Rule 803(2) extend to statements "related to" the startling event or condition that produced the emotional state. The expanded subject matter (permissible content) of Rule 803(2) declarations offers the proponent a greater potential

---

[89]   The personal knowledge requirement does not apply to party-opponent statements (a Rule 801(d)(2) exemption), nor to statements of personal or family history (a Rule 804(b)(4) exception). But it applies to hearsay offered under every other hearsay exception.

[90]   *See Hansel v. Commonwealth*, 260 Ky. 148, 84 S.W.2d 68 (1935) (rape victim dies during childbirth).

for securing a favorable evidentiary ruling. Moreover, there is no requirement that the declarant be unavailable when an excited utterance is offered.

Another possibility for admitting statements that don't quite fit Rule 804(b)(2) is found in Rule 807, the "residual exception." This exception may be invoked when a proffered hearsay declaration does not fit within any of the specific hearsay exceptions contained in Rules 803 and 804, and yet the court finds that it is trustworthy.[91] For example, factors such as the disinterestedness of the speaker, the short duration between the event and her declaration, the likelihood that a false statement would be discovered, and reliance on the statement by persons the declarant would not want to deceive are some of the relevant considerations in determining the trustworthiness of a statement proffered under Rule 807.[92]

Statements Against Interest

The rule that admits statements against a declarant's interest is based on the psychological assumption that a person does not make personally disserving statements unless they are true. The impracticality of assessing the psychological profile of a declarant who makes an against-interest statement has caused courts to resort to a "reasonable person" test in applying this exception. Federal Rule 804(b)(3) explicitly adopts this "reasonable person" approach: the question is whether the statement was so far contrary to the declarant's interest that a reasonable person would not have made the statement unless believing it to be true.

Difference Between Declarations Against Interest and Party-Opponent Statements

It is important at the outset to distinguish declarations against interest from party-opponent statements—which had been referred to, before the restyling of the Federal Rules of Evidence, as "admissions."[93] Although many party-opponent statements are against the party-declarant's interest when made, this disserving element is not an essential feature of the Rule 801(d)(2) exemption. All that is required for a party-opponent statement is that the party

---

[91]   Fed. R. Evid. 807.

[92]   Congress wanted to limit the use of dying declarations in the criminal arena to homicide cases. In Illustration (2) above, a prosecutor could argue that Mae's statement should be admitted under the residual exception, as a "near-miss" of Rule 804(b)(2). See the discussion of Rule 807 and "near misses" later in this Chapter.

[93]   The restyling rejected the term "admissions" and "admissions against interest" because they were confusing and inaccurate. Party-opponent statements need not "admit" anything; they need not be against interest when made; and the term "admission against interest" created confusion with the separate exception for declarations against interest provided by Rule 804(b)(3).

against whom the statement is offered is responsible for the statement.

Recall that "unavailability" is essential to the admissibility of a declaration against interest. This requirement does not, of course, apply to a party-opponent statement. Another important difference between a party-opponent statement and a declaration against interest is this: a party-opponent statement is admissible only against the party responsible for it; a declaration against interest, however, is freely admissible against any or all parties to the suit.

Because admissibility of a declaration against interest is conditioned upon a showing of unavailability, the exception will only apply when the declarant is not a party. As we just observed, when the declarant is a party, she is available to testify and thus the party-opponent exemption is the proper means for her opponent to surmount the hearsay rule. Thus, declarations against interest are disserving statements made by unavailable *nonparty declarants*. It follows that a hearsay statement cannot be both a party-opponent statement and a declaration against interest.

When Is a Statement Against the Declarant's Interest?

We have spoken about a statement against a declarant's interest as if it were apparent when his interest is undermined or threatened by a "disserving" statement. Of course, the nature of a declaration is not always evident. First, it must be determined what kind of interests are embraced within the present exception. There are various possibilities, ranging from a statement inimical to one's social interest ("When I'm drunk, I'm cruel to my wife, when sober, I'm cruel to her dogs")[94] to a statement against penal interest that could lead to criminal punishment "(I shot my business partner"). Most of the common-law cases, especially the early ones, limited the present exception to statements that were directly adverse to the declarant's pecuniary or proprietary interest. Thus, assertions coming within the exception tended to have a business or financial flavor, and thus often were spoken in a context where rational behavior is the expected norm. ("We owe our supplier $50,000.").

Statements against penal interest were usually rejected, primarily because of the suspect context in which they most frequently were proffered. Assume that Alex is prosecuted for the murder of *V*. He offers the testimony of *W* (his cousin) who will testify that Cassius said that he murdered *V*. Cassius cannot be located and is possibly now in another country. The trial judge is apprehensive that Cassius was lying—Cassius is unlikely in fact to be prosecuted,

---

[94]   Although the Federal Rules do not recognize statements against social interest as within the present exception, a few states do. *See, e.g.,* Cal. Evid. Code § 1230 (1966).

and may have made the statement to create evidence on Alex's behalf. In other words, the judge is concerned that false evidence will raise a reasonable doubt in the jury's mind and that Alex will be erroneously acquitted. Common law judges generally responded to this concern by refusing to recognize a hearsay exception for declarations against *penal* interests. But note that not all penal interest statements fit the example. Some declarations against penal interest could be made under reliable circumstances (such as a statement of a declarant to his mother, "Mom, I feel so bad that I murdered *V*," with no hint of influence from the defendant). So the common law bar on against-penal-interest statements was unnecessarily strict.

Modern courts, operating under the Federal Rules or their state counterparts, recognize two kinds of interests that a Rule 804(b)(3) declarant can impair: *pecuniary and penal*. There remains the problem of deciding whether a particular statement is adverse to one of these interests. *This determination is made by the context in which the statement is made.*

Of course, when consideration is given to the context of the statement, it sometimes occurs that the nature of the statement will vary from what appears on its face. Take, for example, the statement, "I owe Alex $5,000." This remark appears to be against the speaker's interest, and usually is. But suppose Alex is claiming that the speaker owes him $10,000, not the $5,000 claimed by the declarant. In this broader context, the speaker's statement is actually self-serving. So, too, would be a declarant's statement to investigators that he committed a crime at noon on day 1 in City X, when he is suspected of committing a more serious crime in City Y at that approximate time.

The point is that statements that appear self-serving sometimes may be disserving; statements that appear disserving sometimes may be self-serving, and "neutral" statements may not in fact be neutral. Consider, for example, a statement by *X* that she is still a member of a certain business partnership. Her statement might be disserving if the partnership were in financial difficulty, but self-serving if the firm were improving its financial posture and she wanted a share of its potential profits.

Text of Rule 804(b)(3)

Federal Rule of Evidence 804(b)(3) provides an exception from the hearsay rule, for the following:

Statement Against Interest. A statement that:

    (A) a reasonable person in the declarant's position would have made only if the person believed it to be true because, when made, it was so contrary to the declarant's proprietary or pecuniary interest or had so great a tendency to invalidate the declarant's claim against someone else or to expose the declarant to civil or criminal liability; and

    (B) is supported by corroborating circumstances that clearly indicate its trustworthiness, if it is offered in a criminal case as one that tends to expose the declarant to criminal liability.

Declarations Against Penal Interest

The major innovation of Rule 804(b)(3) is its recognition of admissibility for declarations against penal interest. But note the proviso at the end of Rule 804(b)(3) that attaches a condition to the admissibility of statements against a hearsay declarant's penal interest when offered in a criminal case. The trial judge may not admit such a statement unless it is supported by "corroborating circumstances that clearly indicate its trustworthiness."[95]

Take a murder case where the accused wants to admit a statement from a declarant taking responsibility for the murder. A variety of circumstances could supply the needed corroborating circumstances—such as the relationship (e.g., animosity) between the declarant and the victim, the motive of the declarant to be truthful, physical evidence (e.g. presence of the declarant's fingerprints or DNA at the scene of the crime), and the testimony of other witnesses. The fundamental point is that the accused (in the example) and the prosecutor (where a statement of an accomplice is offered against the accused) both must establish not only that the statement they offer tends to disserve the declarant's penal interest,

---

[95] Fed. R. Evid. 804(b)(3). As originally adopted, the Rule imposed the corroboration requirement only on the criminal defendant. A 2010 amendment changed this. The Advisory Committee's Note explained: "Rule 804(b)(3) has been amended to provide that the corroborating circumstances requirement applies to all declarations against penal interest offered in criminal cases. A number of courts have applied the corroborating circumstances requirement to declarations against penal interest offered by the prosecution, even though the text of the Rule did not so provide. . . . A unitary approach to declarations against penal interest assures both the prosecution and the accused that the Rule will not be abused and that only reliable hearsay statements will be admitted under the exception."

but also that there are corroborating circumstances clearly indicating that the statement is trustworthy. Those corroborating circumstances are usefully combined into two categories: 1) corroborating evidence (such as forensic evidence supporting the truth of the declarant's account); and 2) circumstantial guarantees of trustworthiness (such as that the statement was made near in time to the event, or made spontaneously with no indication of a litigation motive, etc.).

ILLUSTRATIONS

(1) Harvey and his girlfriend, Ellen, are employed by a successful small business that specializes in selling and laying kitchen and bathroom tile. Harvey, who majored in accounting in college, manages and maintains the company's financial records; Ellen works mostly in the sales department, but sometimes is assigned to help with records and accounting. For more than a year, Harvey has been embezzling small amounts of money from his employer. Recently, he revealed his scheme to Ellen, and enlisted her aid in advancing and covering up his theft. For several months thereafter, the embezzlement scheme worked smoothly, but then a routine outside audit revealed discrepancies in the company's financial records. Both Harvey and Ellen, whose relationship is increasingly acrimonious, fall under suspicion.

As the pressure mounts, Ellen calls the detective from the Fraud Division who has been investigating the case. She reveals her own illegal activities and then explains in detail (and from personal knowledge) exactly how Harvey conceived the scheme, enlisted her aid, and made the false entries that allowed him to embezzle funds. Although Ellen agrees to testify against Harvey, she is killed in an automobile accident prior to trial. The prosecutor offers her statements to the fraud investigator, who is present and willing to testify. Admissible?

Illustration (1) raises difficulty because at least some portions of Ellen's statements are more about Harvey than about Ellen. The problem of "mixed" statements has been variously resolved by courts over the years.

The leading case on the treatment of statements that are not completely disserving to the declarant is *Williamson v. United States*,[96] where the government sought to use certain statements of one Harris, an alleged accomplice, to implicate the defendant,

---

[96]   512 U.S. 594 (1994).

Williamson. Harris was arrested after two suitcases of cocaine were seized from the trunk of his rented car. During custodial interrogation, Harris told a DEA officer that he was transporting the cocaine for Williamson. His statements thus implicated both himself and Williamson. At Williamson's trial, Harris refused to testify and thus was "unavailable" under Rule 804(a). Concluding that Harris's statements were against his penal interest under Rule 804(b)(3), the trial judge allowed the DEA agent to testify concerning what Harris had said about both himself and Williamson.

On appeal, the United States Supreme Court first addressed the meaning of "statement" in the against-interest exception, and concluded that the term should be construed narrowly: even if part of a remark or declaration might be disserving, this does not mean that an entire narrative can be introduced as part of the same "statement." The Court went on to say that parts of a narrative that are not disserving to the declarant are not admissible under Rule 804(b)(3). As applied to Harris's confession, a majority of the Court held that the against-interest exception of subsection (b)(3) did not apply to the confessions insofar as they implicated *Williamson*, because implicating Williamson was not contrary to Harris's interest *given the context in which the statements were made, i.e., made to police officers during an interrogation after an arrest*. The Court cautioned that Harris may have thought that his statements implicating Williamson would ultimately decrease his own punishment—he had the incentive, when arrested and interrogated, to "curry favor" with law enforcement by identifying other criminals; those identifications could not hurt him because he had been caught red-handed, and the only way he could help himself was to cooperate by identifying others.

The *Williamson* Court establishes a cautious approach to statements against penal interest. Narratives, reports, and extended declarations are not to be treated in the aggregate as self-serving or disserving. Each component of a composite narrative requires a discrete analysis. Presumably, this approach would also apply to a single statement with both self-serving and disserving parts. More importantly, *Williamson* stands for the proposition that accusatory statements by alleged accomplices to police officers *are not admissible against the accused under Rule 804(b)(3)* because such accusations are not against the *declarant's* penal interest.

In the cases after *Williamson* there is a critical distinction between statements made to police officers and those made to others such as friends and family. Consider the following hypothetical. Late at night Declarant knocks on the door of a friend's apartment. When admitted, he says, "I've got to hide. Sam and I robbed the convenience store at Seventh and Vine. Someone called the cops, so we ditched the car, split the money, and ran in separate directions." Admissible against Sam? Note that the declarant was not currying favor, was not speaking to the authorities, had no apparent motive to lie, and his statement displays an "insider's" knowledge of the illegal activities, as well as implicates him not only in a crime but also in a *conspiracy* to commit a crime.

This kind of statement has been found sufficiently disserving under Rule 804(b)(3) in all the circuit courts to prove Sam's activities as well as the Declarant's. The reference to Sam is in fact, in this context, disserving to Declarant's penal interest because it indicates inside knowledge of the crime and shows that the declarant was not only involved in a robbery but also in a conspiracy. The same statement made to police officers *upon ar*rest would not be admissible against Sam, given the likelihood at that point that Declarant is currying favor with authorities by identifying an accomplice.

Applying *Williamson* to the facts of Illustration (1), Ellen's declarations would be inadmissible because not sufficiently disserving to her interest. The fact that she made her statements to a law enforcement official and had agreed to testify against Harvey indicates that she may have been currying favor with law enforcement; it also appears that she was attempting to shift most of the blame to Harvey.

Constitutional issues also strongly suggest the inadmissibility of Ellen's proffered statements. The Confrontation Clause contained in the Sixth Amendment of the United States Constitution guarantees to an accused the right "to be confronted with the witnesses against him." A 2004 Supreme Court decision, *Crawford v. Washington*,[97] states that the question for admissibility of hearsay under the Confrontation Clause is whether the hearsay statement is "testimonial" in nature. If so, the statement is inadmissible unless the declarant is available for cross-examination by the accused or, if unavailable, the accused has had a prior opportunity to cross-examine the declarant. The Court has held that statements to police officers during "the course of interrogations [concerning criminal activity] are . . . testimonial" under this standard.[98] Accordingly, statements like Ellen's, made to law enforcement and implicating the accused, violate both the hearsay rule under *Williamson* and the Confrontation Clause under *Crawford*.

(2) Assume that Harvey and Ellen participate in the embezzlement as described in Illustration (1). When the

[97]   541 U.S. 36 (2004).
[98]   Id. at 52.

outside auditor discovers the accounting discrepancies, Ellen confides in her best friend, Ben, that she has been involved in an embezzlement scheme. She also tells him exactly how Harvey conceived and executed the theft, and how she and Harvey tried to cover up their illegal activities. Because Ellen is unavailable at Harvey's criminal trial, the prosecutor calls Ben. Is Ben's testimony about Ellen's description of criminal activity admissible?

The circumstances in Illustration (2) are less likely to provoke constitutional concerns. Ellen's declarations, made to Ben are not testimonial—they are not made to police officers and there is no indication of a primary motive to have the statements used in any criminal prosecution, which as we will see is key to identifying what statements are testimonial after *Crawford*. And three years after deciding *Crawford*, the Supreme Court made clear that if hearsay is not testimonial, then its admission cannot violate the defendant's right to confrontation—that is, the Confrontation Clause is only implicated by testimonial hearsay.[99]

Note that the reason why the statement is not testimonial (it was not made with a primary motive to be used in a criminal prosecution) also supports its admissibility under Rule 804(b)(3) after *Williamson*. The statement obviously is not made to curry favor with law enforcement, as it is made to her trusted friend. Moreover, the statement has a tendency to be disserving, because it implicates *both* Ellen and the accused as acting in concert to commit a crime. When, however, Ellen stops referring to her own conduct with Harvey and provides details of activity solely done by him, then there is a good argument that such statements are not disserving to Ellen—those statements are just shifting blame.

It might be argued that a statement that on its face is disserving ("I have been embezzling funds from my employer") is not against interest when the declarant is confiding in family members, close friends, or other confidants. The argument is that even though the *content* of the statement is disserving, *making* the statement was not disserving because the declarant reasonably believed that her interests were not impaired: she would not expect that her confidant would reveal the statement to anyone. But the courts have rejected this argument.[100] This judicial response can be defended on several grounds. First, it is unlikely that the declarant thought her statements were self-serving, or even neutral. Second, the context of trust and confidentiality suggests that the declarant is likely to be candid—so that is a corroborating circumstance. Third, you can never

---

[99]   *Whorton v. Bockting*, 549 U.S. 406 (2007).

[100]   *See, e.g., United States v. Mock*, 640 F.2d 629 (5th Cir. 1981).

be certain that friends or family members will keep a secret—especially if they find themselves in a situation in which disclosure might be useful to protect themselves from some negative consequence—thus under the terms of Rule 804(b)(3), such a statement, even when made to a trusted person, has a "tendency" to expose the declarant to criminal liability.

In Illustration (2), to the extent the statements are against penal interest, the government will have to establish corroborating circumstances. Such circumstances could probably be found in this case. As stated above, there is a guarantee of trustworthiness because Ellen was confiding to a trusted friend. Secondly, there is likely to be information in the company records that would verify her account—i.e., corroborating evidence.

Personal and Family History (Pedigree Exception)

Modern public records concerning births, deaths, adoptions, divorces, and the like limit the need for this exception for large segments of the population. The Federal Rule in point is 804(b)(4). It has two major parts. In subsection (A), the exception removes from the hearsay ban statements by an unavailable declarant about *his* birth, adoption, ancestry or other aspects of his "personal or family history."[101] In subsection (B), the exception generally addresses the same subject matters,[102] but focuses on declarations by unavailable *family members* (related by adoption, marriage, or blood) and by *family associates* (such as minister or doctor) "likely to be accurate" in light of their relationship with the person's family.[103] Rule 804(b)(4) does not require that the declarant have first-hand knowledge. Thus, an entry in (now unavailable) Uncle's diary that "Niece and Husband called from London to report the birth of their daughter, Alana, 6 pounds, 9 ounces, b. Aug. 2, 2011" would fall within the exception.

This exception is rarely invoked in federal cases, since family law issues tend to be litigated in state courts.

Forfeiture of a Hearsay Objection

Rule 804(b)(6) provides that a party forfeits the right to object to a hearsay statement when the declarant has become unavailable and the party has wrongfully acted, or acquiesced in wrongdoing, that was intended to and did create that unavailability. The most obvious situation for employing this exception is where a criminal defendant

---

[101]   Fed. R. Evid. 804(b)(4)(A).

[102]   Subsection (B) adds "death" to the list of admissible personal and family events and relationships—that would be silly to include in (A), which covers the declarant's statement of his own history.

[103]   Fed. R. Evid. 804(b)(4)(B).

kills a witness, or has him killed, to prevent him from testifying; by engaging in this conduct, the defendant has forfeited the right to object on hearsay grounds to any of the victim's hearsay statements. The Rule is based on the policy that a party should not be able to profit by excluding hearsay that is only necessary because the party has made it impossible to produce the declarant.

The Rule is not limited to criminal defendants. Any party who wrongfully acts, or acquiesces in wrongdoing, with the intent to render a declarant unavailable to testify forfeits the right to object to the unavailable declarant's hearsay statement. So for example, if a prosecutor intentionally intimidates a defense witness so that the witness refuses to testify, the prosecution loses the right to interpose a hearsay objection with respect to any hearsay statement that the witness may have made. The same goes for parties in civil cases. The Rule mandates forfeiture for "wrongdoing" but the conduct need not rise to the level of criminal activity.[104]

Under the Rule, it must be shown that the party against whom the evidence is offered acted *with intent to procure the unavailability of the declarant as a witness*. If the defendant kills a declarant simply because he did not like him, or because he was burned in a drug deal by him, then the defendant has not forfeited his right to object to the declarant's hearsay statement. Assume a murder case in which the victim has made hearsay statements identifying the accused. The government argues that the accused has forfeited his hearsay objection because he murdered the victim. The court will not find forfeiture under these circumstances alone. The government must show that the defendant had the intent to procure the unavailability of the victim *as a witness*.[105] In that way the punishment (forfeiting the right to challenge hearsay) fits the crime (making the witness unavailable so that the adversary is forced to use hearsay).

This does not mean, however, that a forfeiture can be found only if the party wakes up one day and says "I intend to act wrongfully and render the witness unavailable." The intent to render a witness unavailable to testify can be inferred from wrongful activity. Moreover, the exception does not require that the party actually commit the act of wrongdoing that led to the declarant's

---

[104]   *See, e.g., United States v. Scott*, 284 F.3d 758, 762 (7th Cir. 2002) ("Scott argues that his actions were not sufficiently evil because they were not akin to murder, physical assault, or bribery. Although such malevolent acts are clearly sufficient to constitute 'wrongdoing', they are not necessary.").

[105]   In *Giles v. California*, 554 U.S. 353 (2008), the Supreme Court interpreted the Sixth Amendment Confrontation Clause to hold that the accused in a criminal case does not forfeit his right to confront accusers unless the prosecution shows that the accused acted with the intent to prevent a witness from testifying.

unavailability. Acquiescence in the wrongdoing is sufficient under the terms of Rule 804(b)(6).

What if there is a factual dispute about whether the party wrongfully caused the declarant's unavailability? Assume a murder case in which the defendant objects to the hearsay statement of an eyewitness. The government argues that the defendant paid to have the declarant murdered, and he is now unavailable, so the government offers the declarant's hearsay statements. The defendant vigorously denies that he had anything to do with the murder of the declarant. How does the court decide whether forfeiture has occurred? The basic procedure is that the court will hold a hearing (of course outside the jury's presence), and will take evidence on the cause of the declarant's unavailability. As the question of forfeiture is an admissibility requirement, the judge under Rule 104(a) is not bound by the rules of admissibility except for those with respect to privilege. The judge decides whether the defendant has "engaged or acquiesced in wrongdoing" that was designed to, and did, cause the unavailability of the declarant. Under Rule 104(a), the government must prove these facts by a preponderance of the evidence.

If one or more members of a conspiracy successfully engage in wrongdoing with the intention of making a declarant unavailable, all of the conspirators will lose the right to object to statements by the declarant as long as the wrongdoing was a reasonably forseeable object of the conspiracy, and the wrongdoing was during and in furtherance of the conspiracy.[106]

§ 7.10   The Residual Exception—Rule 807

Federal Rule 807 creates an exception for hearsay that is reliable but yet does not meet the admissibility requirements of any of the categorical hearsay exceptions. The text of Rule 807, as amended effective December 1, 2019, describes the statements covered by the exception:

Residual Exception

(a) In General. Under the following conditions, a hearsay statement is not excluded by the rule against hearsay even if the statement is not admissible under a hearsay exception in Rule 803 or 804:

    (1) the statement is supported by sufficient guarantees of trustworthiness—after considering the totality of the

---

[106]   *See, e.g., United States v. Cherry*, 217 F.3d 811 (10th Cir. 2000).

circumstances under which it was made and evidence, if any, corroborating the statement; and

(2) it is more probative on the point for which it is offered than any other evidence that the proponent can obtain through reasonable efforts.

(b) Notice. The statement is admissible only if the proponent gives an adverse party reasonable notice of the intent to offer the statement—including the substance and the declarant's name—so that the party has a fair opportunity to meet it. The notice must be provided in writing before the trial or hearing—or in any form during the trial or hearing if the court, for good cause, excuses a lack of earlier notice.

The important conditions for admissibility under Rule 807 are these: (1) guarantees of trustworthiness, (2) probative force exceeding that of other evidence on the same point that the proponent could secure through reasonable efforts, and (3) notice to the adverse party of intent to offer a hearsay statement under this exception. Only conditions (1) and (2) warrant any further discussion.

As to the "more probative" requirement, the rationale for it is that the residual exception should be narrowly applied and therefore should be used sparingly, only when necessary. The concern is that the residual exception, broadly applied, would allow for too much judicial discretion and perhaps expand to take the place of the categorical exceptions.

In deciding whether the residual hearsay is "more probative" the judge must consider whether other evidence can be procured by reasonable efforts. The other evidence may consist of the declarant's deposition, her appearance as a witness, or testimonial or documentary evidence from other sources. For example, assume that a plaintiff, a former prisoner, is suing prison guards for their role in a prison fight in which the plaintiff was injured. The plaintiff offers the written account of a fellow prisoner describing the guards' actions during the fight. Assume this writing is sufficiently trustworthy. It is nonetheless likely to be excluded because it is not more probative than other evidence reasonably available—specifically, testimony that could be provided by other prisoners with personal knowledge of the event.

Generally speaking, if the declarant is available to testify, the hearsay will be inadmissible under Rule 807 because it is not "more probative" than the trial testimony that the declarant could provide. There are exceptions, however—such as where the witness is a child who would be unlikely to be communicative on the stand—in which the residual hearsay will be more probative than the declarant's trial testimony, because in order to be admissible it will have to be found reliable, and thus it is likely to be more probative than uncommunicative testimony on the stand.

As to the "other evidence" to which Rule 807 makes reference the judge should take into account the inconvenience, time, and expense associated with securing evidence from an alternative source. Central to the judge's determination is the centrality or importance of the hearsay evidence to the main issues in the case.

As we just observed, Rule 807 commands that hearsay admitted under the "residual" exception must have sufficient guarantees of trustworthiness. The original rule required the court to determine that the trustworthiness was "equivalent to" the Rule 803 and 804 exceptions. But the Advisory Committee determined that an "equivalence" analysis was doomed to failure, because the hearsay exceptions are not of uniform reliability. For example, "equivalence" to the ancient document exception would mean that it is not reliable at all.

So the amendment simply requires the court to find that the proffered statement is trustworthy, and it directs the court to two sources that would support trustworthiness. The first is circumstantial guarantees attendant to the making of the statement. Such factors include whether the statement was spontaneous, whether it was affected by a litigation motive, whether it was made while memory was fresh, etc. The second source for trustworthiness is evidence that corroborates the declarant's account—such as actions or statements by others consistent with the declarant's account, or supporting physical evidence. For example, if a child accuses a parent of physical abuse, the injuries found on the child by a physician would provide some corroboration that the child was being truthful.

ILLUSTRATION

Staywich is a town of 30,000 residents. Recently, the heavy clock tower atop the city courthouse came toppling down, crashed through the roof, and virtually destroyed the courtroom below.

Damage to the building was in excess of $100,000. Subsequently, Staywich brings suit against the company that (since 1995) insured the courthouse against loss by *fire or lightning*. Debris from the clock tower contained charred timbers. Several residents testify that the week before the tower collapsed, it had been struck by lightning. The insurance company contends, however, that the tower collapsed due to a faulty design, improper construction, and progressive deterioration. According to the defendant's experts the charred wood and the debris came from a fire in the courthouse tower that occurred sixty years previously, when the courthouse was under construction.

Counsel for the defendant produces an article from the Staywich "Morning Times," the town's only newspaper. The article, which bears the date June 9, 1945, reports that a fire destroyed the unfinished dome of the courthouse, but firemen were able to save the main structure. After counsel authenticates the article as coming from the newspaper's archives, and confirms that she has given the required notice under Rule 807, she offers the newspaper article in evidence. Counsel for the town of Staywich objects on the grounds of hearsay. How should the trial judge rule?

This Illustration is based on a pre-rules case.[107] Although there was no residual exception at common law, the court admitted a newspaper article similar to the one described in the Illustration. It found that hearsay dangers were minimized. The reporter presumably wrote the story soon after the fire when his memory was fresh. Faulty perception was not a significant problem because the fire and its aftermath could easily be observed. The reporter had a motive to be truthful because in a small town the accuracy of his story could be verified by local residents. Moreover, there was a need for this evidence, because the passage of time would make it difficult to find witnesses to the fire and, even if one or more could be located, their memories would have dimmed. All of these factors are, of course, present in the Illustration and, in combination, they strongly suggest that the Illustration meets the criteria of Rule 807. Although that rule does not require unavailability, it does require that the proffered hearsay evidence be "more probative on the point for which it is offered than any other evidence which the proponent can procure through reasonable efforts." Thus, the availability (or unavailability) of live testimony is a relevant consideration in the application of Rule 807.

Near-Misses

Before 2019 there was some federal authority that strictly construed Rule 807 in a way that made it hardly useable. Under the so-called "near miss" construction of Rule 807, the rule was inapplicable if the proffered evidence was addressed by one (or more) of the specific exceptions, but failed to satisfy all of the conditions of admissibility. Thus a statement by a neutral observer to a utility repairman that from his window, five minutes before, he (the

---

[107]   *Dallas County v. Commercial Union Assur. Co.*, 286 F.2d 388 (5th Cir. 1961).

declarant) saw "lightning strike very close to an electrical generator" on a nearby mountainside could not be admitted under Rule 807. The statement would be specifically addressed by Rule 803(1) and (2). The five-minute lapse of time would probably disqualify the statement from admission into evidence as a Rule 803(1), which governs present sense impressions. That rule, you may recall, requires that the declarant speak as he perceives the event or condition he describes or "immediately thereafter." Suppose, further, that the declarant was somewhat taken aback, but not fully "under the stress of excitement"[108] when he spoke, thus ruling out the application of Rule 803(2)—the exception for excited utterances. These "near misses" would make Rule 807 inapplicable under the view of some courts. Another example would be a mother who told her friend "I have been a bad mother to my son, which is why he has murdered so many people." That statement is "against interest" but not admissible under Rule 804(b)(3), because that exception requires the statement to be against the declarant's pecuniary or penal interests—whereas the mother's statements are against a "social" interest, in that the statement harms her social standing. So it would be a "near miss" of Rule 804(b)(3), and not a proper candidate for admission under Rule 807 if that rule is construed to bar "near misses."

The problem with the position that near-misses cannot be admissible under Rule 807 is that almost every hearsay declaration that can be made is addressed, at least peripherally, by one or more of the specific exceptions. One of the reasons for Rule 807 is to provide the courts with some flexibility in applying the hearsay rule; but flexibility is not possible if courts automatically exclude a reliable hearsay statement that comes close to, but does not fit, one of the standard exceptions.

Most courts have rejected the near miss rule, for good reason. The 2019 amendment to Rule 807 makes clear that Rule 807 can be used to admit "near misses" so long as they are trustworthy. The Advisory Committee Note to the amendment explains as follows:

> The rule in its original form applied to hearsay "not specifically covered" by a Rule 803 or 804 exception. The amendment makes the rule applicable to hearsay "not admissible under" those exceptions. This clarifies that a court assessing guarantees of trustworthiness may consider whether the statement is a "near-miss" of one of the Rule 803 or 804 exceptions. If the court employs a "near-miss" analysis it should—in addition to evaluating all relevant guarantees of trustworthiness—take into account the

---

[108]   Fed. R. Evid. 803(2).

reasons that the hearsay misses the admissibility requirements of the standard exception.

ILLUSTRATIONS

(1) Since his graduation from high school a year ago, David has been working as a day laborer for a construction company. Because his wages are low, he has continued to live in the house owned and occupied by his mother. Lately, she has been increasingly concerned about both his excessive drinking and his association with two brothers, known for their violent behavior and substance abuse.

Peter has filed a suit against David, alleging that the latter became intoxicated at a local bar and, egged on by the two brothers, covertly followed Peter (under cover of darkness) from the bar to his (Peter's) car. There he viciously attacked Peter causing serious bodily injury.

David arrived home that night with a bloody nose, and minor cuts and bruises. He managed to drive his motorcycle home, where he dismounted, let the cycle fall on its side, pressed a handkerchief to his nose, and walked unsteadily to the door.

Unbeknownst to David, his mother observed his arrival from her bedroom window. Ten minutes later she quietly went outside, where she saw drops of fresh blood on David's motorcycle tank.

The next morning, after she heard her son "call in sick" and go back to bed, David's mother sought out her pastor. She shared her concerns about David and also disclosed his intoxicated condition the night before, his apparent bloody nose, and the discovery of fresh drops of blood on his motorcycle. A month later, David's mother suffered a massive stroke and died en route to the hospital.

Subsequently, in the civil suit, Peter v. David, for assault and battery, David denies he was Peter's attacker and claims mistaken identity as his defense. During Peter's case-in-chief, he testifies that even though there was no moon on the night in question, he recognized David as his attacker. However, during the case in defense, David and the two brothers testify that the three of them finished their drinks, left the bar together, and immediately drove away— the brothers in their car and David on his motorcycle. During the Plaintiff's case in rebuttal Peter's lawyer, having given the notice required by Federal Rule 807, calls

Pastor who is prepared to testify about David's mother's observations on the night of the attack. David's lawyer immediately enters a hearsay objection. Should the trial judge sustain it?

Illustration (1) appears to meet the criteria of Rule 807. The only evidence possibly more probative on David's likely involvement in the assault is his mother's testimony and it is unavailable. There are circumstantial guarantees of trustworthiness: the short period of time between the mother's disclosures and her perception, her opportunity to observe, and her probable motive to tell the truth to her pastor, from whom she was seeking guidance. Moreover, these are not the kind of statements that would come from a mother unless they were true. (The statements "nearly miss" the declaration against interest exception—because they are against a "parental" interest as opposed to a pecuniary or penal one. But that is not a reason for excluding the statements under Rule 807, and in fact it may be considered by the court as an indication of reliability). It would be another thing if the mother's statement absolved David— that is what mothers would be expected to do. Corroborative evidence supplied by Peter's testimony is an additional guarantee of trustworthiness that the court must consider under the terms of Rule 807, as would be any evidence that David was seen with scrapes and bruises.

(2) Suppose, prior to the civil suit described in Illustration (1), the prosecutor decides to prosecute David for criminal assault causing serious bodily injury. A grand jury is convened, and among the witnesses called before the grand jury are Peter, and David's mother. The latter testifies as to David's intoxicated condition, his handkerchief pressed against his nose, and the drops of fresh blood on his motorcycle. The grand jury indicts David. Because David's mother is unavailable at his criminal trial, the prosecutor (after giving proper notice) offers a transcript of her grand jury testimony. Admissible under Rule 807?

Illustration (2), regarding the admissibility of grand jury testimony under Rule 807, raises constitutional concerns. The former testimony exception cannot be used to introduce grand jury testimony against the accused because he is not represented at the grand jury hearing and, except for the possibility of being called as a witness, is absent from these proceedings. A prosecutor would be unlikely to invoke Rule 807 for the testimony of an unavailable grand jury witness against the accused—admissibility under Rule 807 would be an academic exercise, because the grand jury testimony is inadmissible under the Confrontation Clause.

As we will see in Chapter 8, the Court in *Crawford v. Washington*,[109] held that hearsay that is testimonial cannot be admitted against the accused unless he has the opportunity to cross-examine the declarant. Obviously the accused has no right to cross-examine a declarant at a grand jury; obviously as well, grand jury testimony is the paradigmatic example of testimonial hearsay. It fits the Court's definition of "testimonial" because it is prepared with the motivation that it be used in a criminal prosecution—and for good measure it's even called "testimony." So if the grand jury declarant is not available to testify at trial, admission of the testimony would violate the accused's right to confrontation. It wouldn't matter whether the testimony was reliable. Under *Crawford* the question for the Confrontation Clause is not whether hearsay is reliable but whether it is testimonial. Thus, *Crawford* has served to substantially limit the use of the residual exception as a means of admitting hearsay against the accused. (It does not, of course, alter the trustworthiness analysis as applied to parties other than the accused, because only the accused has a constitutional right to confront adverse witnesses.)

§ 7.11 Applying the Hearsay Exceptions to Multiple Hearsay

Sometimes a hearsay statement includes, or repeats, one or more other hearsay statements. When this occurs, in order for the statement to be admitted into evidence, there must be an applicable hearsay exception or exemption for each hearsay transmission.

Federal Rule 805 provides that:

Hearsay within hearsay is not excluded by the rule against hearsay if each part of the combined statements conforms with an exception to the rule.

Thus, with multiple hearsay, a hearsay exception or exemption must be found for each level of hearsay. Consider, for example, the following illustration: an insurance investigator goes to the scene of an accident and takes the statement of one of several persons involved in the accident. The declarant admits fault, taking the entire blame for the accident. Suppose that the police charge another person with reckless driving, and the declarant is unavailable at trial. If the investigator is also unavailable, an offer of a report by the investigator concerning the declarant's statement would have to overcome two hearsay hurdles; one for the out-of-court statement of

---

[109]   541 U.S. 36 (2004).

the declarant who admitted fault, and one for the investigator's statement (the report). Probably the declarant's statement is a declaration against interest. However, the second hearsay hurdle is not overcome unless the investigator's report meets the requirements of the exception for regularly conducted business activities. (It can't be a past recollection recorded because the investigator is not a witness at trial).

Note that party-opponent statements under Rule 801(d)(2) and certain prior statements of available witnesses under Rule 801(d)(1) are technically defined as not hearsay. So Rule 805—which refers to an "exception" to the hearsay rule—could technically be read to be inapplicable to situations in which statements covered by Rule 801(d) are included within another statement that is hearsay. But courts have held that the technical difference between Rule 801(d) "not hearsay" and Rule 803, 804, and 807 "hearsay subject to exception" cannot control the application of Rule 805's limitation on multiple hearsay. As one court put it: "For the purposes of the hearsay-within-hearsay principle expressed in Rule 805, nonhearsay statements under Rule 801(d) . . . should be considered in analyzing a multiple hearsay statement as the equivalent of a level of the combined statements that conforms with an exception to the hearsay rule."[110] Of course, the mere fact that one level of a multiple level statement qualifies as exempt from the hearsay rule does not excuse the other levels from the Rule 805 requirement that each level satisfy the hearsay rule.[111] Conversely, a statement admissible under Rule 801(d) can be admitted when included in another hearsay statement if the other hearsay statement qualifies under an exception.[112]

---

[110]   *United States v. Dotson*, 821 F.2d 1034, 1035 (5th Cir. 1987).

[111]   *See, e.g., Southern Stone Co. v. Singer*, 665 F.2d 698 (5th Cir. 1982) (even if one level of a double hearsay statement is admissible under Rule 801(d)(2)(A), the second level of hearsay was not subject to an exception, so the document was inadmissible).

[112]   *See, e.g., Wright v. Farmers Co-op*, 681 F.2d 549 (8th Cir. 1982) (a statement by the defendant's employee qualified as statement of an agent, and the transcribed version of the statement that was made by an insurance adjuster who obtained it qualified as a business record).

Chapter VIII

HEARSAY AND THE
CONFRONTATION CLAUSE

The Confrontation Clause: A Primer

An important problem in criminal trials is how to reconcile the accused's Sixth Amendment right "to be confronted with the witnesses against him" with the government's invocation of the various exceptions to the hearsay rule. These escapes from the hearsay ban allow a declarant's statement to be introduced against the accused for the truth of the declarant's assertion. Yet, in most instances, the accused cannot cross-examine the declarant concerning the reliability of her statement. Perhaps she was lying or mistaken; these possibilities cannot be explored through cross-examination when the declarant does not testify.

In the typical hearsay setting *A* (the declarant) makes a statement to *B* who appears as a witness and discloses *A's* statement to the trier of fact. It is true, of course, that the accused can confront and cross-examine *B*, but the "real" witness against the accused is *A*. Yet if the Confrontation Clause were construed to completely forbid the admission of *A's* statement unless she testified, the trier of fact would often be denied probative and reliable evidence.

One possible escape from this dilemma is to equate the accused's constitutional protection with the assumed reliability of the hearsay exceptions. The argument would run: exceptions to the hearsay rule are based on determinations by judges and legislators that some classes of hearsay are reliable. These classes of hearsay may be introduced into evidence even though the opponent has no opportunity to cross-examine the declarant. The accused is given adequate constitutional protection because of the way the hearsay rule is administered—unreliable hearsay is rejected, and the defendant should have no complaint about admission of reliable hearsay, because there is no reason to cross-examine a declarant who has imparted a reliable statement.

[handwritten margin note: assumed reliability of exception]

The problem with this argument is that the tail (the evidence rule) is wagging the dog (the accused's constitutional right). Moreover, it is difficult to assure that every statement within the hearsay exceptions is reliable. Thus, the Supreme Court has rejected this approach and has sought some middle ground between denying the use of hearsay exceptions in criminal trials and placing the constitutional protection of the Confrontation Clause entirely in the hands of the rule-makers and judges who oversee and administer the hearsay rule.

As we will see, the landmark case on the relationship between hearsay and the Confrontation Clause is *Crawford v. Washington*.[1] Understanding *Crawford* requires some consideration of the constitutional doctrine preceding it.

Major Features of Pre-Crawford Confrontation Doctrine

One possible way to protect the right to confrontation is to require a diligent effort by the prosecutor to produce the hearsay declarant for cross-examination by the accused. Under this approach, a hearsay exception could not be invoked by the government against the accused until the prosecutor has made a good-faith, diligent effort to secure the live testimony of the hearsay declarant. The degree of effort required would be dictated by the Confrontation Clause. But although the Court has occasionally used the Confrontation Clause to require the prosecutor to make a diligent effort to produce the declarant,[2] this use of the clause has been sporadic and, so far at least, inconsequential. It is probably safe to assume that the Court will usually defer to the terms of the hearsay exception on the issue of unavailability.[3] Thus, for example, if a hearsay exception does not require as a condition of its application that the declarant be unavailable, such as an excited utterance, the Court is unlikely to impose a constitutional requirement that the prosecutor make a diligent effort to produce the declarant.

Another way to protect the accused's confrontation right is to develop constitutional standards of trustworthiness (reliability) that evaluate the hearsay exceptions for corresponding indications of trustworthiness. From 1980[4] until 2004,[5] the Supreme Court's principal approach to reconciling the textual demand of the Confrontation Clause and the hearsay exceptions was to focus primary attention on newly established hearsay exceptions. If an exception had the imprimatur of many years of judicial experience (that is, was "firmly rooted"), the Court would defer to the collective judgments that had determined the hearsay was reliable and,

---

[1]   541 U.S. 36 (2004).

[2]   *See, e.g., Barber v. Page*, 390 U.S. 719, 723–25 (1968) (state government has obligation to try to produce the declarant who was in federal prison before resorting to testimony declarant gave at a preliminary hearing).

[3]   *See, e.g., White v. Illinois*, 502 U.S. 346, 355–57 (1992) (government may invoke exceptions for excited utterance and statements made to medical personnel without showing unavailability). *United States v. Inadi*, 475 U.S. 387, 394–96 (1986) (prosecutor not required to show coconspirator unavailable before invoking exemption for coconspirator's statements).

[4]   *Ohio v. Roberts*, 448 U.S. 56 (1980).

[5]   *Crawford v. Washington*, 541 U.S. 36 (2004).

accordingly, hold that the Confrontation Clause was satisfied.[6] A hearsay declaration introduced against the accused under an exception that was not firmly rooted would violate the Confrontation Clause unless the prosecutor could show that the hearsay statement was attended by indicia of reliability or "particularized guarantees of trustworthiness."[7] As you can now anticipate, the *Crawford* decision, discussed previously and below, has relegated the reliability-based analysis of hearsay exceptions to the annals of legal history.

There are, however, several areas of pre-*Crawford* confrontation jurisprudence that remain largely unaffected by the *Crawford* decision. IF WITNESS - OUT OF COURT STATEMENTS are OK

First, the Confrontation Clause is not offended by the introduction of a *witness's* own prior statements, assuming the accused has a fair opportunity to cross-examine the witness at trial.[8] After all, the witness can be cross-examined about both her present testimony and her previous declarations and this is sufficient to satisfy the right to confrontation.

Second, the Confrontation Clause requires that the accused and the adverse witness face each other—that is, be in a position to have eye contact during the witness's testimony.[9] (The assumption is that a face-to-face confrontation reduces the likelihood that the witness will lie.) This requirement affects the ability of the government to use electronic transmission, or a "one-way" screen in order to block the witness's view of the accused.[10] If this arrangement were always constitutionally permissible, it would be frequently used when a young child, allegedly victimized by the accused, is called to testify. However, under the Confrontation Clause, blocking the child's view of the accused is constitutionally forbidden—*unless* the trial court makes a determination, *specific to the case before it*, that requiring the child to testify in the presence of the accused is likely to produce trauma.[11]

---

[6]   *See, e.g., White* 502 U.S. at 355 n.8 (excited utterances and statements made for medical treatment); *Bourjaily v. United States*, 483 U.S. 171, 183–84 (coconspirator statements).

[7]   *See, e.g., Roberts*, 448 U.S. at 66.

[8]   *California v. Green*, 399 U.S. 149, 158 (1970). Thus, a statement admitted under the exemption for certain prior statements of a testifying witness would not ordinarily be constitutionally suspect. *See* Fed. R. Evid. 801(d)(1). Even though the Federal Rule limits the types of prior inconsistent statements that may be admitted for their truth, the Supreme Court's *Green* decision indicates that the Confrontation Clause permits all prior inconsistent statements to be admitted for their truth when a witness testifies and is subject to cross-examination.

[9]   *Coy v. Iowa*, 487 U.S. 1012, 1019–20 (1988).

[10]   The accused, and other trial participants, can, of course, see and hear the witness.

[11]   *Maryland v. Craig*, 497 U.S. 836, 857–58 (1990).

Third, the Confrontation Clause precludes the use of a confession to the police by one of the accused's non-testifying confederates against the accused, even in a joint trial. Suppose, for example, *A* and *B* are indicted for kidnapping. Following *A's* arrest, he signs a written statement that admits his guilt and also implicates *B*. In the joint trial of *A* and *B*, the trial judge allows the prosecutor to use *A's* prior statements against *A* as a statement by a party-opponent. Meanwhile *A* exercises his constitutional right not to testify. A constitutional violation occurs because *A's* earlier confession implicates *B* in the charged criminal activity and *B* cannot effectively cross-examine *A*; and the Court has held that a limiting instruction telling the jury that it is to use the statement only against *A* and not against *B* is insufficient to protect *B's* right to confrontation—such "powerfully incriminating" evidence cannot be ignored by lay jurors. Because the limiting instruction is ineffective, the end result is that *A* is an adverse witness against *B*; the hearsay is testimonial vis-a-vis *B*; and *A* is not subject to cross-examination at trial. This is known as the "*Bruton* problem."[12]

The *Bruton* problem is solved if *A* and *B* are given separate trials, in which case *A's* prior statement will only be admitted in *A's* trial (as a statement of a party-opponent). In some cases, it may be possible to delete *B's* name from *A's* hearsay statement, but this technique ("redaction") is constitutionally defective if a jury is certain to infer that the omitted name is that of co-defendant *B*.[13] One possible form of redaction that has worked is to substitute the defendant's name with a neutral pronoun—instead of "defendant and I did the crime", the statement is offered as "another guy and I did the crime." Courts have generally held such a redaction permissible because the redacted statement is no longer "powerfully incriminating" to the defendant.

Of course, if *A* elects to take the stand and testify fully, the Confrontation Clause is satisfied.[14] It does not matter whether *A* admits the prior statements, denies them, or qualifies them, because *B* (*A's* co-defendant) can confront and cross-examine *A* with respect to both *A's* prior statements and his present testimony.

The fourth confrontation principle unaltered by *Crawford* is this: if the out-of-court statement admitted against the accused is not hearsay, because not offered for its truth, then there is no violation of the right to confrontation. This is because confrontation is all about

---

[12]   The cornerstone case is *Bruton v. United States*, 391 U.S. 123, 136–37 (1968).

[13]   *See Gray v. Maryland*, 523 U.S. 185, 192–95 (1998).

[14]   *See Nelson v. O'Neil*, 402 U.S. 622, 629–30 (1971) (prior statement denied; favorable testimony given); *LaFrance v. Bohlinger*, 499 F.2d 29, 35 (1st Cir. 1974) (statement admitted; truth of it denied; police threats alleged).

cross-examination, and if the statement is offered for a purpose other than proving the truth of its contents, there is no point in cross-examining the declarant. For example, in *Tennessee v. Street*,[15] the defendant testified and challenged his own confession, arguing that a police officer first attempted to force him to write out a confession to the crime. When he protested that he couldn't write out a confession because he didn't have any information about the crime, the officer, according to Street, gave him the written confession of his alleged accomplice, Peele, and told him to copy it word-for-word. In rebuttal, the government offered and the court admitted Peele's confession, not for the truth of its contents, but to show that it differed from Street's written confession in several important respects. Peele did not testify at Street's trial, but the Court found no violation of the right to confrontation. Peele's confession was not admitted for the truth of its contents, but only for comparison with Street's confession. When offered for that purpose, it would make no sense to have to call Peele to the stand. He could not answer any relevant question, e.g., "Was your confession used by the officer as the template for Street's confession?" The Court held, therefore, that if an out-of-court statement is not hearsay given the purpose for which it is offered, then it cannot violate the accused's right to confrontation. The Court in *Crawford* specifically approved of the result in *Street*. And it is to *Crawford* that we now turn.

OLD → reliability

Crawford v. Washington: A Crossroads

In 2004 the Supreme Court adopted a new approach to the Confrontation Clause and discarded the constitutional doctrine it had been developing and refining since 1980. The core of that doctrine, set out in the Court's opinion in *Ohio v. Roberts*,[16] was to focus on whether the proffered hearsay was reliable. But the Court in *Crawford* held that the reliability-based approach was too flimsy and subjective to protect the accused's right to confrontation as it was understood by the Framers of the Constitution.

Crawford involved a prosecution for assault and attempted murder. The accused, Michael Crawford, claimed self-defense. An important factual question was whether the victim had drawn a weapon just before the accused stabbed him. Crawford's wife, Sylvia, was present at the assault and indeed participated in the alleged crime by leading Michael to the victim's apartment. However, at Crawford's trial she claimed her privilege not to testify against her spouse, and thus became unavailable. The prosecutor responded by proffering a tape-recorded statement that Sylvia had given to the police. Her statement described the assault in terms that cast doubt

---

[15]   471 U.S. 409 (1985).
[16]   448 U.S. 56 (1980).

on Michael's claim of self-defense. The trial judge admitted the taped statement on the ground that it was a declaration against Sylvia's penal interest that was accompanied by "indicia of reliability" sufficient to overcome Michael's confrontation clause objection. (Note that had Crawford been tried in federal court, Sylvia's statement would not have been admissible under the federal exception for declarations against penal interest—Rule 804(b)(3)—because statements by accomplices to police officers are thought to be made with a motivation to "curry favor" with law enforcement).[17]

Eventually, the case reached the United States Supreme Court where the question posed was whether the admission of Sylvia's hearsay statement to the police violated Crawford's rights under the Confrontation Clause. Justice Scalia, speaking for seven members of the Court, concluded that it did. The Court refused to employ the framework that was established in *Roberts* and its progeny. Instead, the Court began with the premise that the core historical concern of the Confrontation Clause is to assure that unexamined ex parte declarations that are *testimonial* in character are not introduced against an accused, unless the accused has an opportunity for cross-examination. The *Crawford* Court did not precisely define what constitutes a testimonial statement, but Justice Scalia provides considerable guidance at scattered places in his opinion. The paradigm of "testimony" according to the Court is the hearsay admitted in the trial of Sir Walter Raleigh—that hearsay was in the form of affidavits prepared for trial by eyewitnesses, and prepared with the assistance of the prosecution. Following this paradigm, testimonial declarations are directed to proving a fact for the purposes of a criminal prosecution;[18] they are characterized by structure and a certain degree of formality,[19] as opposed, for example, to a casual remark or a spontaneous or excited utterance; and such statements are directed at or prepared by government officials or bodies such as prosecutors, police, judicial officers, grand juries, or other investigative units.[20] Thus, testimonial hearsay is essentially prepared as a substitute for trial testimony of the declarant. In an important passage, the Court said that although it declined to adopt a definitive definition of "testimonial statements," the term

---

[17]   See the discussion of *Williamson v. United States* in § 7.9, supra.

[18]   *Crawford*, 541 U.S. at 61–62.

[19]   Id. at 51–52.

[20]   Justice Scalia mentions other ways of defining testimonial declarations. For example, a statement might be characterized as testimonial if the declarant "would reasonably expect [it] to be used prosecutorially" or, in a variation, if "an objective witness reasonably . . . [would] believe that the statement would be available for use at a later trial." These formulations, however, have been abandoned in the Court's subsequent cases. *White v. Illinois*, 502 U.S. 346, 365 (1992) (Thomas, J., joined by Scalia, J., concurring in part and concurring in judgment).

applies at a minimum to prior testimony at a preliminary hearing, before a grand jury, or at a former trial, and to police interrogations.[21]

These "modern practices," said the Court, have "the closest kinship to the kinds of testimonial abuses at which the Confrontation Clause was historically directed."[22] *ABSOLUTE ban on testimonial statement*

The *Crawford* rule as to testimonial statements is absolute. These hearsay statements cannot be introduced into evidence against the accused if the declarant is unavailable at the accused's trial and the accused never had a prior opportunity to cross-examine the declarant. The Confrontation Clause applies when, and only when, a declarant's statements are offered for their truth, thus implicating the hearsay rule. It is immaterial whether or not a testimonial statement fits within a hearsay exception. *rule*

The only possible deviation from these constitutional requirements set forth in *Crawford* is when the proffered statement is a dying declaration (mentioned in a footnote in *Crawford*). Most such declarations would not be testimonial in nature. However, when *dying declaration* a public official, such as a police officer, conducts a formal or structured interrogation of a dying declarant, the resulting responses would probably be testimonial. Justice Scalia stated that if these statements were nonetheless allowed in evidence, the rationale would be a long historical practice—and dying declarations would be *sui generis*. Because the statement before the Court in *Crawford* was not a dying declaration, the Court left open the question of the admissibility of a testimonial dying declaration.

One question unanswered in *Crawford* was whether the *Roberts* reliability framework remains partially intact and is to be applied to nontestimonial hearsay statements. In the subsequent case of *Whorton v. Bockting*,[23] the Court held that *the Confrontation Clause has no applicability to nontestimonial hearsay statements*.

The First Applications of Crawford

The critical question after *Crawford* is whether a hearsay statement is "testimonial" or not. While the Court did not try to define the term "testimonial" in *Crawford*, it added some explanation in *Davis v. Washington*.[24] The Court addressed two cases involving domestic disputes, one from Washington and the other from Indiana. Both involved 911 calls from women who claimed to have been

---

[21]   *Crawford*, 541 U.S. at 68.

[22]   Id.

[23]   *Whorton v. Bockting*, 549 U.S. 406 (2007).

[24]   547 U.S. 813 (2006). The companion case was *Hammond v. Indiana*.

abused by a former boyfriend and a husband, and then statements made to police who arrived at the scene. Justice Scalia found that the 911 calls were not testimonial. The motivation of the victims calling 911 was not to generate evidence for a criminal prosecution. Rather, the statements were made for the purpose of obtaining protection in an emergency situation. Thus the 911 statements look nothing like the kinds of statements that gave rise to the Confrontation Clause—those statements were generated by prosecutors who brought witnesses in to make formal statements to be admitted at a trial. The Court stated that the test for testimoniality was whether the statement was made with the *primary motivation* that it would be used in a criminal prosecution.

In contrast, the Court held that the written statements made by the wife in the Indiana case were testimonial. They were made after the couple's quarrel was over, and the police placed the defendant in a different room and asked the wife to write out what happened. At that point, "the primary, if not indeed the sole, purpose of the interrogation was to investigate a possible crime."[25]

Development of the Primary Purpose Test

In *Michigan v. Bryant*[26] the Court provided further guidance on the "primary purpose" test of testimoniality. The Court stated that under that test it is not enough that a declarant could *anticipate* that a statement could be used in a criminal investigation or prosecution—the statement must be *primarily motivated* for such use.

In *Bryant,* a shooting victim was approached by police and identified Bryant as the shooter. The Court held that the statement was not testimonial because the officers were responding to an emergency and were obtaining information not primarily for a prosecution, but to protect the public from a person who had just fired a gun—and the victim was motivated as much by an interest in treatment as an interest in prosecution. The Court also noted that the statement was made under informal circumstances, thus making it unlike the formal affidavits and other formal statements that gave rise to the Confrontation Clause.

The Court made the following observations about how to determine testimoniality when statements are made to police officers:

1.   The primary purpose inquiry is objective. The relevant inquiry into the parties' statements and actions is

---

25   Id. at 829–30.
26   562 U.S. 344 (2011).

not the subjective or actual purpose of the particular parties, but the purpose that reasonable participants would have had, as ascertained from the parties' statements and actions and the circumstances in which the encounter occurred.

2.   The existence of an "ongoing emergency" at the time of the encounter is critical in establishing an interrogation's primary purpose. An emergency focuses the participants not on proving past events potentially relevant to later criminal prosecution, but on ending a threatening situation. But there is no categorical distinction between present and past fact. Rather, the question of whether an emergency exists and is ongoing is a context-dependent inquiry. An assessment of whether an emergency threatening the police and public is ongoing cannot narrowly focus on whether the threat to the first victim has been neutralized, because the threat to the first responders and public may continue.

3.   Whether an ongoing emergency exists is simply one factor informing the ultimate inquiry regarding an interrogation's "primary purpose." Another is the encounter's informality. Formality suggests the absence of an emergency, but informality does not necessarily indicate the presence of an emergency or the lack of testimonial intent.

4.   The statements and actions of both the declarant and interrogators provide objective evidence of the interrogation's primary purpose. Looking to the contents of both the questions and the answers ameliorates problems that could arise from looking solely to one participant, because both interrogators and declarants may have mixed motives.

Statements to Non-Law Enforcement Persons

In *Ohio v. Clark*,[27] the Court held that statements by a child made to teachers investigating possible child abuse were not testimonial. Darius Clark sent his girlfriend away to engage in prostitution while he cared for her 3-year-old son L. P. and 18-month-old daughter A. T. L. P.'s preschool teachers noticed marks on his body and asked him about them, and he identified Clark as his abuser. At the trial of multiple charges of abuse of both children, the State introduced L. P.'s statements to his teachers as evidence of Clark's guilt, but L. P. did not testify. The statements were admitted

---

[27]   576 U.S. 237 (2015).

under the Ohio residual exception. The trial court denied Clark's motion to exclude the statements under the Confrontation Clause. The Supreme Court upheld the trial judge's ruling.

Justice Alito's opinion for the Court noted that the case addressed a question that the Court had reserved: i.e., whether statements to persons other than law enforcement officers can be testimonial. The Court rejected a categorical approach, because at least some statements to individuals who are not law enforcement officers could conceivably raise confrontation concerns. It observed, however, that such statements are *extremely unlikely to be testimonial* because if the primary motivation of a speaker is to have a statement used for a criminal prosecution, the person is likely to make that statement to a law enforcement officer, not a private party. The Court concluded that L. P.'s statements clearly were not made with the primary purpose of creating evidence for Clark's prosecution. It also held that the fact that the teachers had a mandatory duty to report child abuse did not make the statements testimonial—they did not become law enforcement officers by having that duty, because it was clear that the teachers would have reported the abuse regardless of any state-imposed duty. Justice Alito also indicated that statements by very young children will rarely violate the Confrontation Clause because young children have little understanding of prosecution.

Laboratory Tests and Confrontation

In *Melendez-Diaz v. Massachusetts*,[28] police officers arrested the defendant and found a powdered substance in his car. It was tested by an analyst at the police lab, and the analyst issued a report indicating that the substance tested positive for cocaine. The analyst executed a certificate which attested to the findings. The report and the certificate were offered at trial, but the prosecution did not call the analyst to testify. The Supreme Court held that the admission of a forensic testing report against an accused, without the testimony of a person who was involved with the testing, violated the accused's right to confrontation. The Court concluded that the report was testimonial because the only reason for preparing it was for use in a criminal investigation and prosecution.

Justice Scalia again wrote for the Court and rejected every argument made against applying the Confrontation Clause to these testing reports. His opinion reasoned that laboratory analysts are as much witnesses in a criminal cases as eyewitnesses to criminal acts. The opinion made clear that it made no difference whether testimonial statements were made nearly contemporaneously with

---

[28]   557 U.S. 305 (2009).

observations; the absence of interrogation is irrelevant as is the fact that a witness volunteers testimony; and the affidavits of lab technicians do not qualify as traditional business or public records. Finally, the opinion rejected the argument that lab analysts should be exempt from confrontation because their statements result from neutral scientific testing and concluded that this was little more than an argument to return to the reliability standard of *Roberts*.

Justice Kennedy's dissent argued that the decision was a sweeping change from precedent. The dissent identified a number of people who participate in the preparation of a laboratory report and warned that there would be confusion as to which of them must testify to satisfy the majority's confrontation approach. (The lower courts after *Melendez* have found that the right to confrontation is satisfied when the analyst who signs the report is produced to testify.)

The Court again found a confrontation violation when a laboratory report was admitted in *Bullcoming v. New Mexico*.[29] The difference from *Melendez-Diaz* was that in *Bullcoming* a witness from the lab did testify but he was not the one who prepared the report and he had not participated in the testing. The Court held that the defendant, charged with driving while intoxicated, had a right to confront the analyst who certified the report. Justice Sotomayor wrote a concurring opinion in which she observed that "this is not a case in which an expert witness was asked for his independent opinion about underlying testimonial reports that were not themselves admitted into evidence."[30]

Justice Sotomayor's observation raised the question whether an *expert* can testify on the basis of a forensic test conducted by an analyst who is not called to testify. She suggested that the Confrontation Clause is then satisfied because the testimony actually admitted against the defendant is that of the expert, who can be confronted, and not the hearsay statements of anyone who conducted the test.

That is the issue that arose in *Williams v. Illinois*,[31] a case that demonstrated that the Court was even more divided (yes, it is possible) than in the two 5–4 decisions in *Melendez-Diaz* and *Bullcoming*. Williams was charged with rape and tried in a bench trial. The prosecution relied upon the testimony of Sandra Lambatos, a forensic specialist at the Illinois State Police lab. She testified that her lab had a done a DNA profile of Williams' blood; she matched that

---

[29]   564 U.S. 647 (2011).

[30]   Id. at 673.

[31]   567 U.S. 50 (2012).

profile with another profile done by Cellmark, an accredited outside laboratory; and business records showed that vaginal swabs taken from the rape victim, L. J., were sent to Cellmark and returned. One bit of the testimony elicited from Lambatos was the following:

Q   Was there a computer match generated of the male DNA profile found in semen from the vaginal swabs of [L.J.] to a male DNA profile that had been identified as having originated from Sandy Williams?

A   Yes, there was.

Lambatos offered no testimony as to how Cellmark handled or tested its sample. The defense claimed that her testimony violated the Confrontation Clause because it required her to rely upon the Cellmark profile, and no witness from Cellmark was produced for cross-examination about that profile. The prosecutor argued that Illinois Rule of Evidence 703 (which is similar to the Federal Rule) permitted an expert to disclose facts on which the expert's opinion is based even if the expert is not competent to testify to those underlying facts, and that any deficiency went to the weight of the evidence, not its admissibility. The trial court admitted the evidence and found Williams guilty. Illinois appellate courts affirmed and concluded that there was no confrontation violation because the Cellmark report was never admitted in evidence. The Supreme Court also affirmed but in a set of opinions that left many questions unanswered.

Justice Alito wrote for four Justices and reached the following conclusions: (1) Lambatos's answer that there was a match to a male profile that had originated from Williams simply assumed that the profile came from Williams—she did not so testify to the source as a fact; (2) there was no plausible explanation as to how Cellmark could have produced a DNA profile that matched Williams's if Cellmark tested any sample other than the one taken from the victim; (3) the question was whether Williams' Confrontation Clause rights were violated, not whether the prosecution laid a sufficient evidentiary foundation to support Lambatos' opinion, so that the absence of proof that Cellmark produced a reliable profile or of the provenance of the profile would go to relevance, not to confrontation; (4) it did not matter whether the facts asserted in the Cellmark report were true because Lambatos simply testified that the two DNA profiles matched, and her testimony was not in any way dependent on the origin of the samples from which the profiles were derived; (5) Lambatos's reference to the Cellmark report did not mean that the contents of the report were offered for their truth, but only that it was part of the basis of the expert's opinion; and (6) even if the report had been admitted for its truth there would be no Confrontation Clause violation because the report was not made for the primary purpose of identifying a targeted individual—at the time of the test, the perpetrator was unknown, therefore it was not testimonial in the first place.[32]   NoT restimonial

Justice Thomas concurred in the result, on the ground that the reports lacked the solemnity and formality associated with testimonial statements—making them unlike the problematic affidavits of witnesses that gave rise to the Confrontation Clause. He wrote, however, that he found no plausible basis for admitting the Cellmark statements other than for their truth, and he rejected the notion that the Confrontation Clause did not come into play until the identity of a suspect was known.[33]

Justice Kagan's dissenting opinion for four Justices viewed the case as "an open-and-shut case" because Illinois prosecuted Williams for rape based in part on a DNA profile created in Cellmark's laboratory and failed to give Williams a chance to question the analyst who produced that evidence. The dissent emphasized that, although the opinion by Justice Alito is referred to as a plurality opinion, "[f]ive Justices specifically reject every aspect of its reasoning and every paragraph of its explication."[34]

In view of the disarray in *Williams*, it is hoped that the Court will take another case in order to provide greater clarity as to what the Confrontation Clause requires when laboratory reports are used as the basis for expert testimony. For now, though, it appears that an expert can rely on testimonial hearsay so long as: 1) the expert is making her own conclusion and not simply parroting the testimonial report; and 2) the report is not read into evidence or disclosed to the jury in any way. Lower courts after *Williams* have found no confrontation violation if both of these requirements are met.

Examples of Testimonial and Non-Testimonial Hearsay

Crawford specifically held that certain hearsay statements—i.e., grand jury testimony, testimony from a prior trial, and statements made in a police interrogation—are testimonial. *Davis* and *Bryant*, as discussed above, refined the testimonial test to require a primary motivation that the statement, when made, would be used in a criminal investigation or prosecution. Generally speaking, lower courts seem to have made sense of *Crawford*, *Davis*, and *Bryant* and have established *the following three factors that must be triggered for the hearsay statement to be testimonial*:

---

[32]   Id. at 71–79.

[33]   Id. at 103–104, 107–108, 114–115.

[34]   Id. at 119–120.

FACTORS FOR TESTIMONIAL

1.   The primary motivation for making the statement was that it would be used in a criminal investigation or prosecution;

2.   Law enforcement officials must be involved in the preparation or making of the statement—otherwise it is not sufficiently *formal* or geared toward a prosecution to qualify as testimonial; and

3.   The statement must be something more than a mere certification or ministerial affidavit prepared to authenticate a document that is not itself testimonial. That is, if the underlying information is something like a business record, which is not testimonial, a ministerial affidavit qualifying the record is not testimonial (even though it is prepared for trial).

Applying these factors, the following is a list of examples that have been reviewed by the federal courts after *Crawford*:

Hearsay Found Testimonial:

1.   Confession of an accomplice made to a police officer.

2.   Grand jury testimony.

3.   Plea allocutions of accomplices, even if specific references to the defendant are redacted.

4.   Statement of an incarcerated person, made to a police officer, identifying the defendant as taking part in a crime.

5.   Report by a confidential informant to a police officer, identifying the defendant as involved in criminal activity.

6.   Accusations made to officers responding to a 911 call, *after* any emergency or public risk has subsided.

7.   Statements made by an accomplice while placed under arrest, but before formal interrogation.

8.   False alibi statements made by accomplices to the police (though while testimonial, they do not violate the defendant's right to confrontation because they are not offered for their truth).

9.   A police officer's count of the number of marijuana plants found during the search of the defendant's premises.

10.   Certificates of nonexistence of a record, prepared solely for litigation (after *Melendez-Diaz v. Massachusetts, supra*).

Hearsay Found Not Testimonial:

1.   Statement admissible under the state of mind exception, made to friends.

2.   Routine autopsy reports—"routine" meaning in contrast to an autopsy report prepared with the participation of law enforcement officers. Law enforcement involvement in the autopsy process will probably render the report testimonial in most courts.

3.   Declaration against penal interest implicating both the declarant and the defendant, made in informal circumstances to a friend or loved one (i.e., statements admissible under the Court's interpretation of Rule 804(b)(3) in *Williamson v. United States, supra*).

4.   Letter written to a friend admitting criminal activity by the writer and the defendant.

5.   Statements by coconspirators during the course and in furtherance of the conspiracy (because the primary motive is to further the conspiracy and not to generate evidence for a criminal prosecution).

6.   Warrants of deportation and other immigration documents.

7.   Entries into a regulatory database.

8.   Statements made for purpose of medical treatment.

9.   911 calls reporting crimes or emergencies.

10.   Statements to law enforcement officers responding to the declarant's 911 call reporting a crime, while the emergency is ongoing.

11.   Accusatory statements in a private diary.

12.   Odometer statements prepared before any crime of odometer-tampering occurred.

13.   A present sense impression describing an event that took place months before a crime occurred.

14.   Business records—including certificates of authenticity of business records prepared for trial, even after *Melendez-Diaz*.

15.   Statements made by an accomplice to his lawyer, implicating the accomplice as well as the defendant.

16.   Judicial findings and orders entered in one case and offered in a different case.

17.   Informal statements made with no law enforcement officers present.

Forfeiture of the Right to Confrontation

In *Giles v. California,*[35] the Supreme Court held that an accused may forfeit his constitutional right to confront testimonial hearsay by making the declarant unavailable for trial—but only if the government shows that the defendant engaged in wrongdoing *designed to keep the witness from testifying at trial.* Giles was charged with the murder of his former girlfriend. A short time before the murder, Giles had assaulted the victim, and she made statements to the police implicating Giles in that assault. The victim's hearsay statements were admitted against the defendant on the ground that he had forfeited his right to rely on the Confrontation Clause—by murdering the victim. The government made no showing that Giles murdered the victim with the intent to keep her from testifying (nor could that have been the case, because you don't murder somebody to keep them from testifying in the very murder prosecution in which the declarant is the victim). Justice Scalia, writing for the Court, found an intent-to-procure unavailability requirement in the common law of forfeiture, and therefore, under the historical analysis mandated by *Crawford,* there is necessarily an intent-to-procure requirement for forfeiture of confrontation rights. Thus, after *Giles,* the standards for forfeiture of a hearsay exception under Federal Rule 804(b)(6)[36] and for forfeiture of the confrontation objection are coterminous.

---

[35]   554 U.S. 353 (2008).

[36]   See § 7.9.

Chapter IX

IMPEACHMENT

Table of Sections

§ 9.1 Competency to Testify

The early common law had a number of restrictive rules that declared various persons incompetent to testify. Included among these were infants, insane persons, atheists, spouses of parties, and even parties themselves. The assumption was that these persons were either unduly biased or incapable of giving reliable testimony. With the passage of time, and especially during the Twentieth Century, statutory reform abolished or modified these incapacities. It became recognized that these strict competency rules were derived from concerns that a witness would not be *credible*—and that questions of credibility should be left to the factfinder.

Federal Rule 601

The opening sentence of Federal Rule of Evidence 601 illustrates the modern rule:

> **General Rule of Competency.** Every person is competent to be a witness unless these rules otherwise provide. But in a civil case, state law governs the witness's competency regarding a claim or defense for which state law supplies the rule of decision.

Rule 601 has two features. First, it states a general rule that every person is a competent witness unless prohibited from testifying by another Federal Rule. Only a scattering of prohibitory rules are found in Article VI of the Federal Rules, the most notable of which disallow testimony by the presiding judge[1] or a member of the jury.[2] But generally speaking, a witness is disqualified only when he is shown to be incapable of understanding the oath requirement—the

---

[1]   Fed. R. Evid. 605.
[2]   Fed. R. Evid. 606.

fact that the witness may be, e.g., a drug addict, an unstable person, biased, or a liar, are issues for the factfinder.

Second, Rule 601 defers to the policy of *Erie R.R. Co. v. Tompkins*[3] which dictates that when a federal court is applying state substantive law (e.g., in "diversity" cases), it should also apply those state procedural rules that potentially could have a significant impact on the outcome of the trial.[4] Thus, suppose State *X* has passed a statute that renders felons convicted of specified crimes incompetent to testify in designated civil trials. If a federal court were entertaining one of these civil suits and applying the substantive law of State *X*, the court must, under Rule 601, apply the "witness competency" rule of State *X*. It should be noted, though, that most states have modernized their rules governing the competency of witnesses, so there are comparatively few instances in which a witness, competent under the general approach of the Federal Rules, is disabled from testifying because of a specific contrary state rule.

The most likely remaining possibility of a state rule of competency is a statute that creates special rules of competency in suits in which one of the parties (usually the defendant) is deceased and thus represented by a fiduciary, such as an executor. The live party litigating against the decedent's estate has the potential advantage of taking the stand and testifying, whereas the decedent is of course denied this opportunity. So-called "Dead Man's Statutes" were once common but are now regarded as a misguided legislative attempt to correct this adversarial imbalance. The most rigid form of Dead Man's Statute provides that the live party is not competent to testify to any conversation or transaction with the decedent. The injustice that results from holding the live party incompetent is apparent in cases where the survivor has a valid claim stemming from an oral agreement with the deceased or, perhaps, from a personal injury caused by the decedent. The living party is prohibited from substantiating his claim by his own testimony. Even in states which retain some version of the Dead Man's statute, there has been widespread reform. For example, the living party may testify, but his testimony triggers the opponent's right to introduce the decedent's hearsay statements pertaining to the event in question. Another technique is to allow the survivor's testimony, but require him to produce corroborative evidence before he can gain a favorable judgment. Finally, the scope of the Dead Man's Statute may be restricted. For example, it is likely to apply only when the *defendant*

---

[3] 304 U.S. 64, 78–80 (1938).

[4] Generally speaking, Congress or the Supreme Court acting pursuant to an enabling statute is free to displace the state "procedural" rule with a uniform federal rule. *See Hanna v. Plumer,* 380 U.S. 460 (1965).

is the deceased party and the statutory prohibition may apply only to *oral communications* between the plaintiff and the decedent. (Older Dead Man's Statutes typically applied to any "transaction" between a live party and the deceased party.)

Limits on Juror Testimony About Deliberations

One rule in Article Six of the Federal Rules might be thought of as an "incompetency" rule, but it is actually based on public policy. That is Rule 606(b), which provides as follows:

(b) During an Inquiry into the Validity of a Verdict or Indictment.

(1) *Prohibited Testimony or Other Evidence.* During an inquiry into the validity of a verdict or indictment, a juror may not testify about any statement made or incident that occurred during the jury's deliberations; the effect of anything on that juror's or another juror's vote; or any juror's mental processes concerning the verdict or indictment. The court may not receive a juror's affidavit or evidence of a juror's statement on these matters.

(2) *Exceptions.* A juror may testify about whether:

(A) extraneous   prejudicial   information   was improperly brought to the jury's attention;

(B) an outside influence was improperly brought to bear on any juror; or

(C) a mistake was made in entering the verdict on the verdict form.

The basic fact situation involving this rule is that a party who lost a jury verdict interviews jurors after the trial, and learns from them that something possibly improper occurred during jury deliberations. Possibilities include jurors flipping a coin to decide a verdict or damage award; jurors ignoring limiting instructions; jurors making comments expressing ignorance of the case, and so forth. Rule 606(b) prohibits jurors from presenting evidence about juror deliberations. Often called the "no-impeachment" rule, it furthers at least five policies. The Third Circuit has described these policies as follows:

(1) discouraging harassment of jurors by losing parties eager to have the verdict set aside; (2) encouraging free and open discussion among jurors; (3) reducing incentives for jury tampering; (4) promoting verdict finality; and

(5) maintaining the viability of the jury as a judicial decisionmaking body.[5]

The rule contains exceptions, but they are really more illustrations of the scope of the rule, which is to prevent jurors from providing evidence about deliberations. So for example jurors *can* testify that the jury received prejudicial information, or that a juror was improperly influenced by, say, a threat, an internet search. But even in these instances, no evidence can be provided about the *effect* of these outside influences on the jury deliberations. Likewise, there is an exception under which jurors are allowed to testify to when an error is made on the jury form (such as a clerical error in entering the amount of the verdict in a civil case). But in this instance the jurors are testifying about *what the actual verdict was,* not about the deliberations.

The limits on proof of jury deliberations may raise constitutional issues in criminal cases. Thus, in *Pena-Rodriguez v. Colorado,*[6] a juror during deliberations made derogatory comments about Hispanics, indicating that he was relying on racial animus in finding the defendant guilty. The Court held that application of the Rule 606(b) bar on proof of jury deliberations violated the defendant's Sixth Amendment right to fair trial. The Court stated that "where a juror makes a clear statement that indicates he or she relied on racial stereotypes or animus to convict a criminal defendant, the Sixth Amendment requires that the no-impeachment rule give way in order to permit the trial court to consider the evidence of the juror's statement and any resulting denial of the jury trial guarantee." The Court also stated, however, that in general it strongly favored the policy of protecting jury deliberations, and that "[n]ot every offhand comment indicating racial bias or hostility will justify setting aside the no-impeachment bar to allow further judicial inquiry." For that inquiry to proceed, "there must be a showing that one or more jurors made statements exhibiting overt racial bias that cast serious doubt on the fairness and impartiality of the jury's deliberations and resulting verdict" and that "racial animus was a significant motivating factor in the juror's vote to convict." Thus, *Pena-Rodriguez* is a narrow exception to the Rule 606(b) bar on proof of jury deliberations.

§ 9.2   Impeachment: In General

We turn now to the subject of impeachment. The rules of impeachment govern the means by which a party tries to weaken or

---

[5]   *United States v. Stansfield*, 101 F.3d 909, 915 (3d Cir. 1996) (holding that Rule 606(b) prohibits inquiry into a partial verdict rendered by a jury).

[6]   137 S.Ct. 855 (2017).

discredit the testimony of adverse witnesses (including hearsay declarants).[7] Some of the techniques of impeachment trace their ancestry to rules governing the competency of witnesses. For example, conviction of a serious crime, once a basis for a potential witness's incompetence, is now a basis for impeaching a witness's testimony.

Types of Impeachment

The term "impeachment" generally refers to all evidence offered to negate or raise doubts about the reliability of a witness's testimony, including evidence that calls into question the accuracy of his observation, his recollection, or the fidelity of his account. The examiner may, for example, try to extract the witness's concession that he was unable to observe clearly the event in question, that his memory has dimmed, or that he was under the influence of an intoxicating substance when he observed the event to which he testified. Note that this type of attack on credibility does not *necessarily* imply that the witness is consciously lying. Rather, the principal thrust of this means of impeachment is to show that, sincere or not, the witness is wrong or mistaken.

A witness's credibility is also impaired by a showing that the witness has made a prior statement that is inconsistent with her present testimony. Another line of attack is directed at the witness's bias. Perhaps the witness is related to one of the parties or has a financial interest in the outcome of the case. Again, the examiner is suggesting testimonial distortions or inaccuracies that hint at, but do not necessarily rest upon, a conscious fabrication. A third approach is to call other witnesses to contradict the first witness's testimony. Contradictory accounts cast doubt on the accuracy of the first witness's testimony. Of course, all of the foregoing methods of impeachment may carry an innuendo of deliberate fabrication; much depends on how the cross-examiner frames her questions and the subtleties of her body language and voice intonations.

Other methods of impeachment more directly impugn a witness's honesty by revealing his disposition to consciously distort or falsify. In other words, the cross-examiner tries to show the witness himself (and not just his testimony), has a defect. Most often, a witness's character for truthfulness is attacked by cross-examining the witness about criminal convictions or misdeeds ("bad acts" that

---

[7]   Fed. R. Evid. 806 provides that when a declarant's hearsay statement has been admitted under an exception or as statutory nonhearsay (under Rule 801(d)(2)(C), (D), or (E)), the "declarant's credibility may be attacked, and then supported, by any evidence that would be admissible for those purposes if the declarant had testified as a witness." The justification for the rule is that if a hearsay statement is admitted, it is as if the declarant is testifying. Therefore, the hearsay declarant should be subject to the same impeachment as witnesses who do testify.

suggest falsity or deceit) or by offering testimony of lay witnesses who know the witness under attack and can speak to his (bad) character for veracity. Although the law of evidence generally disfavors character or "propensity" evidence, there are exceptions,[8] and impeachment is one of them. Because the outcome of most trials depends upon which witnesses are believed by the trier of fact, the law of evidence is crafted to provide the trier with ample information pertaining to the credibility of the witnesses whose testimony is admitted. So it is one thing to prove a person's character to show how they acted on a previous occasion in dispute—the risk there is that you end up trying people, not cases. But it is another thing to prove something about the person who is testifying before the factfinder— there the factfinder needs to know what kind of person the witness is, in order to determine whether the witness should be believed.

Impeaching One's Own Witness

At common law, there was a general rule that prohibited a party from impeaching her own witness. The idea was that by calling a witness to testify, a party "vouched for" the witness's character and credibility. A related notion was based on the perceived unfairness of calling a witness and then attacking her veracity.

The rule against impeaching one's own witness might be defensible if a party had a wide choice of witnesses to the same event. In reality, however, a party has very limited choices—or perhaps no choice at all. A party often subpoenas a particular witness because she has knowledge of relevant facts, not because she has an alliance with the party or because her credibility is beyond reproach. Faced with this reality, common law judges and legislatures began to devise means of avoiding the rule against impeaching "your own witness." Here are some of the common law and statutory escapes from the rule:

1. The court would call the witness, so the rule did not forbid impeachment by either party.

2. The rule had no application if the law required a party to call a certain witness—for example, an attesting witness to a deed or will.

3. The rule had no application when a party called her adversary.

4. The rule was suspended if the party calling the witness was genuinely surprised by her unexpected testimony.

---

[8]   *See, e.g.,* Fed. R. Evid. 413, 414 and 415, allowing propensity (disposition) evidence in connection with certain sexual offenses. *See also* Fed. R. Evid. 404(a) (character of the accused and the victim).

In most jurisdictions today, resort to these escape devices is unnecessary.

Federal Rule 607

The modern approach to impeaching witnesses is contained in Federal Rule 607. It states:

Who May Impeach a Witness. Any party, including the party that called the witness, may attack the witness's credibility.

In the commentary accompanying this provision, the Advisory Committee notes the unreality of the assumption that a party has unfettered choices in selecting witnesses.[9] Generally speaking, Rule 607 clears the way for a party to impeach her own witness by any of the techniques discussed in the next section.

§ 9.3   Techniques of Impeachment

It is helpful to arrange the various techniques of impeachment on a continuum that begins with those methods clearly directed at the witness's character for truthfulness, and proceeds to those methods that speak more to the witness's mistaken testimony than to his mendacity. For example, impeaching a witness by evidence of his criminal conviction impugns his character; impeaching him by evidence of his poor eyesight casts doubt on his perception; impeaching him by evidence of his probable bias falls somewhere between.

Conviction of a Crime

One method of impeaching a witness is to show that he has been convicted of a crime. There are, to be sure, limitations having to do with the nature of the crime and its recency, but this impeachment technique, uniformly recognized, is fairly common, especially in criminal trials where witnesses are more likely to have a criminal record. The desired inference is as follows: if a person has been convicted of a criminal offense it makes it more likely that he has a character of untruthfulness and disrespect for legal standards, and thus is more likely to give false testimony under oath than one who has not been convicted.

Nonetheless, a number of distinctions can be made among convictions. Some offenses are more closely linked to truthfulness than others. For example, convictions for perjury, embezzlement, fraud, or tax evasion yield strong inferences relating to truth-telling, while convictions for manslaughter or reckless driving do not—the latter being probative only to show a disrespect for the law. A distinction might also be drawn between a felony-grade offense and

---

9   Fed. R. Evid. 607 ACN.

a misdemeanor. Further, a distinction might be drawn between old convictions and recent ones, because the older the conviction the less probative it is of the witness's character, in that character is to be assessed at the time of trial. Finally, a distinction could be made between ordinary witnesses and an accused who elects to testify. If the accused can be freely impeached by prior convictions, he probably will decline to take the stand. Even if he does testify, the impeaching evidence—supposedly directed only at his *untruthful* character— might be used by the jury to infer that he has a criminal character (propensity) and thus must be guilty of the crime with which he is charged.

Many lawyers believe that, notwithstanding the presumption of innocence, jurors assume that there must be some merit in a prosecution or it would not be brought. Moreover, they cannot be unaware that an accused has a strong motive to testify favorably for the defense, because it is the accused who has chosen to go to trial and to risk the consequences of a conviction. Thus, it is a fair question whether it is necessary to permit prior convictions of an accused, because the defendant comes to the stand already impeached by self-interest (bias), and because the jury is likely to consider her testimony with some skepticism even without evidence of a conviction. But, if other witnesses in a case are subject to impeachment with their convictions, immunizing the accused might mislead a jury into believing that the accused is morally or ethically superior to other witnesses. Even so, no other witness faces the type of potential prejudice—the misuse of impeachment evidence as substantive evidence of propensity—and so there is a strong argument in favor of providing special protection for the accused from impeachment with prior convictions.

Federal Rule 609

The Federal Rule governing impeachment of a witness's character for truthfulness—by evidence of a prior conviction—is Rule 609. It provides:

(a) **In General.** The following rules apply to attacking a witness's character for truthfulness by evidence of a criminal conviction:

(1) for a crime that, in the [convicting jurisdiction,] was punishable by death or by imprisonment for more than one year, the evidence:

(A) must be admitted, subject to Rule 403, in a civil case or in a criminal case in which the witness is not a defendant; and

(B) must be admitted in a criminal case in which the witness is a defendant, if the probative value of the evidence outweighs its prejudicial effect to that defendant; and *uhndhi*

(2) for any crime regardless of the punishment, the evidence must be admitted if the court can readily determine that establishing the elements of the crime required proving—or the witness's admitting—a dishonest act or false statement.

(b) **Limit on Using the Evidence After 10 Years.** This subdivision (b) applies if more than 10 years have passed since the witness's conviction or release from confinement *10 year* for it, whichever is later. Evidence of the conviction is admissible only if: *limir*

(1) its probative value, supported by specific facts and circumstances, substantially outweighs its prejudicial effect; and

(2) the proponent gives an adverse party reasonable written notice of the intent to use it so that the party has a fair opportunity to contest its use.

(c) **Effect of a Pardon, Annulment, or Certificate of Rehabilitation.** Evidence of a conviction is not admissible if:

(1) the conviction has been the subject of a pardon, annulment, certificate of rehabilitation, or other equivalent procedure based on a finding that the person has been rehabilitated, and the person has not been convicted of a later crime punishable by death or by imprisonment for more than one year; or

(2) the conviction has been the subject of a pardon, annulment, or other equivalent procedure based on a finding of innocence.

(d) **Juvenile Adjudications.** Evidence of a juvenile adjudication is admissible under this rule only if:

(1) it is offered in a criminal case;

(2) the adjudication was of a witness other than the defendant;

(3) an adult's conviction for that offense would be admissible to attack the adult's credibility; and

(4) admitting the evidence is necessary to fairly determine guilt or innocence.

(e) Pendency of an Appeal. A conviction that satisfies this rule is admissible even if an appeal is pending. Evidence of the pendency is also admissible.

Rule 609 governs the use of a prior conviction to cast doubt on the witness's character for truthfulness; the chain of inference is that a conviction indicates a propensity to violate the law, which in turn means that the witness is more willing than others to lie, and a tendency to lie is probative of whether the witness is lying on the stand.[10] It is fair to ask whether this chain of inferences is persuasive. Not surprisingly, there is no empirical evidence to prove that a person who has been convicted is more likely than others to lie. But even if the inference is questionable, the fact is that American courts have long relied upon prior convictions as proper impeachment.

The Rule presently under consideration—609—has the following general structure. Rule 609 draws a distinction between the accused and any other witness. The accused as witness is given somewhat greater protection from impeachment by conviction, primarily because of a special balancing test, contained in Rule 609(a)(1)(B), that applies only to the criminal defendant (discussed below). Rule 609 also distinguishes between a conviction of a prior crime involving "a dishonest act or false statement"[11] and conviction of other crimes such as criminal assault or manslaughter. Prior crimes involving lying or deceit point strongly toward a witness's lack of truthfulness, and Rule 609 provides for automatic admissibility of this class of convictions. Finally, Rule 609 discourages the use of "stale" convictions (more than ten years old) and of juvenile adjudications.

Rule 609(a)(1)—Convictions for Crimes That Do Not Involve Dishonesty or False Statement

Rule 609(a)(1) addresses serious crimes that do not involve dishonesty or false statement. To be candidates for admissibility, these convictions must be punishable by death or imprisonment for

---

[10]   Other uses of a criminal conviction are possible, but implicate other rules. For example, Rule 803(22) addresses the use of a prior conviction as proof of a fact essential to sustain the judgment. And under Rule 404(b), other crimes, wrongs, or acts may be admissible to prove an element of the crime charged, such as motive, identity, or intent.

[11]   Fed. R. Evid. 609(a)(2).

more than one year, i.e., felony-grade offenses.[12] In the case of an ordinary witness in a criminal or civil trial, the judge must balance the probative value of the prior conviction against the counterweights contained in Rule 403. Thus, unless the probative force of the prior conviction on the issue of the witness's truthfulness is *substantially* outweighed by the dangers of unfair prejudice, jury confusion, and waste of time, the prior conviction is admissible—you will recall that the balancing test of Rule 403 is weighed in favor of admissibility, as the bad factors must substantially outweigh probative value for the evidence to be excluded. In contrast, *when the defendant in a criminal case is the witness*, the judge may admit the prior conviction only if its "probative value outweighs its prejudicial effect to that defendant."[13] Thus, the special balancing test of Rule 609 provides an additional measure of protection for the criminal defendant—the balance of factors is set to be more protective than Rule 403, under which the conviction is presumptively admissible.

In applying this special balancing test to the accused, the judge may take into account such factors as the probative value of the prior conviction on the issue of the accused's truthfulness, the nature of the prior offense (in particular, its similarity to the crime charged or the likelihood that it would inflame the jury), the centrality of the accused's credibility to the main issues in the case, the accused's record as a whole, the age of the conviction, the fact that the accused is already impeached by self-interest, and the importance of hearing the accused's account of the charged event (because if the conviction is admitted the accused may decide not to testify for fear of suffering unfair prejudice).

Suppose, for example, the accused is on trial for armed bank robbery. He testifies that he was not one of the robbers (mistaken identity). The prosecutor now offers a certified copy of a prior criminal judgment showing that nine years ago the accused was convicted of the armed robbery of a convenience store. In the exercise of her discretion to admit or exclude this evidence, the trial judge should be particularly attentive to how probative it is on the accused's character for truthfulness, to the span of time between the prior conviction and the accused's testimony (because the longer the time period, the less probative it is to prove the witness's character for veracity at the time of the testimony), and to the similarity of the past offense to the present one. Although it might be true that one who would rob would also lie under oath, the framework of Rule 609

---

[12]　The controlling language in Rule 609(a) is "punishable by death or by imprisonment for more than one year." This is usually, but not always, the dividing line between a felony and a misdemeanor. Thus, for convenience, we will use the term "felony" or "felony-grade" to denote this class of serious crimes.

[13]　Fed. R. Evid. 609(a)(1)(B).

places the greatest probative value on past crimes of falsity or deceit (covered by Rule 609(a)(2)). Furthermore, there is a strong resemblance between the prior offense and the one now charged. That increases the risk that the jurors may use the past crime as propensity evidence to infer the accused's guilt in the case before them (e.g., "once a robber, always a robber"). Finally, the defendant comes to the stand already impeached by self-interest, so the marginal probative value of this prior conviction is low. Therefore, the court should find that the probative value of the conviction as to the accused's character for truthfulness does not outweigh its prejudicial effect to the accused.[14]

Rule 609(a)(2)—Convictions for Crimes That Involve Dishonesty or False Statement

Rule 609(a)(2) states that a prior conviction of a crime involving a dishonest act or false statement *must* be admitted against any witness in *any civil or criminal case*. No distinction is drawn between the accused and other witnesses. Furthermore, the judge *has no discretion to exclude* a conviction that falls within this special category—Rule 403 is inapplicable. Congress made a judgment that convictions that require proof of a dishonest act or false statement are strongly probative of a witness's character for truthfulness. Note that Rule 609(a)(2) mandates admissibility of all convictions, even misdemeanors. Under Rule 609(a)(1), misdemeanor convictions cannot be admitted to impeach the witness.

Thus there is a major distinction between crimes that involve dishonesty or false statement and those that do not. The former are covered by Rule 609(a)(2) which mandates admissibility as to all convictions of all witnesses in all cases. The latter are covered by Rule 609(a)(1), which excludes misdemeanors, and admits felonies depending on a balance of probative value and prejudicial effect. This scheme makes it imperative to determine what crimes are characterized by dishonesty or false statement. The use of the term "dishonest act" causes the most difficult problems, because that word is sometimes broadly associated with illegal or corrupt acts that do not necessarily involve deceit. But the legislative history of Rule 609(a)(2) strongly suggests that as used in the rule, "dishonest act" is an elaboration of "false statement," and that the reference in 609(a)(2) is limited to crimes that necessarily involve deceit, falsification, or untruthfulness.[15] Thus, crimes falling within this special category are those such as perjury, mail fraud, embezzlement,

---

[14]   *See United States v. Brackeen*, 969 F.2d 827 (9th Cir. 1992) (accused charged with bank robbery could not be impeached by a prior conviction for bank robbery).

[15]   *See* H. R. CONF. REP. NO. 93–1597, at 9 (1974). See also the extensive opinion in *United States v. Smith*, 551 F.2d 348, 362 (D.C. Cir. 1976).

forgery, false pretense, counterfeiting, knowingly passing a worthless check, income tax evasion, and larceny by trick.

According to almost all courts, crimes such as drug distribution, burglary, shoplifting and smuggling, while perhaps involving underhanded activity, do not on their face require proof of false statements and so do not fall within Rule 609(a)(2). (To allow these crimes to be automatically admissible would make Rule 609(a)(2) the predominant rule, even though it is contrary to the basic premise of the Federal Rules of Evidence—that they are grounded in judicial discretion.)

The test for the court in distinguishing Rule 609(a)(2) crimes from Rule 609(a)(1) crimes is whether the elements of the crime for which the witness was convicted "required proving—or the witness's admitting—a dishonest act or false statement." (The reference to "admitting" an act refers to convictions entered after a guilty plea). This test demands that the required proof of a dishonest act or false statement must be "readily determined." The court is not required (or allowed) to search the record of the prior case to see whether there was proof or admission of some false statement. Rather, the conviction must be one in which it had to be found that the witness made a false statement—otherwise the witness could not have been convicted of that crime. The commission of most crimes involve some act of lying at some point, so requiring the court to comb the prior record for proof of a false act would probably lead to almost all convictions being automatically admissible. Rule 609(a)(2) is intended to cover only those crimes where it is obvious—usually from the face of the indictment—that the trier of fact *had to* find that there was a lie in order to convict. That will usually be limited to crimes like perjury and fraud. But in some cases the Rule might cover a conviction for obstruction of justice (which does not always require deceit—e.g., intimidation of a witness can constitute obstruction of justice). Yet even in such cases, the judge must be able to readily determine whether proof of deceit was required for the conviction—that will ordinarily be made evident by the indictment.

Proving the Prior Conviction

Under the Federal Rules (and thus in most states) there are two ways of proving a prior conviction: counsel may adduce this evidence, usually during cross-examination, by asking the witness to admit his prior conviction; or counsel may introduce a certified copy of the prior criminal judgment. Neither of these means of proof consumes much time, and thus the introduction of a prior conviction usually poses only the problem of whether the conviction is admissible at all. When a conviction is admissible, judges disallow detailed descriptions of the previous offense, confining counsel to such essentials as the name of the crime, the time and place of the conviction, and the punishment imposed. That is all that a judgment of conviction shows on its face. Because description of details and the like are not on the face of the judgment of conviction, they may be subject to dispute, time-consuming contrary proof, and confusion of the issues (because the issue the jury must decide is not exactly what the witness did at a prior time, but rather whether the witness is telling the truth about the matter in dispute).

In Limine Determinations

Of particular concern to an accused who is considering taking the stand is whether he can be impeached by a prior conviction. In order to make an informed decision about whether to testify, he will often seek (by a motion *"in limine"*)[16] an early ruling on the admissibility of prior conviction(s), tendered by the prosecutor for the purpose of undermining the accused's credibility. An *in limine* ruling, which the judge may provide in the exercise of her authority to manage the trial,[17] is subject to revision until the accused actually testifies at trial.

ILLUSTRATION

Clyde is on trial for the armed robbery of a bank. Eight years ago, he was convicted of breaking into a residence and committing an armed robbery. (At the time of the presently charged offense, he was on parole.) In the current prosecution, [Clyde's defense is alibi.] He admits that he was in the vicinity of the bank robbery on the day of the crime and that he was arrested while fleeing. He insists, however, that the two witnesses who identified him as one of the robbers were mistaken. As to his presence near the bank, Clyde claims that he was waiting there to meet a friend. He explains his flight on the ground that he was afraid he might be arrested on suspicion, and that his parole might then be revoked because he had two unpaid traffic violations.

Prior to trial, Clyde files a motion *in limine*, urging the court to rule that the prosecutor cannot introduce his prior conviction to impeach him. The prosecutor argues that the conviction is admissible automatically under Rule 609(a)(2) and, failing that, it is admissible under (a)(1). The trial judge denies the motion and rules that should Clyde decide

---

[16]   This is a motion made prior to trial or during its early stages in which a party seeks an early ruling, usually to resolve an evidentiary issue.

[17]   *See* Fed. R. Evid. 611(a). *See also Luce v. United States*, 469 U.S. 38, 41 n. 4 (1984).

to testify, his conviction for residential robbery may be used to impeach his credibility.

1. Did the trial judge correctly apply Federal Rule 609?

2. Does Clyde have the option of declining to take the stand, but (assuming he is convicted) nonetheless appealing the ruling of the trial judge?

There is an intentional ambiguity in this Illustration. The trial judge erred if he admitted the prior conviction for residential robbery under subsection (a)(2). The prior offense is not one of "dishonest act or false statement" as that phrase is used in this subsection, because the witness did not have to lie to be convicted of robbery. However, if the trial judge admitted the prior conviction under the special balancing test of Rule 609(a)(1) and entered in the record her considered application of the various factors relevant to a determination under that subsection, she would probably not be reversed on appeal.[18] The reality is that a trial judge could easily justify a ruling admitting or excluding the prior conviction under the Rule 609(a)(1) balancing test.

For example, the trial judge might conclude that the probative value of the prior conviction (a serious offense) is relatively high and that the conviction also has a special informative value in the context of this case. Without knowledge of the prior conviction, the jury might be left with the impression that Clyde, whose good behavior earned his parole from some (unknown) past offense, is the victim of a double misfortune: two traffic tickets and the coincidence of being in the neighborhood where a bank robbery was occurring.

On the other hand, in deciding to exclude the conviction, the judge might emphasize the importance of Clyde's testimony, the age of the prior conviction, and the likelihood that (should his prior conviction be admitted) the jury would infer that his commission of one armed robbery (in a residence) makes it likely that he committed another armed robbery (in a bank). Furthermore, if Clyde has been on parole for several years without committing any significant offenses, the judge might be influenced by his interim good behavior. Finally, Clyde comes to the stand impeached by his self-interest (in avoiding jail) and so adding another form of impeachment can be seen as piling on, and as limited in probative value.

---

[18]   For a case with many features in common with the present illustration, *see United States v. Alexander*, 48 F.3d 1477 (9th Cir. 1995) (trial court did not abuse its discretion in admitting convictions for residential robbery and possessing cocaine for sale to impeach the accused).

Given the relatively protective nature of the Rule 609(a)(1) balancing test as applied to the accused, the stronger argument is that the conviction should be excluded—but this is not at all to say that a trial court would abuse its discretion to admit it.

As to the right to appeal the *in limine* determination: In *Luce v. United States*,[19] the Supreme Court addressed the appealability of *in limine* rulings. These early rulings by the trial judge are not final— that is, they are subject to revision during trial. Suppose, then, that an accused files a motion *in limine* seeking an early ruling by the trial judge that his prior conviction cannot be used to impeach him.[20] The judge determines, however, that the prior conviction may be used to impeach the defendant if he decides to testify. Suppose, further, the judge does not reverse her earlier ruling, the accused testifies, and the prosecutor introduces the prior conviction for impeachment purposes. The defendant, if convicted, can appeal the judge's ruling.

On the other hand if the accused *declines to testify*, the *Luce* Court holds that the accused waives his right to appeal the judge's *in limine* ruling. The Court gave three reasons for this result: 1) The accused has nothing to appeal because no objectionable evidence was actually admitted against him at trial—he didn't testify and so was never impeached. 2) There is no way to verify the accused's argument that his reason for not taking the stand was his fear of impeachment by the objectionable conviction; the accused may have had many reasons for deciding not to testify, so it is impossible under the circumstances to determine whether the error, if any, was harmful. 3) The Court was concerned that an accused might have decided *from the outset* not to testify, and yet would move *in limine* to exclude his prior convictions—hoping that the trial court would make an error that the accused could then use on appeal; the Court would not abide that kind of strategic activity.

Faced with an *in limine* ruling that an accused's prior conviction will be admissible if he testifies, defense counsel will sometimes call the accused to the stand and, during direct examination, have him admit that he has a specified past conviction(s). The idea is that by frankly admitting the prior conviction, the jurors will not judge the defendant as harshly as they would if this evidence were revealed by the prosecutor during impeachment. But while this may be a useful trial tactic, it carries a cost: the defendant waives the right to appeal

---

[19]   469 U.S. 38, 42–43 (1984).

[20]   The prosecution may also ask for an advance ruling, as it may be useful for the prosecution to figure out the strength of its case.

the judge's earlier ruling that the prior conviction is admissible, because the defendant himself introduced this evidence.[21]

Stale Convictions; Pardons; Juvenile Adjudications

Generally speaking, a conviction is not admissible under Rule 609 if "more than 10 years have passed since the witness's conviction or release from confinement for it, whichever is later."[22] Thus, if a witness was not imprisoned for the prior offense, the ten-year period began to run on the date of the conviction.[23] If more than ten years has elapsed since the conviction or release from prison, the judge may nevertheless admit the conviction but only if the probative value of the conviction "*substantially* outweighs its prejudicial effect."[24] While not an absolute bar, this is a very strict test, the reverse of Rule 403, and the result in practice is that old convictions are not going to be admitted to impeach a witness unless three factors are present: 1) lying or deceit was an element of the conviction; 2) the witness's credibility is very important in the case; and 3) the witness is not subject to impeachment with any other evidence (e.g., a newer conviction, a bad act, a prior inconsistent statement, etc.).

A party who proffers a conviction outside the usual ten-year time limit must give her opponent written notice so that the latter can muster his arguments against admissibility.[25]

Rule 609(c) and (d) address other circumstances in which admissibility of a prior conviction is either absolutely barred or is disfavored. A pardon, annulment, or certificate of rehabilitation will render the prior conviction inadmissible if the forgiving act was based on either a finding of innocence or rehabilitation.[26] Generally speaking, juvenile adjudications are inadmissible. There is, however, an exception to this general rule. In criminal trials, the judge can admit a juvenile judgment (adjudication) if "necessary to fairly determine guilt or innocence," *and if a* conviction of the offense would be admissible to attack the credibility of an adult *and if* the witness being impeached is *not the accused*.[27]

---

[21] *Ohler v. United States*, 529 U.S. 753, 756–58 (2000).

[22] Fed. R. Evid. 609(b).

[23] In most courts the ten-year time period is assessed from the time of conviction or release (whichever is later) to the date on which the trial in which the witness will testify begins.

[24] Id. Note that this balancing test differs from the one applied to criminal defendant witnesses in Rule 609(a)(1) and also differs from the balancing test in Rule 403. The Rule 609(b) test is pitched heavily against admitting the old conviction.

[25] Id.

[26] Fed. R. Evid. 609(c).

[27] Fed. R. Evid. 609(d).

608(b) – other-Bad act

Prior Bad Acts

YES even if no conviction BUT subject to balancing of probative value against risk of prejudice or confusion

False vs. Dishonesty knn

Suppose a witness has committed an act in the past that reflects unfavorably upon her character for truthfulness. We have seen that if her prior conduct led to a criminal conviction, Rule 609 often permits the introduction into evidence of that conviction to impeach her credibility. But if there were no conviction, can the "bad" act (the conduct itself) be disclosed to the jury? The current answer is that such impeachment is possible,[28] subject to a balancing of probative value against the risk of prejudice and confusion. The Federal Rule in point is Rule 608(b), with the balancing conducted under Rule 403.

Two difficulties attend this method of impeachment. First, the probative value of bad acts in proving the witness's character for truthfulness is definitely act-dependent. This, of course, is a familiar problem—one that we also encountered in connection with Rule 609—in that some bad acts are more probative of truthfulness than others. Thus, filing false statements on an application for a retail license clearly involves deceit and has relatively strong probative force upon the issue of a witness's character for truthfulness. On the other hand, engaging in drunken or disorderly conduct has little bearing on one's willingness to testify truthfully. Theft, if unaccompanied by falsehood or stealth, falls somewhere between the wrongs discussed above. Given all the possibilities it is not surprising that courts have divided when ruling on the admissibility of various prior bad acts.

A second problem—growing out of the practical aspects of trial administration—arises from the generally shared concern that trials stay focused on the principal issues and not be unduly prolonged. There is resistance to conducting a mini-trial within a trial by adjudicating the circumstances of some alleged act that has relevance *only because it brings into question a witness's character for truthfulness*. In an effort to limit the distraction and expenditure of time associated with impeachment by prior bad acts, common law courts usually ruled that the examiner must settle for the admissions and concessions he is able to adduce during cross-examination. He cannot resort to additional or "extrinsic" evidence to prove the existence of (or circumstances surrounding) the prior bad act. This is the position taken in *Federal Rule 608(b)* which provides in part:

    (b) Specific Instances of Conduct. Except for a criminal conviction under Rule 609, extrinsic evidence is not admissible to prove specific instances of a witness's conduct in order to attack or support the witness's character for

---

[28]   In the past, and in a few jurisdictions today, courts rejected impeachment by prior bad acts on the grounds of limited probative force and (more importantly) distraction from the main issues.

truthfulness. But the court may, on cross-examination, allow them to be inquired into if they are probative of the character for truthfulness or untruthfulness of:

(1) the witness; or

(2) another witness whose character the witness being cross-examined has testified about.

* * *

In determining whether prior bad acts can be inquired into for purposes of impeachment, Rule 608 emphasizes discretionary control by the trial judge. In exercising her discretion, the judge may take into account a number of factors such as the centrality of the witness's testimony (and so the importance of fully assessing credibility), whether the witness is a party to the action, whether the nature of the prior bad act is likely to inflame the jury, and, of course, the probative value of the past act on the issue of truthfulness.

Although the text of Rule 608(b) makes no mention of the cross-examiner's good faith, there is a judicially-imposed requirement that the cross-examiner have a good-faith belief that the event he inquires about actually occurred. The application of this good-faith standard means that the attorney who intends to inquire about a prior bad act must take reasonable steps to confirm its existence.

As we noted above, the range of "bad" acts that may be the subject of the cross-examiner's questions is limited by Rule 608(b)'s requirement that the past conduct be "probative of the character for truthfulness or untruthfulness." Obvious candidates for inclusion within this category are acts such as forgery, bribery, threatening witnesses, using false documents, or making false entries in an application or an official document, such as a tax return. There is at least a rough congruence between the bad acts that can be used to impeach under Rule 608(b) and the convictions that are "automatically" admissible under Rule 609(a)(2) because the underlying offense involved "a dishonest act or false statement." However, under Rule 608(b) the trial judge does have considerable discretion to admit or exclude evidence of a prior bad act that bears on credibility. The court should not be reversed unless it has clearly abused that discretion. In contrast, under Rule 609(a)(2) if an appellate court has ruled that a particular crime is (or is not) one of dishonesty or false statement, the trial judge is without discretion; she must abide by the characterization.

The Extrinsic Evidence Bar for
Bad Act Impeachment

no evidence of other

Recall that Rule 608(b) forbids *extrinsic* evidence of prior conduct that relates to the witness's character for truthfulness or untruthfulness. [Extrinsic evidence is evidence other than the witness's testimony on cross-examination—that is, extrinsic evidence is the testimony of other witnesses or the introduction of documentary evidence.] As to the latter, merely having a document marked as an exhibit and then asking the witness about it does not constitute the introduction of extrinsic evidence. Introducing the document as evidence would, however, violate Rule 608(b)'s prohibition against extrinsic evidence.[29]

ILLUSTRATION

old cw?

Rob, who sells "new and second-hand discount goods," is on trial for receiving stolen property consisting of twenty-five large screen, high definition television sets. He admits that he received the electronic equipment in question, but claims that he had no idea the sets were stolen. Rob's business records show that he paid $20,000 for the twenty-five unused TVs. The prosecutor has a witness (Rob's former employee) who will testify that Rob actually paid only $5,000 for the twenty-five units, but entered a price of $20,000 in his account records.

rules?

Confronted with this alleged disparity on cross-examination, Rob vehemently denies that he paid only $5,000 for the equipment in question. Later in the trial, the prosecutor proffers the former employee who is willing to testify, on the basis of first-hand knowledge, that Rob paid only $5,000 for the television sets, but made false entries reflecting a price of $20,000. Rob's defense attorney points to Rule 608(b) and contends this extrinsic evidence is inadmissible. How should the judge rule?

If the *only* relevance of the former employee's testimony were to show that Rob's past conduct reflected a character for untruthfulness, Rule 608(b)'s prohibition against extrinsic evidence would apply. However, this evidence (false entries to cover up the crime) has another probative role: it undermines Rob's claim that he had no suspicion that the television sets were stolen. This prior act is an integral part of the crime charged, and so the testimony would be admissible evidence of a substantive fact. Thus, Rule 608(b)'s rule

---

[29]   Of course, the document may be admissible under some other rule of evidence. The prohibition against extrinsic evidence applies when the sole purpose of showing the witness's previous conduct is to cast doubt on her character for truthfulness.

against extrinsic evidence is inapplicable. Obviously there cannot be a bar on extrinsic evidence for proving the facts at issue in the case.

Smuggling in Extrinsic Evidence

Can the cross-examiner engaged in bad act impeachment ask, "didn't your *employer fire you* for falsifying time sheets" (as opposed to, "didn't you falsify time sheets")? At first blush, the question about the firing appears proper because it does not involve calling another witness or introducing a document and thus does not have the hallmark of typical extrinsic evidence. But, it clearly is an attempt to elicit testimony about a third party's actions—here, the employer—to prove that the employer believed that the witness falsified the time sheets. The only purpose of the question is to try to get the witness to concede the employer's actions so that the jury will treat the firing as contradicting the witness's denial. This is an attempt to smuggle into evidence what really is extrinsic. The Advisory Committee for the Federal Rules of Evidence recognized this risk of abuse in its 2003 Advisory Committee Note to an amendment to Rule 608, and stated that the practice was barred by the extrinsic evidence rule.

Bad Act Impeachment and the
Fifth Amendment Privilege

Occasionally, a cross-question concerning a witness's prior bad acts calls for an answer that would violate her Fifth Amendment privilege against compelled self-incrimination. This may occur when admitting to a bad act could be used in a subsequent prosecution as evidence of guilt. It is clear that, for all witnesses, the constitutional privilege is available and may be claimed. Indeed, the last paragraph in Rule 608(b) provides that:

> By testifying on another matter, a witness does not waive any privilege against self-incrimination for testimony that relates only to the witness's character for truthfulness.

Of course, should the witness neglect to claim the privilege, her answer disclosing the prior bad act may be freely used to assess her credibility.

A Little More on Extrinsic Evidence

Rule 608(b) is the only Federal Rule of Evidence that bans the use of extrinsic evidence to disprove a witness's denial when confronted with an impeachment attempt. It turns out that this provision in Rule 608(b) has caused considerable confusion over many years. To avoid this confusion, there is a simple rule of thumb to keep in mind: Rule 608's extrinsic evidence bar applies only when a party seeks to offer evidence to contradict a witness's denial of a bad act that was raised *only* for the purpose of challenging the witness's character for truthfulness under Rule 608(b). If the questioning party is offering the evidence for any other relevant purpose, the bar is inapplicable.

The previous Illustration which posited that Rob is on trial for receiving stolen property demonstrates that if there is a legitimate reason to offer evidence for a purpose other than simply to contradict a witness's denial of a Rule 608(b) bad act, the ban on extrinsic evidence does not apply. A few more examples should make the rule of thumb even clearer.

examples of when extrinsic evidence is

- A witness denies a prior conviction that is admissible under Rule 609. The party seeking to impeach the witness may provide extrinsic evidence of the conviction. (This makes eminent sense because proof of a conviction is simple, and indisputable).

- A witness denies making a prior inconsistent statement. The party seeking to impeach may introduce extrinsic evidence to show that the statement was made.

- A witness denies being biased for or against a party. The party seeking to impeach the witness may offer evidence to prove the alleged bias.

- A witness claims to have been sober when an event occurred. The party seeking to impeach the witness may offer evidence that the witness was actually intoxicated.

In short, the extrinsic evidence bar is extremely limited. If the only reason a party is entitled to ask a witness about an act is to challenge the witness's character for truthfulness pursuant to Rule 608(b), then and only then does the extrinsic evidence bar come into play.

This is not to suggest that trial judges will always permit witnesses to be contradicted through extrinsic evidence. If the assertion to be contradicted is of little importance for impeachment or otherwise, or is highly disputed, a court will rely on Rule 403 to prohibit extrinsic evidence. Judges will use Rule 403 to keep trials moving forward without unwarranted forays into disputes about minutia that are far removed from the genuine issues in dispute.

Character Witness Testimony

We have already observed that prior convictions and prior bad acts (not resulting in a conviction) are often admitted into evidence for the ultimate inference that a witness's testimony should not be believed. The trier is invited to draw the following inferences: the witness's prior conduct indicates that his character for truthfulness is defective; therefore his testimony in the present trial is more likely to be false or misleading. Basically, the evidence of past conduct is used to show that the witness has a character trait that predisposes him to falsify.

Another method by which counsel can seek to establish this same character trait is to offer one or more witnesses who testify that they are familiar with the principal witness and that his character for truthfulness is bad. There are two means by which the character witness may establish his familiarity with the principal witness: one means is to be *personally acquainted* with the principal witness; the other is to be acquainted with the principal witness's *reputation* for truthfulness. Of course, in a mobile, largely urban society, the principal witness may not have a reputation bearing upon his truthfulness. The traditional approach of the common law was to require that the principal witness have a reputation concerning truthfulness *in the community* in which he resided. Today, it suffices that he has a reputation concerning truthfulness in some associational setting (such as a work environment) in which more or less the same group of persons frequently interact. Often, however, counsel presents "character evidence" through witnesses who know the principal witness and are thus able to give a personal opinion concerning his character for truthfulness.

The direct examination of a reputation or opinion witness has a ritualistic character. Counsel first establishes the necessary foundation. In the case of a reputation witness, this consists of eliciting testimony that demonstrates that the witness is or has been in a position to learn of the principal witness's reputation for truthfulness, and that he is in fact familiar with this reputation. In the case of an opinion witness, the foundation consists of the character witness's testimony that he is personally acquainted with the principal witness, and that this acquaintance has been sufficiently close to permit the character witness to have an informed opinion of the principal witness's character for truthfulness. Next, with little or no elaboration, the character witness states the principal witness's *reputation* for truthfulness (or "truth and veracity") is bad; or that, in the character witness's *opinion*, the principal witness has bad character with regard to truthfulness. The perfunctory nature of this testimony is caused by Rule 608's limitation on the form of proof—proof cannot be made by reference to specific acts of the witness. Thus a witness cannot say, "my opinion of the witness's bad character is based on the fact that he defrauded me of my life's savings."

Federal Rule 608(a)

The governing Federal Rule of Evidence is Rule 608(a) which states,

(a) Reputation or Opinion Evidence. A witness's credibility may be attacked or supported by testimony about the witness's reputation for having a character for truthfulness or untruthfulness, or by testimony in the form of an opinion about that character. But evidence of truthful character is admissible only after the witness's character for truthfulness has been attacked.

only when attacked

As stated above, proof of the witness's character for truthfulness can only be in the form of opinion or reputation. By negative inference, this means that the character witness cannot testify to specific acts of the principal witness (e.g., "I saw him file a counterfeit form"). Though remember that such bad acts can be raised in questioning the principal witness, subject to Rule 403.

CAN'T reference SPECIFIC ACTS

The last sentence of Rule 608(a) ensures that the opposing parties cannot engage in a "bolstering" contest by having one or more character witnesses support the credibility of another witness whose credibility has not been attacked. Such a practice, if allowed, would be distracting and time-consuming. Thus, every witness who takes the stand is assumed to have a good character for truthfulness—at least, until the witness's character is attacked. For example, the cross-examiner might attack a witness's character for veracity by introducing evidence showing that he has been convicted of a crime that bears on credibility. This attack opens the door for the opposing party's introduction of evidence directed at "rehabilitating" the witness. An example of a proper rebuttal under the rule: the opponent might present an opinion witness who testifies that the principal (attacked) witness has a good character for truthfulness.

CAN'T BOLSTER

Impeachment by Evidence of Bias

The term "bias" denotes a variety of mental attitudes—either conscious or unconscious—that may incline a witness to give misleading or false testimony. In general, bias signifies a witness's interest in the outcome of a trial—including a friendly or hostile association with one of the parties—that could induce him to shade, distort, or falsify his testimony. The cross-examiner can expose a witness's probable bias by probing to discover links between the witness and the case. For instance, the examiner's questions might reveal that the witness is related to a party, is employed by a party, bears a grudge against a party, has an economic stake in the outcome of the trial, received compensation for testifying, was promised immunity from prosecution, received favored treatment from the

BIAS

prosecutor in return for his testimony, or has a strong identification with the subject of the litigation (such as environmental protection). These are simply illustrations; the possible sources of a witness's bias (suspect motive) are almost infinite.

Although there is no Federal Rule of Evidence specifically addressing impeachment by bias, this technique of impeachment is uniformly allowed in both federal and state courts—subject to the familiar balancing of probative value, prejudicial effect, etc. in Rule 403 or its state counterpart. Furthermore, there is general agreement about the evidentiary rules governing this method of impeachment. The cross-examiner probing the possible bias of a witness does not have to "settle for" or "take" the witness's answer on cross, but can introduce (again subject to Rule 403) extrinsic evidence through other witnesses or documents. It is usually unnecessary to lay a foundation for extrinsic evidence by first asking the witness about the sources of his possible bias. Some federal courts,[30] however, do require such a foundation where the evidence showing bias consists of the witness's prior statement ("I hate that SOB [the defendant] and hope the plaintiff reduces him to poverty"). Those judges requiring that the witness be asked about her prior statement before it is proved by extrinsic evidence do so on the grounds of fairness and expedition: the witness should be afforded an opportunity to explain or deny her prior statement; furthermore, if she frankly admits having made it, extrinsic evidence becomes unnecessary. As stated above, the admissibility of extrinsic evidence proffered to prove a witness's bias is governed by Rule 403—the factfinder should receive the information unless its probative value as to bias is substantially outweighed by the risks of prejudice, confusion of the jury, and delay. So for example, if the charge of bias is that the prosecution witness was beaten up by the defendant in a fight on the playground 40 years ago, the probative value of that event to show bias is not high, and the confusion and delay resulting from proving that event if disputed will probably justify its exclusion.

The admissibility of evidence of bias for impeachment purposes in the federal courts was strongly affirmed by the Supreme Court in *United States v. Abel*.[31] In that case, a bank robbery prosecution, the government called witness X, who had earlier entered a guilty plea to the same robbery with which defendant Abel was now charged as a co-participant. X's testimony directly implicated Abel in the bank robbery. Later in the trial, Abel called witness Y in an effort to refute X's damaging testimony: Y testified that X had once admitted to him

---

[30]   Fed. R. Evid. 611(a) gives the judge "reasonable" control over the mode and order of interrogating witnesses and presenting evidence.

[31]   469 U.S. 45, 50–51 (1984).

that X intended to falsely implicate Abel so that X would receive lenient treatment from the government. The prosecution was now faced with the task of rebutting Y's testimony. First, the prosecutor asked cross-examination questions in an unsuccessful attempt to elicit an admission from Y that he and Abel shared membership in a White supremacist gang. Subsequently, the prosecutor recalled X, who testified that Abel, X, and Y had previously belonged to the gang. According to X, membership in that gang required that each member deny the existence of the gang and "lie, cheat, steal [and] kill to protect each other."[32] Thus, X testified, it would have been "suicide" for him to have told Y that he (X) intended to falsely implicate Abel. (Note that the probative force of X's testimony supports both the unlikelihood that he would have disclosed a plan to frame Abel and, more importantly, the likelihood that Y's testimony in Abel's favor was biased.)

Ultimately, the United States Supreme Court approved the trial judge's admission of X's rebuttal testimony. The Court found that the probative force of this testimony on the issue of Y's possible bias (favoring Abel in light of their co-membership in the prison gang) justified its reception. Reverting to first principles, Justice Rehnquist noted that relevant evidence is admissible unless blocked by an exclusionary rule, and that evidence supporting bias clearly meets the test of relevance. Such evidence diminishes the likelihood that the facts to which the biased witness testified are accurate. Here, the membership of Y and Abel in a gang embracing secrecy and falsehood "supported the inference that [Y's] testimony was slanted or perhaps fabricated in . . . Abel's favor."[33] Furthermore, the Court said, the jury was entitled to hear evidence concerning the type of organization in question—closely knit, secret, and sworn to perjury and mutual protection. Knowledge about the gang and its tenets allowed the jury to identify the source of Y's possible bias and to assess its strength. That kind of association is much more probative of bias than, say, common membership in a Book of the Month Club.

Bias Impeachment and the Rule 608(b) Bar on Extrinsic Evidence

Note that Y's membership in the secret prison gang is also a prior bad act bearing on his character for truthfulness—membership was contingent on agreeing to lie on behalf of other members, so Y had to have an untruthful character to qualify. If evidence of gang membership were offered *only* to prove Y's character for untruthfulness, the bar on extrinsic evidence in Rule 608(b) would apply. But evidence of Y's membership *also* discloses his possible

---

[32]   Id. at 48.

[33]   Id. at 52.

bias. On the issue of bias, the cross-examiner need not settle for the witness's denial; extrinsic evidence (i.e., *X's* rebuttal testimony) is admissible, subject to Rule 403. Thus, we see again the familiar principle that evidence admissible for one purpose is usually not rendered inadmissible simply because it would be excluded if offered for some other purpose. Note that the trial court in *Abel did* use Rule 403 to prevent the government from introducing particularly inflammatory and detailed evidence about the witness's association in the gang, including preclusion of the name of the gang, which was the "Aryan Brotherhood."

Impeachment by Prior Inconsistent Statements

A frequently used impeachment technique is to introduce evidence that a testifying witness has made prior statement(s) inconsistent with his testimony. The prior statement might be contained in a writing or it might have been an oral remark. In any event, its impeaching value is obvious: unless the witness has a convincing explanation as to why he gave an earlier contradictory account, the credibility of his trial testimony is weakened.

Of course, the prior statement must actually be inconsistent with the trial testimony to have impeachment value. However, a blatant, irreconcilable contradiction is *not* required. It suffices that the previous statement is sufficiently at variance with the witness's trial testimony to weaken or undermine it. (For example, a statement that the defendant was in the front seat of the car during a drug transaction is inconsistent with a later statement that he was in the back seat—in both cases, the testimony is that the defendant was at the drug transaction, but the witness's conflicting statements tend to undermine his credibility.) It also suffices for impeachment that a significant point that was included in the witness's testimony was omitted from his prior statement.[34] It is likely, however, that the impeachment value of a prior inconsistent statement will depend on the nature and degree of inconsistency; inconsistency on important points will matter more than on lesser points, and large discrepancies between statements will matter more than small ones.

This all seems simple enough; nonetheless, impeachment by prior inconsistent statements is attended by a subtle point or two, and hedged by several restrictions. Recall that a statement other than one made by the declarant while testifying at the trial is hearsay if it is offered to prove the truth of the earlier declaration.[35] Thus,

---

[34]   *United States v. Strother*, 49 F.3d 869, 874–75 (2d Cir. 1995)(witness's testimony included assertion that defendant specifically requested that she make payment on a particular check; earlier written statement omitted any reference to this request).

[35]   Fed. R. Evid. 801(c).

generally speaking, the prior statement of a witness on the stand is hearsay if it is offered for its truth. Of course, sometimes a witness's prior statement fits within an exemption (prior inconsistent statements made at a formal proceeding and subject to the penalty of perjury are exempted from the hearsay rule[36]) or an exception to the hearsay rule. However, if it does not, it can still be used by the trier of fact, *but only for the limited purpose of discrediting the witness's trial testimo*ny. Thus, suppose a witness testifies that the car in question was black; previously she has said that the car was white. She is impeached with evidence of her prior inconsistent statement. Unless her earlier statement is exempted or excepted from the hearsay rule, her prior statement cannot be used to prove the car was white. The sole purpose of the evidence is to show that the witness's testimony ("the car was black") may not be credible because she gave a different account on an earlier occasion. Of course, there is some likelihood that a jury, instructed to use the prior inconsistent statement only for impeachment purposes, will disregard (or not understand) that instruction, and will use the prior statement as proof of a fact.

Extrinsic Evidence of a Prior Inconsistent Statement

There is general agreement that counsel may *cross-examine* a witness about a prior inconsistent statement even if it appears incidental to the substantive facts of the case (e.g., a discrepancy about what the witness said she was eating at the time she saw the crime). The theory in allowing this inquiry is that if the witness has made an inconsistent statement even about comparatively unimportant topics to which she testified, she may have been inaccurate in her account of the central topics. Thus, if she testifies that the bank teller wore an orange dress (a minor point, we will assume), the cross-examiner can ask, "Didn't you tell Detective Larkin, when you spoke with him the day after the robbery, that the teller's dress was green?" If the witness was self-contradictory about the color of the teller's dress, perhaps her description of the getaway car (a central point) is inaccurate.

What happens, though, if the witness denies that she made an inconsistent statement? The cross-examiner would then want to proffer extrinsic evidence (another witness or a document or recording) to prove that the witness made the alleged inconsistent statement. Note that the extrinsic evidence bar of Rule 608(b) is not applicable here, because the prior inconsistent statement is not being offered to prove the witness's *character for untruthfulness*—it's offered to impair the credibility of the witness's trial testimony on the

---

[36]   Fed. R. Evid. 801(d)(1)(A). There are other prior statements by a witness that are exempted from the hearsay rule. *See* Fed. R. Evid. 801(d)(1).

ground that she has been inconsistent in her account. But the inapplicability of Rule 608(b) does not mean that extrinsic evidence of every prior inconsistent statement will be allowed, because proving the statement raises the prospect of confusing the jury and delaying the proceedings. Ultimately, the judge must apply Rule 403 and determine whether the probative value of the proffered extrinsic evidence (its bearing on the witness's credibility) is substantially outweighed by the danger of unfair prejudice, confusion of the issues, and undue delay. The bottom line is that if the prior inconsistency concerns an incidental matter, extrinsic evidence will be forbidden, as it doesn't sufficiently advance the credibility inquiry to justify the risk of confusion and delay involved in proving the statement at trial. In the above example, this would mean that if the witness had been inconsistent about the color of the teller's dress, this inconsistency could be raised on cross-examination, but the judge might bar extrinsic evidence under Rule 403. But if the witness had been inconsistent about the color of the *getaway car*, the inconsistency would go to a central fact and extrinsic evidence would be permitted.

Disclosing the Inconsistent Statement

Federal Rule of Evidence 613(a) provides as follows:

(a) Showing or Disclosing the Statement During Examination. When examining a witness about the witness's prior statement, a party need not show it or disclose its contents to the witness. But the party must, on request, show it or disclose its contents to an adverse party's attorney.

The purpose of this subdivision is to abolish what was known at common law as the Rule in Queen Caroline's case—that a prior written statement had to be shown to the witness before the witness could be questioned about it. The Advisory Committee Note explained Rule 613(a): "Abolished by statute in the country of its origin, the requirement nevertheless gained currency in the United States. The rule abolishes this useless impediment, to cross-examination. . . . Both oral and written statements are included."

You will see that, although the counsel seeking to question a witness about a prior statement need not first disclose its contents to the witness, she must show it to opposing counsel upon request. As the Advisory Committee further explained, "[t]he provision for disclosure to counsel is designed to protect against unwarranted insinuations that a statement has been made when the fact is to the contrary."

Opportunity to Explain or Deny the Inconsistent Statement

Under *Federal Rule 613*, a witness who is impeached by extrinsic evidence of her prior inconsistent statement must ordinarily be afforded an opportunity at some point in the trial to explain or deny it. Specifically, Rule 613(b) provides:

> **(b) Extrinsic Evidence of a Prior Inconsistent Statement.** Extrinsic evidence of a witness's prior inconsistent statement is admissible only if the witness is given an opportunity to explain or deny the statement and an adverse party is given an opportunity to examine the witness about it, or if justice so requires. This subdivision (b) does not apply to an opposing party's statement under Rule 801(d)(2).

Common law judges required that a witness be asked about a prior inconsistent statement *prior* to the introduction of extrinsic evidence offered to prove the content of the statement. Thus, the cross-examiner had to lay a foundation by identifying the prior statement with sufficient detail (e.g., time, place, person spoken to) to allow the witness to explain, deny, or qualify her prior remark.[37] Under Rule 613, it suffices that the witness be afforded an opportunity *at some point in the trial* to address her prior inconsistency and to respond to questions about it by the attorney supporting her credibility.[38] Even this requirement (an opportunity *at some point*) can be waived by the judge "if justice so requires."[39] Furthermore, the requirement of a chance to respond has no application when the out-of-court statement in question is the statement of a party-opponent. Rule 613 does not apply to prior statements that fall within the party-statement exemption, because the statement is admissible for its truth whether or not the declarant testifies.

Despite the fact that Rule 613(b) gives the lawyer who seeks to use a prior inconsistent statement some leeway as to when to give a witness the opportunity to explain or deny the statement, trial tactics

---

[37] This traditional, common law approach explains why some judges still insist that before extrinsic evidence of bias evidenced by a prior statement is offered, the witness must be given an opportunity to explain or deny the bias.

[38] Some federal appellate courts have construed Rule 611 (judges' control over testimony) broadly enough to allow a trial judge, in her discretion, to require that a witness be asked about his prior inconsistency before he is impeached by extrinsic evidence. *See, e.g., United States v. Schnapp*, 322 F.3d 564, 571–72 (8th Cir. 2003).

[39] For example, suppose the witness completes his testimony, leaves the court's jurisdiction, and thereafter counsel discovers that the witness has made a prior inconsistent statement. The court may find that the interest of justice permits impeachment even though the witness was never confronted with the statement. Obviously, the interest of justice exception is narrow.

often provide a powerful incentive for the impeaching lawyer to confront the witness as soon as possible. As a practical matter, letting a witness who could be impeached with an inconsistent statement leave the stand unimpeached might make it more difficult later in a trial for the jury to recall exactly what prior testimony an inconsistent statement is directed at. Moreover, a lawyer who chooses not to use an inconsistent statement while the witness is testifying is likely to be required to ask the judge to direct the witness to remain available to testify and thereby to signal to the witness that he should ready himself for impeachment.

Impeachment by Contradiction

Suppose counsel for the plaintiff has two witnesses to a single-car automobile accident. The principal issue in the case is whether the accident was caused by a defect in the road, or by the plaintiff's negligent driving. Witness A gives an account of the relevant event that, at best, mildly favors the plaintiff's version of the facts; witness B's description of the accident is more favorable to the plaintiff.

This imagined case presents a commonplace sequence of events: the testimony of two or more witnesses vary on one or several points. The fact that B's testimony is not entirely congruent with A's testimony does not mean that A has been impeached. On the other hand, suppose that while A is on the stand, the lawyer who called her seeks and receives the court's permission to examine witness A "as if under cross-examination." He then conducts a hostile examination as to the condition of the road at the time of the accident. Assume that he fails in his attempt to have A retract or alter her account of the condition of the road. Counsel now calls B, and directs his attention to the condition of the road or, perhaps, even to A's testimony. B's testimony conflicts with A's account. A has been impeached by a technique called "contradiction."

Typically, "contradiction" is employed by the cross-examiner who, unable to get the witness to modify her testimony, attempts to impeach her by introducing extrinsic evidence that contradicts that testimony. There is no difficulty if the extrinsic evidence is independently admissible for some relevant purpose—such as the condition of the road; that testimony is admissible as proof of a fact. However, extrinsic evidence is ordinarily not permitted if it is not independently admissible and it contradicts the witness on a tangential or "collateral" point. The cross-examiner will often argue that if the witness is mistaken as to a collateral fact, she may also be mistaken as to the important facts. But the courts have generally held that to receive evidence of contradiction on tangential portions of a witness's testimony exacts too great a price in distraction and time consumption. In other words, the admissibility of extrinsic evidence when offered solely for contradiction is subject to the balancing test of Rule 403. This means, though, that extrinsic evidence that contradicts a witness's assertion is possibly admissible even if it is not a fact that is central to the case. The question is whether the fact is so important to the witness's story that getting it wrong raises substantial doubt about that story.

ILLUSTRATION

Adnan is charged with murdering his girlfriend. The star prosecution witness, Jay, testifies that Adnan called him on the day of the murder and told him to pick him up "at the phone booth in front of the BestBuy." Then, Adnan showed Jay the body of his girlfriend in his trunk, and provided detailed testimony about his and the defendant's movements for the rest of the day. On cross-examination, defense counsel asked Jay if he would be surprised to find out that there was no phone booth in front of the BestBuy. Jay says, "I would be very surprised, because there is a phone booth there, and that is where I picked Adnan up." Defense counsel seeks to introduce an authenticated picture, taken the day of the disputed events, which shows that there is no phone booth in front of the BestBuy.

The picture is offered as extrinsic evidence of contradiction. But it is not offered as proof of any fact in contention in the case—Adnan is not being charged with murdering his girlfriend at the phone booth. So proof of the fact would be offered only to impeach Jay by way of contradiction—because he got this fact wrong, he might be wrong about other facts more central to the dispute.

What the trial judge must do is balance probative value for impeachment against the risk of prejudice, confusion, and delay. Here, the probative value for impeachment should be found to be high. Jay has made the location, the telephone booth, the jumping off point for a detailed account of disputed movements throughout the day. He is also relating a purported statement from Adnan. If he is wrong about the phone booth—where his whole time with Adnan purportedly started—it throws doubt not only on his testimony about the rest of the detailed activity, but also about what Adnan might have said. The prejudicial effect is about zero—the government suffers no unfair prejudice in evidence that there is no phone booth at a BestBuy. Confusion of the jury seems minimal as well. And delay is trivial because it is only a picture that is being admitted—there is not going to be a minitrial about the existence of the phone booth. So, applying Rule 403, the picture should be admitted as proof of contradiction.

The main point about impeachment by contradiction is this: on cross-examination, counsel can seek to have a witness express doubt or retract his testimony on a minor point. But introducing extrinsic evidence to contradict a witness on a point that is not important to the case is usually disallowed. Thus, if a witness testifies that she was returning from church when she saw the accident in question, the cross-examiner can ask in good faith, "Isn't it true that you were actually returning from a card game?" However, if the witness denies the assertion, the cross-examiner will have to "take the answer" on cross. This does not mean that the examiner cannot press the witness; it only means that extrinsic evidence is ordinarily inadmissible if its only value is to impeach this witness on a minor (collateral) point.

Ultimately a trial judge should decide the admissibility of extrinsic evidence on a so-called "collateral" point by applying Rule 403—the use of the term "collateral" as a label often clouds the analysis. For example, the BestBuy phone booth issue in the Illustration is a "collateral" fact because it is not a fact that the government needs to prove to win its case. But its nonexistence is, in context, important evidence of contradiction of the witness.

Sensory Impairments

Here we speak of various impairments that hinder a witness's ability to accurately observe, remember, and relate. The sensory defect may range from a mild impairment (the witness wasn't wearing her glasses) to total incapacity (psychosis). Common impairments are poor eyesight, defective hearing, intoxication, drug use, or memory loss. Although the focus is usually on the witness's condition at the time of the event in question, issues about a witness's capacities can also arise as of the time she is called to testify. (The communication of an earlier sensory perception may be impaired.) For example, some event, such as memory loss or a debilitating condition, may have intervened between the witness's observation and her proffered testimony, or the witness may be under the influence of drugs at the time of her testimony.[40] The availability of extrinsic evidence to prove a sensory defect is controlled by Federal Rule 403. The general practice is to permit extrinsic evidence unless

---

[40]   An issue that sometimes arises is whether a witness may be impeached by showing she is addicted to alcohol or drugs. That is, although counsel has no evidence that the witness was under the influence of an intoxicating substance at the time of the event (or at trial), she does have evidence of the witness's general addiction. Rule 403 is the governing evidentiary provision. The general practice is to exclude evidence of addiction. *See United States v. Ramirez*, 871 F.2d 582, 584 (6th Cir. 1989). *But see United States v. Lochmondy*, 890 F.2d 817, 824 (6th Cir. 1989) (limited inquiry into heroin addiction permissible).

the witness's admission during cross-examination renders unnecessary any further proof.

Psychiatric Condition

Some mental illnesses, often not apparent to the trier of fact, affect a witness's credibility. For example, a mental condition might impair a witness's capacity to perceive accurately or to testify truthfully—a witness may have a mental condition that makes it difficult to separate fantasy from reality. The question before the court is whether a witness may be impeached by existing evidence of a mental illness that could affect his credibility. As this form of impeachment is usually time-consuming (and embarrassing to the witness), courts (applying Rule 403) permit it sparingly. It is certainly not the case that counsel can ask a witness "isn't it true that you have been seeing a psychiatrist for the last ten years?" Four considerations are particularly influential to the Rule 403 analysis: (1) the nexus, according to medical authorities, between the alleged mental condition and testimonial accuracy; (2) the importance of the witness's testimony; (3) the time involved in presenting the psychiatric evidence and any counter-evidence; and (4) the extent to which evidence may be far more embarrassing than probative (a consideration for the judge under both Rule 611(a) and Rule 403).

Impeaching a Hearsay Declarant

We have seen that the hearsay rule applies only to statements that are proffered to prove the truth of the assertions contained within them. Because the trier is asked to believe the hearsay declarant, the credibility of the declarant is important. Federal Rule of Evidence 806[41] allows the credibility of a hearsay declarant to be attacked, as a general rule, by the same impeachment techniques that are available to discredit a testifying witness. In practice, there are minor differences. For example, if the declarant made a statement inconsistent with the hearsay admitted at trial, the inconsistent statement can be admitted without giving the declarant an opportunity to explain or deny it. The reason is obvious—the declarant is generally not at trial, so if an opportunity had to be afforded, few inconsistent statements would ever be admitted to impeach a hearsay declarant. And that result would be contrary to

---

[41] "When a hearsay statement—or a statement described in Rule 801(d)(2)(C), (D), or (E)—has been admitted in evidence, the declarant's credibility may be attacked, and then supported, by any evidence that would be admissible for those purposes if the declarant had testified as a witness. The court may admit evidence of the declarant's inconsistent statement or conduct, regardless of when it occurred or whether the declarant had an opportunity to explain or deny it. If the party against whom the statement was admitted calls the declarant as a witness, the party may examine the declarant on the statement as if on cross-examination."

the basic policy of Rule 806, which is that hearsay declarants can be impeached to the same extent as trial witnesses.

It is also possible that many hearsay declarants cannot be impeached with prior bad acts under Rule 608(b). Rule 608(b) provides that extrinsic evidence cannot be offered to prove such acts, so it would seem necessary that the declarant be present at trial in order to be questioned about the acts, and many hearsay declarants will not be—though some courts have held that extrinsic evidence *is* admissible to impeach a hearsay declarant, because otherwise the hearsay declarant would escape impeachment in a way that an in-court witness could not.[42]

Abusing Impeachment

Suppose counsel knows that a witness, *W*, will give unfavorable testimony. However, counsel has identified an inconsistent statement, made by *W* on a prior occasion, that is favorable to counsel's client. Assume the prior inconsistent statement would be inadmissible hearsay if offered for its truth. However, as we have seen, a prior inconsistent statement is normally admissible for the limited purpose of impeaching the witness who made it. Can counsel call *W* knowing that he will give unfavorable testimony, and then impeach him with a prior inconsistent statement that the jury is not supposed to use for its truth? The risk of abuse is apparent—there is no good reason to call a witness solely to impeach him with a prior statement. If the lawyer knows the witness will give completely unfavorable testimony, then his reason for calling the witness must be to reveal the witness's prior inconsistent statement. Although technically the prior statement can only be introduced for the purpose of impeachment, there is a risk that the jury may use it for the truth of its assertion—which is exactly what the lawyer must intend.

The practice of calling a witness solely to "impeach" him with otherwise inadmissible statements is condemned in both criminal and civil cases; the remedy is to disallow the impeachment by the prior statements.

Of course, if the inconsistent statement *is* admissible for its truth, then there is no abuse and the witness can be called solely for the purpose of admitting it. An example is where the declarant made the prior inconsistent statement under oath at a proceeding, in which case the statement would be admissible not only for impeachment, but also to prove the facts related in the statement, under Rule 801(d)(1)(A). Moreover, situations will arise in which the lawyer was

---

[42]　*See* SALTZBURG, MARTIN & CAPRA, FEDERAL RULES OF EVIDENCE MANUAL, § 806.02 [2] (12th ed. 2019).

not certain about whether the witness would give completely unfavorable testimony—for example the witness tells the lawyer he is thinking about or leaning toward such testimony but did not categorically state that he would so testify. In those cases, courts will not find that the lawyer abused the impeachment rules if the witness ends up testifying unfavorably. The question in all cases is whether the lawyer was in good faith in offering up impeachment evidence that would otherwise be barred by the hearsay rule.

Accrediting the Witness (Rehabilitation)

So far we have considered ways in which a witness's credibility may be attacked. Do the rules permit an attempt to *support* a witness's credibility? The starting point for this discussion is the basic principle that the credibility of a witness may not be supported until it has been attacked. Federal Rule 608(a) makes this general principle clear. The assumption is that most witnesses are conscientious and honest, so there is no reason to prolong the trial by receiving evidence pertaining to credibility when truthfulness has not been questioned.

Generally speaking, when the attacking party impeaches by evidence showing an untruthful character, the party supporting the witness is entitled to respond with evidence that is probative to rehabilitate the witness's character for truthfulness. Regarding other impeachment techniques such as bias, prior inconsistent statements, and contradiction, the trial judge must decide if the proffered rehabilitation evidence actually rebuts the attack. For example, if a witness is impeached with a prior inconsistent statement, it will not be rebutted by the mere fact that the witness has also made a prior statement consistent with his testimony. The impeachment shows that the witness has contradicted himself out of his own mouth—the fact that he has also made a consistent statement does not rebut that attack.

It is important to note that the supporting party is always entitled to use redirect examination to try to rebuild the witness's credibility. The witness may, for example, refute the impeaching evidence, recharacterize it, or offer a benign explanation.

ILLUSTRATION

Zeke, an African-American, is prosecuted for the robbery of a jewelry store. Just as the robber, who was wearing a mask and gloves, was dropping rings, watches, and other items of merchandise into his satchel, a police siren sounded. As the robber ran out of the door to the sidewalk, muscular, athletic Passerby pulled off the robber's ski mask. As Passerby was about to wrench the satchel away from the robber, the latter shot him in the leg and escaped down an alley.

At trial, Passerby is one of the prosecution witnesses. He testifies that he cannot be certain that Zeke was the person running out of the jewelry store. He does state, however, that the robber was a young black male, about six feet. (Zeke fits this description.) On cross-examination, Zeke's defense attorney asks, "Isn't it true that after the robbery you told Officer Clack that the robber was Hispanic?" Passerby's response is a denial: "No, I said the robber's skin color was light enough for him to be Hispanic, but that he was African-American."

Later in the trial, the defense calls Officer Clack, who reluctantly admits that when he interviewed Passerby, an hour after the robbery, the latter had told him that the robber was "Hispanic—rather young and about six feet tall." Still later in the trial, the prosecutor presents Curtis, one of Passerby's friends who belongs to the same health and fitness club as Passerby. Curtis is prepared to testify that he returned from vacation about ten days after the robbery. The day after his return, he and Passerby worked out together, and Passerby described the robber as "fairly young, around six feet, and a black guy." Should the judge sustain a defense objection to Curtis's testimony?

Passerby has, of course, been impeached by the introduction of his prior inconsistent statement. The impeaching evidence, furnished by Officer Clack, was proper, and Passerby was given the opportunity on cross-examination to admit that he made such a statement and to explain it.[43] Note also that the judge was correct in receiving extrinsic evidence (Clack's testimony). On cross, Passerby refused to admit that he had previously said that the robber was Hispanic, which means that Officer Clack's testimony was not redundant or superfluous. Furthermore, because Passerby's testimony addresses a central point—the identity of the robber—extrinsic evidence of the inconsistent statement should be admissible under Rule 403.

The prosecutor's attempt to rehabilitate Passerby by introducing the latter's prior consistent statement will fail. Had the defense attorney charged or insinuated that Passerby had recently fabricated his trial testimony or was responding to some improper influence or motive, the prior consistent statement would be admitted *if an*

43　Fed. R. Evid. 613(b).

important condition were met.[44] It would be essential that the prosecutor convince the judge that the prior consistent statement *predated* the alleged influence, motive, or recent fabrication.[45] If this foundation is provided, the prior consistent statement has heightened relevance in that it has probative value to show that Passerby was not responding to a corrupt or improper stimulus. (He made an earlier statement (to Curtis) that is consistent with his testimony and the prior statement *predated* the alleged influence or fabrication.) In the Illustration, however, the defense attorney simply impeaches Passerby with a prior inconsistency. The trier of fact now has before it Passerby's testimony and evidence of a prior statement inconsistent with that testimony. Producing evidence that Passerby also made a statement consistent with his testimony adds very little: the trier already has before it two conflicting accounts of the robber's race. It's not a question of which account was stated more often.

Methods of Rehabilitation

Often evidence offered to rehabilitate a witness is not barred by any evidence rule and will be admitted as long as it is relevant. One way to rebut impeaching evidence is to produce evidence that the impeaching evidence is false and should not be believed. Counsel may attempt to negate the impeaching evidence during redirect examination or—unless the impeaching evidence is forbidden because it pertains to a minor point—by producing extrinsic evidence. For example, if a witness is impeached by evidence that he was intoxicated at the time he observed the event in question, supporting counsel can offer evidence that the witness was sober.

Sometimes the evidence rules specifically recognize the possibility of rehabilitation evidence being admitted. If, for example, the witness is impeached by opinion evidence that his character for truthfulness is bad pursuant to Rule 608(a), that Rule anticipates that supporting counsel can offer an opinion witness to testify to the principal witness's good character for truthfulness.

A second means of attacking impeachment evidence is to produce evidence that rebuts *the inference of distorted or untruthful testimony that is derived* from the impeaching facts. Suppose, for example, the witness is impeached by evidence that eight years ago he was convicted of a crime that casts doubt on his credibility. Supporting counsel might respond by producing evidence that the witness currently has a good reputation for truthfulness. Obviously, this rebuttal strikes not at the impeaching fact (the conviction), but

---

[44]   The Federal Rule in point is 801(d)(1)(B). If this rule applies, the prior statement is also admitted for its truth. See the discussion in Chapter XI, § 6.2.

[45]   *See Tome v. United States*, 513 U.S. 150, 156–60 (1995).

rather at the inference of untruthfulness that can be derived from the impeaching fact.

This second means of rebutting impeachment evidence—countering the inference of distortion or falsity—often raises issues of relevance. If, for example, impeachment is by evidence of bad reputation for truthfulness, rebuttal evidence that shows the witness has made prior statements consistent with her testimony usually has little or no probative force. The courts would reject it for the obvious reason that the witness's prior assertions may also have been false. A similar result can be expected when the witness is impeached with evidence of bias, and supporting counsel seeks to accredit the witness with evidence of prior consistent statements. Unless these previous accounts predate the alleged inception of the bias, they fail to negate the inference to be drawn from the impeaching evidence.

Chapter X

PRIVILEGE

Table of Sections

§ 10.1 Rationale and Characteristics

As we have seen, the law of evidence generally seeks accuracy in fact-finding by receiving relevant evidence thought to be reliable, while rejecting evidence deemed untrustworthy. Recall, however, that some of the specific evidentiary rules of relevance, such as those that prohibit evidence of post-accident remedial measures or offers of settlement,[1] are based on social policy concerns. In other words, relevant evidence is rejected on the ground that an extrinsic policy is more important than the factfinder's consideration of the excluded evidence. Evidence that reveals a privileged communication bears a kinship to these specific relevance rules, in that extrinsic policies— rather than the law's search for truth—dictate the rejection of probative evidence.

Privileged information is excluded because disclosure would harm a governmental interest or a private relationship that courts and legislatures deem worthy of preserving or fostering. For example, the government has a privilege not to reveal information that would compromise national security,[2] and a client has a privilege not to reveal confidential communications made to her attorney.

---

[1]   *See generally* Chapter IV.

[2]   The President also has a qualified privilege that protects confidential communications with subordinates in the Executive branch. *See United States v. Nixon*, 418 U.S. 683, 708–09 (1974).

The cost of evidentiary privileges is apparent in the courtroom: probative evidence is suppressed, and the trier makes factual determinations without it. This means, of course, that the application of an evidentiary privilege increases the probability of an erroneous trial outcome. On the other hand, the benefits of conferring a privilege are difficult to measure. For example, confidential communications between husband and wife are privileged. It is fair to ask whether this privilege encourages spousal communications—which is said to be its immediate purpose. The answer here, as with many privileges, is uncertain. The most that can be said is that privileges rest largely on unproven assumptions; some of these assumptions are highly probable, others are highly problematic.

There are two justifications for the recognition of privileges. The principal rationale is utilitarian or instrumental: privileges are justified because their existence encourages behavior that is socially desirable. For example, the attorney-client privilege encourages full and candid revelations by the client, thus enabling the attorney to provide the appropriate legal advice. Furthermore, the existence of the privilege encourages persons who need legal advice to seek it. The second rationale for privileges rests upon notions of personal autonomy and privacy. Some privileges are justified because certain intimate relationships, such as those of husband and wife, clergy and penitent, and lawyer and client, should be protected from governmental intrusion and prying.

Assertion of a Privilege

The right to claim a privilege belongs exclusively to the person or persons for whom the privilege was created—that is, the holder(s). The holder may be a party to litigation and thus conveniently situated to claim his privilege if he wishes. Sometimes, however, the holder is not a party litigant; in this event, none of the parties to the suit has standing, in his own right, to object to the introduction of privileged evidence. The claimant's right is reserved for the holder, who might or might not wish to exercise it. Nonetheless, a party or some other person is sometimes permitted to assert the privilege on behalf of the holder—as the holder's agent or representative. This is the case, for example, where the holder gives express authorization to someone else to claim the privilege on the holder's behalf; the same is true where authorization may be fairly implied, as it is when a lawyer invokes the attorney-client privilege on behalf of the client, who is the holder. In still other circumstances, the law may authorize a presiding judge to invoke a privilege on the absent holder's behalf.

If the trial judge erroneously upholds a claim of privilege and *excludes* evidence that is not privileged, the disadvantaged party can object without regard to the identity of the holder. (He stands in the same position, for example, as a party who complains on appeal that the trial judge excluded evidence as hearsay, when it was not.) The appellate court can correct the lower court's error by holding that the claimed privilege was not applicable.

Non-Evidentiary Confidentiality Obligations

Do not confuse privileges with various professional codes that obligate persons such as lawyers and doctors to preserve their clients' and patients' confidences and secrets. Violating these ethical codes can lead to disciplinary action by the appropriate authorities. However, disclosures that violate a professional code are not barred from evidentiary use unless they also fall within a privilege.

§ 10.2 Privileges Under the Federal Rules of Evidence

In the 1970's when the proposed Federal Rules of Evidence were considered and debated in Congress, there was widespread disagreement about what privileges should be recognized and what their proper scope should be. Congress could not agree on the detailed privilege provisions that were prepared by the Advisory Committee and approved by the Judicial Conference and the Supreme Court. So a compromise was reached. Congress deleted the detailed proposed privilege rules, which recognized nine privileges, and in their place passed a single rule, *Federal Rule 501*. It now reads:

Privilege in General

The common law—as interpreted by United States courts in the light of reason and experience—governs a claim of privilege unless any of the following provides otherwise:

- the United States Constitution;

- a federal statute; or

- rules prescribed by the Supreme Court.

But in a civil case, state law governs privilege regarding a claim or defense for which state law supplies the rule of decision.

The key phrase directs that the common law, as determined "in the light of reason and experience" determines the law of privilege in the federal courts. Thus, under federal law, privileges are determined by the case law as it existed when the Federal Rules were enacted, and as it has subsequently developed under federal common law.

Relevance of State Law of Privilege

Of course, pursuant to the Supreme Court's decision in *Erie Railroad Co. v. Tompkins*,[3] federal courts often apply state common and statutory law. They do so, for example, in "diversity cases," that is, civil cases in which the federal courts have jurisdiction to entertain the litigation only because the parties are citizens of different states. Federal courts also apply state law in civil cases where the plaintiff's principal claim is based on federal law, but he "tacks on" a state law claim that arises from the same cluster of facts or events that underlie his federal claim. Federal Rule 501 directs that in civil cases the state law of privileges applies to the trial of claims and defenses based on state law. Thus, if a plaintiff from Virginia sues a defendant from Delaware in a federal court in connection with an automobile collision that occurred in Virginia, the substantive law of Virginia would apply. The federal judge presiding over the case would also apply Virginia's law of privilege, including any Virginia laws that might defer to the privilege law of another state (*i.e.* Delaware). This diversity case is straightforward because it involves only *state* substantive law.

Suppose, however, a plaintiff sues a defendant in federal court and the plaintiff's claim is based on a federal antitrust statute. Suppose further, the plaintiff appends a second claim based on state "unfair competition" law. The federal court can entertain the state claim by invoking its supplemental subject matter jurisdiction,[4] if the events giving rise to the state claim are the same as or closely related to the events that underlie the federal claim. The intertwining of facts supporting jurisdiction over both the federal and state claims makes it likely that some witnesses will give testimony that is relevant to both claims. What happens when the state law of privilege is different from the federal law? For example, suppose state law confers a privilege on part or all of a witness's testimony, but federal law does not. Where the facts to which a witness will testify are relevant to both the federal and state claims, it is clear that one or the other law of privilege must apply to both claims. It would be silly, for example, to tell the jury that it could use a communication for the federal claim (where there is no privilege) but not on the related state claim (because of the state privilege). Where one or the other law of privilege must apply to both claims, federal courts generally apply *federal* privilege law; a contrary rule would mean that the federal court was excessively deferring to state law, by applying the state law of privilege to a federal claim.[5]

---

3   304 U.S. 64 (1938).

4   28 U.S.C. § 1367 is the "supplemental jurisdiction" statute.

5   *See Pearson v. Miller*, 211 F.3d 57, 66 (3d Cir. 2000).

§ 10.3 The Attorney-Client Privilege

The privilege protecting communications between attorney and client is recognized in every American jurisdiction. It is firmly rooted and unqualified—that is, once it attaches, it is not subject to a judicial override. Furthermore, it can be claimed, even after the client's death, by her personal representative. The privilege rests both on privacy concerns and, more importantly, on a utilitarian rationale. The privilege encourages frank and full disclosure by the client, thus improving the quality of legal representation. And because the existence of the privilege is widely known, it may encourage persons in need of legal advice to seek it. That said, it is still not easy to craft the proper bounds of the attorney-client privilege.

Here are some, but by no means all, of the difficulties:

1)   The client may wish to conceal physical evidence, or hide his identity. Note that the protection of information like this is only tenuously connected to the purpose of the privilege—full and frank communications between client and lawyer. Thus the privilege is generally inapplicable in situations like these.

2)   Another difficulty arises because, in the course of legal representation, lawyers and clients necessarily interact with a wide range of third parties, such as investigators, paralegals, accountants, physicians, and consulting attorneys. Thorny problems emerge in determining whether communications with and among these secondary actors fall within the boundaries of the attorney-client privilege.

3)   There is a difficulty in marking the appropriate bounds of this privilege when the holder is a business enterprise, such as a corporation, partnership, or other business association.

4)   Special problems also exist when shareholders in a corporation sue management on behalf of the corporation—an increasingly common practice in American business life.

5)   Other problems arise when a lawyer represents several clients on a common matter and they subsequently become adversaries, or when separately represented clients cooperate and pool their resources.

6)   Demarcation of the privilege is difficult when the lawyer is sought for "mixed" objectives, such as a consultation seeking both business and legal advice.

In resolving these and other problems, it is important to keep in mind the core objective of the attorney-client privilege: to promote full and candid confidential communications between client and attorney so as to facilitate the rendition of legal services. While the development of the attorney-client privilege generally proceeds by case law, courts have been guided by proposed Federal Rule 503. Even though neither this rule nor the other proposed privilege rules were adopted when Congress enacted the Federal Rules of Evidence in 1975, Congress made it clear that its decision to allow the law of privilege to evolve by judicial decision was not a disapproval of any of the proposed enumerated privileges.[6] Proposed Rule 503 is a carefully crafted, detailed provision, covering many aspects of the attorney-client privilege. It has been an influential "standard" in both federal and state courts and its influence has prompted greater uniformity across jurisdictional lines. You should be aware, however, that some differences in the scope of the attorney-client privilege do exist among the jurisdictions and this is particularly true among the various states. Thus, the following textual materials should be viewed as representing the position of most courts and, in particular, of most federal courts.

The Privilege Defined

Proposed Rule 503 broadly defines the attorney-client privilege. Subsection (b) states:

> **General rule of privilege.** A client has a privilege to refuse to disclose and to prevent any other person from disclosing confidential communications made for the purpose of facilitating the rendition of professional legal services to the client, (1) between himself or his representatives and his lawyer or his lawyer's representative, or (2) between his lawyer and the lawyer's representative, or (3) by him or his lawyer to a lawyer representing another in a matter of common interest, or (4) between representatives of the client or between the client and a representative of the client, or (5) between lawyers representing the client.

Representatives of the Attorney and Client

The privilege protects not only the direct communications between attorney and client, but also communications between and among various non-lawyer agents. Legal services often involve non-lawyer specialists such as investigators, physicians, economists, investment bankers, accountants, scientists, and mathematicians. It is important to note, however, that for communications to these non-lawyers to be protected by the attorney-client privilege, these

---

6   S. REP. NO. 93–1277, at 4 (1974).

representatives must either be communicating to the lawyer (or his representative) or the client (or his representative) for the purpose of or assisting the lawyer in delivering legal services. The non-lawyer specialist must be *necessary to the legal representation*. So, for example, communications with a jury consultant could fall within the privilege, but communications with a public relations specialists are unlikely to be protected because promoting the client's public image is ordinarily not necessary to the legal representation.

The following illustrations raise questions about the use of representatives within the attorney-client relationship, as well as a number of other thorny issues in the application of the privilege.

ILLUSTRATIONS

Cusp. Associates is a dental partnership consisting of partners White and Phil and three employees: two hygienists and an administrative assistant. Recently, a successful elderly dentist ("Seller", age 68) has mentioned to friends that he has decided to retire at age 70 and to sell his dental business. Seller owns the modern building in which his office is located and he leases approximately half the square footage in this building to an accounting firm. He has told several of his friends and associates that he intends to sell the building, the one-acre tract on which it is located, all of his office furnishings and dental equipment, and his "goodwill." The asking price will be about four and a half million dollars.

Seller's dental office is just two blocks from Cusp. Associates, and White and Phil are considering making an early bid. To that end, they decide to consult lawyers Todd and Sheila, who specialize in legal work for small businesses. At the initial consultation, the two potential clients discuss with the lawyers the possibility of buying the Seller's practice and moving their own practice into his larger and newer building; they also discuss the possibility of hiring a third dentist and maintaining two offices. One difficulty is that there is considerable animosity between the retiring dentist and White and Phil. Therefore, the partners suggest that their identity as potential buyers remain secret. Near the conclusion of this initial consultation, the four participants (White, Phil, Todd and Sheila) discuss fee arrangements, the advantages and disadvantages of changing from a dental partnership to a professional or Limited Liability Corporation, various ways in which the contemplated acquisition might be financed, and the general terms of a contract for sale. Overwhelmed by the complexities of the purchase, White and Phil say they need a "few days to think everything over" before they decide to go forward.

(1)   Assume the two dentists abandon their tentative plan to acquire Seller's business. Assume further that Todd and Sheila provide an initial consultation to potential clients without charge. Only if they (the lawyers) are retained do they enter into a formal fee agreement with new clients. Are the initial conversations among White, Phil, Todd, and Sheila within the attorney-client privilege?

The attorney-client privilege is available not only to individual clients, but also to partnerships, various business entities (such as associations and corporations), and to governmental officers and agencies. Proposed Rule 503(a)(1), tracking federal common law, defines "client" as a person or entity "who is rendered professional legal services by a lawyer, or who consults a lawyer with a view to obtaining professional legal services from him." The availability of the privilege is thus not dependent on the payment of legal fees or on a formal contract between client and attorney. And the privilege applies to an initial attorney-client consultation, even if the client[7] (or the attorney) declines representation.

The Legal Advice Requirement

What about the fact that the initial conversations between the dental partners and their attorneys addressed some topics that, viewed in isolation, related primarily to business (as opposed to legal) matters? The privilege requires that the client must be seeking *legal advice* from the lawyer; that requirement emphasizes the obvious fact that not everything said to a lawyer, even in confidence, is privileged. (If that were the case, lawyers would be quite popular at bars and parties). That said, clients often seek lawyers for assistance on complex matters that involve a *mixture* of law, business, policy, and other subjects that are not strictly "legal." But if including any non-legal subject within a broader legal discussion would lose the privilege, then the attorney-client relationship would suffer. Accordingly, the courts have generally held that if the *dominant intent* of the client is to seek legal advice, the privilege is not lost if advice is also sought on related business, financial, or other not strictly legal matters. (Some courts have held that a "significant" motivation to obtain legal advice is sufficient.) In the illustration, the

---

[7]   If the privilege did not apply, the client seeking the benefit of the privilege would be in the awkward position of having to retain the lawyer before revealing his legal problem. Also, the lawyer would be in the equally awkward position of having to agree to represent the client before knowing the facts giving rise to the client's legal difficulties.

subjects discussed were intimately associated with rendering legal services such as the structure of the combined dental offices and the general terms of a contract for sale. When rendering legal services to a business, lawyers often require information about the business enterprise itself. The context for providing legal advice or legal services must be fully developed in order for the consulting attorney to give the appropriate legal advice. Thus, the privilege probably attaches generally to the communications in Illustration (1), and it certainly attaches to some of them, such as the terms of the contract of sale and the possible legal restructuring of Cusp.'s business. The key factor is the dominant purpose of the consultation.

Two-Way Protection

What about the fact that the statements in Illustration (1) are not only by the clients but also by the lawyers? Although the attorney-client privilege was initially formulated to protect only the client's confidential communications, modern courts recognize that the privilege must also apply to the attorney's confidential communications to the client—in order to promote a full exchange of information between client and lawyer. This is especially so because the client's statements and the attorney's statements often interlock. If the privilege did not attach to the attorney's statements, her disclosures could often be used to infer at least the general content of the client's confidential communications to the attorney. Thus, considerations of both practicality and preserving confidentially have prompted courts to apply the privilege to the confidential communications of both client and attorney.

---

(2) Assume White and Phil decide to make an early bid on the Seller's dental business. Thus, they return to Todd and Sheila and engage them "to handle the whole transaction." Here are some of the events that follow:

(a) White and Phil send Cusp., Associates' [hereafter "CA"] latest financial statements to Todd and Sheila. In order to expedite delivery, CA's administrative assistant puts the relevant statements in a file, marks the file "confidential," and hand-delivers it to the dental firm's new lawyers.

(b) Sheila personally contacts the managing partner of the accounting firm that currently leases half of the building owned by Seller. In the privacy of the partner's office, they discuss the general terms of the accounting firm's current lease, whether the accountants may need additional space, the probability that the accountants will want to renew their lease, and their willingness to accept a clause that ties the rent to the rate of inflation.

(c) Todd and Sheila engage Real Estate Associates to conduct "a highly confidential appraisal" of Seller's lot and office building. The firm is to consult tax records, compare the selling price of comparable property, evaluate the soundness of the building, calculate its total and usable square footage, gain access to the interior by using some pretext such as seeking accounting or dental services, and, finally, the firm is to prepare a confidential report, summarizing findings, to be delivered to Todd and Sheila.

(d) Todd and Sheila dispatch a young associate from their law firm to the offices of White and Phil. There, over lunch with the two dentists, their hygienists and their administrative assistant, the associate describes and explains a bill pending in the state legislature that, if passed, would change the tax liability of business partnerships.

(e) Subsequently, the bill is amended and passed. The young associate prepares a memorandum in which he discusses and analyzes the potential tax liability of CA if, (a) it remains a partnership and if, (b) it becomes a professional corporation. This memorandum is delivered to Todd, who reviews it and forwards a copy (marked "confidential") to White and Phil.

(f) Later, with the assistance of Todd and Sheila and the Seller's attorney, CA ("Buyer") and the retiring dentist ("Seller") close the deal. However, the real identity of White and Phil is not revealed. Instead, the contract of sale is signed by Seller and "Dental Associates, P.C." a corporation controlled by White and Phil. The contract calls for a certified check at closing. It also contains a number of conditions, one of which is that the Seller agrees to allow an accountant or other financial expert retained by the Buyer (Dental Associates) to conduct an in-depth financial analysis of the Seller's dental business. A copy of this report is to be delivered to Seller's attorney. Since this report could affect the final selling price, the Seller is given 75 days to have his own report prepared. If the parties thereafter fail to agree, an arbitrator will be appointed.

(g) The bank that is financing the Buyer's purchase insists that White and Phil have adequate life and health insurance. Thus, both men undergo a thorough physical conducted by a Dr. Brooke. The doctor sends a copy of his confidential report to the bank, with copies to White, Phil, Todd and Sheila.

Suppose, prior to closing, Seller learns the true identity of the buyers. Thereafter, the deal sours as animosity develops and the contracting parties accuse each other of misrepresentation and bad faith. Subsequently, Seller brings suit for breach of contract, naming as defendants CA, Dental Associates, P.C., and White and Phil as individuals.

Which, if any, of the conversations and documents described in Illustration (2)(a)–(g) are protected by the attorney-client privilege?

Pre-Existing Documents

As to Illustration (2)(a): the attorney-client privilege *does not apply* to letters, documents (such as CA's financial statements), or other inscribed items that were not prepared for the purpose of facilitating legal services. If the rule were otherwise, a client could place all "preexisting" documents beyond the reach of discovery by the simple expedient of turning them over to her attorney. The fact that such documents end up being useful to the lawyer is beside the point—the question is whether the communications were *initially* made to the lawyer for the purpose of securing legal advice. Of course, if the client prepares a confidential letter to the attorney telling her, for example, how to interpret the documents or suggesting trends reflected in the data contained in them, this letter would be protected by the privilege.[8] Furthermore, if an attorney gives confidential legal advice to a client that is based on the attorney's review or analysis of unprotected documents, the *communication from the attorney* to the client is protected by the privilege (while the underlying documents are not). And finally, while the content of a pre-existing document is not protected by the privilege, the *fact* that the client sent it to the lawyer, confidentially, for purposes of legal advice, is privileged. That is because the production to the lawyer is itself a communication ("I think this document is relevant to the legal matter on which you are representing me."). This means that the opponent could offer the

---

[8]   We are assuming, of course, that the documents and cover letter are transmitted primarily for a legal, not a business purpose.

document as evidence but could not offer proof that the document was exchanged between the client and the lawyer.

Statements Outside the Attorney-Client Relationship

In Illustration (2)(b), the privilege should not apply. The accountant is neither a representative of the client, nor of the attorney. Indeed the accountant could even be the agent of the seller—so the statement goes to one completely outside the attorney-client relationship. Furthermore, content of the communications appears to be addressed predominantly, and perhaps solely, to business concerns—whether, and under what conditions the accounting firm would renew its lease.

Possibility of Work Product Protection

Students of civil procedure may recall the so-called "work-product" doctrine, traceable to the Supreme Court's decision in *Hickman v. Taylor*.[9] The central features of the work product doctrine have been codified in Federal Rule of Civil Procedure 26(b)(3), which sets forth the basic rules of work-product; subsection (b)(4) extends the work-product doctrine (or at least its rationale) to experts engaged by a party to assist in trial preparation. Generally speaking, the work-product doctrine extends *qualified immunity from discovery* by an opponent to written materials prepared in "anticipation of litigation." (It is a rule of discovery, which is why work product is generally not covered by the Evidence Rules). Typically, the protected materials are prepared by the lawyer, but materials prepared by others—such as an investigator, agent, consultant, or the party himself—are also conditionally immune if prepared for litigation. Familiar examples of a lawyer's work-product would be her notes about a witness's statement or his investigator's recorded measurements of skid marks at the scene of an automobile accident. Like the attorney-client privilege, the work-product doctrine protects the *materials or communications* generated by the lawyer, or by a client who is a party to a suit, or by a representative of either. However, the work-product doctrine *does not protect the client's knowledge*, which includes facts known to his attorney who is his agent. In other words, the client would have to answer an interrogatory: "How far were you from the 'Hazard' sign when you first saw it?" Furthermore, the court may order discovery of work-product materials if the party seeking them shows a substantial need. Unlike the privilege, work product protection is not absolute. The requisite showing of need varies with the particular context, by the type of work product ("opinion" or "fact") and also depends on the discovering party's ability to secure unprotected evidence that is the

---

9   329 U.S. 495, 510–11 (1947).

substantial equivalent of the materials sought. Note that unlike the privilege, which extends to all confidential communications where the dominant intent is to seek legal advice—whether or not related to the prospects of litigation—the work product doctrine protects *only those materials prepared in anticipation of litigation*. So for example, a lawyer's work in preparing an estate is not work product; but confidential communications between a client and lawyer in furtherance of estate planning are covered by attorney-client privilege.

Suppose in Illustration (2)(b), Sheila had made notes of her conversation with the managing partner of the accounting firm. Of course, it is uncertain whether the notes would have any bearing on a subsequent suit between Seller and Buyer. Even if the notes were relevant to subsequent litigation, they probably would *not be conditionally protected* by the work-product doctrine. That doctrine would apply *only* if Sheila could convince the judge that she prepared the notes "in anticipation of litigation."[10] This seems highly unlikely because, when the notes were made, there was no indication of forthcoming litigation.

Agents Necessary to the Representation

Illustration (2)(c) raises the question whether Real Estate Associates is a non-legal agent of the lawyer covered by the attorney-client privilege. Courts have held that the non-lawyer must be *necessary to the legal representation* for communications to or from the non-lawyer to be privileged. This is a contextual judgment requiring more information than is included in the Illustration. Sheila and Todd would have to convince the judge that the legal advice or legal services rendered to the client depend upon the condition and market value of the target property. There are some plausible possibilities. For example, perhaps the terms of the contract of sale, or advice as to tax considerations, or the business form[11] of CA are closely linked to the value of Seller's real property. A more obvious case of a non-lawyer necessary to the business representation is an environmental engineer in a case involving complex questions of pollution and causation; another example is an accountant in a case involving complex financial transactions.

Reasonable Expectation of Confidentiality

In Illustration (2)(d), the associate is clearly a representative of the lawyers, because his communications bear on legal matters. The problem is with confidentiality. The informal occasion, attended by all of the dental firm's employees, strongly suggests that there was

---

[10]   Fed. R. Civ. Proc. 26(b)(3).

[11]   For example, whether to remain a partnership or to incorporate.

no reasonable expectation that the luncheon communications would be kept confidential. Thus, the presence of third parties—the hygienists and assistant—nullifies the privilege.

Illustration (2)(e) involves, first, a communication from an attorney's representative (the associate) to the attorney, and, second, a direct communication from attorney to client. The communication is clearly legal in nature, and the requisite confidentiality is maintained. This context should be distinguished from one in which a lawyer simply prepares a client's income tax return and the client supplies the necessary financial information. That information would not be privileged. The mere preparation of an income tax return is not legal in nature; indeed most income tax preparers are not attorneys. On the other hand, tax lawyers routinely render legal services, creating many occasions on which communications from their clients (and their communications to their clients) are within the attorney-client privilege.

While in some circumstances, an accountant or financial expert could be a representative of an attorney (or of a client), in Illustration (2)(f) the parties agree that the report of the financial auditor will be shared by the Buyer and Seller. Thus, the attorney-client privilege is inapplicable because there is no reasonable expectation of confidentiality. There is a second point to be made: note that attorneys Todd and Sheila create a corporation controlled by their clients in order to shield White and Phil's identity. The lawyers would have an attorney-client relationship with both CA and the new entity, Dental Associates, P.C.

Incidentally, a question sometimes arises as to whether the name of a client is protected by the attorney-client privilege.[12] For example, a grand jury or the IRS invokes a process such as a summons or subpoena addressed to a lawyer, demanding the identity of the lawyer's client. In most cases, the client has no intention to conceal her identity—disclosure of her identity to the lawyer is preliminary to and independent from any communications made to secure legal advice. Even if a client desired anonymity, sound public policy usually militates against granting it. Occasionally, however, protection of a client's identity is justified, as when a whistleblower seeks legal advice in connection with revealing wrongdoing or when

---

[12] Similar questions arise with respect to whether a client has consulted an attorney and what fee arrangements have been made. These incidental subjects, usually unconnected to the facts on which legal advice is based, are normally outside the attorney-client privilege for essentially the same reasons that the identity of the client is unprotected.

revealing the client's name would disclose the general content of a confidential communication.[13]

Illustration (2)(g) appears to be far afield from the concerns underlying the attorney-client privilege. The communications in question essentially concern business arrangements between White and Phil, on one hand, and the bank on the other. The bank is not a representative of either the client or the attorney. The copies to Todd and Sheila serve to keep them informed, but insofar as the Illustration reveals, are not the basis for giving legal advice or rendering legal services.

The Corporate Client and the Attorney-Client Privilege

Suppose that the client is a corporation (or other business entity) and that the communication in question is made by a corporate agent to the corporation's attorney. Because the corporation can speak only through individuals, the question is whether the corporation—the client and holder of the privilege—is the communicant. Depending on the context and a particular court's view of the proper scope of the attorney-client privilege, the statements of the agent could be either, (1) communications from the corporate client and within the corporation's privilege or, (2) statements of a person who is speaking as an individual witness and whose communications are not within the corporation's privilege.

Note that if the privilege extends far down into the corporate personnel structure—to middle management or even below—the reach of the privilege may unjustifiably hinder the efforts of an opponent to support its claim or defense. It also makes it difficult to discover discrepancies between what a corporate employee says (in a deposition, for example) to the opponent and what he told the corporate attorney.

The application of attorney-client protection in the corporate setting often strains some of the basic doctrines of privilege law, rooted as they are in the context of the individual client. The requirement of confidentiality, for example, meshes poorly with the layered structure of the large corporation, where statements may be passed through many hands before reaching counsel or counsel's advice may be widely shared within the corporation. In addition, the often indistinct boundary between legal and business advice is likely to be blurred in the corporate context, and this is especially true as

---

[13]   For example, in *United States v. Liebman*, 742 F.2d 807, 809–10 (3d Cir. 1984), the IRS was pursuing taxpayers who had used certain tax shelters thought by the IRS to be illegal. The Service issued a summons that directed a law firm to name all clients who had paid fees for legal services in connection with establishing or using such shelters. Held: the identity of the clients is privileged because their identity reveals the substance of their communications.

to communications between a corporate spokesman and in-house counsel.

On the other hand, the modern corporation could not realize the full potential of legal advice without some application of the privilege. It, like the individual client, needs to communicate freely and fully with its attorneys, preferably through the corporate agents with the most knowledge. The problem, therefore, is one of drawing a line that sensibly balances the corporation's need for an attorney-client privilege and the opponent's need for fair access to evidence generated within the corporate structure. The extremes are easily recognized and managed. Clearly protected is a confidential communication from the CEO to the attorney, made for the purpose of receiving legal advice for the corporation. Clearly unprotected is a routinely prepared statement by a lower-level employee, about a transaction made in the normal course of business, but subsequently sent to the corporate attorney. The difficulties lie in the shadowy area between these polarities. For communications to corporate counsel, two general tests have been devised.

Some states still adhere to the "control-group test" for determining which corporate agents are considered part of the client when communicating to the corporation's attorney. Under this test, the privilege attaches only if the corporate officer speaking with the attorney is vested with authority both to seek legal advice for the corporation and to participate significantly in the corporation's response to the attorney's recommendations. The analogy is to the individual client, who can obtain legal advice and then, if he wishes, tailor his conduct consistently with that advice.

The second approach to the corporate attorney-client privilege is often referred to as the "subject-matter test." It was adopted for the federal courts in *Upjohn Co. v. United States*,[14] and is the prevailing approach in most states. The facts before the *Upjohn* Court were these: the Upjohn Corporation, through its general counsel, undertook an investigation to discover whether the company made illegal payments to certain foreign governments. Subsequently, the IRS issued a summons demanding production of files pertaining to the investigation, including questionnaires prepared by counsel and answered by various corporate managers. The IRS also demanded records of interviews between counsel and some Upjohn managers. The Court noted that in the letter accompanying the questionnaires, Upjohn's Chairman of the Board stated that the investigation was under the direction of counsel, that responses were highly

---

[14]   449 U.S. 383 (1981).

confidential, and that the completed questionnaires should be returned to counsel.

The Court then turned to the question of what approach should guide federal judges in determining the scope of the corporate attorney-client privilege. It rejected as too restrictive the control-group test, because a corporate lawyer often finds it necessary to get information from lower-level personnel in order to effectively represent the company—and under the control group test the lawyer would be discouraged from seeking such information as it would not be privileged. The *Upjohn* Court extended privilege protection when the facts show that: (1) the communication in question was pursuant to a corporate purpose to obtain legal advice, (2) the communication "concerned matters within the scope of the employee's corporate duties," (3) the employee knew that he was making a confidential statement and was doing so at the direction of the employer (or employer's counsel), and (4) the statements were kept confidential or disclosed on a limited basis consistent with maintaining the privilege.[15]

The last requirement—limited disclosure—can apply in two contexts: disclosure *within* or *outside* the corporate firm. Because corporations depend heavily upon information, there is a practical need that corporate records be accessible to those individuals or groups who need access. Yet, there is a risk that information collected under the umbrella of the attorney-client privilege may be so widely shared that the privilege is lost. Generally, privileged communications may be disclosed within the corporation only to persons who need access—to those who *"need to know"* the confidential information in order to do their jobs—and care must be taken to ensure that these persons understand the need to maintain confidentiality. If privileged documents are kept in a general filing system, access must be restricted. Otherwise the corporate privilege will be lost.

Voluntary disclosures outside the company pose an even greater risk of losing the privilege. Here, it is important to ensure the disclosure is made only to those who are "necessary to the legal representation"—a concept discussed above.[16] Common sense dictates the importance of signaling the confidential nature of the disclosure through the use of labels, cover letters, or other precautionary measures.

Because litigation often deals with events that occurred several or more years before suit was filed, some of the employees or officers

---

[15]   Id. at 394–95.

[16]   Proposed Fed. R. Evid. 503(a)(3), (4).

who gave privileged communications on the corporation's behalf may
have died or left the company. Their departure from the corporate
staff does not affect the availability of the privilege for
communications made at the time of their employment. A closer
question attends *post-employment* statements by a former employee
to corporate counsel. In his concurring opinion in *Upjohn*, Chief
Justice Burger suggested that the privilege did embrace these
statements because a former employee, like a current employee, may
have information that is necessary for the lawyer to give sound legal
advice[17]—and lower courts have so held.[18]

Several other issues surrounding the corporate attorney-client
privilege warrant brief mention. As we have seen, the holder of the
privilege is the corporation. The privilege can be waived only by
management; sometimes the board of directors will reserve for itself
the right to claim or waive the privilege. The power to waive resides
with the current board, regardless of when the privileged
communications were made. Thus if a corporation changes
management (or is acquired, taken over by a receiver, etc.) the power
to waive the privilege as to prior communications is transferred to
the new management.

Note the anomaly that arises when a corporate agent speaks to
the corporate lawyer about a matter that would incriminate him
personally. Those communications are privileged, but it is the
corporation that holds the privilege. If the corporation decides to
waive its privilege as to those communications—most commonly to
cooperate with the government in order to avoid fines or other
penalties—the agent is unprotected, and his own statements can be
admitted against him at his trial. This is because there is no personal
attorney-client relationship with the corporate lawyer—nor can there
be, because a lawyer representing both the corporation and the agent
in circumstances of possible corporate/agent wrongdoing would be
operating under a conflict of interest, for the very reason that the
corporation may find it beneficial to waive its privilege and cooperate
with the government, leaving its agent unprotected.[19]

---

[17]   *Upjohn*, 449 U.S. at 403.

[18]   ˙ *See, e.g., In re Allen*, 106 F.3d 582, 605–06 (4th Cir. 1997).

[19]   When lawyers conduct an internal investigation for a corporation, it is
imperative that they make clear to the employees that they represent only the
company and not the employees. If the individual employees reasonably believe that
the lawyers represent them, the lawyers might inadvertently create a "joint client"
relationship in which the corporation cannot waive the privilege unless their co-client
employees also agree to waive. Moreover, ethics rules require disclosure to the
corporate agent that the lawyer is representing the entity, and not the agent. See ABA
Model Rules of Professional Conduct 1.13.

Shareholder Suits

Shareholder suits ("derivative suits") are a common feature of corporate America. In these suits, a group of disaffected shareholders sues corporate management on behalf of the corporation, typically on grounds of self-dealing or some other breach of fiduciary duty. Who should control the privilege for corporate communications to counsel in this setting? On the one hand, it seems odd that shareholders could not have access to these communications, because management is supposed to be operating on the shareholders' behalf. On the other hand, well-intentioned managers may communicate with counsel less freely if they believe the corporate privilege can be easily stripped by minority stockholders in a derivative action. Clearly, if the trial judge finds that the communications in question furthered a crime or fraud, the privilege should give way. Beyond this, the best reasoned cases discourage frivolous suits, but allow shareholders to defeat the privilege for *good cause*. The trial judge considers such factors as the plaintiffs' need, the seriousness of the alleged misconduct, the plausibility of claims that wrongdoing occurred, the number of shareholders joining as plaintiffs, and the availability from other sources of the communications sought.[20] Note that this flexible approach creates an exception to the general rule that once the attorney-client privilege attaches, it is absolute and cannot be overcome by judicial "balancing" of factors peculiar to the case before the court. Of course, communications by management to corporate counsel related to the shareholder suit itself will remain protected by the privilege.

Underlying Factual Information

The attorney-client privilege protects *communications*, not factual information that was the subject of a communication between the lawyer and the client—as shown in the following Illustration.

ILLUSTRATION

Clyde, whose expensive luxury car is only two years old, has just been told by his mechanic that the car will soon need costly repairs. Doubtful that the mechanic is correct, Clyde (who is mechanically inclined) verifies for himself the imminent repairs. Because the manufacturer's warranty on the car has expired, Clyde decides to sell it without disclosing its defects.

Subsequently, the buyer sues Clyde and Clyde retains a defense lawyer. He tells his attorney about the mechanic's

---

[20]   *See Garner v. Wolfinbarger*, 430 F.2d 1093, 1100–04 (5th Cir. 1970), a leading case.

report and about his own confirmation of the impending mechanical failures. During discovery, the plaintiff's lawyer takes Clyde's deposition. He asks Clyde the following questions.

(1) Q: "Did you know this car had these [named] serious mechanical defects?"

(2) Q: "Did your mechanic, at Bosch Bros. Luxury Cars, inform you on June 3 that the car had these [named] defects?"

(3) Q: "Isn't it true that on or about June 5 you personally verified that the car you sold to the plaintiff had precisely the defects and problems identified by the Bosch Bros. mechanic?"

Clyde's attorney objects to these questions on the ground that they call for responses that are protected by the attorney-client privilege. How should the judge rule?

None of these questions is improper, and Clyde must provide answers to each. The attorney-client privilege does not apply to facts or events that are the subject of, or described in, a confidential communication. If it did, there would be little or no evidence for the jury to consider. A client could simply relate all the relevant facts to his attorney and thereby insulate the client's knowledge of the underlying events from discovery. Of course, the attorney-client privilege does protect Clyde's *communications* to his lawyer.

Communications by Multiple Clients and Attorneys Pursuing a Common Interest

It sometimes happens that several clients with a common problem retain a single lawyer or firm to represent them. For example, one lawyer may represent both *A* and *B* in a matter of joint or common interest, such as their purchase of real estate or their common dispute with an insurance company. The rule in such situations provides that the statements of both clients and those of the lawyer are privileged if made for purposes of seeking legal advice on the common objective. It seems plain enough that, as against outsiders, *each client* is entitled to claim the privilege as to statements *she has made*, as well as to the attorney's responsive statements. But can client *A* invoke the privilege (as against outsiders) so as to prevent disclosure of *B's* statements to the attorney as well as the attorney's responsive statements to *B*? The issue usually does not arise because *A* and *B* have a common objective and thus each is likely to claim the privilege or agree to waive it. However, should they disagree, most courts hold that all clients remain bound by the common interest arrangement—that is, *A* will not be permitted to disclose any communications made by either party in pursuit of the common interest. (Note that the parties can contract in their common interest arrangement either to bind all parties or to allow parties to waive the protection as to their own communications—but the default rule is that all parties are bound and the privilege is retained.)

In subsequent litigation in which *A* and *B*, having fallen out, become adversaries, the rule is that privilege is lost as to all of their statements. (Here, no "outsider" is involved.) First, when they were joint clients, neither client intended that his communications would be shielded from the other. Second, even if, say, *A* "secretly" communicated with the attorney, the communication would not be privileged as to *B* because the attorney would have an ethical duty to share it with her other joint client and *A* cannot in any event reasonably anticipate that the communication would remain confidential as to *B* given the joint client representation.(Again, though, the parties can contract with each other to protect against disclosure in a subsequent litigation between them).

The rule protecting joint-client discussions has also been extended to protect confidential communications where two or more clients, *each with his own attorney,* agree to pool or share information in order to conserve resources and mount a more effective case— either a defensive or an offensive one. These allied clients have both a mutual and an individual interest: they are sharing information (and perhaps resources) with respect to their common interests, yet each participating client is represented by his own lawyer or firm. These sharing arrangements would seldom materialize if outsiders could successfully argue that confidential disclosures within the group lost the protection of the attorney-client privilege because dissemination went beyond the individual attorney-client units that comprise the pool. Thus, it is not surprising that courts protect the confidential communications of separately represented parties who pursue a common legal objective. Protection under the common-interest doctrine applies, however, only if the parties claiming the attorney-client privilege can show that they have agreed (orally or, preferably, in writing) to assume an allied position. It is thus advisable for the parties to a pooling arrangement who wish to protect the attorney-client privilege to enter into a formal, preferably written, agreement. Again, however, if the parties pursuing a common interest later end up suing each other, the communications previously made can be freely used by the parties in that subsequent litigation—this is because there was no expectation of confidentiality vis-a-vis the member of the common interest "unit" at the time the statements were made. (But the parties can, by contract, provide for protection against use of the statements in a subsequent litigation between or among them.)

Duration of the Attorney-Client Privilege

Traditionally, courts have held that the attorney-client privilege survives the death of the client. It can be claimed by the executor or some other proper successor in interest. In 1998, the Supreme Court endorsed this principle for the federal courts.[21] The Court was persuaded that if the privilege did not survive the client, at least some clients would be inhibited in their communications with counsel. For example, "[c]lients may be concerned about reputation, civil liability, or possible harm to friends or family."[22]

There is, however, one situation in which courts agree that the privilege will be terminated. In disputes between persons claiming property or an entitlement through the decedent—"disputes among insiders," so to speak—claims of privilege by the executor or other successor (such as next of kin) are rejected. Suppose, for example, one group of disputants claims under the decedent's will, the other group, by intestacy. Various combinations of claimants can be imagined, but the point is that relevant communications otherwise within the privilege are subject to disclosure. The privilege is inapplicable "regardless of whether the claims are by testate or intestate succession or by inter vivos transaction."[23] The assumption made in the law is that the deceased would probably approve of the privilege's termination, because the resulting evidence will shed additional light on the property distribution he favored.

The Crime-Fraud Exception to the Attorney-Client Privilege

Judicial systems in free societies adhere to the principle that every person, guilty or not, is entitled to a fair hearing and adequate representation by counsel. As a consequence, communications about *past* crimes are shielded to allow lawyers and clients to communicate freely and plan legitimate defenses. Yet the system is subverted, and the privilege properly lost, when lawyer-client communications are made with the intent to *advance* criminal or fraudulent activity. The *client's* objective is critical and the privilege does not attach if he "sought or obtained [the attorney's services] to enable or aid anyone to commit or plan to commit what the client knew or should have known to be a crime or fraud."[24]

---

[21]   *Swidler & Berlin v. United States*, 524 U.S. 399, 410–11 (1998).

[22]   Id. at 407.

[23]   Proposed Fed. R. Evid. 503(c)(2).

[24]   Proposed Fed. R. Evid. 503(d)(1).

It is not always easy to determine if the crime-fraud exception applies. For example, the client's communications might disclose past misdeeds, but also allude to concealment or contemplate some future illegality. The party who seeks to negate the privilege must first provide the judge with evidence of a prima facie case—that is, evidence from which a reasonable person could find that the client communicated with the lawyer for the purpose of furthering a plan of crime or fraud. If that standard is met then the court may, pursuant to the Supreme Court's decision in *United States v. Zolin*,[25] conduct an *in camera* review to determine if the privilege is applicable; and in that review, the judge can consider the statements claimed to be privileged as part of the crime-fraud showing. The ultimate burden is on the party seeking disclosure to prove more likely than not that the client was communicating with the lawyer for purposes of perpetrating a crime or fraud. There is some authority expanding the crime-fraud exception to embrace other forms of future illegal behavior, such as willful torts.[26]

Waiver of the Attorney-Client Privilege

While a confidential communication between a client and a lawyer on a legal matter is protected by the privilege, that privilege can be waived in a number of circumstances. The basic question of waiver is whether the client has—by some statement or action subsequent to the making of the privileged communication— explicitly or implicitly acted in such a way that justifies a finding that the party no longer wishes to, or should, retain the privilege.

The most obvious form of waiver is a knowing and voluntary disclosure of the privileged information. That waiver-by-disclosure most often occurs when the client determines that the benefits of the disclosure outweigh the risks that the privileged information will be used against the client. A common example is a corporation that is being investigated by a government regulator or prosecutor for possible internal corporate misconduct (e.g., accounting violations). Assume that the corporation had previously hired a law firm to conduct an internal investigation, and the law firm prepared a report. That report is confidential. But the corporation may decide to voluntarily disclose it to the government investigator. By doing so the corporation has determined that the benefits of disclosure— cooperating with the government and thereby avoiding or ameliorating fines and penalties—outweigh the risk that the report, now waived, will be used against the corporation in some litigation.

---

[25]   491 U.S. 554, 568–75 (1989).

[26]   *See Commodity Futures Trading Comm. v. Weintraub*, 471 U.S. 343, 354 (1985) (collecting authorities).

Disclosure pursuant to such a cost-benefit analysis constitutes a voluntary waiver.

Other situations arise in which waiver is *implied* from the client's conduct. Implied waiver is likely to be found when the client acts in such a way that it would be unfair to the adversary to uphold the privilege. When a client sues her lawyer for malpractice, for example, the lawyer can use relevant confidential statements made during the representation to defend herself—it would be unfair for the client to attack the lawyer's performance and yet leave the lawyer unable to rebut the charges by showing that, for example, he was instructed by the client to do the act for which he is now criticized. Similarly, if a client refuses to pay his attorney, the attorney can support her claim for fees with confidential information. In other words, the privilege is suspended as to any "communication relevant to an issue of breach of duty by the lawyer to . . . [her] client or by the client to his lawyer."[27] This is because it would be unfair for the client to contest the value of the lawyer's services, and yet not allow the lawyer to defend by offering communications by the client that affected those services.

In a related context also indicating unfairness, a client waives his privilege if he asserts an affirmative defense of "reliance on advice of counsel."[28] It would be unfair for the client to raise the attorney-client discussions as a defense, but then to prevent the adversary from inquiring into just what was said between the client and the attorney on the matter.

Selective Waiver

Recall that corporations often find it useful to cooperate with government investigations by turning over privileged information. While that is a waiver, should it extend to allowing private parties to use the information? Here is an example: a corporation is being investigated by the SEC for securities fraud. It turns over a confidential report on the fraud to the SEC. Then private parties sue the corporation, and argue that they are entitled to the report, because the corporation waived the privilege by disclosing it to the SEC. The question in such a case is whether the waiver is *selective* or general. The policy argument for finding the waiver to be selective is that it would encourage corporations to cooperate with the government, because it would limit the costs of that cooperation; and the protection of selective waiver could also limit the costs of government investigations into potential corporate misconduct,

---

27   Proposed Fed. R. Evid. 503(d)(3).

28   *See, e.g., Chevron Corp. v. Pennzoil Co.*, 974 F.2d 1156, 1162–63 (9th Cir. 1992).

because the government would be able to rely on the report instead of having to do its own investigation from square one.

But almost all courts have rejected the notion of selective waiver—meaning that a voluntary disclosure to anyone operates as a waiver to everyone.[29] The courts reason that corporations are *already*—in the absence of selective waiver—cooperating with the government by turning over confidential reports. This is because the benefits of cooperation with the government, in avoiding criminal fines and penalties, generally outweigh the costs—even including the cost that the privileged material can be used by private parties. Thus, selective waiver protection is not necessary to encourage cooperation (except, perhaps, for corporations at the margin, but the consequence of establishing selective waiver would be that *all* corporations would be protected, even those that would cooperate anyway.) Moreover, the courts frown upon strategic activity in the use of the privilege; it seems to be gaming the privilege for a client to say, "I will waive to you, but not to you—it depends on how advantageous the waiver will be to me."

Mistaken Disclosures of Privileged Information

In litigation, it is often the case that a party will mistakenly disclose privileged information during discovery. This is especially true in cases involving electronic discovery, where the explosion of information raises substantial challenges for an accurate "privilege review" of documents subject to discovery and increases the likelihood of mistaken disclosures. In recent years, the costs of electronic discovery have skyrocketed, and most of those costs have been attributed to the resources necessary to make sure that no e-mail, spreadsheet, metadata, etc. contains privileged information. The consequences of mistaken disclosure of privileged information, at least in some common law courts, was to find a waiver no matter how careful the privilege review. And some courts even found a *subject matter* waiver in these circumstances—meaning that all privileged documents related to the subject matter of the mistakenly disclosed documents would also have to be disclosed to the adversary.

Federal Rule 502, enacted by Congress in 2008, seeks to reduce the costs of privilege review by providing some measure of protection against a finding of waiver after a mistaken disclosure. Three provisions of the Rule are especially important:

1) Rule 502(a) precludes the court from finding a subject matter waiver unless the waiver of the privileged information was *intentional* and results in unfairness to the

[29]   *See* SALTZBURG, MARTIN & CAPRA, FEDERAL RULES OF EVIDENCE MANUAL § 501.02[5][k][iii] (12th ed. 2019).

adversary. (See the advice of counsel example above). Thus, a mistaken disclosure in discovery will never result in a subject matter waiver. The worst consequence would be a loss of privilege as to the documents actually disclosed.

2)	Rule 502(b) provides that a mistaken disclosure in a federal proceeding will not be a waiver at all if the party took "reasonable steps" to prevent the disclosure and acted reasonably promptly to retrieve the information once the party learns about the mistaken disclosure. Thus, while a party cannot be careless, it need not undertake herculean efforts to protect against mistaken disclosures in discovery.

3)	Rule 502(d) provides that if a federal court enters an order that disclosure of privileged information in a proceeding is not a waiver, then that order is binding on all subsequent courts, state and federal. So obtaining a court order can allow parties on each side to limit the costs of preproduction privilege review, because there will not be a waiver if privileged material is disclosed in the litigation. Most importantly, the protection against waiver can apply even to *intentional* production of privileged material to the adversary—this is a recognition that a party may not be concerned about disclosure of the information to the adversary in a particular litigation, but would remain concerned that the disclosure would be treated as a waiver in other lawsuits. Of course the parties and the court must carefully determine the wording of the Rule 502(d) order, so that it covers such matters as intentional disclosures and waiver of work product as well as privilege.[30]

## § 10.4	Spousal Privilege for Confidential Communications

There are two privileges that protect the marital relationship. One is the privilege protecting confidential communications between married partners—marriage is assessed as of the time that the confidential communication was made and is determined, even in federal courts, by reference to applicable state law. The most frequently	invoked	justification	for	the	"confidential communications" privilege is that it encourages marital partners to share their innermost thoughts and secrets, thus adding to the

---

[30]	Rule 502 specifically covers disclosures of work product as well as attorney-client privileged material. Many times the protected information will be both work product and privileged, so in terms of protection of mistaken disclosure, it would make no sense to protect only privilege. Moreover, the costs of reviewing data would not be reduced if the rule covered only privileged material—the parties would still have to engage in expensive review for fear of disclosing work product.

intimacy and mutual support that strengthens marriage. This rationale is not convincing. It is probably safe to assume that most married couples are unaware of the privilege and so don't rely on it in deciding whether to speak to each other. Unlike most privileges, this one does not involve a professional such as a doctor, lawyer, or clergyman who is schooled in a particular privilege and can give advice about its existence. Furthermore, even on the improbable assumption that the existence of the privilege is widely known among marriage partners, it is doubtful that it has a significant impact on the flow of information between them. Most people would not take the privilege into account when deciding what to say or not to say to their spouse.

Justification for the marital-confidence privilege may, however, rest upon a different footing. There is something to be said for the notion that certain aspects of one's private life should be free from public disclosure. This is especially desirable in light of today's diminished privacy in general and the wide availability of sophisticated electronics that can collect, store, and transmit private information. The argument supporting the privilege is that the intrusion into marital communications is an indelicate and distasteful undertaking that should be carefully circumscribed. The counterargument is that the privilege does not protect the marriage—rather, it protects a communicating spouse (usually a criminal defendant, and usually a man) at the expense of a spouse who wishes to testify. So the privilege can be looked at as preserving an outdated patriarchy.

The privilege for marital confidential communications extends to any *confidential* statement made *between spouses* during the existence of a legal marriage. The general rule is that courts will not inquire into the "quality" of the marriage, although courts hold that communications made after a formal or permanent separation or after one spouse has filed for divorce are not privileged.[31] In other words, while courts are not going to determine the quality of a marital relationship, they are willing to look for objective evidence that the marriage is not viable. But if the confidential communications are made during a viable marriage, they retain their privileged status no matter what happens to the relationship thereafter—meaning that even if the witness is divorced from the party at the time of a trial, confidential statements made between them during their marriage will not be admissible. The focus is on promoting the marital relationship at the time the statement is made.

---

[31] *See United States v. Porter*, 986 F.2d 1014, 1019 (6th Cir. 1993); *United States v. Treff*, 924 F.2d 975, 982 n.11 (10th Cir. 1991).

The scope of the privilege is restricted: it protects only "confidential communications"—that is, communications reasonably anticipated to remain secret between the spouses. Thus, if a third person (including the couple's child) capable of understanding the communication is present, the privilege does not attach, even if the spouses did not want their communication revealed. "Communications" are written or verbal statements, as well as gestures (such as a nod of the head or a hand signal) that are intended to substitute for words.[32] Some state courts go further and broaden the privilege to include non-communicative actions—such as unpacking firearms—of one spouse in the presence of the other, at least where it reasonably can be inferred that the actor-spouse did not want his activity revealed. But applying the privilege to "disclosive acts" is ill-conceived because it extends the privilege beyond its policy of fostering communication between the spouses; if this kind of observation deserves protection at all, that protection should be afforded by the other spousal privilege, discussed in the next section.

The courts have carved out exceptions to the confidential communications privilege. First, the privilege does not attach to a marital communication made for the purposes of furthering an ongoing or future crime—a rule analogous to the crime-fraud exception to the attorney-client privilege. (Thus, if the husband asks the wife in confidence to destroy evidence of a crime, this communication will not be protected by the privilege). Second, the privilege does not protect communications that pertain to a past or planned *crime against immediate family members*, such as a spouse or child.

§ 10.5   The Spousal Testimonial Privilege

The second privilege protecting the marital relationship is broader when applicable than the privilege protecting confidential communications. This privilege, called the "adverse testimonial privilege," is recognized in the federal system and in most states. Unlike the marital communications privilege, which may be invoked in civil and criminal cases, the adverse testimonial privilege is usually confined exclusively to criminal proceedings such as trials and grand jury investigations. The privilege is based on society's interest in preserving marital harmony, which would be impaired when one spouse testifies adversely to the other. Where it applies, it protects a witness-spouse from having to provide *any* adverse testimony against a spouse—it's not limited to confidential communications.

---

[32]   *See, e.g., United States v. Estes*, 793 F.2d 465, 467–68 (2d Cir. 1986).

The focus of the testimonial privilege is on 1) one spouse (the "witness-spouse") 2) having *adverse information* against the other 3) in a *criminal proceeding* 4) when the couple *are married at the time* the prosecutor *seeks to call* the witness-spouse. Generally speaking, in these circumstances the witness-spouse can claim the privilege, thus preventing her from having to take the stand.[33] Under the majority view, the availability of the privilege is not dependent on the source or timing[34] of the witness-spouse's knowledge (i.e., whether the adverse information concerns activity before or after the marriage began). Rather, the privilege is concerned with the *negative effect* on the marriage of her (or his) adverse testimony during the marriage—thus it protects the marriage at the time the testimony is demanded.

The privilege has no application if a spouse is called to the stand to give favorable testimony. Furthermore, when the spouse testifies on direct in the party's favor, the spouse is subject to cross-examination like any other witness—any question within the scope of the direct that calls for adverse testimony will be permitted. Notice particularly that whereas the privilege for marital confidential communications is selectively claimed during testimony, the testimonial privilege, when applicable, keeps the witness-spouse off the witness stand.

In the federal system, the leading case setting the contours of the spousal privilege against adverse testimony is *Trammel v. United States*,[35] decided by the Supreme Court in 1980. In *Trammel*, the Court overturned a sizeable body of federal precedent[36] and adopted the rule that the *witness-spouse is the sole holder of the privilege*.[37] The Supreme Court reasoned that in cases in which one spouse is willing to testify against the other, the marriage is probably beyond repair—there is no marital harmony to preserve. It followed from this assumption that the witness-spouse should be the sole holder. The witness-spouse's decision to testify or not was thought to be a good indication of the state of marriage. So, while the defendant can keep his spouse from testifying to a confidential communication he made during the marriage, he cannot prevent his spouse from testifying to

---

[33]   The privilege should be claimed before the witness-spouse is sworn in; if not, the court may rule that the privilege has been waived. It is clearly waived if the spouse begins her testimony.

[34]   A minority view refuses the privilege as to matters pre-dating the marriage. *See United States v. Clark*, 712 F.2d 299, 302 (7th Cir. 1983).

[35]   445 U.S. 40 (1980).

[36]   In earlier cases, the Supreme Court had adopted the minority rule that *both spouses* were holders and either could claim the privilege. *See, e.g., Hawkins v. United States*, 358 U.S. 74, 77–79 (1958).

[37]   Some state courts adhere to different views and hold that the accused is the holder or, alternatively, that both spouses are holders.

acts that are not communicative. So for example, the spouse could not testify that the defendant told her in confidence that he robbed a bank. But she could testify that the defendant came home with a ski mask and a gun.

Doubts have been raised about whether the *Trammel* rule affords adequate protection of the marriage when both spouses are implicated in a crime. The prosecutor can then offer lenient treatment to one spouse, but only on the condition that the spouse give adverse testimony against the defendant-spouse. This hard choice ("testify or go to prison") undermines *Trammel*'s point that if one spouse is "willing" to testify the marriage is, for practical purposes, already over. But perhaps this is acceptable, because the bottom line is that the adverse testimonial privilege is exceedingly costly—a spouse with intimate knowledge of a crime can simply refuse to testify. The privilege is not limited to confidential communications, like other privileges. It is a serious cost to the search for truth, and so there is merit in limiting the privilege to where it is certain that it is necessary for preserving marital harmony. Marital harmony is questionable where the witness spouse is willing to take a deal, knowing that the probable result will be that the defendant will be sent to prison.

Some federal courts have established an exception to the testimonial privilege if the trial judge finds (out of the jury's presence and by a preponderance of the evidence) that the witness-spouse was a "joint participant" in the defendant-spouses crime.[38] The asserted justification for the exception is that joint participants in crime are acting more like a criminal conspiracy than a married couple. But most courts have rejected this exception to the privilege, on the ground that joint participants may well have marital harmony.

There is an occasional problem when, just before trial or just prior to the expected testimony, the accused marries the potential witness. The holder then claims the testimonial privilege. If the trial judge is convinced that the marriage is a ruse or sham, she can declare the privilege inapplicable. However, the artificial nature of the marriage is not always easy to discern, as in one case where the newlyweds had lived together for two years before judicial proceedings began and they were married.[39] A scattering of federal case law endorses a minority position that refuses recognition of the adverse-testimony privilege if the acts or conduct under interrogation

---

[38]   This was the holding by the lower court in *Trammel. Contra, In re Koecher,* 755 F.2d 1022, 1024–28 (2d Cir. 1985).

[39]   *See In re Grand Jury Proceedings* No. 84–5, 777 F.2d 508, 509 (9th Cir. 1985) (adverse testimony privilege upheld).

predated the marriage.[40] While this approach avoids the "sham-marriage" problem, it erodes the purpose of the testimonial incapacity privilege because it pits against each other spouses who are lawfully married (perhaps for many years) at the time of trial. Moreover, the incentive for a sham marriage has been dampened by the *Trammel* decision, which places the privilege in the hands of the witness-spouse—a prospective criminal defendant has no guarantee that a sham spouse can be kept off the stand.

The privilege is uniformly denied if the accused spouse is charged with a crime against the witness-spouse or their children. Thus, in domestic violence cases the adverse testimony privilege is usually unavailable, and the prosecutor can call even a reluctant spouse to testify—and that spouse can be required to testify on pain of contempt. Query whether that result makes sense when the case involves spousal abuse.

The Illustration below tests several of the principles of both spousal privileges—the confidential communications privilege (protecting confidential communications, but only those made during the marriage, and held by the communicating spouse) and the adverse testimonial privilege (protecting against disclosure of all adverse information, but only if the parties are married when the testimony is demanded, and held by the witness-spouse).

ILLUSTRATION

Henry and Anne's relationship was stormy at times, although they have lived together, relatively happily, for almost three years. Two subjects have occupied center stage in most of their arguments: Anne's attraction to Thomas (which infuriated the jealous Henry) and Henry's dismal failure to help provide adequate income to sustain the couple. Eventually, in the face of Anne's threat to leave him, Henry promised to provide for the two of them, and in the next several months he earned a surprising amount of money as a "salesman." Unbeknownst to Anne, Henry was making and selling methamphetamine ("meth"), a profitable activity until Henry was arrested and indicted. Two weeks prior to his arrest, Henry confided in Anne and revealed the details of how he and a friend were making and selling "meth."

After Henry's arrest, he pleaded with Anne to marry him. She agreed and the two were married in a civil

---

[40]   The leading minority case is *United States v. Clark*, 712 F.2d 299 (7th Cir. 1983). The majority view is adopted in *United States v. Lofton*, 957 F.2d 476, 477 (7th Cir. 1992).

ceremony held near the cell in which Henry was incarcerated, awaiting trial. In the two months that intervened between Henry's marriage and his trial, Anne fell in love with Thomas, although their relationship was hidden from everyone, including Henry, who received frequent visits from Anne. On the eve of trial, however, Anne told the prosecutor she would testify against Henry. When Anne was called to the stand, Henry's attorney objected, citing both the spousal testimonial privilege and the spousal privilege protecting confidential communications. How should the judge rule?

The privilege that protects marital confidential communications applies only to communications made during a legal marriage, so it has no application to premarital communications. The availability of the privilege against adverse testimony in a criminal prosecution poses a closer question. In the federal system and most states, the witness-spouse is the sole holder and can claim or waive the privilege as she wishes. Thus, in these jurisdictions, Anne may testify against Henry over his objection. In the *Trammel* case, the Supreme Court found the willingness of one spouse to testify against the other was ample reason to make the witness-spouse the sole holder of the testimonial privilege. If Anne *did* refuse to testify, she could properly invoke the privilege. The joint participant exception (recognized by some courts) would not be applicable because Anne was not a participant in Henry's illegal activity.

§ 10.6 Psychotherapist-Patient Privilege

Effective psychotherapy depends upon a relationship of candor and trust between the patient and the therapist. Full disclosure by the patient is essential, and to encourage that disclosure the federal courts, as well as those of all the states, recognize a psychotherapist-patient privilege. This privilege was included in Proposed Federal Rule 504, which can serve as a "standard" for the development of federal common law. (As we have seen, federal common law usually controls the law of privilege in the federal courts.)[41] Proposed Rule 504(b), approved by the Supreme Court in 1972 but not enacted by Congress as part of the Federal Rules, describes the "general rule" governing the psychotherapist-patient privilege:

> A patient has a privilege to refuse to disclose and to prevent any other person from disclosing confidential communications, made for the purposes of diagnosis or

---

[41]   Fed. R. Evid. 501. Federal statutes or rules of court passed pursuant to statutory authority will supersede the common law, thus modifying the law of privilege.

treatment of his mental or emotional condition, including drug addition, among himself, his psychotherapist, or persons who are participating in the diagnosis or treatment under the direction of the psychotherapist, including members of the patient's family.

A number of persons, in addition to the patient, himself, can claim the privilege. These include his guardian or conservator, and, in the event of the patient's death, his personal representative. The psychotherapist who treated the patient may also claim the privilege, but only on behalf of the patient.[42]

In *Jaffee v. Redmond*[43] the Supreme Court established the psychotherapist-patient privilege under federal common law, and held that it applied beyond psychiatrists and psychologists to also include confidential communications to licensed clinical social workers.[44] Moreover, the Court held that the privilege was unqualified, in the sense that it was not subject to judicial nullification through a case-by-case balancing test. The Court reasoned that a qualified privilege was little better than none at all, because the patient couldn't confidently rely upon it.

The *Jaffee* Court stated that federal courts can establish a privilege where the costs of that privilege (the loss of reliable evidence) are outweighed by the social policy benefits. As to the psychotherapist-patient privilege, the Court asserted that its cost was minimal because, without it, patients would often refuse to make disclosures against their interests—thus, there would be no statement for possible evidential use at any rate. Moreover, even if some evidence were lost by recognition of the privilege, the benefits of the privilege were thought to outweigh that loss—the patient is usually helped, thus serving her private interest, and the public is also benefitted because "[t]he mental health of [the] citizenry, no less than its physical health, is a public good of transcendent importance."[45]

The federal psychotherapist privilege does not, under *Jaffee's* terms, extend to social workers generally, but only to duly licensed clinical social workers who are providing psychological therapy and counseling in roughly the same fashion as it would be offered by a psychologist or psychiatrist. And despite its unqualified nature, the

---

[42]   Proposed Fed. R. Evid. 504(c). The psychotherapists' authority to do so is presumed. Id.

[43]   518 U.S. 1, 15 (1996).

[44]   The specific issue was whether the plaintiff could discover communications between a police officer and a clinical social worker. The officer had sought therapy after she fatally shot the plaintiff's decedent.

[45]   *Jaffee*, 518 U.S. at 11.

psychotherapist privilege has exceptions. The Supreme Court recognized this in its *Jaffee* opinion, commenting it had no "doubt that there are situations in which the privilege must give way, for example, if a serious threat of harm to the patient or others can be averted only by means of disclosure by the therapist."[46] Proposed Rule 504(d) listed three exceptions: hospitalization or commitment proceedings, a court-ordered mental examination, and litigation in which the patient asserts his mental condition as "an element of his claim or defense. . . ." Courts have also found a future crime-or-fraud exception to the psychotherapist-patient privilege.[47]

§ 10.7 Physician-Patient Privilege

A privilege for confidential communications between a patient and a medical doctor is recognized in most states, but not by the federal courts. Privileges in the federal courts, if not granted by statute, are developed under common law. The physician-patient privilege has been a creature of statute in the states, but Congress has never enacted a physician-patient privilege. Moreover, in *Jaffee, supra,* the Court found that the psychotherapist-patient relationship was *solely based* on confidential communications, so recognition of a privilege was necessary—and the Court negatively compared the physician-patient relationship, which was less dependent on communications. All this has led the federal courts to uniformly reject a physician-patient privilege as a matter of federal common law. But of course, as we have seen, federal courts apply state privilege law to claims or defenses based on state law.[48]

Variations among the states make generalizations about the physician-patient privilege rather hazardous. The privilege is usually justified on the now familiar ground that it is needed to ensure that a patient will speak candidly to his physician. Such candor, it is said, is essential to the physician's diagnosis and the patient's effective treatment. Whether a patient seeking treatment from his doctor would withhold information without the assurance of a judicial privilege is highly doubtful. A privacy rationale for the privilege provides a better fit: the intimate nature of communications about

---

[46]   Id. at 18 n.19. In the wake of *Jaffee*, some courts have recognized a "dangerous patient" exception. The temporal focus for applying this exception is the time when a demand by a court or other official body is made. For example, if a demand is made in connection with a proceeding to involuntarily commit the patient on ground of dangerousness, the exception would apply. *See United States v. Glass*, 133 F.3d 1356, 1359 (10th Cir. 1998).

[47]   *See In re Grand Jury Proceedings (Violette)*, 183 F.3d 71, 74–78 (1st Cir. 1999).

[48]   *See* Fed. R. Evid. 501. Federal courts have authority to prevent "fishing expeditions" into private medical records by granting motions for protective orders pursuant to Fed. R. Civ. P. 26(c).

one's bodily condition may arguably justify the law's assurance of confidentiality.

The essence of the physician-patient privilege is this: it applies when the patient is seeking *treatment* and it clearly covers communications between the patient and the doctor that are pertinent to diagnosis and treatment. Many jurisdictions expand the privilege to include information secured by the doctor through examination and tests. Note, however, that a patient's consultation with a physician for the purpose of securing a medical evaluation unrelated to treatment is usually outside the privilege. Thus, an examination to secure life insurance, a court-ordered examination, and an examination solely for the purpose of litigation are typically outside the boundaries of the privilege. And because the privilege rests upon either a policy of encouraging full disclosure or the protection of privacy, courts require that the information subject to the privilege be confidential—or at least so intended by the patient. However, courts are reasonable in their recognition that certain persons may share the presumably privileged information without destroying its confidential status. For example, nurses and other medical personnel associated with the physician may share the confidential information. But the casual sharing of information with third parties before, during, or after the consultation will probably prevent the privilege from attaching or, if it has attached, result in its waiver.

Most jurisdictions provide that the physician-patient privilege survives the death of the patient. The privilege can then be claimed by a fiduciary (or, perhaps by the next of kin) acting on behalf of the patient who, during her life, was the *sole holder of the privilege*. This postmortem reflects the judgment a patient—who took all reasonable measures to assure that the most private medical facts she disclosed to or were discovered by the doctor while she was alive—might well want those private facts to remain secret forever. However, the harmful consequences of generally permitting the survival of the privilege are leavened by statutory provisions (or, sometimes, judicial constructions) that certain circumstances permit postmortem disclosure. For example, in actions by the estate or next of kin to recover money or property from third persons, as in the case of a wrongful death action, the privilege is lifted as to relevant doctor-patient communications. Furthermore, in suits where both litigants are claiming an entitlement or inheritance through the decedent (as for example, in a will contest) the privilege is lifted.

Even more telling are the numerous exceptions that apply during the lifetime of the patient-holder. Often, the privilege is found inapplicable in criminal proceedings and even in certain civil proceedings such as workman's compensation, sanity, or child abuse hearings. Inroads into the privilege are also made by statutory provisions that compel physicians and hospitals to report to the proper authorities certain physical conditions such as gunshot wounds, venereal diseases, sexual abuse, child abuse, or the ingestion of controlled substances.

Sometimes, of course, the fragility of the doctor-patient privilege can be overcome by demonstrating that the physician-patient exchange is an integral part of the attorney-client privilege. That is, if the physician is a necessary representative of the client or the lawyer, and communications between the doctor and the patient are part of a larger network of communications "made for the purpose of facilitating the rendition of professional legal services to the client. . . ."[49], the attorney-client privilege would protect the communication. In order to establish protection on this ground, it is essential to show that the medical consultation between patient and physician was arranged by the lawyer for the purpose of obtaining legal advice or services.

§ 10.8 The Privilege Against Compelled Self-Incrimination: A Primer

Most readers are probably aware that the privilege against compelled self-incrimination is a constitutional privilege contained in the Fifth Amendment of the United States Constitution. The privilege is founded on the principle that our system of government rests upon an accusatorial, not an inquisitorial, foundation. Furthermore, it is considered unseemly for the government to place a person in the "cruel trilemma" by forcing him to incriminate himself (and go to jail), or lie (and go to jail), or remain silent and be subjected to contempt proceedings (and go to jail).[50]

The privilege is enforceable against both the federal and state governments.[51] The applicable constitutional language reads, "No person . . . shall be compelled in any criminal case to be a witness against himself."[52] This provision (and the privilege it secures) is

---

[49] Proposed Fed. R. Evid. 503(b). A leading state case, pre-dating the Federal Rules of Evidence, is *San Francisco v. Superior Court of San Francisco*, 37 Cal.2d 227, 231 P.2d 26, 29–31 (1951).

[50] *See Murphy v. Waterfront Comm'n of New York Harbor*, 378 U.S. 52, 55–57 (1964).

[51] Although the Fifth Amendment originally applied only to the federal government, it (and most other liberties contained in the first eight amendments) was made applicable to the states through the "due process" clause of the Fourteenth Amendment which expressly applies to the states. The Supreme Court decision that "incorporated" the privilege against self-incrimination into the due process clause of the Fourteenth Amendment is *Malloy v. Hogan*, 378 U.S. 1, 6 (1964).

[52] U.S. Const. amend. V.

usually given extensive coverage in criminal procedure courses. However, the basic features of the privilege are often addressed in evidence classes, which accounts for this brief introduction.

The succinct constitutional language conferring the privilege suggests its outlines. It is concerned with "compulsion" in the context of a "criminal case" that induces a "person" to become "a witness against himself." Although "person" in some constitutional provisions means both individuals and business entities such as corporations, here it means just what the noun suggests—*individuals* (and not corporations or partnerships). And even though the context for the application of the privilege is criminal, the privilege may be invoked outside the context of a criminal trial. Any proceeding or inquiry, civil or criminal, is within its embrace if official compulsion is used in an attempt to coerce an individual to respond to inquiries that could potentially be a link in a chain of evidence that *could lead* to criminal prosecution or criminal liability.

If an individual's statement cannot be used to impose criminal liability on him, then the privilege is not available. Thus, if one has been acquitted[53] of the crime that is the subject of the official inquiry, and testimony would not raise a risk of incrimination for some other crime, the privilege does not attach. Similarly, if the statute of limitations for a particular offense has expired or the person claiming the privilege has been granted immunity from prosecution,[54] the privilege does not apply.

The privilege offers protection only from compelled *communicative, testimonial* statements. It is not available where official compulsion is used to secure non-testimonial evidence, such as blood samples, other bodily fluids, or fingerprints. Nor does it apply to other non-communicative activity such as participation in a lineup or wearing certain items of apparel.[55] A suspect can also be compelled to speak for purposes of voice identification, or to provide a handwriting sample, so long as what is compelled is not a statement

---

[53] The double jeopardy provision of the Constitution, contained in Amendment V would prevent a second prosecution.

[54] There are two kinds of immunity: "use" and "transactional." A potential criminal defendant prefers the latter, for it ensures that he will not be prosecuted for any part of the *transaction* to which his testimony relates. The more narrow "use" immunity shields the potential accused from the use of his protected ("immunized") statements—or the fruits thereof—in any future prosecution against him. Thus, when only use immunity is granted, the government might be able to successfully prosecute the witness by using independent (non-shielded) evidence. Either kind of immunity suffices to allow testimony to be compelled on the ground that the witness had no risk of incrimination. *See Kastigar v. United States*, 406 U.S. 441, 457–58 (1972).

[55] The principal case concerning non-communicative evidence is *Schmerber v. California*, 384 U.S. 757, 760–65 (1966) (blood sample). *See also, United States v. Wade* 388 U.S. 218, 222–23 (1967) (lineup) *and Gilbert v. California*, 388 U.S. 263, 266–67 (1967) (handwriting sample).

that is an incriminating assertion. All this is because the privilege protects against the cruel trilemma of incrimination, lying, and punishment for silence—providing a fingerprint, for example, raises no cruel trilemma because it cannot be true or false.

We noted above that only individuals, not separate business entities, are entitled to claim the privilege. Thus, a corporate officer or employee who is subpoenaed to turn over corporate records cannot decline to do so on the ground that the records would incriminate him. The subpoena is directed to the corporation and the individual producing the records is acting as a corporate agent.[56] Because the corporation has no privilege, its records must be turned over to the proper authorities. Even preexisting records of an *individual* must normally be produced, for no compulsion attended their creation and their mere production is usually not a communicative act.

The privilege also gives way when the government seeks records which it requires to be kept for *regulatory* purposes, at least when the records are regularly maintained and have a "public aspect" in that they serve a public interest and thus bear a resemblance to public documents.[57] This is called the "required records" exception to the Fifth Amendment privilege.

ILLUSTRATION

James Bradley is the sole proprietor of a small convenience store which, in addition to selling a variety of foods and beverages, sells lottery tickets. Law enforcement officials suspect that James is also engaged in an illegal bookmaking trade in which his customers phone in bets on various sporting events. On the basis of sworn statements from two disgruntled customers, the authorities serve a subpoena on James for the production of all records prepared between January 1, 2020 and January 1, 2021 "containing statements, dates, figures, names, addresses, or other information pertaining to bets placed on any collegiate or professional sporting event." James's lawyer advises his client that unless the government grants James

---

[56] We do not go into detail here, but it is important to note that an individual who produces corporate records as the corporate agent could potentially incriminate himself as a result of producing (e.g., indicating that he knows of the records and has access to them) corporate records. The Supreme Court recognized the potential unfairness to the individual and held in *Braswell v. United States*, 487 U.S. 99 (1988), that because the agent must produce the records for the corporation that has no privilege, no use of the individual's act of production may be made against the individual.

[57] See *Grosso v. United States*, 390 U.S. 62, 68 (1968).

immunity, he can successfully resist production. Is the lawyer correct?

James is the sole proprietor of the convenience store, and the Court has held that a sole proprietorship is distinguishable from other businesses such as corporations, partnerships, and labor unions which, as separate entities representing common interests, are not "persons" within the meaning of Fifth Amendment's privilege against self-incrimination. However, James's standing as a "person" to claim the privilege does not mean that he is entitled to it on the facts. While it is true that the records sought could subject James to criminal liability, the records in question were not subjected to official compulsion *when they were prepared*. The government did not compel James to prepare the records. As the courts have put it: the Fifth Amendment does not protect the contents of documents that were prepared without compulsion. The remaining question is whether the *production* of documents, which *is* being compelled, raises concerns about compelled *testimony* that tends to incriminate the producing party. Does the production itself communicate anything? The answer is yes,[58] but in most cases the communication from the act of production is not incriminating and so is not protected by the Fifth Amendment.

The act of production is a concession by the producer *that the records exist and that the producing person had custody of them*. But it is often the case that the mere existence of records, or the mere possession of them, is not incriminating. Even when the act of production might be incriminating, the government might well have independent evidence of the existence of the documents sought, their location, and the identity of the party possessing them, and if the trial judge determined that this evidence was accurate, then production by the possessor would not be within the privilege. The argument against the application of the privilege is that delivering the documents sought would not constitute a communication of heretofore unknown incriminating evidence. The trial judge has made a factual determination, based upon independent evidence, that the government already possessed particularized knowledge of the existence, possession, and general content of the reports sought.[59]

---

[58]   The clearest example of how producing evidence could be incriminating would be a grand jury subpoena duces tecum to a suspect to appear before the grand jury and bring with him "the knife he used to stab John Doe to death." Were the suspect to arrive at the grand jury with a knife, the suspect would essentially be saying "this is the knife I used to stab John Doe to death." It is hard to imagine a more incriminating act.

[59]   In *United States v. Doe*, 465 U.S. 605, 614 n.11 (1984), the trial judge found that the government had failed to "satisfy this court" that it had adequate independent proof of the "existence, possession and authenticity" of the "documents it sought". The Supreme Court took note of this determination and refused to disturb it. Therefore,

Even more clearly, if the documents in question were discovered and lawfully seized during a proper search of the possessor's premises, the privilege has no application because the individual is not being compelled to testify.

The Illustration presents an exceptional situation, in which there is no indication that the existence of the records sought was conceded by James or that the government had convincing proof of their existence. The government's knowledge, so far as the Illustration discloses, is based on the statements of several disgruntled customers who would be unlikely to have any knowledge about James's records. James's production of the records described in the subpoena would thus be communicative because it would affirm the existence of the records, his possession of them, and their genuineness—in the sense that the records conform to the description contained in the subpoena. Therefore, the privilege against self-incrimination would attach and the government would not be able to compel the defendant to produce the records. But the *contents* of the documents remain unprotected, so if the government found them in a lawful search it could use them.[60]

Several other features of the Fifth Amendment's self-incrimination clause should be noted. *First*, there is a difference in the way the privilege is applied to an accused, on the one hand, and a witness (not the accused), on the other. The privilege of the accused not to be a witness against herself has been construed to confer a right to remain completely off the witness stand—that is, the prosecutor cannot call the accused to testify. Nor can the prosecutor emasculate the privilege by forcing the accused to claim it in the jury's presence or by commenting to the jury that the defendant has refused to testify.[61] Of course, the defendant can waive the privilege and elect to testify. If she does, the privilege is lifted as to her testimony on direct and cross. However, the constitutional protection

---

one can draw the inference that had the government's proof satisfied the trial judge, the compelled production would not have offended the Fifth Amendment's self-incrimination privilege.

[60]   *See* Id. (privilege applies to government's attempt to compel production of various telephone, banking, and business records because the government did not offer immunity and failed to show by independent evidence the necessary foundational facts). The other leading cases are *Fisher v. United States*, 425 U.S. 391, 397–98 (1976) (accountant's work papers producible) and *United States v. Hubbell*, 530 U.S. 27, 34–38 (2000) (accused's disclosure of documents was communicative and prosecutor improperly used evidence to which the disclosure led him).

[61]   *See Griffin v. California*, 380 U.S. 609, 613–15 (1965) (privilege may be freely exercised and adverse comment by prosecution or judge's instruction that adverse inferences may be drawn from accused's failure to testify will not be permitted). However, in civil cases, when a party refuses to answer a question on Fifth Amendment grounds, there is no constitutional prohibition against adverse comment. *Baxter v. Palmigiano*, 425 U.S. 308, 318 (1976).

afforded by the privilege is probably determined by the non-constitutional evidentiary rule limiting the scope of cross-examination. In the federal system and in a majority of states, cross-examination is ordinarily limited to the direct examination and matters affecting the witness's credibility.[62]

A *second* notable feature of the self-incrimination privilege is that only the accused is entitled to avoid testifying altogether. In civil proceedings, and in criminal trials in which the witness is not the accused, the privilege must be selectively claimed. It is available to an ordinary witness only if the witness's response would tend to incriminate him. The presiding judge must decide, on the basis of the interrogator's inquiry and all of the surrounding circumstances, whether there is a reasonable possibility that the response sought would tend to incriminate the claimant. It is sufficient to sustain the privilege that the expected response, though not incriminating on its face, appears to form a part of the circumstantial evidence potentially available to convict the claimant or that the claimant's response may lead to incriminating evidence.[63]

*only
accused
must
is
avoid
to
entirely*

A *third* aspect of the privilege against self-incrimination concerns the obligation of one sovereign to respect a grant of immunity conferred on a witness by another sovereign. The starting point for the discussion is that an individual is entitled to claim the privilege if the answer or response sought by the government would tend to subject him to criminal liability under the laws of another sovereign *within the United States.* Suppose a federal court, at a prosecutor's request, grants immunity to a witness who claims that (without immunity) his answer would be incriminating under the law of a state. A similar pattern emerges when a state court, at a prosecutor's request, grants immunity to a witness on the ground that his response would be incriminating under federal law. These grants of immunity would be ineffectual unless the "other" (non-granting) sovereign had to respect the immunity granted. Therefore, grants of immunity within the United States must be respected by other governments *within the United States.* This means, for example, that a grant of immunity by State *A* must be acknowledged by State *B* as well as by the federal government.[64] The non-granting sovereign is prohibited from using the immunized incriminating

---

[62]   Fed. R. Evid. 611(b).

[63]   The Supreme Court has recognized that even though a person denies any wrongdoing, she may claim the privilege because "truthful responses of an innocent witness, as well as those of a wrongdoer, may provide the government with incriminating evidence from the speaker's own mouth." *Ohio v. Reiner,* 532 U.S. 17, 21 (2001) (per curiam).

[64]   The leading Supreme Court case is *Murphy v. Waterfront Comm'n of New York Harbor,* 378 U.S. 52, 77–79 (1964).

statements, and this prohibition includes using evidence ("fruits") *derived* from the incriminating testimony.[65]

But what happens if an individual is allegedly involved in an *international* drug conspiracy? Assume that he is subpoenaed to testify before a grand jury investigating the drug trade. He invokes the Fifth Amendment privilege, and the prosecutor (who wants his testimony in order to prosecute other conspirators) obtains from the court an immunity grant. But the individual still refuses to testify on the ground that the grant of immunity will not stop *foreign* governments from prosecuting him on the basis of his statements about the drug conspiracy. (In the absence of a treaty or an executive agreement, a foreign country is free to prosecute an individual who has been given immunity from prosecution within the United States.) The Supreme Court held that the Fifth Amendment does not protect against the risk of foreign prosecution.[66] The Court noted that the Fifth Amendment trade-off is that the government *can* compel incriminating testimony so long as it gives the witness immunity—prosecutorial objectives are not completely stifled, as the government can use the compelled testimony to proceed against other individuals. But if a person could invoke the risk of foreign prosecution, immunity would not be available—thus completely forestalling the government's interest in prosecution. Accordingly, an immunized individual can be forced to testify even if there is a risk of foreign prosecution—and if he does not testify, he can be imprisoned for contempt.

§ 10.9 Analyzing Privilege Law: A Suggested Approach

There are many other privileges, both public, such as the privilege ("state secrets") protecting sensitive military and diplomatic information, and private, such as the privilege protecting confidences between clergyman and parishioner.[67] Generally speaking, privileges

---

[65]   There are generally two types of immunity. One is "transactional." That immunity guarantees that no prosecution will be brought against the individual based on any transaction covered by the individual's testimony. The other is "use-fruits" immunity. It guarantees that no use will be made of any testimony or the fruits thereof, but leaves open the possibility that a prosecution could be based on independent evidence. If State *A* has granted immunity (regardless of whether it was transactional or use-fruits immunity) to *X*, State *B* may still prosecute *X* as long as it does not use the compelled testimony obtained by State *A* or its fruits. This assures that the privilege is honored while each sovereign is treated equally. *Murphy v. Waterfront Comm'n of New York Harbor*, 378 U.S. 52, 79 (1964).

[66]   *United States v. Balsys*, 524 U.S. 666, 695–98 (1998).

[67]   Other notable privileges include a presidential (executive) privilege providing a qualified protection for confidential presidential communications, *see United States v. Nixon*, 418 U.S. 683, 708–09 (1974), and in an increasing number of states, a qualified journalist's privilege protecting confidential sources, *see, e.g.,* N.J. Stat. Ann.

share a common framework. Putting aside the privilege protecting against self-incrimination and the spousal privilege against adverse testimony, privileges are usually designed to encourage the free flow of information between or among those persons within the protected circle or certain privacy interests. Of course, there are significant variations, but despite these differences, shared characteristics provide a common theme and suggest a common approach to the analysis of privilege law.

The initial step in this suggested approach is to discover the *purpose, rationale, or justification* for the recognition of the particular privilege. The accepted rationale usually provides arguments for or against its application in a particular case. Of course, sometimes there are several justifications for a single privilege, and these several purposes usually support multiple arguments for, or occasionally against, the attachment of a privilege in a specific set of circumstances.

Observe how the identification of the justification for a particular privilege leads naturally to an identification of the *persons within the protection of the privilege.* For example, the privilege may extend beyond the lawyer and her client to the representatives of each. Somewhere within the circle of protected persons is the holder (or holders) of the privilege and her identification is critical for only the holder(s) or someone authorized to act on her or their behalf can claim or waive the privilege. Finally, if the privilege in question does attach, it is necessary to determine *its duration.* Here, the inquiry focuses on such issues as whether the privilege survives death, whether it can be overridden by court order, and most importantly, whether it has been waived. The most common basis for waiver is disclosure of the privileged statements by the holder to persons ("outsiders") not within the protected circle.

---

§ 2A:84A–21.1—which some federal courts recognize as a qualified privilege as a matter of federal common law. "Qualified" means that the privilege applies unless substantial countervailing interests require disclosure. In *Nixon,* the Court held that the executive privilege was qualified by the grand jury's interest in investigating crime.

Chapter XI

EXPERT TESTIMONY

Table of Sections

§ 11.1   Role and Qualification of the Expert Witness

By definition, an expert witness possesses knowledge and skills that distinguish her from an ordinary witness. The expert is in a position superior to other trial participants, and in particular the jury, to draw inferences and reach conclusions within her field of expertise. She may gain that expertise though either education, training, or experience. The point is that she has abilities that are not shared—or at least not fully shared—by lay persons. Thus, if a witness qualifies as an expert, she may render an opinion concerning subjects within her expertise. Even if she does not express her opinion about contested facts, her testimony can still provide assistance to the trier of fact, for she can help *facilitate the understanding* of scientific or technical or other specialized information.

When one of the parties presents a witness who will testify as an expert, the judge, upon objection, must determine whether the witness has the necessary qualifications. In addition to resolving that question, the judge must decide whether the subject matter of the proposed testimony is sufficiently removed from common experience that the expert opinion will be helpful to the jury. The trier of fact does not need an expert to testify that persons wearing gloves do not leave fingerprints,[1] or that compulsive gamblers characteristically

---

[1]   *See United States v. Booth*, 669 F.2d 1231, 1240 (9th Cir. 1981) (an expert is not permitted to testify that the reason no fingerprints were on the getaway car was because the occupants "had either used gloves or wiped [off] the fingerprints").

mismanage their finances.[2] In older cases, the courts often required that the subject matter in question be outside the reach ("beyond the ken") of the trier of fact, thus emphasizing the highly specialized nature of the subject. Modern courts are less demanding and require only that the expert's testimony *be helpful* to the trier of fact—as is provided by Rule 702. When the subject concerns an aspect of such specialized fields as medicine, economics, statistics, science, engineering, or investment banking, there is usually no question about the legitimacy of expert opinion. But other, less technical subjects, such as burglars' tools, the effect on livestock of drinking salt water, bricklaying, strategies and code words used by drug dealers, trucking practices, and techniques for controlling motorcycles are also appropriate subjects for expert testimony.

Federal Rule 702

Rule 702 of the Federal Rules of Evidence states:

Testimony by Expert Witnesses

A witness who is qualified as an expert by knowledge, skill, experience, training, or education may testify in the form of an opinion or otherwise if:

(a) the expert's scientific, technical, or other specialized knowledge will help the trier of fact to understand the evidence or to determine a fact in issue;

(b) the testimony is based on sufficient facts or data;

(c) the testimony is the product of reliable principles and methods; and

(d) the expert has reliably applied the principles and methods to the facts of the case.

Before turning to the last three of the lettered sub-parts of the Rule, it is useful to briefly look to three aspects of the introductory language together with sub-part (a): (1) "qualified as an expert by knowledge, skill, experience, training or education"; (2) "in the form of an opinion or otherwise"; and (3) "knowledge will help the trier of fact to understand the evidence or to determine a fact in issue."

The rule makes it clear that one does not need a Ph.D. in nuclear physics to qualify as an expert on some issues. Indeed, such a degree would not likely qualify its holder as an expert on most of the issues we explore in this Chapter. When aspects (1) and (3) are combined, it

---

[2]   *United States v. Shorter*, 809 F.2d 54, 61 (D.C. Cir. 1987) (trial judge properly excluded "expert" testimony that financial mismanagement is characteristic of a compulsive gambler).

appears that the basic requirement is that the person put forward as an expert must have knowledge, skill or something special that lay jurors are unlikely to have, and that special something must be helpful to the jury. "Thus, experience may be a crucial component for one type of expert opinion, whereas academic training may be essential for another. For yet other types, no particular basis is required, so long as one of the bases in the rule is established."[3]

Expert testimony can be helpful in one of two ways. Sometimes the expert may provide background information that is helpful to the jury in understanding the evidence that the parties will present, without the expert offering any views on the disputed facts in the case. For example, a DNA expert could simply explain DNA testing to set the stage for another expert to testify about a specific test. Or, the expert might weigh in on a disputed fact, such as whether exposure to a particular substance can cause cancer.

How highly skilled must an expert be? There are two answers to this question. The evidence answer is that the expert must simply be qualified by education, experience, or training to give the opinion that is offered. There is no requirement that the highest or best qualified witness be called.[4] The tactical answer is for a party to put the most impressive expert, who often will be best qualified, before the jury, because that expert will be more likely to impress the jury than someone less qualified, although very experienced trial lawyers report that some experts with middling credentials can be very persuasive witnesses.

§ 11.2 Background of Current Rule 702

Some background is necessary for a fuller understanding of Rule 702 which, along with Rules 701 and 703,[5] was amended in 2000. A persistent question under the original version of Rule 702 was how to determine whether proffered "scientific" evidence was sufficiently reliable to be admitted. The main battleground was the validity of the scientific principles on which the proffered expert based his opinion, although admissibility also hinged on the sufficiency of facts,

---

[3]   SALTZBURG, MARTIN & CAPRA, FEDERAL RULES OF EVIDENCE MANUAL § 702.02 [3] (12th ed. 2019).

[4]   "[C]ourts have not required a party to show that the witness is an outstanding expert, or to show that the witness is well-known and respected in the field; these are generally questions of weight." Id.

[5]   Rule 701 was amended to ensure that the requirements for expert testimony in Rule 702 could not be evaded by having an expert testify as a lay witness. Rule 703 was amended to address the admissibility of evidence reasonably relied upon by the expert, but not independently admissible.

as well as methodology in applying the scientific principles to the disputed issues in the case.

The Frye Test

As to the validity of the underlying principles, an early federal case, *Frye v. United States,*[6] was widely recognized as setting the standard before the adoption of the Federal Rules of Evidence: a scientific principle or process would not be recognized in the federal courts unless it had "gained general acceptance in the particular field in which it belongs."[7] General acceptance in the field was thought to be a proxy for reliability.

One virtue of the *Frye* test is that it is relatively easily applied. The trial judge does not have to actually figure out whether an expert's methodology is actually scientifically valid. Rather the trial judge relies on the community of scientists for that determination.

Most state courts accepted the "*Frye* Test" and some states continue to use it today. But the language of the original[8] (and current) Rule 702 does not appear to embrace *Frye*, for the rule speaks of "scientific, technical, or other specialized knowledge [that] will help the trier of fact * * *." Further doubt was cast on the continuing validity of *Frye* because the original Advisory Committee Note to Rule 702 failed to mention the *Frye* standard.

The unclear position of the Federal Rule, and its reference to assisting the trier, opened the way for renewed debate regarding the proper standard governing the admissibility of scientific evidence. Some courts and commentators feared that abandoning the *Frye* test in favor of a more liberal standard would result in admitting questionable and misleading "science" (so called "junk science"). Critics of *Frye*, including many courts, found its standard vague and hard to apply. (For example, when is a principle "generally accepted" in the relevant field? And what is the relevant field?) More importantly, they pointed out that *Frye*'s demand for general acceptance requires a protracted waiting period during which a newly discovered principle or technique gains its footing. In the interim, courts are deprived of useful scientific evidence that is in fact reliable, even though not yet recognized to be so. Not surprisingly, federal lower court opinions were in disarray.

---

6   293 F. 1013 (D.C. Cir. 1923).

7   Id. at 1014.

8   The Federal Rules, and thus the original text of Rule 702 became effective in 1975.

The Daubert Test of Reliable Methodology

The Supreme Court settled the debate about the applicability of the *Frye* "general acceptance" test, at least for the federal judiciary, in a 1993 case, *Daubert v. Merrell Dow Pharmaceuticals, Inc.*[9] There, two sets of parents and their minor children sued Merrell Dow for the children's birth defects, allegedly resulting from the mother's ingestion during pregnancy of Bendectin, an anti-nausea drug. The defendant presented experts who testified that on the basis of a large number of epidemiological studies and other scientific tests (such as animal studies) causation could not be established. The plaintiffs then offered their own experts to testify that based on a reanalysis of the defendant's epidemiological studies, as well as several non-human studies, there was a causal link between Bendectin and the children's birth defects. The plaintiffs' evidence was rejected by the trial judge on the ground that it failed to meet *Frye*'s "general acceptance" test. The Ninth Circuit affirmed, but the Supreme Court reversed and, after holding that the *Frye* test was not controlling, remanded the case.

Speaking through Justice Blackmun, the Court held that the *Frye* test was at odds with the "liberal thrust" of the Federal Rules of Evidence and did not survive the passage of Rule 702.[10] The Court went on to set out a new standard governing the admissibility of scientific evidence in the federal courts. Particular emphasis was placed on the language of Rule 702 which allows the introduction of "scientific . . . knowledge" that will "assist the trier" in understanding the evidence or resolving a disputed fact. The adjective "scientific" is important, said the Court, for it connotes knowledge that is the product of the methods and procedures of science, such as testing a hypothesis, careful measurement, replication of results, peer review, scientific acceptance,[11] and so forth. The focus for determining if evidence is "scientific" is on the principles embraced and the methodology employed. Rule 702, the Court emphasized, also makes it clear that the proffered scientific evidence must "assist the trier of fact." This requirement is closely related to the first essential

---

[9]   509 U.S. 579 (1993). The trial judge's opinion in *Daubert* may be found at 727 F.Supp. 570 (S.D. Cal. 1989).

[10]   It is extremely ironic that Justice Blackmun relied on the "liberal thrust" of the Rules, since *Daubert* and its progeny have generally made it more difficult than it previously had been to persuade a court to admit expert testimony.

[11]   "Scientific acceptance" is a legacy of the *Frye* test. Under *Daubert*, general acceptance by the scientific community is still a factor, but not the *only* factor, influencing admissibility.

("*scientific* knowledge"),[12] but has a different focus. The focus here is on the relevancy or "fit" of the scientific knowledge (evidence presented by an expert) to the disputed issues in a particular case. It is quite possible that a reliable body of scientific knowledge would not be helpful in resolving the disputed issues before the court. To use an example suggested by the *Daubert* Court:

> The study of the phases of the moon . . . may provide valid scientific "knowledge" about whether a certain night was dark. . . . However (absent credible [scientific] grounds. . .), evidence that the moon was full on a certain night will not assist the trier of fact in determining whether an individual was unusually likely to have behaved irrationally on that night.[13]

Trial Judge as Gatekeeper

The application of Rule 702, as that rule was construed in *Daubert*, places a heavy responsibility on the trial judge. Gatekeeping is critical because the concern is that the jury will not be able to determine whether an expert's testimony is reliable. After all, the very reason that an expert is needed—to help the jury understand something beyond their knowledge—means that jurors are unlikely to be able to determine whether the expert is really providing a reliable opinion. The accepted premise is that jurors may simply be wowed by the expert's scientific-sounding testimony, which is in fact nothing but "junk science."

In her "gatekeeping" role the judge must evaluate the reliability and relevance of evidence that may pertain to a scientific field—in which the judge probably has no expertise. It is no longer enough to poll the scientific community to determine whether the expert's methodology is generally accepted (that is now just one factor in the reliability enquiry). The trial judge must determine whether the expert's methodology is actually reliable. The proponent of the expert must prove by a preponderance of the evidence that the expert's testimony is reliable.

The trial court, in exercising its gatekeeping responsibility, is assisted by a number of factors that the court laid out in *Daubert*. These factors are not exclusive, but they do assist the trial judge in determining reliability. Those factors are: 1) whether the expert's

---

[12] Knowledge that is not scientific would presumably be speculative or unsupported by scientific theory or methodology and hence would not "help" the factfinder.

[13] *Daubert*, 509 U.S. at 591. This example also illustrates the close connection between the requirement that evidence be scientifically based and the requirement that it be helpful.

methodology is objective and testable, as opposed to subjective and idiosyncratic; 2) whether the methodology has been reviewed; 3) whether standards and controls are in place for applying the methodology; 4) whether there is a documentable rate of error that is sufficiently low; and 5) whether the methodology is generally accepted as reliable by other scientists (which is the *Frye* test, but which is no longer dispositive).

The burden of the judge's gatekeeping responsibility is increased because the decision she makes will be sustained on appeal unless she "abused her discretion."[14] Often, she will find it necessary to conduct a *"Daubert* hearing," out of the jury's presence, for the purpose of considering data and arguments for and against the admissibility of scientific evidence. In cases in which expert testimony is important and each side's partisan experts reach completely different conclusions, she may wish to invoke Federal Rule 706 and select a "court appointed expert witness."

Gatekeeper Function Applies to Non-Scientific Expert Testimony

Recall that Federal Rule 702 speaks of "scientific, technical, or other specialized knowledge. . . ." The issue in *Daubert* was whether the admissibility of evidence based on "scientific" knowledge was to be governed by *Frye* or some other standard. Many observers predicted that the gatekeeping function established in *Daubert* would be extended to "technical or other specialized knowledge." Their prediction was confirmed by the Supreme Court in *Kumho Tire Co., Ltd. v. Carmichael.*[15] In *Kumho* the Supreme Court held that *Daubert's* "gatekeeping" test of reliability and relevance applied not only to scientific knowledge, but to "technical or other specialized knowledge" as well. In *Kumho* a proffered "tire expert" (an engineer) claimed that through a visual and tactile inspection of the tire in question, he could determine whether the tire's failure was caused by a manufacturing or design defect, on the one hand, or consumer mistreatment (under-inflation or overloading), on the other.

Applying *Daubert's* evaluative factors, such as the testability of the expert's hypothesis, peer review, and acceptance by other technicians, the trial judge rejected the proposed testimony. The Eleventh Circuit Court of Appeals reversed, concluding that *Daubert's* approach applied to scientific testimony, not to testimony resting on "experience" and "skill-based" observations. The Supreme Court, however, agreed with the trial judge, although it noted that factors bearing upon the reliability and relevance of non-scientific

---

[14]   *See General Electric Co. v. Joiner,* 522 U.S. 136, 152 (1997).

[15]   526 U.S. 137 (1999).

testimony might vary from factors pertinent to scientific testimony. For example, peer review,[16] quite common in the world of science, may have limited or no application to technical or specialized evidence—one would not expect an expert car mechanic to have published his methodology in a peer reviewed journal. And in some cases involving specialized or technical testimony, the observations and experience of the expert may weigh more heavily on the admissibility decision than these factors would in assessing the proposed testimony of an expert scientist.

According to the Court in *Kumho*, the *basic question for the judge as to all experts is to determine whether the expert is employing the same "intellectual rigor" in reaching her opinion as you would expect her to employ in her real life as an expert*. Thus, one of the major concerns of the gatekeeper is whether the expert, in preparing testimony for trial, is making assumptions and cutting corners in a way that the expert would not do outside the context of litigation.

Note that the standard of proof that the judge must employ in assessing an expert's opinion for reliability is *a preponderance of the evidence*. The *Daubert* Court explicitly so stated. Thus, for example, the trial court must find that the expert employed a methodology that is more likely than not reliable and that the expert more likely than not applied the method reliably.

§ 11.3 Amended Rule 702

Rule 702 was amended in 2000 so as to more accurately capture the Supreme Court's approach to expert testimony as set forth in *Daubert* and *Kumho Tire*. The rule now specifies that an expert may testify to "scientific, technical, or other specialized knowledge" only if,

- the testimony is based upon sufficient facts or data (i.e. the expert had done enough research and investigation to render a reliable opinion);

- the testimony is the product of reliable principles and methods; and

- the expert has reliably applied the principles and methods to the facts of the case.

The Advisory Committee's Note to Amended Rule 702 emphasizes both the trial judge's "gatekeeping" function and the

---

[16]   The Court also pointed out that there may be some instances in which "a claim made by a scientific witness has never been the subject of peer review, for the particular application at issue may never previously have interested any scientist." Id. at 151.

variety of factors relevant to the decision to admit or exclude expert testimony. No single list of relevant concerns will suffice for all cases. A partial list includes:

- objective testing of the expert's methods

- peer review

- potential (or known) rate of error

- careful standards and controls

- acceptance by other persons in the field

- whether the methodology was developed especially for litigation (in which case it is less likely to be reliable)

- whether alternative explanations are adequately addressed and accounted for

- the depth of the expert's knowledge and experience

- whether the expert used the same care in developing an opinion as experts use outside of court

- whether the expert—including experts who base their testimony solely on experience—can adequately explain how their methods lead to their conclusions.[17]

The Advisory Committee also notes that even though the main focus for evaluating scientific evidence rests upon "principles and methodology," as opposed to conclusions, it is still important to consider whether the conclusion reached by the proffered expert departs sharply from that of his peers. If it does, there is reason to be concerned that the relevant principles and methodologies "have not been faithfully applied."[18] An unreliable application of a reliable methodology results in an unreliable opinion. So the gatekeeper must look to how the expert has applied the methodology.

§ 11.4 The Expert Witness: Sources of Knowledge and Direct Examination

The factfinder, of course, is always faced with questions of what evidence to believe and what inferences to draw. The use and evaluation of expert testimony, however, poses special difficulties. The first is determining exactly what factual assumptions underlie

---

[17]   Thus, an expert on car accidents cannot simply say, "Based on my review of 10,000 accidents, I conclude that the plaintiff was not paying attention at the time of the accident." The expert's experience may make her qualified, but under *Daubert* a trial judge may not accept an expert's conclusion simply because she is qualified and says it is so.

[18]   Fed. R. Evid. 702 ACN (2000 amendment).

an expert opinion; the second is deciding which (if any) of the expert's specialized inferences or conclusions should be accepted as true. The trier's task is made more difficult because the expert often uses technical language that describes principles and methodologies foreign to most lay persons. To complicate matters even more, there is usually opposing expert opinion that reaches different conclusions. The starting point, however, is for the trier to identify the facts (or factual assumptions) that underlie an expert's opinion. If these facts are contested—and often they are—the basis of the expert's opinion will be negated or weakened if the trier rejects the foundational facts in whole or in part. It thus becomes essential *that there be some means by which the trier can identify the factual assumptions underlying an expert's opinion.*

A simple example will make the point. A physician testifies that the plaintiff has a certain illness or injury. Three symptoms of the illness are persistent headaches, dizziness, and nausea. Earlier in the trial, the plaintiff testified that she had experienced all of these ill effects. Subsequently, however, the defendant introduces conflicting evidence, provided by estranged family members, that challenges the plaintiff's assertions. It is important for the trier of fact to know the extent to which the doctor's opinion rests upon the presence of these symptoms. If the trier rejects all or part of the plaintiff's testimony, it will take this into account in evaluating the accuracy of the expert physician's opinion. It is possible that experts come to contrary conclusions based on different factual assumptions. The jury will then determine the facts and decide which expert to believe on the basis of which expert's factual assumptions have been proven.

There are various means by which an expert can gain knowledge of the facts that underlie his opinion. Take as an example a physician in a case involving the plaintiff's personal injuries: (1) the expert may have knowledge acquired through first-hand observation or examination; (2) she may have learned the facts prior to trial by studying the plaintiff's medical records and, perhaps, by consulting with others who have treated the patient; (3) she may learn the facts during the courtroom proceedings by observing and hearing the evidence bearing on the plaintiff's condition, and; (4) she may learn the facts when he takes the witness stand and is asked a "hypothetical" question that contains a recitation of the assumed facts. For example, counsel for the plaintiff may say, "Assuming, Doctor, that during the four weeks before the plaintiff was hospitalized, and while he was working in close proximity to the liquid chemical known as Benzene, he experienced, with increasing frequency, persistent headaches, dizziness, and nausea, do you have an opinion, within a reasonable degree of medical certainty, as to what caused these symptoms?" The hypothetical question, as you can see, not only informs the witness of the pertinent underlying "facts" but it also identifies the assumed facts on which the expert bases his opinion.

Consider further the third possibility noted above: suppose one or even several witnesses who precede the expert's testimony give all of the evidence on which the expert bases his opinion. Instead of using a hypothetical question, the direct examiner may simply ask his expert to assume, for purposes of giving his opinion, that all of the facts to which the preceding witnesses testified are true. The examiner would then, for example, continue, "Now, Doctor, do you have an opinion. . . ." This reliance on one or more prior witnesses works effectively when the prior testimony is consistent. It is not usually practical when a single witness recants or qualifies her direct testimony, or when several witnesses are inconsistent. Then, the assumed facts underlying the expert's testimony become unclear, and a hypothetical question may be desirable. Of course, as we have noted, the expert is sometimes able to supply the underlying facts based on personal knowledge. For example, a physician who has examined the patient may base an opinion on the "facts" discovered during the examination. Finally, because it is common practice in every profession to rely frequently on the work of others, especially other professionals in the same or a related field, a testifying expert may rest his opinion on facts or data that others in the field would rely upon.

Federal Rule 703

All the various means described above that *could* be used to provide the expert witness with a factual basis for his opinion *are allowed* by Federal Rule 703. It reads:

Bases of an Expert's Opinion Testimony

An expert may base an opinion on facts or data in the case that the expert has been made aware of or personally observed. If experts in the particular field would reasonably rely on those kinds of facts or data in forming an opinion on the subject, they need not be admissible for the opinion to be admitted. But if the facts or data would otherwise be inadmissible, the proponent of the opinion may disclose them to the jury only if their probative value in helping the jury evaluate the opinion substantially outweighs their prejudicial effect.

The rule's formulation is broad, for it embraces facts and data personally perceived by the witness, as well as facts and data of which the expert has been "made aware." And note there is no time frame for obtaining that information. Thus the expert can rely on acts and data obtained at any time—either at or before the trial. Finally, factual materials that are not admissible may still underlie the expert's inferences and opinions, provided these materials are those that "experts in the particular field would reasonably rely on." In other words, an expert's opinion may be based on his first-hand knowledge, on facts that are revealed during the trial or hearing, or on "out-of-court" facts of the sort used by professionals in the expert's field. *This latter category allows the expert to rely on hearsay information if other experts in the field would do so.* For example, a psychiatrist preparing an opinion on a party's mental state may interview the party's friends, relatives, etc. If the accounts from such people were offered for their truth at trial, they would be hearsay. But under Rule 703, the accounts are only being relied upon by the expert as a basis for her opinion. The question under Rule 703 is whether other psychiatrists would rely on such accounts in assessing the party's mental condition, and the answer to that question in this example is undoubtedly yes.

Federal Rule 705

You need to examine Rule 703 in conjunction with the other Federal rules governing expert testimony. Rule 705 is particularly important, for it specifies the testimonial form in which an expert may state his opinion or conclusion. Consider, especially, the impact of Rule 705 on the traditional means of securing expert testimony: the hypothetical question. Rule 705 states:

DISCLOSING THE FACTS OR DATA UNDERLYING AN EXPERT'S OPINION

Unless the court orders otherwise, an expert may state an opinion—and give the reasons for it—without first testifying to the underlying facts or data. But the expert may be required to disclose those facts or data on cross-examination.

———————

Analyze the following hypothetical, keeping in mind both Rule 703 and Rule 705.[19]

———————

[19]   Rule 704(a) provides that if an expert opinion is helpful, it may not be excluded simply because it embraces an ultimate issue in the case. Rule 704(b) carves out a single exception to the *general rule*, embodied in Rule 704(a), that an expert *may give* a helpful opinion as to the *ultimate issue* in a case. Under Rule 704(b), an expert is

ILLUSTRATION

Assume that in a suit against an insurance company, the issue is whether a warehouse fire had an incendiary origin (arson) or is traceable to other causes. The defendant puts Fire Marshal on the stand, qualifies him as an expert witness on the cause and origin of fires, and then asks, "Are you familiar with, and have you investigated, the warehouse fire at 914 Cargo Street, on August 23, 2017?" After receiving an affirmative answer, counsel asks, "Do you have an opinion on what caused this fire?" Over plaintiff's objection that defense counsel must use a hypothetical question, Fire Marshal answers, "I do." When counsel then asks, "What is your opinion?", Marshal replies (over objection), "My opinion is that the source of the fire was arson." On cross, counsel for the plaintiff asks questions that elicit the factual basis for Fire Marshal's opinion. The underlying facts or data were:

(1)   A personal inspection of the debris from the fire, including evidence indicating the areas of greatest heat intensity, the pattern of the flames, and the condition of the warehouse electrical system.

(2)   A report containing the results of a chemical analysis of the soil under the warehouse where the fire probably started. [The chemist's report states that minute traces of gasoline residue were embedded in the soil near the most likely point of the fire's origin.]

(3)   Conversations with three eyewitnesses (night watchmen guarding other buildings) who told Marshal that they first observed the fire and smoke on the east side of the warehouse.

(4)   A report prepared by another expert (privately retained), as well as conversations with that expert, whose findings, analysis, and conclusions were consistent with those of Fire Marshal.

Counsel for the plaintiff moves to strike Fire Marshal's direct testimony on the ground that his opinion is based on hearsay that is not in evidence and, in any event, is inadmissible, and on the further ground that Marshal's opinion is based on the opinion of another

---

barred from giving his opinion as to whether the defendant in a criminal case did or did not have the mental state required as an element of the crime charged. Subsection (b) was a reaction to the "not-guilty-by-reason-of-insanity" verdict rendered in the trial of John Hinckley for the attempted assassination of President Reagan.

expert. The trial judge again rules against the plaintiff on both grounds.

Were the judge's rulings correct?[20]

Hypothetical Questions

The parties are, first, arguing over whether the expert's opinion must be elicited through a hypothetical question. Although asking a hypothetical question might appear to be the ideal means of eliciting an expert's opinion, experience has shown that often it is not. There are many problems in accommodating the hypothetical question to the adversary system. The lawyer asking a hypothetical often crafts it in partisan terms, and includes extraneous facts that are not relevant to the expert's opinion. Furthermore, counsel sometimes omits unfavorable relevant facts or states the relevant facts in such argumentative terms that the hypothetical partakes of closing argument. Undue length (and resulting confusion) is another problem: it is not unusual for a hypothetical question to occupy several or even a dozen pages in a trial transcript.

Traditionally, rigid requirements have attended the use of hypothetical questions. The hypothetical question was considered defective—and an appellate reversal could result—if a relevant fact was omitted from the question. The same was true if a relevant fact included in the hypothetical was not supported by *admitted* evidence in the record. Modern courts are somewhat more forgiving in their review of "defective" hypothetical questions. Today, for example, appellate judges are more diligent in trying to assess the probable harm caused by the defect. They will forgive the omission of a relevant fact that is not very significant. Furthermore, they conduct their review with greater awareness of the cross-examiner's opportunity to reveal (assumed) facts omitted from the hypothetical and to ask cross-examination questions containing additional or fewer assumed facts.[21] Nonetheless, the common-law framework of the hypothetical remains largely intact, and the most that can be said is that sometimes the hypothetical question is more helpful to the jury than other means of eliciting expert testimony.

---

[20] For two somewhat similar cases, *see Ferrara & DiMercurio v. St. Paul Mercury Ins. Co.*, 240 F.3d 1 (1st Cir. 2001) and *United States v. Lundy*, 809 F.2d 392 (7th Cir. 1987).

[21] "Doctor, would you change your opinion about the cause of the plaintiff's neck injury if you assumed that two days before the automobile accident in question he fell from a stepladder onto a concrete stairs, sustained a blow to the forehead, and was rendered unconscious?"

In any event, the use of a hypothetical question is not required by Federal Rule 705 unless the court orders otherwise.[22] The elimination of a general requirement that the examiner use a hypothetical question is accomplished by Rule 705's allowance of an expert's opinion without the need to first reveal "the underlying facts or data." When a hypothetical question is used, the expert testifies that he has an opinion based on the preceding assumed facts recited by counsel, and only then does the expert render an opinion grounded on those facts. In the Illustration, counsel chose not to use a hypothetical question, the court did not rule otherwise, and the expert properly gave his opinion.

Leaving the Expert's Basis to Cross-Examination

The first point to be made about the judge's refusal to strike Marshal's direct testimony is that allowing an expert to give his opinion without first revealing its factual basis might well not be an appropriate procedure *unless* the opponent is able to use pre-trial discovery to learn what the expert's opinion or conclusion will be *and* the data, facts, principles, and methodologies (the "foundation" or "basis") that support the expert's opinion. Without this information, the cross-examiner is in the untenable position of asking questions designed to reveal the basis of the expert's opinion without knowing in advance what that basis is. Suppose, for example, the cross-examiner asks the expert whether his opinion rests in part on conversations with persons who observed the outbreak of the fire. And, suppose, further, the expert answers, "I spoke with eyewitnesses, yes." Is the cross-examiner now to ask, "What did they say?" Or is the cross-examiner to move to a different inquiry and ask about another basis for the expert's opinion, thus leaving the jury wondering what these eyewitnesses said and whether the cross-examiner is avoiding the disclosure of helpful evidence?

Fortunately, in almost all jurisdictions, modern discovery provisions, such as those contained in the Federal Rules of Civil and Criminal Procedure (which require expert reports from which the expert may not depart at trial), allow adequate discovery of an opposing expert's opinion, as well as the basis on which it rests.[23] The opportunity to review these reports permits opposing counsel to file *in limine* motions to exclude expert testimony, usually on the ground that it is insufficiently reliable and therefore fails to satisfy *Daubert* and Rule 702. In many civil cases the opponent will depose the

---

[22] Judges do not often require that the direct examiner interrogate an expert witness only through the use of a hypothetical. If the examiner declines to use a hypothetical question, the cross-examiner is entitled to ask questions that will reveal the factual assumption underlying the expert's opinion.

[23] *See* Fed. R. Civ. Proc. 26(a)(2) and (b)(4)(A); Fed. R. Crim. P. 16(a)(1)(G).

expert, and sometimes in both civil and criminal cases the expert will testify before the judge during a *Daubert* hearing. By the time of trial, the cross-examiner—armed with prior knowledge about the basis of an expert's opinions or conclusions and in some cases with prior experience in cross-examining the expert—is free to explore only those parts of the expert's foundation that he believes are weak, or to identify certain factual assumptions and ask the expert if he would change or modify his opinion if different factual assumptions were made.[24] Rule 705 therefore allows an expert to testify on direct without disclosing his basis, leaving the issues of the sufficiency of the expert's basis to cross-examination.

Disclosure to the Jury of Inadmissible Facts Relied on by the Expert

Note the closing sentence of Rule 703. It provides that if facts or data relied upon by the expert would otherwise be inadmissible, the proponent of the opinion may not disclose them to the jury unless *"their probative value in helping the jury evaluate the expert's opinion substantially outweighs their prejudicial effect."* This is a very strict— reverse Rule 403—balancing test, meaning that the inadmissible evidence relied on by the expert can rarely be disclosed to the jury on direct examination. Two factors are at play here. First, there is the question of how much the jury will be aided in weighing the expert's opinion if the "inadmissible" underlying facts and data are revealed. Second, there is a concern that the jury will improperly use the underlying materials not only to evaluate the expert's opinion, but also for the truth of assertions contained in these materials (e.g., the fire started where the hearsay declarants said it did). Of course, the test applies only to the *proponent* of the expert's opinion; and, as we have seen, the test applies only to facts or data otherwise inadmissible. Therefore (in the Illustration above) evidence resulting from Marshal's personal inspection is unaffected by the special balancing test. Knowledge gained through personal observations of the testifying witness is admissible; the proponent (or for that matter, the cross-examiner) can elicit Marshal's testimony relating to his observations. The same might be true of the chemist's report, for it could escape the hearsay rule and be received in evidence if it was a properly prepared business or public record.

Marshal's conversations with eyewitnesses and his communications with the other expert (including use of the other's

---

[24]   The different assumptions must, however, rest on a permissible foundation such as evidence in the record or facts reasonably relied on by persons in the field in question.

expert's report)[25] appear to be "otherwise . . . inadmissible" under Rule 703, because they are hearsay if offered for their truth. Let us assume that conversations with eyewitnesses and consultations with other experts constitute evidentiary sources that are "inadmissible" but nonetheless are "reasonably relied upon by experts" in the field of fire detection. Under this assumption (generally an accurate one), these sources are a proper basis for an expert opinion, but the evidentiary *content* of these sources (witnesses' statements about where the fire started; the other expert's findings and conclusions) cannot be disclosed to the jury unless Rule 703's special balancing test is satisfied—and that is certainly unlikely.

Note that the last sentence of Rule 703 does *not* prohibit an expert from *relying* on inadmissible information in reaching an opinion. That last sentence only addresses whether the inadmissible information may be *disclosed* to the jury under the guise that it is only being offered to illustrate the expert's basis. Rule 703 cautions that the risk of misuse of this evidence is so high—and the possibility that an expert may be used as a pretense in order to get such evidence before the jury so real—that disclosure will be permitted on direct examination only rarely.

The course and tenor of cross-examination often affects the trial judge's decision on the disclosure of "inadmissible" evidence for the purpose of assisting the jury in understanding and evaluating the expert's opinion. Suppose, for example, the cross-examiner reveals the source of some of the inadmissible evidence (facts, data, or other expert's opinions) underlying the expert's opinion. Without disclosing the content of this evidence, he suggests its unreliability. ("Are you telling the jury that part of your opinion that this fire was caused by arson is based on hearsay conversations with night watchmen, untrained in fire detection, and not even present at the building that burned?") Tactics like this, suggesting that the "inadmissible" basis of the expert's opinion is not credible, can "open the door" to disclosure of the underlying (and otherwise inadmissible) evidence on redirect examination.

§ 11.5   The Expert Witness: Cross-Examination and Impeachment

The technique of cross-examining an expert will vary somewhat depending largely upon which of the various modes of direct examination is used. For example, if the direct examiner does not ask

---

[25]   If the other expert was a public official, his report (as opposed to his informal conversations) could probably be admitted into evidence as a public report. *See* Fed. R. Evid. 803(8)(A)(iii). This report might also qualify as a business record. *See* Fed. R. Evid. 803(6).

a hypothetical question or does not fully explore the bases for the expert opinion, the cross-examiner may want to ask questions designed to reveal the underlying basis of the expert's opinion. If the expert himself has supplied the underlying facts or data, the cross-examiner may want to ask questions designed to reveal the expert's lack of thoroughness, or defects in his observations or memory. There are several additional possibilities for weakening the force of the expert's testimony. As we have already noted, the cross-examiner may ask the expert to assume different facts from those assumed during direct examination, and to state whether these new factual assumptions would alter his opinion. The interrogator may also probe aspects of the expert's education or experience in an attempt to show that the expert's background is not well suited to developing a high degree of expertise in the particular specialty pertinent to the present case.

And like other witnesses, the expert is subject to any of the usual methods of impeachment such as bias, prior inconsistent statements, or prior "bad" acts reflecting on credibility. Bias, in particular, may be an available technique because, for example, the expert usually is paid a fee by the party who engages him. Evidence that an expert frequently testifies in trials and invariably aligns herself with one point of view or one kind of litigant (such as personal injury plaintiff) also suggests bias. Furthermore, the examiner may confront the expert with a treatise, text, or other reliable authority and, after extracting a concession (or providing other evidence) that the proffered work is a reliable authority, point to passages that contradict the expert's opinion. For example, if the expert testifies on direct that a "whiplash" injury is always manifested within several weeks after a blow is sustained, the cross-examiner may read (or have the expert read) passages from a standard text or professional periodical that indicate a longer period. Under the Federal Rules, the "learned" treatise or periodical may be used not only to challenge the expert's opinion, but also as substantive proof that the statement in the reference work is true.[26]

Cross-examination will also, in some cases, cover whether the expert relied on sufficient facts or data, and employed a reliable methodology in a reliable manner. For example, in a toxic tort case, where the expert relies on a study for his conclusion on causation, the expert can be asked about *other* contrary studies and be pressed to explain why he didn't read or rely on them. And if an expert testifies about handwriting identification, he can be questioned about the methodology of such identification—which is based on assumptions

---

[26]   *See* Fed. R. Evid. 803(18) and the discussion in Chapter VII.

(that all people have a unique way of writing and that nobody can write a signature that is identical to another person) that have not been validated.

§ 11.6 Scientific and Technical Evidence: A Sample

There are many occasions for the application of science (including social science) and other specialized disciplines, such as statistics, in the courtroom. Some of these applications involve principles and methodologies that are rigorous and precise, yielding results that are usually highly reliable. For example, blood testing, blood typing, and the application of genetic and DNA principles, if properly conducted, produce results that are highly refined and quite dependable. In contrast, handwriting analysis, ballistics testimony, hair identification, the identification and meaning of various kinds of syndromes (such as battered woman and rape trauma), and the psychology of eyewitness identification involve more speculative principles, greater subjectivity, and—though often admitted—rest on less certain footing.

In many of these latter situations, the problem is that experts overstate their conclusions—they express a confidence that is not supported by the methodology. For example, a ballistics expert who calls himself a "scientist" is overstating the support for his conclusion, because ballistics is not a scientific endeavor. And if such an expert says that his rate of error is "zero" or that the bullet he tested "matches" the bullet found at the scene, these are overstatements—because there *is* a rate of error based on subjective judgment, and because it has not been established that each gun makes a unique marking on a bullet, and so the expert cannot validly testify to a "match."[27]

Assuming the *topic* on which an expert will testify is appropriate, a trial judge must make four related inquiries when deciding whether to admit the testimony of an expert proffered to share her "scientific technical, or other specialized knowledge."[28] First, the judge must be satisfied that the witness has the necessary expertise; second, that the principles, data, scientific laws, or studies that underlie the expert's testimony are sound and that the expert

---

[27]   *See generally* National Research Council, Committee on Identifying the Needs of the Forensic Sciences Community, Strengthening Forensic Science in the United States: A Path Forward, 5–20 (2009); President's Council of Advisors on Science and Technology, *Forensic Science in Criminal Courts: Ensuring Scientific Validity of Feature Comparison Methods* (2016) (concluding that the only forensic technique supported by the scientific method is DNA identification).

[28]   Fed. R. Evid. 702.

has done a sufficient investigation; third, that the methodology or application of these principles is acceptable, and fourth, that the expert has reliably applied the methodology. Some examples of how courts treat certain types of expert testimony will now be discussed.

Polygraph Tests

Polygraph evidence has traditionally been held inadmissible because application of the *Frye* test for admitting scientific evidence has led to the conclusion that polygraph testing had not gained sufficient "standing and scientific recognition among physiological and psychological authorities."[29] Since the decision in *Frye*, a majority of states have followed the traditional practice and embraced the rule that polygraph evidence is per se inadmissible. With the passage of the Federal Rules of Evidence and the *Daubert* decision (holding that lack of general acceptance is not dispositive) courts have revisited the admissibility of polygraph evidence, but have usually come to the same conclusion—polygraph evidence is not sufficiently reliable to be admissible.

Polygraph, or "lie detector," tests are based on the premise that a lying subject's fear of detection sets in motion a series of involuntary physical responses that can be measured. Specifically, modern polygraph machines record a number of physical responses: galvanic skin responses, sweating of the palms, blood pressure, respiration, and sometimes, changes in the flow of blood to the tip of the index finger.[30] There are two main techniques used to elicit these involuntary responses: the "relevant-irrelevant" test and the more modern, control question technique. In the relevant-irrelevant test, questions of no moment (such as "Are you over 21?") are used to measure the subject's physiological state while telling the truth. The results from these questions are then compared to the subject's answers to relevant questions. If they match, the subject is telling the truth. In the control question technique, a general and vague control question is posed to the subject that usually deals with an illegal activity (such as "Have you ever stolen anything?"). Innocent subjects respond more fully and readily to these control questions than to relevant questions about the event in question; while the opposite is true for guilty subjects.

Critics of the polygraph test point out that it does not measure "fear of detection of lying" but rather it measures any form of anxiety.

---

[29]   *Frye v. United States*, 293 F. 1013 (D.C. Cir. 1923), which established the "general acceptance" test (*see* text at note 5) involved the admissibility of lie detector results derived from an early, less sophisticated polygraph machine.

[30]   Sheila K. Hyatt, *Developments in the Law of Scientific Evidence: The Admissibility of Polygraph Evidence*, 18 J. NAT'L ASS'N ADMIN. L. JUDGES 171, 179 (1998).

Thus, the subject may have feelings of anxiety unrelated to the truthfulness of a particular response. Additionally, a trained subject can be coaxed into simulating these feelings of anxiety in order to minimize variations or otherwise distort the results of the polygraph test.[31]

One appellate decision suggested that *Daubert* may have opened the door to polygraph evidence in criminal cases if it is offered by the defendant.[32] In this case, the Fifth Circuit found polygraph evidence reliable because there had been significant technological advances in polygraphic techniques. Research now shows that the tests are reliable 70–90% of the time (though these are lab studies as opposed to real-life testing), that the technique is subject to extensive publication and research, and that polygraphy is widely used by private employers and government agencies.[33] But most federal courts, even after *Daubert*, have found polygraph evidence to be unreliable because of the lack of standards, the ability of testees to beat the polygraph, and the inability to determine the rate of error.[34]

Another form of "truth-detection" has arisen, called the "functional MRI." The MRI measures brain waves and the theory is that if a person is lying there will be increased activity in certain parts of the brain. Courts at both the federal and state level have not admitted functional MRI testimony; they are concerned not only with the reliability of the method (no established rate of error, etc.), but also with the consequences to the jury's role in assessing the credibility of witnesses.

Syndrome Testimony: Battered Woman Syndrome

Testimony from psychologists and other social scientists is sometimes offered to explain personal behavior in specific situations by showing that people "typically" respond to a particular stimulus in a patterned and predictable manner. This type of evidence is usually referred to as "syndrome testimony."

Battered Woman Syndrome (BWS) was one of the first forms of syndrome testimony to gain evidentiary access in American courts. BWS describes the typical pattern of a woman's reaction to an

---

[31]   *See United States v. Cordoba*, 991 F.Supp. 1199, 1204 (C.D.Cal. 1998).

[32]   *United States v. Posado*, 57 F.3d 428 (5th Cir. 1995).

[33]   Id. at 433–36.

[34]   See the cases cited in SALTZBURG, MARTIN & CAPRA, FEDERAL RULES OF EVIDENCE MANUAL § 702.03[89] (12th ed. 2019). *See also United States v. Scheffer*, 523 U.S. 303 (1998) (upholding an evidence rule providing a per se exclusion of polygraph evidence against a constitutional challenge; noting that "there is simply no consensus that polygraph evidence is reliable," so the exclusionary rule was "a rational and proportional means of advancing the legitimate interest in barring unreliable evidence.").

abusive relationship. Experts commonly characterize BWS as consisting of three phases: the tension phase, the violent phase, and the quiet or loving phase.[35] The tension phase involves minor incidents of battering, eventually leading the victim to the belief that she deserves physical, sexual, or verbal abuse. The violent phase sets in as the abuser inflicts increasing, and perhaps more frequent injury. During this phase, the woman withdraws emotionally and refuses to seek help—her behavior in this phase is analogous to a disaster victim. In the final phase, the abuser becomes remorseful and makes promises not to inflict more injury. During this phase, the woman is induced to continue the relationship; however, her rapprochement is often the prelude for a cyclical repetition, characterized by more episodes and increased violence.[36]

Courts generally allow BWS evidence because it is reliable and its foundation rests upon considerable research.[37] The most common context for the introduction of BWS evidence is its admission to dispel commonly held notions concerning a woman's apparent failure to take protective steps. As one court put it, "[e]xpert testimony explaining why a person suffering from the battered woman syndrome would not leave her mate, would not inform police or friends, and would fear increased aggression against herself would be helpful to a jury in understanding a phenomenon not within the competence of an ordinary lay person."[38] However, courts have been wary of routinely extending the use of BWS testimony, and they continue to assess the relevance and reliability of this testimony on a case-by-case basis. For example, in one case the defense tried to use BWS to bolster a claim of duress, but the court held that the testimony was not helpful because the duress defense requires the application of an objective test, and the introduction of BWS evidence would change the inquiry into a subjective one.[39]

BWS is not the only syndrome testimony that frequently appears in cases. Two other diagnoses receiving court recognition are Child Sexual Abuse Accommodation Syndrome (CSAAS) and Rape Trauma Syndrome (RTS). Since the advent of *Daubert*, defendants have sought to introduce a variety of sociological and psychological

---

[35]　*See United States v. Brown*, 891 F.Supp. 1501, 1505 (D. Kan. 1995).

[36]　Id.

[37]　While BWS has generally gained scientific acceptance, it is not without criticism. For a detailed analysis on the flaws of BWS *see* Faigman & Wright, *Battered Woman Syndrome in the Age of Science*, 39 ARIZ. L. REV. 67 (1997).

[38]　*State v. Allery*, 101 Wash.2d 591, 682 P.2d 312, 316 (1984).

[39]　*United States v. Willis*, 38 F.3d 170, 177 (5th Cir. 1994). *But see, Dunn v. Roberts*, 963 F.2d 308, 313–14 (10th Cir. 1992) (accused suffering BWS was entitled to expert assistance in order to develop a duress defense).

evidence.[40] However, much of this proposed testimony does not have as firm a grounding in research and study as does CSAAS, RTS, and BWS. It seems likely, however, that as more social and psychological research becomes available, "syndrome testimony" will find increased receptivity in the courtroom.

A Note on Mathematical Evidence

Mathematical evidence can be useful in helping a trier of fact embrace or reject a factual specific proposition. Nonetheless, courts have struggled with the question of admissibility. The difficulty arises because there is often a risk that the trier will exaggerate the reliability of mathematical proof. Furthermore, the jury might fail to appreciate fully the assumptions that underlie the application of a statistical or other mathematical formula. When correctly used in the proper context, though, the problems generally associated with mathematical evidence can often be minimized.

A basic, but sometimes useful mathematical principle is the "product rule." This rule involves assessing the separate probability (expressed as a fraction) of the occurrence of each of a number of independent events (or conditions) and then, because these events allegedly concurred, multiplying these individual probabilities. The product of these two or more probabilities represents the probability of the joint occurrence of these separate events or conditions. For example, suppose that a witness reported seeing an interracial couple drive away from the crime scene in a yellow car. Assume that the probability was 1 in 10 that any given car would be yellow and 1 in 500 that an interracial couple would be in the same car. The odds that such a couple would be in a yellow car would be 1 in 5,000 (1/10 × 1/500). This result suggests that the couple later apprehended—an African-American and a Caucasian occupying a yellow car—is the same couple that the witness saw earlier. The product rule indicates that there is a comparatively remote chance that the couple apprehended is another interracial couple in a yellow car that, by chance, happened to be in the same area.[41]

Close examination of this example, however, will reveal some of the problems that attach to probability evidence. The first difficulty is determining the separate probability of a particular component of the composite event. How is it known that 1 in 10 cars are yellow? And what is the geographic area for this figure? Perhaps there are

---

[40] See, e.g., State v. Foret, 628 So.2d 1116, 1128 (La. 1993) (court disallowed expert testimony that said the defendant's "personality profile" was inconsistent with that of a murderer because the proposed testimony was unreliable).

[41] See generally, People v. Collins, 68 Cal.2d 319, 66 Cal.Rptr. 497, 438 P.2d 33 (1968) (a leading case in the use—and misuse—of mathematical evidence).

more yellow cars in Southern California than in Northern California (or Montana). Even more difficult is determining the probability of an interracial couple occupying the same car. It is doubtful that a reliable statistic exists that would fairly represent this probability. Again, the geographic area in which to gather data on interracial couples in the same car would have to be defined. Moreover, how certain is it that the couple was actually interracial given that some individuals might not be readily classified and that some observations of individuals within a car might be fleeting? Without a reliable probability for the happening of each of the component events, the final product will not accurately reflect the actual chance of the joint occurrence.

The second difficulty is that the validity of the final product depends upon the independence of the separate events or characteristics. Suppose that the two characteristics to which a separate probability must be assigned are a male wearing a beard and a male wearing a mustache. Since many men with beards also have mustaches, these conditions are not independent of each other and, if treated as independent, would lead to faulty results.

While these problems are significant hurdles to the admission of simple probability evidence, they can sometimes be avoided. The probability of some independent events can be satisfactorily determined. In appropriate circumstances, courts have admitted statistical data that reveal the estimated probability of an event based on the joint occurrence of two (or more) events or conditions that comprise the principal event or condition.[42] For example, assume a company is sued under Title VII for promoting men over equally qualified women. The company defends on the ground that it could not have intended to discriminate because it used a procedure of "blind" promotion—the names of all qualified individuals were put into a hat and the CEO picked out of the hat. Assume further that the number of qualified men and women were equal, and the company made 100 promotion decisions—all of them men. The plaintiffs would be allowed to call an expert to testify to the unlikelihood that 100 blind drawings would turn out to be men. (A very small probability).

A more sophisticated form of mathematical evidence involves the application of Bayes' Theorem.[43] The purpose of Bayes' Theorem

---

[42] See *Rachals v. State*, 184 Ga.App. 420, 361 S.E.2d 671 (1987) (probability of large number of cardiac arrests occurring by chance during defendant-nurse's duty hours).

[43] The formula can be expressed as follows:

$O(G \mid E) = (P(E \mid G)/P(E \mid \text{not } G)) \times O(G)$

is to reduce to mathematical terms the final probative effect when *new* evidence is added to *pre-existing* evidence. The resulting probability, expressed as a percentage, represents the "odds" that a specified conclusion is true, after the new evidence is considered in light of the pre-existing evidence.[44] Suppose, for example, that in a criminal trial a rational factfinder believes, on the basis of the evidence already admitted, that the odds that the defendant is guilty are 50%. Subsequently, additional evidence is produced showing that the perpetrator of the crime has brown hair. Assume 50% of the population has brown hair and so does the defendant. If the defendant did commit the crime, the probability that the perpetrator's hair would be brown is 100%. The probability of brown hair if someone else committed the crime is 50%. If Bayes' Theorem is applied to these percentages, the result is 67%. This means that based on this new evidence, a *rational* factfinder should now believe that the odds that the defendant is guilty are 67%.

The application of Bayes' Theorem presents at least two problems. The first is determining the probabilities associated with the pre-existing evidence, and the second is finding an accurate and helpful way to communicate the Bayes' Theorem results, especially in a jury trial. The first problem is shown in the example above where we assumed (as does Bayes' Theorem) that the factfinder initially believed that the odds that the defendant was guilty were 50%. This is just an assigned estimate based upon the assumed evaluation by the trier of the evidence already before it (the "pre-existing" evidence). It's a fake number. Mathematicians customarily assign the arbitrary figure of 50% to the pre-existing evidence because it is deemed a neutral figure that does not favor either party. The problem is that it is abstractly and arbitrarily derived and has no relationship to the actual evidence in the case or, more importantly, to that particular trier's belief in the reliability of that pre-existing evidence. Thus, the normal role of the factfinder, to evaluate and weigh the pre-existing evidence, is ignored. As to the second problem, it is easy to see how Bayes' Theorem can mislead a jury. Frequently, the effect of the "new evidence," when expressed mathematically, is dramatic. Furthermore, there is a supposed certainty to a mathematical result that can be misleading—the result is no better than its arithmetic

---

This equation says that the odds that a defendant is guilty (G) taking into account newly introduced evidence (| E) equals the probability that the evidence would be presented to the jury if the defendant is found guilty, divided by the probability that the same evidence would be presented to the jury if the defendant is found not guilty, times the prior odds of the defendant's guilt. The prior odds are the odds that the defendant was guilty if the new evidence had not been introduced.

[44]   Most of the decided cases consider the application of the Theorem to paternity cases in which blood test results are introduced. *See* 1 McCORMICK § 211, at 962–68.

input. For these reasons, Bayes' Theorem has not been widely used in the courts.

Another form of mathematical evidence—one that often finds favor with the courts—is regression analysis. Regression analysis can help determine if a postulated relationship exists between two events or characteristics and what the strength of that relationship is. Regression analysis, however, does not, by itself, explain causation; it just reveals the correlation between the events. That is, it is possible to falsely conclude that A caused B, simply on the ground that A is associated with B.

The mechanics of regression analysis, to which we now turn, can be illustrated through an example. Suppose you postulated that the more apples you ate the better your vision would be. To test this hypothesis, you asked 100 people how many apples they ate a week and the condition of their eyesight (e.g. 20/40). You could plot this information on a graph, with the number of apples eaten on the X-axis (the independent variable) and eyesight figures on the Y-axis (the dependent variable). By so doing, you could determine whether there is a correlation between the two. If more apples ingested does correlate to better eyesight, the graph would appear as an upward curving line.

This illustration, of course, is a quite simple example. Often, many more variables are included in the analysis. Regression analysis has been received in evidence by courts to illustrate a variety of relationships. In one case, for instance, regression analysis was used to show the relationship between major league baseball players' contract value, the players' game statistics, and their salary level.[45] In other cases, regression analysis is used to determine the damages suffered by a defendant's wrong (as a way of excluding alternative causes for the damage).

One problem with regression analysis is that the expert selects the variables to be included in the analysis. By adding or subtracting a variable, an expert can greatly alter the results of the analysis. Thus, the expert may be engaged in a process of "torturing the data until they confess." That is a concern that the gatekeeper will have to assess at a *Daubert* hearing. Another problem is that the expert may have to depend on others to determine whether an item is classified one way or another—for example, in a price fixing case an expert may use as two of the variables "urban" and "rural" to identify the geographic-based data. The expert may have no expertise in distinguishing various towns and cities and appropriately labeling

---

[45]   *Selig v. United States*, 565 F.Supp. 524, 537–38 (E.D.Wis. 1983).

them. Thus, the expert may rely upon someone who claims this expertise—e.g., a state contracting officer. Whether the expert has improperly added or ignored a variable is a Rule 702 gatekeeper question, because it goes to whether the regression methodology was reliably applied. Whether the expert has properly relied upon third persons is a Rule 703 question. If a motion to exclude a regression analysis is made, the trial judge will answer both questions when they are properly raised.

Chapter XII

BURDENS AND PRESUMPTIONS

Table of Sections

---

§ 12.1   Burdens of Persuasion and Production

In an adversarial system, the burden is upon each of the opposing parties to gather evidence, present it at trial, and to attempt to persuade the trier of fact of its efficacy. The responsibility for dispute resolution lies in the hands of neutral participants—the judge and jury. In a jury trial, the judge instructs or "charges" the jurors concerning the elements of a claim or defense and directs them, first, to ascertain the historical (adjudicative) facts from the evidence, and, then, by applying the law as described in the charge, to determine whether the claim or defense is established. For example, the judge may instruct the jury that slander consists of a defamatory statement [which would be further defined], that was communicated or "published" to one other than the person allegedly defamed, (the plaintiff), and that caused the plaintiff to sustain monetary damage or harm to reputation. Depending upon what defenses are asserted, the judge also may instruct the jury, for example, that if it finds that the statement is true or that it is privileged [which would be further explained], there is no liability. Of course, in a nonjury trial, the judge alone determines the historical facts and applies the governing legal principles—that is, she alone determines the existence or nonexistence of the elements.

In both judge and jury trials, there is a need to specify the consequences of the trier's determination that all (or alternatively only some) of the elements of a claim or defense are satisfactorily proved. This specification takes the form of allocating to the parties their respective obligations with regard to proving the elements of a claim or defense. Thus, in a civil trial for slander the judge should make it clear to the jurors that the plaintiff, if he is to recover, must convince them of the existence of all of the contested elements of slander: for example, the defamatory statement, its publication, and the resulting damage or harm. The assertion of certain defenses (called "affirmative" defenses) requires additional instructions that make it clear that as to these defenses the defendant has the responsibility of proof. If, for example, the defendant pleads the affirmative defense of truth, the judge will charge the jury that *if the defendant* convinces them that the defamatory statement is true, he is not liable.

This allocation of the responsibility for proof is not made on an ad hoc basis, but in accordance with precedent or statutory provisions. In most instances, especially in civil cases, a party is obligated to *plead* those elements for which he bears the responsibility of proof. A number of considerations influence the rules allocating the burden of proof, such as which party seeks to have the court alter the status quo, whether one party alleges an event that appears improbable, whether any social or public policy militates for or against recovery, and whether certain evidence is more readily available to one party than to the other.

It is no simple matter to predict which of these factors may be dominant, but it is relatively easy to determine from statute or precedent the allocative rules of a particular jurisdiction. The rules loosely are spoken of as governing the "burden of proof"; the preferred and more precise phrase is "burden of persuasion" (or, alternatively, "the risk of nonpersuasion"), because it connotes that the party with the responsibility for particular elements has the burden of persuading (or bears the risk of not persuading) the trier that each of these particular elements exists.[1] The burdened party must persuade the trier of the existence of these elements according to a standard or degree of certainty mandated by the type of proceeding: in a criminal trial, the government must prove the elements of an offense beyond a reasonable doubt; in a typical civil case, a party must prove the

---

[1] The phrase "burden of proof" often has been used to refer to two separate and distinct responsibilities of the parties: the "burden of persuasion" and the "burden of production." These two burdens typically fall upon the party with the burden of pleading her claim or, in the case of the defendant, counterclaim or affirmative defense. It is important to stress that, as noted in the text above, the "burden of producing evidence" refers to the obligation of producing sufficient evidence for the trier of fact to find each contested element that is necessary to sustain a claim, counterclaim, or affirmative defense. The "burden of persuasion" refers to a party's obligation to persuade the trier of fact that it has met whatever standard of persuasion is required of it.

elements of his claim by a preponderance of the evidence (sometimes expressed by the phrases "greater weight of the evidence" or "more probable than not").[2] There also are occasional intermediate standards, the most common of which is "clear and convincing" proof, that apply in particular kinds of civil cases or to particular elements within them. For example, when a party claims that his opponent engaged in fraudulent conduct, he may be required to prove the elements of fraud by clear and convincing evidence.

These standards are intended to indicate the convincing force of the evidence required to meet the burden of persuasion, not quantitatively to measure the evidence. A defendant who presents five witnesses will not always prevail over a plaintiff who presents only one. What is important is the factfinder's belief in the existence or nonexistence of the disputed factual elements. Believability is not necessarily associated with the number of witnesses or quantity of evidence presented.

The diagrammatic framework that we will examine shortly illustrates an allocation of the burdens of persuasion to the respective parties for the various factual elements of the foregoing defamation case. To establish the framework for a particular case, one must know or assume the elements of the claims or defenses asserted. Here, assume the plaintiff must plead and prove three elements by a preponderance of the evidence: the existence of the defamatory statement [A], the communication or publication to a third party [B], and the resulting damage (or harm) [C]. Assume that the defendant, first, denies that he made the statement and second, pleads the affirmative defense that the alleged defamatory statement is true. As to this and other affirmative defenses (such as contributory negligence or assumption of risk), the defendant normally bears the

---

[2]   In criminal cases, an accused may be assigned the burden of persuading the trier of the existence of certain affirmative defenses. *See Patterson v. New York*, 432 U.S. 197, 206 (1977). However, there are some limits upon the state's power to allocate a burden of persuasion to the accused. *In re Winship*, 397 U.S. 358, 364 (1970), held that the prosecutor was obliged to prove beyond a reasonable doubt each element or fact necessary to constitute the crime charged. *Winship*, as applied in *Mullaney v. Wilbur*, 421 U.S. 684, 700–01 (1975), was construed to prohibit Maine from assigning to the accused the burden of proving provocation. The case turned, however, on the fact that under Maine law provocation was classified as simply a means of disproving "malice aforethought—an essential element of the offense charged". *See Patterson*, 432 U.S. at 215–16. Thus, a state retains considerable latitude to place upon the accused the burden of persuasion for specified defenses. However, care must be taken to define the defense (or the criminal offense itself) so that the defense assigned to the accused does not simply negate or rebut an essential element of the crime charged, but rather consists of new facts that negate or reduce criminal responsibility. This distinction has been the subject of considerable debate. For a discussion of the complicated law on shifting burdens of production and persuasion in criminal cases, *see* SALTZBURG & CAPRA, AMERICAN CRIMINAL PROCEDURE 1107–42 (11th ed. 2018). We also discuss *Mullaney* and some burden shifting issues that arise in conjunction with presumptions in the last section of this Chapter.

burden of persuasion which, in the case before us, means that he must convince the factfinder that the statement is true. Thus, each party has an affirmative responsibility of proof, although the defendant will prevail if *either* the plaintiff fails to persuade the trier of the existence of elements A, B, or C *or* the defendant does persuade the trier that the alleged statement is true (element D).

Because the jury resolves only those questions that reasonably can be disputed, the plaintiff, as a first step, must offer (*evidence* sufficient to allow jury consideration of the existence of each element (this is his "burden of production"). That evidence must be at least adequate to permit a reasonable jury, viewing the evidence most favorably to the plaintiff, to find that the existence of the essential elements is more probable than their nonexistence—the "preponderance" standard. In the diagram below, the evidence at a minimum must justify the jury resolution signified by Block II. If evidence pertaining to the disputed elements is insufficient to raise a jury question (that is, insufficient to move all disputed elements in the plaintiff's case to Block II), the judge, on proper motion, will direct a verdict against the plaintiff ("grant a judgment as a matter of law") on the ground that he failed to produce sufficient evidence to support his case. Put otherwise, if plaintiff's evidence has failed to create a *reasonable* dispute as to one or more disputed elements, the case is resolved by the judge (Block I).

Plaintiff's Elements	Existence of Element Reasonably Disputable	Defendant's Element
I.	II.	III.
[Judge Resolution in Favor of D]	[Jury Resolution Based on the Evidence]	[Judge Resolution in Favor of P]
A (defamatory statement)		
B (publication)		
C (damage or harm)		
		D (truth)

Thus, ultimately to meet his burden of persuasion, the plaintiff must first satisfy the essential requirement of producing evidence sufficient to move all the elements necessary to his recovery from Block I (resolution by the judge) to Block II (resolution by the jury). Unless his opponent has conceded the existence of one or more elements (thereby rendering proof unnecessary),[3] the plaintiff begins this process in his case in chief by *producing* evidence to support each element. (In other words, he strives to meet his burden of production).

---

[3]   The element might be conceded, for example, in the pleadings, by stipulation, or by an admission made during discovery. Furthermore, if the facts constituting a particular element were judicially noticed, no production of evidence would be necessary. Fed. R. Evid. 201.

By meeting the immediate responsibility imposed by the burden of production, the plaintiff avoids a directed verdict (often called, "judgment as a matter of law")[4] and moves the dispute at least as far as Block II. In short, he paves the way toward meeting his second and greater burden, that of persuasion.

Of course, the plaintiff, if he can, will present evidence so convincing on one or more elements that no reasonable jury could find the nonexistence of the element(s). Absent persuasive rebuttal evidence by the defendant as to those elements thus firmly established, there would be a resolution by the judge (Block III) *in favor* of the plaintiff. The judge either would impose a judgment for the plaintiff (if all elements indisputably were present) or would take from jury consideration, through a peremptory instruction, those elements that were proven indisputably. If the plaintiff, during his case in chief, were able to produce evidence of such convincing force that the existence of all the necessary elements was indisputable, the state of the evidence would be reflected as follows:

Plaintiffs Elements	Existence of Element Reasonably Disputable	Defendant's Element
I.	II.	III.
[Judge Resolution]	[Jury Resolution]	[Judge Resolution]
A (defamatory statement)	—	————————→ A
B (publication)		————————→ B
C (damage or harm)		————————→ C
		D (truth)

[handwritten margin note: PLAINTFF GOES → then DEF GOES]

Before the judge resolves the presence of any or all elements in plaintiff's favor, however, he must give the defendant the opportunity to rebut plaintiff's evidence. The depicted state of the evidence, therefore, requires that the defendant take steps toward rebuttal or else face a judge-imposed outcome. The burden of *producing evidence now has shifted to the defendant,* although the burden of persuasion has remained fixed upon the plaintiff. Because the plaintiff must show the existence of all three elements in order to recover, the defendant can avoid a directed verdict (that is, he can meet the shifted burden of production) by rebutting at least one element so that he raises a jury question as to that element.[5] The defendant's "evidence" might be developed during cross-examination of witnesses produced by the plaintiff. The fact that the plaintiff calls witnesses

---

[4]   This is the terminology of the Federal Rules of Civil Procedure. *See* Fed. R. Civ. Proc. 50.

[5]   As to those elements not rebutted (i.e., not moved out of Block III by the defendant), the judge will give a peremptory instruction that these elements shall be taken as established.

does not necessarily mean that their testimony must be believed by the jury.

Ideally, after the plaintiff offers sufficient evidence to meet the burden of production, the defendant strives to present evidence that is so much stronger than the plaintiff's that one or more elements would be resolved in his favor by the judge (Block I of diagram), thus entitling *him* to a directed verdict. If the defendant were thus successful, the burden of production on the element(s) he was able to move to Block I would shift to the plaintiff, who would attempt to produce sufficient rebuttal evidence to move the issue of the existence of the element(s) back into Block II. As a practical matter, however, multiple shifts in the burden of production are unusual because it is not often that the state of the evidence fluctuates back and forth between the extremes represented by Blocks I and III. Furthermore, at the close of the evidence, it is frequently the jury, as opposed to the judge, that determines whether an element (that has not been conceded) exists. Often, the conflicting evidence results in a pattern (Block II) that justifies a reasonable jury in finding for either party.

The defendant, of course, is not limited to evidence that negates the plaintiff's evidence concerning elements A, B, and C. In the case before us, he also can avoid liability by establishing the affirmative defense of truth. To do so, he must first meet *his* burden of production by providing sufficient evidence of the truth of his statement to raise a jury question (that is, to move element D into Block II). If the evidence of truth were highly convincing (for example, the plaintiff had been convicted of the alleged misconduct described in the "defamatory" statement), thus moving the affirmative defense to Block I, the defendant could shift the burden of production for this element to the plaintiff. Note, however, that the burden of *persuasion* on the element of truth would not shift to the plaintiff, but would remain fixed upon the defendant, where it was originally assigned.

Various assumptions about the state of the evidence, including the allocation of the burdens of production and persuasion, can be depicted by using the basic diagram above. Suppose, for example, that *at the conclusion* of the case, the following state of the evidence exists:

Plaintiffs Elements	Existence of Element Reasonably Disputable	Defendant's Element
I.	II.	III.
[Judge Resolution]	[Jury Resolution]	[Judge Resolution]
A (defamatory statement)	———————————————————————→ A
B (publication)	———————————————————————→ B
C (damage or harm)	—————————→ C
	D ◄————————— D (truth)

The judge would instruct the jury that it shall take as an established fact that the defendant uttered (published) a slanderous statement to a third person (elements A and B). Jury questions exist, however, as to whether the plaintiff incurred damage or harm (element C) and as to whether the defendant's statement was true (element D). Regarding these reasonably disputed elements, both plaintiff and defendant have discharged their respective *burden of production* and each must now attempt to meet his *burden of persuasion*. Accordingly, it is necessary that the judge instruct the jury that the plaintiff has the burden of persuasion on the element of damage or harm and the defendant has the burden of persuasion on the element of truth. If the jury does not believe that damage or harm occurred, it should render a defendant's verdict. If it finds (by a preponderance of the evidence) that there was damage or harm and if it is not persuaded by the defendant that the statement was true, it will return a verdict for the plaintiff. On the other hand, if the jury is persuaded that the statement was true, it will return a defendant's verdict regardless of whether the plaintiff sustained damage or harm.

Suppose, however, that the jury is in a state of indecision or equipoise regarding the issue of damage (harm) or the issue of truth.[6] When the jury agrees that the probabilities of the existence or nonexistence of an element are equal, the *allocation of the burden of persuasion becomes decisive in determining who prevails.* Because the party to whom that burden is allocated has failed to convince the jury affirmatively of the existence of the element(s) for which she is responsible, she has not discharged his burden of persuasion and the jury, in obedience to proper instructions from the court, should find against her. Thus, if the jury concludes that it is equally likely that

---

[6]   The problem of a jury in a state of decisional balance can arise regarding the existence of any element of a claim or defense that, because of the state of the evidence, is the proper subject of jury resolution. As to any element in Block II, the jury may conclude that the probability of the existence of the element is equal to the probability of its nonexistence. Of course, if the judge is the factfinder—that is, there is no jury—the judge also resolves disputed issues of fact in accordance with the allocation of the burden of persuasion. Note again that in the illustration above, the defendant prevails if either the plaintiff fails to carry his burden of persuasion on all essential elements or the defendant carries his burden of persuasion on the element of truth.

plaintiff did or did not suffer damage (or harm) from the defamatory statement, the plaintiff loses. She has failed to meet her burden of persuading the jury that it is more likely than not (the "preponderance" standard) that she sustained a loss. Correspondingly, if the jury believes that the probabilities of the truth or falsity of the defamatory statement are equal, the defendant has failed to carry his burden of persuasion on the affirmative defense.

As noted earlier, the substantive law dictates what elements constitute a civil or criminal offense and what element(s) comprise an affirmative defense. It is usually easy to determine which party bears the ultimate responsibility of proving by the applicable standard the elements of a claim or defense. Whether a party who has met his burden of producing sufficient evidence (by moving his case to Block II) has also met his burden of persuasion depends simply upon whether the trier, at the conclusion of the case, is persuaded by the evidence favoring that party.

In a jury trial, the verdict will signify the trier's determination of whether or not a party has carried his burden. Of course, a general verdict ("We find for the defendant") may not be completely informative about which party discharged his burden of persuasion. If the defendant has denied the plaintiff's allegations supporting a recovery and also has offered an affirmative defense (e.g., truth), a verdict for the defendant can mean either that the plaintiff failed to carry her burden on her contested elements or that the defendant successfully carried his burden on the affirmative defense. In a trial to the judge, there is usually a more explicit indication in the record (often contained in an opinion, memorandum, or statement of findings and conclusions) disclosing the basis upon which a judgment is given.

The section that follows will explore the effects of a presumption upon the burden of persuasion and the burden of production. A true presumption always affects the burden of production, but in most jurisdictions, including the federal system, a presumption does not, generally speaking, reallocate the burden of persuasion. It remains where it was originally assigned.

§ 12.2 Presumptions: General Nature and Effect

A trial involves many instances in which the trier of fact makes a factual determination by a process of inference. The factfinder first finds the existence of a certain fact or set of facts and then infers the existence of a related fact or facts. Human experience yields countless situations in which one fact or group of facts, if believed to exist, can by the process of inferential reasoning lead to a related factual conclusion. For example, if there is evidence that a letter was addressed properly and thereafter stamped and posted, it may be inferred that the addressee received it. As further examples: if a vehicle is labeled with the name of a person or company, it may be inferred that the name is that of the owner; if a person cannot be found and neither family nor acquaintances have heard from him for many years, it may be inferred that he is dead. In each of these situations certain *basic* facts (proper mailing, name on vehicle, absence without word) support a finding of the *inferred* facts (receipt, ownership, death).

Although the number and variety of basic facts that can lead to inferential conclusions are countless, certain patterns, such as those in the foregoing illustrations, frequently recur. The courts and legislatures have singled out many sets of basic and inferred facts, such as mailing-receipt, absence-death, labeling-ownership, and have given to them the status of *presumptions*. In many of these recurring instances, there appears to be a strong likelihood of the validity of the presumed conclusion. In other instances, the probative force of the basic facts may not be very convincing, yet some policy rationale or procedural consideration (such as superior access to evidence) may make the presumed conclusion desirable. Thus, when an article is found to be damaged after having been transported by more than one carrier, a presumption is raised that the last carrier caused the damage. Here, as among several carriers, the probative value of the presumption that the damage occurred while the property was in the custody of the last carrier may appear weak. Absent any evidence that pinpoints the cause of damage, it could be argued that it is no more probable that damage occurred while the goods were on the terminal carrier than it is that the damage occurred on one of the prior carriers. On the other hand, if the goods already were damaged at the time the last carrier took custody, it perhaps is probable that the last carrier would have noted or recorded the damaged condition. More importantly, the presumption here serves as a procedural device that gives to the plaintiff (who in the setting just described is disadvantaged in ascertaining the facts) a fair chance to recover by tentatively placing the damage with the last carrier. (The last carrier is in a better position to prove that it did not damage the goods.)

Let us now distinguish a presumption from an inference. Although the language used with reference to presumptions is often indiscriminate, a genuine presumption is raised by a basic fact or facts that, when accepted as true by the trier, give rise to a *mandatory* inference, properly called a *presumed fact*. That is, *once the basic fact or facts are established,* the resulting presumed fact must be accepted by the trier *unless* it is rebutted by contravening evidence. An *inference* (if that term is properly applied) never has such a compulsory effect. The trier always is at liberty either to accept or reject an inferred fact. Note further that because a presumption founded on established facts creates a compulsory finding that remains obligatory until the presumed fact is rebutted, the raising of a presumption has a mandatory procedural effect: generally, it shifts to the opposing party at least the *burden of producing evidence*. This is not true of an inference, which results only in creating a jury question whether the inferred fact exists.

A simple example can help you understand the difference between a presumption and a permissible inference. Consider proof by a plaintiff that a letter to the defendant was addressed properly and thereafter stamped and posted. The plaintiff wants a jury to believe that the defendant actually received it. If there is no presumption applicable, the plaintiff may ask the jury to draw an inference of receipt based on its experience with the mails. But the jury is free to reject that inference. If, however, there is a presumption applicable to the mailing, the defendant must rebut the fact that the letter was received. Absent rebuttal evidence the judge will instruct the jury that if it believes that the letter was addressed properly and stamped and mailed, it *must* find that the defendant received the letter.

Although the terms "presumption" and "inference" as defined above have gained general usage, terminology in this area is not uniform. For example, judges and lawyers sometimes speak of "permissive presumptions" by which term they usually mean inferences. The cases also contain the term "presumption of law," which usually means a rebuttable presumption of the kind here called simply a presumption. A "conclusive presumption," often encountered in statutes, is not really a presumption at all, but rather is a rule of substantive law. This "presumption" declares that certain basic facts, once established, give rise to an *irrebuttable* conclusion. For example, it may be presumed conclusively that a child under the age of seven years (basic fact) cannot commit a felony (presumed fact). This rule, although stated in presumptive language, is merely a substantive principle that serious criminal responsibility may not be imposed upon one under the age of seven.

§ 12.3   Some Sample Presumptions

Although presumptions are found in all jurisdictions, what one jurisdiction considers a presumption, another may classify as an inference. Since there are dozens and dozens of presumptions, the illustrative list that follows is but a small sample.

Basic Fact(s)	Presumed Fact
1. Letter regularly addressed and mailed	Received by addressee
2. Vehicle lawfully stopped is struck in rear by second vehicle	Driver of second vehicle was negligent
3. Violent death from external means	Death was accidental (not a suicide)
4. Absent for 7 years without explanation or any communication with family or friends; inquiries unavailing	Absentee deceased
5. Will cannot be found	Revoked by testator
6. Employee in accident while driving vehicle owned by employer	Employee was acting within scope of employment
7. Goods delivered to bailee in good condition; damaged when returned	Bailee negligent
8. Goods damaged during transit provided by more than one carrier	Last carrier caused damage

There is a measure of probative force in each of the groupings above. Other considerations, however, including superior knowledge or easier access to the evidence (numbers 1, 2, 6, 7, 8) and policies favoring the settlement of estates (4, 5), the protection of survivors (3, 4), or the recovery of damages in cases of accident (2, 6), appear to be operative. The next section will examine the dispute over the power of a presumption. Does a presumption merely shift the burden of producing evidence, or does it shift the burden of persuasion?

§ 12.4 Presumptions: Impact upon Opponent and Effect of Rebuttal Evidence

There are two dominant views regarding the general effect of a presumption. The majority view, which was first associated with Professor James Bradley Thayer,[7] holds that when a presumption arises after the establishment of the basic fact(s), its only procedural effect is to shift the burden of producing evidence to the opponent. The opponent must meet the shifted burden of producing evidence,

---

[7]   JAMES THAYER, PRELIMINARY TREATISE ON EVIDENCE (1898). See especially pp. 314, 336–37.

but he does not bear the ultimate burden of convincing the trier of fact of the nonexistence of the presumed fact; rather, if the opponent produces enough contrary evidence to allow a reasonable person to believe that the presumed fact does not exist, the presumption "bursts"—meaning it drops out of the case, leaving the proponent with the burden of proving the fact. The Thayer "bursting bubble" view of presumptions is the default rule found in Federal Rule of Evidence 301. ("Default" because there are different (stronger) presumptions set forth in a number of federal statutes).

The second view, embraced by a minority of jurisdictions, holds that the procedural effect of establishing the basic facts is usually to shift the burden of persuasion. This latter position, often called the Morgan view because of its advocacy by the late Professor Edmund Morgan,[8] places great weight both on the probative link between basic and presumed facts and on the supposed utility of presumptions in advancing desirable social policy.

Professor Morgan's minority approach gives considerably greater effect to most presumptions: a shift in the burden of persuasion results in placing upon the opponent the burden of convincing the trier that the nonexistence of the presumed fact is more probable than its existence. Simply providing enough rebuttal evidence to allow a reasonable jury to find the nonexistence of the presumed fact is insufficient to negate the "Morgan" presumption because the burden of persuasion has shifted to the party against whom the presumption operates. This shift in the persuasion burden occurs if the existence of the basic facts is conceded; it also occurs if the proponent of the presumption convinces the judge that the basic facts cannot be reasonably disputed (i.e. no jury question exists). And, of course, as we have seen, the existence of the basic facts of a presumption is sometimes an issue for the jury. If so, the proponent attempts to carry his burden of convincing the trier of the truth of the basic facts so that the presumption will arise. If the presumption does arise, and the jurisdiction applies Morgan's approach, the burden of persuasion to show the nonexistence of the presumed fact will be cast upon the opponent of the presumption.[9] The rationale behind the Morgan view is that presumptions ought to mean something—if a presumption can be burst with a minimal showing of contrary evidence, then it is hardly worth having.

---

[8]   EDMUND MORGAN, SOME PROBLEMS OF PROOF UNDER THE ANGLO-AMERICAN SYSTEM OF LITIGATION, 74–81 (1956).

[9]   For a trenchant criticism of the Morgan approach, pointing out the confusion that can attend its implementation, see Ronald Lansing, *Enough is Enough: A Critique of the Morgan View of Rebuttable Presumptions in Civil Cases*, 62 OR. L. REV. 485 (1983).

It is important to recognize, however, that few if any jurisdictions invariably adhere either to the Thayer (majority) or Morgan (minority) view of the effect of presumptions. The marked tendency is to endorse generally one view or the other, but to make occasional departures in case law or statutes for selected presumptions. Thus, a jurisdiction adopting Thayer's position may nonetheless determine that, in the case of a certain presumption, special considerations warrant the greater presumptive effect of shifting the burden of persuasion. Some departures, often contained in statutory enactments, are likely to be found in every jurisdiction.

The debate over which general approach to presumptions—Thayer or Morgan—is the more desirable one is not likely to be decisively concluded. The difficulty is that such a variety of reasons underlie presumptions that a single approach to all presumptions seems destined to fail. Thus, the majority (Thayer) approach, which does not reassign the burden of persuasion, can be criticized when it is applied to certain presumptions—for example, those that are supported both by convincing probative force and strong policy grounds. Once the basic facts are established, the cogent considerations of policy and probability that were instrumental in the initial assignment of the burden of persuasion arguably support a reallocation of this burden. The argument for reassigning the burden of persuasion—that is, rejecting Thayer's view—can be advanced (and often is) when *either* probative force *or* policy considerations associated with a particular presumption appear quite strong. On the other hand, the minority (Morgan) view, that shifts the burden of persuasion, can be criticized when it is applied to some presumptions because its procedural effect on many routine presumptions might be greater than desirable.[10]

Thus, the continuing problem faced by legislatures and courts is whether to adopt, with some exceptions, the Thayer approach or the Morgan approach or, alternatively, to adopt an intermediate scheme that somewhat favors one view or the other but does not coincide with either. One scheme, for example, is to shift the burden of persuasion when there is a substantial probative relationship between the basic facts and the presumed fact. In the absence of such a nexus, a presumption shifts only the burden of production. Another approach, usually associated with the California Evidence Code, is to shift the burden of persuasion for those presumptions identified by the legislature or courts as based upon "public policy"; presumptions outside the public-policy category shift only the burden of producing evidence. Because many presumptions have at least some public

---

[10]   *See, e.g.*, Fed. R. Evid. 301, Comment from the Report No. 93–650 of the House Committee on the Judiciary.

policy underpinnings, the determination of which presumptions are within the persuasion-shifting category is not easy. Obviously, any dual approach to presumptions necessitates careful inquiry by student and practitioner as to the procedural effect assigned to a particular presumption.

Caution must be exercised even in a jurisdiction that purports to adhere to a single view of the effect of presumptions. As previously noted, several exceptions will usually be found; that is, some presumptions will be singled out by statute or judicial opinion for special treatment. (For example, the Supreme Court has held in securities cases that the presumption of investor reliance on a fraud on the market shifts the burden to the defendant to show by a preponderance of the evidence that the plaintiffs did not actually rely.[11]) The reasons for this departure from the normal scheme will vary, but factors (singly or in combination) such as policy concerns, fairness, or probative force may justify singling out certain presumptions for special treatment. For example, the forceful policy favoring the legitimacy of children, coupled with strong probability, gives a special strength to the presumption that a child born during a couple's marriage is the legitimate offspring of the husband, and not the child of another man (a presumption that once had considerable importance but has diminished with the use of DNA evidence). And the importance of transparency in the securities market, which underlies the fraud on the market theory of liability, justifies imposing the burden of proving lack of reliance on the defendant.

One must be alert for yet another variance. As noted below, even among those jurisdictions that adopt the general view of Professor Thayer (and thus to shift only the burden of production), there may be differences in the measure of rebuttal evidence that is ordinarily considered sufficient to negate the presumed fact. Fortunately, most jurisdictions that adhere to Thayer's view—including the Federal Rules of Evidence—also endorse his position concerning the measure of counter-evidence necessary to rebut the presumption. That position is that a presumption *disappears after the introduction of*

---

[11]   In *Goldman Sachs Group, Inc., v. Arkansas Teacher Retirement System,* 141 S.Ct. 1951 (2021), the Court considered the effect of the "fraud on the market" presumption of reliance on a misstatement, under which a plaintiff would not have to show individual reliance on the misstatement, but rather could rely on the presumption that investors rely on a functioning market. The defendants argued that this presumption could be "burst" by a minimal showing that the individual plaintiffs did not rely. But the Court held that the presumption shifted to defendants the burden of persuasion to prove a lack of price impact by a preponderance of the evidence. The Court reasoned that the benefit of the presumption, and the rationale of the presumption to protect investors, would be meaningless if it could be easily rebutted by some evidence of lack of reliance.

rebuttal evidence that is sufficiently probative to allow a reasonable trier to find the nonexistence of the presumed fact. In practical terms, this usually means that the opponent has produced evidence sufficient for the trier to find the opposite of the presumed fact—for example, to find the *nonreceipt* of a properly mailed letter.[12] Once adequate rebuttal evidence is presented, a true Thayer presumption *disappears from the case.* The trier ultimately decides the issue in question—the existence or nonexistence of the fact that was the subject of the presumption—just as if no presumption was ever raised. Under this pure Thayerian approach, the presumption is extinguished by the presentation of rebuttal evidence that the *judge* deems *sufficient* to support a finding that the presumed fact does not exist. It is of no consequence *to the disappearance of the presumption* that neither the judge nor the trier *believed* the counter-evidence. The judge simply determines whether the rebuttal evidence was sufficient to reasonably support a finding contrary to that expressed in the presumed fact. Of course, even if the presumption disappears, any remaining probative value that naturally links the basic fact to the presumed fact remains intact.

As previously suggested, it is difficult to support a single approach that applies to all presumptions. Thus, a flexible scheme that treats differently various presumptions within a jurisdiction can be appealing. Yet disparate approaches introduce further complexity and confusion to an area already cluttered with ambiguity and misunderstanding. Perhaps a practical compromise, admittedly imperfect, offers the best solution. As a starting point, there is much to be said for adopting a general approach that applies to all presumptions except those relatively few that for compelling reasons are singled out (presumably by legislative determination) for different treatment. This concession to uniformity avoids the difficulty of classifying a large number of presumptions into different procedural categories.

As a general approach, Thayer's position, which has been adopted by the Federal Rules of Evidence (Rule 301) and by a majority of states, suffers no greater disadvantages than the competing theories. It is true, as the critics point out, that Thayer's approach does not always give a sufficient effect to presumptions. As we have seen, an opponent need only present enough rebuttal evidence to permit a reasonable trier to find the nonexistence of the presumed fact. On the other hand, Thayer's view is easy to understand and administer. It avoids the problem of confusing juries

---

[12] The burden of presenting rebuttal evidence can be slight in some cases. For example, a defendant who takes the stand and swears "I never got the letter" ordinarily has offered sufficient rebuttal evidence.

by dividing the burden of persuasion (basic fact to proponent; presumed fact to opponent) on what is essentially a single factual issue—a division that is necessary under the Morgan view. You will see in the next Section just how confusing the jury instructions can be under the Morgan view.

Further, the disappearance of a Thayer presumption does not usually dissipate the force of the presumption altogether: because almost all presumptions are supported by a logical relationship between the basic and presumed fact,[13] the destruction of the presumption does not negate the residual probative force yielded by the basic facts. That is, the disappearance of a presumption only removes its compulsory effect; after a presumption vanishes, there still remains the inference that arises from the basic facts. And the judge may, in her discretion, instruct the jury concerning the existence of this residual inference. It seems especially desirable to give such an instruction in cases where either the probative relationship between the basic and presumed fact is very strong or the rebuttal evidence is barely sufficient to eliminate the presumption. Such a practice may represent the best compromise in an area marked by both intense disagreement and a host of practical difficulties.

§ 12.5   Presumptions: Instructing the Jury

In civil cases, under both the predominant Thayer view of presumptions and the minority Morgan view, it is not necessary to use the term "presumption" in instructing the jury. Avoiding this term is desirable because the jury may misunderstand a presumption's function and effect. Under Thayer's approach, if there is no rebuttal evidence and the existence of the basic fact is undisputed, the judge either directs a verdict (if the presumed fact is dispositive) or instructs the jury that it must consider the presumed fact as proven. In the latter instance, use of the term "presumption" is unnecessary. The judge simply describes the presumed fact: "You must find that the letter in question, written by *A* and addressed to *B*, was received." If the basic fact is contested, but there is no evidence rebutting the presumed fact,[14] it still is unnecessary to mention the word "presumption": the judge simply instructs the jury that "If from the evidence you believe that the letter in question was regularly

---

[13]   Even some presumptions commonly thought to originate only in procedural convenience or fairness (e.g., goods damaged during transit: damage caused by last carrier in the series) may be regarded as based upon logical inferences. *See In re Wood's Estate*, 374 Mich. 278, 132 N.W.2d 35, 42 (1965); *See* § 12.3.

[14]   As a practical matter, this is unlikely to occur because the opponent will probably also offer evidence rebutting the presumed fact. But it could occur (as, for example, where the addressee is not available as a witness) that there is no evidence available to rebut the presumed fact.

addressed and mailed, you must find that it was received." Finally, if there is sufficient rebuttal evidence directed at the presumed fact so as to entitle a reasonable jury to find the nonexistence of that fact, the presumption disappears from the case in a Thayer jurisdiction. In recognition of any residual inference, however, the judge, has discretion to instruct the jurors that if they conclude that the letter was properly addressed and mailed, they *may* find that it was received.[15]

In jurisdictions that hold that presumptions shift the burden of persuasion (Morgan's view), the jury also may receive the case without mention of the term "presumption." If, for example, the basic facts are admitted or indisputably established and the opponent of the presumption attacks only the presumed fact, the judge should instruct the jury [to continue the example above] that "you will find that the letter in question was received, unless from the evidence you believe its nonreceipt is more probable than its receipt." This instruction gives the maximum effect to the presumption by shifting the burden of persuasion on the issue of receipt to the party against whom the presumption operates. If the opponent attacks both the basic fact and the presumed fact, the judge should instruct "that if from the evidence you believe that the letter in question was accurately addressed and thereafter properly mailed, then you also must find that it was received, unless you believe that its nonreceipt is more probable than its receipt."[16]

ILLUSTRATIONS

Henry, aged 38, was a wealthy, but restless, husband and father. In April, 2013, he embarked on a fishing trip. The plan was, or so he told his wife and two children, to fly to Argentina, where he would meet an old friend. The two of them, with the help of a guide, would then spend two weeks fishing. But, alas, Henry did not appear at the designated meeting place—a hotel in Buenos Aires—although he was listed among the passengers on board a flight from Washington, D.C. to Buenos Aires. Nor did Henry return to his wife and family, or send them any word of his whereabouts.

Seven and a half years later (in October, 2020), his wife—or perhaps his widow—sued the Safeguard Insurance

---

[15]   The most appealing case for judicial comment on the residual inference is where there is a strong probative link between the basic fact(s) and the presumed fact.

[16]   If you find this instruction confusing (as most people untrained in presumptions do), imagine how confusing it must be for a jury that hears a set of instructions for the first time. The difficulty of instructions arising from the Morgan view is one reason why it is the minority view.

Co. to collect the face value ($2,000,000) of two insurance policies covering Henry's life. The defendant answered the wife's complaint with allegations denying that Henry was dead. At trial, the wife, who under the applicable law had the burden of establishing Henry's death, testified that neither she nor the children had heard from Henry for more than seven years. Nor had they been able to locate him. Other friends, relatives, and business associates gave similar testimony, either in person or by deposition. The law of the relevant jurisdiction establishes a presumption that a person who cannot be located and has not been heard from for a period of seven years is presumed dead.

(1) Assume that the defendant, Safeguard, offers no counter evidence, but simply argues that Henry's silence is insufficient proof of his death, especially as there have been no reports of his death, no circumstances suggesting an accident, and no evidence that his body has been found. Should the judge nonetheless direct a plaintiff's verdict (enter judgment for the wife as a matter of law)? If not, how should the judge instruct the jury?

Safeguard offers no rebuttal evidence. Thus, the basic fact appears to be established. If cross-examination had cast doubt on the basic fact (so that a reasonable jury could disbelieve it), then the jury would have to decide if the basic fact—that no one had heard from or seen Henry—was established. Assuming it is established, the judge would direct a verdict (enter judgment as a matter of law) for the wife. (Once it is established that no one had heard or seen from Henry, the presumption requires a conclusion that he is dead when there is no rebuttal evidence under both the Thayer and Morgan views.)

Suppose that Safeguard's cross-examination of the wife and her witnesses is sufficient to cause the judge to conclude that a jury could disbelieve them. Yet, there is no evidence offered by Safeguard that Harry actually is alive. What does the judge tell the jury? The judge would instruct that the wife has the burden of proving by a preponderance of the evidence that Harry has not been seen or heard from in seven years, and if the jury believes this to be true it must return a verdict for the wife. The instruction would be the same in Thayer and Morgan jurisdictions.

(2) Assume that Safeguard offers the testimony of Barry, the old friend that Henry was supposed to meet in Buenos Aires. Barry testifies that in March, 2017, he traveled to Budapest, Hungary, on business. (Budapest also happens to have been Henry's favorite city.) There, while

walking down one of the main streets, he is sure that he spotted Henry who was waiting to board a bus, about forty yards from Barry. When Barry called Henry's name, the latter turned his head toward Barry, pulled his fedora down over his forehead and quickly climbed aboard the bus, which pulled away from the curb. Should the judge direct a verdict? If not, how should she instruct the jury?

This is an unusual situation in which Safeguard's rebuttal evidence challenges both the basic fact and the presumed fact. Barry's testimony is sufficient to justify a jury in finding both that Harry has been seen and that Harry is alive. So what does the judge tell the jury? In a Thayer jurisdiction, the judge simply tells the jury that the burden is on the wife to prove by a preponderance of the evidence that Henry is dead; and the judge might add that if the jury believes that Harry has not been seen or heard from in seven years the jury *may* infer from this that he is dead.

In a Morgan jurisdiction, the wife has offered sufficient evidence to shift the burden of persuasion *if her evidence is believed*. But in this unusual situation, the jury cannot believe that no one has seen or heard from Harry in seven years if it believes Barry. So, while technically the burden shifts to Safeguard to prove by a preponderance of the evidence that Harry is alive if the jury believes that no one has seen or heard from Harry in seven years, the jury cannot believe this if it also believes Barry. Thus the judge might give the following jury instruction: [If you believe that it is more probable than not that no one has seen or heard from Harry for seven years, your verdict must be for the wife. Otherwise it must be for Safeguard. The logic behind this instruction is as follows: (1) The only evidence the wife has that Harry is dead is her claim that no one has seen or heard from him in seven years. (2) If the jury does not believe this, the burden does not shift to Safeguard, and the wife has no other evidence to prove that Harry is dead and therefore cannot meet the burden of persuasion which remains on her. (3) If the jury believes that she has proved the basic fact, it must disbelieve Barry, and there is no other evidence to prove that Harry is alive.

(3) Assume that Safeguard does not challenge the wife's evidence that no one has seen or heard from Harry in seven years, but Safeguard offers its own evidence that (a) Harry owed $1 million dollars in gambling debts to some very dangerous individuals at the time he disappeared, (b) Harry had a wealthy girlfriend who disappeared at the same time Harry did, and (c) earlier in his life when Harry was suspected of involvement in illegal gambling he disappeared for several years, was thought to be dead, and

reappeared to the surprise of many after the investigation ended.

Assume also that the judge determines that Safeguard's evidence is sufficient to prove a motive for Harry to be hiding out rather than to be dead and that this is sufficient rebuttal evidence.[17] What does the judge tell the jury? In a Thayer jurisdiction, the judge instructs the jury that the wife must prove it more likely than not that Harry is dead; and the judge may add that the if the jury finds that no one has heard or seen Harry for seven years it *may* infer that he is dead. In a Morgan jurisdiction, since Safeguard has conceded that no one has seen or heard from Harry in seven years, the judge will tell the jury that Safeguard must prove that it is more likely than not that Harry is alive.[18]

§ 12.6 Presumptions Under the Federal Rules of Evidence

Rules 301 and 302 of the Federal Rules of Evidence deal with presumptions. No provision is made for presumptions in criminal cases, largely because at the time of the passage of the Federal Rules these presumptions were being considered in connection with a revision of the federal criminal code (which was never enacted) and more importantly out of concern about the constitutionality of presumptions in criminal cases (discussed below). In addressing civil cases, the Federal Rules neither define nor enumerate presumptions, but only state their function and probative effect. In proceedings where federal substantive law governs the claim or defense, Rule 301 adopts the Thayer view, specifying that "the party against whom a presumption is directed has the burden of producing evidence to rebut the presumption. But this rule does not shift the burden of persuasion, which remains on the party who had it originally." Although Rule 301 does not expressly adopt Thayer's view of the measure of rebuttal evidence that is required to negate the presumption (evidence "sufficient" to permit a reasonable trier to find the nonexistence of the presumed fact), most courts and commentators have concluded that Rule 301 adopts the Thayer approach in its entirety.

---

[17]   There is reason to doubt whether this would qualify as "rebuttal" evidence, since it does not actually rebut the evidence that no one has heard from or seen Harry during the relevant seven year period.

[18]   If you wonder why this instruction is so clear as compared to others we have seen, it is because the basic fact is unchallenged. Instructions in Morgan jurisdictions become complicated when the party against whom a presumption operates challenges both the basic and the presumed facts. The complication is that the burden of persuasion does not shift until there is a determination that the basic fact has been proved, and the judge must explain this in jury instructions.

The Federal Rules also contain an accommodation to the varying state approaches to presumptions. Rule 302 specifies that in a civil case, "state law governs the effect of a presumption regarding a claim or defense for which state law supplies the rule of decision." Students of civil procedure will recognize that this accommodation accords with the principles and policy of *Erie Railroad Co. v. Tompkins.*[19] The Rule defers to state law only as to those presumed facts that constitute an element of a claim or defense; presumptions of lesser impact are governed by the Thayer approach of Federal Rule 301— even in diversity cases where state law is applicable.

Rule 301 does not, of course, mean that all civil presumptions arising under federal law are treated in accordance with the Thayer approach. Congress may enact a particular statutory presumption and specify its effect, for example, by stipulating that it will persist until rebutted by clear and convincing evidence[20] or that it will shift the burden of persuasion.[21] It should be noted that despite the passage of Rule 301, the federal courts have occasionally upheld the continuing validity of certain presumptions with early statutory or common law origins that, usually for compelling policy or probative reasons, have been consistently construed as shifting the burden of persuasion.[22]

§ 12.7 Conflicting Presumptions

It occasionally happens that evidence admitted in a case provides a foundation for establishing two sets of basic facts which then give rise to conflicting presumptions. For example, when there is evidence of a legal marriage between *H* and *W,* there often is a presumption that their marital status continues. Another presumption often arises when the basic fact of a ceremonial marriage between *H* and *W-2* is shown: any prior marriage is presumed to have been dissolved. In a case where evidence supporting both sets of basic facts is introduced, how is the court to handle the "conflicting presumptions"? It is obvious that both presumptions cannot operate with full force.

---

[19] 304 U.S. 64 (1938); *see Dick v. New York Life Ins. Co.,* 359 U.S. 437, 446 (1959). (*Erie* doctrine embraces presumptions).

[20] *See, e.g.,* 26 U.S.C.A. § 6653 (underpayment of tax treated as presumptively negligent unless taxpayer shows otherwise by clear and convincing evidence).

[21] *See Alabama By-Products Corp. v. Killingsworth,* 733 F.2d 1511, 1514–15 (11th Cir. 1984).

[22] *James v. River Parishes Co., Inc.,* 686 F.2d 1129, 1132–33 (5th Cir. 1982) (longstanding presumption of maritime common law that a vessel found adrift was operated negligently shifts the burden of persuasion; unaffected by Rule 301); *Plough, Inc. v. Mason & Dixon Lines,* 630 F.2d 468, 472 (6th Cir. 1980) (Rule 301 does not affect prior statutory presumption of the 1906 Carmack Amendment imposing on common carriers the burden of persuasion in rebutting the presumption of carrier liability).

One solution, favored by Thayer and adopted by many courts, is simply to ignore both presumptions. In essence, the presumptions negate each other. Thus, it is possible in the context of conflicting presumptions to give some effect to the presumption raised against the party who normally has the burden of persuasion: the opposing presumption can at least have the effect of negating his presumption and of forcing him to produce evidence of the fact (that would have been presumed) without the added force of a presumption. Permitting such an effect, that is, allowing the opposing presumption to dispel the presumption that favors the party with the burden of proof, reaches the result favored by Thayer. Both presumptions disappear from the case.

Those jurisdictions that do not routinely negate both presumptions usually inquire whether one of the two presumptions is supported by the greater weight of policy or probability, or perhaps both. If one of the presumptions is so supported to a greater extent than the other, it is given preference and the lesser presumption is ignored. Assuming the surviving presumption is in favor of the party with the burden of persuasion, the case goes forward with one operative presumption. In the example above, the presumption favoring the legality of the current marriage has strong support on both policy and probability grounds, and it would be preferred in many jurisdictions.

§ 12.8 Presumptions in Criminal Cases: Constitutional Problems

In criminal cases, special considerations limit the scope of allowable presumptions. A directed verdict against the accused is never permitted (due to the accused's constitutional right to a jury trial); further, a conviction must rest upon the trier's belief beyond a reasonable doubt that each element of the charged offense exists.[23]

In the discussion that follows, you should carefully distinguish between two types of presumptions. As used by the Supreme Court a "mandatory presumption" is one that, once the basic facts are shown, *requires* the factfinder to find the presumed fact *unless* the defendant introduces at least some contrary evidence; a "permissive presumption" (also called an inference) is one that permits but *never* requires the factfinder to infer the presumed fact from the basic facts.

In *Mullaney v. Wilbur*,[24] the Court held unconstitutional Maine's mandatory presumption that shifted to the accused the burden of proving provocation. The judge had instructed the jury that if they

---

[23]   *In re Winship*, 397 U.S. 358, 364 (1970).

[24]   421 U.S. 684 (1975).

found that the accused unlawfully and intentionally killed the victim, they should presume malice aforethought unless they were convinced by the accused by a preponderance of the evidence that he acted from sudden provocation. It was significant that under Maine law a showing of provocation was viewed as negating malice aforethought—an essential element of murder.[25] Thus, provocation can plausibly be distinguished from an affirmative defense as the latter does not negate an essential element of the prosecution's case, but rather introduces *new facts* that, if believed by the trier, relieves or reduces the defendant's criminal responsibility. In the Court's view, the effect of the presumption in *Mullaney* was to relieve the prosecution of the burden, imposed by the leading case of *In Re Winship*,[26] of proving malice aforethought (an element of the crime charged) beyond a reasonable doubt.

Mullaney, decided in 1975, was not the first case in which the Supreme Court invalidated a criminal presumption. However, the tenor of the Court's *Mullaney* opinion and its emphasis upon the state's inescapable duty to prove all elements of the crime charged raised the question whether a mandatory presumption could *ever* be used against an accused. As interpreted in later cases, *Mullaney* meant *at least* that a presumption may not, consistent with the requirements of due process, shift to the accused the burden of proof—even under a preponderance standard—with regard to an element of the crime. Beyond that, the decision was ambiguous. It was, of course, possible to read the *Mullaney* opinion narrowly: the presumption in that case operated to shift the burden of persuasion (not simply the burden of production); furthermore, there was not an especially strong probative nexus between the basic facts (illegal and intentional killing) and the presumed fact (malice aforethought). But a broad application of *Mullaney* could render unconstitutional any presumption that shifted a procedural burden (persuasion or production) to the accused. The precise effect of *Mullaney* still remains somewhat uncertain, but the overall picture, as developed in subsequent cases, is now relatively clear.

The Supreme Court has sometimes gauged the constitutional validity of a criminal presumption by assessing the probative nexus between the basic facts and the presumed facts while on other occasions, the Court has focused upon whether or not the presumption under review operates to relieve the prosecution of its burden of proving each element of the offense charged. The Court has

---

[25]   Id. at 686–87. *Patterson,* 432 U.S. at 215–16, upholding the constitutionality of an affirmative defense almost identical to the *Mullaney* presumption, distinguished *Mullaney* on this ground.

[26]   397 U.S. 358 (1970).

also been concerned with the actual effect of a presumption, as opposed to the formal or statutory effect. That is, when jury instructions might have led jurors to the belief that they were obligated to find a presumed fact, the Court has intervened. The focus is on the jury instructions, not on the statutory or judicial articulation of the presumption. The leading Supreme Court cases suggest that mandatory presumptions will be subjected to a very rigorous analysis, while permissive inferences will be evaluated under a more lenient standard that takes account of the factual context in which the presumption operates. A sample of leading cases follows.

In 1979 the Supreme Court considered the constitutionality of criminal permissive inferences. *County Court of Ulster County v. Allen*[27] involved the prosecution by New York authorities of four persons (three male adults and a female minor) for various offenses, including the illegal possession of handguns. A car occupied by the defendants was stopped for speeding. The investigating officer noticed that the open handbag of the sixteen-year-old passenger was in the front seat area, and he observed within it two large-caliber handguns. At trial, the prosecutor relied upon a statutory "presumption" that *allowed an inference* of illegal possession by all persons occupying a vehicle upon a showing of the basic fact that a firearm, not on the person of any particular occupant, was within the automobile. The trial judge instructed the jury that it was permissible to infer possession by all of the defendants from their presence in the vehicle containing the handguns, but that such an inference was not mandatory; it could be ignored even if the defendants produced no rebuttal evidence. It was thus clear that, in the terminology used by the Supreme Court, the inference was permissive, not mandatory.

The defense attacked the statute as so broad on its face that it failed to satisfy due process. By its terms, it was argued, it would sweep within the presumption (1) occupants who may not know that the vehicle in which they are riding contains a gun, and (2) persons who, even though aware of the gun, were not permitted access to it. Thus, the argument continued, the statutory provision, even if only creating a permissible inference, lacked the minimal probative force essential to its constitutionality.

The Court held that, as applied to the circumstances in *Allen*,[28] the inference of possession by all of the defendants was "entirely

---

[27]   442 U.S. 140 (1979).

[28]   The opinion emphasized that the defendants were not hitchhikers or casual passengers, the guns were in plain view, it was improbable that a sixteen-year-old was sole custodian of two large-caliber handguns, and circumstances suggested an inept attempt to conceal the weapons when the defendants' vehicle was stopped for speeding. *Allen*, 442 U.S. at 163–64.

rational"—that is, the inferred fact was "more likely than not to flow from the ... [basic facts]." It is not appropriate, held the Court, to require that a permissive inference meet a reasonable doubt standard: that more stringent measure of proof applies to the evidence as a whole and has no applicability to a permissive inference that constitutes only part of the proof.[29]

Ulster County thus teaches that permissive inferences are allowable if the basic facts, taken in the context of the other evidence in the case, would permit a jury to find the inferred fact more likely than not. In contrast, mandatory presumptions, bear upon the elements of an offense, shift an evidentiary obligation to the accused, and so come within the constitutional prohibition set out in *Ulster County* and other cases.

A consistent theme of the Supreme Court's cases is the important difference between a permissive inference and a mandatory presumption. And the Supreme Court has been concerned with the actual, not the formal or statutory effect of a presumption. A permissive inference, for example, is judged in the context of the surrounding evidence. Furthermore, the constitutionality of any inference or presumption is judged by the way it is actually communicated to the jury. As we shall see below, where the jury instructions might have led jurors to believe that they were *obliged* to find the presumed fact if the basic facts were established, that is the equivalent of a mandatory presumption that is barred because it imposes on the defendant's right to a jury trial. In other words, the Court looks to jury instructions rather than statutory or case law to determine the nature and probable effect of a presumption.

In *Sandstrom v. Montana*,[30] decided two weeks after the *Ulster County* case, the accused was charged with purposely or knowingly causing the victim's death, an offense that Montana denominated "deliberate homicide." The accused admitted the killing, but claimed that he did not act with the requisite purpose or knowledge and, therefore, was guilty of a lesser offense. At the conclusion of the evidence, the trial judge instructed the jury that "[t]he law presumes that a person intends the ordinary consequences of his voluntary acts." Under state law the intended effect of the *Sandstrom* presumption was to shift to the accused only the burden of producing some contrary evidence; the burden of persuasion remained with the prosecution. However, the Supreme Court concluded that there was a significant risk that the instruction given to the jury had been

---

[29] It would be a different matter if the permissively inferred fact were the *sole* basis for a finding of guilt, since a reasonable doubt standard would necessarily apply. Id. at 167.

[30] 442 U.S. 510 (1979).

misunderstood: the jurors might have thought that they were peremptorily directed to find the requisite intent or, at least, that they were directed by a mandatory presumption shifting the burden of persuasion to find intent unless the defendant proved the contrary. Under either of these possible constructions, the presumption had unconstitutional consequences. First, because the state is obliged to prove beyond a reasonable doubt *"every fact* necessary to constitute the crime . . . charged"[31] and because there is no doubt that intent is an essential element of "deliberate homicide," a *conclusive* (peremptory) presumption would be unconstitutional. According to the Court, such a presumption would have the untoward effects of lifting from the prosecution its assigned burden of proving intent and of abrogating the defendant's status of innocence until proven guilty of each element of the offense charged.[32] Second, constitutional infirmities would also result from a presumption that shifted to the accused the burden of persuasion pertaining to the requisite state of mind. When the state proved the basic fact of homicide—a fact that did not itself establish that the killing was knowing or purposeful— the jury might erroneously have presumed the element of intent unless persuaded otherwise by the accused.

In the 1985 case of *Francis v. Franklin,*[33] the Court again condemned a jury instruction that embodied a presumption. The *Francis* instruction, unlike the instruction that was invalidated in *Sandstrom,* posed no risk that the jury might have construed the presumption in question as preemptive. Nonetheless, the Court ruled that there was a reasonable possibility that the jury had interpreted the trial court's instruction as shifting the burden of persuasion on the essential element of intent, in violation of *Mullaney* and *Sandstrom.* The *Francis* Court expressly refused to rule on the constitutionality of presumptions that shift only the burden of production. But observe that if the production burden did shift and if a defendant failed to meet that burden, the prosecution is in fact relieved of its task of proving each element, even though technically there has been no shift in the burden of persuasion. There is an additional difficulty in cases where the defendant himself is the only person who can provide the rebuttal evidence; as a practical matter, he must testify even though he might prefer to exercise his Fifth Amendment right not to take the stand. It is thus highly likely that the Court's decisions, taken as a whole, invalidate *all* mandatory presumptions, except, perhaps, those mandatory presumptions addressed to a minor point or those that have such a strong probative

---

[31] *In re Winship,* 397 U.S. 358, 364 (1970).

[32] *Sandstrom,* 442 U.S. at 521–23.

[33] 471 U.S. 307 (1985).

link with the basic facts that the presumed fact *must* exist beyond any reasonable doubt. In any event, the Court is clear that there remains a significant difference between a mandatory presumption that shifts some burden to the accused and a permissive inference.

A legislature can probably achieve some of the same effects in criminal trials that the Court has seemingly condemned in its treatment of presumptions. Suppose that a statutory reform resulted in converting a fact formerly the subject of a presumption into one that constituted an affirmative defense in the sense that *additional facts* would excuse or reduce the offense. For example, suppose that the Maine legislature, confronted with the *Mullaney* ruling, redefined murder as simply unlawful and intentional killing (excising the "malice aforethought" element), and transformed lack of malice aforethought from its role as negating an essential element to an affirmative defense consisting of additional facts which, if proved, would reduce the grade of the crime to second degree murder.[34] Affirmative defenses, even those that call upon the accused to carry the burden of persuasion, are usually found constitutional. It will thus be seen that, despite the Supreme Court's rather stringent requirements surrounding presumptions, a sovereign is still permitted considerable latitude in allocating elements of an offense (or defense). First, it may take an element that could be used to define the crime (e.g., lack of provocation) and denominate it an affirmative defense (provocation justifying the act charged). Furthermore, the state apparently has rather broad authority to eliminate altogether one or, perhaps, more elements of an offense.[35] For example, the state might define a crime as the illegal entry [element 1] into a dwelling [element 2] in the nighttime [element 3] with the intent to commit a felony therein [element 4] or it might state the offense more broadly, for example, by including only elements 1 and 2, or some other combination of fewer than four.

There may be limits, however, to what a legislature can do. It is unclear if the Supreme Court would permit a radical departure from

---

[34]   The Supreme Court upheld a murder statute essentially identical to that described in the hypothetical above in *Patterson v. New York*, 432 U.S. 197 (1977).

[35]   For example, American legislatures have sometimes created strict liability offenses by eliminating the state's burden of establishing any *mens rea* on the part of the accused. *See* John Jeffries & Paul Stephan, *Defenses, Presumptions, and the Burden of Proof in Criminal Law*, 88 YALE L.J. 1325, 1373–76 (1979). The authors urge that legislatures should be free to employ any affirmative defenses, mandatory presumptions, or inferences, free of restrictive constructions by the courts, so long as the remaining elements of the offense are proven beyond a reasonable doubt and comprise a constitutionally adequate basis for the punishment contemplated. Id. at 1365. Thus, if a legislature could constitutionally (i.e., consistent with principles of substantive due process and proportionality) define a felony of illegal entry without including element (3) (see text above), then courts should not concern themselves with whether element (3) is cast as a presumption or an affirmative defense.

common law principles and permit a legislature to define crimes with extremely broad definitions and require a defendant to prove most facts that typically distinguished greater from lesser offenses.[36]

In light of the ability of the state to avoid some and perhaps much of the impact of the Supreme Court's decisions restricting presumptions, it is not clear why the Court has insisted upon such strict constitutional requirements. Perhaps the answer lies in the Court's view of the jury's role, especially in criminal cases. That role is not, of course, one of simply finding facts by relying upon credible evidence and drawing rational inferences. The jury's historic protective role—its interposition between the power of the state and the individual accused—carries with it the unfettered right of acquittal. Presumptions, created by the state and administered by an authoritative state official, may have undue influence and effect on the jury. Thus, while the Court generally will allow the state legislature to redefine a crime or allocate to the defendant an affirmative defense, a majority of the Justices are uneasy with any procedure that seems to slant the trial court's fact-finding process against the accused. For this reason, mandatory presumptions are particularly suspect and are unlikely to survive constitutional challenge.[37]

---

[36] *See* Stephen A. Saltzburg, *Burdens of Persuasion in Criminal Cases: Harmonizing the Views of the Justices*, 20 AMERICAN CRIMINAL LAW REVIEW 393–421 (1983).

[37] *See, e.g., Government of Virgin Islands v. Parilla*, 7 F.3d 1097 (3d Cir. 1993) (statute criminalizing maiming, which provided that the infliction of serious injury is presumptive evidence of intent, constitutes an impermissible mandatory presumption, invalid on its face).

The difficulty of clearly instructing a lay jury about the nature and effect of a presumption may also help explain the Supreme Court's hostility toward presumptions in criminal cases.

Chapter XIII

THE BEST EVIDENCE RULE

(PROVING THE CONTENT OF WRITINGS, RECORDINGS, AND PHOTOGRAPHS)

Table of Sections

§ 13.1   In General: The Rule and Its Purpose

The "Best Evidence Rule" is something of a misnomer: parties are generally free to prove propositions with whatever relevant evidence they want, subject to any applicable exclusionary rules. When making choices among relevant items of evidence to prove a proposition, self-interested parties usually balance considerations of cost and persuasiveness. In other words, there is no general requirement that parties produce the "best" or most probative evidence of a proposition—though they often find it advantageous to do so. But such a requirement does exist when proving the contents of a document or certain other recordings. *Rule 1002* provides as follows:

Requirement of the Original

An original writing, recording, or photograph is required in order to prove its content unless these rules or a federal statute provides otherwise.

At common law, the original was preferred because its use eliminated the risk of mistranscriptions that could arise in a copy. It may now be asked whether there is any longer much need for the Best Evidence Rule, given the reliability of modern means of reproduction. Because of technological accuracy, it is untenable to base one's choice between the original and a copy (as opposed to a choice between the original and verbal testimony) on the ground that the copy lacks reliability because it more likely contains accidental inaccuracies or omissions. Recognizing the accuracy of most reproductions, the drafters, in Federal Rule 1003, permit the admission of a reliable "duplicate" in lieu of the original unless the authenticity of the original is in question, or unfairness would result.[1] The term "duplicate" encompasses photocopies, electronic re-recordings, chemical reproductions, and other reliable means of making accurate copies.[2]

Today, the principal impact of the Best Evidence Rule is to exclude *oral testimony* about the contents of a document or other recording, not to exclude duplicates. Insisting on an "original" instead of a "duplicate" seldom results in more accurate factfinding, with the exceptions, already noted, embodied in Federal Rule 1003. The same cannot be said of preferring a writing, recording, or photograph, whether original or duplicate, to oral testimony describing or reciting its contents.[3] In short, the Best Evidence Rule still serves its original purpose of enhancing accurate factfinding, but grants more flexibility to litigants and judges in light of modern technology.

§ 13.2 Application: Proving the Contents of a Writing

Before determining if the Best Evidence Rule is satisfied, you must determine if it applies at all. Recall that the rule applies only when a writing, recording, or photograph is offered "to prove its content." Whether an item is a "writing" can be disputed at the margins—e.g., does a product's serial number or a car's odometer reading qualify?—but few unclear applications actually arise. In theory, any inscribed chattel can constitute a writing, but courts have exercised discretion under Rule 1001(a) in deciding if such items should be treated as writings or ordinary chattels. If application of the Best Evidence Rule to a chattel would not serve the Rule's purposes, the court need not apply it.[4] Moreover, an inscribed chattel is sometimes found to be a writing, yet the inscription is far removed from the controlling issues of the case and thus is exempted from the requirements of the Best Evidence doctrine by Rule 1004(d). That

---

[1]   Unfairness might result, for example, where only part of the original is reproduced and the uncopied section modifies the copied section, or where the duplicate is otherwise misleading. Unfairness would also result in the unlikely event that there was genuine concern as to whether the duplicate faithfully reproduced the original.

[2]   Specifically, a "duplicate" is "a counterpart produced by a mechanical, photographic, chemical, electronic, or other equivalent process or technique that accurately reproduces the original." Fed. R. Evid. 1001(e).

[3]   Of course, a recording is not always more reliable evidence of a fact to which it is addressed than is oral testimony. The document is only clearly preferable when used solely as evidence of its own contents.

[4]   *See United States v. Duffy*, 454 F.2d 809, 812 (5th Cir. 1972) (oral testimony about laundry mark on defendant's shirt proper).

subsection states that if a writing, recording, or photograph "is not closely related to a controlling issue" it is collateral and the Best Evidence Rule is inapplicable.

Subtle issues sometimes arise in determining whether a writing is being offered to prove its content—an essential element for the application of the Best Evidence Rule. This question can arise in a number of contexts. Sometimes proof of a writing's content is required by the substantive law, as when its content is the element of a charge, claim or defense. The most obvious example is an action for libel. Furthermore, the substantive law sometimes prescribes that a writing subsumes, so to speak, any prior events; in other words, the law requires that the transaction in dispute be evidenced by a writing. A deed, a will, certain contracts, or a judicial judgment are transactions the law regards as essentially written, and the proponent must make his proof by the writing if it is available. In these instances, the proponent does not have the option of simply proving the oral declarations that preceded the written instrument— the oral declarations are "merged" into it.

Note, however, that often a writing or recording merely recites or records a perceivable event or condition such as a marriage (marriage certificate), payment of money (receipt), utterance of certain words (transcript) or an accident (videotape). Here, the proponent wishing to prove the underlying event may proceed in either of two ways: (1) offer the testimony of an observer, or (2) offer a writing, recording, or photograph that records or recites the event. The first approach does not involve the Best Evidence Rule because the proponent is not attempting to prove the terms of the writing or recording,[5] but merely is presenting evidence of an event perceived by a witness with first-hand knowledge. It makes no difference that the occurrence of the event is recited in a subsequent writing or recording, because the recording does not, so far as legal rules of proof are concerned, "erase" or supplant the preceding event.

§ 13.3 Application: Identifying an "Original"

Once it is clear that the Best Evidence Rule applies (i.e. the evidence is a writing, recording, or photograph, and is proffered to prove the content of the recordation), an "original"—or, in most instances, a duplicate—must be identified. Often, deciding if a document is an "original" is straightforward. We have already noted that Rule 1003 usually permits the use of duplicates (subsequent reliable copies) in lieu of originals. It should also be noted that parties can create *multiple* originals. In determining if they have done so, the crucial question is the parties' intent. For example, if several copies

---

[5]   *See, e.g., Allstate Ins. Co. v. Swann*, 27 F.3d 1539, 1543 (11th Cir. 1994).

of a contract, will, or other agreement are duly executed (*i.e.* signed and, if necessary, attested), the parties have shown an intention to give equal status to all of the identical writings, regardless of their mechanical or surface characteristics.

Besides the execution of multiple copies, other circumstances sometimes suggest the creation of several originals as, for example, when one receipt is given to a customer and the other is retained by the seller (as in many sales transactions). In this retail setting, both documents are likely to be deemed originals. Beyond this kind of "intent" determination, reference to the substantive law is often necessary to ascertain what constitutes an original for purposes of the Best Evidence Rule. Suppose, for example, a defendant types an original of a libelous document; she then makes a photocopy but publishes only the latter. The copy is the operative document under the substantive law, and as such, constitutes the original with respect to the Best Evidence Rule. In situations like these, the result usually turns not upon which document was created first (or even upon a party's intent), but rather the answer is found by identifying the record that has the operative legal effect.

In addition to the problems created by substantive legal doctrines, modern technology often blurs the line between an original and a copy. As you know, data can be entered and stored in computers and printed out on command. All such printouts of one computer file should be considered multiple originals and each should be afforded equal evidentiary status. Unexecuted photocopies of originals are considered duplicates, absent evidence that the parties intended to treat them as originals, which is unlikely if the copies are unsigned. Oral testimony purporting to give the terms of the original is quintessential secondary evidence.

§ 13.4 Application: Recordings and Photographs; Statutory Modifications

As we have seen, the Federal Rules extend application of the Best Evidence Rule beyond writings to include sound recordings and photographs. This broadening of the rule, a relatively modern development, can be traced to similar "pre-rules" extensions in several states,[6] and should not be viewed as a far-reaching or problematic change. The extension is justified because testimony about the contents of a photograph or recording may be inferior in probative value to a visual or auditory examination by the factfinder. Moreover, as with documents, insisting on original photographs and

---

[6]   *People v. King,* 101 Cal.App.2d 500, 225 P.2d 950, 955 (1950) (recording); *Cellamare v. Third Ave. Transit Corp.,* 273 A.D. 260, 77 N.Y.S.2d 91, 91 (1948) (X-rays).

recordings reduces somewhat the potential for fraud in the reproduction process.

Commonly, photographic and video evidence is admitted as a graphic representation of a scene or subject that a testifying witness has observed and is describing from the stand. This illustrative use of photographic evidence does not involve proving the contents of the picture; rather, it is an attempt to establish the scene itself by testimony, aided by a visual background. But *if* the proponent *is attempting* to prove the content of a photograph (as in the case of an X-ray, or a surveillance camera photograph),[7] the Best Evidence Rule applies. The same is true of a photograph alleged to be libelous, obscene, violative of a copyright, or of an individual's privacy. In instances such as these, the photographic material is offered for its content and testimony about that content is secondary evidence.

When Is Secondary Evidence Permitted?

If the original is lost or destroyed (excepting bad faith destruction by the proponent himself) then production is excused and under Rule 1004, secondary evidence (usually, oral testimony) is permitted.[8] Records are often destroyed in the ordinary course of business, and in most cases, showing that the destruction was a business practice should suffice to establish absence of bad faith by the proponent.[9] The same result obtains when the original is in the hands of the opponent and, after due notice, he fails to produce it— another permissible excuse for secondary evidence under Rule 1004.[10] The proponent has afforded his opponent the opportunity to have the original admitted and the latter has declined.

Is There a Hierarchy of Secondary Evidence?

A few states create classes of secondary evidence, preferring one class to another. The Federal Rules, however, contain no provision for classes of secondary evidence. If the proponent is required to produce the original under Rules 1002 and 1003, but production is excused under Rule 1004, than any probative secondary evidence will suffice.[11] Nonetheless, the proponent's self-interest will usually

---

[7]   A common example is a security (surveillance) camera that photographs customers or intruders.

[8]   Fed. R. Evid. 1004(a). Production is also excused if the "original cannot be obtained by any available judicial process." Fed. R. Evid. 1004(b).

[9]   Note that this would not be the case if litigation had commenced and a party was aware that documents might be sought in discovery. Once involved in litigation, a party must abandon routine document destruction.

[10]   Fed. R. Evid. 1004(c).

[11]   Fed. R. Evid. 1004 ACN. *See also United States v. Ross*, 33 F.3d 1507, 1513 (11th Cir. 1994).

result in placing before the trier the most reliable secondary evidence.

ILLUSTRATION

Law enforcement authorities have information that *D* plans to rob a bank, so FBI agents plant "bait money" with known serial numbers at the target bank. *D* does, in fact, carry out the robbery. During an initial search of *D's* house, the bait money is allegedly discovered and examined by police. When the police return a second time, however, the bills cannot be found. At trial, the prosecution offers the testimony of a police officer who will testify that the bills with the bait money serial numbers were present in the defendant's home. The defense raises a best evidence objection. What result?

The facts in the Illustration are based on *United States v. Marcantoni.*[12] There, the Fifth Circuit concluded that the Best Evidence Rule applied and that the testimony was secondary evidence. Production was excused, however, by Rule 1004 because the bills were either unavailable or withheld by the defendant. Therefore secondary evidence (officer testimony) was permissible.

§ 13.5   Role of Judge and Jury; Classes of Secondary Evidence

Typically, questions about which records are originals, duplicates, or secondary evidence is a preliminary question of fact decided by the trial judge pursuant to Rule 104(a). However, *Rule 1008* provides:

FUNCTIONS OF THE COURT AND JURY

Ordinarily, the court determines whether the proponent has fulfilled the factual conditions for admitting other evidence of the content of a writing, recording, or photograph under Rule 1004 or 1005. But in a jury trial, the jury determines—in accordance with Rule 104(b)—any issue about whether:

(a) an asserted writing, recording, or photograph ever existed;

(b) another one produced at the trial or hearing is the original; or

(c) other evidence of content accurately reflects the content.

---

[12]   590 F.2d 1324 (5th Cir. 1979).

Often, the court's resolution of the issues described in Rule 1008 would go beyond mere trial administration and effectively dictate the outcome of the case. The drafters of the Federal Rules intended to protect the jury's factfinding role in these situations, subject to the court's management and the usual requirement that conditionally relevant facts be accompanied by sufficient evidence of the conditioning (underlying) facts.[13]

ILLUSTRATION

Pope, a self-employed auto mechanic, purchases a diagnostic computer from Swift Co. for use in his business; the computer subsequently malfunctions, and Pope sues Swift for breach of warranty. At trial, Pope produces a written sales contract containing ordinary UCC warranty terms. Swift then produces a written sales contract disclaiming all warranties. Each claims that his document is the original and that the other party has modified its copy. Neither writing is obviously fraudulent.

The court, pursuant to Rule 1008(b), should allow the jury to decide which document's terms control—that is, which is the original. If the judge decides which document is the original, she effectively supplants the jury's factfinding role and dictates the outcome of the case.

---

[13]   *See* Fed. R. Evid. 1008 ACN; Fed. R. Evid. 104(b).

Appendix I

IS IT HEARSAY?

A Short Quiz

Unless otherwise noted, in the following hypotheticals, "W" refers to the witness on the stand and "DC" is the off-the-stand declarant.

1. On the issue whether Cherubino's military commission (now lost or destroyed) had an official seal, W's testimony that the Chief of Records said it did not. *ves*

2. On the issue whether Madam Butterfly was depressed, Butterfly's statement to W, "Where is Pinkerton? Can't he see that I am in a state of despair!" *→ ves b next*

3. On the same issue, Military Commander's statement to Butterfly in W's presence, "I must inform you, as Pinkerton's commander that he will never return to you." *→ nor neal*

4. On the issue whether Lt. Pinkerton and Kate were married, W's testimony that at the wedding ceremony, attended by a few friends and presided over by Minister, Pinkerton and Kate had each said, "I take you to be my wedded [wife; husband]", and the Minister then said. "I now pronounce you husband and wife." *no →*

5. On the same issue, W's testimony that just as the ceremony was beginning, DC (Suzuki) rushed into the chapel and said, "I object to this marriage! Pinkerton is a cheat and a bigamist! He is already married to Butterfly." *hot nc*

6. In a defamation suit by Pinkerton against Suzuki, W's testimony that Suzuki called Pinkerton a "cheat and a bigamist." *- nc*

7. In the same defamation suit, in which Suzuki's defense is truth, her pre-trial statement to W, "Pinkerton can't marry Kate he is still married to Butterfly." *nc →*

8. In the same defamation suit and for the same purpose as in 7, above, Suzuki, herself, testifies to her statement to W. *- nc*

9. In a bigamy prosecution of Pinkerton, on the issue whether Pinkerton knew before he married Kate that he was legally married to Butterfly, his statement to W (prior to his marriage to Kate), "I was totally distressed when my commanding officer

449

told me that my Japanese marriage to Butterfly was actually valid." [There is other evidence supporting the validity of the Japanese marriage.]

10. In the same bigamy prosecution, on the issue whether Pinkerton knew when he married Kate that he was legally married to Butterfly, his statement to W (made a month after the marriage to Kate), "I was absolutely shocked when my commanding officer told me yesterday that my Japanese marriage to Butterfly was valid." [There is other evidence supporting the validity of the Japanese marriage.]

11. On the issue whether Scarpia, a sheriff, ordered the torture of Mario, Scarpia's statement to his deputy, in the presence of W, "Bind him with wire and chain him to the rafters by his feet until he either talks or passes out."

12. On the issue whether Scarpia used duress to force Tosca to have sex with him, his statement to Tosca (W); "Yield or your Mario will die, for even now he is swinging in chains from the prison rafters."

13. On the issue whether Mario was chained to the prison rafters, the statement in 12 above.

14. On the issue whether Mario disliked Scarpia, Mario's statement to W, "That bastard, Scarpia, he arrested me on a false charge, tortured me, and raped my dearest Tosca."

15. On the issue whether Tosca was justified in stabbing Scarpia (self-defense), W's earlier statement to Tosca, "Watch out for Scarpia, he said he would rape you before the night was over."

16. On the issue whether Don José impersonated the famous toreador, Escamillo, in order to gain entry into Carmen's skybox, the statement by José to Carmen's doorkeeper (W), "I am Escamillo; please open the door."

17. On the issue whether Faust made a pact with Satan, testimony by W that Satan said to Faust, "If you will agree to do my bidding after your death, I will obey all of your earthly commands."

18. On the issue whether Sacristan violated securities laws by falsely announcing to English stockjobbers that Napoleon had won the Battle of Waterloo, testimony by Rothschild that his messenger in an excited state came to him and said, "I just heard from Sacristan that Napoleon won the Battle of Waterloo!"

19. On the issue whether Violetta had tuberculosis, testimony by W, a nurse, that the treatment administered by Violetta's physician was the standard treatment for tuberculosis.

20. On the same issue, an authenticated page from Violetta's diary: "Again, last night I suffered chest pains and constant coughing, and when I awoke I found blood spots on my pillow."

21. On the same issue (tuberculosis), on which P has the burden of proof, D calls Violetta's physician who testifies that she was "suffering from emphysema, not tuberculosis." To discredit Physician, P calls N, a nurse, who testifies that two weeks before the trial, Physician told her that "Violetta has tuberculosis."

ANSWERS AND COMMENTS

The tacit assumption in these problems is fundamentally important: in each instance, it is assumed that the evidence points to (helps prove or disprove) a consequential fact. Thus, for example, if Madam Butterfly's depression (question 2) were not consequential under the substantive law governing the case, evidence that tended to make her depression more (or less) likely would be irrelevant. Thus, in considering the admissibility of evidence, you should first resolve the relevance question. Only if the evidence is relevant do you need to inquire whether some other rule, such as the hearsay rule, bars admission.

1. Hearsay. This evidence, an out-of-court statement, is offered to prove there was no seal.

2. Hearsay. Madam Butterfly's statement, offered for its truth, asserts her state of mind. Note that if Butterfly were a party and her statement were offered against her by her party-opponent, that statement would be "exempted" from the *general* definition of hearsay (Rule 801(c)) by reason of FRE 801(d)(2). Note also that the statement is admissible despite the fact it is hearsay, under the state of mind exception to the hearsay rule.

3. Nonhearsay. The evidence is offered to show the probable effect of the declarant's statement on Butterfly's state of mind.

4. Nonhearsay. These are words of independent legal significance, often referred to by courts as constituting a "verbal act."

5. Nonhearsay. These statements are offered not for their truth, but rather for their probable effect on the listeners, especially Kate. The accusations decrease the likelihood that the marriage ceremony continued. Note, however, that if Suzuki's last sentence were offered to prove Pinkerton was already married, it would be hearsay.

6. Nonhearsay. There are words of independent legal significance constituting a verbal act.

7. Hearsay. Assuming, as the problem suggests, that this evidence is offered *by Suzuki* and not *against her* (See FRE 801(d)(2)), the evidence is hearsay. It is offered to prove that Pinkerton was in fact a bigamist.

8. Hearsay, as noted above in 7. The fact that Suzuki testifies as to her own prior out-of-court statement does not change its hearsay character. The statement meets the general definition of hearsay (FRE 801(c)) and does not fit within FRE 801(d)(1) (an exemption from the hearsay rule). In other words, it is not exempted from the general definition of hearsay.

9. Nonhearsay. There are several explanations. If the prosecution offers the statement against Pinkerton, the statement comes in as a party-opponent statement and so is exempt from the hearsay rule. Further, if the statement were offered for the limited purpose of showing Pinkerton's awareness or knowledge that his earlier marriage was valid, the statement would not be offered for its truth, but for its effect on the listener.

10. Hearsay. This declaration is an out-of-court statement made by Pinkerton and presumably offered by him for its truth, namely, his good-faith ("innocent" state of mind) when he married Kate. It is not a statement of a "then-existing" state of mind and so is not admissible under Rule 803(3).

11. Nonhearsay (with qualifications). If Scarpia were a party, and the statement were offered against him, it would be a party-opponent statement and so exempt from the hearsay rule. Also, if the substantive law makes it illegal for a sheriff to order the torture of an arrestee, Scarpia's words would have independent legal significance.

12. Nonhearsay. The threats to the survival of Mario are offered to show their probable coercive effect on Tosca.

13. Hearsay. But note that if these statements are offered against Scarpia by a party-opponent, they are admissible over a hearsay objection. (See FRE 801(d)(2) governing hearsay exemptions or "definitional" nonhearsay)

14. Nonhearsay. None of the assertions are offered to prove what Scarpia did; they are offered to show that Mario did not like Scarpia.

15. Nonhearsay. The warning is offered to show that Tosca was apprehensive and fearful of Scarpia and thus was justified in using a knife to defend herself. (Put otherwise: the declaration is offered not for its truth, but rather for its tendency to influence the listener's state of mind.)

16. Nonhearsay. The words have independent legal significance (verbal act). The false words constitute the impersonation.

17. Nonhearsay. Same rationale as 16, above. This is an offer.

18. Hearsay. There is a statement embedded in a statement. Rothschild is testifying to (1) what his messenger told him that (2) Sacristan said about the battle. What Sacristan said is a statement by a party-opponent when offered against him and is not hearsay in any event because it is not offered for its truth (quite the opposite). But, to believe that Sacristan made the statement, one must believe that what the messenger said was true. If the messenger's statement was an excited utterance then Rothschild's testimony is admissible despite a hearsay objection.

19. Nonhearsay. The physician probably did not intend to make the assertion "Violetta has tuberculosis," but was simply treating her. If there was no intended assertion, the nonassertive nature of the evidence keeps it outside the general definition of hearsay under FRE 801(a) and (c) because the doctor did not intend to make a "statement."

20. Hearsay. Although Violetta may not have been speaking to someone when she made the diary entry, she was consciously making an assertion about her physical condition. The trier of fact is asked to believe Violetta's statement and then to infer that she suffered from tuberculosis. Quite often, hearsay statements do not state directly a consequential proposition, but rather the statements are ultimately directed toward a consequential proposition. The consequential proposition is established by drawing inferences. Nonetheless, if a conscious (intended) out-of-court statement must be accepted as true in order to infer the existence of a consequential fact, the out-of-court statement meets the general definition of hearsay (FRE 801(c)). Note that the statement looks backward in time and so does not fit the hearsay exception for state of mind, Rule 803(3).

21. Nonhearsay. The nurse's testimony is not offered for its truth, but only to impeach—that is, to cast doubt on Physician's testimony. A witness's prior inconsistent statement cannot be used for the truth of the matter asserted unless the statement fits either an exemption or an exception to the hearsay rule. The exemption would cover an inconsistent statement made under oath at a formal proceeding. But that is not the case here. The statement may, however, be used for the limited (nonhearsay) purpose of impeachment. Note, however, that under Fed. R. Evid. 613(b), Physician must be given a chance to deny or explain the prior statement.

Appendix II

FEDERAL RULES OF EVIDENCE FOR UNITED STATES COURTS

ARTICLE I. GENERAL PROVISIONS

Rule 101.   Scope; Definitions

(a) Scope. These rules apply to proceedings in United States courts. The specific courts and proceedings to which the rules apply, along with exceptions, are set out in Rule 1101.

(b) Definitions. In these rules:

    (1) "civil case" means a civil action or proceeding;

    (2) "criminal case" includes a criminal proceeding;

    (3) "public office" includes a public agency;

    (4) "record" includes a memorandum, report, or data compilation;

    (5) a "rule prescribed by the Supreme Court" means a rule adopted by the Supreme Court under statutory authority; and

    (6) a reference to any kind of written material or any other medium includes electronically stored information.

Rule 102.   Purpose

These rules should be construed so as to administer every proceeding fairly, eliminate unjustifiable expense and delay, and promote the development of evidence law, to the end of ascertaining the truth and securing a just determination.

Rule 103.   Rulings on Evidence

(a) Preserving a Claim of Error. A party may claim error in a ruling to admit or exclude evidence only if the error affects a substantial right of the party and:

    (1) if the ruling admits evidence, a party, on the record:

        (A) timely objects or moves to strike; and

        (B) states the specific ground, unless it was apparent from the context; or

(2) if the ruling excludes evidence, a party informs the court of its substance by an offer of proof, unless the substance was apparent from the context.

(b) Not Needing to Renew an Objection or Offer of Proof. Once the court rules definitively on the record—either before or at trial—a party need not renew an objection or offer of proof to preserve a claim of error for appeal.

(c) Court's Statement About the Ruling; Directing an Offer of Proof. The court may make any statement about the character or form of the evidence, the objection made, and the ruling. The court may direct that an offer of proof be made in question-and-answer form.

(d) Preventing the Jury from Hearing Inadmissible Evidence. To the extent practicable, the court must conduct a jury trial so that inadmissible evidence is not suggested to the jury by any means.

(e) Taking Notice of Plain Error. A court may take notice of a plain error affecting a substantial right, even if the claim of error was not properly preserved.

Rule 104. Preliminary Questions

(a) In General. The court must decide any preliminary question about whether a witness is qualified, a privilege exists, or evidence is admissible. In so deciding, the court is not bound by evidence rules, except those on privilege.

(b) Relevance That Depends on a Fact. When the relevance of evidence depends on whether a fact exists, proof must be introduced sufficient to support a finding that the fact does exist. The court may admit the proposed evidence on the condition that the proof be introduced later.

(c) Conducting a Hearing So That the Jury Cannot Hear It. The court must conduct any hearing on a preliminary question so that the jury cannot hear it if:

(1) the hearing involves the admissibility of a confession;

(2) a defendant in a criminal case is a witness and so requests; or

(3) justice so requires.

(d) Cross-Examining a Defendant in a Criminal Case. By testifying on a preliminary question, a defendant in a criminal case does not become subject to cross-examination on other issues in the case.

(e) Evidence Relevant to Weight and Credibility. This rule does not limit a party's right to introduce before the jury evidence that is relevant to the weight or credibility of other evidence.

Rule 105. Limiting Evidence That Is Not Admissible Against Other Parties or for Other Purposes

If the court admits evidence that is admissible against a party or for a purpose—but not against another party or for another purpose—the court, on timely request, must restrict the evidence to its proper scope and instruct the jury accordingly.

Rule 106. Remainder of or Related Writings or Recorded Statements

If a party introduces all or part of a writing or recorded statement, an adverse party may require the introduction, at that time, of any other part—or any other writing or recorded statement—that in fairness ought to be considered at the same time.

ARTICLE II. JUDICIAL NOTICE

Rule 201. Judicial Notice of Adjudicative Facts

(a) Scope. This rule governs judicial notice of an adjudicative fact only, not a legislative fact.

(b) Kinds of Facts That May Be Judicially Noticed. The court may judicially notice a fact that is not subject to reasonable dispute because it:

(1) is generally known within the trial court's territorial jurisdiction; or

(2) can be accurately and readily determined from sources whose accuracy cannot reasonably be questioned.

(c) Taking Notice. The court:

(1) may take judicial notice on its own; or

(2) must take judicial notice if a party requests it and the court is supplied with the necessary information.

(d) Timing. The court may take judicial notice at any stage of the proceeding.

(e) Opportunity to Be Heard. On timely request, a party is entitled to be heard on the propriety of taking judicial notice and the nature of the fact to be noticed. If the court takes judicial notice before notifying a party, the party, on request, is still entitled to be heard.

(f) Instructing the Jury. In a civil case, the court must instruct the jury to accept the noticed fact as conclusive. In a criminal case, the court must instruct the jury that it may or may not accept the noticed fact as conclusive.

ARTICLE III. PRESUMPTIONS IN CIVIL CASES

Rule 301. Presumptions in Civil Cases Generally

In a civil case, unless a federal statute or these rules provide otherwise, the party against whom a presumption is directed has the burden of producing evidence to rebut the presumption. But this rule does not shift the burden of persuasion, which remains on the party who had it originally.

Rule 302. Applying State Law to Presumptions in Civil Cases

In a civil case, state law governs the effect of a presumption regarding a claim or defense for which state law supplies the rule of decision.

ARTICLE IV. RELEVANCE AND ITS LIMITS

Rule 401. Test for Relevant Evidence

Evidence is relevant if:

(a) it has any tendency to make a fact more or less probable than it would be without the evidence; and

(b) the fact is of consequence in determining the action.

Rule 402. General Admissibility of Relevant Evidence

Relevant evidence is admissible unless any of the following provides otherwise:

- the United States Constitution;
- a federal statute;
- these rules; or
- other rules prescribed by the Supreme Court.

Irrelevant evidence is not admissible.

Rule 403. Excluding Relevant Evidence for Prejudice, Confusion, Waste of Time, or Other Reasons

The court may exclude relevant evidence if its probative value is substantially outweighed by a danger of one or more of the following: unfair prejudice, confusing the issues, misleading the jury, undue delay, wasting time, or needlessly presenting cumulative evidence.

Rule 404.   Character Evidence; Other Crimes, Wrongs, or Acts

(a) Character Evidence.

(1) *Prohibited Uses.* Evidence of a person's character or character trait is not admissible to prove that on a particular occasion the person acted in accordance with the character or trait.

(2) *Exceptions for a Defendant or Victim in a Criminal Case.* The following exceptions apply in a criminal case:

(A) a defendant may offer evidence of the defendant's pertinent trait, and if the evidence is admitted, the prosecutor may offer evidence to rebut it;

(B) subject to the limitations in Rule 412, a defendant may offer evidence of an alleged victim's pertinent trait, and if the evidence is admitted, the prosecutor may:

(i) offer evidence to rebut it; and

(ii) offer evidence of the defendant's same trait; and

(C) in a homicide case, the prosecutor may offer evidence of the alleged victim's trait of peacefulness to rebut evidence that the victim was the first aggressor.

(3) *Exceptions for a Witness.* Evidence of a witness's character may be admitted under Rules 607, 608, and 609.

(b) Other Crimes, Wrongs, or Acts.

(1) *Prohibited Uses.* Evidence of any other crime, wrong, or act is not admissible to prove a person's character in order to show that on a particular occasion the person acted in accordance with the character.

(2) *Permitted Uses.* This evidence may be admissible for another purpose, such as proving motive, opportunity, intent, preparation, plan, knowledge, identity, absence of mistake, or lack of accident.

(3) *Notice in a Criminal Case.* In a criminal case, the prosecutor must:

(A) provide reasonable notice of any such evidence that the prosecutor intends to offer at trial, so that the defendant has a fair opportunity to meet it;

(B) articulate in the notice the permitted purpose for which the prosecutor intends to offer the evidence and the reasoning that supports the purpose; and

(C) do so in writing before trial—or in any form during trial if the court, for good cause, excuses lack of pretrial notice.

Rule 405. Methods of Proving Character

(a) By Reputation or Opinion. When evidence of a person's character or character trait is admissible, it may be proved by testimony about the person's reputation or by testimony in the form of an opinion. On cross-examination of the character witness, the court may allow an inquiry into relevant specific instances of the person's conduct.

(b) By Specific Instances of Conduct. When a person's character or character trait is an essential element of a charge, claim, or defense, the character or trait may also be proved by relevant specific instances of the person's conduct.

Rule 406. Habit; Routine Practice

Evidence of a person's habit or an organization's routine practice may be admitted to prove that on a particular occasion the person or organization acted in accordance with the habit or routine practice. The court may admit this evidence regardless of whether it is corroborated or whether there was an eyewitness.

Rule 407. Subsequent Remedial Measures

When measures are taken that would have made an earlier injury or harm less likely to occur, evidence of the subsequent measures is not admissible to prove:

- negligence;
- culpable conduct;
- a defect in a product or its design; or
- a need for a warning or instruction.

But the court may admit this evidence for another purpose, such as impeachment or—if disputed—proving ownership, control, or the feasibility of precautionary measures.

Rule 408. Compromise Offers and Negotiations

(a) Prohibited Uses. Evidence of the following is not admissible— on behalf of any party—either to prove or disprove the validity or amount of a disputed claim or to impeach by a prior inconsistent statement or a contradiction:

(1) furnishing, promising, or offering—or accepting, promising to accept, or offering to accept—a valuable consideration in compromising or attempting to compromise the claim; and

(2) conduct or a statement made during compromise negotiations about the claim—except when offered in a criminal case and when the negotiations related to a claim by a public office in the exercise of its regulatory, investigative, or enforcement authority.

(b) Exceptions. The court may admit this evidence for another purpose, such as proving a witness's bias or prejudice, negating a contention of undue delay, or proving an effort to obstruct a criminal investigation or prosecution.

Rule 409.   Offers to Pay Medical and Similar Expenses

Evidence of furnishing, promising to pay, or offering to pay medical, hospital, or similar expenses resulting from an injury is not admissible to prove liability for the injury.

Rule 410.   Pleas, Plea Discussions, and Related Statements

(a) Prohibited Uses. In a civil or criminal case, evidence of the following is not admissible against the defendant who made the plea or participated in the plea discussions:

(1) a guilty plea that was later withdrawn;

(2) a nolo contendere plea;

(3) a statement made during a proceeding on either of those pleas under Federal Rule of Criminal Procedure 11 or a comparable state procedure; or

(4) a statement made during plea discussions with an attorney for the prosecuting authority if the discussions did not result in a guilty plea or they resulted in a later-withdrawn guilty plea.

(b) Exceptions. The court may admit a statement described in Rule 410(a)(3) or (4):

(1) in any proceeding in which another statement made during the same plea or plea discussions has been introduced, if in fairness the statements ought to be considered together; or

(2) in a criminal proceeding for perjury or false statement, if the defendant made the statement under oath, on the record, and with counsel present.

Rule 411.   Liability Insurance

Evidence that a person was or was not insured against liability is not admissible to prove whether the person acted negligently or otherwise wrongfully. But the court may admit this evidence for another purpose, such as proving a witness's bias or prejudice or proving agency, ownership, or control.

Rule 412. Sex-Offense Cases: The Victim's Sexual Behavior or Predisposition

(a) Prohibited Uses. The following evidence is not admissible in a civil or criminal proceeding involving alleged sexual misconduct:

(1) evidence offered to prove that a victim engaged in other sexual behavior; or

(2) evidence offered to prove a victim's sexual predisposition.

(b) Exceptions.

(1) *Criminal Cases.* The court may admit the following evidence in a criminal case:

(A) evidence of specific instances of a victim's sexual behavior, if offered to prove that someone other than the defendant was the source of semen, injury, or other physical evidence;

(B) evidence of specific instances of a victim's sexual behavior with respect to the person accused of the sexual misconduct, if offered by the defendant to prove consent or if offered by the prosecutor; and

(C) evidence whose exclusion would violate the defendant's constitutional rights.

(2) *Civil Cases.* In a civil case, the court may admit evidence offered to prove a victim's sexual behavior or sexual predisposition if its probative value substantially outweighs the danger of harm to any victim and of unfair prejudice to any party. The court may admit evidence of a victim's reputation only if the victim has placed it in controversy.

(c) Procedure to Determine Admissibility.

(1) *Motion.* If a party intends to offer evidence under Rule 412(b), the party must:

(A) file a motion that specifically describes the evidence and states the purpose for which it is to be offered;

(B) do so at least 14 days before trial unless the court, for good cause, sets a different time;

(C) serve the motion on all parties; and

(D) notify the victim or, when appropriate, the victim's guardian or representative.

(2) *Hearing.* Before admitting evidence under this rule, the court must conduct an in camera hearing and give the victim and parties a right to attend and be heard. Unless the court orders otherwise, the motion, related materials, and the record of the hearing must be and remain sealed.

(d) Definition of "Victim." In this rule, "victim" includes an alleged victim.

Rule 413. Similar Crimes in Sexual-Assault Cases

(a) Permitted Uses. In a criminal case in which a defendant is accused of a sexual assault, the court may admit evidence that the defendant committed any other sexual assault. The evidence may be considered on any matter to which it is relevant.

(b) Disclosure to the Defendant. If the prosecutor intends to offer this evidence, the prosecutor must disclose it to the defendant, including witnesses' statements or a summary of the expected testimony. The prosecutor must do so at least 15 days before trial or at a later time that the court allows for good cause.

(c) Effect on Other Rules. This rule does not limit the admission or consideration of evidence under any other rule.

(d) Definition of "Sexual Assault." In this rule and Rule 415, "sexual assault" means a crime under federal law or under state law (as "state" is defined in 18 U.S.C. § 513) involving:

    (1) any conduct prohibited by 18 U.S.C. chapter 109A;

    (2) contact, without consent, between any part of the defendant's body—or an object—and another person's genitals or anus;

    (3) contact, without consent, between the defendant's genitals or anus and any part of another person's body;

    (4) deriving sexual pleasure or gratification from inflicting death, bodily injury, or physical pain on another person; or

    (5) an attempt or conspiracy to engage in conduct described in subparagraphs (1)–(4).

Rule 414. Similar Crimes in Child-Molestation Cases

(a) Permitted Uses. In a criminal case in which a defendant is accused of child molestation, the court may admit evidence that the defendant committed any other child molestation. The evidence may be considered on any matter to which it is relevant.

(b) Disclosure to the Defendant. If the prosecutor intends to offer this evidence, the prosecutor must disclose it to the defendant, including witnesses' statements or a summary of the expected testimony. The prosecutor must do so at least 15 days before trial or at a later time that the court allows for good cause.

(c) Effect on Other Rules. This rule does not limit the admission or consideration of evidence under any other rule.

(d) Definition of "Child" and "Child Molestation." In this rule and Rule 415:

    (1) "child" means a person below the age of 14; and

    (2) "child molestation" means a crime under federal law or under state law (as "state" is defined in 18 U.S.C. § 513) involving:

        (A) any conduct prohibited by 18 U.S.C. chapter 109A and committed with a child;

        (B) any conduct prohibited by 18 U.S.C. chapter 110;

        (C) contact between any part of the defendant's body—or an object—and a child's genitals or anus;

        (D) contact between the defendant's genitals or anus and any part of a child's body;

        (E) deriving sexual pleasure or gratification from inflicting death, bodily injury, or physical pain on a child; or

        (F) an attempt or conspiracy to engage in conduct described in subparagraphs (A)–(E).

Rule 415. Similar Acts in Civil Cases Involving Sexual Assault or Child Molestation

(a) Permitted Uses. In a civil case involving a claim for relief based on a party's alleged sexual assault or child molestation, the court may admit evidence that the party committed any other sexual assault or child molestation. The evidence may be considered as provided in Rules 413 and 414.

(b) Disclosure to the Opponent. If a party intends to offer this evidence, the party must disclose it to the party against whom it will be offered, including witnesses' statements or a summary of the expected testimony. The party must do so at least 15 days before trial or at a later time that the court allows for good cause.

(c) Effect on Other Rules. This rule does not limit the admission or consideration of evidence under any other rule.

ARTICLE V.   PRIVILEGES

Rule 501. Privilege in General

The common law—as interpreted by United States courts in the light of reason and experience—governs a claim of privilege unless any of the following provides otherwise:

- the United States Constitution;

- a federal statute; or

- rules prescribed by the Supreme Court.

But in a civil case, state law governs privilege regarding a claim or defense for which state law supplies the rule of decision.

Rule 502. Attorney-Client Privilege and Work Product; Limitations on Waiver

The following provisions apply, in the circumstances set out, to disclosure of a communication or information covered by the attorney-client privilege or work-product protection.

(a) Disclosure Made in a Federal Proceeding or to a Federal Office or Agency; Scope of a Waiver. When the disclosure is made in a federal proceeding or to a federal office or agency and waives the attorney-client privilege or work-product protection, the waiver extends to an undisclosed communication or information in a federal or state proceeding only if:

     (1) the waiver is intentional;

     (2) the disclosed and undisclosed communications or information concern the same subject matter; and

     (3) they ought in fairness to be considered together.

(b) Inadvertent Disclosure. When made in a federal proceeding or to a federal office or agency, the disclosure does not operate as a waiver in a federal or state proceeding if:

     (1) the disclosure is inadvertent;

     (2) the holder of the privilege or protection took reasonable steps to prevent disclosure; and

     (3) the holder promptly took reasonable steps to rectify the error, including (if applicable) following Federal Rule of Civil Procedure 26(b)(5)(B).

(c) Disclosure Made in a State Proceeding. When the disclosure is made in a state proceeding and is not the subject of a state-court order concerning waiver, the disclosure does not operate as a waiver in a federal proceeding if the disclosure:

     (1) would not be a waiver under this rule if it had been made in a federal proceeding; or

     (2) is not a waiver under the law of the state where the disclosure occurred.

(d) Controlling Effect of a Court Order. A federal court may order that the privilege or protection is not waived by disclosure connected with the litigation pending before the court—in which event the disclosure is also not a waiver in any other federal or state proceeding.

(e) Controlling Effect of a Party Agreement. An agreement on the effect of disclosure in a federal proceeding is binding only on the parties to the agreement, unless it is incorporated into a court order.

(f) Controlling Effect of this Rule. Notwithstanding Rules 101 and 1101, this rule applies to state proceedings and to federal court-annexed and federal court-mandated arbitration proceedings, in the circumstances set out in the rule. And notwithstanding Rule 501, this rule applies even if state law provides the rule of decision.

(g) Definitions. In this rule:

(1) "attorney-client privilege" means the protection that applicable law provides for confidential attorney-client communications; and

(2) "work-product protection" means the protection that applicable law provides for tangible material (or its intangible equivalent) prepared in anticipation of litigation or for trial.

ARTICLE VI.   WITNESSES

Rule 601.   Competency to Testify in General

Every person is competent to be a witness unless these rules provide otherwise. But in a civil case, state law governs the witness's competency regarding a claim or defense for which state law supplies the rule of decision.

Rule 602.   Need for Personal Knowledge

A witness may testify to a matter only if evidence is introduced sufficient to support a finding that the witness has personal knowledge of the matter. Evidence to prove personal knowledge may consist of the witness's own testimony. This rule does not apply to a witness's expert testimony under Rule 703.

Rule 603.   Oath or Affirmation to Testify Truthfully

Before testifying, a witness must give an oath or affirmation to testify truthfully. It must be in a form designed to impress that duty on the witness's conscience.

Rule 604. Interpreter

An interpreter must be qualified and must give an oath or affirmation to make a true translation.

Rule 605. Judge's Competency as a Witness

The presiding judge may not testify as a witness at the trial. A party need not object to preserve the issue.

Rule 606. Juror's Competency as a Witness

(a) **At the Trial.** A juror may not testify as a witness before the other jurors at the trial. If a juror is called to testify, the court must give a party an opportunity to object outside the jury's presence.

(b) **During an Inquiry into the Validity of a Verdict or Indictment.**

   (1) *Prohibited Testimony or Other Evidence.* During an inquiry into the validity of a verdict or indictment, a juror may not testify about any statement made or incident that occurred during the jury's deliberations; the effect of anything on that juror's or another juror's vote; or any juror's mental processes concerning the verdict or indictment. The court may not receive a juror's affidavit or evidence of a juror's statement on these matters.

   (2) *Exceptions.* A juror may testify about whether:

      (A) extraneous prejudicial information was improperly brought to the jury's attention;

      (B) an outside influence was improperly brought to bear on any juror; or

      (C) a mistake was made in entering the verdict on the verdict form.

Rule 607. Who May Impeach a Witness

Any party, including the party that called the witness, may attack the witness's credibility.

Rule 608. A Witness's Character for Truthfulness or Untruthfulness

(a) **Reputation or Opinion Evidence.** A witness's credibility may be attacked or supported by testimony about the witness's reputation for having a character for truthfulness or untruthfulness, or by testimony in the form of an opinion about that character. But evidence of truthful character is admissible only after the witness's character for truthfulness has been attacked.

(b) Specific Instances of Conduct. Except for a criminal conviction under Rule 609, extrinsic evidence is not admissible to prove specific instances of a witness's conduct in order to attack or support the witness's character for truthfulness. But the court may, on cross-examination, allow them to be inquired into if they are probative of the character for truthfulness or untruthfulness of:

(1) the witness; or

(2) another witness whose character the witness being cross-examined has testified about.

By testifying on another matter, a witness does not waive any privilege against self-incrimination for testimony that relates only to the witness's character for truthfulness.

Rule 609. Impeachment by Evidence of a Criminal Conviction

(a) In General. The following rules apply to attacking a witness's character for truthfulness by evidence of a criminal conviction:

(1) for a crime that, in the convicting jurisdiction, was punishable by death or by imprisonment for more than one year, the evidence:

(A) must be admitted, subject to Rule 403, in a civil case or in a criminal case in which the witness is not a defendant; and

(B) must be admitted in a criminal case in which the witness is a defendant, if the probative value of the evidence outweighs its prejudicial effect to that defendant; and

(2) for any crime regardless of the punishment, the evidence must be admitted if the court can readily determine that establishing the elements of the crime required proving—or the witness's admitting—a dishonest act or false statement.

(b) Limit on Using the Evidence After 10 Years. This subdivision (b) applies if more than 10 years have passed since the witness's conviction or release from confinement for it, whichever is later. Evidence of the conviction is admissible only if:

(1) its probative value, supported by specific facts and circumstances, substantially outweighs its prejudicial effect; and

(2) the proponent gives an adverse party reasonable written notice of the intent to use it so that the party has a fair opportunity to contest its use.

(c) Effect of a Pardon, Annulment, or Certificate of Rehabilitation. Evidence of a conviction is not admissible if:

(1) the conviction has been the subject of a pardon, annulment, certificate of rehabilitation, or other equivalent procedure based on a finding that the person has been rehabilitated, and the person has not been convicted of a later crime punishable by death or by imprisonment for more than one year; or

(2) the conviction has been the subject of a pardon, annulment, or other equivalent procedure based on a finding of innocence.

(d) Juvenile Adjudications. Evidence of a juvenile adjudication is admissible under this rule only if:

(1) it is offered in a criminal case;

(2) the adjudication was of a witness other than the defendant;

(3) an adult's conviction for that offense would be admissible to attack the adult's credibility; and

(4) admitting the evidence is necessary to fairly determine guilt or innocence.

(e) Pendency of an Appeal. A conviction that satisfies this rule is admissible even if an appeal is pending. Evidence of the pendency is also admissible.

Rule 610.   Religious Beliefs or Opinions

Evidence of a witness's religious beliefs or opinions is not admissible to attack or support the witness's credibility.

Rule 611.   Mode and Order of Examining Witnesses and Presenting Evidence

(a) Control by the Court; Purposes. The court should exercise reasonable control over the mode and order of examining witnesses and presenting evidence so as to:

(1) make those procedures effective for determining the truth;

(2) avoid wasting time; and

(3) protect witnesses from harassment or undue embarrassment.

(b) Scope of Cross-Examination. Cross-examination should not go beyond the subject matter of the direct examination and matters affecting the witness's credibility. The court may allow inquiry into additional matters as if on direct examination.

(c) Leading Questions. Leading questions should not be used on direct examination except as necessary to develop the witness's testimony. Ordinarily, the court should allow leading questions:

(1) on cross-examination; and

(2) when a party calls a hostile witness, an adverse party, or a witness identified with an adverse party.

Rule 612. Writing Used to Refresh a Witness's Memory

(a) Scope. This rule gives an adverse party certain options when a witness uses a writing to refresh memory:

(1) while testifying; or

(2) before testifying, if the court decides that justice requires the party to have those options.

(b) Adverse Party's Options; Deleting Unrelated Matter. Unless 18 U.S.C. § 3500 provides otherwise in a criminal case, an adverse party is entitled to have the writing produced at the hearing, to inspect it, to cross-examine the witness about it, and to introduce in evidence any portion that relates to the witness's testimony. If the producing party claims that the writing includes unrelated matter, the court must examine the writing in camera, delete any unrelated portion, and order that the rest be delivered to the adverse party. Any portion deleted over objection must be preserved for the record.

(c) Failure to Produce or Deliver the Writing. If a writing is not produced or is not delivered as ordered, the court may issue any appropriate order. But if the prosecution does not comply in a criminal case, the court must strike the witness's testimony or—if justice so requires—declare a mistrial.

Rule 613. Witness's Prior Statement

(a) Showing or Disclosing the Statement During Examination. When examining a witness about the witness's prior statement, a party need not show it or disclose its contents to the witness. But the party must, on request, show it or disclose its contents to an adverse party's attorney.

(b) **Extrinsic Evidence of a Prior Inconsistent Statement.**
Extrinsic evidence of a witness's prior inconsistent statement is
admissible only if the witness is given an opportunity to explain
or deny the statement and an adverse party is given an
opportunity to examine the witness about it, or if justice so
requires. This subdivision (b) does not apply to an opposing
party's statement under Rule 801(d)(2).

Rule 614.   Court's Calling or Examining a Witness

(a) **Calling.** The court may call a witness on its own or at a party's
request. Each party is entitled to cross-examine the witness.

(b) **Examining.** The court may examine a witness regardless of
who calls the witness.

(c) **Objections.** A party may object to the court's calling or
examining a witness either at that time or at the next
opportunity when the jury is not present.

Rule 615.   Excluding Witnesses

At a party's request, the court must order witnesses excluded so that
they cannot hear other witnesses' testimony. Or the court may do so
on its own. But this rule does not authorize excluding:

(a) a party who is a natural person;

(b) an officer or employee of a party that is not a natural person,
after being designated as the party's representative by its
attorney;

(c) a person whose presence a party shows to be essential to
presenting the party's claim or defense; or

(d) a person authorized by statute to be present.

ARTICLE VII. OPINIONS AND EXPERT TESTIMONY

Rule 701.   Opinion Testimony by Lay Witnesses

If a witness is not testifying as an expert, testimony in the form of an
opinion is limited to one that is:

(a) rationally based on the witness's perception;

(b) helpful to clearly understanding the witness's testimony or to
determining a fact in issue; and

(c) not based on scientific, technical, or other specialized knowledge
within the scope of Rule 702.

Rule 702. Testimony by Expert Witnesses

A witness who is qualified as an expert by knowledge, skill, experience, training, or education may testify in the form of an opinion or otherwise if:

(a) the expert's scientific, technical, or other specialized knowledge will help the trier of fact to understand the evidence or to determine a fact in issue;

(b) the testimony is based on sufficient facts or data;

(c) the testimony is the product of reliable principles and methods; and

(d) the expert has reliably applied the principles and methods to the facts of the case.

Rule 703. Bases of an Expert's Opinion Testimony

An expert may base an opinion on facts or data in the case that the expert has been made aware of or personally observed. If experts in the particular field would reasonably rely on those kinds of facts or data in forming an opinion on the subject, they need not be admissible for the opinion to be admitted. But if the facts or data would otherwise be inadmissible, the proponent of the opinion may disclose them to the jury only if their probative value in helping the jury evaluate the opinion substantially outweighs their prejudicial effect.

Rule 704. Opinion on an Ultimate Issue

(a) **In General—Not Automatically Objectionable.** An opinion is not objectionable just because it embraces an ultimate issue.

(b) **Exception.** In a criminal case, an expert witness must not state an opinion about whether the defendant did or did not have a mental state or condition that constitutes an element of the crime charged or of a defense. Those matters are for the trier of fact alone.

Rule 705. Disclosing the Facts or Data Underlying an Expert's Opinion

Unless the court orders otherwise, an expert may state an opinion— and give the reasons for it—without first testifying to the underlying facts or data. But the expert may be required to disclose those facts or data on cross-examination.

Rule 706. Court-Appointed Expert Witnesses

(a) **Appointment Process.** On a party's motion or on its own, the court may order the parties to show cause why expert witnesses should not be appointed and may ask the parties to submit nominations. The court may appoint any expert that the parties agree on and any of its own choosing. But the court may only appoint someone who consents to act.

(b) Expert's Role. The court must inform the expert of the expert's duties. The court may do so in writing and have a copy filed with the clerk or may do so orally at a conference in which the parties have an opportunity to participate. The expert:

(1) must advise the parties of any findings the expert makes;

(2) may be deposed by any party;

(3) may be called to testify by the court or any party; and

(4) may be cross-examined by any party, including the party that called the expert.

(c) Compensation. The expert is entitled to a reasonable compensation, as set by the court. The compensation is payable as follows:

(1) in a criminal case or in a civil case involving just compensation under the Fifth Amendment, from any funds that are provided by law; and

(2) in any other civil case, by the parties in the proportion and at the time that the court directs—and the compensation is then charged like other costs.

(d) Disclosing the Appointment to the Jury. The court may authorize disclosure to the jury that the court appointed the expert.

(e) Parties' Choice of Their Own Experts. This rule does not limit a party in calling its own experts.

ARTICLE VIII. HEARSAY

Rule 801. Definitions That Apply to This Article; Exclusions from Hearsay

(a) Statement. "Statement" means a person's oral assertion, written assertion, or nonverbal conduct, if the person intended it as an assertion.

(b) Declarant. "Declarant" means the person who made the statement.

(c) Hearsay. "Hearsay" means a statement that:

(1) the declarant does not make while testifying at the current trial or hearing; and

(2) a party offers in evidence to prove the truth of the matter asserted in the statement.

(d) Statements That Are Not Hearsay. A statement that meets the following conditions is not hearsay:

(1) *A Declarant-Witness's Prior Statement.* The declarant testifies and is subject to cross-examination about a prior statement, and the statement:

    (A) is inconsistent with the declarant's testimony and was given under penalty of perjury at a trial, hearing, or other proceeding or in a deposition;

    (B) is consistent with the declarant's testimony and is offered:

        (i) to rebut an express or implied charge that the declarant recently fabricated it or acted from a recent improper influence or motive in so testifying; or

        (ii) to rehabilitate the declarant's credibility as a witness when attacked on another ground; or

    (C) identifies a person as someone the declarant perceived earlier.

(2) *An Opposing Party's Statement.* The statement is offered against an opposing party and:

    (A) was made by the party in an individual or representative capacity;

    (B) is one the party manifested that it adopted or believed to be true;

    (C) was made by a person whom the party authorized to make a statement on the subject;

    (D) was made by the party's agent or employee on a matter within the scope of that relationship and while it existed; or

    (E) was made by the party's coconspirator during and in furtherance of the conspiracy.

The statement must be considered but does not by itself establish the declarant's authority under (C); the existence or scope of the relationship under (D); or the existence of the conspiracy or participation in it under (E).

Rule 802. The Rule Against Hearsay

Hearsay is not admissible unless any of the following provides otherwise:

    • a federal statute;

- these rules; or

- other rules prescribed by the Supreme Court.

Rule 803. Exceptions to the Rule Against Hearsay— Regardless of Whether the Declarant Is Available as a Witness

The following are not excluded by the rule against hearsay, regardless of whether the declarant is available as a witness:

(1) *Present Sense Impression.* A statement describing or explaining an event or condition, made while or immediately after the declarant perceived it.

(2) *Excited Utterance.* A statement relating to a startling event or condition, made while the declarant was under the stress of excitement that it caused.

(3) *Then-Existing Mental, Emotional, or Physical Condition.* A statement of the declarant's then-existing state of mind (such as motive, intent, or plan) or emotional, sensory, or physical condition (such as mental feeling, pain, or bodily health), but not including a statement of memory or belief to prove the fact remembered or believed unless it relates to the validity or terms of the declarant's will.

(4) *Statement Made for Medical Diagnosis or Treatment.* A statement that:

(A) is made for—and is reasonably pertinent to—medical diagnosis or treatment; and

(B) describes medical history; past or present symptoms or sensations; their inception; or their general cause.

(5) *Recorded Recollection.* A record that:

(A) is on a matter the witness once knew about but now cannot recall well enough to testify fully and accurately;

(B) was made or adopted by the witness when the matter was fresh in the witness's memory; and

(C) accurately reflects the witness's knowledge.

If admitted, the record may be read into evidence but may be received as an exhibit only if offered by an adverse party.

(6) *Records of a Regularly Conducted Activity.* A record of an act, event, condition, opinion, or diagnosis if:

(A) the record was made at or near the time by—or from information transmitted by—someone with knowledge;

(B) the record was kept in the course of a regularly conducted activity of a business, organization, occupation, or calling, whether or not for profit;

(C) making the record was a regular practice of that activity;

(D) all these conditions are shown by the testimony of the custodian or another qualified witness, or by a certification that complies with Rule 902(11) or (12) or with a statute permitting certification; and

(E) the opponent does not show that the source of information or the method or circumstances of preparation indicate a lack of trustworthiness.

(7) *Absence of a Record of a Regularly Conducted Activity.* Evidence that a matter is not included in a record described in paragraph (6) if:

(A) the evidence is admitted to prove that the matter did not occur or exist;

(B) a record was regularly kept for a matter of that kind; and

(C) the opponent does not show that the possible source of the information or other circumstances indicate a lack of trustworthiness.

(8) *Public Records.* A record or statement of a public office if:

(A) it sets out:

　(i) the office's activities;

　(ii) a matter observed while under a legal duty to report, but not including, in a criminal case, a matter observed by law-enforcement personnel; or

　(iii) in a civil case or against the government in a criminal case, factual findings from a legally authorized investigation; and

(B) the opponent does not show that the source of information or other circumstances indicate a lack of trustworthiness.

(9) *Public Records of Vital Statistics.* A record of a birth, death, or marriage, if reported to a public office in accordance with a legal duty.

(10) *Absence of a Public Record.* Testimony—or a certification under Rule 902—that a diligent search failed to disclose a public record or statement if

    (A) the testimony or certification is admitted to prove that:

        (i) the record or statement does not exist; or

        (ii) a matter did not occur or exist, if a public office regularly kept a record or statement for a matter of that kind; and

    (B) in a criminal case, a prosecutor who intends to offer a certification provides written notice of that intent at least 14 days before trial, and the defendant does not object in writing within 7 days of receiving the notice— unless the court sets a different time for the notice or the objection.

(11) *Records of Religious Organizations Concerning Personal or Family History.* A statement of birth, legitimacy, ancestry, marriage, divorce, death, relationship by blood or marriage, or similar facts of personal or family history, contained in a regularly kept record of a religious organization.

(12) *Certificates of Marriage, Baptism, and Similar Ceremonies.* A statement of fact contained in a certificate:

    (A) made by a person who is authorized by a religious organization or by law to perform the act certified;

    (B) attesting that the person performed a marriage or similar ceremony or administered a sacrament; and

    (C) purporting to have been issued at the time of the act or within a reasonable time after it.

(13) *Family Records.* A statement of fact about personal or family history contained in a family record, such as a Bible, genealogy, chart, engraving on a ring, inscription on a portrait, or engraving on an urn or burial marker.

(14) *Records of Documents That Affect an Interest in Property.* The record of a document that purports to establish or affect an interest in property if:

    (A) the record is admitted to prove the content of the original recorded document, along with its signing and its delivery by each person who purports to have signed it;

(B) the record is kept in a public office; and

(C) a statute authorizes recording documents of that kind in that office.

(15) *Statements in Documents That Affect an Interest in Property.* A statement contained in a document that purports to establish or affect an interest in property if the matter stated was relevant to the document's purpose— unless later dealings with the property are inconsistent with the truth of the statement or the purport of the document.

(16) *Statements in Ancient Documents.* A statement in a document that was prepared before January 1, 1998, and whose authenticity is established.

(17) *Market Reports and Similar Commercial Publications.* Market quotations, lists, directories, or other compilations that are generally relied on by the public or by persons in particular occupations.

(18) *Statements in Learned Treatises, Periodicals, or Pamphlets.* A statement contained in a treatise, periodical, or pamphlet if:

(A) the statement is called to the attention of an expert witness on cross-examination or relied on by the expert on direct examination; and

(B) the publication is established as a reliable authority by the expert's admission or testimony, by another expert's testimony, or by judicial notice.

If admitted, the statement may be read into evidence but not received as an exhibit.

(19) *Reputation Concerning Personal or Family History.* A reputation among a person's family by blood, adoption, or marriage—or among a person's associates or in the community—concerning the person's birth, adoption, legitimacy, ancestry, marriage, divorce, death, relationship by blood, adoption, or marriage, or similar facts of personal or family history.

(20) *Reputation Concerning Boundaries or General History.* A reputation in a community—arising before the controversy—concerning boundaries of land in the community or customs that affect the land, or concerning general historical events important to that community, state, or nation.

(21) *Reputation Concerning Character.* A reputation among a person's associates or in the community concerning the person's character.

(22) *Judgment of a Previous Conviction.* Evidence of a final judgment of conviction if:

    (A) the judgment was entered after a trial or guilty plea, but not a nolo contendere plea;

    (B) the conviction was for a crime punishable by death or by imprisonment for more than a year;

    (C) the evidence is admitted to prove any fact essential to the judgment; and

    (D) when offered by the prosecutor in a criminal case for a purpose other than impeachment, the judgment was against the defendant.

The pendency of an appeal may be shown but does not affect admissibility.

(23) *Judgments Involving Personal, Family, or General History, or a Boundary.* A judgment that is admitted to prove a matter of personal, family, or general history, or boundaries, if the matter:

    (A) was essential to the judgment; and

    (B) could be proved by evidence of reputation.

(24) [*Other Exceptions.*] [Transferred to Rule 807.]

Rule 804. Exceptions to the Rule Against Hearsay—When the Declarant Is Unavailable as a Witness

(a) Criteria for Being Unavailable. A declarant is considered to be unavailable as a witness if the declarant:

    (1) is exempted from testifying about the subject matter of the declarant's statement because the court rules that a privilege applies;

    (2) refuses to testify about the subject matter despite a court order to do so;

    (3) testifies to not remembering the subject matter;

    (4) cannot be present or testify at the trial or hearing because of death or a then-existing infirmity, physical illness, or mental illness; or

(5) is absent from the trial or hearing and the statement's proponent has not been able, by process or other reasonable means, to procure:

    (A) the declarant's attendance, in the case of a hearsay exception under Rule 804(b)(1) or (6); or

    (B) the declarant's attendance or testimony, in the case of a hearsay exception under Rule 804(b)(2), (3), or (4).

But this subdivision (a) does not apply if the statement's proponent procured or wrongfully caused the declarant's unavailability as a witness in order to prevent the declarant from attending or testifying.

(b) **The Exceptions.** The following are not excluded by the rule against hearsay if the declarant is unavailable as a witness:

    (1) *Former Testimony.* Testimony that:

        (A) was given as a witness at a trial, hearing, or lawful deposition, whether given during the current proceeding or a different one; and

        (B) is now offered against a party who had—or, in a civil case, whose predecessor in interest had—an opportunity and similar motive to develop it by direct, cross-, or redirect examination.

    (2) *Statement Under the Belief of Imminent Death.* In a prosecution for homicide or in a civil case, a statement that the declarant, while believing the declarant's death to be imminent, made about its cause or circumstances.

    (3) *Statement Against Interest.* A statement that:

        (A) a reasonable person in the declarant's position would have made only if the person believed it to be true because, when made, it was so contrary to the declarant's proprietary or pecuniary interest or had so great a tendency to invalidate the declarant's claim against someone else or to expose the declarant to civil or criminal liability; and

        (B) is supported by corroborating circumstances that clearly indicate its trustworthiness, if it is offered in a criminal case as one that tends to expose the declarant to criminal liability.

(4) *Statement of Personal or Family History.* A statement about:

> **(A)** the declarant's own birth, adoption, legitimacy, ancestry, marriage, divorce, relationship by blood, adoption, or marriage, or similar facts of personal or family history, even though the declarant had no way of acquiring personal knowledge about that fact; or

> **(B)** another person concerning any of these facts, as well as death, if the declarant was related to the person by blood, adoption, or marriage or was so intimately associated with the person's family that the declarant's information is likely to be accurate.

(5) *[Other Exceptions.]* [Transferred to Rule 807.]

(6) *Statement Offered Against a Party That Wrongfully Caused the Declarant's Unavailability.* A statement offered against a party that wrongfully caused—or acquiesced in wrongfully causing—the declarant's unavailability as a witness, and did so intending that result.

Rule 805. Hearsay Within Hearsay

Hearsay within hearsay is not excluded by the rule against hearsay if each part of the combined statements conforms with an exception to the rule.

Rule 806. Attacking and Supporting the Declarant's Credibility

When a hearsay statement—or a statement described in Rule 801(d)(2)(C), (D), or (E)—has been admitted in evidence, the declarant's credibility may be attacked, and then supported, by any evidence that would be admissible for those purposes if the declarant had testified as a witness. The court may admit evidence of the declarant's inconsistent statement or conduct, regardless of when it occurred or whether the declarant had an opportunity to explain or deny it. If the party against whom the statement was admitted calls the declarant as a witness, the party may examine the declarant on the statement as if on cross-examination.

Rule 807. Residual Exception

(a) **In General.** Under the following conditions, a hearsay statement is not excluded by the rule against hearsay even if the statement is not admissible under a hearsay exception in Rule 803 or 804:

(1) the statement is supported by sufficient guarantees of trustworthiness—after considering the totality of circumstances under which it was made and evidence, if any, corroborating the statement; and

(2) it is more probative on the point for which it is offered than any other evidence that the proponent can obtain through reasonable efforts.

(b) Notice. The statement is admissible only if the proponent gives an adverse party reasonable notice of the intent to offer the statement—including its substance and the declarant's name— so that the party has a fair opportunity to meet it. The notice must be provided in writing before the trial or hearing—or in any form during the trial or hearing if the court, for good cause, excuses a lack of earlier notice.

ARTICLE IX.   AUTHENTICATION AND IDENTIFICATION

Rule 901.   Authenticating or Identifying Evidence

(a) In General. To satisfy the requirement of authenticating or identifying an item of evidence, the proponent must produce evidence sufficient to support a finding that the item is what the proponent claims it is.

(b) Examples. The following are examples only—not a complete list—of evidence that satisfies the requirement:

(1) *Testimony of a Witness with Knowledge.* Testimony that an item is what it is claimed to be.

(2) *Nonexpert Opinion About Handwriting.* A nonexpert's opinion that handwriting is genuine, based on a familiarity with it that was not acquired for the current litigation.

(3) *Comparison by an Expert Witness or the Trier of Fact.* A comparison with an authenticated specimen by an expert witness or the trier of fact.

(4) *Distinctive Characteristics and the Like.* The appearance, contents, substance, internal patterns, or other distinctive characteristics of the item, taken together with all the circumstances.

(5) *Opinion About a Voice.* An opinion identifying a person's voice—whether heard firsthand or through mechanical or electronic transmission or recording—based on hearing the voice at any time under circumstances that connect it with the alleged speaker.

(6) *Evidence About a Telephone Conversation.* For a telephone conversation, evidence that a call was made to the number assigned at the time to:

(A) a particular person, if circumstances, including self-identification, show that the person answering was the one called; or

(B) a particular business, if the call was made to a business and the call related to business reasonably transacted over the telephone.

(7) *Evidence About Public Records.* Evidence that:

(A) a document was recorded or filed in a public office as authorized by law; or

(B) a purported public record or statement is from the office where items of this kind are kept.

(8) *Evidence About Ancient Documents or Data Compilations.* For a document or data compilation, evidence that it:

(A) is in a condition that creates no suspicion about its authenticity;

(B) was in a place where, if authentic, it would likely be; and

(C) is at least 20 years old when offered.

(9) *Evidence About a Process or System.* Evidence describing a process or system and showing that it produces an accurate result.

(10) *Methods Provided by a Statute or Rule.* Any method of authentication or identification allowed by a federal statute or a rule prescribed by the Supreme Court.

Rule 902.   Evidence That Is Self-Authenticating

The following items of evidence are self-authenticating; they require no extrinsic evidence of authenticity in order to be admitted:

(1) *Domestic Public Documents That Are Sealed and Signed.* A document that bears:

(A) a seal purporting to be that of the United States; any state, district, commonwealth, territory, or insular possession of the United States; the former Panama Canal Zone; the Trust Territory of the Pacific Islands; a political subdivision of any of these entities; or a department, agency, or officer of any entity named above; and

(B) a signature purporting to be an execution or attestation.

(2) *Domestic Public Documents That Are Not Sealed but Are Signed and Certified.* A document that bears no seal if:

(A) it bears the signature of an officer or employee of an entity named in Rule 902(1)(A); and

(B) another public officer who has a seal and official duties within that same entity certifies under seal—or its equivalent—that the signer has the official capacity and that the signature is genuine.

(3) *Foreign Public Documents.* A document that purports to be signed or attested by a person who is authorized by a foreign country's law to do so. The document must be accompanied by a final certification that certifies the genuineness of the signature and official position of the signer or attester—or of any foreign official whose certificate of genuineness relates to the signature or attestation or is in a chain of certificates of genuineness relating to the signature or attestation. The certification may be made by a secretary of a United States embassy or legation; by a consul general, vice consul, or consular agent of the United States; or by a diplomatic or consular official of the foreign country assigned or accredited to the United States. If all parties have been given a reasonable opportunity to investigate the document's authenticity and accuracy, the court may, for good cause, either:

(A) order that it be treated as presumptively authentic without final certification; or

(B) allow it to be evidenced by an attested summary with or without final certification.

(4) *Certified Copies of Public Records.* A copy of an official record—or a copy of a document that was recorded or filed in a public office as authorized by law—if the copy is certified as correct by:

(A) the custodian or another person authorized to make the certification; or

(B) a certificate that complies with Rule 902(1), (2), or (3), a federal statute, or a rule prescribed by the Supreme Court.

(5) Official Publications. A book, pamphlet, or other publication purporting to be issued by a public authority.

(6) Newspapers and Periodicals. Printed material purporting to be a newspaper or periodical.

(7) Trade Inscriptions and the Like. An inscription, sign, tag, or label purporting to have been affixed in the course of business and indicating origin, ownership, or control.

(8) Acknowledged Documents. A document accompanied by a certificate of acknowledgment that is lawfully executed by a notary public or another officer who is authorized to take acknowledgments.

(9) Commercial Paper and Related Documents. Commercial paper, a signature on it, and related documents, to the extent allowed by general commercial law.

(10) Presumptions Under a Federal Statute. A signature, document, or anything else that a federal statute declares to be presumptively or prima facie genuine or authentic.

(11) Certified Domestic Records of a Regularly Conducted Activity. The original or a copy of a domestic record that meets the requirements of Rule 803(6)(A)–(C), as shown by a certification of the custodian or another qualified person that complies with a federal statute or a rule prescribed by the Supreme Court. Before the trial or hearing, the proponent must give an adverse party reasonable written notice of the intent to offer the record—and must make the record and certification available for inspection—so that the party has a fair opportunity to challenge them.

(12) Certified Foreign Records of a Regularly Conducted Activity. In a civil case, the original or a copy of a foreign record that meets the requirements of Rule 902(11), modified as follows: the certification, rather than complying with a federal statute or Supreme Court rule, must be signed in a manner that, if falsely made, would subject the maker to a criminal penalty in the country where the certification is signed. The proponent must also meet the notice requirements of Rule 902(11).

(13) Certified Records Generated by an Electronic Process or System. A record generated by an electronic process or

system that produces an accurate result, as shown by a certification of a qualified person that complies with the certification requirements of Rule 902(11) or (12). The proponent must also meet the notice requirements of Rule 902(11).

(14) *Certified Data Copied from an Electronic Device, Storage Medium, or File.* Data copied from an electronic device, storage medium, or file, if authenticated by a process of digital identification, as shown by a certification of a qualified person that complies with the certification requirements of Rule 902(11) or (12). The proponent also must meet the notice requirements of Rule 902(11).

Rule 903.   Subscribing Witness's Testimony

A subscribing witness's testimony is necessary to authenticate a writing only if required by the law of the jurisdiction that governs its validity.

ARTICLE X.   CONTENTS OF WRITINGS, RECORDINGS, AND PHOTOGRAPHS

Rule 1001.   Definitions That Apply to This Article

In this article:

(a) A "writing" consists of letters, words, numbers, or their equivalent set down in any form.

(b) A "recording" consists of letters, words, numbers, or their equivalent recorded in any manner.

(c) A "photograph" means a photographic image or its equivalent stored in any form.

(d) An "original" of a writing or recording means the writing or recording itself or any counterpart intended to have the same effect by the person who executed or issued it. For electronically stored information, "original" means any printout—or other output readable by sight—if it accurately reflects the information. An "original" of a photograph includes the negative or a print from it.

(e) A "duplicate" means a counterpart produced by a mechanical, photographic, chemical, electronic, or other equivalent process or technique that accurately reproduces the original.

Rule 1002.   Requirement of the Original

An original writing, recording, or photograph is required in order to prove its content unless these rules or a federal statute provides otherwise.

Rule 1003.   Admissibility of Duplicates

A duplicate is admissible to the same extent as the original unless a genuine question is raised about the original's authenticity or the circumstances make it unfair to admit the duplicate.

Rule 1004.   Admissibility of Other Evidence of Content

An original is not required and other evidence of the content of a writing, recording, or photograph is admissible if:

(a)   all the originals are lost or destroyed, and not by the proponent acting in bad faith;

(b)   an original cannot be obtained by any available judicial process;

(c)   the party against whom the original would be offered had control of the original; was at that time put on notice, by pleadings or otherwise, that the original would be a subject of proof at the trial or hearing; and fails to produce it at the trial or hearing; or

(d)   the writing, recording, or photograph is not closely related to a controlling issue.

Rule 1005.   Copies of Public Records to Prove Content

The proponent may use a copy to prove the content of an official record—or of a document that was recorded or filed in a public office as authorized by law—if these conditions are met: the record or document is otherwise admissible; and the copy is certified as correct in accordance with Rule 902(4) or is testified to be correct by a witness who has compared it with the original. If no such copy can be obtained by reasonable diligence, then the proponent may use other evidence to prove the content.

Rule 1006.   Summaries to Prove Content

The proponent may use a summary, chart, or calculation to prove the content of voluminous writings, recordings, or photographs that cannot be conveniently examined in court. The proponent must make the originals or duplicates available for examination or copying, or both, by other parties at a reasonable time and place. And the court may order the proponent to produce them in court.

Rule 1007.   Testimony or Statement of a Party to Prove Content

The proponent may prove the content of a writing, recording, or photograph by the testimony, deposition, or written statement of the party against whom the evidence is offered. The proponent need not account for the original.

Rule 1008.   Functions of the Court and Jury

Ordinarily, the court determines whether the proponent has fulfilled the factual conditions for admitting other evidence of the content of a writing, recording, or photograph under Rule 1004 or 1005. But in a jury trial, the jury determines—in accordance with Rule 104(b)— any issue about whether:

(a) an asserted writing, recording, or photograph ever existed;

(b) another one produced at the trial or hearing is the original; or

(c) other evidence of content accurately reflects the content.

ARTICLE XI.   MISCELLANEOUS RULES

Rule 1101.   Applicability of the Rules

(a) To Courts and Judges. These rules apply to proceedings before:

- United States district courts;

- United States bankruptcy and magistrate judges;

- United States courts of appeals;

- the United States Court of Federal Claims; and

- the district courts of Guam, the Virgin Islands, and the Northern Mariana Islands.

(b) To Cases and Proceedings. These rules apply in:

- civil cases and proceedings, including bankruptcy, admiralty, and maritime cases;

- criminal cases and proceedings; and

- contempt proceedings, except those in which the court may act summarily.

(c) Rules on Privilege. The rules on privilege apply to all stages of a case or proceeding.

(d) Exceptions. These rules—except for those on privilege—do not apply to the following:

   (1) the court's determination, under Rule 104(a), on a preliminary question of fact governing admissibility;

   (2) grand-jury proceedings; and

   (3) miscellaneous proceedings such as:

- extradition or rendition;

- issuing an arrest warrant, criminal summons, or search warrant;

- a preliminary examination in a criminal case;

- sentencing;

- granting or revoking probation or supervised release; and

- considering whether to release on bail or otherwise.

(e) Other Statutes and Rules. A federal statute or a rule prescribed by the Supreme Court may provide for admitting or excluding evidence independently from these rules.

Rule 1102. Amendments

These rules may be amended as provided in 28 U.S.C. § 2072.

Rule 1103. Title

These rules may be cited as the Federal Rules of Evidence.

Table of Cases

Index

References are to Pages